Cloud Database Development *and* Management

Cloud Database Development *and* Management

Lee Chao

CRC Press
Taylor & Francis Group
Boca Raton London New York

CRC Press is an imprint of the
Taylor & Francis Group, an **informa** business
AN AUERBACH BOOK

CRC Press
Taylor & Francis Group
6000 Broken Sound Parkway NW, Suite 300
Boca Raton, FL 33487-2742

Printed on acid-free paper
Version Date: 20130515

International Standard Book Number-13: 978-1-4665-6505-0 (Hardback)

Library of Congress Cataloging-in-Publication Data

Chao, Lee, 1951-
Cloud database development and management / Lee Chao.
pages cm
Includes bibliographical references and index.
ISBN 978-1-4665-6505-0 (hardback)
1. Cloud computing. 2. Database management. I. Title.

QA76.585.C44 2013
004.67'82--dc23 2013018420

Visit the Taylor & Francis Web site at
http://www.taylorandfrancis.com

and the CRC Press Web site at
http://www.crcpress.com

Contents

Preface

Today's e-commerce depends on various types of databases used to store and manage business information. In the e-commerce environment, users across the world should be able to access the databases from anywhere and at anytime through the Internet. A large number of IT infrastructures have been developed to support e-commerce. Developing and maintaining IT infrastructures can be difficult and expensive, especially for small companies. As a solution for supporting business activities in e-commerce, the cloud computing platform has been adopted by many companies. Internet-based databases and their applications can particularly benefit from cloud computing. The development of databases and applications in a cloud environment is motivated by the following factors.

Motivation

Owing to its flexibility, security, availability, scalability, and affordability, cloud computing has attracted the attention of the IT industry. The features provided by cloud computing are especially beneficial to small businesses and educational institutions that lack funding to maintain their own IT services.

Cloud computing is a type of Internet-based computing platform. With public clouds, companies and educational institutions do not have to invest in expensive IT infrastructures, which can significantly reduce the cost of IT expenditure. Although the use of cloud computing in supporting business activities gives some relief to this kind of burden, many IT professionals are not familiar with the cloud computing platform. For many small companies, there are still a handful of challenges in developing databases and applications in a cloud environment.

The potential of cloud computing and the challenges IT professionals are facing have inspired the author to write this book that includes enough knowledge to create database systems on the cloud platform.

Today's job market requires IT professionals to understand cloud computing theories and have hands-on skills for developing real-world database systems. Therefore, many IT professionals prefer a book that integrates database development and cloud computing at the same time, and they want the book to be easy to follow and the instructions for hands-on practice to be step by step. The book should also include instructions on setting up the database development environment in a cloud. To help IT professionals to catch up with the trend in cloud computing, this book will demonstrate how to integrate cloud computing into the database and application development process.

With the above motivation, this book is designed with the following objectives to help IT professionals to get a quick start in developing cloud-based database systems.

Objectives of the Book

The fundamental goal of this book is to prepare students and IT professionals to develop and manage databases in a cloud computing environment. This book is designed to provide the necessary knowledge and hands-on skills for developing a fully functioning database system and applications with the Microsoft Windows Azure cloud service. The content in the book is suitable for IT professionals to do self-study on developing cloud-based database systems.

This book will help readers to set up a cloud-based database development environment where they can carry out all the hands-on activities covered in this book. The cloud-based database development environment will allow readers to develop database systems collaboratively or individually at home through the Internet.

This book prepares students and IT professionals for developing cloud-based database systems. The process of database system development involves database design, implementation, and management. This book covers the knowledge related to all three aspects. The content covered in this book helps readers to create database systems that can be used for daily business activities.

With the cloud environment, we can speed up the implementation of databases and database applications. By taking advantage of the cloud-based database development environment, readers will be able to implement database systems and other data storage services in a short time.

Another intention of this book is to help readers understand how a database system works. It is written so that the database-related concepts are introduced in an orderly fashion and progress step by step.

Features of the Book

The author wrote this book for the convenience of readers. The book is self-contained. It provides detailed instructions that are suitable for self-study while covering all the important topics to meet the requirements of the database development process in the cloud. The following briefly describes the features of the book.

- *Self-contained content*: For the convenience of readers, the book is self-contained. It includes some necessary basic database concepts and theories, hands-on activities, and information about cloud-based database development tools.
- *Suitable for self-study*: This book provides detailed instructions that are suitable for self-study. It not only states the concepts and theories, but also explains them through examples, illustrations, and hands-on activities.
- *Designed for Windows Azure*: The book is specially designed for cloud-based database development. All the hands-on activities can be done with a Windows Azure's 3-month trial account.
- *A wide range of coverage*: This book covers a wide range of topics in database system development: database design, database implementation, and database deployment to the cloud environment. It also covers other topics such as data storage services: Table storage service, Blob storage service, and Queue storage service. It also discusses database application development.

- *Step-by-step instructions*: For the hands-on activities, the book provides step-by-step instructions and illustrations. The book also provides instructions on setting up the cloud environment for hands-on practice.
- *Real-world approach*: Examples, illustrations, and hands-on practice projects are included in each chapter. These materials are designed to help readers gain confidence and skills in developing cloud-based database systems that can be used in real-world businesses.

With these features, the book is suitable for IT professionals who do self-study on developing cloud-based database systems with Windows Azure.

Organization of the Book

This book includes 12 chapters. Each chapter contains an introduction of the content to be covered by that chapter, the main body of the chapter, a summary section to summarize the discussion in the chapter, and a review questions section to help readers review the knowledge learned from the chapter. Each chapter also includes hands-on activities to help readers practice the skills learned in the chapter.

Chapter 1 introduces the readers to database systems and cloud computing. It outlines what a database can do and the components included in the database. It presents a process used by the database developer to develop a database system. This chapter also gives an overview of cloud computing. It introduces several well-known computing services such as Software as a Service (SaaS), Infrastructure as a Service (IaaS), and Platform as a Service (PaaS). For the hands-on activity, this chapter provides instructions on creating a Windows Azure 3-month free account, developing a virtual machine with Windows Server 2012 as the guest operating system, and downloading Windows Azure SDK to the virtual machine.

The topics related to database design are presented in Chapter 2. This chapter deals with all three aspects of database design: conceptual design, logical design, and physical design. The physical design section emphasizes the cloud computing environment. The hands-on practice covers database logical design and the development of a Windows Azure SQL Database server as part of the physical design.

Once a database is designed, the next step is to convert a data model to a relational database. Before converting a data model to a relational database, the first task is to make sure that the tables are well defined to avoid anomalies. This leads to the coverage of normalization. Chapter 3 covers the topics related to the normalization process. The hands-on practice of this chapter creates a cloud-based relational database with Windows Azure SQL Database.

Chapter 4 introduces the SQL language and demonstrates how to use SQL to create database objects. It provides technical details about creating database objects on Widows Azure. During the hands-on activities, the reader will be creating database objects with SQL on the Windows Azure SQL Database portal. With SQL statements, the reader can manage the database objects. The SQL statements are also used to populate the database tables.

After the database is created, Chapter 5 introduces the migration of the database between Windows Azure and the on-premises SQL Server. The hands-on activities in this chapter cover several database migration tools: SQL Server Management Studio, Data-tier Application, Windows Azure SQL Database Migration Wizard, and SQL Server Integration Services. The hands-on practice also introduces and uses data transfer tools such as a bulk copy program and Extensible Markup Language (XML).

Chapter 6 demonstrates how to retrieve information from a database. The SQL language is used to select data from a database and properly present the data. This chapter introduces basic SQL statements for querying data from a single table. Then, the subquery and join are introduced to query data from multiple tables. Some of the built-in functions are also used to query data. In the hands-on activities, readers will experiment with various queries in the Windows Azure cloud environment.

For more sophisticated database querying tasks, Chapter 7 introduces programming units such as functions, stored procedures, and triggers. This chapter first explains how ANSI SQL is extended to T-SQL to meet some programming requirements. It then introduces various functions including built-in functions and user-defined functions. The stored procedure is another program unit covered in this chapter, which discusses how to view, execute, and modify stored procedures. To automatically carry out database management tasks, the programming unit "trigger" is presented in this chapter, which explains how triggers work and how to create triggers. The hands-on activities for this chapter include creating, modifying, and deleting programming units such as functions, stored procedures, and triggers in the Windows Azure cloud environment.

More database objects are introduced in Chapter 8. They are views, indexes, and federations. These database objects are used to support front-end database applications, which will be discussed in Chapter 9. The hands-on activities provide opportunities and instructions on how to create and manage these database objects in the Windows Azure cloud environment.

Once the SQL database is made available on Windows Azure, it is time to develop database applications. Through these applications, users can interact with the database to perform tasks such as importing and exporting data, enforcing constraints and security, and implementing business logic. Chapter 9 first discusses issues related to database application design. Then, database applications such as forms and reports are developed in the cloud environment emulated with the Windows Azure Software Development Kit (SDK) on a local computer. Packages such as Microsoft Visual Studio are used to create database applications. The hands-on practice in this chapter details the creation of a Web form.

Beginning with Chapter 10, the focus of the book switches to the deployment of database applications to Windows Azure. Chapter 10 demonstrates how to deploy database applications to Windows Azure. Once the database applications are deployed to Windows Azure, these applications become available on the Internet. They can be opened in a Web browser. The hands-on activities are carried out to deploy the Web form and report to Windows Azure.

Chapter 11 introduces Windows Azure storage services, including Table storage, Blob storage, and Queue storage. The Windows Azure storage services are used to store nonrelational data. The chapter discusses the features provided by these storage services and provides step-by-step instructions for the hands-on practice to develop these storage services.

Chapter 12 is about Windows Azure SQL Database management. This chapter discusses the management tasks that keep Windows Azure SQL Database running smoothly. The chapter first introduces database security and the management of user accounts. It also discusses issues related to monitoring and diagnostics. The hands-on activities use several database management tools: Windows Azure Management Portal, Service Management API, and Windows Azure Service Management PowerShell. This chapter's hands-on activities cover these tools for SQL Database management, user management, and service monitoring.

One or more hands-on activities are included in each of the chapters. It is recommended that readers complete the activities in the previous chapters before starting a hands-on activity in the next chapter because some of the hands-on activities may depend on the ones in the previous chapters.

For real-world cloud solutions, this book provides the tools and knowledge to create a cloud-based database system. The book demonstrates to IT professionals how to take advantage of the cloud environment to develop a fully functioning database system with minimal cost. It shows how to properly design, implement, and manage database systems in Windows Azure. It also provides enough technical details to help readers develop database systems on their own. The book introduces a number of database tools that can make database development more efficient and flexible.

Acknowledgments

I would like to thank my family for their continuous and loving support, patience, and understanding during the course of my work.

My special gratitude goes to my students and Dr. Jenny Huang for their participation in the proofreading process. They carefully reviewed the content of the manuscript. Their constructive suggestions and corrections greatly improved the quality of the book.

I would also like to thank the outstanding editorial staff members and other personnel at Auerbach Publications of Taylor & Francis Group for supporting this project. I truly appreciate the encouragement and collaboration of John Wyzalek, senior acquisitions editor, David Fausel, project coordinator, and all the other people who have been involved in the book's production. The book would not be possible without their inspiration and great effort.

Author

Lee Chao, PhD, is a professor in the Science, Technology, Engineering, and Mathematics division at the University of Houston–Victoria, USA. He earned his PhD at the University of Wyoming, USA.

Dr. Chao has been teaching IT courses for over 20 years. His current research interests are database system development and cloud computing. Dr. Chao is the author of over a dozen research articles and books in various areas of IT.

Chapter 1

Introduction to Database Systems and Cloud Computing

Objectives

- Become familiar with major database components
- Understand database functions
- Be introduced to cloud computing

1.1 Introduction

Today's e-commerce has brought many new challenges for data storage and management. The number of new data generated by e-commerce has grown exponentially. Recently, over 65,000 petabytes of new data have been processed by various businesses each year. One petabyte is equal to one thousand terabytes. Web-based businesses can generate mega-scale datasets in a very short time, such as those on sale events around holidays. The data storage is required to quickly respond to these events. For the applications scaled out all over the world, the traditional databases inevitably face the difficulty of scalability. With the growth of datasets, the cost to store and manage the data increases accordingly. Facing the challenges in data storage and management, cloud computing has emerged as an efficient solution. By taking advantage of the cloud computing technology, companies are able to overcome difficulties in scalability and cost. Built on highly scalable infrastructure, the cloud can take care of the sudden increase of the data volume.

As cloud computing provides an ideal environment for processing data generated by today's online businesses, introducing the development of databases in a cloud environment is therefore the goal of this chapter, which discusses the components of a database, the tasks that can be accomplished by a database, and database management systems (DBMSs). It also provides an overview of cloud computing and cloud services such as Software as a Service (SaaS), Infrastructure as a Service (IaaS), Platform as a Service (PaaS), and the personal cloud.

1.2 Overview of Database Management Systems

For the creation and management of a database, computer software packages are created. A computer software package may also include tools for data analysis for business decision makers. Such a software package is known as database management system. In the early 1970s, IBM developed a DBMS known as SQL/DL, which was later developed into DB2. IBM also invented the data querying language, structured query language (SQL), which is used for data retrieval and database development and management. By the late 1970s, other DBMS vendors such as Oracle and Sybase were established. In the 1980s, user-friendly personal DBMSs such as dBASE, Access, and Lotus were developed for PCs. In the late 1980s, SQL Server 1.0 developed by Sybase for Microsoft was released.

The DBMS to be covered by this book is Microsoft Windows Azure SQL Database, which extends the capabilities of Microsoft SQL Server to the cloud. Microsoft SQL Server was built by Sybase and later was further developed by Microsoft. The choice of Microsoft Windows Azure SQL Database is because it is very similar to Microsoft SQL Server. Microsoft SQL Server is widely available. Users can create and test the databases locally and then migrate the database objects to the Microsoft cloud platform, Windows Azure. SQL Server is included in the Windows Azure Software Development Kit (SDK), which can be downloaded for free. With the Windows Azure SDK, users can develop and test database applications locally in an emulated cloud environment. Once tested, these applications can be uploaded to Windows Azure. Another advantage of SQL Server is that it can be seamlessly integrated with other Microsoft products. For example, it can be integrated with Microsoft Visual Studio for application development. By being integrated with Microsoft Visio, it can be used to accomplish tasks in database design. There are some other factors that have also contributed to the decision. First, Microsoft Windows Azure SQL Database is a user-friendly product. The easy-to-use feature is important for users who do not have previous experience with DBMS products. By working with Microsoft Windows Azure SQL Database, users will not be overwhelmed by the complexity of a DBMS.

The creation of a database in Windows Azure SQL Database is relatively easy. Once the database is created on the cloud platform, users can get a quick start on the hands-on practice included in this book. On the other hand, Windows Azure SQL Database is sophisticated enough to handle most of the enterprise-level database tasks. Windows Azure SQL Database includes the components listed in Table 1.1 that can be used to accomplish various tasks in database system development.

These components are often included in other sophisticated DBMS systems too. The management tools listed in Table 1.1 are commonly used by database developers to create and manage database objects, extract information from existing databases, implement data access schemes, develop database applications, perform data analyses, and exchange data over the Internet. The DBMS provides a unified working environment to allow database professionals to accomplish all the above tasks. In later chapters, you will learn, in more detail, about these components.

1.3 Database Components

With a DBMS, a database professional can create various database objects. This section introduces some commonly used database objects. These database objects are used to store data, manage data, configure database properties, implement database security, and set up database constraints. Figure 1.1 displays databases hosted by an SQL Database Server in Windows Azure SQL Database.

Table 1.1 Windows Azure SQL Database Components

	Components	*Descriptions*
Database	SQL Database	It is used for storing, processing, and securing data. It includes tools for the management of relational and XML data.
	Reporting Services	Reporting Services is used for developing, managing, and deploying tabular, matrix, and graphical reports.
	Data Access	Data Access is used by database applications for moving, copying, and transforming data in and out of databases.
Management Tools	SQL Server Management Studio	SSMS is an integrated environment used to access, configure, manage, administer, and develop components of SQL Database.
	Security Management	It provides tools for configuring access to database servers, databases, and database roles.
	Deployment Management	It deploys the databases and database applications from the on-premises SQL Server to the cloud.
	Connectivity Components	This tool provides the database accessing tools for managing the communication between clients and servers.
Database Server	SQL Database Server	It hosts databases, manages database log-ins, establishes connections, specifies database locations, and sets up firewalls.

Databases: As shown in Figure 1.1, there are some databases in SQL Server. The data stored in a database are systematically arranged so that they can be retrieved with some kind of query language. Database professionals can use the tools provided by a DBMS to manage and analyze the data stored in a database. Each database consists of objects such as tables, views, and stored procedures.

Tables: As shown in Figure 1.2, in a database, the data are stored in tables. The data related to the same subject are stored in the same table. A table is constructed with columns and rows. Each column represents an attribute that is used to describe the subject. For example, the column LastName in Figure 1.2 is the attribute used to describe the subject STUDENT. Here, the table STUDENT is one of the tables created in the database Class_Registration. Normally, a database contains multiple tables, each related to a subject with its information stored in the database.

Views: Similar to a table, a view is also a database object. It collects data from tables. Sometimes, a database application may need data from multiple tables. Instead of searching these data during an operation, the data are often preselected and stored in a database object called a view, as shown in Figure 1.3. A view serves as intermediate storage between tables and database applications. Using views can improve the performance and security.

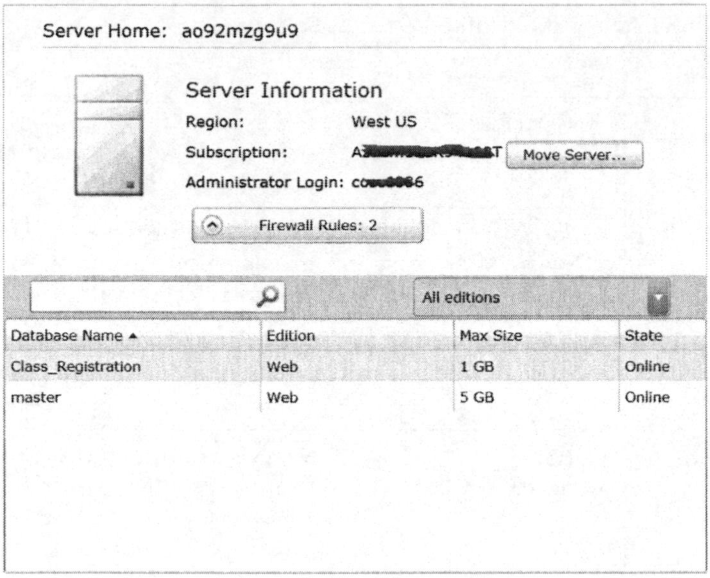

Figure 1.1 Databases hosted by an SQL Database Server in Windows Azure SQL Database.

Stored Procedures: A stored procedure contains programming code to perform a sequence of operations or call other procedures. It is precompiled and stored in SQL Server for better performance and security. Figure 1.4 shows a stored procedure.

Functions: A function also contains programming code to perform a sequence of operations. It can be called by its name by other programs and returns a single value to the calling program. Windows Azure SQL Database provides many built-in functions to assist the development of databases.

Database Triggers: A database trigger is a specific kind of stored procedure. It will be executed automatically when a specific database event occurs.

In this section, you have briefly gone over some of the commonly used database objects. There are more to come in later chapters. You will learn in more detail about these database objects.

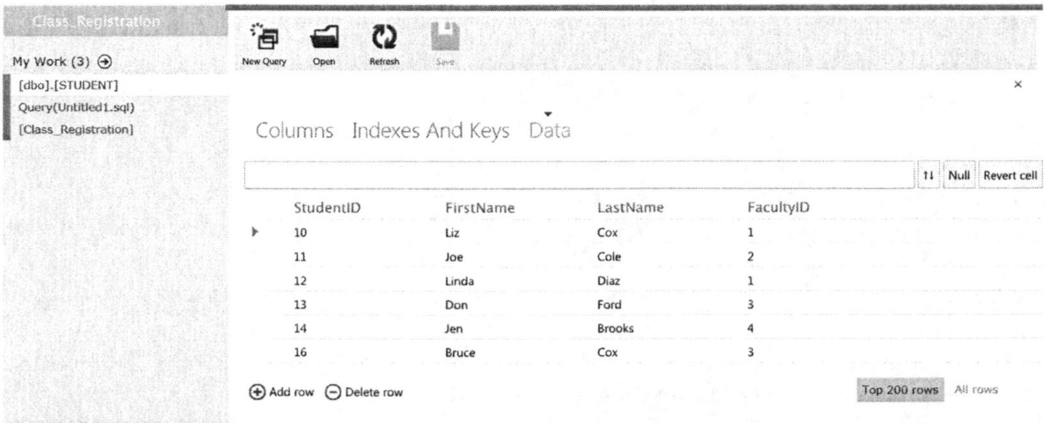

Figure 1.2 STUDENT table.

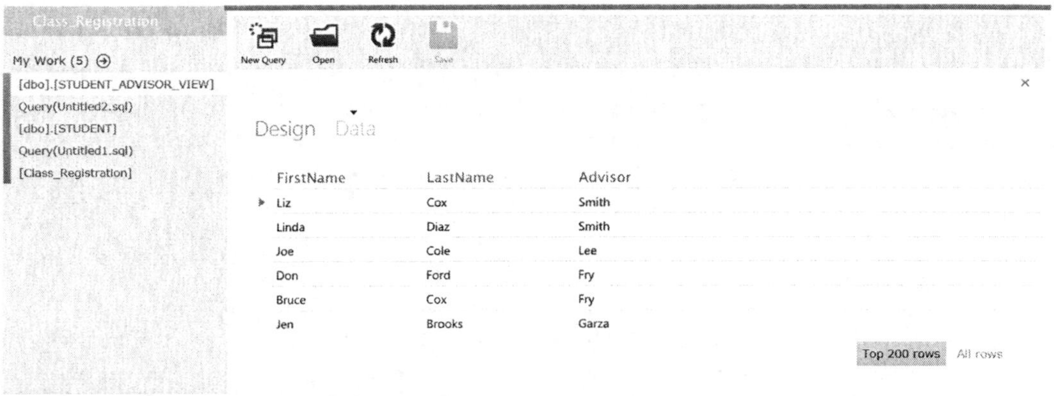

Figure 1.3 View.

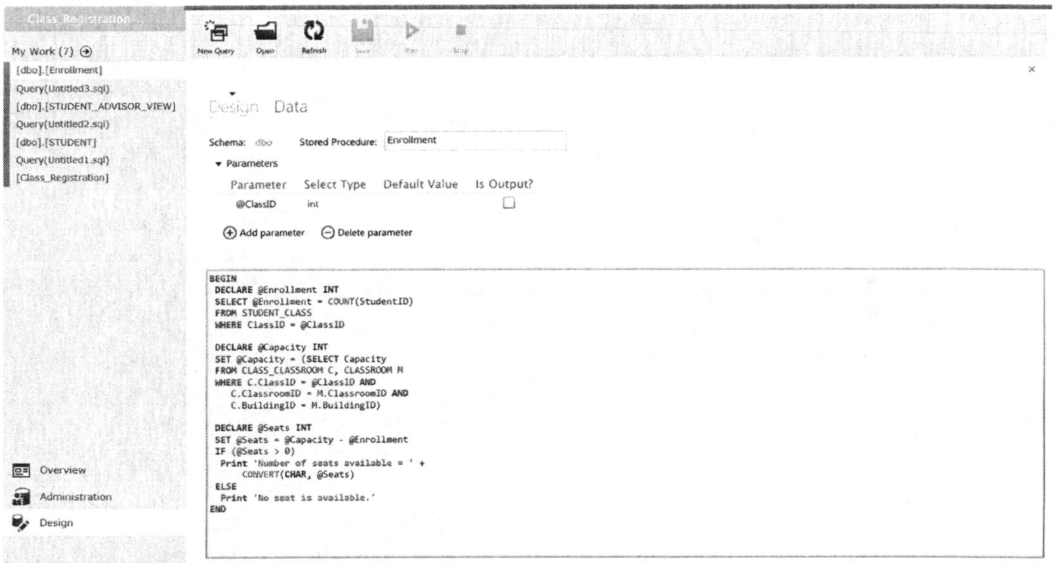

Figure 1.4 Stored procedure.

1.4 Database Development Process

A database system, as the heart of an information system, can be very complicated. For such a complicated project, a divide-and-conquer approach is often used to develop a database system. Often, a group of IT professionals are involved in the database system development and management. The process of database development normally includes several major steps: requirement analysis for the to-be-built database system, design of the database system based on the requirements, development of the database system according to the design, deployment of the database system, development of database applications, database management and maintenance, and development of data analysis services. To get the whole picture of a database development process, let us take a brief look at each database development phase.

The first task is to investigate the requirements for the database to be developed. The requirement analysis is based on a thorough understanding of a business process. Always keep this in mind: a well-designed database is based on a good understanding of the business process. To understand the business process, database designers should answer questions such as: What will a business do with the future database? What are the business rules and limitations related to the future database? What information does the business want to keep track of? What improvement should be made by the future database? Several methods can help the database designers to collect the needed information. The database designers can conduct interviews with key players of the business process. They can also examine the company's documents to see how data are used in the business process. Tracking the data flow in the business process is a way to figure out how the future database will be used to support the ongoing business.

Once the first task is accomplished, it is to time to sort out the collected information, interpret the collected information in technical terms, and figure out the relationships among the things to keep track of. To represent the things to keep track of and the relationships among them, the database designers will develop a data model that serves as the blueprint for the future database. Once the data model is created, it can be used to verify if the future database will meet the database requirements. It may take several rounds of modifications before the design goals can be achieved logically. Both the database designers and the company they serve should be satisfied with the data model before they can physically implement the database. The database designers may need to prepare a contract with the company they are serving and draft a timeline to fulfill the contract.

During the database development phase, the database designers need to select a proper DBMS and create database objects according to the design. The choice of a DBMS will depend on the requirements of the future database. The chosen DBMS should be able to create a database system that meets all the database management, data analysis, and data storage requirements. By using the DBMS, the database designers can transfer their data model to a relational database. The business data will be stored in the well-defined database and be organized according to the specifications made in the data model. The programming units will be created to implement the constraints and to retrieve data from the database. To allow the users to access the database remotely, the database should be hosted by a database server. The network infrastructure should be so built that the users can securely access the database through the Internet. Or, instead of developing the network infrastructure, we can deploy the database to a cloud environment. For the database to handle intense data volume change and support database applications across the world, a cloud computing environment should be considered.

Once the database is constructed, before the newly developed database can be used in the business process, it needs to be tested to see if the database is able to meet all the requirements. The database administrators (DBAs) and users should be involved in the testing process. Based on the testing results, the database will be modified again by the database designers to meet the users' needs. Successful deployment of the database requires training and technical support. First, there should be some operation instructions written for the users. The users should be trained on how to use the database. The technical support team should be organized to help the users with troubleshooting.

Once the database is implemented, it is necessary to create some database applications that are used to help front-end users interact with the database. The database applications may include forms, reports, web pages, as well as apps for mobile devices. To support front-end users' interaction with the database through the local network or through the Internet, the database must be built to support remote access. With cloud computing, a collaboration environment can also be built to allow the developers to participate in the application development remotely throughout the world.

To keep the database running and providing services continuously, the database should be managed by a group of experienced DBAs. The DBAs perform tasks such as creating user accounts, performing data transformation, database backup, restoration, and doing performance tuning. It is the DBAs' responsibility to enforce security measures. For a large corporation, the DBAs may also perform tasks such as database partitioning and managing network utilities for distributed databases. A cloud platform can significantly reduce the workload of the DBAs since the tasks such as database backup can be taken care of by a cloud provider.

The data stored in a database can be used to provide useful information for decision making. To extend the usage of data stored in a database, an enterprise-level DBMS provides data analysis services to support business decision making. Through the analysis services, an information analyst can develop data analysis projects with online analytical processing (OLAP), data mart or data warehouse, and data mining. The information analyst supports the decision-making team with necessary analytical information such as customer behaviors, market trends, and patterns hidden in the daily business operation data.

The above paragraphs give a brief description of the database development process. More specific coverage on database development will be covered in the following chapters. Each major step of the database development process will be discussed in detail. Examples and hands-on practice will be used to enhance the understanding of the theories and techniques involved in the database development process. In this book, some of the examples and hands-on practice are for learning purposes, and they may not be necessarily the best solution for some specific business tasks.

1.5 Overview of Cloud Computing

It is mentioned above that the cloud computing environment is ideal for developing a database system that is dynamically scalable depending on the needs. Cloud computing has the potential to significantly reduce the cost for developing and managing a database as well. The cloud computing technology can be a great solution for those small businesses that lack resources to support their own IT infrastructure.

Cloud computing is an Internet-based computing platform that provides services and computing resources to subscribers who only pay for the services and computing resources they use. In such a way, a small company does not have to develop its own IT infrastructure to support its e-commerce activities. All the company needs to do is to subscribe some services and computing resources from a cloud provider to get a quick start. Instead of constructing a network and a server to host the DBMS package, the company can create database objects with the DBMS package right after the computing resources have been subscribed from the cloud provider. There will be no upfront expenditure on IT infrastructure. As the business grows, the company can subscribe more services and computing resources. The daily IT infrastructure maintenance will be handled by the cloud provider. This means that the cost for IT service personnel can be significantly reduced. E-commerce can fully take advantage of cloud computing since the services and computing resources provided by the cloud provider can be accessed anywhere and anytime.

There are three types of cloud computing platforms: private cloud, public cloud, and hybrid cloud. Based on the business requirements, the company can create its own cloud services. A private cloud is constructed on the existing IT infrastructure owned by a company. Both the cloud provider and subscribers are working within the company. Cloud servers are built by the IT service department. The services and computing resources are provided by the company's IT department. The data will be stored in the data center located on the company's private network. The private cloud allows the company to have a total control of the data. The company can decide what security measures to be enforced on the private cloud. The cloud subscribers are authenticated by the company.

By establishing a private cloud, a company can take advantage of the flexibility and availability provided by cloud computing without paying subscription fees to a third-party cloud provider. Since the data are stored on a private network, the company is less worried about its private data being exposed to the public. On the other hand, it requires the company to have a group of skilled technical personnel and adequate computing resources to develop and manage the private cloud.

In a public cloud, the services and computing resources are provided by a third-party cloud provider. The data center and IT infrastructure used to support cloud computing are developed and managed by the third-party cloud provider. Some of the well-known ones are Amazon Elastic Compute Cloud (EC2), IBM Blue Cloud, Microsoft Windows Azure, and so on. Based on the needs of a cloud subscriber, the third-party cloud provider dynamically provisions computing resources. Companies or individuals subscribe and pay for cloud services and computing resources. By subscribing to cloud services and computing resources, a company does not have to develop its own IT infrastructure to support its e-commerce. Without investing in IT infrastructure, the company can significantly reduce the initial cost and can start its business right away. The drawback of a public cloud is that cloud subscribers have no control over where the data are stored. The data center of a public cloud can store the data anywhere around world. The lack of knowledge about where the data are stored may cause some concerns about the public cloud. For example, an educational institution is required to keep the students' privacy. If the student data are stored in a data center located in a foreign country, it may violate state or federal government regulations. Also, it is always a concern to place an organization's financial system entirely on a third party's public cloud without knowing where the data are stored.

To take advantage of the public cloud and to keep the data safe, a third type of cloud, hybrid cloud, is accepted by many companies. For many companies, they have the existing IT infrastructure for their daily business operations. These companies can keep their financial systems on their own private clouds and use the public cloud to support the less sensitive business processes such as the companies' web applications. On the other hand, by using the hybrid cloud, a company may end up paying fees for subscribing the services and computing resources to the third-party cloud provider as well as for developing and managing the private cloud. If the cost of using both the private cloud and the public cloud is too high, the company may consider the private cloud option.

There are three major types of cloud services: SaaS, IaaS, and PaaS. Recently, the personal cloud has also become available in cloud computing. A brief introduction of these types of cloud services is given below.

1.5.1 Software as a Service

This type of cloud service provides application software running on a cloud infrastructure to cloud subscribers. It allows companies to use web-based application software and pay for the usage of the software. As subscribers, the companies do not need to manage the IT infrastructure, including networks, servers, operating systems, and databases, to support the application software. Since the application software is running on a cloud-based server, the software is accessible through web browsers. The personal computing devices such as notebook computers or even smart phones can be used to run a company's daily business. Commonly used application software provided by cloud providers are web-based e-mail, document processing software, multimedia software, web development software, application development software, and digital games.

Some of the well-known cloud IT organizations have been providing SaaS services for years. For example, Google is currently providing cloud-based application software such as Google Mail, Google Doc, Google Cloud Print, and Google Calendar. Google's application software is supported by Google App Engine.

Microsoft also provides cloud-based applications such as Microsoft Office 365. In addition to the web-based office software such as Word, Excel, PowerPoint, and OneNote, Microsoft Office 365 also includes software for cloud-based e-mail, shared calendars, PC-to-PC calling, video conferencing, and antivirus and antispam filters.

1.5.2 Platform as a Service

This service provides a web-based application development platform for cloud subscribers. A company can use this service to design, develop, test, deploy, upgrade, and host web-based application software. Application developers can also use this service to form a community to carry out collaborative work on a project. To support application development, cloud providers provide the application development environments, which include the necessary IT infrastructure as well as the software such as server operating systems, databases, middleware, web servers, and project management tools.

One of the well-known PaaS services is implemented with Microsoft Windows Azure. Windows Azure provides a cloud computing environment that consists of a large number of virtual machines. It supports data storage and network infrastructure for application development. With Windows Azure, application developers are able to create web-based applications that are scalable and highly available to customers. To help with the application development, Microsoft provides the free application development package, Windows Azure SDK. Windows Azure SDK allows application developers to develop application collaboratively in the cloud as well as individually on their local computers. For data storage, Windows Azure offers data storage service for storing and managing nonrelational data. For applications that require relational data, Microsoft provides the cloud version of Microsoft SQL Server, Windows Azure SQL Database. With Windows Azure SQL Database, application developers can handle tasks such as data storage, data management, data transfer, and data querying. Windows Azure SQL Database provides almost the same working environment as that of Microsoft SQL Server. Like SQL Server, Windows Azure SQL Database supports Transact-SQL for programming. That is why the Windows Azure SDK includes a version of SQL Server Express for processing relational data. SQL Server application data accessing tools such as ODBC and ADO.NET are also included in the Windows Azure SDK.

IBM Blue Cloud provides similar services called IBM SmartCloud Application Services. IBM Blue Cloud provides the data center and Linux virtual machines to form an environment for developers to develop, test, and run the distributed applications. Application developers can share the cloud infrastructure provided by IBM. IBM Blue Cloud can also be used to test the migration of the existing traditional IT infrastructure to the cloud-based IT infrastructure. The application lifecycle service provided by IBM PaaS offers a test-based real-time collaborative development and deployment environment. With the application lifecycle service, application developers can collaborate on agile planning, change management, and software configuration management. The application resource service offers a centralized environment that can be shared by application developers. Centralized database service is an example of such an environment. IBM PaaS provides application environments that are used for application deployment. The application environments can perform automatic scaling for an application and manage the application with purpose-built services. IBM PaaS is able to provide application development environments tailored for different application types. The application management service offers the environments for the management of packaged applications. It can be used to accomplish the tasks such as fast upgrade and back-up of installations, data change management, and the deployment of packaged applications with automated and managed services. The integration service provided by IBM PaaS synchronizes data and processes among multiple applications. With the integration service, application developers can synchronize applications without custom coding or manual processes.

1.5.3 Infrastructure as a Service

This cloud service provides an IT infrastructure that consists of servers, network connections, and data storage. Tools for managing the IT infrastructure are also provided by cloud providers. The cloud-based IT infrastructure is created in a virtual computing environment to fulfill the requirements of e-commerce. With IaaS, cloud subscribers can run their own operating systems and set up their own application development platforms. The cloud subscribers can decide how to construct their own databases for data storage and analysis.

Amazon is such a cloud provider that provides the IaaS service. It is a pioneer for popularizing the cloud computing platform. Through Amazon Web Services (AWS), cloud subscribers can get virtual network servers, virtual desktop computers, data storage, and IP addresses. The IaaS service provided by AWS does not have to tie to a specific cloud provider's software. The cloud subscribers can install their own existing software on the infrastructure provided by AWS. This advantage provides an opportunity for a cloud subscriber to install free or open source software such as open source database MySQL. Another key feature provided by AWS is the Virtual Private Cloud (VPC) technology. The VPC technology allows cloud subscribers to create their own private network in a cloud. The virtual machines with properly assigned IP addresses can still be reached through the Internet Gateway and remote desktop connection. AWS also provides the Moonwalk program, which is a large-scale data management solution for cloud subscribers. Through Moonwalk, cloud subscribers can move their data from one platform such as Windows to another platform such as Linux, or vice versa. Another advantage of AWS is that it can integrate a company's private cloud with Amazon's public cloud. The IaaS service provided through AWS is very flexible. It even allows another third-party cloud provider to provide SaaS and PaaS services through AWS.

1.5.4 Personal Cloud

In addition to the SaaS, PaaS, and IaaS cloud services, the personal cloud has become a new trend in cloud computing. Through a personal cloud, cloud subscribers are able to access all of their personal data anywhere and anytime. The personal cloud subscribers can share their personal data such as photos, movies, contacts, e-mail, and documents with their friends, family, and coworkers online. With the services provided by the personal cloud, the subscribers are able to store, retrieve, and organize their own data online. With the personal cloud, a subscriber can update, backup, and replicate all the personal data across his/her mobile devices.

iCloud is this type of cloud to allow a subscriber to store his/her music, photos, documents, and more, and it wirelessly pushes them to all his/her devices automatically, effortlessly, and seamlessly.

More than an online storage service, iCloud keeps a person's data content available on all his/her computing devices including iPhone, iPad, iPod touch, Mac, or PC. It also keeps a person's e-mail, contacts, and calendars up to date across his/her devices. The iCloud service does everything for the subscriber to manage his/her personal data.

Windows Live SkyDrive is the Microsoft Version of the personal cloud. The subscribers of SkyDrive can store, organize, and download their files, photos, and favorites on Windows Live servers. They can access the data stored on SkyDrive from any computer with an Internet connection. SkyDrive allows the subscribers to organize their data by creating folders and to collaborate on document editing. The subscribers can move, copy, delete, rename, and caption their files. They can also create a contact list and grant permissions to access specific folders so that friends and family members can share photos, videos, music, and other data content. The multimedia files can be displayed in multiple formats such as JPG, JPEG, GIF, BMP, PNG, TIF, and TIFF. From their blogs or web pages, the subscribers can create links to their files stored on SkyDrive or embed the data stored on SkyDrive.

As described above, cloud computing is everywhere now. Database system development can particularly benefit from the features provided by cloud computing. The goal of this book is to develop a cloud-based database system and its applications by taking advantage of the cloud computing environment. The PaaS service provided by Windows Azure is particularly suitable for accomplishing the goal of this book. Throughout the book, Windows Azure and Windows Azure SQL Database will be used for the hands-on activities. To prepare for the database development, one needs to first install the Windows Azure SDK, which will be covered in the next section.

ACTIVITY 1.1 WINDOWS AZURE SOFTWARE DEVELOPMENT KIT INSTALLATION ON WINDOWS 7

To simplify the development, deployment, and management of cloud-based applications on the Windows Azure platform, Microsoft provides the application developers with a set of rich application development tools such as the Windows Azure SDK. The Windows Azure SDK provides an application development environment for Windows Azure. The SDK package includes APIs, tools, documentations, and samples needed to develop cloud applications that run on Windows Azure. With the SDK package, application developers can create and test applications locally before deploying the applications to a cloud. The Windows Azure SDK comes with the compute and storage emulators that simulate the cloud computing environment. To develop the project covered in this book, you will need to download and install the Windows Azure SDK package.

TASK 1: WINDOWS AZURE SDK INSTALLATION PREPARATION

Before the installation of the Windows Azure SDK, make sure that your computer meets the following requirements:

1. To install the Windows Azure SDK, your computer needs to have one of the following or later versions of the software:
   a. Windows Server 2008 or Windows 7
   b. SQL Server 2012

   c. Microsoft Visual Studio 2010 with SP1
   d. Microsoft Visio or other database design software

   If Windows Server 2008 is used as the operating system, you also need to install .NET Framework 3.5. The early versions of the above software may also work. However, more configurations may be required.
2. You need to find out if your computer runs on a 32-bit or 64-bit operating system. Later, you need to download the Windows Azure SDK that matches your operating system.
3. To develop web applications, **Internet Information Services (IIS) 7.0** should be enabled. Suppose that you have the 64-bit Windows 7 Professional operating system running on your computer. To verify if IIS is enabled on your machine, click the **Start** button, **Control Panel**, Programs and Features, and **Turn Windows features on or off**. You should be able to see if the node **Internet Information Services** is checked. If not, you need to check the node to enable IIS.
4. To make sure that ASP.NET as well as other features is enabled, click **Start, Control Panel, Programs and Features**, and **Turn Windows features on or off**. Expand the **IIS** node. Edit the nodes **Web Management Tools**, **Application Development Features**, and **Common HTTP Features** as shown in Figure 1.5.
5. If you have a previous version of the Windows Azure SDK, make sure to remove all its components in the Control Panel before installing the SDK.

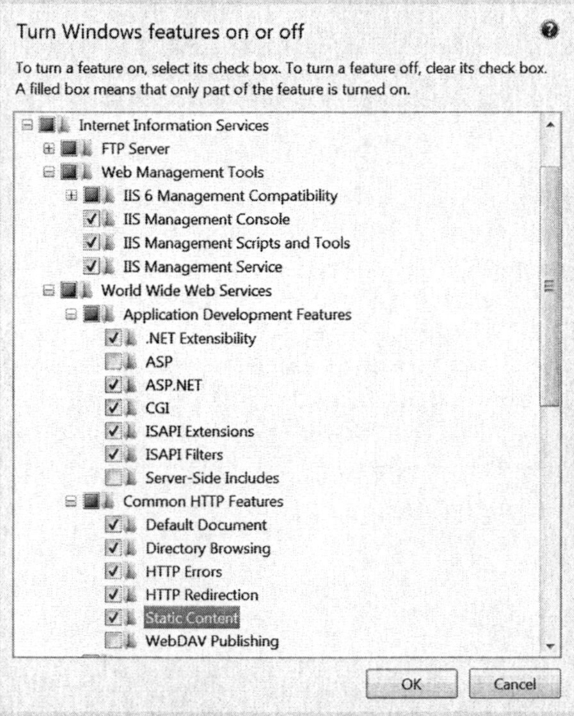

Figure 1.5 Configure Internet Information Services.

6. To accept the pop-ups from the Windows Azure website, you need to configure Internet Explorer (IE) as the following:
   a. In the IE window, click the **Tools** menu, select **Pop-up Blocker**, and then click **Pop-up Blocker Settings**.
   b. In the address bar of the website, type **windows.azure.com**, click **Add**, and then click **Close**.

TASK 2: WINDOWS AZURE SOFTWARE DEVELOPMENT KIT INSTALLATION

After the above preparation, you are now ready to download and install the Windows Azure SDK package with the following steps:

1. The first step is to download the Windows Azure SDK. You can download the Windows Azure SDK from the following website: http://www.microsoft.com/windowsazure/sdk
2. On this website, you can find different versions of SDKs. For full installation, under the label **.NET**, select a version of SDK to install. If Microsoft Visual Studio 2010 is installed on your machine, click **VS 2010** as shown in Figure 1.6. Then, click **Save**.
3. After the package is downloaded, navigate to the **Downloads** directory where the file is downloaded. Then, double click the downloaded file to start the installation process. The installation may take some time.
4. Now that the SDK is installed. You should have a new item related to the Windows Azure SDK as shown in Figure 1.7.

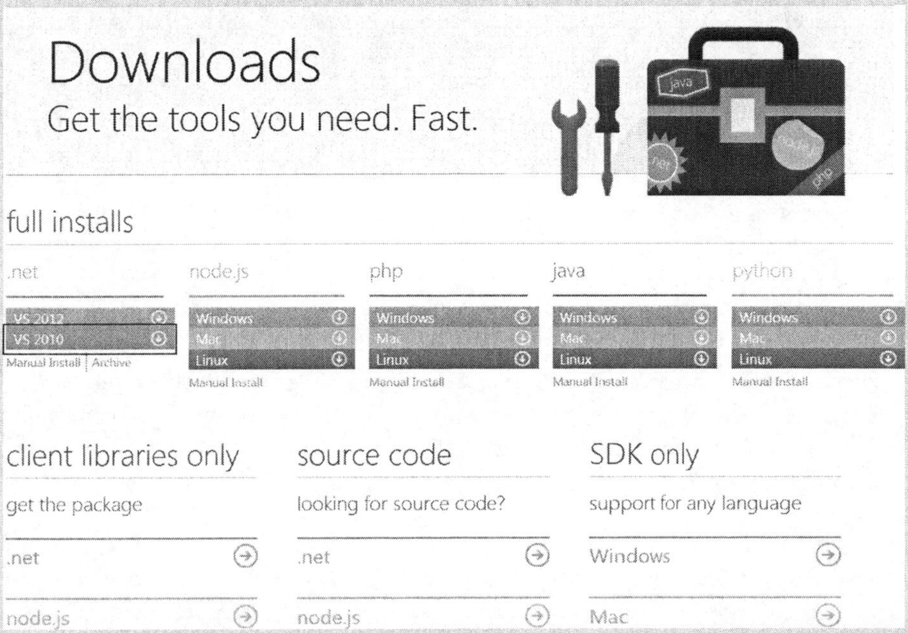

Figure 1.6 Download SDK installation package.

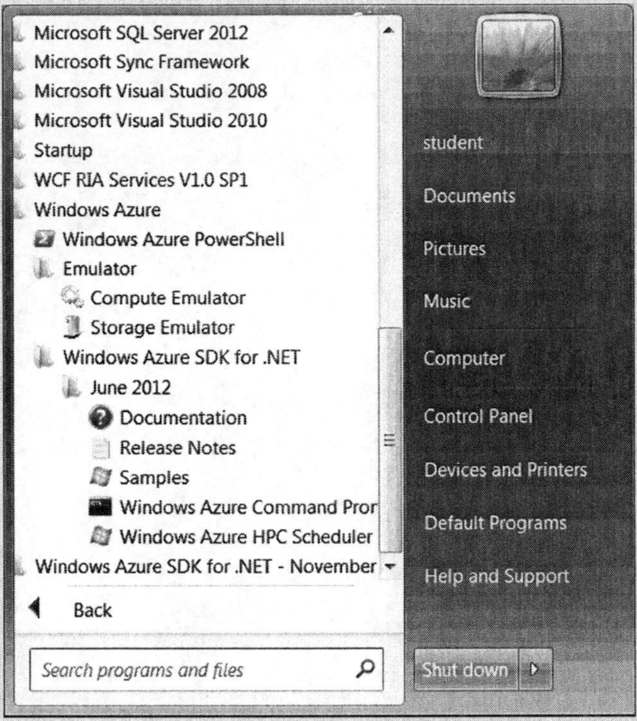

Figure 1.7 Packages installed.

5. After the installation process is completed, to test the SDK, click **Start, All Programs**, and expand the **Microsoft Visual Studio 2010** node. Right click **Microsoft Visual Studio 2010** and select **Run as administrator.** After Microsoft Visual Studio is opened, click **File, New Project,** and click **Cloud** under the Visual C# node. In the Templates pane, you should be able to see **Windows Azure Project** as shown in Figure 1.8. Click **Cancel** to exit.
6. You can now start SQL Server Management Studio (SSMS). To do so, click **Start, All Programs, SQL Server 2012**, and **SQL Server 2012 Management Studio.** After the Connect to Server dialog is opened, in the **Server name** dropdown list, select the server on your local server as shown in Figure 1.9. (On your computer, the name of the SQL server will be different.) Select **Windows Authentication** as the method of authentication. After the server name is selected, click the **Connect** button.
7. You should be able to log on to SSMS as shown in Figure 1.10.
8. By default, the database named master is installed for database management. Expand the **Databases** node and double click **master.** You should be able to see the database objects such as Tables, Views, and Programmability. In addition, Microsoft SQL Server also includes Service Broker, Storage, Security, Users, Roles, Schemas, and Symmetric Keys.

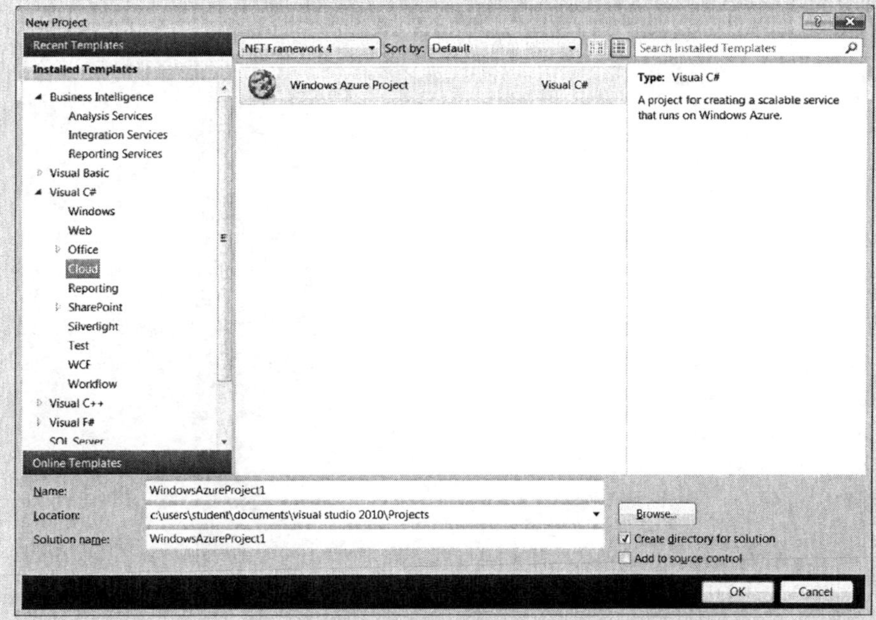

Figure 1.8 Visual Studio.

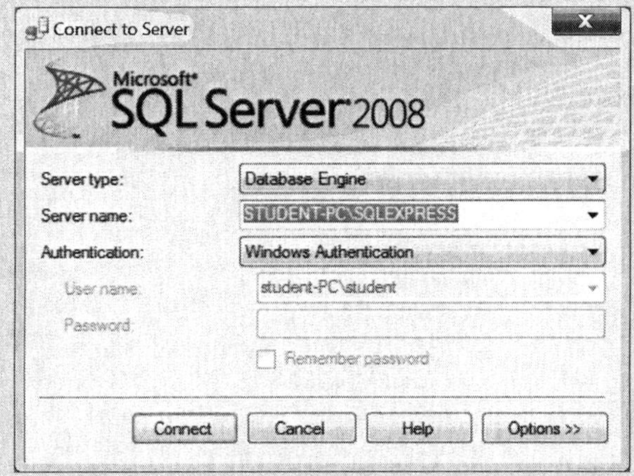

Figure 1.9 Connect to Server Dialog.

Service Broker: Service Broker provides messaging services. It can be used to let applications send and receive messages among multiple SQL Server instances. The components of Service Broker are given in Figure 1.11.

Storage: Storage contains Full Text Catalogs for storing Full Text indexes, Partition Schemes for mapping partitions to a set of filegroups, and Partition Functions for mapping tables or indexes into partitions. The components of Storage are given in Figure 1.11.

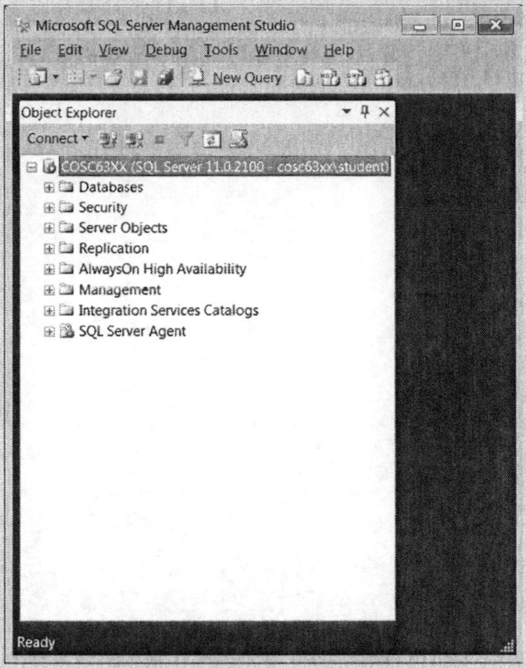

Figure 1.10 Microsoft SQL Server Management Studio.

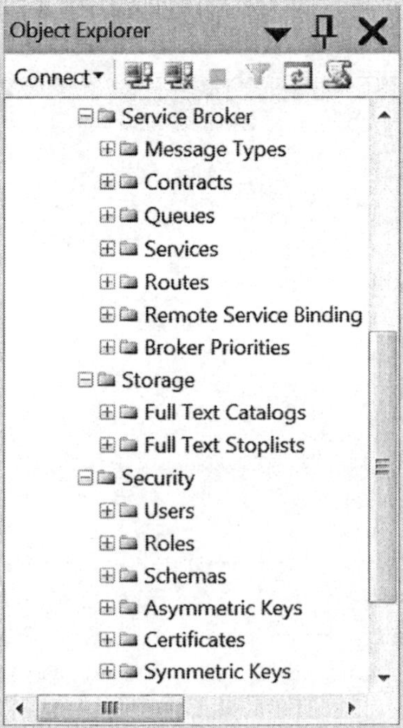

Figure 1.11 Service Broker, Storage, and Security.

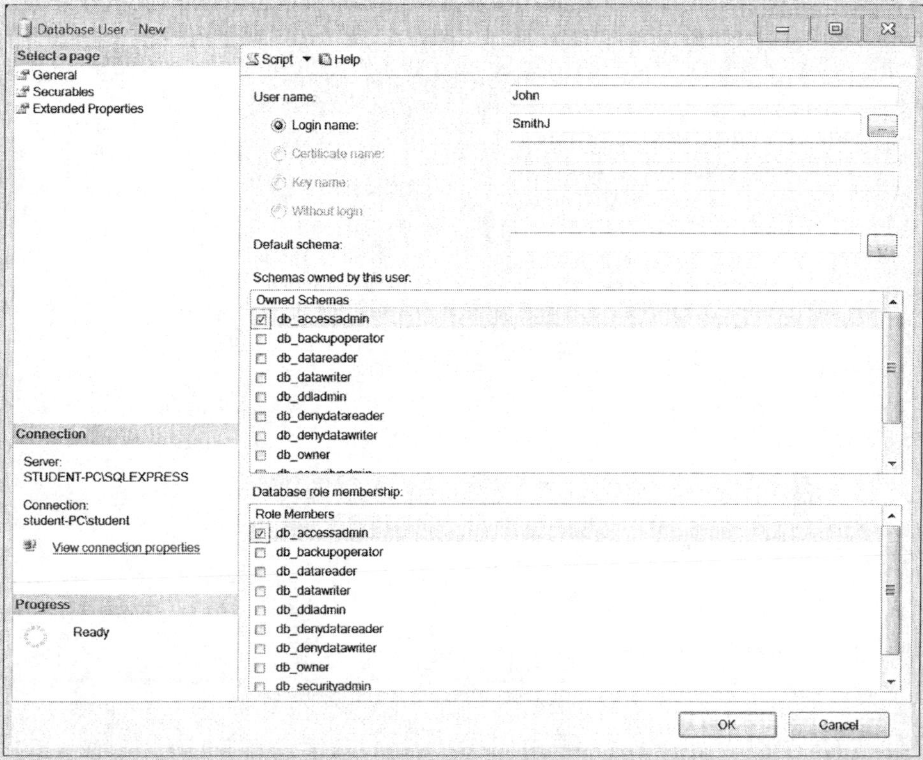

Figure 1.12 Database user.

Security: With Security, you can configure database security measures for databases. The main security components are Users, Roles, Schemas, and Symmetric Keys.

Users: The Users object defines users in a database. It is used to create user accounts. A user account is created to identify each individual user. A user can access his/her account with his/her user name and password. After logging on to a database, the user can access database objects with properly assigned ownership and permissions. You can grant and modify permissions on objects in a database for users with this component. The user configuration for a new user is shown in Figure 1.12.

Roles: The Roles object allows you to group users with the same set of permissions. Roles can be used to simplify administrative tasks. For example, when modifying permissions, instead of changing the permissions for each individual user, you can modify the permissions for the role. Once the role's permissions are changed, the permissions for all the users with the same role will be modified automatically. When a group of users perform the same kind of job, you should assign these users to the same role and then configure the same set of permissions to the role. Figure 1.13 shows the configuration of a role.

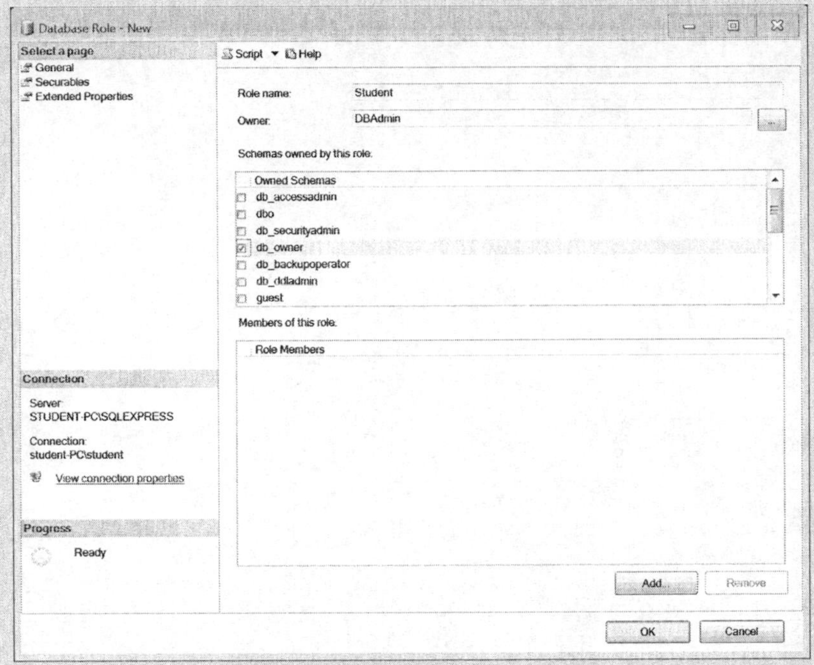

Figure 1.13 Database role.

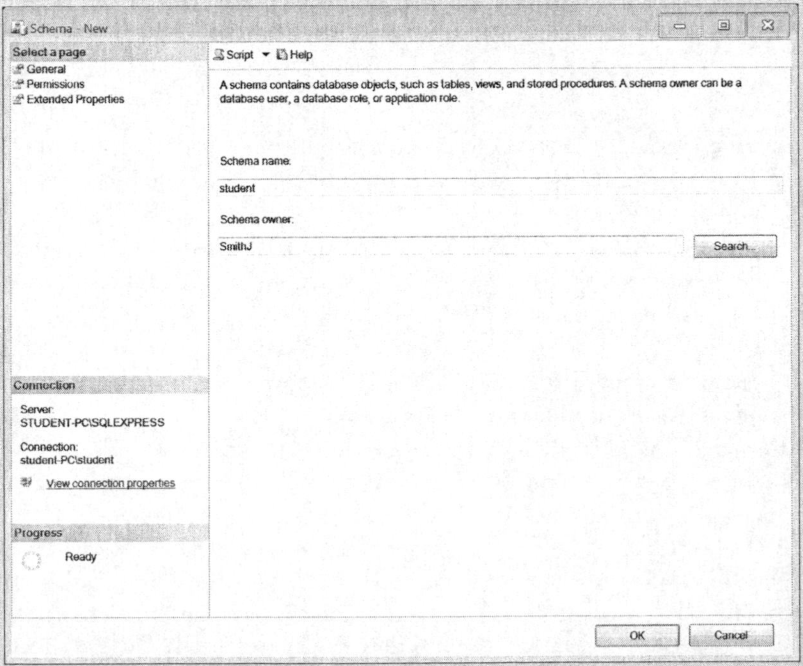

Figure 1.14 Schema.

Schemas: The Schemas component is a container that includes a set of database objects. A schema can have its own set of permissions. A database user can own several schemas. In contrast, you can assign several users to the same schema. If a database user is not assigned a schema, the default schema for the user is dbo (database owner). Figure 1.14 shows the configuration of a schema.

Symmetric Keys: This component is used to configure symmetric keys for encryption.

9. Click **File** and **Exit**. At this point, your installation is completed.

ACTIVITY 1.2 WINDOWS AZURE SOFTWARE DEVELOPMENT KIT INSTALLATION ON WINDOWS SERVER 2012

For those who prefer to use Windows Server 2012 to host SQL Server 2012 and Visual Student 2012, the following provides instruction for installing the Windows Azure SDK on a virtual machine. Windows Server 2012 can be installed on a PC with a minimum of 1 GB RAM and a 30 GB hard drive. Or, one can simply create a virtual machine on Windows Azure. With the 3-month free trial Windows Azure account, you can create a virtual machine with Windows Server 2012 installed. You are able to log on to the virtual machine anywhere and anytime through the Internet. By using the virtual machine, you do not have to spend money for a PC and network hardware.

TASK 1: CREATING VIRTUAL MACHINE ON WINDOWS AZURE

To create a virtual machine on Windows Azure, follow the steps below:

1. Log on to your Windows Azure Management Portal through the following URL: http://widows.azure.com
2. Once you have logged on to the Windows Azure Management Portal, click **VIRTUAL MACHINES** and then **NEW** as shown in Figure 1.15.
3. After the virtual machines page is opened, click **FROM GALLERY** as shown in Figure 1.16.
4. On the Virtual machine operating system selection page, click **Windows Server 2012** as shown in Figure 1.17 and then click the **Next** arrow.
5. On the virtual machine configuration page, enter your virtual machine name, the password for administrator, and the size of your virtual machine as shown in Figure 1.18. The small size is adequate for the hands-on activities in this book. Then, click the **Next** arrow.

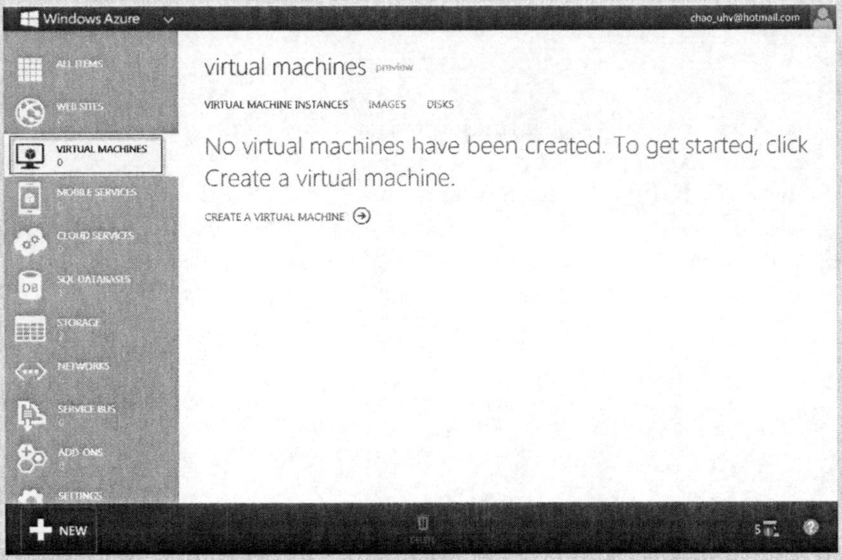

Figure 1.15 Create new virtual machine.

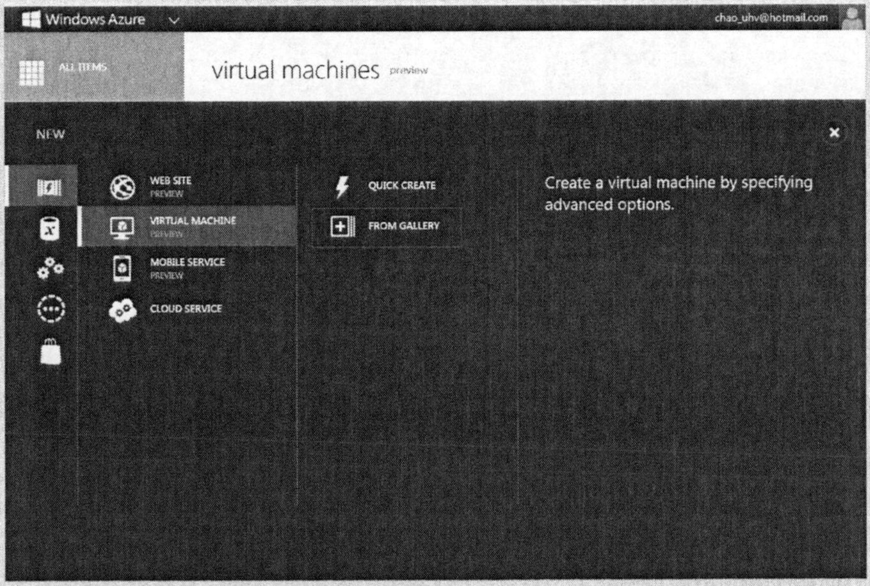

Figure 1.16 Create virtual machine from gallery.

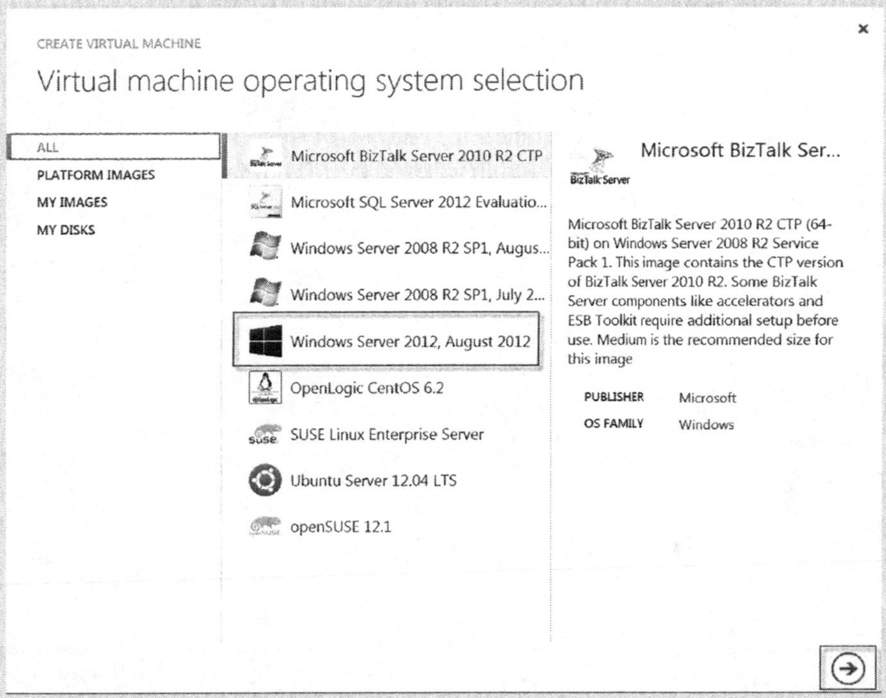

Figure 1.17 Select operating system.

6. On the Virtual machine mode page, specify **DNS NAME**, **STORAGE ACCOUNT**, and **REGION/AFFINITY GROUP/VIRTUAL NETWORK** as shown in Figure 1.19. Then, click the **Next** arrow.
7. On the Virtual machine option page, click the check mark at the lower-right corner to create the virtual machine.
8. After the virtual machine is created, click the **CONNECT** link at the bottom of your screen as shown in Figure 1.20. Enter the password for Administrator and then click **OK** to log on to the virtual machine.

TASK 2: PREPARING FOR INSTALLING WINDOWS AZURE SDK

1. Since the Windows Server 2012 installed on the virtual machine is only the core, it can be managed with the Windows PowerShell command line tool. However, for beginners, the graphic user interface (GUI) may be more intuitive. To install the GUI, start Windows PowerShell by clicking the Windows PowerShell icon at the bottom

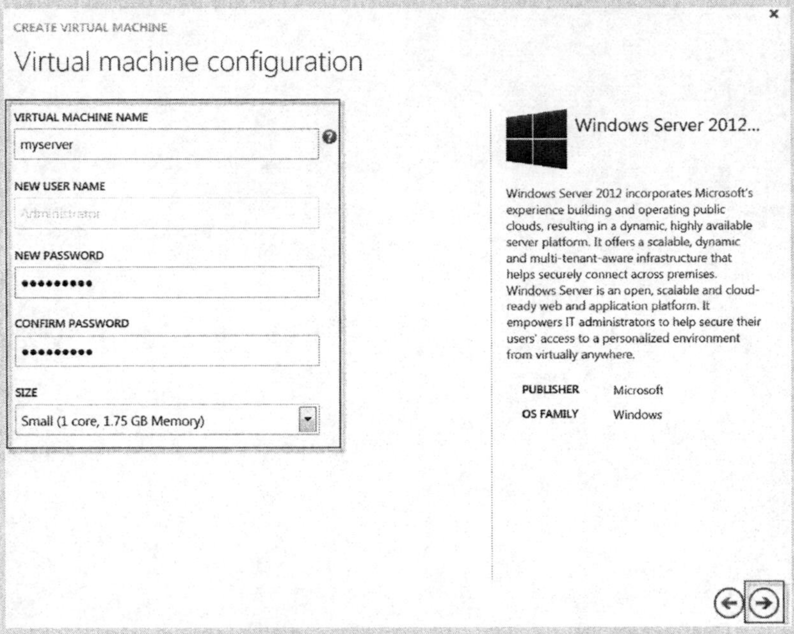
CREATE VIRTUAL MACHINE
Virtual machine configuration
VIRTUAL MACHINE NAME
myserver
NEW USER NAME
Administrator
NEW PASSWORD
CONFIRM PASSWORD
SIZE
Small (1 core, 1.75 GB Memory)
Windows Server 2012...
Windows Server 2012 incorporates Microsoft's experience building and operating public clouds, resulting in a dynamic, highly available server platform. It offers a scalable, dynamic and multi-tenant-aware infrastructure that helps securely connect across premises. Windows Server is an open, scalable and cloud-ready web and application platform. It empowers IT administrators to help secure their users' access to a personalized environment from virtually anywhere.
PUBLISHER Microsoft
OS FAMILY Windows

Figure 1.18 Configure virtual machine.

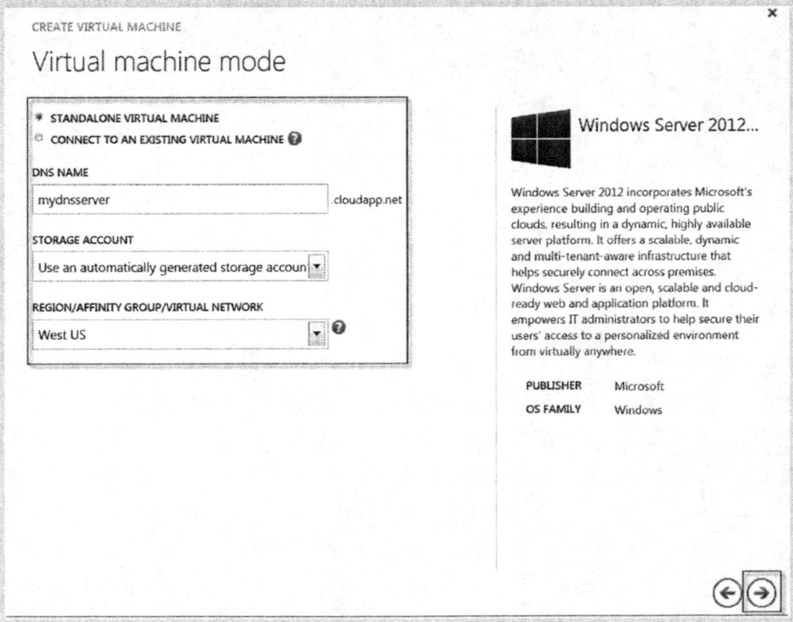
CREATE VIRTUAL MACHINE
Virtual machine mode
STANDALONE VIRTUAL MACHINE
CONNECT TO AN EXISTING VIRTUAL MACHINE
DNS NAME
mydnsserver
.cloudapp.net
STORAGE ACCOUNT
Use an automatically generated storage accoun
REGION/AFFINITY GROUP/VIRTUAL NETWORK
West US
Windows Server 2012...
Windows Server 2012 incorporates Microsoft's experience building and operating public clouds, resulting in a dynamic, highly available server platform. It offers a scalable, dynamic and multi-tenant-aware infrastructure that helps securely connect across premises. Windows Server is an open, scalable and cloud-ready web and application platform. It empowers IT administrators to help secure their users' access to a personalized environment from virtually anywhere.
PUBLISHER Microsoft
OS FAMILY Windows

Figure 1.19 Configure virtual machine mode.

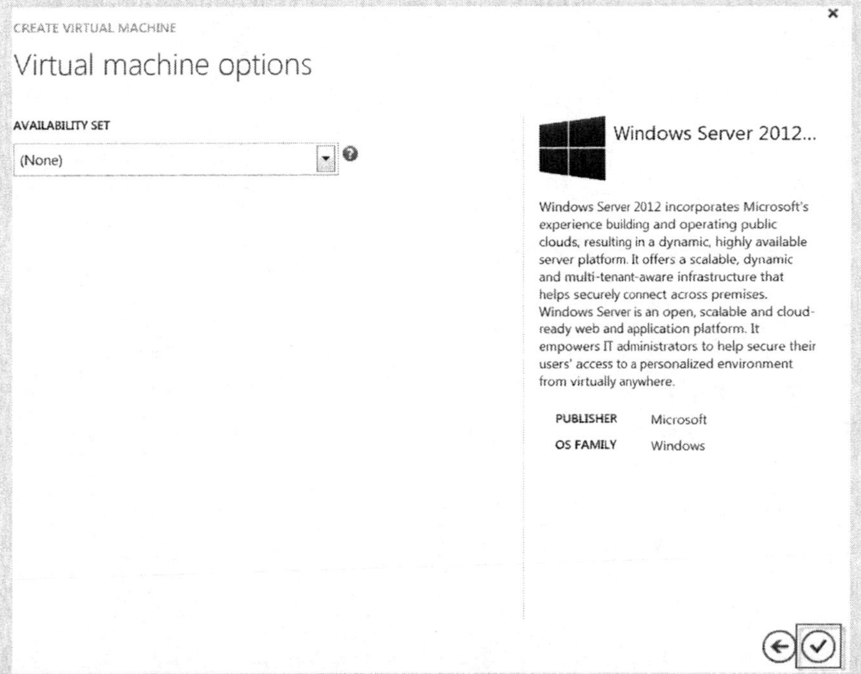
CREATE VIRTUAL MACHINE
Virtual machine options
AVAILABILITY SET
(None)
Windows Server 2012...
Windows Server 2012 incorporates Microsoft's experience building and operating public clouds, resulting in a dynamic, highly available server platform. It offers a scalable, dynamic and multi-tenant-aware infrastructure that helps securely connect across premises. Windows Server is an open, scalable and cloud-ready web and application platform. It empowers IT administrators to help secure their users' access to a personalized environment from virtually anywhere.
PUBLISHER
Microsoft
OS FAMILY
Windows

Figure 1.20 Log on to virtual machine.

of your screen. When the Windows PowerShell window is opened, run the following commands.

```
Import-Module Dism

Enable-WindowsOptionalFeature -online -Featurename ServerCore-
FullServer,Server-Gui-Shell,Server-Gui-Mgmt
```

2. You may also need to get on the Internet to download the iso files for the installation of SQL Server 2012 and Visual Studio 2012. To enable Internet Explorer 10 (IE10), run the following command in Windows PowerShell.

```
dism/online/Disable-Feature/FeatureName:Internet-Explorer-
Optional-amd64
```

3. After IE10 is enabled, you may need to temporarily turn off IE Enhanced Security Configuration to make the download process go smoothly. To do so, click **Local Server** in Server Manager. Then, click **IE Enhanced Security Configuration form On** and check the option **Off** for **Administrators** as shown in Figure 1.21. Then, click **OK**.
4. To open the IE, press the combination key **Ctrl + Esc** to view the desktop tile as shown in Figure 1.22. You can also view the desktop tile by pressing the **Windows logo** key or hovering the mouse cursor over the upper right corner of the screen, and then clicking the **Start** menu.

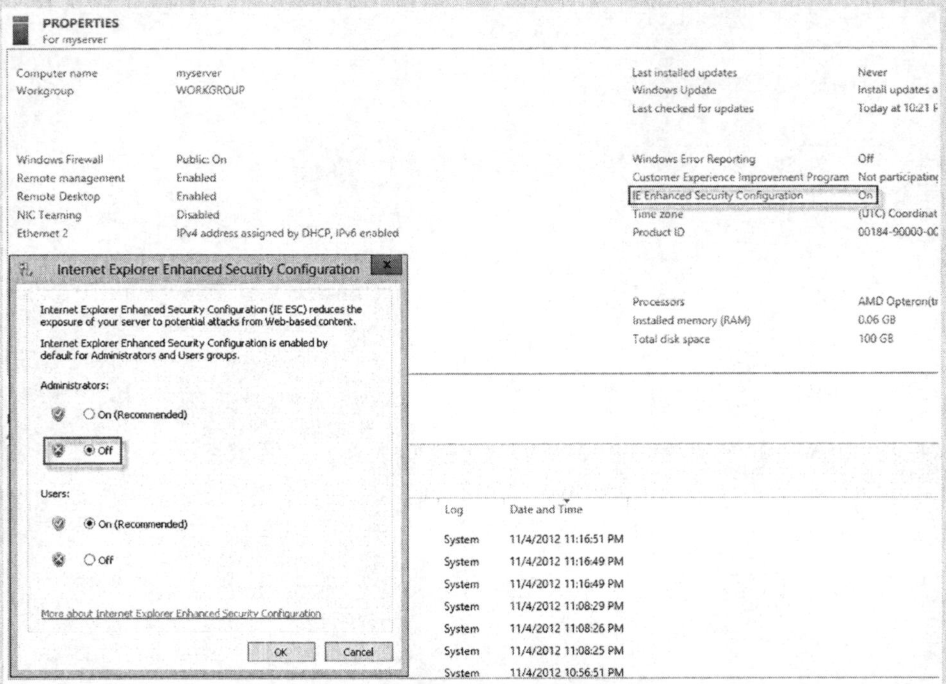

Figure 1.21 Turn off IE Enhanced Security Configuration.

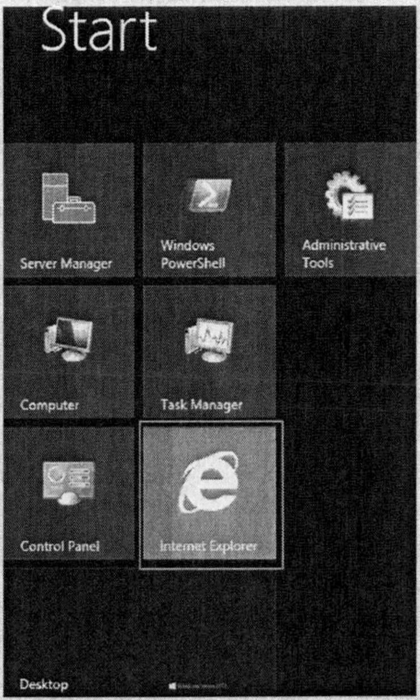

Figure 1.22 Start menu.

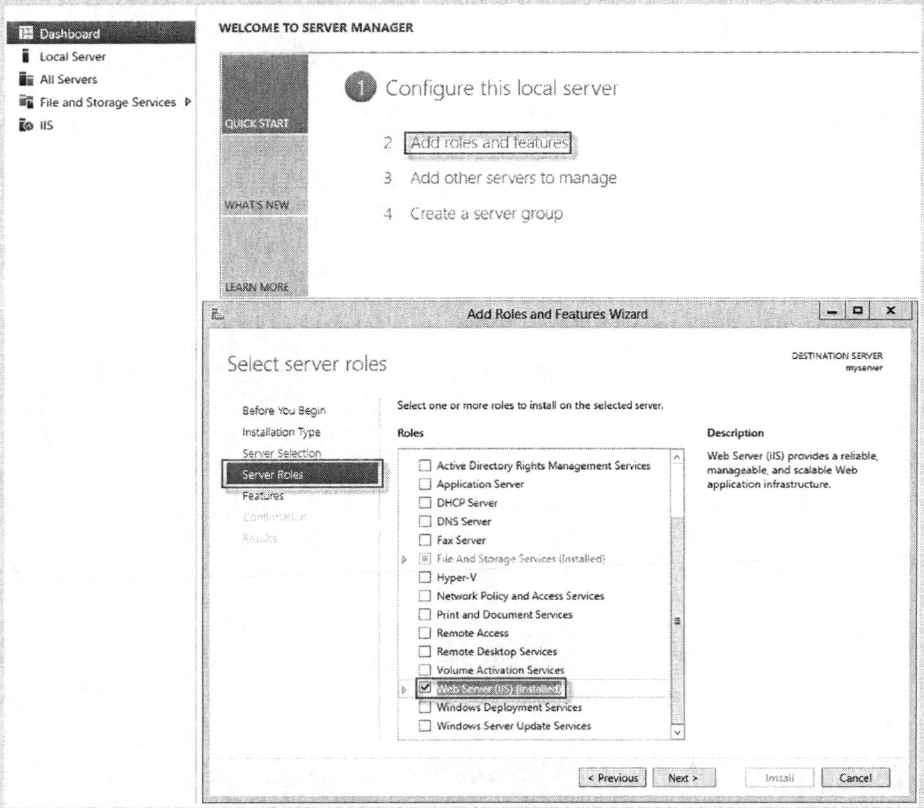

Figure 1.23 Configure IIS.

5. Click the IE icon to start the web browser. From the web browser, you can download the SQL Server 2012 and Visual Studio 2012 installation files. Since the size of the default C drive for a small virtual machine is 30 GB, you should move the downloaded files to the D drive, so you can have more space on the C drive.
6. As in Activity 1.1, you will need to configure IIS. To do so, click the Server Manager icon at the bottom of your screen. In Server Manager, click **Add Roles and Features** and select **Web Server (IIS)** in **Server Roles** as shown in Figure 1.23.
7. Click **Next** to go to the **Select features** page. Make sure that **.NET Framework 3.5 Features** and **.NET Framework 4.5 Features** are checked as shown in Figure 1.24.
8. Click **Next** a few times to go to the **Select role services** page. Check the services as shown in Figure 1.25. Then, click **Next** to the end of the configuration.

TASK 3: INSTALLING WINDOWS AZURE SDK

1. To install the Windows Azure SDK, browse the website http://www.microsoft.com/windowsazure/sdk as shown in Figure 1.26 and select **VS 2012**. Then, click **Run** to install the SDK package.

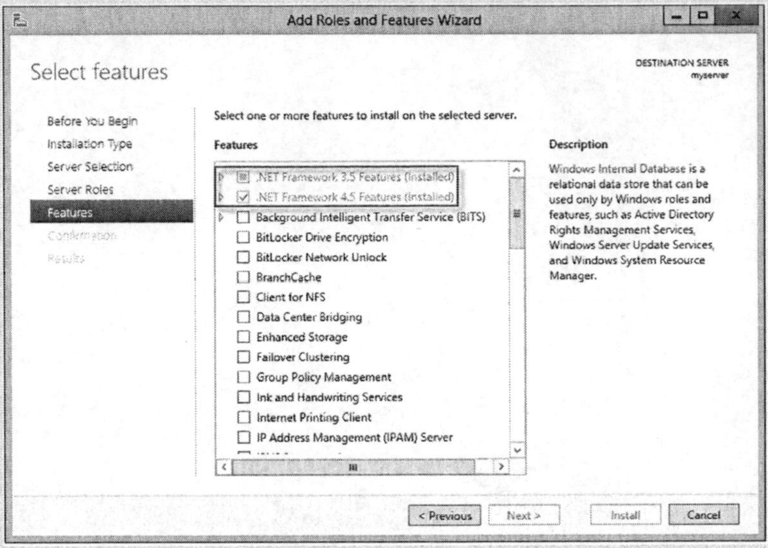

Figure 1.24 Select features to install.

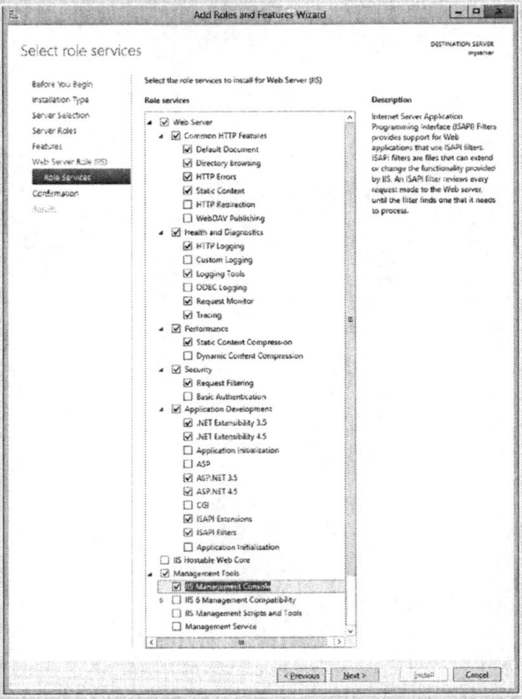

Figure 1.25 Configure IIS features.

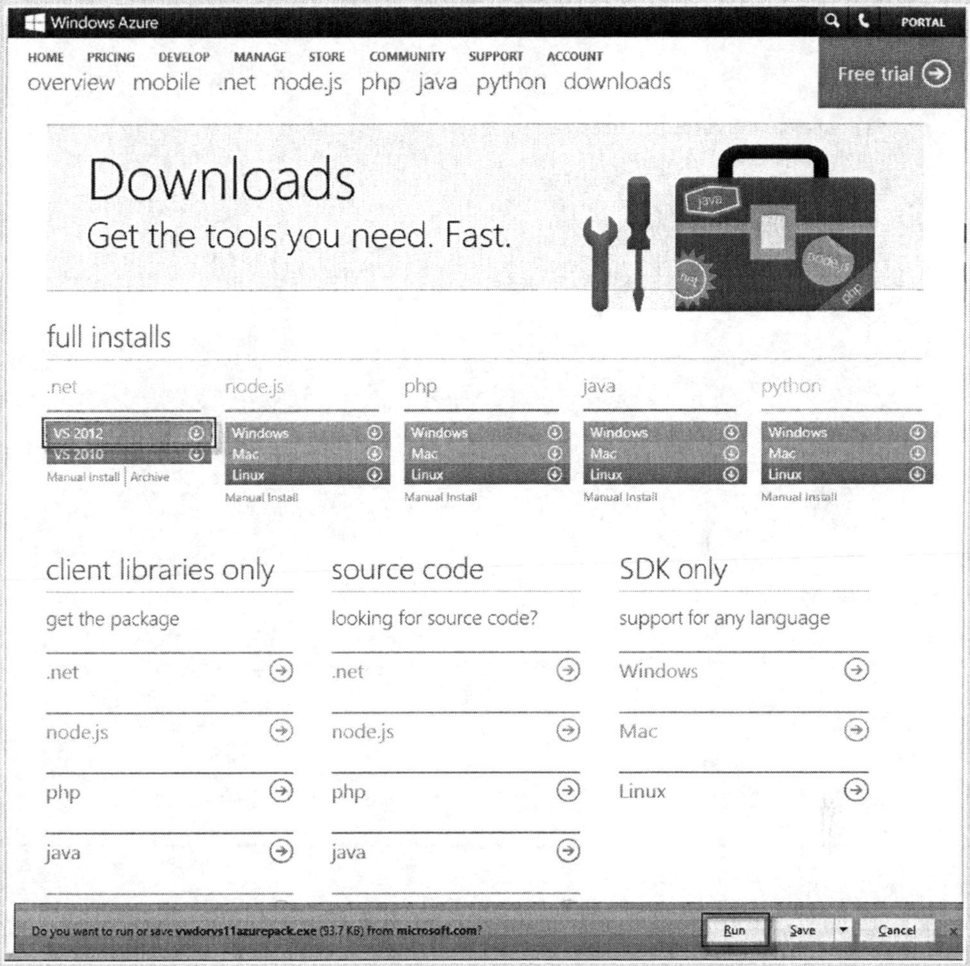

Figure 1.26 Install Windows Azure SDK for VS 2012.

2. After the SDK package is installed, you can also install some tools such as Windows Azure PowerShell.
3. After the installation, you should be able to see the installed items on your server's desktop tile as shown in Figure 1.27.

In this activity, you have installed the Windows Azure SDK on a virtual machine provided by Windows Azure. The virtual machine can be used as the on-premises server to communicate with Windows Azure SQL Database. Starting from next chapter, our focus will be on the developing databases in Windows Azure SQL Database.

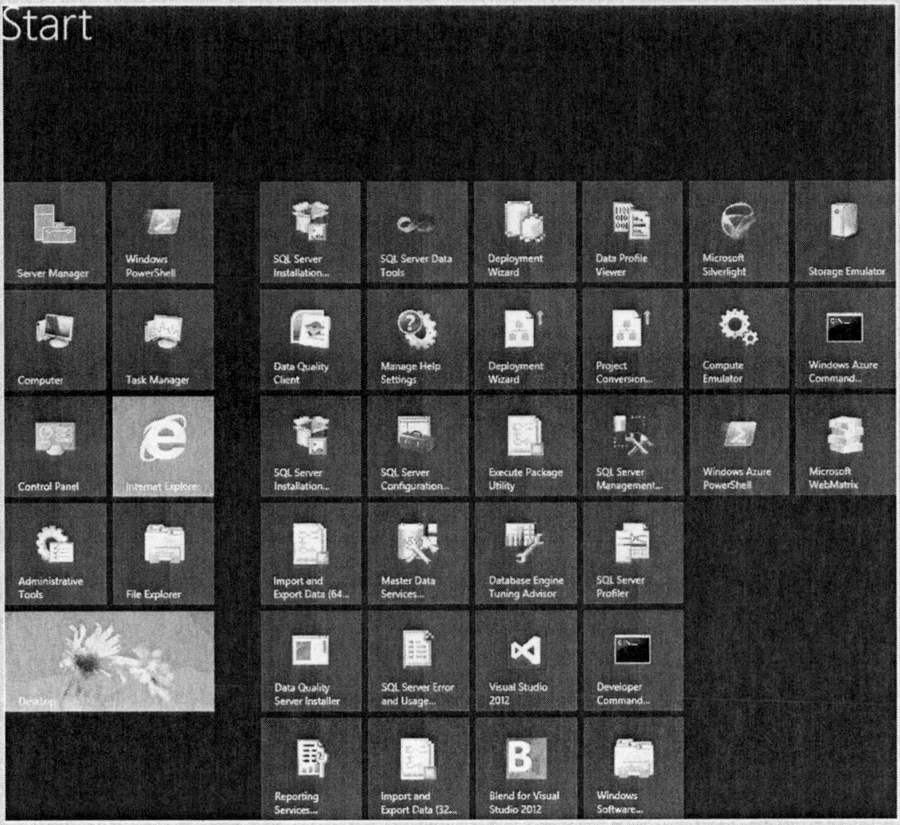

Figure 1.27 Software installed.

1.6 Summary

This chapter provides a general picture of a database system. It explains the role played by a database in a business process. It introduces several DBMS packages. It also describes the components of a DBMS, including tables, views, stored procedures, triggers, functions, schemas, roles, and users. An overview of the major steps in a database development process was given in this chapter. The role of cloud computing in database development is also described. This chapter introduces three types of clouds and four types of cloud services. The last section of this chapter provides some hands-on activities on the installation of the Windows Azure SDK.

Review Questions

1. What is a database?
2. Describe the advantages of SQL Server.
3. Name the items included in Server Components.

4. Name the items included in SQL Server Management Tools.
5. What objects are included in a database?
6. Describe tables and their structures.
7. What is a view in a database?
8. What is a database trigger?
9. What are the major steps in database development?
10. Name three types of cloud computing platforms.
11. Describe the advantages and disadvantages of the private cloud.
12. How can a small business benefit from the public cloud?
13. What are the concerns about public cloud?
14. Name four types of cloud services?
15. What service can SaaS provide?
16. What service can PaaS provide?
17. What service can IaaS provide?
18. Give two examples of SaaS.
19. Give two examples of PaaS.
20. Give two examples of the personal cloud.

Chapter 2

Database Design and Windows Azure Data Storage

Objectives

- Become familiar with relational databases
- Understand database design and data modeling
- Learn how to use database development tools

2.1 Introduction

As the center of an information system, a database is used to store and manage data generated by day-to-day business processes. As pointed out by many experienced information system professionals, if a database is not carefully designed, it will cause chaos for an entire enterprise. In many cases, it may be too difficult to make changes in database structures after a database is populated with terabytes or even petabytes of data. Therefore, we must take database design seriously.

A well-built database should meet the needs of business requirements. To achieve the goal, a database designer needs to investigate the database requirements and to structure database objects to meet the requirements. These tasks can be accomplished through a database design process, which includes the phases of conceptual design, database design, and physical design. The flowchart in Figure 2.1 lists the activities in each design phase.

The definition of conceptual design, database design, and physical design may vary from one author to another. In the flowchart (Figure 2.1), we consider the logical design phase as software-independent and the physical design phase as software-dependent. The detailed description of each phase is given in the following sections.

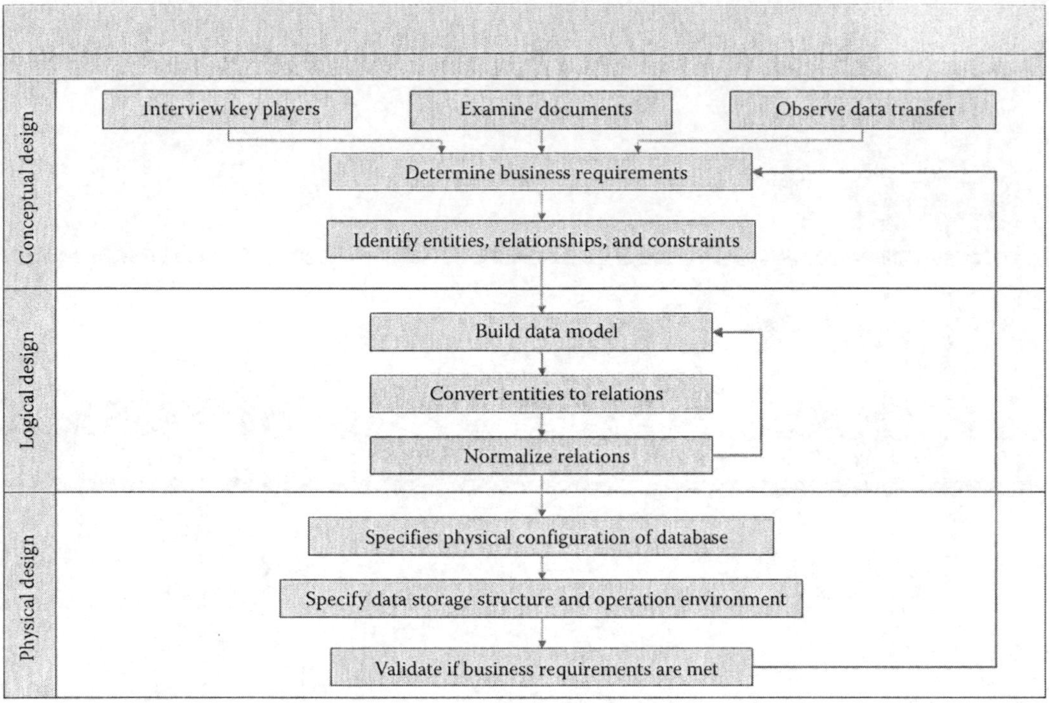

Figure 2.1 Database design process.

2.2 Database Conceptual Design

Since the goal of database design is to meet the business requirements, clearly identifying the business needs is the key to success. In this section, several methods that you can use for your investigation are introduced.

First, let us list the information that needs to be collected during the investigation. We should focus on the objects whose information needs to be stored in a database. For example, the objects involved in a class registration process may be student, professor, class, and classroom. The following is the object information we want to collect:

- The objects to keep track of
- The attributes describing the objects
- The type and amount of data associated with the objects
- The relationships among the objects
- The business rules imposed on the objects
- The roles played by the objects in the business process

The following are commonly used methods to collect the information listed above:

- Interview the key players who are involved in the business process. Find out what works and what does not in the current business process, the requirements for the future database, and what the motivation is for developing the new database. A successful interview depends on careful preparation and good interpersonal and communication skills.

- Observe how data are used in a business process. Use a flowchart to document the transactions of data in the business process. Data transaction flowcharts are helpful in implementing database activities later.
- Examine the company's documents about its business process. For example, the currently used forms and reports are a good source. The company's documents also provide information about the business rules. You can also find useful information from existing spreadsheets, database backups, and security measures imposed on the business process.

To illustrate the information collection process, a case study on information collection is given below.

2.2.1 Interview Key Players

As an example, let us consider the class registration process for Jackson University. Currently, Jackson University's registration office is still using the traditional way for class registration. The office is planning to provide an online registration system to replace the current paper-based registration system. To keep track of student and class information, a database must be developed to support the online registration system. As a database designer, you are asked to collect the requirements for the future database.

The investigation starts with interviewing key players: students, registration clerks, registration director, and faculty members involved in the business process. The following are the key players' responses.

Registration Director: Currently, students have to drive to campus to register for classes. Jackson University is located in a rural area. Some students may have to travel over 100 miles for class registration. An online registration system will greatly help those students. The registration records are currently stored in a file cabinet. The registration information is also partially stored in an Access database, which is created on a personal computer. The Access database is less secure and does not have enough room to hold a lot of information. Each semester, we need to print thousands of copies of new class schedules; this costs us a lot of money. We want the new database to be able to support online registration, to be more secure, and to store all the information we want to keep track of.

Registration Clerks: The paper-based registration is not efficient. Manually entering tons of students' information into the personal computer is tedious. We would like to have electronic forms so that information entered by students can be directly saved to the database. Our current Access database can only store limited student information. We would like our next database to store all the registration-related information, including courses, classes, classrooms, class schedules, students, and professors.

Students: The current registration system is not convenient for us. Some of us have to drive for hours for registration. We have to search for class information through various printed materials that are only available on campus. On registration days, there could be hundreds of students waiting in line for registration. An online registration system is really what we need.

Faculty Members: We would like to use the online registration system to obtain information about our advisees and the settings of our classes.

2.2.2 Observe How Data Are Used in Business Processes

First, a student needs to find a class that is offered next semester by searching the class schedule. The student may also need to check the course catalog to learn about the course content and

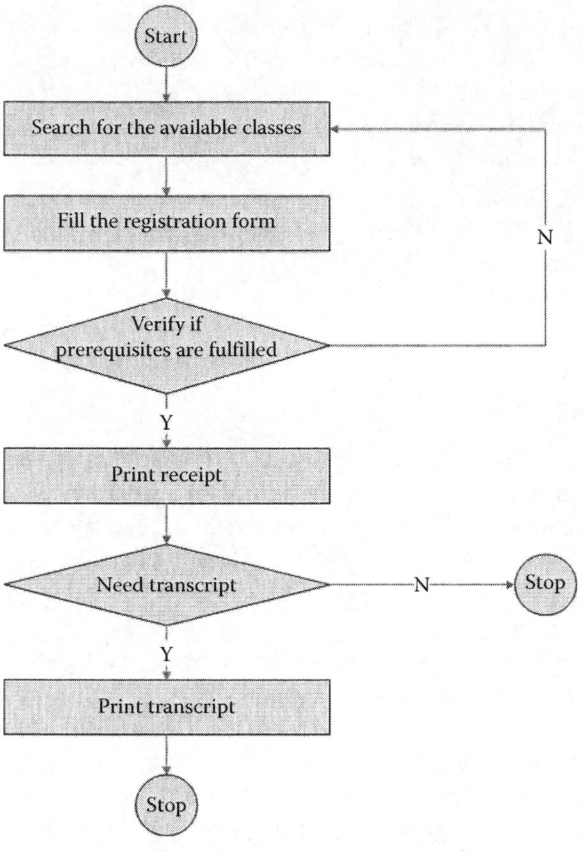

Figure 2.2 Class registration process.

prerequisites. Once the student decides which classes to take, she/he needs to fill the class registration form and submit the form to one of the registration office clerks who will verify if the prerequisites have been fulfilled and if there are seats available for that class. After it is confirmed, the office clerk registers the student, prints the registration information, and places the registration form alphabetically in the file cabinet. When students ask for their transcripts, the clerks will print transcripts including the information about the classes and the grades. The accumulated GPAs earned by the students are also included in the transcripts. The business process is demonstrated by the flowchart in Figure 2.2.

2.2.3 Examine Documents Used in Business Processes

For learning purposes, let us look at a simplified version of documents used in the registration (see Tables 2.1 through 2.5). Before the registration process begins, the class schedule will be available for students to review the classes offered for the new semester.

For detailed information about a course, the students can either talk to their advisors or check the course catalog shown in Table 2.2.

If a student has decided which classes to take, he/she will fill out the form shown in Table 2.3 for class registration.

Table 2.1 Class Schedule

Class ID	*Course Name*	*Class Time*	*Instructor*	*Room/Building*
1000	Visual Basic	1:00–4:00 pm, M	Smith	103 West
1001	Database	4:00–7:00 pm, T	Lee	105/109 South
1002	E-Commerce	1:00–4:00 pm, W	Smith/Lee	206 North
1003	Database	7:00–10:00 pm, M	Garza	103/121 West
1004	Info-Systems	1:00–4:00 pm, TH	Fry	Online
1005	Visual Basic	4:00–7:00 pm, TH	Fry	201 East
1006	Database	1:00–4:00 pm, W	Smith	206/109 South

Table 2.2 Course Catalog

ISC 2301 Visual Basic (Prerequisite: None) *Credits: 3* An introduction to Visual Basic programming; topics include variables, data types, control structures, arrays, object-oriented programming, GUI, and database access.
ISC 3311 Database (Prerequisite: ISC2301) *Credits: 3* An introduction to database systems; topics include database design and implementation, SQL programming, database access, and database management.
ISC 3321 Info-Systems (Prerequisite: ISC3311) *Credits: 3* An introduction to information systems; topics include IS functions and structures, decision theory, and system design and application.
ISC 4301 E-Commerce (Prerequisite: ISC3311) *Credits: 3* An introduction to electronic commerce; topics include architecture of web-based computing, data communication over the Internet, XML and script languages, and web database.

Table 2.3 Class Registration Form

Student Information:	
Student ID: 10	Major: CIS
First Name: Liz	Last Name: Smith
Signature:______	
Class Information:	
Class ID: 1002	Semester: Fall08
Course ID: ISC4301	Prerequisite: ISC3311
Class Information:	
Class ID: 1004	Semester: Fall08
Course ID: ISC3321	Prerequisite: ISC3311

Table 2.4 Class Registration Receipt

Student ID: 10 The following classes have been registered:	
Class ID	*Course ID*
1004	ISC3321
1002	ISC4301

Table 2.5 Transcript

Student ID: 10 First Name: Liz Last Name: Smith		
Semester: Spring07		
Course ID:	Course Name:	Grade:
ISC2301	VB	A
	Semester Average: 4.0	
Semester: Summer07		
Course ID:	Course Name:	Grade:
ISC3311	Database	B
	Semester Average: 3.0	
Semester: Fall07		
Course ID:	Course Name:	Grade:
ISC3321	Info-Systems	
ISC4301	E-Commerce	
	Semester Average	
Grade Accumulate Average: 3.5		

The registration clerks will verify that the prerequisites are satisfied. If a prerequisite is not satisfied or a class is full, the student will be asked to choose a different class. If the registration is confirmed, the student will get a receipt like the one shown in Table 2.4.

The class id is necessary since the same course may be taught in more than one class. If asked by the student, the registration clerk will print the transcript in the format shown in Table 2.5.

After the information is collected, the next task is to extract the useful components for the database design.

2.2.4 Analyze Collected Information

To identify the information that is useful for designing the database, the analysis will focus on the following areas.

Identify objects to keep track of: From the class schedule, we can identify the objects: **class, class time, classroom, building, instructor**, and **course**. Both the Class Registration Form and Transcript indicate that the **student** and **semester** objects should also be included. By examining the results of the interviews and the observation of the registration process, those are the objects to keep track of.

Identify specifications of objects: Let us examine each of the objects identified in the above step.

- **Class**: According to the class schedule, a class can be described by its ID, the course content to be covered in this class, the class meeting time, the instructor, and the classroom. The middle section of the Transcript gives more description about the **class** object. There, a class is described by its course ID, course name, and the student's grade.
- **Course**: Course catalog indicates that we can use course ID, credit, prerequisite, and course description to describe the **course** object.
- **Classroom and Building**: From the class schedule, a classroom can be specified by its number and the name of the building. By observing how data are used in a business process, we should also include the capacity of the classroom as the attribute of the **classroom** object. The **building** object can be described by its ID and name.
- **Student**: From the Transcript, the object **student** can be described by the ID, first name, and last name. The Class Registration Form also shows the student's major, which is also a characteristic of the student.
- **Faculty**: In the class schedule, the object **instructor** is described by the last name. Through the interviews, we found out that the faculty members need to be related to their advisees. It is better to describe a faculty member by both the last name and the first name so that it is easier for advisees to identify their advisors in case some professors have the same last name. From the course catalog, you can find which department a professor belongs to.
- **Class Time**: The object **class time** is specified by time blocks and weekdays as shown in the class schedule.
- **Semester**: According the Class Registration Form and Transcript, this object can be described by its name.

Identify type and amount of data: Let us check the type of data used in each object.

- For the **class** object, the class ID can be the integer data type. The class time, course name, instructor, and grade can all be character strings. Each semester, there may be hundreds of classes scheduled. The data accumulated for many years of classes can add up to a significant number.
- For the **student** object, the student ID is the integer type. The first name, last name, and major can be described by character strings. Hundreds or even thousands of new students may be added to the **student** table each semester. The growth rate of data for this object is high.
- For the **course** object, the data type for credit can be an integer. The course ID, prerequisite, and course description can all be defined as character strings. The growth rate of data is relatively low. Each year, only some courses are added or modified.

- For the **classroom** and **building** objects, the classroom number and capacity are of the integer type. The building name can be defined as character strings. There are few changes in classrooms and buildings. Therefore, the data increase rate is very low.
- For the **faculty** object, the faculty ID can be the integer type, and the first name and last name should be character strings. The faculty is relatively stable, so its growth rate is low.
- For the **class time** object, time blocks and week days are a set of predefined character strings. The values for these objects are fixed, so there is almost no data growth for this object.
- For the **semester** object, the data type for the semester is defined as character strings. Since semester values need to be accumulated each year, there will be some data growth for this object.

Identify relationships among objects: Our next task is to find out how the objects are related to each other in a business process. Since the class object is related to course, class time, semester, classroom, instructor, and student, we have the relationships Class–Course, Class–Student, Class–Faculty, Class–Time Block, Class–Week Day, Class–Semester, and Class–Classroom. From the interviews, we know that the faculty object is related to the student object. We should have the relationship Faculty–Student. Also, by examining the class schedule, we can see that the relationship Classroom–Building should also be included.

Identify business rules imposed on objects: The university has some rules related to the objects in this database project. These rules will have an impact on the relationships among the objects.

By examining the course catalog, we list the following related rules for our database objects.

- The minimum enrollment for each class is 10 students. If an undergraduate class is <10 students enrolled, the class will be canceled.
- The maximum number of students for a class will depend on the classroom capacity.
- A course may or may not have a prerequisite. Some courses can have the same prerequisite and several prerequisites can be required for one course.
- Credits for each course range from 1 to 12.
- A new student may not be assigned an advisor immediately. Therefore, a student may or may not have an advisor in the database. Each student can only have one advisor and each faculty member can have zero, one, or many advisees.

From the class schedule, the following rules can be observed:

- Two classrooms may have the same number if they located in different buildings. Therefore, when listing classroom information in the class schedule, we are required to attach building names to classrooms.
- Sometimes, one class may need two classrooms. For example, a computer science class may need a classroom for lecture and another classroom for lab.
- A classroom can hold multiple classes scheduled for different time blocks.
- The teaching load for a full-time faculty member is four classes per semester. For example, Smith is teaching multiple classes in the class schedule print out.
- Sometimes, a class may be taught by more than one professor. For example, e-commerce is taught by both Smith and Lee; each teaches the topics from their own research.
- A building may have one or more classrooms.
- Each classroom should have one class at a time. We cannot schedule two classes in the same classroom at the same time.

- Many classes are scheduled in one semester.
- Multiple classes can be scheduled on one weekday.
- Different classes can be scheduled for the same time block but in different classrooms.

From the Transcript, we can obtain the following rules:

- A grade is specified by student ID, semester, and course. Since both semester and course are included in the class information, the student ID and class ID together can be used to find a student's grade from a class.
- Each student can enroll in more than one class. As seen in the sample transcript, Liz enrolled in two classes in fall 2008. By the university' rule, a student can take as many as 21 credit-hour classes per semester.

So far, we have carefully analyzed the results from the interviews, the observation of the registration process, and the examination of the documents. The next step is to logically present the class registration process. This task will be accomplished in the next section.

2.3 Entity–Relationship Data Model

From the above analysis, we have found that the registration office wants to store the information of the objects student, class, course, timeblock, weekday, semester, classroom, building, and faculty. Before you can physically build a database to store the information, you should first draw a sketch, also called data model, to represent the database. It is similar to first drawing a blueprint of a house before you can physically build it. A data model consists of logical representations of the objects and the relationships among these objects. You can use the data model to verify that the new database will meet the business requirements. If changes on the database structure are needed, it is much easier to do it on the data model. Once a database is built and populated with data, it is much harder to make any change on the database structure.

Since the 1970s, several data modeling tools have been developed. One of the widely used modeling tools is the entity–relationship model (E–R model) introduced by Peter Chen in 1976. The E–R data model consists of entities, attributes, and relationships to represent the logical structure of a database. Another widely used modeling tool is unified modeling language (UML), which includes components such as classes, attributes, and operations.

2.3.1 Integration Definition for Information Modeling

Before we develop an E–R data model, we will first become familiar with the components of the E–R model. An E–R model can be represented by several ways. One of the commonly used E–R model representations is the **Integration Definition for Information Modeling (IDEF1X)**, which is based on the national standard called Federal Information Standard published in 1993 due to the following advantages:

- E–R model components such as entities, attributes, relationships, and domains can be represented by the icons provided by IDEF1X.
- The IDEF1X standard can be used to represent most of the logical structures in a data model.

- Data models compliant with the IDEF1X standard can be easily converted into a physical database.

Because of these advantages, some popular database modeling software packages such as ERwin and Microsoft Visio include IDEF1X as one of their data modeling standards. The IDEF1X standard will be used for the development of the E–R model in this section. The following are the descriptions of **entities**, **attributes**, **domains**, **relationships**, and **business rules**.

2.3.2 Entities

An entity is a generic name for an object such as a person, a computer, or a location involved in a business process. In a class registration process, we are interested in keeping track of the information about the objects such as class, student, course, faculty, semester, timeblock, weekday, building, and classroom. These objects will be entities in the E–R model. According to the IDEF1X standard, each entity can be represented by an icon as shown in Figure 2.3.

Graphically, an entity is represented by a rectangle with the entity name printed on top of the rectangle in capital letters. The rectangle is divided into two parts. The top part is used to display the identifier of the entity. The bottom part is used to display other attributes of the entity. For the STUDENT entity, each individual student is an **instance** of the STUDENT entity. A group of students is called an **entity class**. By the requirement analysis, the other possible entities for this database project are CLASS, COURSE, CLASSROOM, BUILDING, TIMEBLOCK, SEMESTER, and FACULTY.

2.3.3 Attributes, Identifiers, and Domains

Attributes are used to describe an entity. For the entity STUDENT, a student can be described by his/her student ID, first name, last name, and major, which are the attributes of the entity. Figure 2.4 shows the IDEF1X icon for the entity STUDENT with its attributes.

As shown in Figure 2.4, the entity identifier StudentID is displayed in the top part of the rectangle, and other attributes are displayed in the lower part of the entity rectangle. As an identifier, a

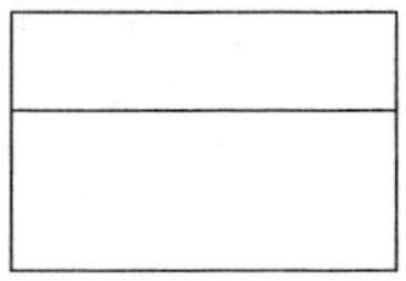

Figure 2.3 IDEF1X icon representing an entity.

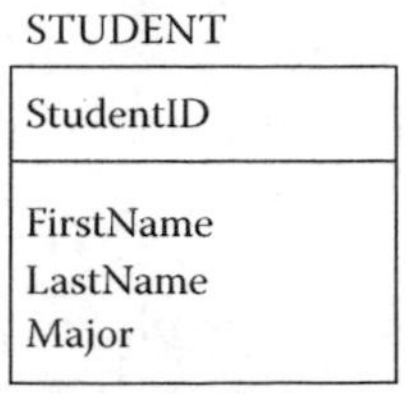

Figure 2.4 IDEF1X icon representing entity STUDENT and its attributes.

value of StudentID identifies an instance of the entity STUDENT, which is an individual student. Sometimes, an identifier may consist of more than one attribute, for example, a combination of the first name and last name.

When an identifier can uniquely distinguish each individual entity instance, it is called a **key**. In general, an identifier does not have to be unique. For example, if the last name attribute is used as an identifier, there may be several students that have the same last name. When there is no attribute in an entity that can serve as a unique identifier, you can use a sequence of unique integers as the key, which is often called a **surrogate key** and the integers used by this type of key can be generated automatically by a DBMS.

A **domain** is a set of possible values that an attribute can use. For example, possible values for the attribute Grade are A, B, C, D, and F. Then, the domain for the attribute Grade is a set of characters {A, B, C, D, F}. A domain is used to specify the data type and constraints for an attribute. In Table 2.6, domains are defined for each attribute in the entity STUDENT.

From the requirement analysis, we come up with the attributes for the other entities CLASS, COURSE, CLASSROOM, BUILDING, TIMEBLOCK, SEMESTER, and FACULTY listed in Figure 2.5.

For some of the entities such as SEMESTER, an integer ID attribute is added as the key instead of using SemesterName as the key. A semester name could be a long string. It is not as convenient as using an integer. Also, an integer key can be automatically generated by the DBMS.

Table 2.6 Attributes and Their Domains

Attribute	*Domain Definition*
StudentID	A set of distinct positive integers
First Name	A set of character strings with variable length
Last Name	A set of character strings with variable length
Major	A set of character strings with variable length

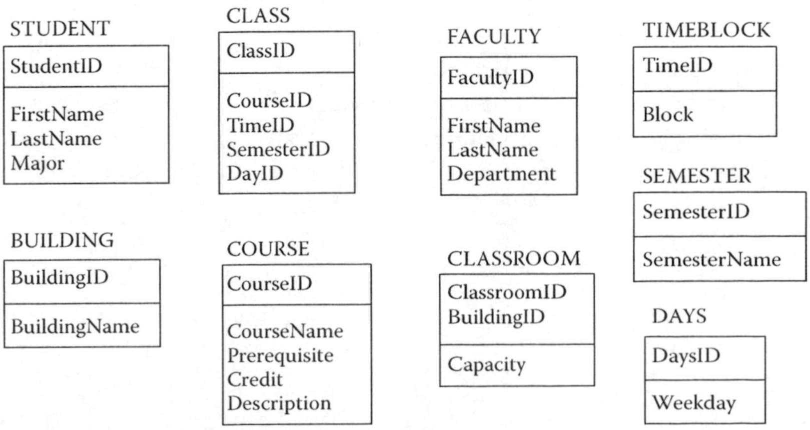

Figure 2.5 IDEF1X icon representing entities and their attributes.

2.3.4 Relationships

Objects in a business process are often related as shown in the requirement analysis section. Therefore, entities' relationships are logically represented in the data model according to how they are related in the business process. The **relationship** component in the E–R model is used to describe how entities are associated with each other. In the IDEF1X standard, relationships are classified into several different types. The descriptions of some of the commonly used relationships are given below. We will start with the identifying relationship.

Identifying relationship: To understand this kind of relationship, let us examine how the entity CLASSROOM is related to the entity BUILDING. Since two classrooms in two different buildings may have the same classroom number, the business rule requires that the CLASSROOM entity should include the building identifier as part of its own identifier. That is, the classroom identifier depends on the existence of the building identifier. In such a case, the CLASSROOM entity is called a **weak entity**. An **identifying relationship** relates two entities and one of them is a weak entity. In our example, the CLASSROOM entity is the **weak** entity that depends on the existence of the **parent** entity BUILDING. To represent the identifying relationship in IDEF1X, use the symbols in Figure 2.6.

In Figure 2.6, the parent entity is represented by a rectangle, and the weak entity is represented by a round-cornered rectangle. The identifying relationship is represented by a solid line. The entity attached to a filled-in black dot is the child entity. The attribute BuildingID is the key for the entity BULDING. The combination of ClassroomID and BuildingID is the key for the entity CLASSROOM. The symbol (FK) indicates that the key attribute BuildingID is from a foreign entity called a foreign key. In the identifying relationship, it is required that the key of the child entity always includes the key of the parent entity, which makes the child entity a weak entity.

Nonidentifying relationship: From the requirement analysis, we have discovered that the entity STUDENT is related to the entity FACULTY. A faculty member may advise zero, one or many students and a student may or may not have an advisor. Such a relationship is different from the identifying relationship. In this relationship, each student, that is, an instance of the entity, is given zero or one faculty ID. The key attribute of the STUDENT entity does not need to include the key attribute from the FACULTY entity. This kind of relationship is called a **nonidentifying relationship**. The IEDF1X representation of the nonidentifying relationship is given in Figure 2.7.

Notice that, to relate these two entities, the attribute FacultyID is added to the STUDENT entity. In the IDEF1X standard, the two entities are associated by a relationship sharing a common attribute. Again, a filled-in black dot indicates that STUDENT is the child entity. The dashed line means that the relationship is a nonidentifying relationship. The diamond sign on the side of the FACULTY entity indicates that an advisor is optional. Usually, a nonidentifying relationship is used to represent a relationship where one entity instance in an entity relates to several entity instances in another entity. This type of relationship is often a one-to-many (1:*N*) relationship,

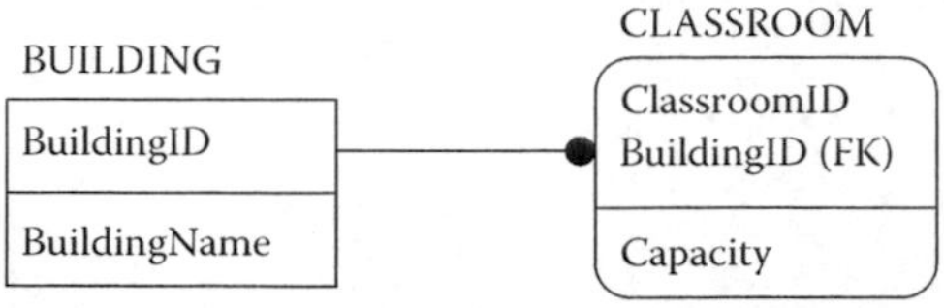

Figure 2.6 Identifying relationship.

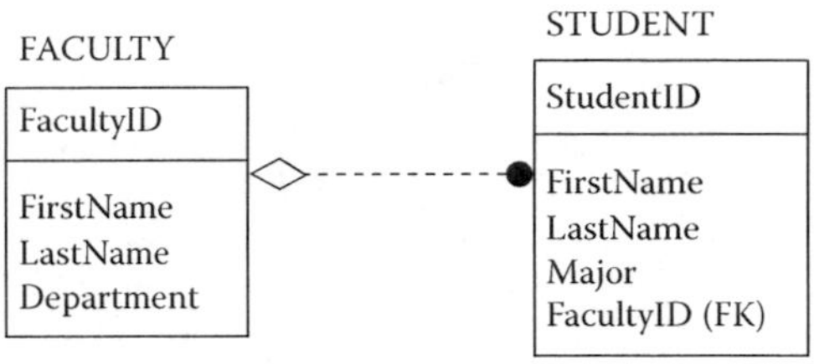

Figure 2.7 Nonidentifying relationship with optional parent.

where *N* can be zero, one, or many. In our example, the FACULTY entity is on the 1 side of the relationship and the STUDENT entity is on the *N* side of the relationship.

Nonspecific relationship: From the requirement analysis, we have learned that a student can take several classes and a class should have at least 10 students. This is a many-to-many (*M*:*N*) relationship. Since such a relationship does not have a direction from a parent entity to a child entity, it is called a **nonspecific relationship**. Physically, you cannot directly place a key value such as an ID of one entity to the other entity as the foreign key like what we did in a 1:*N* relationship. If you do so, several IDs from the first entity placed in the second entity will relate to the same ID in the second entity. This behavior forces the second entity to generate nonunique ID values. The same is true if several IDs from the second entity are placed in the first entity. To overcome this difficulty, a nonspecific relationship is often represented by two 1:*N* relationships that will relate the two entities with an intersection entity as shown in Figure 2.8.

As seen in Figure 2.8, a new entity STUDENT_CLASS is added to connect the entity STUDENT and the entity CLASS. The intersection entity STUDENT_CLASS contains the keys from both entities involved in the nonspecific relationship. It is required that all the key attributes are not null. We will further discuss the *M*:*N* relationship when we get to the physical implementation of a database.

Categorization relationship: Categorization relationship is used to represent a relationship between a **super type** (also called **generic**) entity and a group of **subtype** (also called **specific**) entities. In our requirement analysis, we did not find this type of relationship. But, we can use another example. Consider the entity FACULTY that includes professors and instructors who have some unshared attributes such as Rank, which only applies to a full-time professor. If we place all the unshared instances in the FACULTY entity, the unshared attributes will contain a large number of null values. For example, if the Rank attribute is included in the FACULTY entity, all the corresponding Rank values for instructors will be NULL. To avoid this problem, we can place the shared attributes in the generic entity FACULTY and the unshared attributes in the

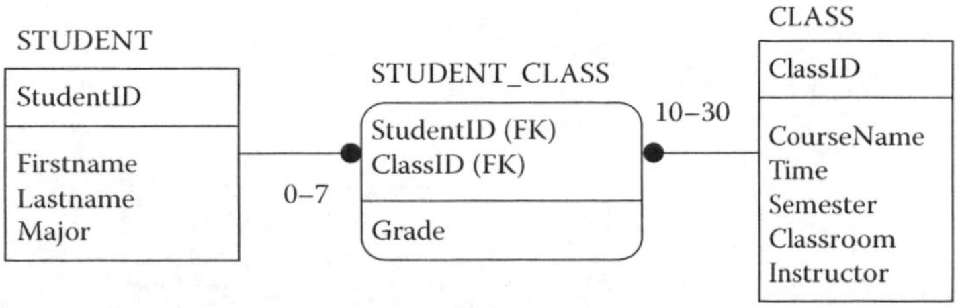

Figure 2.8 Nonspecific relationship with intersection entity.

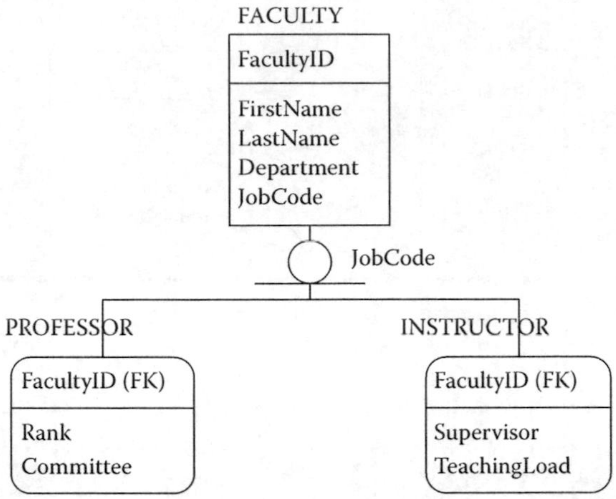

Figure 2.9 Incomplete categorization relationship.

specific entities PROFESSOR and INSTRUCTOR. Such a relationship is called a **categorization relationship**. Figure 2.9 shows one type of categorization relationship in the IDEF1X standard.

In Figure 2.9, the super type entity FACULTY is represented by a rectangle. The subtype entities PROFESSOR and INSTRUCTOR are represented by round-cornered rectangles. Here, the attribute Supervisor refers to the faculty who supervises the instructor. The **Category** icon is a **discriminator** that distinguishes a faculty member as a professor or an instructor. The attribute JobCode is used for classification. There are two types of categorization relationships. If at least one subtype entity is not included in the relationship, the categorization relationship is **incomplete**, which is represented by a single horizontal line in the Category icon as shown in Figure 2.9. When all the subtype entities are included in the relationship, the categorization relationship is **complete**, which is denoted by two horizontal lines in the **Category** icon. For example, suppose that we have one more FACULTY category, researcher. By adding this category, we have generated a complete categorization relationship as shown in Figure 2.10.

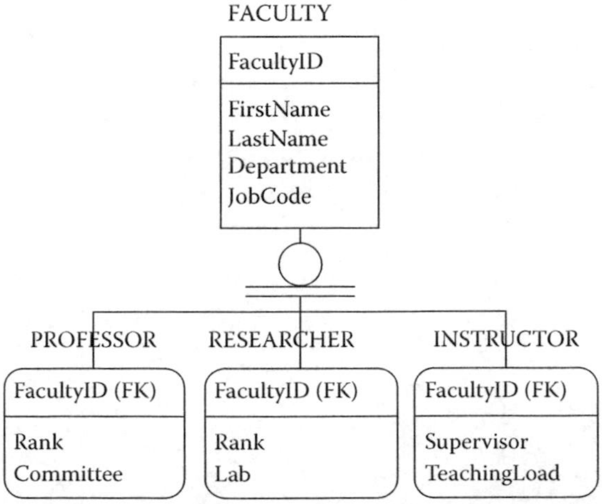

Figure 2.10 Complete categorization relationship.

In the categorization relationship, the key of the super type entity is also used as the key for the subtype entities. A faculty member can be a professor, an instructor, or a researcher. If a faculty member cannot be in two categories at the same time, the relationship can also be called an **Exclusive OR** relationship.

When two entities related by a relationship are of two different logical types, the relationship is a **HAS-A** relationship. For example, the nonidentifying relationship between the entities FACULTY and STUDENT is a HAS-A relationship. In contrast, if the related entities have the same logical type, we say the relationship is an **IS-A** relationship. An IS-A relationship can be used to represent the relationship that connects a super type to a subtype. For example, the categorization relationship that relates the entities FACULTY and PROFESSOR is an IS-A relationship.

The number of entities associated by a relationship is the **degree** of the relationship. For example, the nonidentifying relationship that connects the entities FACULTY and STUDENT has a degree of 2. Relationships with a degree of 2 are the most used relationships. There are other relationships with degrees different from 2. These relationships will be described in the following paragraphs.

Recursive relationship: A recursive relationship relates an entity to itself. It represents a self-join relationship. For example, suppose that each faculty member is related to the dean who is also a faculty member. The relationship between the dean and the group of faculty members is a recursive relationship shown in Figure 2.11.

Since the dean is managing many other faculty members, this recursive relationship is a 1:*N* relationship. The dashed line indicates that the relationship is nonidentifying. There can be a *M*:*N* recursive relationship (nonspecific). In such a case, an intersection entity is used to connect an entity to itself. As an example, consider the COURSE entity. By the requirement analysis, a course can have many prerequisites and a prerequisite can be used by many courses. The *M*:*N* recursive relationship is displayed in Figure 2.12.

Notice that the attribute Prerequisite pairs up with the CourseID attribute to form a key. One instance of CourseID can be paired up with multiple Prerequisite instances or multiple CourseID instances can be paired up with a Prerequisite instance. Since it is required that all the

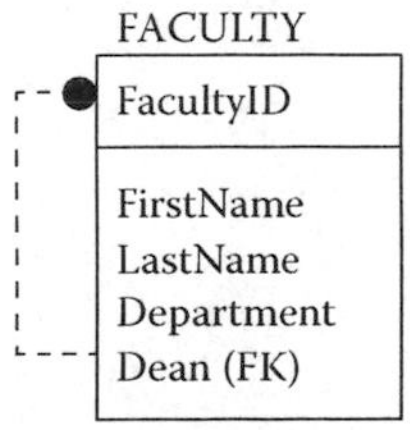

Figure 2.11 Recursive relationship.

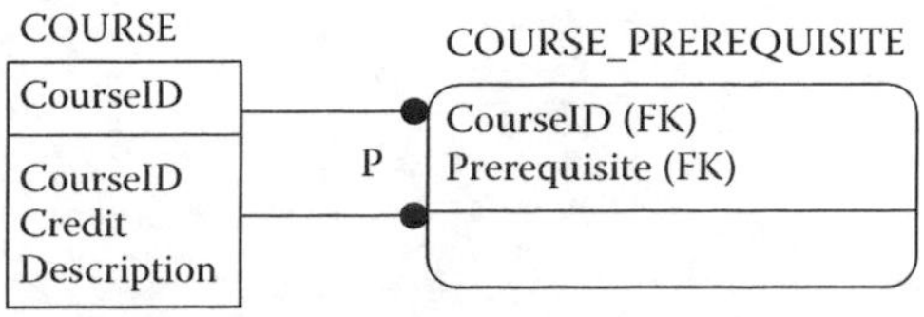

Figure 2.12 *M*:*N* recursive relationship.

Table 2.7 Symbols for Relationships

Symbol	*Description*
	Child entity with zero or more children
Z	Zero or one child
P	One or more children
n-m	Ranging from *n* to *m* children
1	Exactly one child
	Optional parent
—	Identifying relationship
- - -	Nonidentifying relationship

key attributes are not null, the courses that do not have a prerequisite will not be present in the intersection entity. For the meaning of the letter **P**, refer to Table 2.7.

Ternary relationship: There are three entities involved in a ternary relationship. For example, from the requirement analysis, one or more instances of the FACULTY entity are associated with one or more instances of the CLASS entity and one or more instances of the CLASSROOM entity. This relationship is a many-to-many-to-many ternary relationship shown in Figure 2.13.

In some cases, a ternary relationship can be treated as two separate binary relationships. In this case, consider using binary relationships first for simplicity. It is possible to break a ternary relationship into binary relationships. In the above example, we can treat the ternary relationship as two binary relationships shown in Figure 2.14.

There are some other types of ternary relationships. Let us consider the following examples that are not included in our requirement analysis. Suppose that each course can only be taught

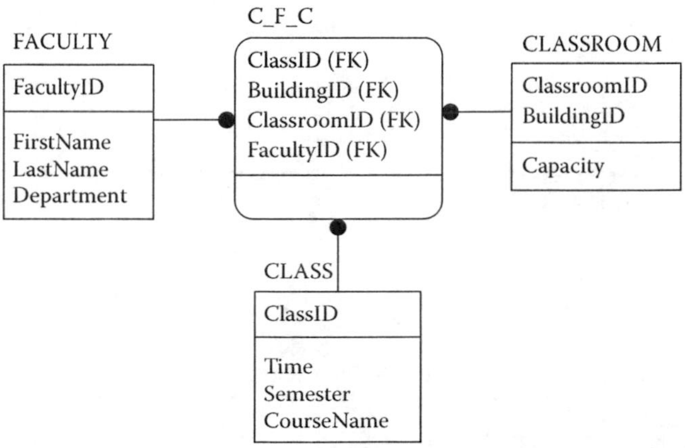

Figure 2.13 Many-to-many-to-many ternary relationship.

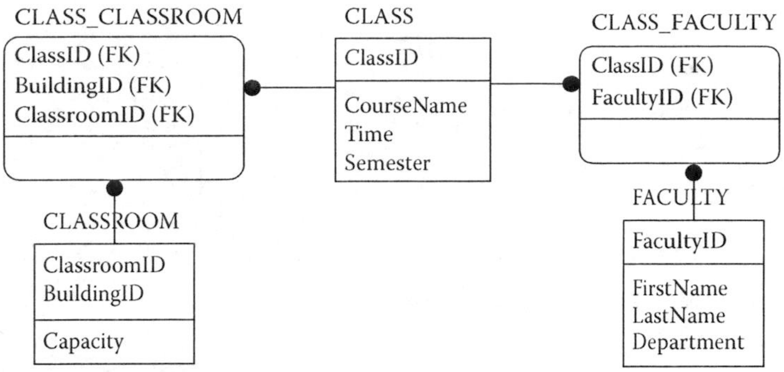

Figure 2.14 Ternary relationship represented by binary relationships.

by a dedicated professor in a dedicated classroom, we have a one-to-one-to-one ternary relationship. In the case that a particular course can only be taught in a dedicated classroom by different professors, we then have a one-to-one-to-many ternary relationship. As another example, if some courses can only be taught by one professor in several different classrooms, the relationship is a one-to-many-to-many ternary relationship. In the case that more than three entities are associated in a relationship, the relationship is an *N*-ary relationship, where *N* is an integer greater than three.

Cardinality: Cardinality is used to specify the number of entity instances involved in a relationship. As an example, let us consider the cardinality for the relationship connecting the entities COURSE and CLASS. From the requirement analysis, the same course can be taught in different classes and each class can only teach one course. Therefore, we have a nonidentifying relationship. Figure 2.15 shows the cardinality for this relationship.

Notice that we have modified the entities CLASS and COURSE. For instance, we removed some attributes that will be in other entities. We changed the attribute CourseName in the CLASS entity to CourseID due to the fact that course names may not be unique if they are offered by different departments. Also, it is easier to deal with IDs with integer values. Therefore, we use TimeID for Time and SemesterID for Semester. As shown in Figure 2.15, the course instance is required for the nonidentifying relationship since the diamond icon is not on the side of COURSE. This means that a course ID is required for each class. The cardinality symbol **P** indicates that each course ID is associated with one or more class instances on the child side.

As another example, let us consider the nonspecific relationship that relates the entities STUDENT and CLASS. According to the requirement analysis, each student can take 0–7 classes and a class has to have at least 10 students. The cardinality for CLASS is (0, 7), and the cardinality for STUDENT is (10, *M*). Here, *M* is an integer greater than or equal to 10 and less than the classroom capacity. In our example, let *M* be equal to 30. Figure 2.16 shows the IDEF1X representation of these cardinalities.

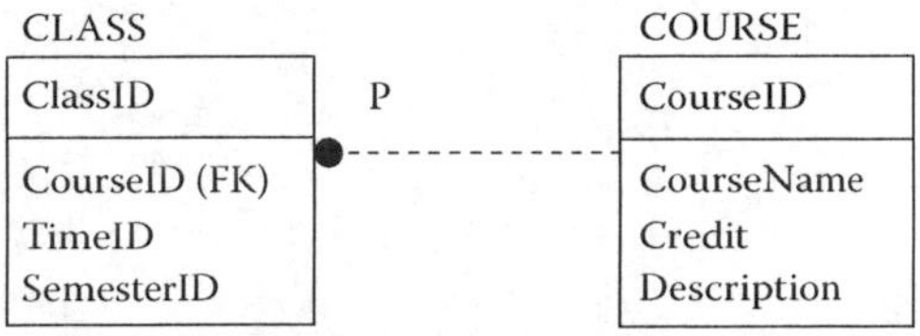

Figure 2.15 One-or-more cardinality.

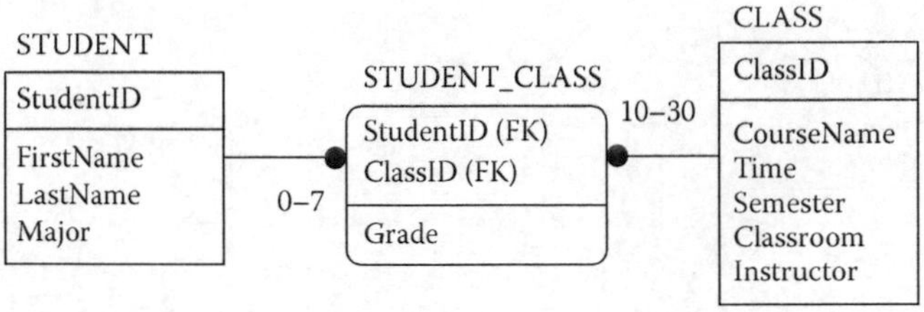

Figure 2.16 Cardinality of nonspecific relationship.

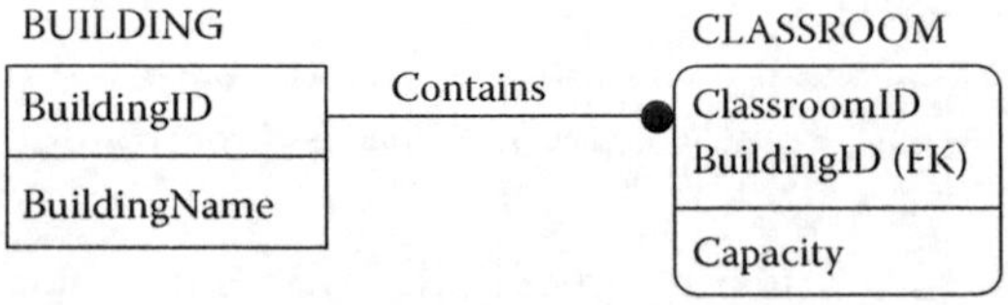

Figure 2.17 Relationship naming from parent to child.

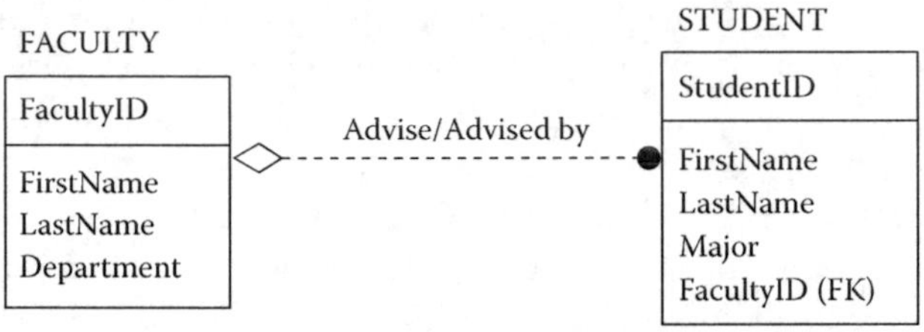

Figure 2.18 Relationship naming from parent to child and from child to parent.

Figure 2.16 shows that a class can enroll 10–30 students and a student can take 0–7 classes.

So far, you have seen some symbols such as those for cardinality representations used in a relationship. Table 2.7 lists some commonly used relationship symbols.

Relationship labeling: A relationship can be labeled by a word or phrase. For example, to emphasize the identifying relationship connecting the entities BUILDING and CLASSROOM, where CLASSROOM is a weak entity, you may label the relationship with a verb "Contains" from the parent to the child as shown in Figure 2.17.

Sometime, by including both verb phrases from the parent to the child and vice versa, the meaning of a relationship may be clearer. To demonstrate this, let us name the relationship connecting the entity FACULTY and STUDENT by including two verb phrases as shown in Figure 2.18.

ACTIVITY 2.1 CREATING ENTITY-RELATIONSHIP MODEL

Now that you have learned about the components of a data model, it is time to integrate these components to represent the class registration process. Table 2.8 summarizes the relationships among the entities involved in the class registration process.

For the nonidentifying relationships, Course–Class, Weekday–Class, Time Block–Class, and Semester–Class, we may group them together as a ternary relationship with an

Table 2.8 Summary of Relationships

Relationship	*Type*	*Related Entities*	*Cardinality*
Course—Class	Nonidentifying	COURSE CLASS	One course is related to one or more classes
Course—Prerequisite	Many-to-many recursive	COURSE COURSE_PREREQUISITE	One or more courses are related to zero or more prerequisites and vice versa
Weekday—Class	Nonidentifying	DAYS CLASS	One weekday is related to zero, one, or more classes
Time Block—Class	Nonidentifying	TIMEBLOCK CLASS	One time block is related to zero, one, or more classes
Semester—Class	Nonidentifying	SEMESTER CLASS	One semester is related to one or more classes
Faculty—Student	Nonidentifying	FACULTY STUDENT	One faculty advisor is related to zero, one, or more students
Building—Classroom	Identifying	BUILDING CLASSROOM	One building is related to one or more classrooms
Class—Student Class—Classroom Class—Faculty	Many-to-many-to-many *N*-ary	STUDENT CLASS CLASS_STUDENT CLASSROOM CLASS_CLASSROOM FACULTY CLASS_FACULTY	At least 10 students are related to 0–7 classes, zero or more instructors, and one or more classrooms and vice versa

intersection entity CLASS that contains the attributes CourseID, DayID, TimeID, and SemesterID. However, as shown in later chapters, by doing so, this will make the intersection entities for the many-to-many relationships Class–Student, Class–Classroom, and Class–Faculty include all the attributes in the entity CLASS, which will cause a large number of redundancies.

Some of the relationships in Table 2.8 have been defined before. The Course–Class relationship is defined in Figure 2.15. The Course–Prerequisite relationship is defined in Figure 2.12. The Faculty–Student relationship for advising is defined in Figure 2.18. The Building–Classroom relationship is defined in Figure 2.17. The *N*-ary relationship can be represented by multiple binary relationships shown in Figure 2.19.

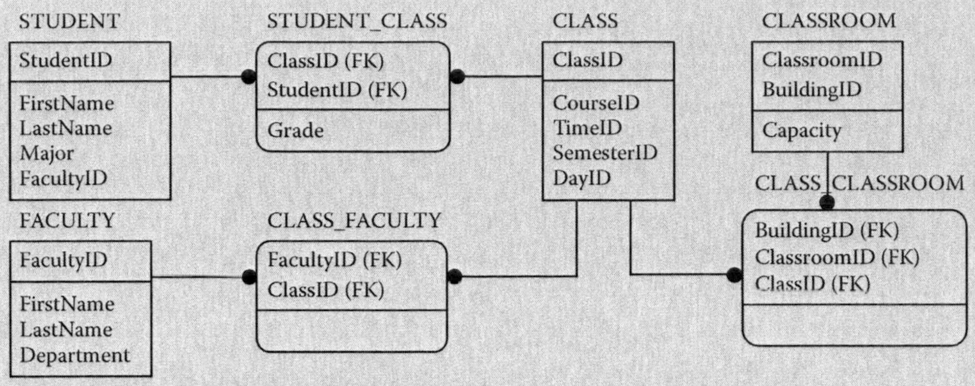

Figure 2.19 Relationship of CLASS, STUDENT, FACULTY, and CLASSROOM.

The relationships that we have not defined are Time Block–Class, Semester–Class, and Weekday–Class. Their definitions are given in Figures 2.20 through 2.22. For each time block, there can be many classes. To represent this nonidentifying relationship, we need the attribute TimeID in the CLASS entity. Similarly, to represent the nonidentifying relationship connecting CLASS and SEMESTER, we need the attribute SemesterID in CLASS. The same is true for the nonidentifying relationship connecting CLASS and DAYS.

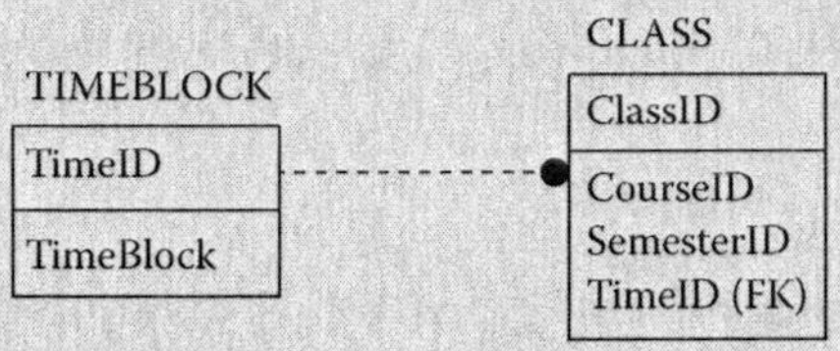

Figure 2.20 Relationship between TIMEBLOCK and CLASS.

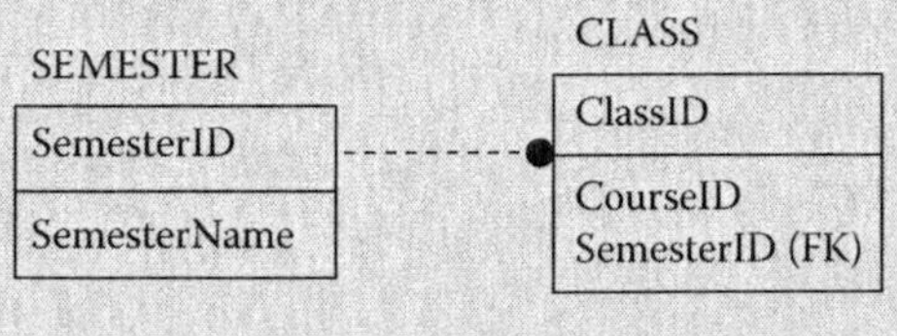

Figure 2.21 Relationship between SEMESTER and CLASS.

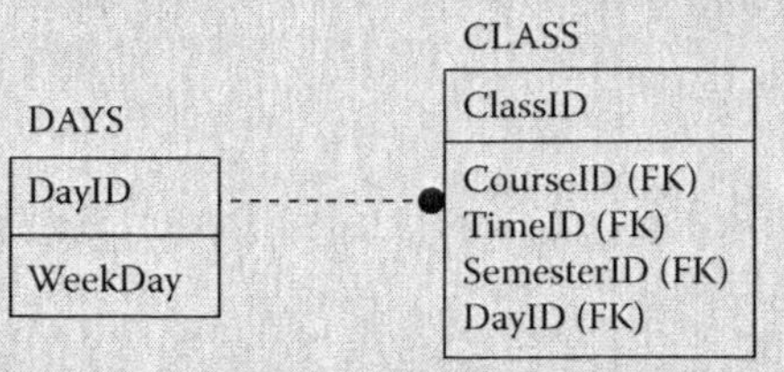

Figure 2.22 Relationship between DAYS and CLASS.

Now, all the relationships among the entities have been defined. It is time to create the class registration data model with Microsoft Visio. The IDEF1X standard will be used to create all the components in the class registration data model.

Create entities: In the following process, a bold-lettered word or phrase means that it is an item you need to click or type. It may also be used to represent a container or a dialog box where you can conduct activities. To get started, follow the steps given below:

1. Suppose that Microsoft Visio 2007 has been installed on your machine. Start **Visio** in **Microsoft Office**. Click **File**, **New**, **Software and Database**, and **Database Model Diagram**.
2. To match the icons used in the examples in this chapter, you need to set the following options for your data model: click **Database** on the menu bar and select **Options** and then **Document.** Under the **General** tab, check the **IDEF1X** option for **Symbol set** (see Figure 2.23). Click the **Table** tab and uncheck the **Show** option for **IDEF1X optionality '(O)'**. Under the **Relationship** tab, check the option **Cardinality**, and then click **OK**.
3. To add an entity to the drawing page, click the **Entity** icon in the **Entity Relationship** pane, hold the mouse and drag the **Entity** icon to the drawing page.
4. To specify the entity just added to the drawing page, right click the entity and select **Database Properties**. The **Database Properties** dialog will be open for configuration. In the **Categories** list box, select **Definition** and enter **STUDENT** in the **Physical name** textbox as shown in Figure 2.24.
5. To specify the attributes, click **Columns** in the **Categories** list box. Enter attribute names such as **StudentID**, **FirstName**, **LastName**, **Major**, and **FacultyID**. Double click the corresponding data type to change the character length; for example, change the length of FirstName and LastName to 30 from the default length of 10. Specify StudentID as the primary key shown in Figure 2.25.

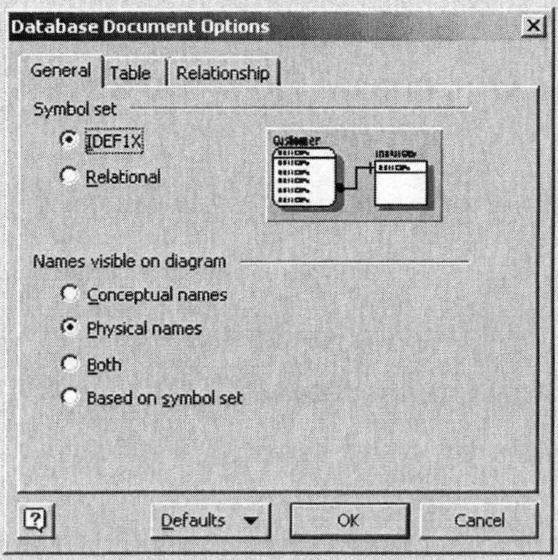

Figure 2.23 Database model diagram options.

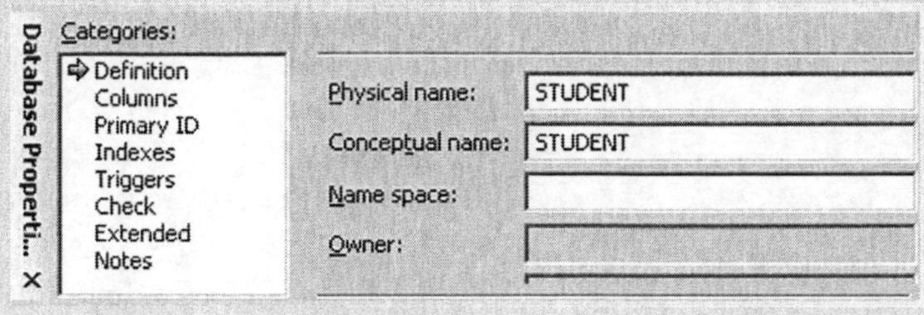

Figure 2.24 Database properties dialog.

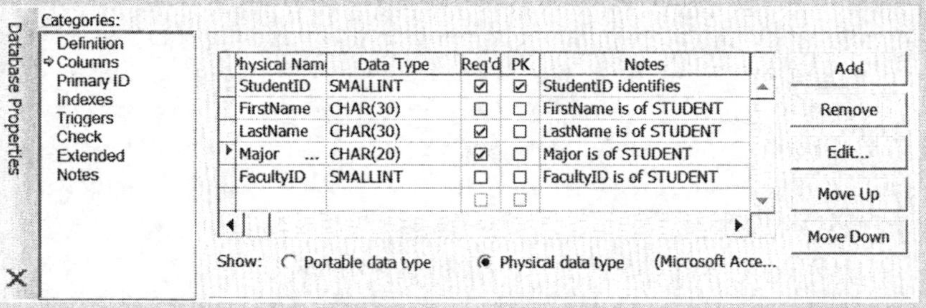

Figure 2.25 Specify attributes.

6. To view the result, drag the **Database Properties** window to the bottom of the screen and zoom the diagram to 100%.

Similarly, you can create other entities based on Figure 2.31.

Note: The above steps are performed on Windows 7 Professional with Microsoft Visio 2007 installed. You may use other database design software to obtain similar E–R diagrams.

Create relationships: With Microsoft Visio, you can create relationships. The following steps show how you can create relationships involved in the class registration data model:

1. **Creating identifying relationship**: Use the following steps to create an identifying relationship connecting the entities BUILDING and CLASSROOM.
   - Assume that you have created BUILDING and CLASSROOM entities as shown in Figure 2.6. Click the **Connector Tool** icon on the tool bar. Move the mouse cursor over the parent entity **BUILDING**. When a red rectangle appears, press the mouse. Then, hold the mouse and move the cursor over to the child entity **CLASSROOM**. When a red rectangle appears around the CLASSROOM entity, release the mouse. An identifying relationship connector is automatically drawn from the parent entity to the child entity.
   - To specify the cardinality, double click on the relationship connector line between the entities BUILDING and CLASSROOM to open the Database Prosperities dialog. Select **Miscellaneous** in the **Categories** pane. Check the option **One or more** as shown in Figure 2.26.

   The letter **P** should appear near the relationship connector line.

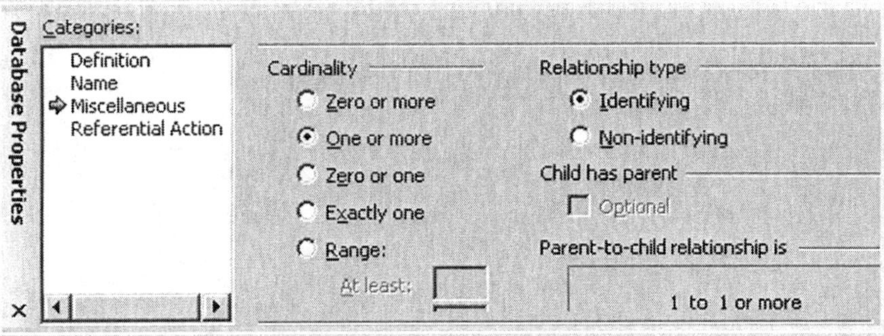

Figure 2.26 Configure cardinality.

2. **Creating nonidentifying relationship**: In the class registration data model, there are several nonidentifying relationships: Course–Class, Course–Prerequisite, Weekday–Class, Time Block–Class, Semester–Class, and Faculty–Student. The following steps show you how to create a nonidentifying relationship between the entities COURSE and CLASS.
   - Assume that both COURSE and CLASS in Figure 2.15 have been created. Click **Connector Tool** on the tool bar. Move the mouse cursor over the parent entity **COURSE**. When a red rectangle appears, press the mouse. Then, hold the mouse and move the cursor over to the child entity **CLASS**. When a red rectangle appears around the child entity, release the mouse. A nonidentifying relationship connector is automatically drawn from the parent entity to the child entity.
   - If a diamond icon appears on the relationship connector line near the COURSE side, it means that a course is optional. In our data model, a course is required for a class. To fix the problem, right click **CLASS** entity and select **Database Properties**. Select **Columns** in the **Categories** pane. Make the column **CourseId** required by checking the **Req'd** option as shown in Figure 2.27. The diamond icon should disappear.
   - To specify the cardinality, double click the newly created relationship connector line. In the **Database Properties** dialog, select **Miscellaneous** in the **Categories** pane. Check the **One or more** option. You should have the result shown in Figure 2.15.

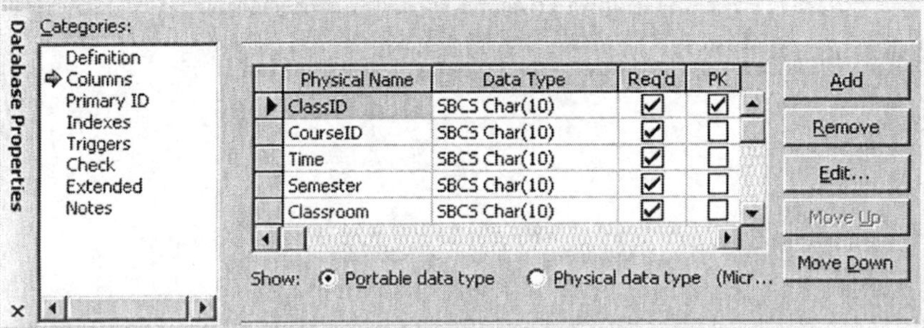

Figure 2.27 Configure required attributes.

Similarly, you can create nonidentifying relationships for the entity pairs Course–Prerequisite, Time Block–Class, Weekday–Time Block, Semester–Class, and Faculty–Student.

3. **Creating nonspecific relationship**: The class registration data model has several nonspecific relationships: Class–Student, Class–Faculty, and Class–Classroom. As an illustration, we will create a Class–Student nonspecific relationship, which is implemented by two identifying relationships with an intersection entity. The following steps show you how to create a nonspecific relationship.
   - Assume that all three entities CLASS, STUDENT, and STUDENT_CLASS in Figure 2.19 have been created. First, create an identifying relationship to connect STUDENT and STUDENT_CLASS. Make STUDENT the parent entity and STUDENT_CLASS the child entity.
   - Then, create an identifying relationship to connect CLASS and STUDENT_CLASS. Make CLASS the parent entity and STUDENT_CLASS the child entity.
   - To specify the cardinality for the relationship connecting STUDENT and STUDENT_CLASS, double click the relationship connector line to open the **Database Properties** dialog. Select **Miscellaneous** in the **Categories** pane. Check the **Range** option. Specify the minimum value as 0 and the maximum value as 7 as shown in Figure 2.28.

   Similarly, you can specify the cardinality range for the relationship that connects the entities CLASS and STUDENT_CLASS as shown in Figure 2.29.

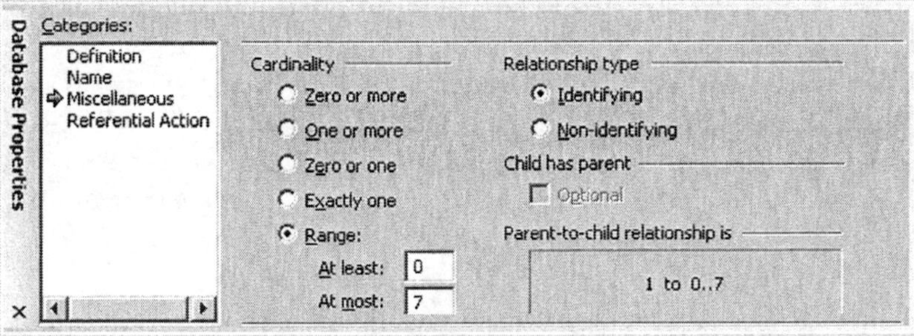

Figure 2.28 Configure cardinality range for class instances.

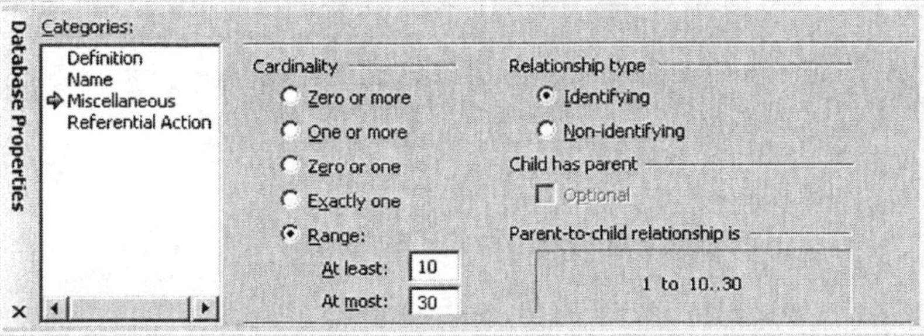

Figure 2.29 Configure cardinality range for student instances.

By using the same steps, you can create other nonspecific relationships.

4. **Creating recursive relationship**: In the class registration data model, there is a many-to-many recursive relationship. The intersection entity is COURSE_PREREQUISITE. The following are the steps to show you how to create the recursive relationship.
   - Suppose that both the COURSE and the COURSE_PREREQUISITE entities in Figure 2.12 have been created. Click **Connector Tool** on the tool bar. Move the mouse cursor over the parent entity **COURSE**. When a red rectangle appears, press the mouse. Then, hold the mouse and move the cursor over to the child entity **COURSE_PREREQUISITE**. When a red rectangle appears, release the mouse.
   - Move the mouse cursor over the parent entity **COURSE** again. When a red rectangle appears, press the mouse. Then, hold the mouse and move the cursor over to the child entity **COURSE_PREREQUISITE**. When a red rectangle appears, release the mouse.
   - While the second relationship connector is selected, make sure that **Definition** is selected in the **Categories** pane. In the **Parent: COURSE** list box, select **CourseID** and select **Prerequisite** in the **Child** list box. Click the **Associate** button to associate CourseID to Prerequisite (Figure 2.30).
   - To configure the cardinality, click the first relationship connector line. In the Database Properties dialog, select **Miscellaneous** in the **Categories** pane. Check the cardinality option **One or more**. Do the same for the second connector line.

Create data model: Now, you have created all the entities and the relationships that associate them. By connecting the components together, you can form a data model shown in Figure 2.31.

Figure 2.31 shows the E–R model for the class registration process. The data model includes entities, attributes, and relationships. The entity CLASS has the most relationships. This type of entity is called a **central entity**.

The above case study has been used to demonstrate the process of developing a data model. It is for illustration purposes only. A real-world registration system can be much more complicated.

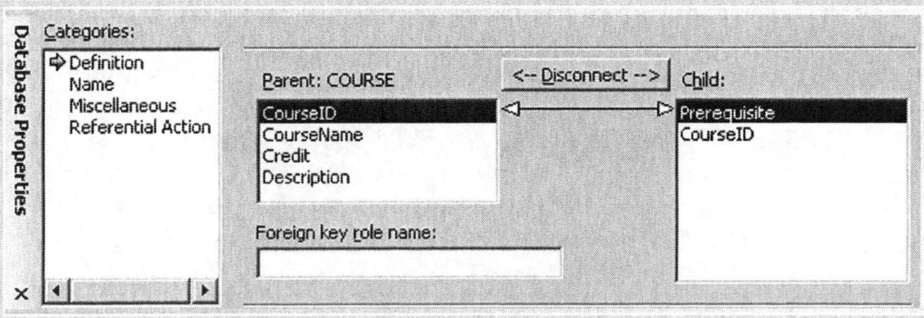

Figure 2.30 Associate CourseID to prerequisite.

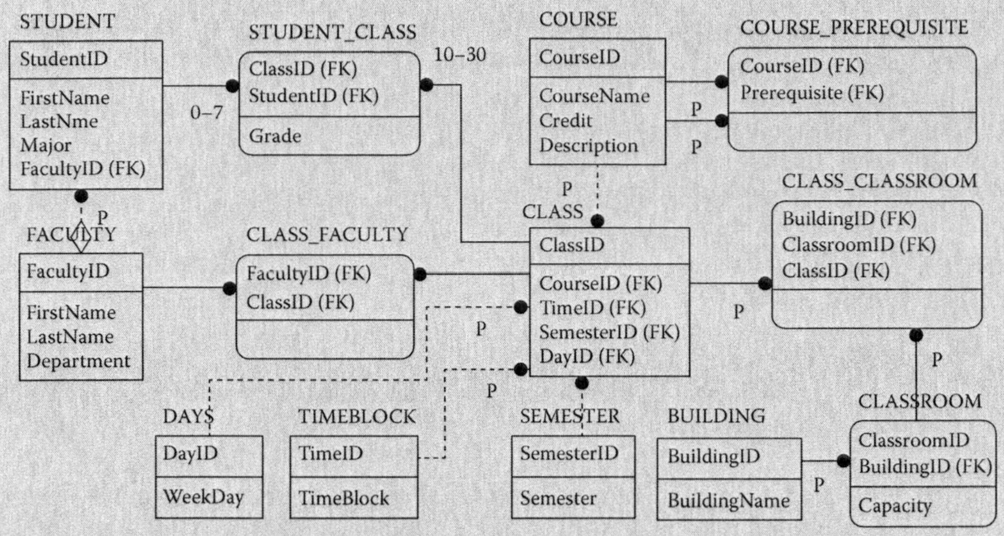

Figure 2.31 Data model for class registration process.

2.4 Database Physical Design

Before you can implement a database physically, careful consideration should be given on some physical design issues. In your physical design, you need to specify the IT infrastructure that will host the future database. For example, if you are designing a database for a company, you need to find out how the users can access the data stored in the database. If the users need to access your database through a local area network or through the Internet, you need to carefully specify the capacity and security of the network. At the physical design stage, you need to choose a server that has enough room for adding more hard drives. It is risky to physically implement a database without much thinking and hope everything will turn out alright. If something goes wrong, it is too costly or too late for you to start all over again.

2.4.1 Database System Architecture

Before implementing a database, as a database designer, you need to know what type of system architecture your future database will be built on. It is important to know if your database will be hosted by a web-based system, a three-tier client–server system, or another type of system. For example, if the database is network-based, you need to address the physical design issues such as the capacity of the network, the security measures imposed on the network, the ability of the network server to handle data transactions, Internet access facilities, and network-based storage and printing equipment. To quickly identify physical implementation problems, let us categorize them below:

- Issues related to system architecture
- Issues related to data characteristics
- Issues related to database access
- Issues related to server and data storage equipment

Issues related to server and data storage equipment: Your database server and data storage devices should be adequate to support all the business activities. Based on the number of users who will be using the database and how many of them will simultaneously log on to the same database, and the time requirements for operations, your decision on the selection of hardware will be quite different. For example, for a database to be used to store information for a large company, database reliability, availability, and security are the major concerns. You may be required to mirror your database on multiple servers and store data on a redundant array of inexpensive disks (RAID) storage structure. Additional devices may also be needed for database backup and recovery. Protecting data stored on your database is another important issue to be addressed. For valuable data, extra equipment should be added for data protection.

Issues related to database access: The way in which users access a database also influences the physical design. For example, if your database users need to access the database through the Internet or local area network, you need to specify the interface for accessing remote data from the client side. Accessing data through GUI often requires more network capacity. Knowing the data transaction rate will help you decide if the network can handle the data communication tasks. There are some design issues involved in data sharing by different types of database applications over different types of computer systems. You need to determine what software and hardware to install to support the communication needs. It is also helpful if you know how the data are used in the business process. The requirements for the hardware and software are different depending on whether your database will be used for decision support or for data transactions. You need to choose the right tools in your database for data conversion. Also, for users to log on to your database, you need to determine which groups of users are allowed to access what kinds of data. Tools used to limit accessing certain sensitive data should be included in your database system.

Issues related to data characteristics: Knowing the characteristics of data in your future database will help you select the server and storage hardware. As a database designer, you need to know how large the existing data sets are and what the annual growth rate is. The data type is also an important factor in helping you determine what kind of server to use. For example, if your database will be used to store data with the blob data type, which requires more storage space than other types and whose growth of data size is fairly fast, you need to build your database on a server with high expandability. If your database can only store a limited amount of data, you need to determine how long the data will have to be stored in the database and find a way to move the old data out of the database and place them in another data storage facility.

Windows Azure: Traditionally, the physical design is carried out around a company's IT infrastructure. In a cloud computing environment, the physical design can be greatly simplified. The required IT infrastructure will be provided by the cloud provider. Especially, Windows Azure provides not only hardware such as networks, servers, and data storage equipment, but also software such as the server operating system and DBMS. It also provides security protection and remote access mechanism. Most of the physical design issues are addressed by Windows Azure, which provides the environment where IT professionals can focus on the development and management of databases and applications. IT professionals who are familiar with the Windows development environment will have no difficulty working in the Windows Azure development environment. The database design tools, database application development software, and database management utilities are about the same. IT professionals can continue to use their knowledge and skills in cloud-based database development. Windows Azure provides a highly available development environment. With Windows Azure, developers can work on their projects from anywhere and at any time. The Windows Azure development environment is highly scalable. Additional database capacity can be added as desired until the subscription limit is reached. Data may be distributed to multiple servers for better scalability and reliability. There is no initial cost on IT infrastructure development and management. However, users need to pay monthly for the storage and server usage.

2.4.2 Windows Azure Data Storage Overview

Windows Azure offers two types of storage services, Windows Azure SQL Database and Windows Azure Storage Services. A brief introduction to these two storage services is given in the following sections.

2.4.2.1 Windows Azure SQL Database

For storing and managing relational data, Windows Azure provides Windows Azure SQL Database. Windows Azure SQL Database is the cloud version of Microsoft SQL Server. With Windows Azure SQL Database, there is no need for a company to conduct tasks such as database backup and recovery. Windows Azure SQL Database automatically replicates databases across multiple servers so that companies do not have to worry about databases server failure. Figure 2.32 illustrates how database replication can be done in Windows Azure.

Windows Azure SQL Database is designed to work with Microsoft data centers. Windows Azure SQL Database also provides tools for database management. Many client databases may share the same physical storage device, and a client database may be stored in different physical storage devices. As for the client side, the detail of the physical storage architecture is hidden from the user. All the user can access is a logical database that abstracts the physical storage architecture. Figure 2.32 illustrates the architecture of the Windows Azure SQL Database.

As shown in Figure 2.32, the application clients interact with the logical server that serves as the data source for the client applications. Behind the logical server, there are actually multiple physical servers. Each server hosts multiple Windows Azure SQL Databases. The logical server distributes the client requests to the client's own database in Windows Azure and prevents other

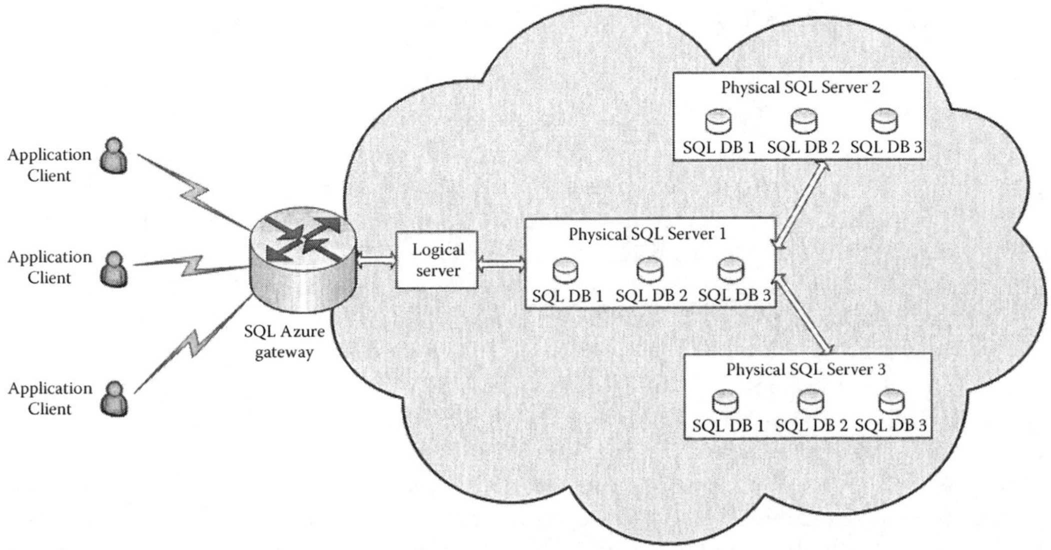

Figure 2.32 Windows Azure SQL Database abstraction.

clients from accessing the database. Each Windows Azure SQL Database replicated to multiple physical servers for better reliability and security. The logical server replicates all the transactions conducted by the applications to all the replicas on different physical servers. In Figure 2.32, there is one primary replica and two secondary replicas. Physical SQL Server 1 has the primary replica, and the other two have the secondary replicas. A transaction made by an application is first sent to the primary replica. Then, changes made to the database in the primary replica will be replicated to the secondary replicas when the system is not too busy. In reality, a Windows Azure SQL Database such as SQL DB 1 in Figure 2.32 can also be distributed to multiple physical servers for better performance. The front-end users will not see the details of the distribution. All they see is their own database hosted by the logical server.

The Windows Azure SQL Database plus Windows Azure SQL Database service and front-end application are the three main components of the Windows Azure SQL Database architecture. Figure 2.33 illustrates the Windows Azure SQL Database architecture, including these three components.

Users on the client side can directly access applications such as programming code, forms, reports, or web pages. Through the front-end applications, the users are able to access the Windows Azure SQL Database services. The applications can be hosted either by the clients' local computers or by Windows Azure in the Microsoft cloud. Some of the services authenticate the requests and manage the bills. The other services monitor and replicate the databases.

The actual SQL Server databases are hosted by the computers in a data center. A data center consists of a large number of computers with the same configuration and low-to-medium performance. In case a computer fails, it can be quickly replaced. At the data center, these computers form a cluster, which includes up to 1000 computers. For some large jobs that require more than 1000 computers, more clusters can be allocated to meet the requirement. Each of these computers serves as a data node in the data center. Each data node is installed with an instance of SQL Server. Each SQL Server instance hosts up to 650 partitions; databases created by users are installed in one or more partitions, as a primary or secondary replica. All these partitions share one log file stored on the data node. Each data node hosts several fabric processes. These fabric processes can

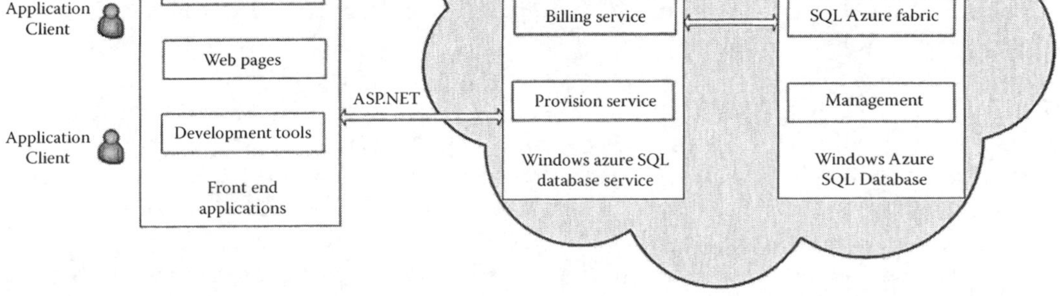

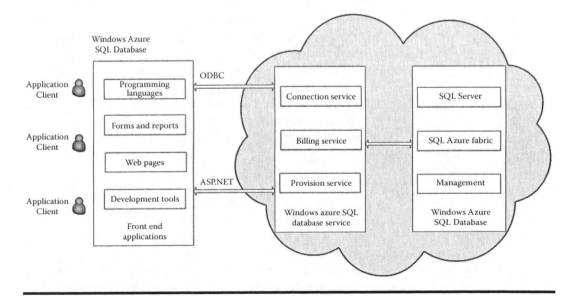

Figure 2.33 Windows Azure SQL Database architecture.

detect an unavailable primary or secondary replica. They can re-establish the primary or secondary replica after a data node failure. In the data center, each data node is monitored by six peers installed on different racks. In case a data node fails, the peers report the problem. A reconfiguration process will be performed on those databases that have a replica on the failed data node. When a primary replica fails, a secondary replica with the least load is selected to be the new primary replica. When a secondary replica fails, a new secondary replica is created with the primary replica. The new secondary replica will be built on a data node that has sufficient disk space and CPU capacity. The gateway will immediately attempt to reconnect the newly created replica. Owing to the replication and effective recovery of the primary replica, Microsoft Windows Azure SQL Database is able to maintain 99.9% availability even when 15% of the replicas fail.

Windows Azure SQL Database and SQL Server have a lot in common. Both SQL Server and Windows Azure SQL Database are used to store and manage the relational data. They can use Transact-SQL (T-SQL) to create database objects, manage databases, and query information out of databases. Many database application development tools work on SQL Server as well as on Windows Azure SQL Database. Similar to SQL Server, Windows Azure SQL Database includes SQL Server components such as stored procedures, views, multiple indices, joins, aggregation, and so on. Windows Azure SQL Database is also able to do some of the administration tasks such as creating logins, users, roles, and so on. They support data migration tools such as SQL Server Integration Services (SSIS), the bulk copy utility (BCP.exe), the System.Data.SqlClient, SqlBulkCopy class, and the scripts that use INSERT statements to load data into the database. Like SQL Server, Windows Azure SQL Database also provides functionalities for the server side processing to reduce network traffic and improve performance. Both of them can use database access technologies such as ADO.NET and ODBC. However, the database access technology OLE DB is not supported by Windows Azure SQL Database.

Unlike SQL Server, Windows Azure SQL Database does not provide the functionalities that directly access the underlying hardware. As cloud-based data storage, Windows Azure SQL Database is not able to determine where to place a database file on a data storage device. The database files will be automatically placed by the Windows Azure platform. Windows Azure SQL Database does not support database replication or backup-related technologies such as Mirror Server, RESTORE statement, or Attach Database. Windows Azure SQL Database does not support SQL Server Agent or jobs, and it does not support distributed transactions. To support SQL Server, a company needs to develop an IT infrastructure, including the network and powerful computers installed with server operating system and application software. The company also needs to take care of security and system update. While using Windows Azure SQL Database, all these things can be done by cloud providers. Windows Azure SQL Database allows database developers to work in an environment that is similar to that of SQL Server. The developers can continue to use the skills learned in the development of SQL Server to develop databases on Windows Azure SQL Database.

When creating a database on Windows Azure SQL Database, a user can specify the name, edition, and the maximum size of the database. The user can choose one of the two database editions, the web edition and the business edition. When the web edition is specified, a database can have 1 or 5 GB storage space. When the business edition is specified, a database can have 10, 20, 30, 40, or 50 GB storage space. When the maximum size is reached, the user can only read, delete, and truncate tables, drop database objects, and rebuild indexes. The activities such as creating database objects, inserting new data, and executing stored procedures will be prohibited. There is a limit on the number of databases that can be created in Windows Azure SQL Database. The maximum number of databases that can be created on each Windows Azure SQL

Database server is 150, including the system database master. Each row in a Windows Azure SQL Database table can contain 1024 columns, which can be up to 8 MB in size. For security reasons, some of the commonly known user names such as admin, administrator, guest, root, and sa cannot be used in Windows Azure SQL Database. To efficiently use Windows Azure SQL Database resources, the connection to Windows Azure SQL Database will be automatically closed under circumstances such as idle for 30 min or longer, failover due to server failures, or excessive resource usage.

Most of the remote access tools and database management tools available to Microsoft SQL Server are also available to Windows Azure SQL Database. When a company needs a database that is accessible anywhere and anytime, Windows Azure can serve that purpose nicely. Also, Windows Azure SQL Database allows databases to be scaled up or scale down along with time. Therefore, it can provide a highly scalable data source to support web-based applications.

2.4.2.2 Windows Azure Storage

In addition to Windows Azure SQL Database, Windows Azure provides Windows Azure Storage service for handling nonrelational data. Also, Windows Azure can use storage space on local computers.

1. **Local Storage**: A running Windows Azure application project uses local storage as temporary storage. Local computer data generated by an application instance are temporally stored on the local hard drive. The data are only accessible by the application on the local machine and is not transferable when the application is moved to a different local computer. The data can be lost when rebooting the local computer. The default local storage size is 1 MB. An application instance can have multiple local data stores.
2. **Windows Azure Storage**: Unlike local storage, Windows Azure Storage Services are accessible anywhere and anytime. Windows Azure Storage Services include three components, Windows Azure Table Service for efficiently storing a large amount of data, Windows Azure Queue Service for the storage of messages, and Windows Azure Blob Service for the storage of large binary objects such as video and audio files. The maximum of 100 TB storage space is available for each Windows Azure Table Service storage or Windows Queue Service storage. The maximum of 1 TB storage space is available for each Windows Azure Blob Service storage.
   a. **Windows Azure Blob Storage**: Multimedia content such as video, audio, and image is usually saved as binary data. Windows Azure Blobs are used to store the binary content. The snapshots of the Blob can be used for backup. The Blob can also be cached at the nearby data center for fast data access.
   b. **Queue Storage**: Similar to Microsoft Message Queuing (MSMQ), Windows Azure Queue Storage is used to process messages between applications. The messages are first placed in a queue and then processed in a first-in-first-out (FIFO) manner. In case an application fails to process a message, the message will be kept in the queue and wait to be processed by another application. While one application is reading the message, the message is marked as invisible until the message is deleted or a specified reading interval is reached. By doing so, it prevents a message from being processed by multiple applications simultaneously. By default, the size of a message is limited to 8 kB.
   c. **Table Storage**: Windows Azure offers Table Storage for storing a large amount of structured data. The data in Table Storage are structured as rows and columns. According to Windows Azure's terminology, rows are also called entities and columns are called

properties. The term entity used in Windows Azure has a different meaning from the entity used in an E–R data model. The entity in Windows Azure is similar to the term entity instance in an E–R model. The concept of table in Windows Azure is also different from the table concept in a relational database. Unlike the relational database where the rows in a table are defined with the same number of columns, the entities in Table Storage can have different numbers of properties with different data types. Here, the entities with different properties and data types can be sequentially placed in one table. The entities in a Windows Azure table are more like the rows in a spreadsheet. There is no relationship that is defined to link one set of entities to another set of entities. Windows Azure Table Storage does not support foreign keys, triggers, stored procedures, and join statements. However, it does support the insert, update, and select statements. A Windows Azure table can store as many as 100 TB of data. The maximum size of each entity in a Windows Azure table is 1 MB.

The cloud computing environment can greatly simplify the physical design. To take advantage of cloud computing, let us create a database server on Window Azure in the following activity.

ACTIVITY 2.2 CREATING A WINDOWS AZURE SQL DATABASE SERVER

In this activity, an SQL Database server will be created on Windows Azure to host the Class_Registration database. Then, you will practice how to remotely access the database server through the database management tool, SQL Server Management Studio. To create a database and SQL Database server on Windows Azure, follow the steps given below.

TASK 1: CREATING SQL DATABASE SERVER ON WINDOWS AZURE

1. In Internet Explorer, enter the following URL to the Windows Azure Management Portal: https://windows.azure.com.
2. If you do not have a user account yet, create one and log in to your Windows Azure Management Portal.
3. Once you have logged on to Windows Azure, your first task is to create a database server. To do so, click **STORAGE** on the left-hand side of your screen and then click **NEW** as shown in Figure 2.34.
4. After the **STORAGE** page opens, select **SQL DATABASE** and click **CUSTOM CREATE** as shown in Figure 2.35.
5. On the Specify database settings page, enter the database name and select the database server as shown in Figure 2.36.
6. Click the **Next** arrow to go to the **SQL Database server settings** page. Specify your login name, password, and region as shown in Figure 2.37. You can have your own login name. However, do not use your email address as the login name. The special character in the email address such as @ is not allowed in the login name.
7. Click the check mark icon to complete the configuration of the new server.
8. To view your newly created database server, click the **SQL DATABASE** link and then click the **SERVERS** tab (Figure 2.38). The name of your server is a random name assigned by Windows Azure. Write down the server name for remote access later.
9. Click the newly created server to open the server's Dashboard shown in Figure 2.39.

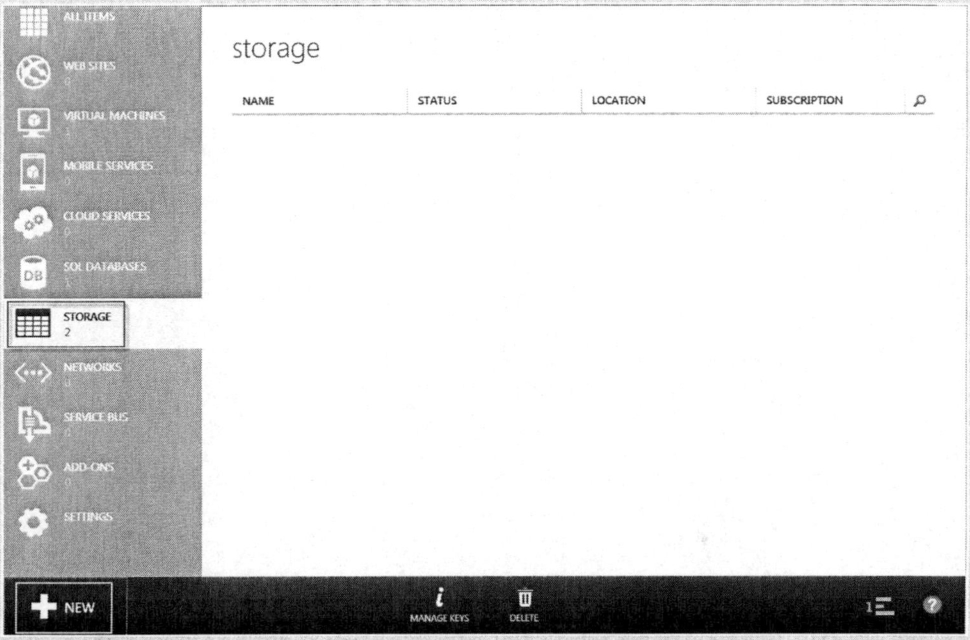

Figure 2.34 Create storage.

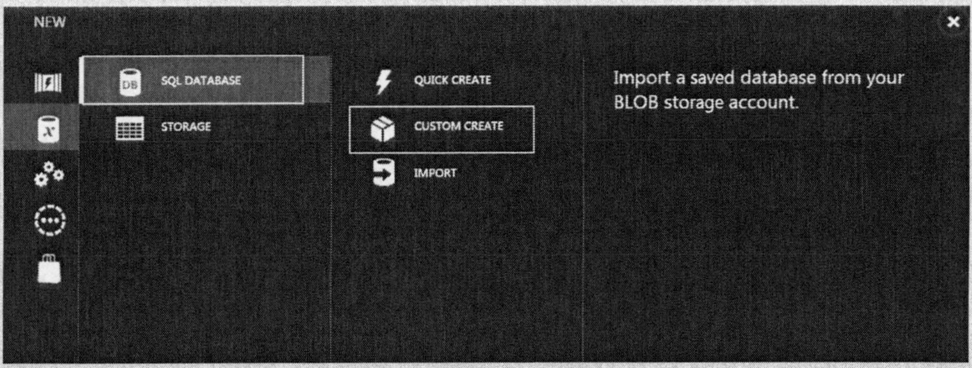

Figure 2.35 Create SQL Database.

10. Click the **CONFIGURE** tab to open the configuration page. On this page, your current local computer's IP address is added to the Allowed IP Addresses list. The computers with IP addresses listed in Allowed IP Addresses are allowed to access the SQL Database server.
11. To allow the connection from the server, myserver created in Chapter 1, to access the SQL Database server, you can add the IP address of myserver to the list of Allowed IP Addresses. To do so, click the **VIRTUAL MACHINES** icon on the left-hand side of your screen. Highlight **myserver** and click the **CONNECT** icon as shown in Figure 2.40.

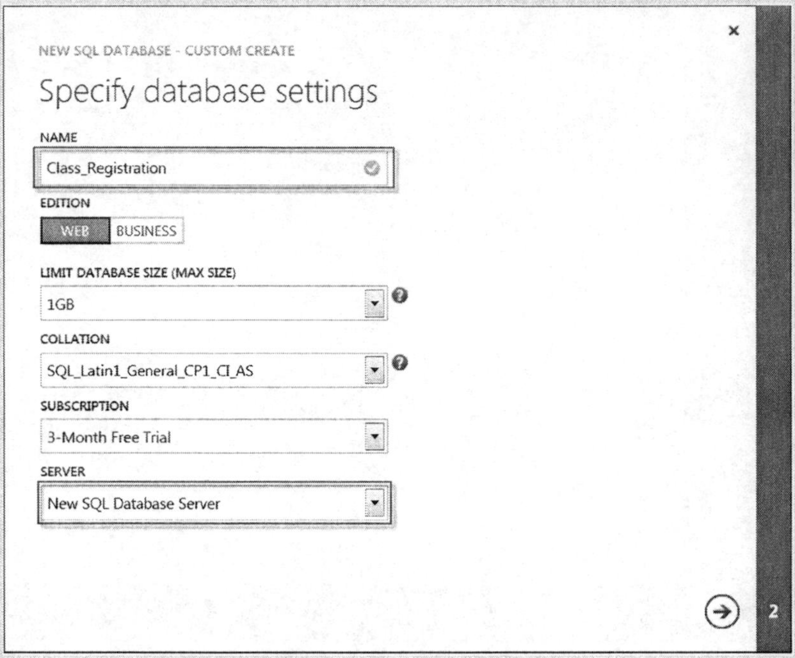

Figure 2.36 Specify database settings.

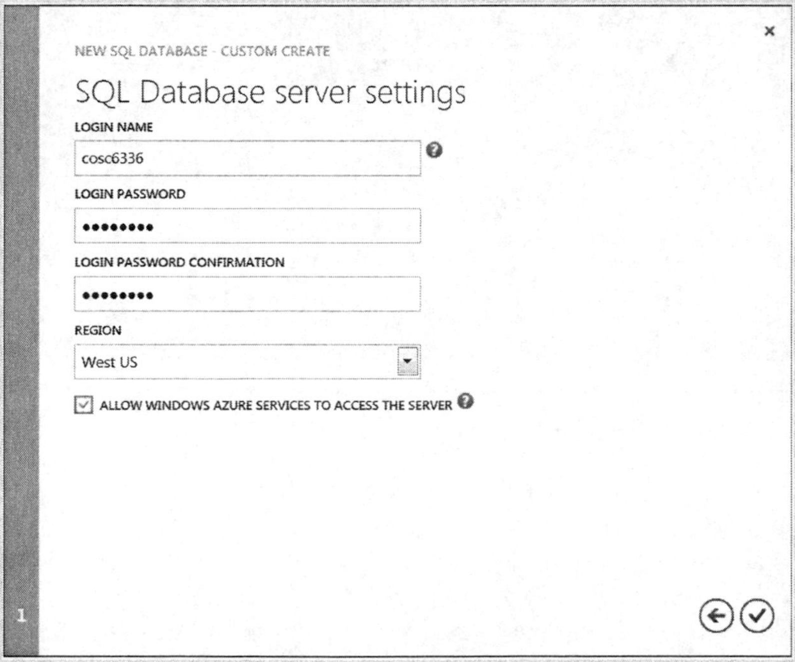

Figure 2.37 Specify SQL Database server setting.

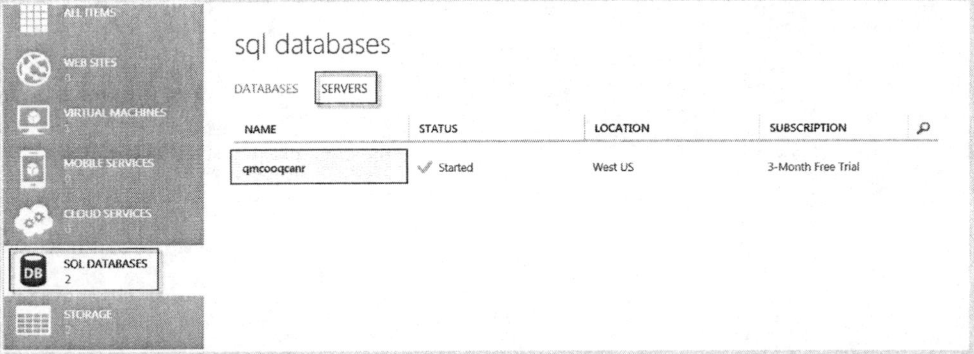

Figure 2.38 SQL Database server.

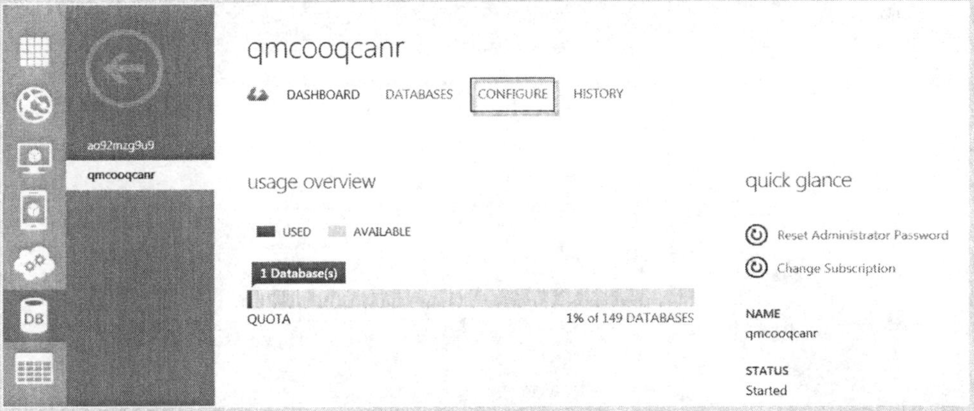

Figure 2.39 Server dashboard.

12. After the virtual machine is connected, press the **Windows Icon** key to open the **Desktop tile.** On the tile, click on the **Developer Command Prompt** icon as shown in Figure 2.41.
13. Once the command prompt is opened, enter the command **ipconfig** and write down the IP address of your server as shown in Figure 2.42.
14. Go back to the server configuration page on the Windows Azure Management Portal; specify the rule name as **myserver**, the start IP address as **10.215.28.42**, and the end IP address as **10.215.28.42** (Figure 2.43).
15. Finally, to view your newly created database, click the **DATABASES** tab as shown in Figure 2.44. You can see that the database Class_Registration is created.

TASK 2: REMOTELY ACCESSING SQL DATABASE SERVER

Once an SQL Database server is created, users can access the server through a web browser or through a database management tool such as SQL Server Management Studio, which is

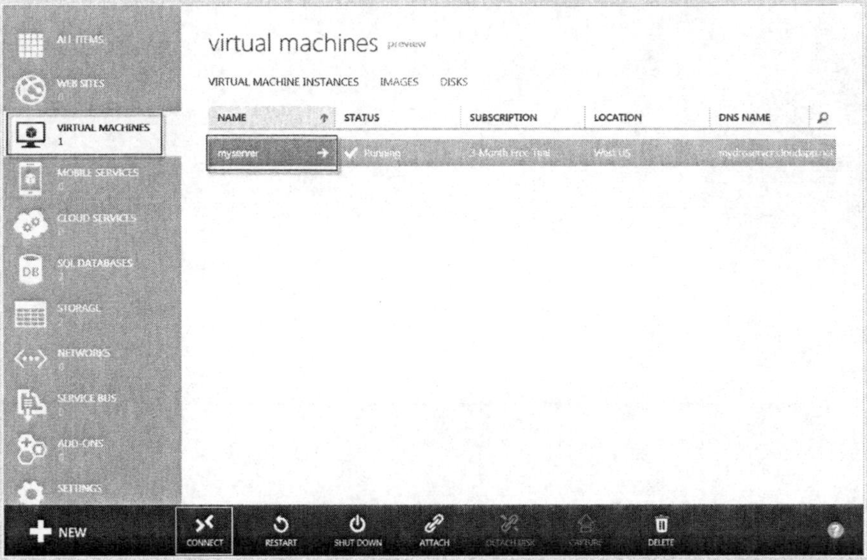

Figure 2.40 Connect to virtual machine.

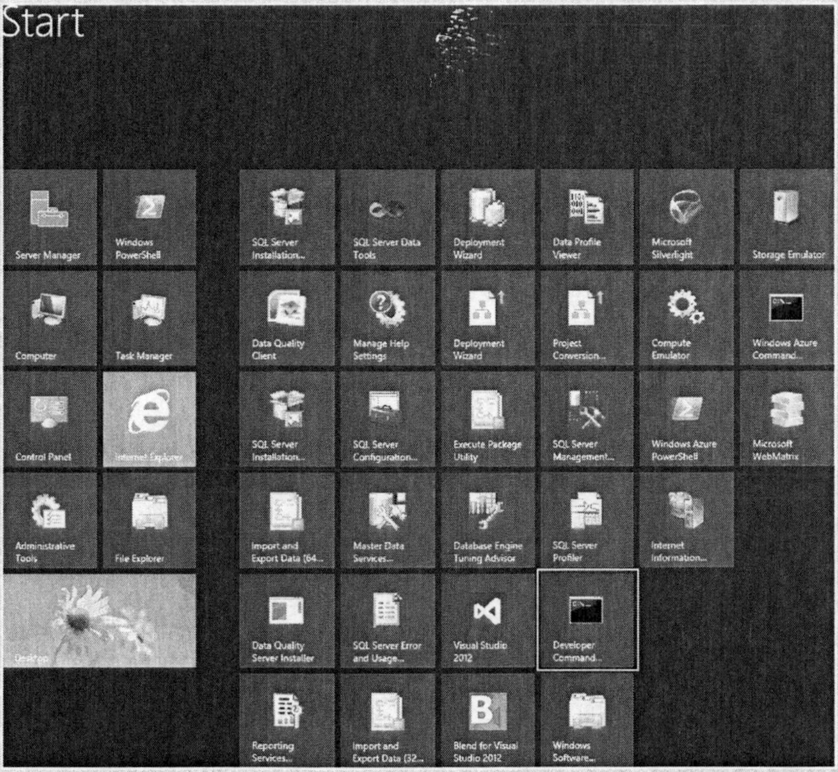

Figure 2.41 Open developer command prompt.

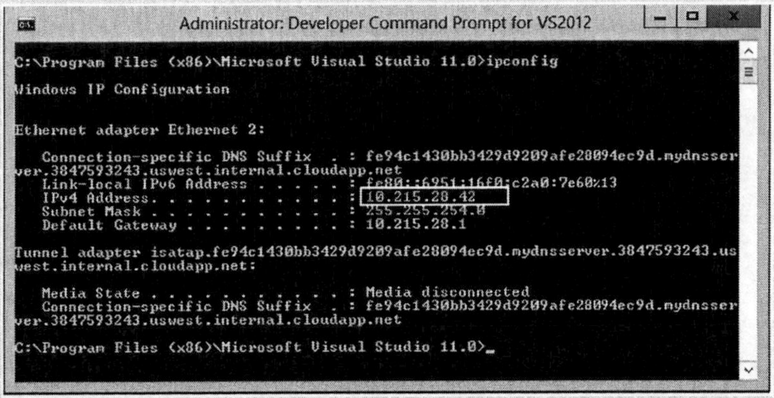

Figure 2.42 IP address of the virtual machine.

Figure 2.43 SQL Database server configuration.

familiar to many database professionals. In the following, we will demonstrate how to access the newly created SQL Database server through SQL Server Management Studio:

1. Assume that your virtual machine is still open. On the tile, click the SQL Server Management Studio icon as shown in Figure 2.45.
2. Once SQL Server Management Studio is opened, in the Server name combo box, enter the name of your SQL Database server. In the Authentication dropdown list, select **SQL Server Authentication**. Then, enter your user name and password as shown in Figure 2.46.

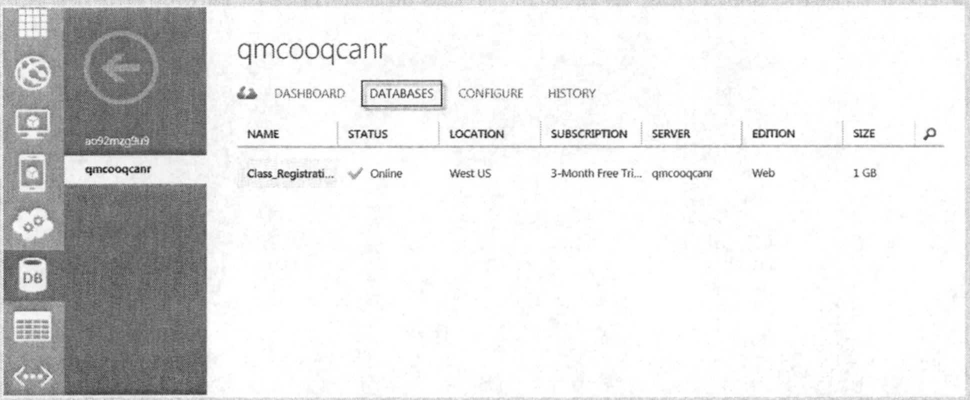

Figure 2.44 Class_Registration Database.

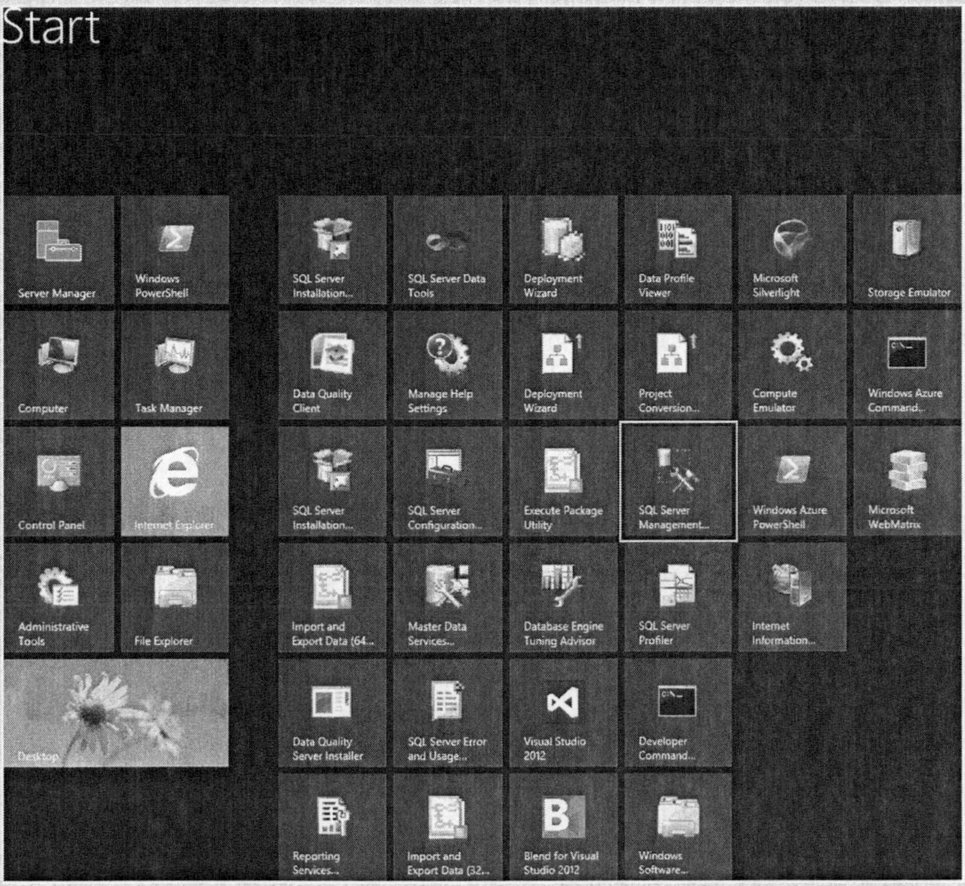

Figure 2.45 Open SQL Server Management Studio.

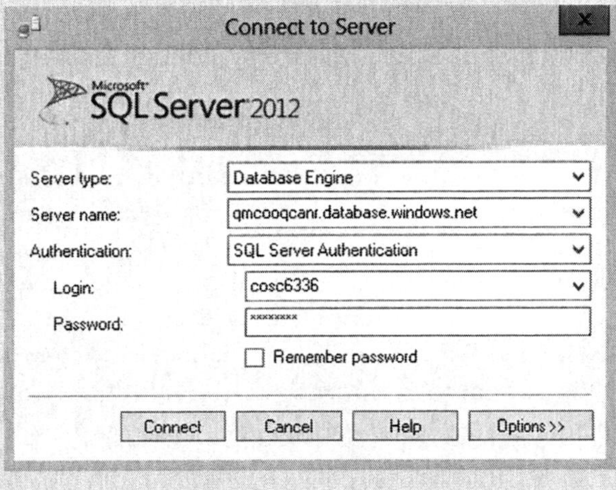

Figure 2.46 SQL Server login.

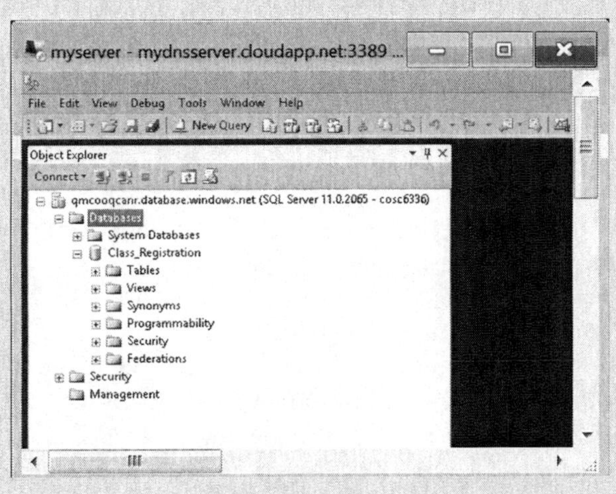

Figure 2.47 Class_Registration Database.

3. After you log on to the SQL Database server, expand the **Databases** node, you should be able to see the newly created database **Class_Registration** as shown in Figure 2.47.

In this activity, you have created a fully functional database server on Windows Azure without creating your own IT infrastructure. With cloud computing, the process of creating a database server is quick and easy, not to mention that the server is highly flexible, scalable, reliable, and secure. Through the Internet connection, the server is available anywhere and anytime.

Although the database Class_Registration is created, it is empty since we have not created any database objects yet. In the next chapter, we will create some database objects such as tables in the Class_Registration database.

2.5 Summary

In this chapter, you have learned about database design, including conceptual design, logical design, and physical design. The first task of database design is to investigate business requirements. A case study is used to illustrate the investigation process. The case study is about a class registration process. The investigation can be accomplished by interviewing the key players, observing the underlying business process, and examining the documents used in the business process. By analyzing the investigation results, the database designer can extract the information useful for developing a data model. For the logical design, data modeling is introduced in this chapter. The IDEF1X standard is used for E–R modeling. IDEF1X is a national standard representing data models in database development. For creating highly scalable databases that are accessible anywhere and anytime, Microsoft Windows Azure is introduced. Cloud computing provides an ideal environment for companies that need dynamically scalable databases. For the physical design, two types of Storage Services, Windows Azure SQL Database and Windows Azure Storage, are discussed in this chapter.

Review Questions

1. What information about objects should be collected before designing a database?
2. How do you collect information needed for the conceptual design?
3. Why is data modeling important in a database development process?
4. What is an entity? Give an example of an entity.
5. Explain the difference between an entity class and an entity instance.
6. What is an attribute? Give an example of an entity with some attributes.
7. What is an identifier? Give an example of an identifier.
8. Explain what a surrogate key is.
9. What is a domain? Give an example of a domain.
10. Describe the identifying relationship and give an example about it.
11. Describe the nonidentifying relationship and give an example of it.
12. Describe the many-to-many relationship and give an example of it.
13. What is a categorization relationship? Give an example of a categorization relationship.
14. What is cardinality? Give an example of cardinality.
15. What does the letter Z stand for as a cardinality symbol?
16. What issues are related to physical design?
17. What is Windows Azure SQL Database?
18. What are the three components included in Windows Azure Storage Services?
19. What type of data does Windows Azure Blob storage store?
20. What type of data does Windows Azure Table storage store?

Chapter 3

Table Normalization and Windows Azure SQL Database

Objectives

- Learn in detail about database tables
- Identify problems in table structures
- Normalize tables
- Convert a data model to a relational database

3.1 Introduction

Once a data model is developed, the next task is to convert the data model to a relational database. The goal of this chapter is to prepare for and carry out the conversion of a data model to a relational database. A relational database is constructed with tables and relationships among these tables. Your first task is to study table structures. Concepts such as relations, keys, and functional dependency will be studied in this chapter. Then, you will learn how to normalize the table structures to avoid database operation problems. Next, you will modify your data model according to the desired table structures. Lastly, the modified data model will be ready to be converted to a relational database.

3.2 Overview of Relational Database

In the 1970s, Edgar Codd introduced the relational database concept. In his proposal, the data model components, entity, attribute, and entity instance have the corresponding names relation, attribute, and tuple, respectively. The words relation, attribute, and tuple are from a mathematical set theory from which Edgar Codd developed the relational database. For business application, less rigorous names are used for entity, attribute, and entity instance. In a relational database, an entity is represented by a table, which is a logical structure containing a set of related entity instances. A column in a table is corresponding to an attribute in an entity. A row in a table is an entity instance in a data model. Another set of names corresponding to entity, attribute, and entity instance are called file, field, and record, often used in file system processing and programming languages by programmers.

A converting process from a data model to a relational database converts the data model components to the database objects and implements the relationships among the database objects. Figure 3.1 shows a table that consists of rows and columns.

As seen in Figure 3.1, each cell in the table contains a data value. For each column, the data values have the same data type. The data type of the column LocationID is integer. The data type of the column Name is character. The data type for the column CostRate is money, and the data type for the column Availability is decimal. For the column ModifiedDate, the data type is datetime. The definition of the table is shown in Figure 3.2.

It is easy to confuse the word **relation** with the word **relationship** in an E–R model. The word **relation** is closely related to **table**. For a **table** to be a **relation**, each cell in the table must contain a single value, there should be no duplicated rows, and all the cells in a column must contain the

	LocationID	Name	CostRate	Availability	ModifiedDate
1	1	Tool Crib	0.00	0.00	1998-06-01 00:0..
2	2	Sheet Metal Racks	0.00	0.00	1998-06-01 00:0..
3	3	Paint Shop	0.00	0.00	1998-06-01 00:0..
4	4	Paint Storage	0.00	0.00	1998-06-01 00:0..
5	5	Metal Storage	0.00	0.00	1998-06-01 00:0..
6	6	Miscellaneous Storage	0.00	0.00	1998-06-01 00:0..
7	7	Finished Goods Storage	0.00	0.00	1998-06-01 00:0..
8	10	Frame Forming	22.50	96.00	1998-06-01 00:0..
9	20	Frame Welding	25.00	108.00	1998-06-01 00:0..
10	30	Debur and Polish	14.50	120.00	1998-06-01 00:0..
11	40	Paint	15.75	120.00	1998-06-01 00:0..
12	45	Specialized Paint	18.00	80.00	1998-06-01 00:0..
13	50	Subassembly	12.25	120.00	1998-06-01 00:0..

Results | Messages

Figure 3.1 Example of table.

Column Name	Data Type	Allow Nulls
LocationID	smallint	☐
Name	Name (nvarchar)	☐
CostRate	smallmoney	☐
Availability	decimal	☐
ModifiedDate	datetime	☐

Figure 3.2 Table definition.

same type of data. In this chapter, if a table is qualified as a relation, we may use the word **relation** in the process of improving the table structure. The word **relationship** refers to the association between tables.

3.2.1 Functional Dependency

In a table, the data values in some columns determine the data values in other columns. For example, in Figure 3.1, each value in the column LocationID can determine a value in the column CostRate. On the other hand, a single value in CostRate cannot determine a value in the column LocationID. That is, the value 0 in the column CostRate corresponds to several different values in the column LocationID. On the basis of the above discussion, we say that LocationID determines CostRate but not the other way around. LocationID is called a **determinant**, and CostRate that is determined by LocationID is called a **dependent.** The notation used to represent the dependency is shown below:

$$\text{LocationID} \rightarrow \text{CostRate}$$

The above notation means that CostRate is **functionally dependent** on LocationID. By examining Figure 3.1, there is another functional dependency.

$$\text{LocationID} \rightarrow \text{Name, CostRate, Availability, ModifiedDate}$$

This indicates that Name, CostRate, Availability, and ModifiedDate are **functionally dependent** on LocationID.

In a data model, **functional dependency** is a relationship among attributes where one attribute or a combination of attributes determines another attribute. The concept of functional dependency can be defined more formally in the following theorem:

> If an attribute X determines another attribute Y, the attribute Y is **functionally dependent** on the attribute X.

Sometimes, a determinant is formed by a combination of attributes. As shown in Figure 3.3, lname or fname alone is not a determinant for other columns since the repeated value Anderson in lname cannot be used to determine the values Ben and Donna in fname and the repeated value Mary in fname cannot be used to determine the values Collins and Garza in lname. If you

fname	lname	phone	address	city	zip
Ben	Anderson	(361)470-6618	231 Ork St.	Victoria	77901
Donna	Anderson	(361)470-6618	231 Ork St.	Victoria	77901
Dan	Smith	(281)375-3029	879 Alen Dr.	Sugarland	77435
Luke	Fischer	(281)560-2207	523 Tree St.	Sugarland	77435
Dan	Erwin	(361)389-3725	101 Nelson St.	Victoria	77901
Mary	Collins	(979)369-2451	340 Ernst Ln.	Wharton	77698
Greg	Moore	(361)783-9371	635 Miori Ln.	Victoria	77901
Mary	Garza	(281)572-2828	275 Julia Ln.	Sugarland	77435
Andy	Wang	(281)254-2258	10 Forest Dr.	Sugarland	77435
Kevin	Harper	(979)458-8376	487 Fox Ln.	Wharton	77698
Roeann	Smith	(281)349-6725	1029 Austin St.	Sugarland	77435

Figure 3.3 Combination determinant.

combine the lname and fname columns, the combination becomes a determinant for the rest of the columns. That is

(fname, lname) → phone, address, city, zip

The notation indicates that the columns phone, address, city, and zip are functionally dependent on the combination (fname, lname).

In the above functional dependency, phone depends on the combination (fname, lname), but fname alone does not determine phone. The discussion leads to another concept, **fully functional dependency**, in the data modeling theory.

If the attribute Y is functionally dependent on the combination X which consists of multiple attributes but not on any subset of the attributes of X, then, Y is fully functionally dependent on X.

In this section, the concepts of functional dependency have been introduced. Later in this chapter, functional dependency will be used to establish the relationships among tables.

3.2.2 Keys

In Chapter 2, you learned that an attribute or a group of attributes that can uniquely identify entity instances in an entity is called a **key**. In the previous section, the column LocationID uniquely determines the rest of the columns. Therefore, LocationID is a **key** for the table. This means that a key is a determinant; however, in general, a determinant may not necessarily be a key. For example, in Figure 3.1, CostRate determines Availability. Any attribute that determines the values of another attribute is a determinant. Although CostRate is a determinant, it is not a key column because the values in it are not unique.

Since a key is a determinant and functional dependency specifies the relationship between two tables, the concept of keys plays an important role in the process of converting a data model to a relational database. Tables in a relational database will be connected with key columns.

To get ready for the converting process, let us do a quick review about keys. First, to be unique, each value in a key column can only occur once. For a table to be a relation, the table must include a **key** column since no relation allows duplicated rows. The concept of keys is summarized in the following:

Candidate key: A nonredundant column or a set of columns that can uniquely identify each row in a table is called candidate key. For the table in Figure 3.1, both LocationID and Name can serve as a key to determine each row in the table. Therefore, the attributes LocationID and Name are both qualified as the candidate key attributes:

LocationID → Name, CostRate, Availability, ModifiedDate

Name → LocationID, CostRate, Availability, ModifiedDate

Primary key: In a relation, a **primary key** is a **candidate key** selected by the user to uniquely identify other columns in the relation.

Foreign key: In a relation, a foreign key is a column or a set of columns whose values match the values of the **primary key** in another relation.

Combination key: A combination key consists of more than one column that can be used as a key.

Now that you have learned the concept of keys, the next step is to use keys to represent relationships.

(a)

pub_id	pub_name	city	state	country
0736	New Moon Books	Boston	MA	USA
0877	Binnet & Hardley	Washington	DC	USA
1389	Algodata Infosyste	Berkeley	CA	USA
1622	Five Lakes Publishir	Chicago	IL	USA
1756	Ramona Publishers	Dallas	TX	USA
9901	GGG&G	München	<NULL>	Germany
9952	Scootney Books	New York	NY	USA
9999	Lucerne Publishing	Paris	<NULL>	France

(b)

emp_id	fname	minit	lname	job_id	job_lvl	pub_id
PMA42628M	Paolo	M	Accorti	13	35	0877
PSA89086M	Pedro	S	Afonso	14	89	1389
VPA30890F	Victoria	P	Ashworth	6	140	0877
H-B39728F	Helen		Bennett	12	35	0877
L-B31947F	Lesley		Brown	7	120	0877
F-C16315M	Francisco		Chang	4	227	9952
PTC11962M	Philip	T	Cramer	2	215	9952
A-C71970F	Aria		Cruz	10	87	1389
AMD15433F	Ann	M	Devon	3	200	9952
ARD36773F	Anabela	R	Domingues	8	100	0877

Figure 3.4 (a) PUBLISHERS table, (b) EMPLOYEES table.

3.2.3 Linking Tables

In a data model, entities are associated by relationships. To implement these relationships in a relational database, two tables involved in a relationship should share a common column. As an example, consider the two linked tables in Figures 3.4a and 3.4b. There is a nonidentifying relationship between these two tables. That is, a row of the PUBLISHERS table is related to one or more rows in the EMPLOYEES table. This relationship can be implemented by adding the pub_ID column to the table EMPLOYEES. The column pub_ID in the table PUBLISHERS is the primary key. It is used to uniquely identify each row in PUBLISHERS. The column pub_ID in EMPLOYEES is a foreign key. As a foreign key, the values in the column pub_ID in the table EMPLOYEES do not have to be unique. In such a way, the relationship is implemented by a primary/foreign key pair.

From the functional dependency point of view, the column pub_ID in the table EMPLOYEES is determined by the column pub_ID in the table PUBLISHERS. This functional dependency specifies the relationship between PUBLISHERS and EMPLOYEES. Not only can a functional dependency be used to specify a relationship, it can also be used to normalize a table structure so that the tables can be used to build a properly defined relational database. The next section discusses table normalization.

3.3 Normalization

A relational database consists of tables and relationships. A properly designed table structure will greatly improve database performance, reduce the size of data storage, and ensure correct database operations. In this section, you will learn about the concepts of table structure and the process of normalizing tables.

3.3.1 Why Table Normalization

A normalization process is a process to eliminate anomalies that occur in a database operation. To see what those anomalies are, let us consider the CLASS_REGISTRATON_INFO table shown in Table 3.1.

In Table 3.1, information about students, faculty members, courses, and classes are stored in a single table CLASS_REGISTRATON_INFO. This fact indicates that the primary key has to be a combination of several columns. Indeed, StudentID alone cannot determine the column Course. For example, the value 11 in the StudentID column cannot determine the values in the Course column. The same 11 relates to two different values, Database and E-Commerce. By the same argument, StudentID cannot determine ClassID. On the other hand, the column Course alone cannot determine StudentID and some other columns. Some students may take the same course more than once. In such a case, the values of ClassID cannot be determined by the combination (StudentID, Course). Therefore, the primary key is a combination of three columns (StudentID, Course, ClassID) for the table CLASS_REGISTRATON_INFO.

The table displayed in Table 3.1 is in fact a relation. Each cell has only a single data value, the values in each column have the same data type, and there are no duplicated rows. Unfortunately, a table that satisfies the requirements of a relation is far from ideal in a relational database. The table CLASS_REGISTRATON_INFO has a data redundancy problem. For example, the name Smith in the Faculty Name column is repeated three times. Data redundancy such as this will cost extra labor for data entry and waste storage space on the hard drive.

In addition to the data redundancy problem, the table CLASS_REGISTRATON_INFO has other more serious problems. The structure of the table is not good enough to avoid problems that will occur during a data modification process. When you modify the existing data in the table, the current table structure may cause undesired results, which are called **modification anomalies.** There are three types of **modification anomalies.**

Update anomalies: Update anomalies occur during the process of updating the existing data in a table. Suppose that you want to change the faculty for the student with ID 11 from Lee to Boyd.

Table 3.1 CLASS_REGISTRATON_INFO Table

Student ID	*Student Name*	*Faculty ID*	*Faculty Name*	*Grade*	*Course*	*Pre-requisite*	*Class ID*
10	Liz	1	Smith	A	VB	None	1000
11	Joe	2	Lee	C	Database	VB	1001
12	Linda	1	Smith	B	E-Commerce	Database	1002
13	Don	3	Fry	C	VB	None	1000
14	Jan	4	Garza	B	Database	VB	1001
10	Liz	1	Smith	A	Database	VB	1003
16	Bruce	3	Fry	B	Info-Systems	Database	1004
11	Joe	2	Lee	B	E-Commerce	Database	1006
13	Don	3	Fry	A	Database	VB	1005

You must first find the rows that contain the value Lee as the value for FacultyName. In Table 3.1, there are two rows with Lee as the faculty name. Then, you need to change the value Lee to Boyd for the rows that contain the student with ID 11. This is called an update anomaly. For a large table, you may end up changing the values in thousands of rows. A full table search has to be performed to locate the rows that need to be updated. It is time consuming. Update anomalies can slow down database performance significantly. You should avoid update anomalies as much as possible.

Insertion anomalies: Suppose you want to add information about a new course called Internet computing. You cannot do so unless a class has been scheduled for the Internet computing course, and some students have already enrolled in at least one class of that course. Without the information about students and classes, the new row cannot be inserted into the table. This type of anomaly is called an insertion anomaly.

Deletion anomalies: Suppose that you want to remove the student with ID 16 from the table CLASS_REGISTRATON_INFO. After the row is deleted, you lose the course information about Info-Systems and the information about the class 1004. This type of anomaly is called a deletion anomaly.

With the knowledge of functional dependency, we can detect what causes a modification anomaly. The table CLASS_REGISTRATON_INFO has a combination key (StudentID, Course, ClassID). That is

(StudentID, Course, ClassID) → StudentName, FacultyID, FacultyName, Grade, Prerequisite

In the above functional dependency, the nonkey column FacultyID is determined by StudentID, which is only a part of the combination key. Such a dependency is called a **partial dependency**. It is also true that Prerequisite depends on Course, which is only a part of the combination key. With the existence of two partial dependencies, when you modify the information about a student, you must modify the corresponding course information and vice versa. To solve the problem, we should break up the table by removing the data that are related to the course from the current table. After the breakup, one table only contains the information related to courses, and the other one contains the information related to students and classes. The two resulting tables are shown in Tables 3.2 and 3.3.

The COURSE table contains course names and prerequisites. The column Course is the primary key. Since no student is involved, duplicated rows are no longer needed to match a student with multiple courses. For the table STUDENT_CLASS, the combination of StudentID and ClassID can be used as the primary key. You can represent the two tables by the notation commonly used for relations as shown below:

STUDENT_CLASS(<u>StudentID</u>, StudentName, FacultyID, FacultyName, Grade, <u>ClassID</u>)
COURSE(<u>Course</u>, Prerequisite)

Table 3.2 COURSE Table

CourseName	*Prerequisite*
VB	None
Database	VB
E-Commerce	Database
Info-Systems	Database

Table 3.3 STUDENT_CLASS Table

StudentID	*StudentName*	*FacultyID*	*FacultyName*	*Grade*	*ClassID*
10	Liz	1	Smith	A	1000
11	Joe	2	Lee	C	1001
12	Linda	1	Smith	B	1002
13	Don	3	Fry	C	1000
14	Jan	4	Garza	B	1001
10	Liz	1	Smith	A	1003
16	Bruce	3	Fry	B	1004
11	Joe	2	Lee	B	1006
13	Don	3	Fry	A	1005

The underlined columns in the above notation represent primary keys. After the breakup, the tables appear to have a better structure. Now, if you want to insert a new course in the table COURSE, you do not have to enter student information. On the other hand, for the table STUDENT_CLASS, if you decide to remove the student with ID 16, you do not have to worry about deleting the information about the course Info-Systems. The process of breaking up a table to get a better table structure is called table **normalization**. A normalization process helps eliminate modification anomalies and reduce data redundancy.

Usually, modification anomalies still exist after the first breakup. For example, in the table STUDENT_CLASS, to insert information about a new class, you have to wait until a student is enrolled in the class. This modification anomaly is caused by a functional dependency between the student and the class. In such a case, the normalization process has to carry on. The ultimate goal of table normalization is to make each table contain only a single dependency.

After a sequence of table break-ups, the original table will be broken into a set of small tables. There are some disadvantages of splitting a table into many smaller tables. One disadvantage is that you have to establish a relationship between each pair of these small tables. When retrieving information from a database consisting of many small tables, you have to go through many small tables to search for the required information. Searching many tables slows down database performance and search queries will become very complicated. Well normalized tables are necessary for databases that are used to handle update-intensive tasks, for instance, databases handling credit card transactions. On the other hand, if a database is used mainly for providing information for decision support, the database will not be updated frequently. Its tables should be constructed to be more efficient for information retrieval and more understandable for users. In such a case, tables that are not fully normalized can do a better job.

3.3.2 Normal Forms

From the discussion in the previous section, you can see that tables should be normalized at different levels to handle different tasks. A table may be normalized in the following normal forms:

- First normal form (1NF)
- Second normal form (2NF)
- Third normal form (3NF)
- Boyce–Codd normal form (BCNF)
- Fourth normal form (4NF)
- Domain-key normal form (DKNF)

These normal forms range from the lowest level, 1NF , to the highest level, DKNF. The higher the level, the fewer the modification anomalies. At the DKNF level, all the modification anomalies will be eliminated. There is a nested relationship among the normal forms; that is, if a table is in 2NF, it is also in 1NF. If a table is in DKNF, then it is in all the other normal forms. For many business applications, 3NF is sufficient. However, for some other business applications, higher-level normal forms are required. For decision support tasks, higher-level normal forms are less likely to be used.

In the following, you will learn the details of each level of the normal forms. You are going to learn how to identify the functional dependencies that cause malfunction and how to eliminate anomalies caused by these functional dependencies.

First normal form: If a table is qualified as a relation, it is in 1NF. That is, it meets the following requirements of 1NF:

- Each cell in the table contains a single value.
- Each column has a unique column name and all the data entries in the column have the same data type.
- No duplicated rows. The primary key is used to uniquely identify the rows in the table.

On the basis of the above specification of 1NF, the table CLASS_REGISTRATON_INFO is in 1NF.

Second normal form: As we have discussed earlier, a table in 1NF contains partial dependencies, which cause various modification anomalies. For the table displayed in Table 3.1, there are two partial dependencies in the combination primary key (StudentID, Course, ClassID):

$$\text{StudentID} \rightarrow \text{FacultyID}$$

$$\text{Course} \rightarrow \text{Prerequisite}$$

Let us try to understand how partial dependencies cause data redundancy and update anomalies. In the above partial dependencies, StudentID determines FacultyID. Each value of StudentID uniquely determines a value in FacultyID. On the other hand, since Course does not determine FacultyID, one faculty ID may be related to multiple courses. For example, in Table 3.1, the faculty with ID 2 is related to two courses, E-Commerce and Database. The faculty with ID 2 and the related student information have to be used twice to match the two courses. Consequently, data redundancy occurs. As a result of data redundancy, the update of faculty information, such as faculty name, has to be done in multiple locations. This causes the update anomaly.

To eliminate modification anomalies caused by partial dependencies, you have to get rid of the partial dependencies by splitting the table into two tables. This leads to the definition of 2NF whose requirements are listed below:

- The table is a relation; that is, it meets all the requirements for 1NF.
- There is no partial dependency in the table.

The two tables resulting from the table split are displayed in Tables 3.2 and 3.3. The table COURSE displayed in Table 3.2 has a single-column primary key; this means it is impossible for a partial dependency to occur. The violation of 2NF is only relevant when a table has a combination key. Thus, any relation that has a single-column primary key is in 2NF.

The table STUDENT_CLASS displayed in Table 3.3 is also in 2NF even though it has functional dependencies as shown below:

$$\text{StudentID} \rightarrow \text{StudentName}$$

$$\text{StudentName} \rightarrow \text{StudentID}$$

Why is the dependency StudentID → StudentName not a partial dependency? Since StudentID uniquely determines StudentName and vice versa, there are two combination candidate keys (StudentID, ClassID) and (StudentName, ClasssID). This indicates that StudentName is considered as part of a key. Remember that a partial dependency happens between a key column and a nonkey column. Therefore, the dependency StudentID → StudentName is not considered a partial dependency.

Third normal form: Being in 2NF, a table may still have modification anomalies. As an example, let us consider the modification anomalies that occurred during data modification in the table STUDENT_CLASS displayed in Table 3.3.

Update anomalies: In the STUDENT_CLASS table, there is data redundancy among the columns FacultyID and FacultyName. For example, a change to the faculty name related to the faculty with the ID 1 has to be done in multiple locations; this causes the occurrence of an update anomaly.

Insertion anomalies: Suppose we want to add a new student into the table STUDENT_CLASS. You would not be able to do so until information about the faculty is provided.

Deletion anomalies: Suppose that the student with the ID 14 is removed from the table STUDENT_CLASS. The information about the faculty Garza is lost.

The above modification anomalies are caused by another type of functional dependency called **transitive dependency**. In the table STUDENT_CLASS, the nonkey column FacultyName is determined by another nonkey column FacultyID. The transitive dependency can be represented with the following relation notation:

$$(\text{StudentID, ClassID}) \rightarrow \text{StudentName, FacultyID, FacultyName, Grade}$$

$$\text{FacultyID} \rightarrow \text{FacultyName}$$

When a nonkey column determines another nonkey column in a table, the table is not in 3NF. For a table to be in 3NF, we must eliminate the **transitive dependency**. 3NF is specified by the following rules:

- It is in 2NF.
- It contains no **transitive dependency**.

The transitive dependency can be eliminated by splitting the table. In our example, we split the table STUDENT_CLASS into two tables, FACULTY and STUDENT_CLASS as shown in Tables 3.4 and 3.5.

Table 3.4 FACULTY Table

FacultyID	*FacultyName*
1	Smith
2	Lee
3	Fry
4	Garza

Table 3.5 STUDENT_CLASS Table

StudentID	*StudentName*	*Grade*	*ClassID*
10	Liz	A	1000
11	Joe	C	1001
12	Linda	B	1002
13	Don	C	1000
14	Jan	B	1001
10	Liz	A	1003
16	Bruce	B	1004
11	Joe	B	1006
13	Don	A	1005

The table FACULTY uses the column FacultyID as the primary key. Since there is only one nonkey column in the table, this means that there is no transitive dependency in the table. Therefore, the table FACULTY is in 3NF.

In general, a table has no transitive dependency if each nonkey column except the foreign key column in the table directly depends on the primary key. This means that even if we add the foreign key column FacultyID to the table STUDENT_CLASS (Table 3.6), it is still in 3NF.

Now, if you want to change a faculty name, you can do it in the FACULTY table displayed in Table 3.4 instead of in the table STUDENT_CLASS displayed in Table 3.3. This will avoid the update anomaly caused by the transitive dependency FacultyID → FacultyName.

As mentioned earlier, tables in 3NF are acceptable for many databases. For some databases, tables in 3NF are still not good enough. In such a case, the normalization process should continue.

Boyce–Codd normal form: First, let us take a close look at the modification anomalies that cannot be eliminated by 3NF. Consider the table STUDENT_CLASS displayed in Table 3.5. The table has a combination primary key (StudentID, ClassID). In addition, there is a combination candidate key (StudentName, ClassID). Here, we have two combination candidate keys, and they have a common element ClassID. That is, we have the following functional dependency:

(StudentID, ClassID) → StudentName, FacultyID, Grade

StudentName → StudentID

Table 3.6 STUDENT_CLASS Table

StudentID	*StudentName*	*FacultyID*	*Grade*	*ClassID*
10	Liz	1	A	1000
11	Joe	2	C	1001
12	Linda	1	B	1002
13	Don	3	C	1000
14	Jan	4	B	1001
10	Liz	1	A	1003
16	Bruce	3	B	1004
11	Joe	2	B	1006
13	Don	3	A	1005

or

(StudentName, ClassID) → StudentID, FacultyID, Grade

StudentID → StudentName

As you can see, StudentName determines StudentID or vice versa. But, the determinant StudentName itself is not a candidate key. The functional dependency can cause the following modification anomalies:

Update anomalies: In the STUDENT_CLASS table, the update of the student name Joe has to be done at multiple locations; this causes the occurrence of update anomalies.

Insertion anomalies: You cannot add a new student into the table STUDENT_CLASS until you provide information about a class.

Deletion anomalies: If the student with the ID 13 is removed from the table STUDENT_CLASS, the class ID 1005 is lost.

To solve the problem, we need to further split the table STUDENT_CLASS to get to the next level of normalization called **Boyce–Codd normal form**. A table is in BCNF if it meets the following requirements:

- It is in 3NF.
- Every determinant is a candidate key.

The requirements listed above indicate that a table in 3NF with only a single key column and a single nonkey column is already in the BCNF because the only determinant is the primary key; that is, every determinant is a candidate key. In our example, to be in the BCNF, the STUDENT_CLASS table is split and multiple tables are created as shown in the following relation notation:

STUDENT(<u>StudentID</u>, StudentName, *FacultyID*)
STUDENT_CLASS(*StudentID*, *ClassID*, Grade)
CLASS(<u>ClassID</u>, TimeBlock, WeekDay, Semester)

In the table CLASS, more specific information about a class is added to the table. We did not add the information in Table 3.1 earlier so that we can focus on the normalization process.

As mentioned earlier that a table has no transitive dependency if each nonkey column (except the foreign key column) directly depends on the primary key. Although we still have StudentName → FacultyID in the STUDENT table, FacultyID is a foreign key. Therefore, there is no transitive dependency. Now, the table STUDENT_CLASS is broken up into three tables STUDENT, STUDENT_CLASS, and CLASS as shown in Tables 3.7 through 3.9.

In the STUDENT table, the determinant StudentName is now a candidate key. Therefore, the table STUDENT is in the BCNF. By the same argument, the tables STUDENT_CLASS and CLASS are in the BCNF. Also, the size of the above tables has been significantly reduced.

Tables in BCNF can still have other types of dependencies that cause modification anomalies. The next level normal form is 4NF, which will be discussed in the following:

Fourth normal form: Being in 4NF, a table should be in the BCNF and should not have **multivalue dependency. Multivalue dependency** is different from functional dependency. To illustrate the multivalue dependency, let us consider the following tables.

Table 3.7 STUDENT Table

StudentID	*StudentName*	*FacultyID*
10	Liz	1
11	Joe	2
12	Linda	1
13	Don	3
14	Jan	4
16	Bruce	3

Table 3.8 STUDENT_CLASS Table

StudentID	*ClassID*	*Grade*
10	1000	A
11	1001	C
12	1002	B
13	1000	C
14	1001	B
10	1003	A
16	1004	B
11	1006	B
13	1005	A

Table 3.9 CLASS Table

ClassID	*TimeBlock*	*WeekDay*	*Semester*
1000	9 am–12 pm	Monday	Fall
1001	1 pm–4 pm	Monday	Spring
1002	7 pm–10 pm	Tuesday	Fall
1003	9 am–12 pm	Tuesday	Spring
1004	1 pm–4 pm	Wednesday	Spring
1006	7 pm–10 pm	Wednesday	Fall
1005	9 am–12 pm	Thursday	Fall

Table 3.10 Table with Multivalue Dependency

StudentID	*TimeBlock*	*Weekday*
10	9 am–12 pm	Monday
10	1 pm–4 pm	Monday
10	1 pm–4 pm	Tuesday
10	9 am–12 pm	Tuesday
11	1 pm–4 pm	Monday
11	1 pm–4 pm	Tuesday
12	7 pm–10 pm	Wednesday

Table 3.10 is about the schedule for three students with the student IDs 10, 11, and 12. The student ID 10 is related to two TimeBlock values, 9 am–12 pm and 1 pm–4 pm. It is also related to two WeekDay values, Monday and Tuesday. Now, for the rows (10, 9 am–12 pm, Monday) and (10, 1 pm–4 pm, Monday), switch the TimeBlock values, and we have two rows (10, 1 pm–4 pm, Monday) and (10, 9 am–12 pm, Monday). Notice that, these two rows with the TimeBlock values switched are not new rows. They are the existing rows in the original table. That is, by switching the TimeBlock values, we do not generate extra rows in the table. Similarly, for the two rows (10, 9 am–12 pm, Monday) and (10, 9 am–12 pm, Tuesday), switch the WeekDay values and you have two rows, (10, 9 am–12 pm, Tuesday) and (10, 9 am–12 pm, Monday). Again, no extra rows are generated in the table by switching the WeekDay values. Keep doing this for every possible combination of TimeBlock and WeekDay values related to a pair of duplicated Student ID. If no extra row is generated after the value switching, we have the multivalue dependency between the columns StudentID and Timeblock as well as StudentID and WeekDay in the table.

In Table 3.11, switching the TimeBlock values in the two rows (11, 1 pm–4 pm, Monday) and (11, 9 am–12 pm, Tuesday), we have (11, 9 am–12 pm, Monday) and (11, 1 pm–4 pm, Tuesday). Notice that those two new rows do not match any rows in the original table. Therefore, there is

Table 3.11 Table with No Multivalue Dependency

StudentID	*TimeBlock*	*WeekDay*
10	9 am–12 pm	Monday
10	1 pm–4 pm	Monday
10	1 pm–4 pm	Tuesday
10	9 am–12 pm	Tuesday
11	1 pm–4 pm	Monday
11	9 am–12 pm	Tuesday
12	7 pm–10 pm	Wednesday

no multivalue dependency between the columns StudentID and TimeBlock. Similarly, you can verify that there is no multivalue dependency between the columns StudentID and WeekDay.

Note that the above analysis should be done in a table with three or more columns. For a table with two columns, multivalue dependency is called trivial multivalue dependency. For a table with nontrivial multivalue dependency, it is not qualified as in 4NF. A modification anomaly can occur in this type of table.

In the above normalization process, modification anomalies are gradually removed as the table is normalized to a higher level. The ultimate goal of table normalization is to eliminate all kinds of anomalies. Now, the question is whether there is a normal form that can achieve this goal. Theoretically, the answer is yes. DKNF will eliminate all types of anomalies.

Domain-Key normal form: Being in the DKNF, a table has no modification anomaly. In other words, if a table has no anomaly, it is in the DK/NF. Theoretically, that is great. However, unlike the normalization process shown above, the process to normalize a table to have the DK/NF is mostly based on the designer's knowledge about the business requirements and his/her design experience. There is no predefined rule to follow. In general, the DK/NF cannot be achieved by a normalization process shown in the previous sections. The key to the converting process is the designer's understanding of the business rules and constraints. It is a crucial step to identify the requirements and constraints of an underlying business. Once business requirements and rules are identified for a database project, the designer can construct tables and relationships to meet the requirements and rules. There may be some business rules that cannot be implemented at this stage; you, as a database designer, can implement those rules later in database application.

In 1981, Ronald Fagin defined the **Domain-Key normal form** as the following:

> A relation is in DK-NF if and only if every **constraint** on the relation is a logical consequence of **key** constraints and **domain** constraints.

The definition seems a bit abstract. Indeed, in Fagin's definition of the DK/NF, the words such as constraints, keys, and domains have very general meanings. A domain constraint is a rule that specifies the format, type, or range of allowed values for a column. That is why domain constraints are also called attribute constraints. A key constraint checks the uniqueness of the rows in a table. The word "constraints" means rules to be enforced on functional dependency, multivalue dependency, interrelation dependency, and intravalue dependency, except time-related dependency. These rules can be identified by examining business requirements and restrictions. The above DK/NF definition says that by enforcing the key constraints and domain constraints, all the constraints on the table should be automatically enforced.

The procedure to create a DK/NF table starts with the determination of business requirements and constraints observed from a business process. Then, all the business requirements will be fulfilled by enforcing the keys and domains in the tables. Even though the DK/NF converting process is complicated and is depending on the specific requirements of a business process, proper use of the DK/NF converting process will help you understand the database design theory.

3.3.3 Denormalization

For a database used in a decision support system, fully normalized DK/NF tables may not always be desirable. In a decision support system, the data in a table are rarely modified. The main task for a decision support system is to search for data that meet certain criteria. Using not fully normalized tables can improve search performance. For example, by using the STUDENT_CLASS table displayed in Table 3.3, once a student is selected based on a given student ID, you will get other information about the student, such as the student's advisor and the grades for his/her classes, at the same time. If tables with a higher level of normalization are used, the search will have to go through tables such as STUDENT, STUDENT_CLASS, CLASS, FACULTY_CLASS, and FACULTY to get the information that meets a given search criterion. For the purpose of information presentation, it is better to use the STUDENT_CLASS table in Table 3.3 so that the faculty and class information related to a student can be retrieved at once without searching other tables. In general, for a decision support system, you can get information faster if low-level normalization tables are used.

In this section, we have looked at the normalization process. After the table structures are normalized, we are ready to convert the data model to a relational database.

3.4 Transferring Data Model to Relational Database

In the previous sections, you learned how to get better structured tables by using normalization. This section is about converting a data model to a relational database.

A data model consists of components such as entities, attributes, and relationships. In the process of transforming a data model to a relational database, you need to represent these components with corresponding objects in a relational database. With the selected database management system (DBMS), you can transform a data model to a relational database by performing the following tasks:

- Represent the entities as tables in a relational database.
- Represent the attributes as columns.
- Represent the relationships with foreign keys and primary keys.
- Specify domains by enforcing constraints on columns when creating tables with a DBMS.

In the following subsections, you will accomplish these tasks.

3.4.1 Representing Entities

When representing entities with tables created in Windows Azure SQL Database, you need to follow the naming rules for identifiers used in T-SQL. The rules for naming tables, columns, or other database objects are listed below:

- A name can include up to 128 characters, numbers, or symbols.
- A name must start with one of [a-z], [A-Z],_ , @, #, or letter characters from other non-English languages defined by Unicode Standard 2.0.
- The subsequent symbols can be the combination of [a-z], [A-Z], #, @, $,_ , numbers, or letter characters from other non-English languages defined by Unicode Standard 2.0.
- A name cannot use a reserved key word such as System for an object.
- An object name cannot use embedded spaces except for a database.

If you have to use names that do not follow these rules, delimit these names with either double quotation marks " " or brackets [] when you use them in your programming code. For example, if you have to use a table name such as CLASS FACULTY in the code, you must reference it in an SQL statement as [CLASS FACULTY] or "CLASS FACULTY."

When an object name starts with the symbols # or @, the name has a special meaning. For example

- A name that starts with the symbol @ represents a local variable or parameter.
- A name that starts with the symbol # represents a temporary table or procedure.
- A name that starts with the symbol ## or @@ represents a global temporary object.

To be consistent in a database development process, the naming rules or naming convention should be established before a database development process starts. Everyone in the development team should follow the naming rules. The examples of the naming rules in this book are listed in Table 3.12. All the database objects in this book will be named with these rules.

Each development team may have its own naming convention. It is important to keep the naming convention consistent and not conflict with the business rules. Even though you may be able to include spaces in an identifier's name, it is not a good idea to use a space or a reserved key word to name database objects except the name of a database. It may cause confusion when executing programming code.

Table 3.12 Naming Convention

Database Object	*Naming Example*
Database	Computer Service or ComputerService
Table	CLASSFACULTY or CLASS_FACULTY
Intersection table	CLASS_CLASSROOM
Column	StudentID

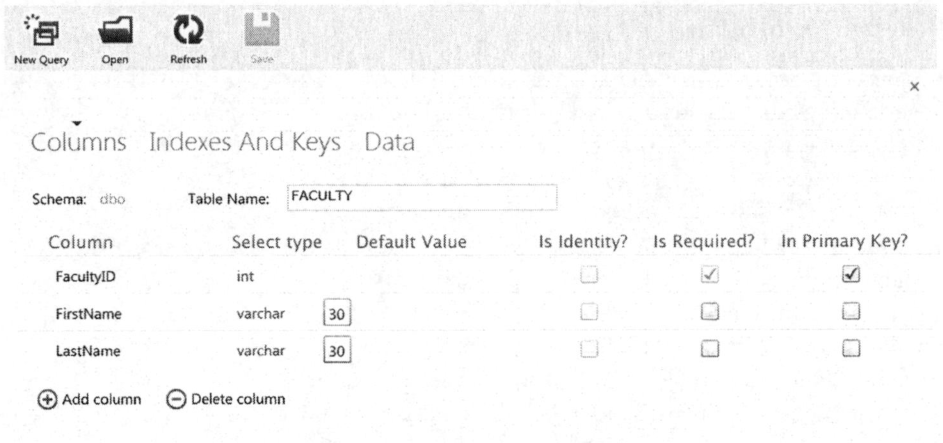

Figure 3.5 Table definition in Windows Azure SQL Database.

Now that you have learned about the naming convention, let us take a closer look at the structure of a table created in Windows Azure SQL Database. The definition of a table in Windows Azure SQL Database is shown in Figure 3.5.

In Windows Azure SQL Database, you can define columns in a table, and each column can be specified by its name, data type, and other properties as listed below:

- *Is Required*: A column does not allow null values.
- *Column Name*: The name of a column.
- *Data Type*: The data type of a column. The commonly used data types are listed in Table 3.13.
- *Default Values*: Values automatically assigned to a column when a new row is inserted.
- *Identity*: A system-generated number that is used as a row identifier. It will be automatically incremented when each new row is inserted.
- *Length*: The length of a character string.
- *Precision*: The maximum number of digits used in decimal data values.
- *Scale*: The maximum number of digits used to the right of the decimal point.

Next, let us represent an entity with a relation notation. For the entity STUDENT created in Chapter 2 (Figure 3.6), the corresponding relation is

STUDENT(<u>StudentID</u>, FirstName, LastName, *FacultyID*)

where the underline is used to indicate that the column is a primary key column. The italic letters indicate that the column is a foreign key column. On the basis of the relation definition, the table structure can be specified with Windows Azure SQL Database as shown in Figure 3.7.

Figure 3.7 shows that the column StudentID is the primary key and is checked under the In Primary Key column. The data type is defined for each column.

Besides the entity component, relationship is another component used in a data model. In the next subsection, you will represent a relationship with a pair of a primary key and a foreign key.

Table 3.13 Commonly Used Data Types

Data Type	*Default Length*	*Description*
Char	10	Fixed-length non-Unicode character data type with a maximum of 8000 characters.
Datetime	8	Date and time data from January 1, 1753, to December 31, 9999.
Decimal or numeric	9	Fixed precision and scale numeric data type ranging from $-10^{38}+1$ to $10^{38}-1$.
Float	8	Floating-precision number data type ranging from –1.79E + 38 to –2.23E–38, 0 and 2.23E–38 to 1.79E + 38.
Image	16	Variable-length binary data representing an image. The maximum length is 2^{31}–1 bytes.
Int	4	Integer data type ranging from -2^{31} through 2^{31}–1.
Money	8	Monetary data values from -2^{63} to 2^{63}–1 with accuracy to the ten-thousandth of a monetary unit.
Text	16	Variable-length non-Unicode data type with a maximum of 2^{31}–1 characters.
Varchar	50	Variable-length non-Unicode data type with a maximum of 8000 characters.
Ntext	16	Variable-length Unicode data with a maximum of 2^{30}–1 characters.
Nchar	10	Fixed-length Unicode data with a maximum of 4000 characters.
Table		A special data type that can be used to store a result set for later processing.
XML		The name of an xml schema collection.
Sql_variant		A data type that stores values of various SQL Server supported data types (except text, ntext, image, timestamp, and sql_variant).

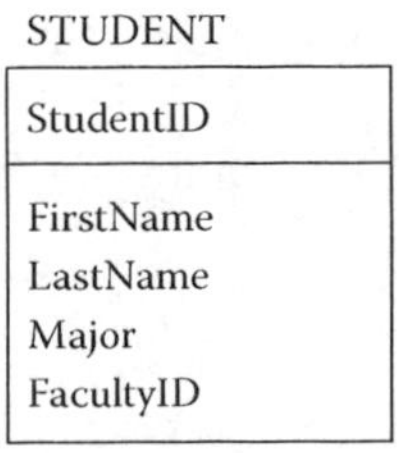

Figure 3.6 STUDENT entity.

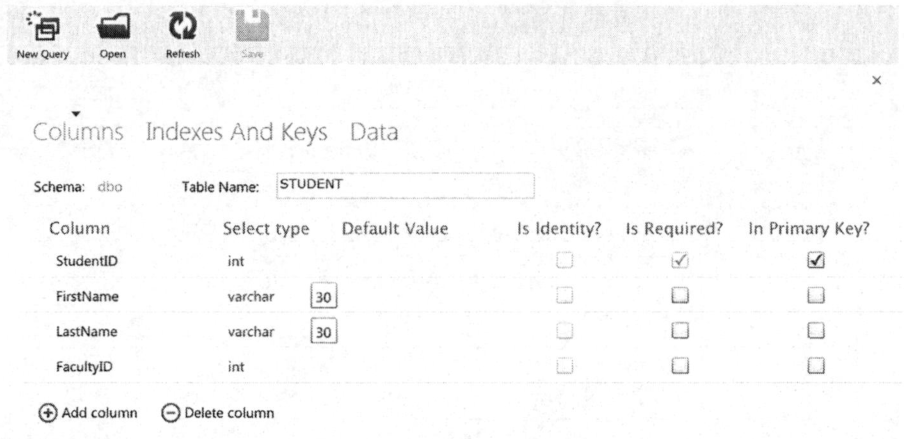

Figure 3.7 STUDENT table design in Windows Azure SQL Database.

3.4.2 Representing Relationships

Chapter 2 described some commonly used relationships: identifying relationship, nonidentifying relationship, nonspecific relationship, categorization relationship, recursive relationship, and ternary relationship. As entities are represented by relations, the relationship between two relations will be represented by a shared column. That is, the primary key of one relation is shared by another relation as a foreign key. The following shows how to represent each type of relationship by sharing the key:

1. *Identifying relationship*: In Chapter 2, we discussed the identifying relationship between the entities CLASSROOM and BUILDING. The relationship between these two entities is shown in Figure 3.8.

   In the above identifying relationship, the entity BUILDING is the parent and the entity CLASSROOM is the child. The identifying relationship can be represented by letting both the parent relation BUILDING and the child relation CLASSROOM share the column BuildingId. BuildingId is the primary key in the parent relation BUILDING and is the foreign key and part of the combination primary key in the child relation CLASSROOM. The relation notation representing the identifying relationship is shown below:

   BUILDING(BuildingId, BuildingName)

   CLASSROOM(ClassroomId, *BuildingId*, Capacity)

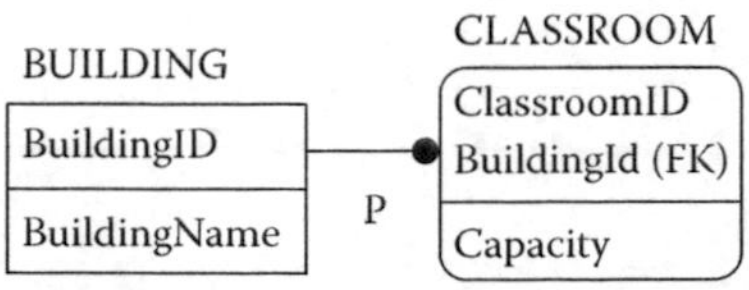

Figure 3.8 Identifying relationship.

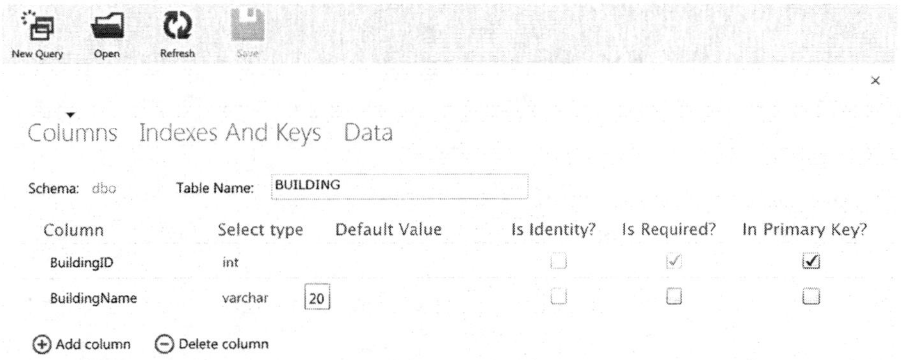

Figure 3.9 Table design of BUILDING.

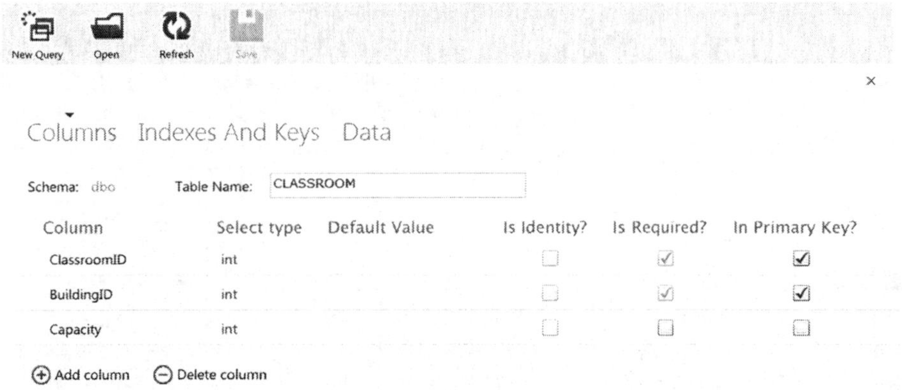

Figure 3.10 Table design of CLASSROOM.

CLASSROOM relates to BUILDING through the column BuildingId. For a given classroom ID, you will be able to find the related building ID located in the same row in the child relation. By matching the building ID found in the child relation to the building ID in the parent relation, you can get the building name in the relation BUILDING. On the other hand, for a given building ID, you can look for all the classrooms in that specified building in the CLASSROOM relation. In Windows Azure SQL Database, these two relations are constructed as shown in Figures 3.9 and 3.10.

As seen in Figure 3.10, the combination primary key in the table CLASSROOM includes two columns, ClassroomId and BuildingId. Make sure that the definition of the column BuildingId in the table CLASSROOM is consistent with the definition of BuildingId in the table BUILDING.

2. *Nonidentifying relationship*: As described in Chapter 2, the relationship between the entities FACULTY and STUDENT is a nonidentifying relationship (Figure 3.11).

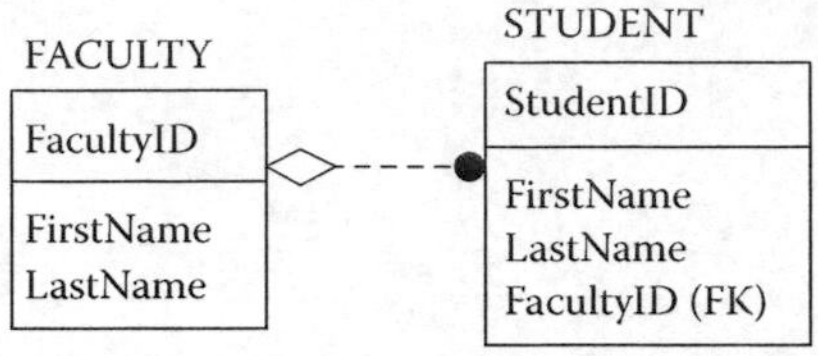

Figure 3.11 Nonidentifying relationship.

The corresponding relations with the shared column FacultyID are given as the following:

FACULTY(<u>FacultyID</u>, FirstName, LastName)

STUDENT(<u>StudentID</u>, FirstName, LastName, *FacultyID*)

To find a student's advisor's name for a given student ID from the above relations, you first look for the faculty ID that is in the same row as the given student ID in the STUDENT relation. Then, search for the faculty ID in the FACULTY relation that matches the faculty ID from the STUDENT relation. Once the faculty ID is found in the FACULTY relation, you can get the advisor's name in the same row. On the other hand, to find all the students who are advised by a faculty whose ID is given, first look up the FacultyID column in the STUDENT relation to find all the values that match the given faculty ID. Then, you can get the students' names in those rows that have the matching faculty ID.

As pointed out in the previous chapter, a nonidentifying relationship is often used to represent a 1:N relationship where N can be 0, 1, or any positive integer. When N is equal to 1, you have a 1:1 relationship. In such a case, you can put the primary key values of one relation to the other relation to represent the relationship. When N is a positive integer that is greater than 1, you have a one-to-many relationship. In this case, the foreign key must be placed in the relation on the many side, not the other way around. In Windows Azure SQL Database, the two tables implementing the relations involved in this nonidentifying relationship are shown in Figures 3.12 and 3.13.

For the FacultyID column in the table STUDENT, no check mark under the Is Required heading indicates that the faculty ID is optional, which matches the specification defined in the nonidentifying relationship shown in Figure 3.11.

3. *Nonspecific relationship*: For the nonspecific relationship described in Chapter 2, there is a many-to-many (M:N) relationship between the entities STUDENT and CLASS. You need an intersection entity to implement a many-to-many relationship as shown in Figure 3.14, where the intersection entity STUDENT_CLASS contains the key attributes from the entities on both sides of the M:N relationship. With the intersection entity, a many-to-many relationship can be represented with a 1:M relationship between STUDENT and STUDENT_CLASS and a 1:N relationship between CLASS and STUDENT_CLASS.

   With Windows Azure SQL Database, you can define the tables STUDENT, CLASS, and STUDENT_CLASS. In Figures 3.15 and 3.16, the tables CLASS and STUDENT_CLASS are defined. The table STUDENT has been defined in Figure 3.13.

   In Figure 3.16, the combination key (<u>StudentID</u>, <u>ClassID</u>) is created. In Figures 3.15 and 3.16, notice that the definitions of the ClassID column in both CLASS and

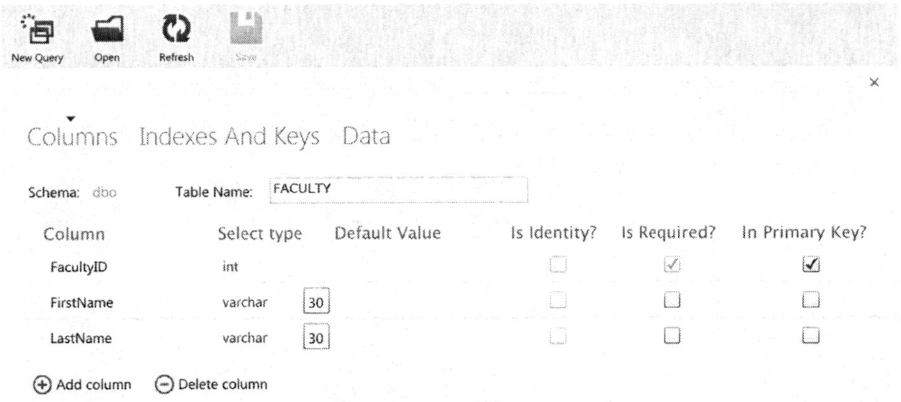

Figure 3.12 Table design of FACULTY.

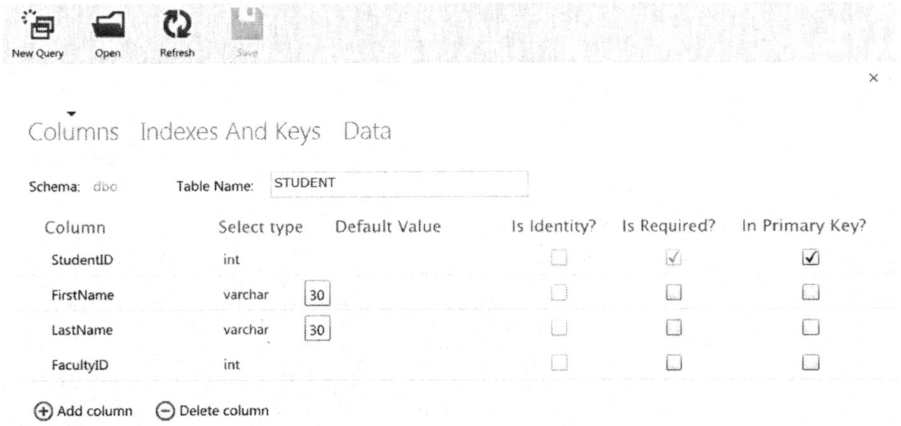

Figure 3.13 Table design of STUDENT.

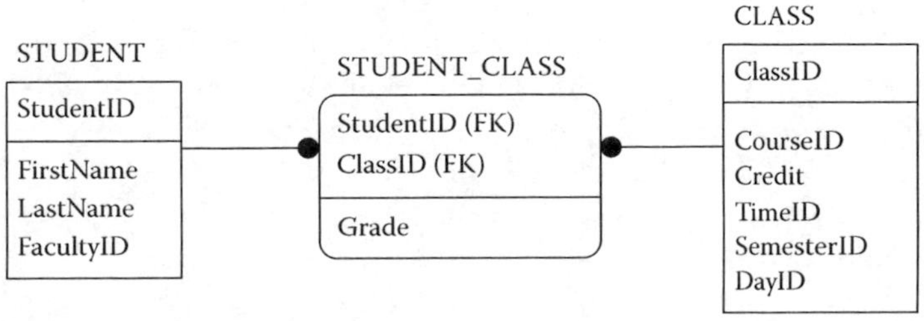

Figure 3.14 Nonspecific relationship.

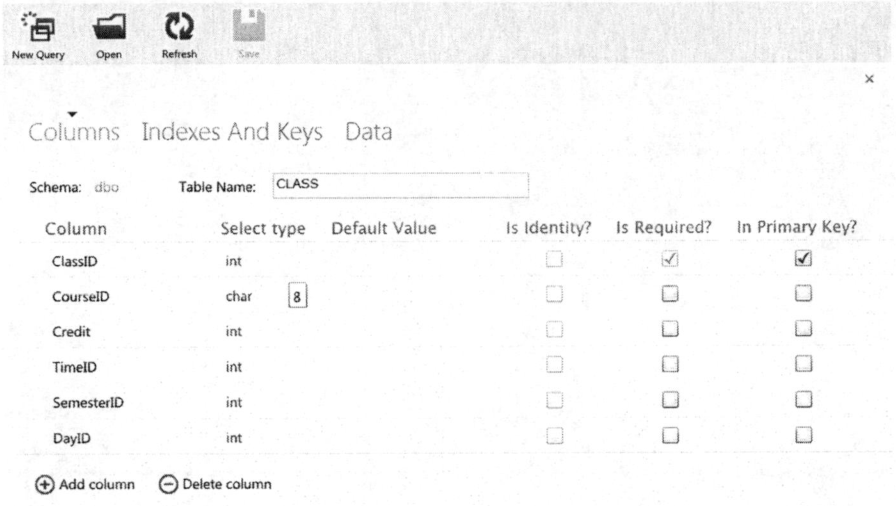

Figure 3.15 Table design of CLASS.

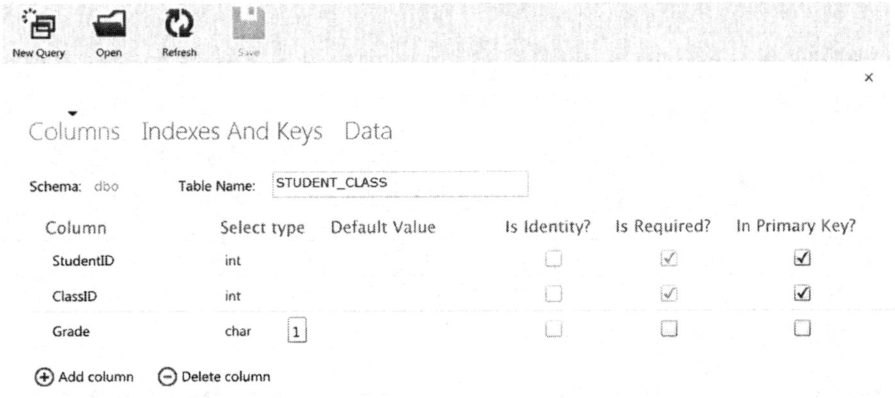

Figure 3.16 Table design of STUDENT_CLASS.

STUDENT_CLASS are consistent. Make sure that the same is true for the StudentID column in both the STUDENT_CLASS and STUDENT tables.

4. *Categorization relationship*: In Chapter 2, we examined the categorization relationship among the entities of FACULTY, PROFESSOR, and INSTRUCTOR as shown in Figure 3.17.

   The entities involved in the above categorization relationship can be represented by the following relations:

FACULTY(FacultyID, FirstName, LastName, JobCode)

PROFESSOR(FacultyID, Rank, OfficePhone)

INSTRUCTOR(FacultyID, Position, HomePhone)

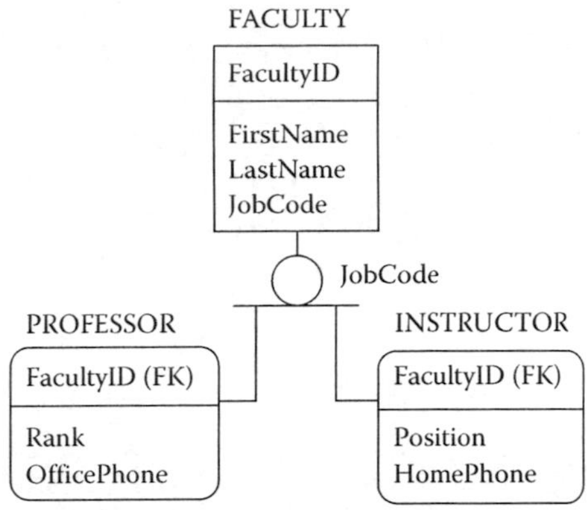

Figure 3.17 Categorization relationship.

As indicated in the definition of the relations, the key column FacultyID is shared by the **generic** relation FACULTY and the **specific** relations PROFESSOR and INSTRUCTOR. In each specific relation, the identifier of each row is the same identifier used in the generic relation. Each row in the specific relations PROFESSOR and INSTRUCTOR corresponds to a row in the generic relation FACULTY.

In a categorization relationship, if you want to insert a new row to the specific table, you have to insert the new row in the generic table first. For example, to insert a record about a new professor in the table PROFESSOR, you need to first insert a row with the FacultyID and other general information about the new professor in the generic table FACULTY. Then, you need to insert specific information about the new professor in the table PROFESSOR. Also, to query the information about the faculty, you need to first query the general information about the professors from the tables FACULTY and PROFESSOR, then query the information about the instructors from the tables FACULTY and INSTRUCTOR, and get the final result by merging the information from the two queries. Although this is doable, the use of the categorization relationship slows down database performance. If the attributes in the specific tables are similar, you may consider eliminating the use of the categorization relationship for better performance.

5. *Recursive relationship*: The recursive relationship defined in Chapter 2 involves only a single entity FACULTY. As shown in Figure 3.18, faculty members are related to the dean, who is also a faculty member, through the foreign key Dean.

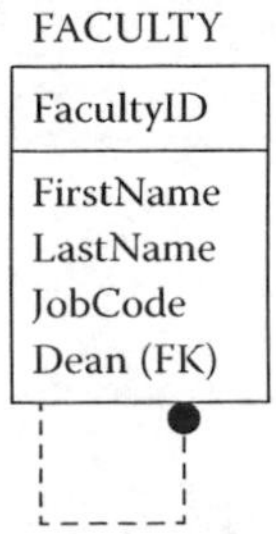

Figure 3.18 Recursive relationship.

The value in the column Dean is the faculty ID. The relationship is a nonidentifying relationship. Since each faculty member is related to the dean, the column Dean cannot have a null value.

Sometimes, you may encounter a many-to-many recursive relationship. For example, in a course catalog, a course may have several prerequisite courses and many courses may require the same course as a prerequisite. The relationship between the courses and the prerequisites is an *M*:*N* recursive relationship. To represent the *M*:*N* recursive relationship, you have to add an intersection relation in the relationship as shown below:

COURSE (CourseId, CourseName)

COURSE_ PREREQUISITE (*CourseId*, *Prerequisite*)

The intersection relation PREREQUISITE_COURSE contains two columns, CourseId and Prerequisite (which is CourseId itself), as the combination key. Like other intersection tables, these two columns are the foreign keys from two parent tables, which, in this example, are the same table COURSE. Each row in the relation PREREQUISITE_COURSE has a course ID and its prerequisite course ID. If a course has no prerequisite or a course is not the prerequisite of any other course, it will not be listed in the table PREREQUISITE_COURSE. The table structures for COURSE and PREREQUISITE_COURSE are defined in Figures 3.19 and 3.20.

For the *M*:*N* recursive relationship, two tables are involved in the relationship and one of them is the intersection table. For a given course ID, search the intersection table to find all matching course ids in the CourseId column. From all the rows that contain the matching course ids, you can find the prerequisite course ids. With these prerequisite course ids, you can obtain the course names in the COURSE table.

6. *Ternary relationship*: A ternary relationship relates multiple entities. Often, a number of binary relationships are used to implement the ternary relationship. Since database designers are more familiar with binary relationships, converting a ternary relationship to binary relationships is a better design. Figure 3.21 shows the ternary relationship introduced in Chapter 2.

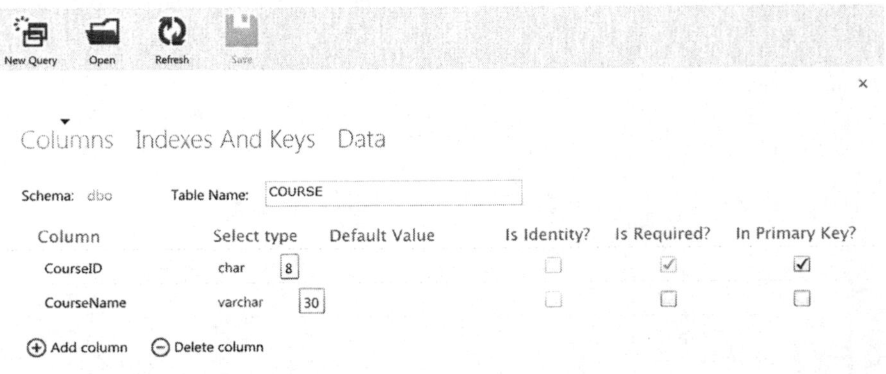

Figure 3.19 Table design of COURSE.

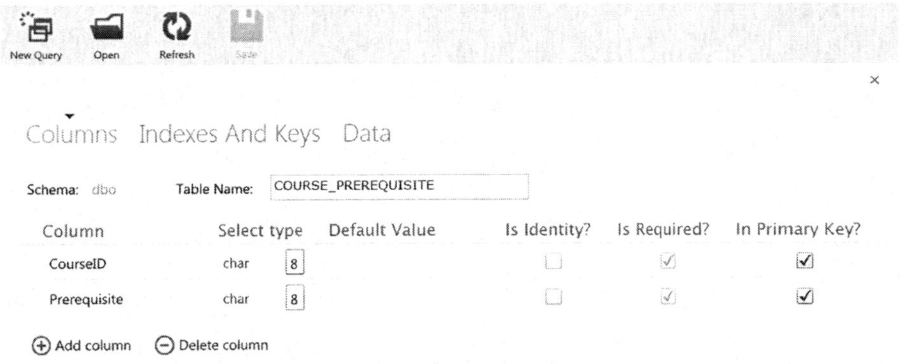

Figure 3.20 Table design of PREREQUISITE_COURSE.

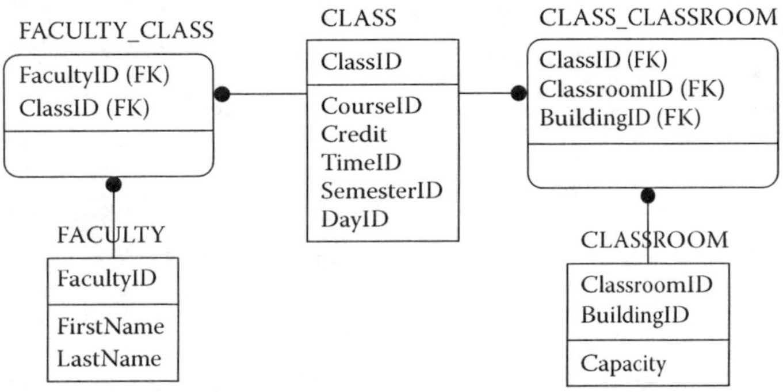

Figure 3.21 Ternary relationship.

The ternary relationship consists of two nonspecific binary relationships. The corresponding relations involved in this ternary relationship are

FACULTY(FacultyID, FirstName, LastName)
FACULTY_CLASS(*FacultyID*, *ClassID*)
CLASS(ClassID, CourseID, Credit, TimeID, SemesterID, DayID)
CLASS_CLASSROOM(ClassID, ClassroomID, BuildingID)
CLASSROOM(ClassroomID, *BuildingID*, Capacity)

There are two intersection relations, FACULTY_CLASS and CLASS_CLASSROOM, used to implement the two *M*:*N* relationships. To find the classrooms for a given professor, the search starts in the intersection relation FACULTY_CLASS to find all the class ids related to the given faculty ID. With these class ids, you can look for the classroom ids in the intersection relation CLASS_CLASSROOM. Once these classroom ids are available, you can use them to query the information about these classrooms for the given professor. On the other hand, if you want to know which professors are teaching in a given classroom, you can first look for the class ids that match the given classroom ID in the relation CLASS_CLASSROOM. With these matching class ids, you will be able to find the corresponding faculty ids in the relation FACULTY_CLASS. By using the faculty ids, you can get the professors' names in the relation FACULTY. In Figures 3.22 through 3.24, the table

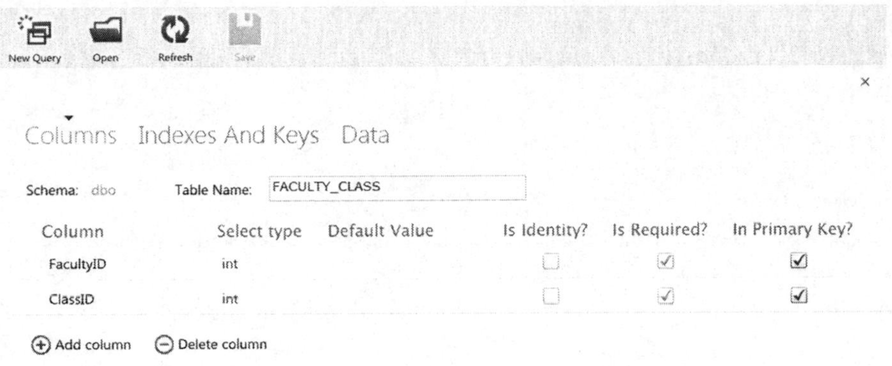

Figure 3.22 Table design of FACULTY_CLASS.

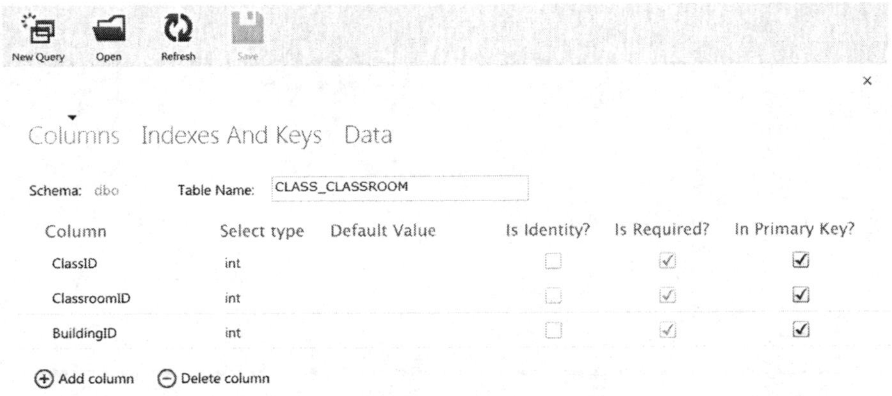

Figure 3.23 Table design of CLASS_CLASSROOM.

designs for the tables FACULTY_CLASS, CLASS, CLASS_CLASSROOM, and CLASSROOM are given. The table design of FACULTY is given in Figure 3.12, the design of CLASSROOM is given in Figure 3.10, and the design of CLASS is given in Figure 3.15.

A ternary relationship may not always be represented by a set of binary relationships. If this happens, you may have to enforce constraints with programming in a database application.

At this point, you have done the first two tasks, representing entities with relations and representing relationships with primary key and foreign key pairs. The next task is to enforce constraints, discussed in the next section.

3.4.3 Enforcing Constraints

By using constraints, you will be able to implement relationships that link the tables in a database. Constraints are widely used in a database to make sure that tables work together properly, so modifications made in one table will not cause malfunctions in other tables. Constraints are also used to verify data entered in a table to make sure that the data are in a proper format. There are four types of commonly used constraints:

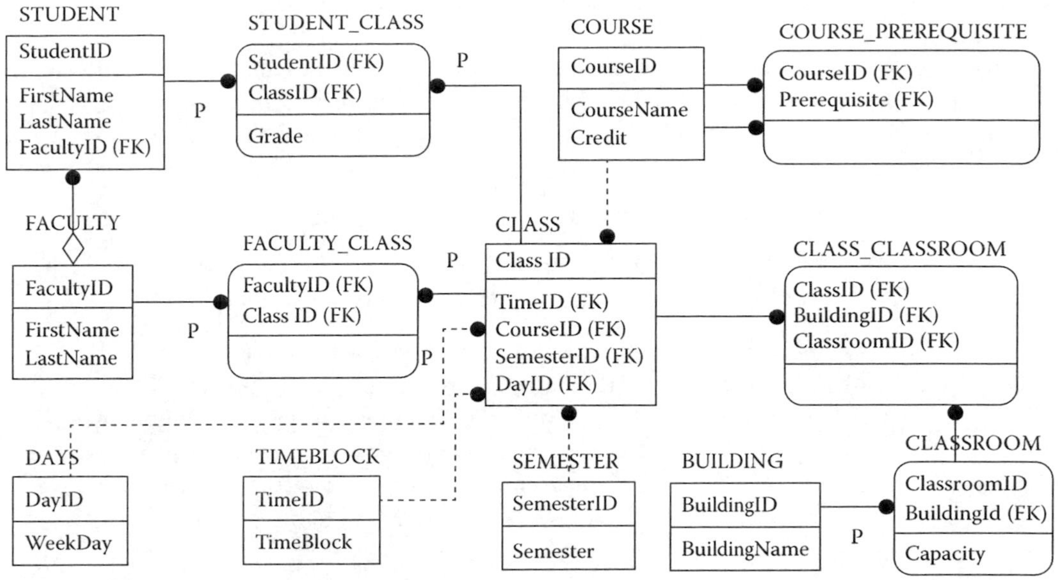

Figure 3.24 Class registration data model.

- *Relationship constraints*: Used to implement relationships by enforcing referential integrity and cardinality among the related tables.
- *Uniqueness constraints*: Used to enforce uniqueness for the values entered in a column.
- *Domain constraints*: Used to control the values entered in a column.
- *Business rules*: Used to enforce a company's policies and regulations.

There are two types of relationship constraints: the **integrity constraint** and **cardinality constraint.** The foreign key and primary key constraint is used to enforce the integrity constraint. As described in the previous sections, a relationship can be represented by a primary key and foreign key. Therefore, a relationship can be implemented by enforcing the integrity constraint. When creating tables, you can enforce the integrity constraint by creating the primary key and foreign key constraint. When defining the foreign key constraint, you can specify the parent table and the column shared by the primary key and the foreign key. After the integrity key constraint is created, the connection between the parent table and child table is established.

When you insert, update, or delete data in a table, some measures may be needed to protect the integrity of the database. For example, when a new row is inserted into a table, you want to make sure that there are no duplicated rows in the table. Or, when a row is updated in the child table, you want to be sure that the foreign key value matches one of the primary key values in the parent table. Most DBMSs provide options that allow you to configure the constraints needed to prevent undesirable values from being entered in a table. Windows Azure SQL Database can automatically enforce the integrity constraint if an integrity constraint violation occurs during a process of inserting, deleting, or updating.

When specifying how many rows in one table can be associated with each row in another table, you need to enforce a cardinality constraint. Cardinality constraints are often created based on business rules. Programming is commonly used to implement the complex logic enforced by a cardinality constraint. You will learn how to create this type of constraint in the chapters that discuss SQL procedures and triggers.

A database should be built to accommodate business policies and regulations. Most business rules are application dependent. Therefore, they are often implemented in database applications. In later chapters, triggers and stored procedures will be used to implement business rules in the chapter activities.

ACTIVITY 3.1 DATABASE IMPLEMENTATION WITH WINDOWS AZURE SQL DATABASE

In this activity, by following the step-by-step instructions, you will learn how to use Windows Azure SQL Database to create a database that consists of tables, relationships, and constraints. For this activity, let us create a database based on the data model displayed in Figure 3.24.

To use Windows Azure SQL Database to implement the database designed in Figure 3.24, you need to first create a Windows Azure account, a database server, and a connection to Windows Azure SQL Database. If you have not done so, refer to Activity 2.2 in Chapter 2 to complete these steps.

TASK 1: CREATING DATABASE TABLES

1. Log on to the **Windows Azure Management Portal**. Click the **SQL DATABASE** link on the left-hand side of your screen. Then, select the database **Class_Registration** and click **MANAGE** as shown in Figure 3.25.

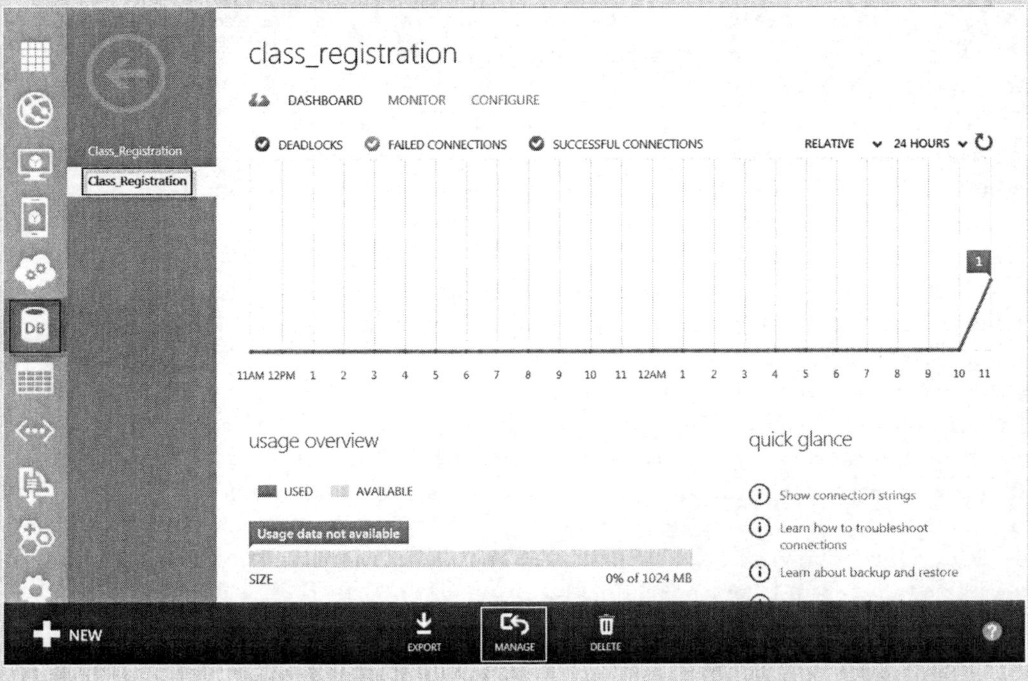

Figure 3.25 Database DASHBOARD.

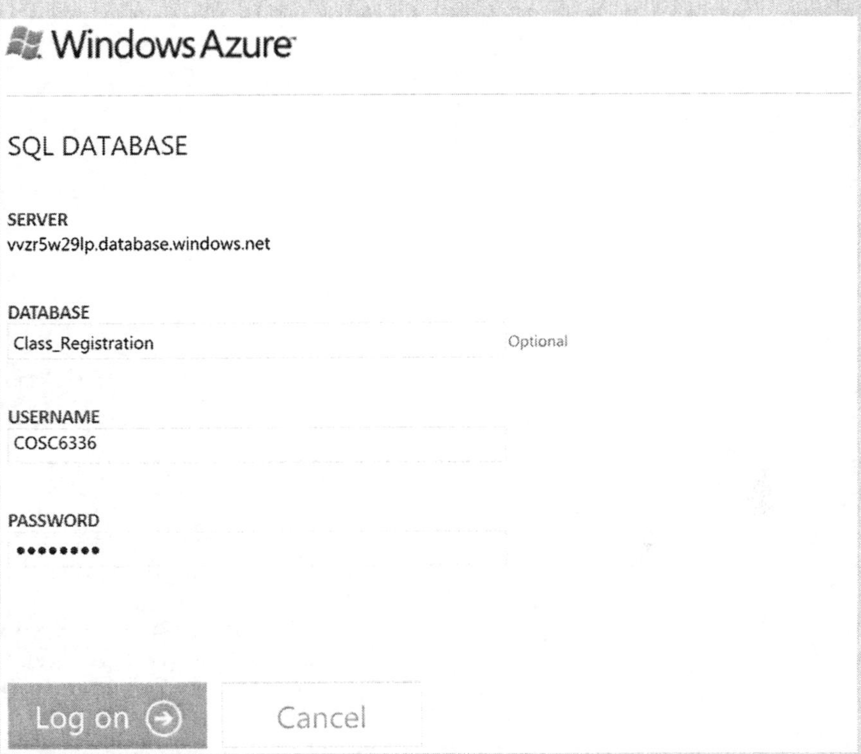

Figure 3.26 Remotely log on to Windows Azure SQL Database.

2. You will be prompted to enter the authentication information for the remote login through the **SQL Database** portal. Enter your server administrator's user name and password created in the previous chapter, and then click **Log on** as shown in Figure 3.26.
3. If the login is successful, you should see the administration page. Click the **Design** icon on the left-hand side of your screen. Click the **New table** link. You will be prompted to design a new table. For example, the BUILDING table can be designed as shown in Figure 3.27. After the configuration is done, click the **Save** icon.
4. Similarly, you can create other tables without foreign keys, such as COURSE, FACULTY, DAYS, SEMESTER, and TIMEBLOCK as shown in Figures 3.28 through 3.32.
5. After the tables without foreign keys are created, you can create other tables with foreign keys. To do so, click **Tables** on the top of your screen and click **New table**. Then, follow the screenshots shown in Figures 3.33 through 3.39 to create these tables.

Now, your database is ready to be populated with data. You can enter data manually through GUI (graphical user interface).

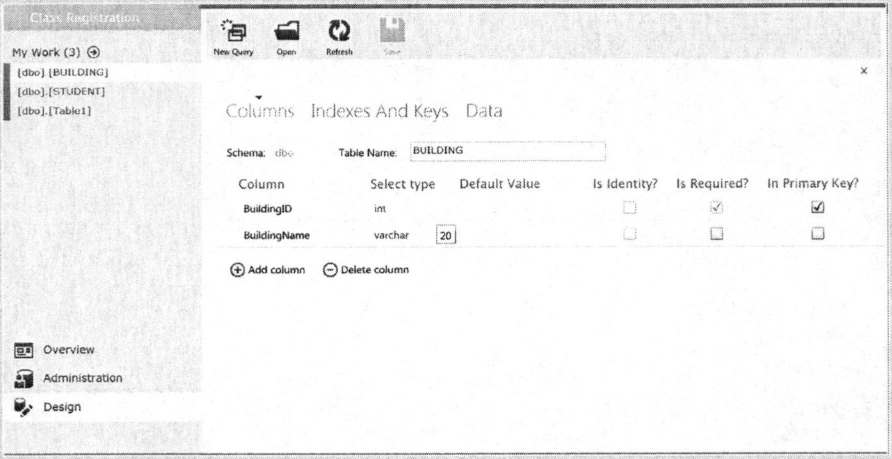

Figure 3.27 Design of BUILDING table.

TASK 2: POPULATING DATABASE WITH DATA

You can enter data into database tables in two ways. You can enter data manually as shown in the following. Or, you can enter data using an SQL statement that will be discussed in the next chapter. If you prefer not to enter data manually, you can wait for the next chapter.

1. Click **Design** to switch back to the design window. Click the **Edit** icon next to the table **BUILDING**. Click the **Data** link. You will be prompted to add data manually. By clicking the **Add Row** link, you can enter the data shown in Figure 3.40. Then, click the **Save** icon to save the data in the table BUILDING.
2. Similarly, you can enter the data in the other tables as shown in Figures 3.41 through 3.52.

After the data are entered, your first database is physically implemented.

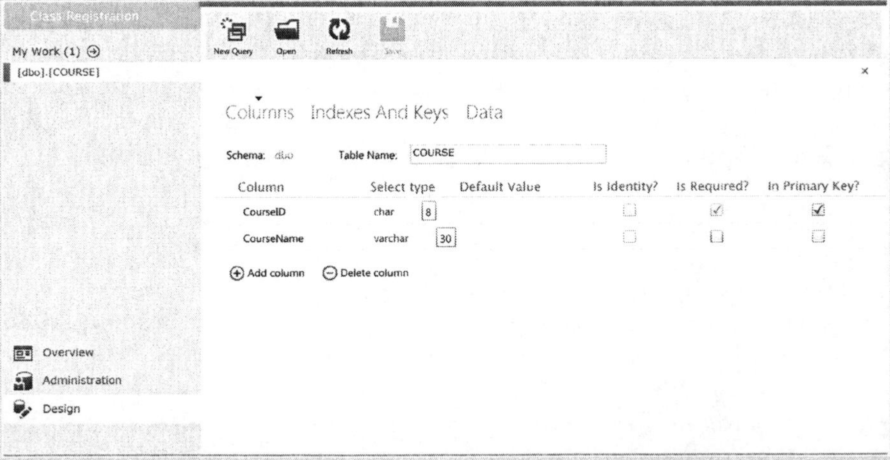

Figure 3.28 Design of COURSE table.

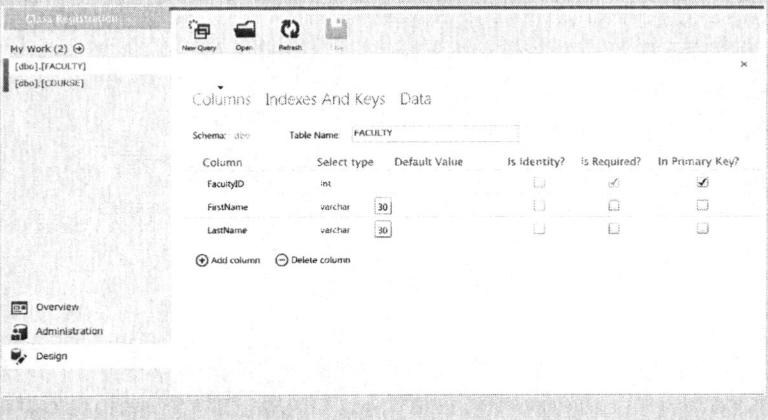

Figure 3.29 Design of FACULTY table.

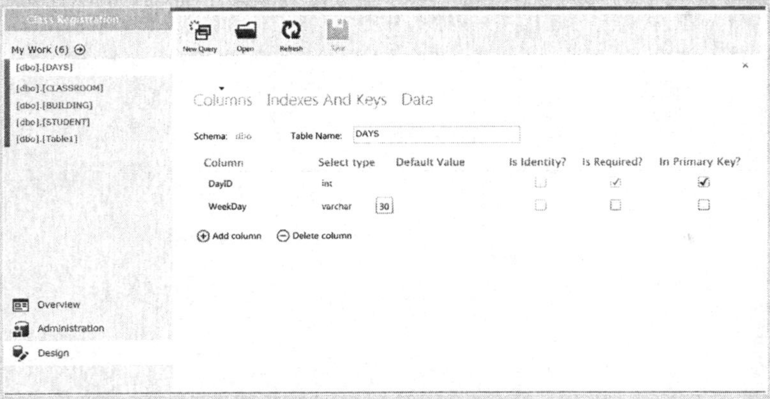

Figure 3.30 Design of DAYS table.

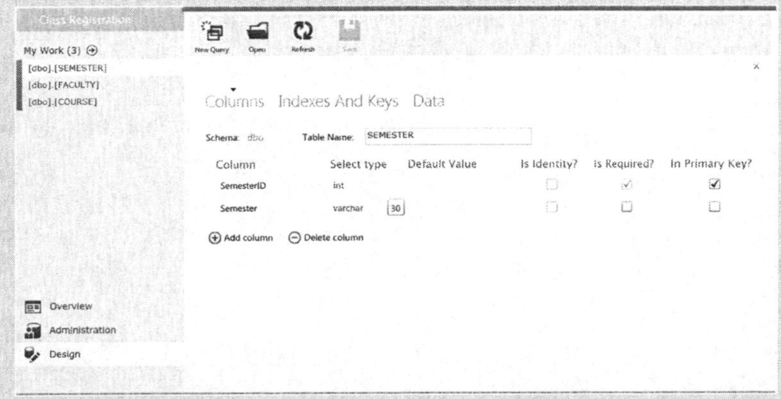

Figure 3.31 Design of SEMESTER table.

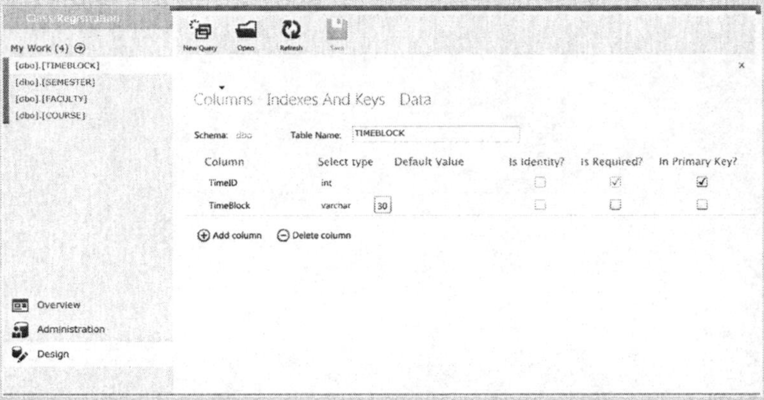

Figure 3.32 Design of TIMEBLOCK table.

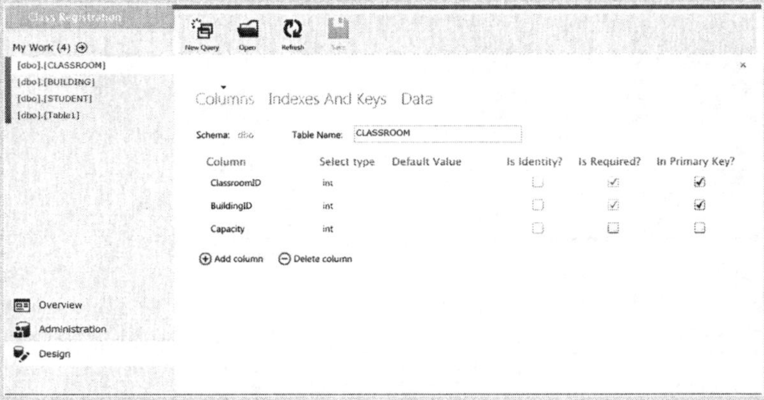

Figure 3.33 Design of CLASSROOM table.

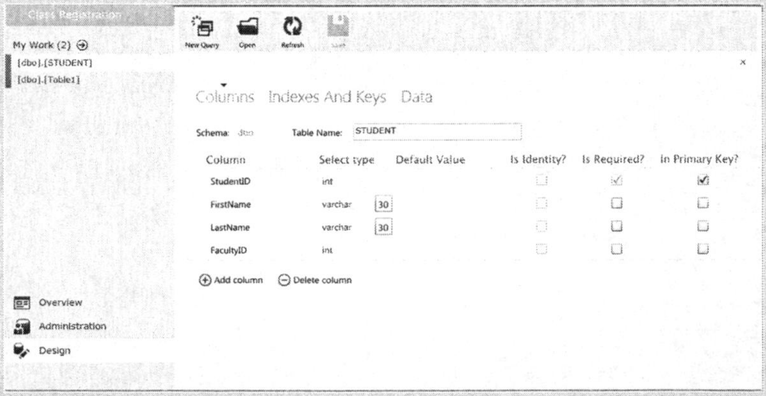

Figure 3.34 Design of STUDENT table.

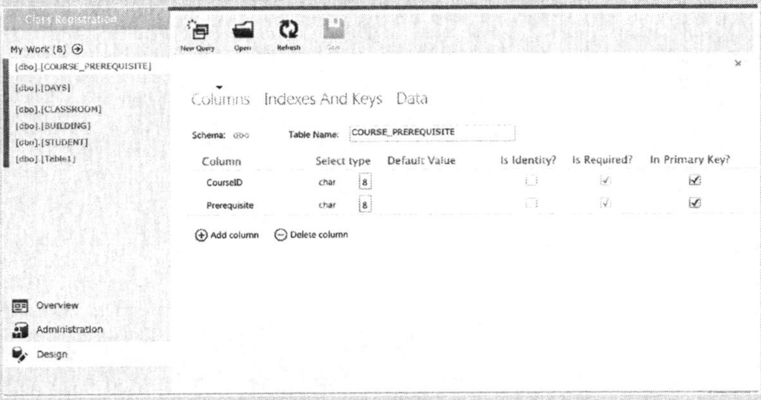

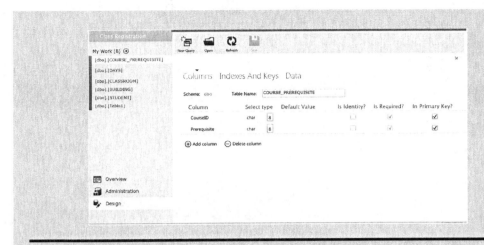

Figure 3.35 Design of COURSE_PREREQUISITE table.

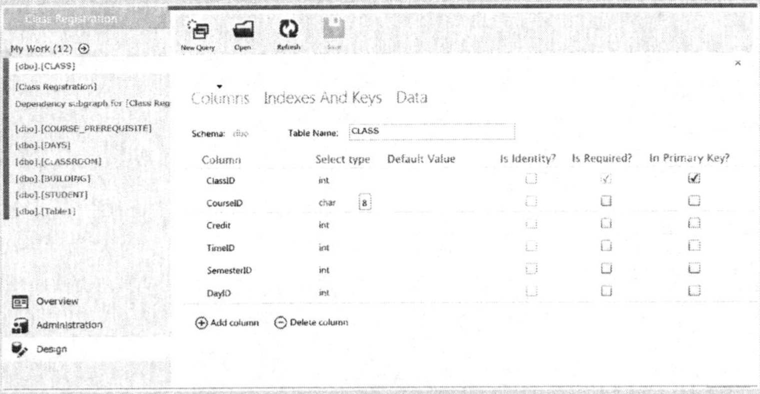

Figure 3.36 Design of CLASS table.

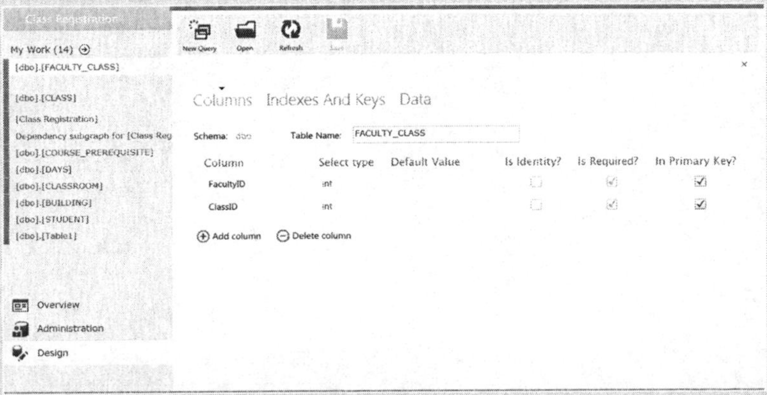

Figure 3.37 Design of FACULTY_CLASS table.

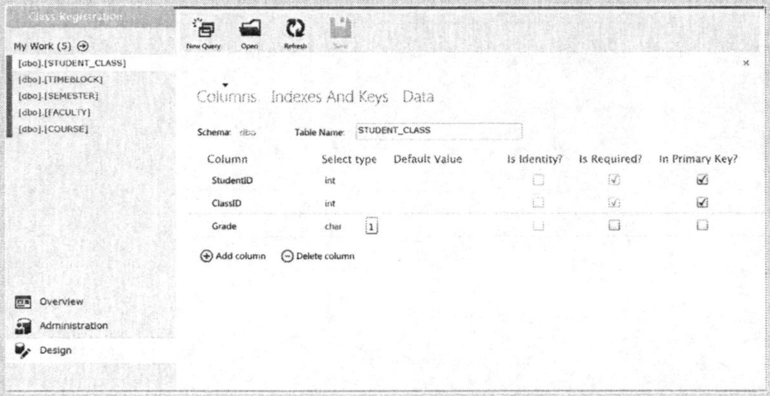

Figure 3.38 Design of STUDENT_CLASS table.

Figure 3.39 Design of CLASS_CLASSROOM table.

Figure 3.40 Data value in BUILDING table.

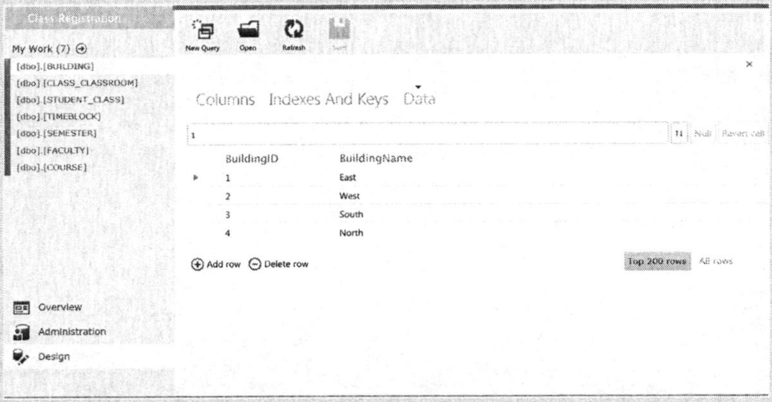

Figure 3.41 Data value in CLASSROOM table.

Figure 3.42 Data value in COURSE table.

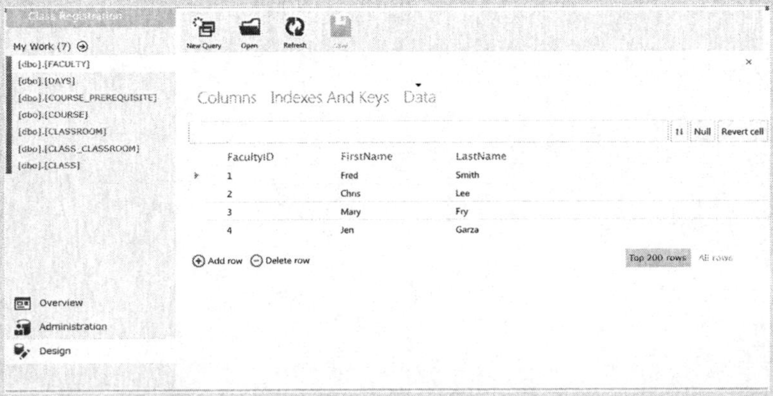

Figure 3.43 Data value in FACULTY table.

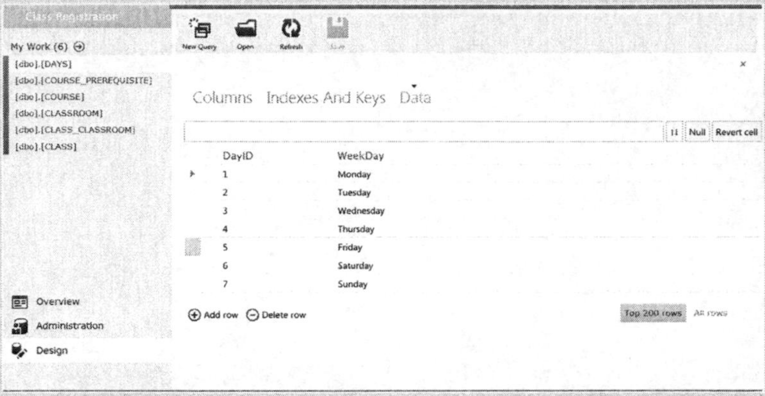

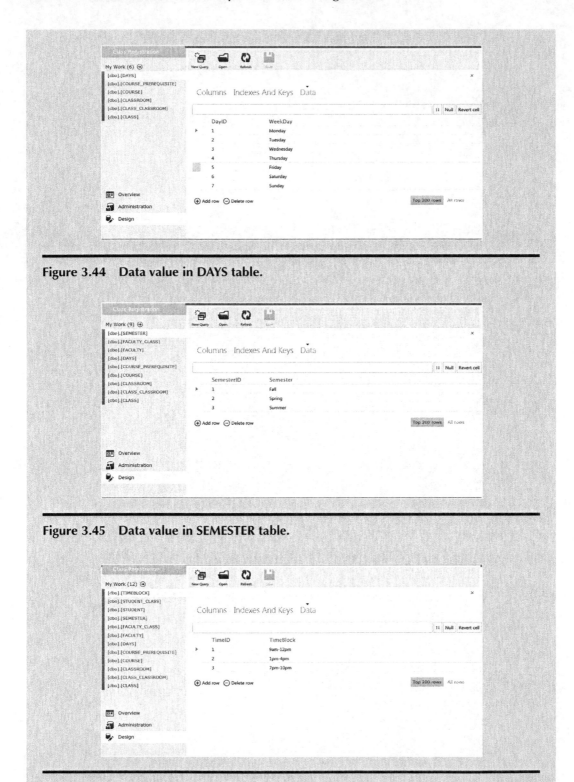

Figure 3.44 Data value in DAYS table.

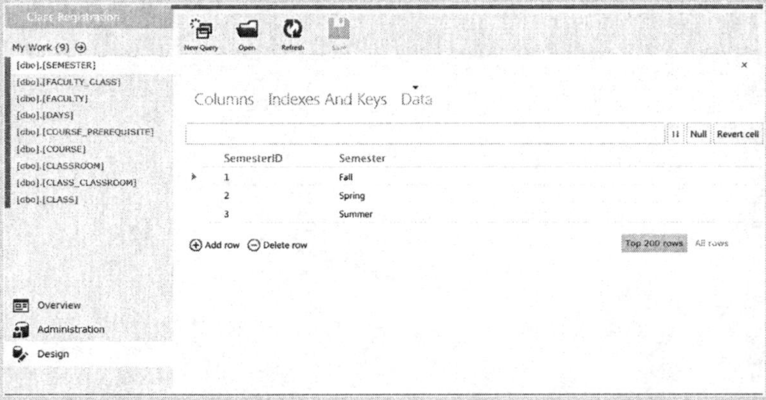

Figure 3.45 Data value in SEMESTER table.

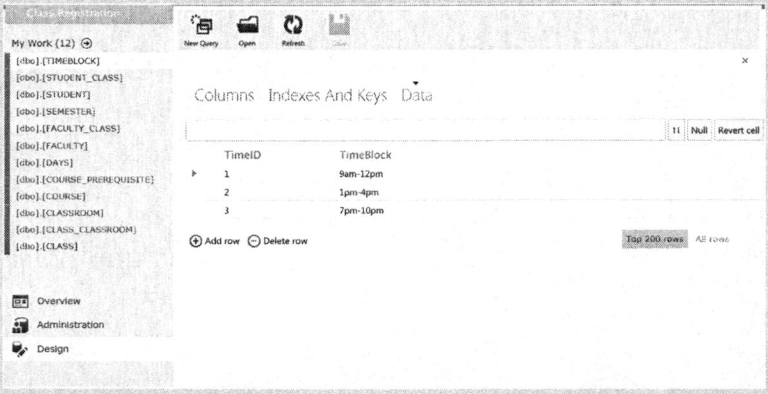

Figure 3.46 Data value in TIMEBLOCK table.

StudentID	FirstName	LastName	FacultyID
10	Liz	Cox	1
11	Joe	Cole	2
12	Linda	Diaz	1
13	Don	Ford	3
14	Jen	Parker	4
15	Mark	Lopez	2
16	Bruce	Cox	3
17	Sarah	Hudson	2

Figure 3.47 Data value in STUDENT table.

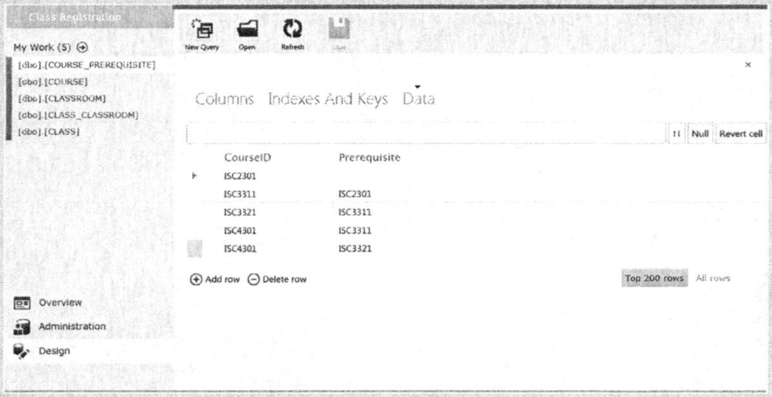

CourseID	Prerequisite
ISC2301	
ISC3311	ISC2301
ISC3321	ISC3311
ISC4301	ISC3311
ISC4301	ISC3321

Figure 3.48 Data value in COURSE_PREREQUISITE table.

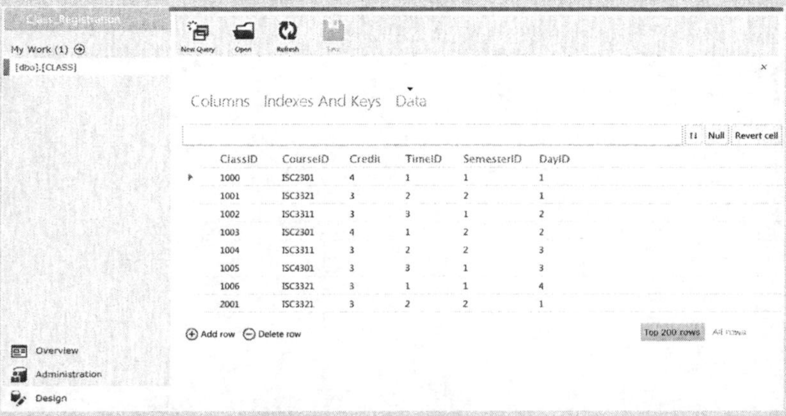

ClassID	CourseID	Credit	TimeID	SemesterID	DayID
1000	ISC2301	4	1	1	1
1001	ISC3321	3	2	2	1
1002	ISC3311	3	3	1	2
1003	ISC2301	4	1	2	2
1004	ISC3311	3	2	2	3
1005	ISC4301	3	3	1	3
1006	ISC3321	3	1	1	4
2001	ISC3321	3	2	2	1

Figure 3.49 Data value in CLASS table.

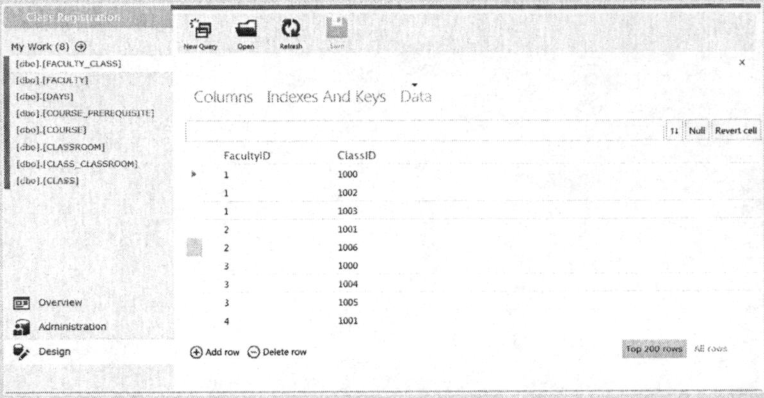

Figure 3.50 Data value in FACULTY_CLASS table.

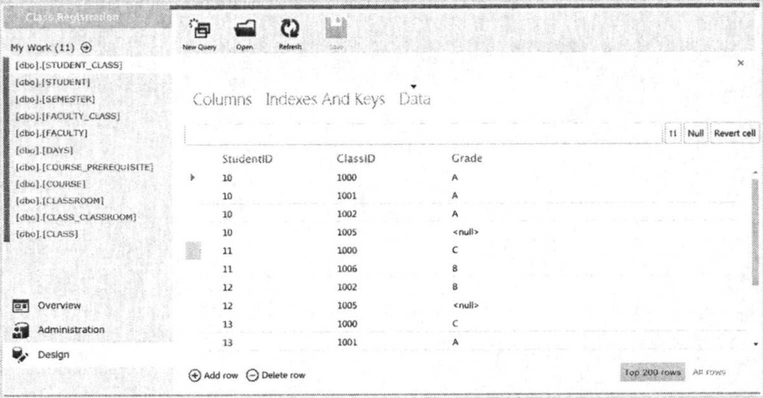

Figure 3.51 Data value in STUDENT_CLASS table.

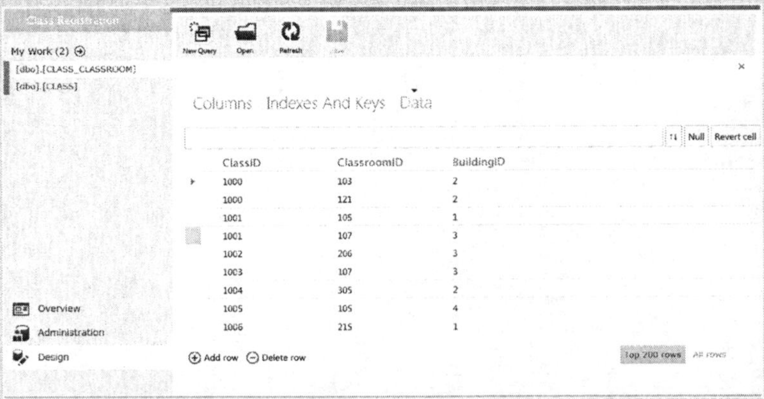

Figure 3.52 Data value in CLASS_CLASSROOM table.

3.5 Summary

In this chapter, we have discussed tables, table normalization, and transferring a data model to a relational database. At the beginning of the chapter, the concepts of tables and functional dependencies were introduced. We discussed the table components and how to link two tables with a shared column. The definitions of primary keys and foreign keys were presented. Before a data model can be converted to a relational database, you need to properly normalize the table structures. During the normalization process, you may need to modify the initial E–R model. You may need to add or remove some of the entities or attributes based on the result of normalization. In a normalization process, a table is split to eliminate modification anomalies. Step by step, you learned in detail about the normal forms 1NF, 2NF, 3NF, BCNF, 4NF, and DK/NF. Denormalization was also discussed in this chapter. After the data model has been modified based on the result of the normalization, you are ready to convert the data model to a relational database. In this chapter, you have learned how to represent entities and relationships with relations and pairs of primary and foreign keys. In the hands-on practice section, you learned how to create tables on Windows Azure SQL Database and how to enter data into tables manually.

Review Questions

1. What are the conditions for a table to be a relation?
2. How do you link a table to another table?
3. What is functional dependency? Give an example of functional dependency.
4. What is a primary key?
5. What is a foreign key?
6. Describe update anomalies by using an example.
7. Describe insertion anomalies by using an example.
8. Describe deletion anomalies by using an example.
9. Why do tables need to be normalized?
10. Why is the highest-level normalization not always desirable?
11. What are the requirements for 1NF?
12. What are the requirements for 2NF?
13. What is 3NF?
14. What is BCNF?
15. List the naming rules used in this book.
16. What do you do with the delimiters " " and []?
17. When a name starts with the symbol @, what does the symbol represent?
18. Use an example to explain how to represent a nonidentifying relationship with tables.
19. Use an example to represent a nonspecific relationship with tables.
20. How do you implement a referential constraint?

Chapter 4

Database Development and Management with SQL

Objectives

- Get started with SQL
- Create database objects with SQL
- Manage database objects with SQL
- Control database object privileges with SQL

4.1 Introduction

In this chapter, SQL, a commonly used database development tool, will be introduced. You will learn some often-used SQL commands and use them to create and manage database objects. You will use SQL to create database objects such as tables, constraints, users, and roles. You will learn how to modify the database structure and data content with SQL commands.

4.2 Structured Query Language

As shown in the previous chapter, you can use Windows Azure SQL Database to create database objects with a graphical tool. Like Microsoft, some other DBMS products also provide graphical tools for database development and management. It is relatively easy to learn how to use graphical tools. Especially for beginners, graphical database development tools can help avoid many mistakes due to lack of experience.

On the other hand, experienced database developers prefer a more popular database development tool called SQL. There are some advantages to using SQL instead of graphical database development tools. For example, a DBMS product does not share its graphical tools with another DBMS product. Also, a graphical database development tool requires interactivity with users.

Therefore, it is not good for bulk operations. On the other hand, SQL code is portable and can be executed by bulk operations.

With SQL, database developers can create database objects such as tables and views. They can also use SQL to perform operations such as inserting, updating, and deleting records in a table. SQL provides functions and procedures to help you implement database security measures and performance tuning. SQL commands can be used to manage databases such as defining constraints to maintain database integrity. Since the early 1970s, SQL has been a primary tool in database development.

As the most important database development tool, SQL is supported by various DBMS products. It has been modified in many ways to serve the special needs of each individual DBMS product. To set up a common ground, the American National Standards Institute (ANSI) published the standard for SQL. In 1986, the ANSI standardized the database querying language and named it ANSI SQL-86. Since then, the SQL standard has been updated several times. SQL has been formally adopted as an International Standard by the International Organization for Standardization (ISO), the International Electrotechnical Commission (IEC), and it has also been adopted as a Federal Information Processing Standard (FIPS) for the U.S. federal government. There are important new features added to this latest version such as the support for XML and additional collection data types.

Even with the added features, ANSI-based SQL is still a very basic query language. DBMS vendors have added their own extensions on top of the basic ANSI-based SQL. The extended SQL language used by Microsoft SQL Server is called Transact-SQL, which supports ANSI SQL. In addition, Transact-SQL has added some commands for procedural programming. In this chapter, let us first study the basic commands for creating and managing database objects.

There are three major types of commands for creating and managing database objects:

- **Data Definition Language (DDL)**: Statements in DDL can be used to create, modify, and delete database objects such as databases, tables, columns, and constraints. The commonly used DDL statements are
  CREATE: Used to create database objects
  ALTER: Used to modify database objects
  DROP: Used to delete database objects
- **Data Control Language (DCL)**: Statements in DCL can be used to grant or revoke permissions on database objects. The commonly used DCL statements are
  GRANT: Used to grant permissions for a user to use a database object or execute some SQL commands
  REVOKE: Used to remove previously granted permissions
- **Data Manipulation Language (DML)**: Statements in DML can be used to select, insert, update, and delete data in a database object. The commonly used DML statements are
  SELECT: Used to query information from a database
  INSERT: Used to insert new rows of data into database tables
  UPDATE: Used to modify data values in database tables
  DELETE: Used to delete existing rows in database tables

SQL statements by various DBMS vendors may be different. Often, the difference is minor. SQL code conversion from one DBMS to another DBMS does not take much effort. This makes SQL almost portable across DBMS products from different database vendors. Some companies may own multiple DBMS products. In such a case, learning SQL is particularly important for those who will work with different DBMS products.

To work with SQL statements, Windows Azure SQL Database provides tools for you to edit, debug, and execute Transact-SQL statements. In the following sections, you will use SQL statements to create database objects such as tables and constraints with DDL. You will also learn how to modify the structures of database objects. You will use DML to insert, update, and delete data for database objects created by you. To accomplish some database management tasks, you will use DCL to grant and revoke permissions.

4.3 Creating Database Objects

In this section, as a case study, a data model called Computer_Store will be converted to a relational database with SQL. The Computer_Store data model is given in Figure 4.1.

4.3.1 Defining Data Types

When creating a table, you need to specify the data type for each column. Let us first take a look at the data types before creating tables. Some commonly used data types are listed below. Data types were introduced in the previous chapter. Here, we review some of them and focus on how to define the data types with SQL statements. For each data type, there is an example to demonstrate how to specify the data type for a column.

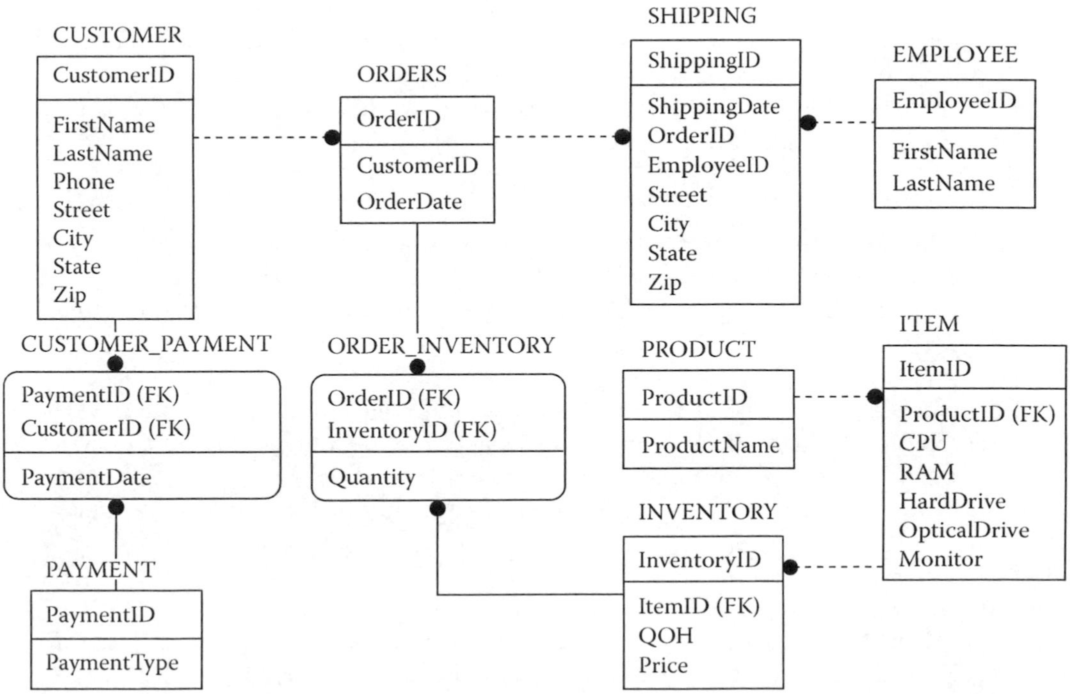

Figure 4.1 Computer_Store data model.

1. Character data types: Character data consist of any combination of letters, symbols, and numeric characters.
   a. **CHAR**: It is a fixed-length character data type.

      Example: To specify the column, Street, and to have the CHAR data type with length 30, use

      Street CHAR(30)
   b. **VARCHAR**: It is a variable-length character data type.
      Example: To specify the column, Description, and to have the VARCHAR data type with the maximum length of 300, use

      Description VARCHAR(300)
   c. **VARCHAR(MAX)**: This data type allows you to define a character data type with a length up to 2^{31} bytes of data.

      The difference between the data type CHAR and the data type VARCHAR is that a column specified by CHAR may have many blank spaces if the data values do not fill up the column width. The advantage of CHAR is that it runs faster when processing data stored in a fixed-length column.

      Corresponding to CHAR, VARCHAR, and VARCHAR(MAX), there are NCHAR, NVARCHAR, and NVARCHAR(MAX) data types for Unicode characters. Unicode characters are used for some special characters in languages such as Chinese and Japanese. Each Unicode character takes two bytes. Therefore, the lengths of NCHAR, NVARCHAR, and NVARCHAR(MAX) are half of CHAR, VARCHAR, and VARCHAR(MAX).
2. Number data types: Number data types include integers and decimals.
   a. **INT**: The INT data type consists of positive, zero, and negative whole numbers. The range of INT is from –2,147,483,648 to 2,147,483,647.
      Example: Integers can be used as the data type for a key column. In the following, we specify the primary key column ClassID with the INT data type:

      ClassID INT PRIMARY KEY
   b. **DECIMAL (or NUMERIC)**: The DECIMAL data type includes positive and negative decimal numbers. The values of DECIMAL data are from – 10^38 + 1 through 10^38 – 1.
      Example: The following statement specifies the column GPA with the DECIMAL data type:

      GPA DECIMAL
3. Date and Time data type: It represents date and time values.
   a. **DATETIME**: This data type specifies a column to contain date and time values from 1-1-1753 to 12-31-9999.
      Example: To define the column ExpirationDate to have date and time values, use

      ExpirationDate DATETIME
4. Monetary data type: It represents amounts of money.
   a. **MONEY**: This data type specifies a column to contain money values.
      Example: To define the money data type for the column Price, use

      Price MONEY

   More data types are supported by Windows Azure SQL Database.

4.3.2 Constraints

When creating a table, you also need to specify constraints for some of the columns. Constraints can be used to keep the integrity of your database, define the range of values to be entered into a column, and specify the properties of a column. Let us take a look at the commonly used constraints.

1. *Referential Constraints*: Referential constraints are used to keep the relationship between tables. The commonly used foreign key constraint and primary key constraint belong to referential constraints.
   a. **Primary Key Constraint**: This constraint is used to specify a column or a group of columns as a primary key. There are two ways to define a primary key. If the primary key is defined on a single column, you can specify the column as a primary key without the keyword CONSTRAINT. For example, to make the column ProductID the primary key, use the SQL statement:

      ProductID INT PRIMARY KEY

      A constraint enforced on a single column is classified as a column constraint.
      If a primary key is defined on multiple columns, it is called a combination primary key and you need to use the keyword CONSTRAINT to define it. The syntax for defining a primary key by using the keyword CONSTRAINT is

      CONSTRAINT constraint_name PRIMARY KEY (multiple_column_names)

      To illustrate the use of the keyword CONSTRAINT, consider the example that defines the combination primary key on the columns OrderID and InventoryID:

      CONSTRAINT OrderID_InventoryID_pk PRIMARY KEY (OrderID, InventoryID)

      If a constraint is enforced on multiple columns, it is called a table constraint. When more than one column is included in a constraint, you should use the table constraint.
   b. **Foreign Key Constraint**: A foreign key constraint can be defined on a single column or multiple columns. When defining it on a single column, you can use either an unnamed or a named constraint. For an unnamed foreign key constraint, consider the following example that makes the column ProductID the foreign key:

      FOREIGN KEY (ProductID) REFERENCES PRODUCT (ProductID)

      The word ProductID after the keyword phrase FOREIGN KEY is the foreign key column name in the child table. The parent table name and the primary key column in the parent table are placed behind the keyword REFERENCES. You can also use a named foreign key constraint by using the keyword CONSTRAINT. When a foreign key is defined on multiple columns, you should use a named foreign key constraint. The syntax for the named foreign key constraint is

      CONSTRAINT constraint_name FOREIGN KEY (fk_column_name)
      REFERENCES parent_table_name (primary_key_column)

      The constraint name is a character string. To make the name meaningful, you can name the constraint as TableName_ColumnName_fk. The keyword phrase FOREIGN KEY indicates that the constraint is a type of foreign key. The keyword REFERENCES specifies the name of the parent table whose primary key column is used as the foreign key column in the child table. For example, if you want to specify the column ItemID as a foreign key, use the SQL statement below:

```
CONSTRAINT Inventory_ItemId_fk FOREIGN KEY (ItemID)
REFERENCES ITEM (ItemID)
```

As indicated in the above SQL statement, the constraint name is Inventory_ItemId_fk, which should be unique in the database. The name of the foreign key column is ItemID. The parent table is ITEM, and the primary key column in the parent table is ItemID. As you can see in the above SQL statement, two tables are connected by a foreign key constraint. If the primary key column in the parent table is referenced by a foreign key in the child table, its content values cannot be deleted or changed. If you really need to delete or change a value of the primary key referenced by a foreign key, you have to delete the foreign key constraint first and then make a change.

2. Domain Constraints: A domain constraint determines the values to be entered into a column. Constraints such as CHECK, NOT NULL, and UNIQUE are domain constraints.
   a. **CHECK Constraint**: A CHECK constraint can be used to limit the values entered into a column to enforce domain integrity. The syntax of the constraint is shown below:

      ```
      CONSTRAINT constraint_name CHECK(constraint_conditions)
      ```

      Logical operators such as AND or OR can be used to enforce multiple conditions. As an example, let us include only the values that are greater or equal to zero in the column Quantity. The SQL statement is given below:

      ```
      CHECK(Quantity >= 0)
      ```

      Or, we can use the named CHECK constraint shown below:

      ```
      CONSTRAINT Quantity_ck CHECK(Quantity >= 0)
      ```

   b. **UNIQUE Constraint**: A UNIQUE constraint can be used to enforce uniqueness on nonprimary key columns. For example, we can make the values in the column ProductName unique with the following SQL statement:

      ```
      CONSTRAINT ProductName_unique UNIQUE(ProductName)
      ```

      You can also use an unnamed unique constraint by using the keyword UNIQUE.
   c. **DEFAULT Constraint**: This constraint specifies the default value for a column. For example, suppose that you want the default value for the column Quantity be 0; you can do this by using the following SQL statement:

      ```
      Quantity INT DEFAULT 0
      ```

   d. **NOT NULL Constraint**: This constraint can be used to prevent null values in a column. If you want to make sure that the column has no null value, use the following SQL statement:

      ```
      OrderDate DATETIME NOT NULL
      ```

e. **Uniqueidentifier**: This constraint can be used to create a surrogate key, which is a column with automatically generated unique integers. Suppose you want to let the machine generate a unique number for the column ProductID every time a new product is added to the table PRODUCT. You can use the following SQL statement to accomplish this task:

   ProductID uniqueidentifier NOT NULL

Now that you have learned about data types and constraints, you can create tables. You will create the database and tables corresponding to the entities displayed in Figure 4.1.

4.3.3 Creating Database

The first task is to create database objects such as tables. In Windows Azure SQL Database, the database can be created in the Windows Azure Management Portal. Later in this chapter, we will demonstrate how to create databases Computer_Store with the Windows Azure Management Portal.

4.3.4 Creating Tables

For each entity in Figure 4.1, we will first define a corresponding table.

Then, we will create the table with SQL statements based on the table definition. Let us start with the tables that do not have foreign key columns. The tables CUSTOMER, EMPLOYEE, PAYMENT, and PRODUCT belong to this type. The column definitions for the table CUSTOMER are given in Table 4.1.

The SQL statement to create the table is

```
CREATE TABLE CUSTOMER
(
      CustomerID INT PRIMARY KEY,
      FirstName VARCHAR(50),
      LastName VARCHAR(50) NOT NULL,
      Phone CHAR(12),
      Street VARCHAR(50),
      City VARCHAR(50),
      State VARCHAR(50),
      Zip CHAR(5)
)
```

The keyword phrase PRIMARY KEY indicates that a column is defined as a primary key. In the above SQL statement, the keywords are capitalized only for clarity. In fact, keywords in an SQL statement are not case sensitive.

For the table EMPLOYEE, the definitions of the columns are listed in Table 4.2.

The SQL statement for creating the table EMPLOYEE is given below:

```
CREATE TABLE EMPLOYEE
(
      EmployeeID INT PRIMARY KEY,
      FirstName VARCHAR(50),
      LastName VARCHAR(50) NOT NULL
)
```

Table 4.1 Column Descriptions for CUSTOMER Table

Column Name	*Data Type*	*PK or FK*	*Reference Table*
CustomerID	INT	PK	
FirstName	VARCHAR(50)		
LastName	VARCHAR(50)		
Phone	CHAR(12)		
Street	VARCHAR(50)		
City	VARCHAR(50)		
State	VARCHAR(50)		
Zip	CHAR(5)		

Table 4.2 Column Descriptions for EMPLOYEE Table

Column Name	*Data Type*	*PK or FK*	*Reference Table*
EmployeeID	INT	PK	
FirstName	VARCHAR(50)		
LastName	VARCHAR(50)		

Table 4.3 gives the definition for the table PAYMENT.

The following is the SQL statement for creating the table PAYMENT:

```
CREATE TABLE PAYMENT
(
      PaymentID INT PRIMARY KEY,
      PaymentType VARCHAR(50) NOT NULL
)
```

For the table PRODUCT, you have the table definition in Table 4.4.

Table 4.3 Column Descriptions for PAYMENT Table

Column Name	*Data Type*	*PK or FK*	*Reference Table*
PaymentId	INT	PK	
PaymentType	VARCHAR(50)		

Table 4.4 Column Descriptions for PRODUCT Table

Column Name	*Data Type*	*PK or FK*	*Reference Table*
ProductID	INT	PK	
ProductName	VARCHAR(50)		

The SQL statement for creating the table PRODUCT is listed below:

```
CREATE TABLE PRODUCT
(
            ProductID INT PRIMARY KEY,
            ProductName VARCHAR(50),
)
```

For the tables ITEM, INVENTORY, SHIPPING, and ORDERS, the table definition contains foreign keys. To implement a foreign key, you need to specify a foreign key constraint in the SQL statement.

Starting with the table ITEM, we will define a foreign key. The ITEM table definition is given in Table 4.5.

Using the following SQL statement, you can create the table ITEM:

```
CREATE TABLE ITEM
(
      ItemID INT PRIMARY KEY,
      ProductID INT,
      CPU VARCHAR(50),
      RAM VARCHAR(50),
      HardDrive VARCHAR(50),
      OpticalDrive VARCHAR(50),
      Monitor VARCHAR(50),
      CONSTRAINT Item_ProductId_fk
                  FOREIGN KEY (ProductID)
                  REFERENCES PRODUCT (ProductID)
)
```

As indicated in the above SQL statement, the foreign key constraint name is Item_ProductId_fk, which should be unique. The name of the foreign key column is ProductID. The entry after the REFERENCES is the name of the parent table. The parent table is PRODUCT, and the primary key in the parent table is ProductID.

After the table ITEM is created, you can create the table INVENTORY that has a foreign key column ItemID. The table definition is given in Table 4.6.

Table 4.5 Column Descriptions for ITEM Table

Column Name	*Data Type*	*PK or FK*	*Reference Table*
ItemID	INT	PK	
ProductID	INT	FK	PRODUCT
CPU	VARCHAR(50)		
RAM	VARCHAR(50)		
HardDrive	VARCHAR(50)		
OpticalDrive	VARCHAR(50)		
Monitor	VARCHAR(50)		

Table 4.6 Column Descriptions for INVENTORY Table

Column Name	*Data Type*	*PK or FK*	*Reference Table*
InventoryID	INT	PK	
ItemID	INT	FK	ITEM
QOH	INT		
Price	Money		

The following code can be used to create the table INVENTORY. In the SQL statement, you need to add the code for the foreign key constraint.

```
CREATE TABLE INVENTORY
(
        InventoryID INT PRIMARY KEY,
        ItemID INT,
        QOH INT DEFAULT 0 CHECK(QOH >= 0) NOT NULL,
        Price MONEY DEFAULT 0 CHECK (Price >= 0) NOT NULL,
        CONSTRAINT Inventory_ItemId_fk
                    FOREIGN KEY (ItemID)
                    REFERENCES ITEM (ItemID)
)
```

The table definition of ORDERS is given in Table 4.7.

To create the table ORDERS, use the following SQL statement:

```
CREATE TABLE ORDERS
(
        OrderID INT PRIMARY KEY,
        CustomerID INT NOT NULL,
        OrderDate DATETIME NOT NULL,
        CONSTRAINT Orders_CustomerId_fk
              FOREIGN KEY (CustomerID)
              REFERENCES CUSTOMER (CustomerID)
)
```

The table definition for SHIPPING is shown in Table 4.8.

In Table 4.8, there are two foreign key columns. To implement these two foreign keys, you need to specify two foreign key constraints. The SQL statement used to create the table SHIPPING is given below:

Table 4.7 Column Descriptions for ORDERS Table

Column Name	*Data Type*	*PK or FK*	*Reference Table*
OrderID	INT	PK	
CustomerID	INT	FK	CUSTOMER
OrderDate	DATETIME		

Table 4.8 Column Descriptions for SHIPPING Table

Column Name	*Data Type*	*PK or FK*	*Reference Table*
ShippingID	INT	PK	
OrderID	INT	FK	ORDERS
EmployeeID	INT	FK	EMPLOYEE
ShippingDate	DATETIME		
Street	VARCHAR(50)		
City	VARCHAR(50)		
State	VARCHAR(50)		
Zip	CHAR(5)		

```
CREATE TABLE SHIPPING
(
        ShippingID INT PRIMARY KEY,
        OrderID INT NOT NULL,
        EmployeeID INT NOT NULL,
        ShippingDate DATETIME NOT NULL,
        Street VARCHAR(50) NOT NULL,
        City VARCHAR(50) NOT NULL,
        State VARCHAR(50) NOT NULL,
        Zip CHAR(5) NOT NULL,
        CONSTRAINT Shipping_OrderId_fk
                      FOREIGN KEY (OrderID)
                      REFERENCES ORDERS (OrderID),
        CONSTRAINT Shipping_EmployeeId_fk
                      FOREIGN KEY (EmployeeID)
                      REFERENCES EMPLOYEE (EmployeeID)
)
```

There are two intersection tables in the Computer_Store database, ORDER_INVENTORY and CUSTOMER_PAYMENT. These two tables contain multiple foreign key columns that are also used in a combination primary key. In Table 4.9, we have the definition of the intersection table ORDER_INVENTORY.

In the SQL statement, you will have three constraints, two for the foreign keys and one for the combination primary key. To create the table ORDER_INVENTORY with these constraints, consider the SQL statement below:

Table 4.9 Column Descriptions for ORDER_INVENTORY Table

Column Name	*Data Type*	*PK or FK*	*Reference Table*
OrderID	INT	PK, FK	ORDERS
InventoryID	INT	PK, FK	INVENTORY
Quantity	INT		

Table 4.10 Column Descriptions for CUSTOMER_PAYMENT Table

Column Name	*Data Type*	*PK or FK*	*Reference Table*
CustomerID	INT	PK, FK	CUSTOMER
PaymentID	INT	PK, FK	PAYMENT
PaymentDate	DATETIME		

```
CREATE TABLE ORDER_INVENTORY
(
      OrderID INT,
      InventoryID INT,
      Quantity INT DEFAULT 0 CHECK(Quantity >= 0) NOT NULL,
      CONSTRAINT OInventory_OrderID_fk
                    FOREIGN KEY (OrderID)
                    REFERENCES ORDERS (OrderID),
      CONSTRAINT OInventory_InventoryID_fk
                    FOREIGN KEY (InventoryID)
                    REFERENCES INVENTORY (InventoryID),
      CONSTRAINT OrderID_InventoryID_pk
                    PRIMARY KEY (OrderID, InventoryID)
)
```

For the table CUSTOMER_PAYMENT, you have the definition in Table 4.10.

Similar to the SQL statement used to create the table ORDER_INVENTORY, the keyword CONSTRAINT is used to define a combination primary key shown in the following code:

```
CREATE TABLE CUSTOMER_PAYMENT
(
          CustomerID INT,
          PaymentID INT,
          PaymentDate DATETIME NOT NULL,
          CONSTRAINT CustPayment_CustomerID_fk
                    FOREIGN KEY (CustomerID)
                    REFERENCES CUSTOMER (CustomerID),
          CONSTRAINT CustPaymant_PaymentID_fk
                    FOREIGN KEY (PaymentID)
                    REFERENCES PAYMENT (PaymentID),
          CONSTRAINT CustomerID_PaymentID_pk
                    PRIMARY KEY (CustomerID, PaymentID)
)
```

Now, all the tables are defined. With the SQL statements given in this section, you should be able to create the tables in Windows Azure SQL Database. Next, you will enter and execute the SQL statements in Windows Azure SQL Database.

ACTIVITY 4.1 CREATING DATABASE OBJECTS WITH SQL IN WINDOWS AZURE SQL DATABASE

Windows Azure SQL Database provides a query tool to run SQL statements. In the following, we will use the query tool to execute SQL statements:

1. In **Internet Explorer**, enter the following URL to the Windows Azure Management Portal: https://windows.azure.com
2. Click the **SQL DATABASES** link on the left-hand side of your screen. Then, click **NEW**.
3. Select SQL DATABASE and CUSTOM CREATE.
4. After the **Specify database settings** dialog is opened, enter the database name **Computer_Store** and select your database server as shown in Figure 4.2. Then, click the check mark to create the database.
5. On the sql databases page, select the newly created database **Computer_Store** and click **MANAGE**.
6. Enter your user name and password as shown in Figure 4.3. Then, click the **Log on** arrow to log on to the SQL Database portal.
7. Once the SQL Database portal is opened, on the toolbar, click **New Query**. As shown in Figure 4.4, the SQL Query pane is open and is ready for you to enter the SQL statements.

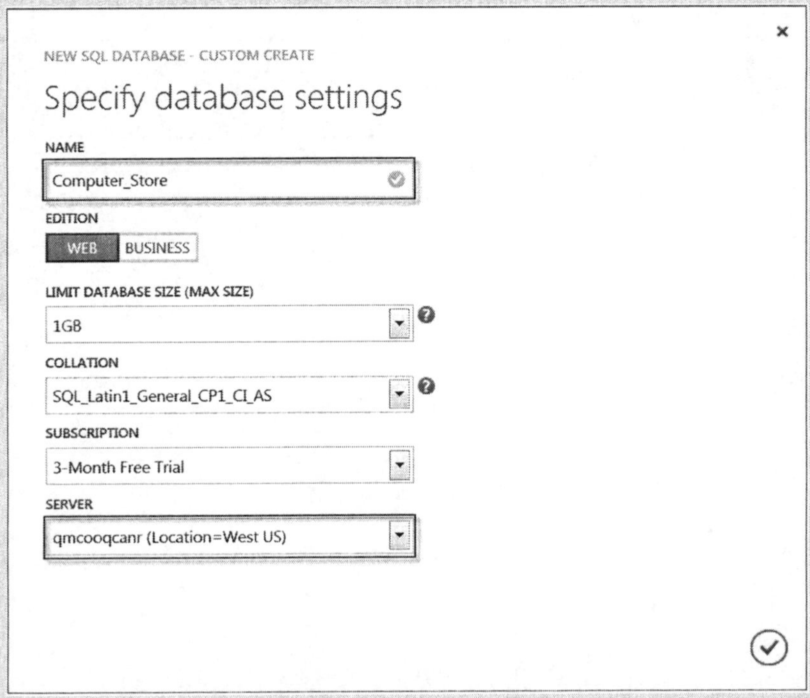

Figure 4.2 Create Computer_Store database.

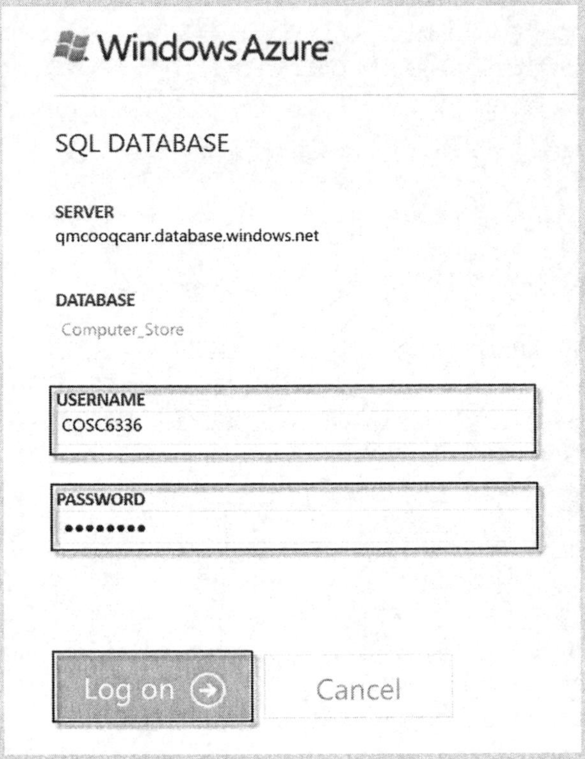

Figure 4.3 Log on to SQL database portal.

Figure 4.4 SQL query editor.

8. Let us enter the following SQL statements to create tables. After the SQL statements are entered, click **Run**.

```
– -Create tables
CREATE TABLE CUSTOMER
(
      CustomerID INT PRIMARY KEY,
      FirstName VARCHAR(30),
      LastName VARCHAR(30) NOT NULL,
      Phone CHAR(12),
      Street VARCHAR(30),
      City VARCHAR(30),
      State VARCHAR(30),
      Zip CHAR(5)
)
GO

CREATE TABLE EMPLOYEE
(
      EmployeeID INT PRIMARY KEY,
      FirstName VARCHAR(30),
      LastName VARCHAR(30) NOT NULL
)
GO

CREATE TABLE PAYMENT
(
      PaymentID INT PRIMARY KEY,
      PaymentType VARCHAR(30) NOT NULL
)
GO

CREATE TABLE PRODUCT
(
      ProductID INT PRIMARY KEY,
      ProductName VARCHAR(30),
)
GO

CREATE TABLE ITEM
(
      ItemID INT PRIMARY KEY,
      ProductID INT,
      CPU VARCHAR(30),
      RAM VARCHAR(30),
      HardDrive VARCHAR(30),
      OpticalDrive VARCHAR(30),
      Monitor VARCHAR(30),
      CONSTRAINT Item_ProductId_fk
                  FOREIGN KEY (ProductID)
                  REFERENCES PRODUCT (ProductID)
```

```
)
GO

CREATE TABLE INVENTORY
(
	InventoryID INT PRIMARY KEY,
	ItemID INT,
	Qoh INT DEFAULT 0 CHECK(Qoh >= 0) NOT NULL,
	Price MONEY DEFAULT 0 CHECK (Price >= 0) NOT NULL,
	CONSTRAINT Inventory_ItemId_fk
			FOREIGN KEY (ItemID)
			REFERENCES ITEM (ItemID)
)
GO

CREATE TABLE ORDERS
(
	OrderID INT PRIMARY KEY,
	CustomerID INT NOT NULL,
	OrderDate DATETIME NOT NULL,
	CONSTRAINT Orders_CustomerId_fk
		FOREIGN KEY (CustomerID)
		REFERENCES CUSTOMER (CustomerID)
)
GO

CREATE TABLE SHIPPING
(
	ShippingID INT PRIMARY KEY,
	OrderID INT NOT NULL,
	EmployeeID INT NOT NULL,
	ShippingDate DATETIME NOT NULL,
	Street VARCHAR(30) NOT NULL,
	City VARCHAR(30) NOT NULL,
	State VARCHAR(30) NOT NULL,
	Zip CHAR(5) NOT NULL,
	CONSTRAINT Shipping_OrderId_fk
			FOREIGN KEY (OrderID)
			REFERENCES ORDERS (OrderID),
	CONSTRAINT Shipping_EmployeeId_fk
			FOREIGN KEY (EmployeeID)
			REFERENCES EMPLOYEE (EmployeeID)
)
GO

CREATE TABLE ORDER_INVENTORY
(
	OrderID INT,
	InventoryID INT,
	Quantity INT DEFAULT 0 CHECK(Quantity >= 0) NOT NULL,
	CONSTRAINT OInventory_OrderID_fk
```

```
                    FOREIGN KEY (OrderID)
                    REFERENCES ORDERS (OrderID),
      CONSTRAINT OInventory_InventoryID_fk
                    FOREIGN KEY (InventoryID)
                    REFERENCES INVENTORY (InventoryID),
      CONSTRAINT OrderID_InventoryID_pk
                    PRIMARY KEY (OrderID, InventoryID)
)
GO

CREATE TABLE CUSTOMER_PAYMENT
(
      CustomerID INT,
      PaymentID INT,
      PaymentDate DATETIME NOT NULL,
      CONSTRAINT CustPayment_CustomerID_fk
                    FOREIGN KEY (CustomerID)
                    REFERENCES CUSTOMER (CustomerID),
      CONSTRAINT CustPaymant_PaymentID_fk
                    FOREIGN KEY (PaymentID)
                    REFERENCES PAYMENT (PaymentID),
      CONSTRAINT CustomerID_PaymentID_pk
                    PRIMARY KEY (CustomerID, PaymentID)
)
```

9. As shown in Figure 4.5. If everything works properly, you should get the message "Command(s) completed successfully."

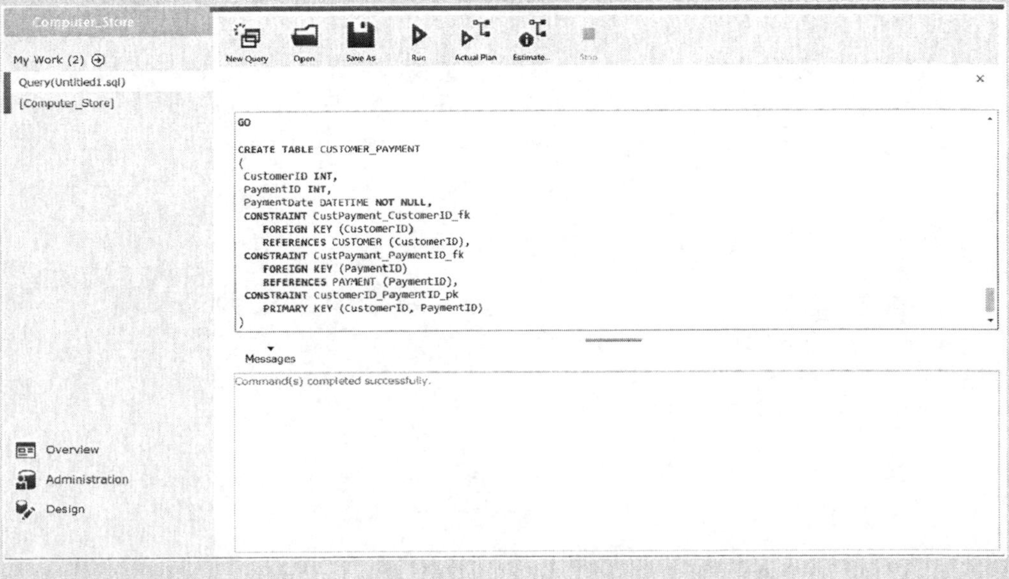

Figure 4.5 Create tables.

Figure 4.6 Tables created by SQL statements.

10. To verify that the tables are indeed created in the database **Computer_Store**, click the **Design** link. The created tables should be listed as shown in Figure 4.6.
11. In Figure 4.7, each table name is attached to the word **dbo** that stands for database owner and is the default schema name. A schema is a container that may hold several database objects that are owned by the same schema. It can be used to manage database object ownerships and security. In Windows Azure SQL Database, each schema may have several owners and each owner may own several schemas. You can grant a set of permissions to a schema and assign a group of users as the owners of the schema. In this way, you can avoid assigning permissions to each individual user, which is time consuming. In the next section, you will learn how to grant permissions to schemas.
12. To check the dependencies among tables, click the icon **Dependencies**. As shown in Figure 4.7, the table CUSTOMER is related to the tables ORDERS and CUSTOMER_ PAYMENT.
13. Click **Design** to switch back to the design window. Click the **Edit** icon next to the table CUSTOMER as shown in Figure 4.8.
14. Figure 4.9 shows the definitions of the columns for the CUSTOMER table. You can modify the column definitions here.

After the tables are created, SQL statements can be used to enter data in those tables. The data entry process will be covered later in this chapter.

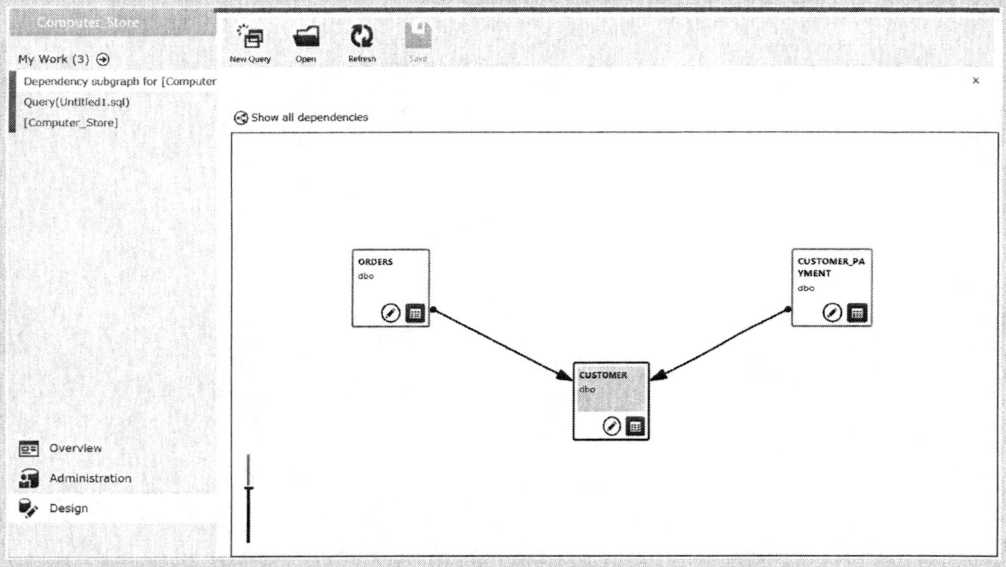

Figure 4.7 Dependencies on CUSTOMER table.

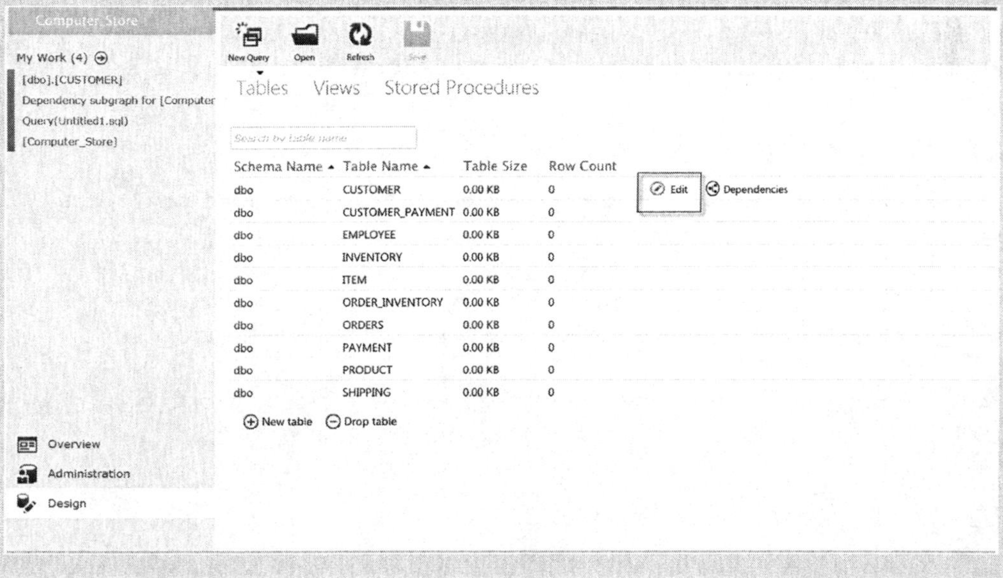

Figure 4.8 Edit tables.

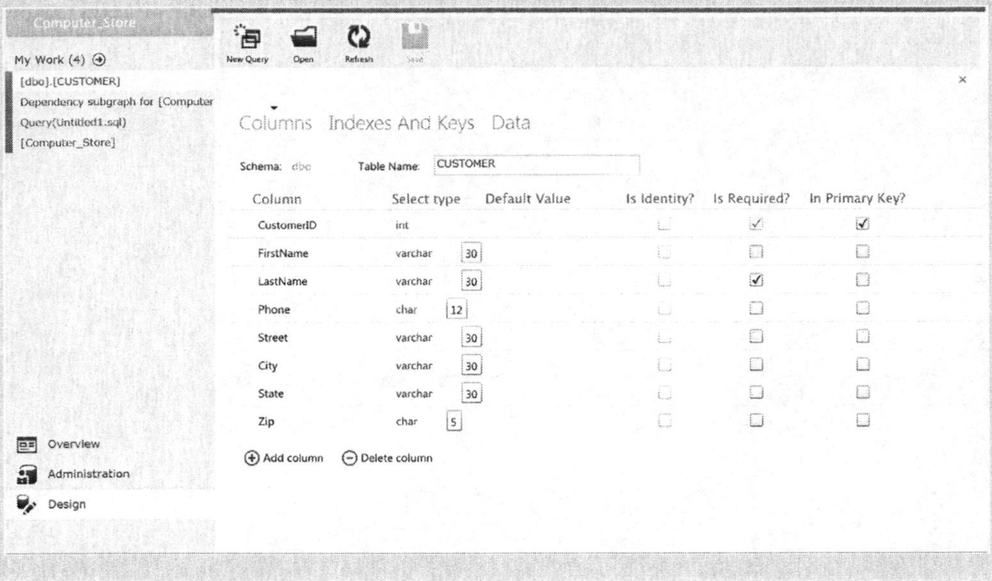

Figure 4.9 Column definitions.

4.4 Managing Database Objects

After the tables have been created, the table structures can be viewed and modified with SQL statements or the built-in stored procedures.

4.4.1 Viewing Table Structures

To view the table properties, you can use the following stored procedures and commands provided by Windows Azure SQL Database:

- sp_help: a built-in stored procedure used to view table definitions
- sp_depends: a built-in stored procedure used to view table dependencies

When running the stored procedure sp_help to view the table definition for the table PRODUCT, you should be able to see the detailed table definition as shown in Figure 4.10.

4.4.2 Modifying Table Structures

SQL statements can be used to modify the structure of database objects. You can change the data type of a column, rename a column or a table, modify constraints, add new columns, or assign permissions to schemas.

The ALTER TABLE statement is used to change the table structure. For example, if you want to add a foreign key constraint to the column EmployeeID in the table SHIPPING, you can use the following SQL statement:

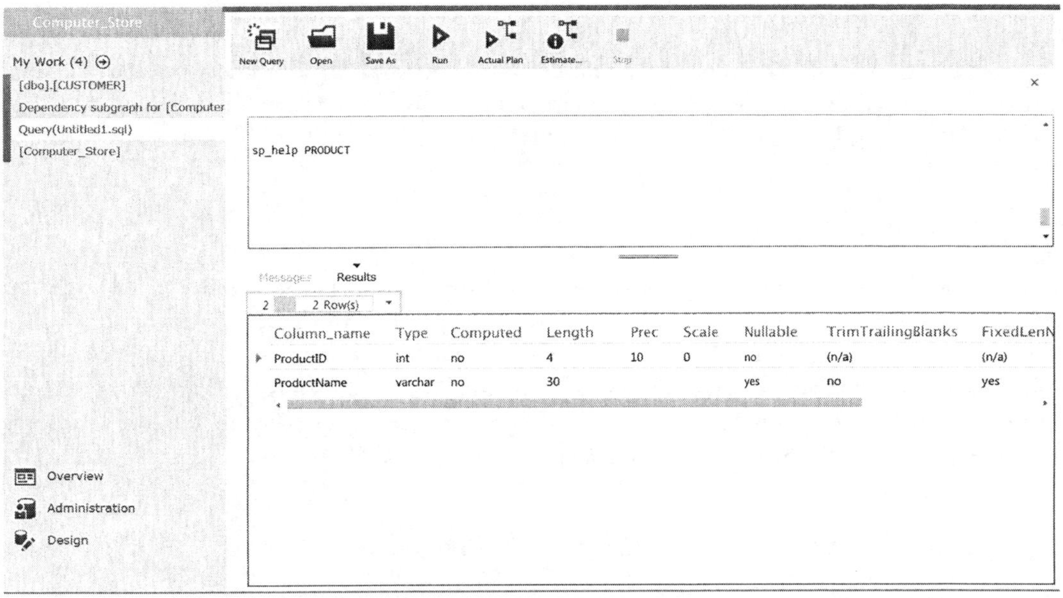

Figure 4.10 Use stored procedure to obtain table definition.

```
ALTER TABLE SHIPPING ADD
CONSTRAINT Shipping_EmployeeID_fk
      FOREIGN KEY (EmployeeID)
      REFERENCES EMPLOYEE (EmployeeID)
```

To add a check constraint to the column Qoh in the INVENTORY table, use

```
ALTER TABLE INVENTORY ADD
      CONSTRAINT Inventory_ck CHECK(Qoh >= 0)
```

With the ALTER TABLE constraint, you can also add and delete columns in a table. For example, if you want to add a column ShelfID to the table INVENTORY, use the following code:

```
ALTER TABLE INVENTORY ADD ShelfID INT
```

You can also delete the column ShelfID from the table INVENTORY with the following code:

```
ALTER TABLE INVENTORY Drop COLUMN ShelfID
```

The ALTER TABLE keyword phrase can also be used to change the data type of the column. For example, if you want to change the data type of the column Qoh from INT to BIGINT, use the following SQL statement:

```
ALTER TABLE INVENTORY ALTER COLUMN Qoh BIGINT
```

When changing the column properties, make sure that the column is not used by constraints and referenced by other columns. For example, the column Qoh in the above code has a domain constraint Inventory_ck built on it. Simply running the above ALTER TABLE SQL statement will cause an error.

You can also modify the length of a column. As the length of a column is reduced, the data in that column will be truncated to fit in that column. This is also true for changing data types. The DROP keyword can be used to drop a table. The following SQL statement drops the table INVENTORY:

```
DROP TABLE INVENTORY
```

If a table is referenced by a foreign key column from another table, deleting the rows in the table or dropping the table will cause errors. Updating the rows in the referenced table can also cause similar problems. Windows Azure SQL Database prevents you from dropping a table referenced by another table. You must drop the referencing table first before you can drop the referenced table. Windows Azure SQL Database allows you to view the dependency of the tables. As an example, Figure 4.7 shows the dependencies on the CUSTOMER table.

4.4.3 Controlling Database Object Privileges

The database objects created by one Windows Azure SQL Database user cannot be accessed by another Windows Azure SQL Database user without permission. The database object owner can grant permissions to other users by using DCL commands. For example, to allow the public to update the table PRODUCT, use the following SQL statement:

```
GRANT UPDATE
ON PRODUCT
TO PUBLIC
```

To remove a previously granted privilege on a database object, use the DCL command REVOKE. Since it is not a good idea to grant the update permission to the public on the PRODUCT table, it needs to be removed. To do that, run the following SQL statement:

```
REVOKE UPDATE
ON PRODUCT
TO PUBLIC
```

If you log on to a database as a database administrator, you have the privilege to grant and revoke database object access privileges to other users.

ACTIVITY 4.2 DATABASE MANAGEMENT WITH SQL

In Chapter 3, you created the Class_Registration database. In this activity, you will create relationships among the tables created for the Class_Registration database according to Figure 4.11. The ALTER TABLE statement will be used to carry out the task.

1. Assume that you have logged on to the Windows Azure Management Portal. Select the database **Class_Registration** and click **MANAGE**. Then, log on to the SQL Database portal with your user name and password.

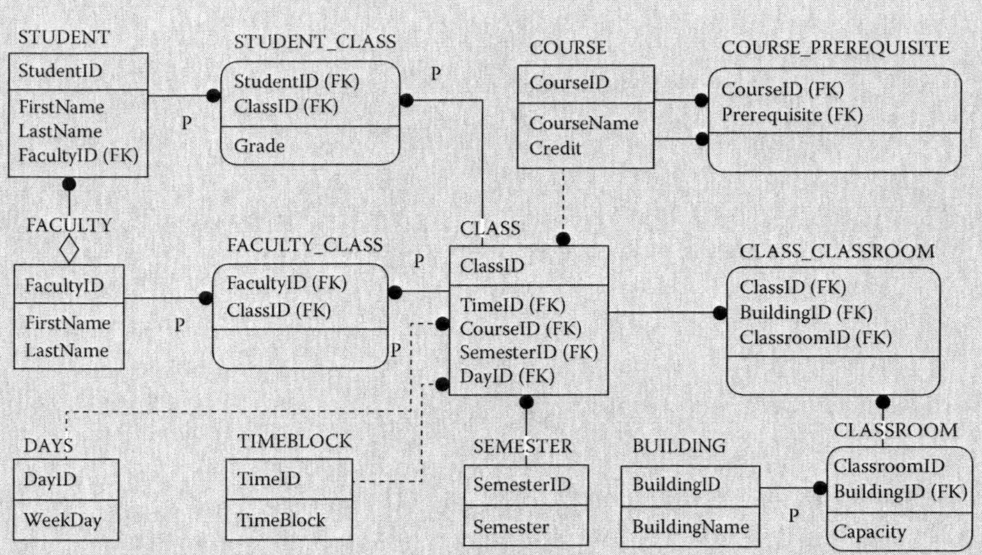

Figure 4.11 Class_Registration data model.

2. Click **New Query** to open the query tool. To create a foreign key constraint on the table STUDENT, enter the following SQL statement. Then click **Run** as shown in Figure 4.12.

Figure 4.12 Create foreign key on STUDENT table.

```
ALTER TABLE STUDENT ADD
CONSTRAINT Student_FacultyID_fk
      FOREIGN KEY (FacultyID)
      REFERENCES FACULTY (FacultyID)
```

3. Similarly, you can enter the following SQL statements to create the rest of the foreign key constraints. Then, highlight each SQL Statement and click **Run**.

```
ALTER TABLE STUDENT_CLASS ADD CONSTRAINT SC_StudentID_fk
  FOREIGN KEY (StudentID) REFERENCES STUDENT (StudentID)

ALTER TABLE STUDENT_CLASS ADD CONSTRAINT SC_ClassID_fk
  FOREIGN KEY (ClassID) REFERENCES CLASS (ClassID)

ALTER TABLE COURSE_PREREQUISITE ADD CONSTRAINT CP_CourseID_fk
  FOREIGN KEY (CourseID) REFERENCES COURSE (CourseID)

ALTER TABLE COURSE_PREREQUISITE
  ADD CONSTRAINT CP_Prerequisite_fk
  FOREIGN KEY (Prerequisite) REFERENCES COURSE (CourseID)

ALTER TABLE FACULTY_CLASS ADD CONSTRAINT FC_FacultyID_fk
  FOREIGN KEY (FacultyID) REFERENCES FACULTY (FacultyID)

ALTER TABLE FACULTY_CLASS ADD CONSTRAINT FC_ClassID_fk
  FOREIGN KEY (ClassID) REFERENCES CLASS (ClassID)

ALTER TABLE CLASS ADD CONSTRAINT CLASS_CourseID_fk
  FOREIGN KEY (CourseID) REFERENCES COURSE (CourseID)

ALTER TABLE CLASS ADD CONSTRAINT CLASS_DayID_fk
  FOREIGN KEY (DayID) REFERENCES DAYS (DayID)

ALTER TABLE CLASS ADD CONSTRAINT CLASS_TimeID_fk
  FOREIGN KEY (TimeID) REFERENCES TIMEBLOCK (TimeID)

ALTER TABLE CLASS ADD CONSTRAINT CLASS_SemesterID_fk
  FOREIGN KEY (SemesterID) REFERENCES SEMESTER (SemesterID)

ALTER TABLE CLASSROOM ADD CONSTRAINT CLASS_BuildingID_fk
  FOREIGN KEY (BuildingID) REFERENCES BUILDING (BuildingID)

ALTER TABLE CLASS_CLASSROOM ADD CONSTRAINT CC_ClassID_fk
  FOREIGN KEY (ClassID) REFERENCES CLASS (ClassID)

ALTER TABLE CLASS_CLASSROOM ADD CONSTRAINT CC_ClassroomID_fk
  FOREIGN KEY (ClassroomID, BuildingID)
  REFERENCES CLASSROOM (ClassroomID, BuildingID))
```

4. To view a newly created constraint, click **Design** on the left-hand side of the screen. Select the table **CLASS_CLASSROOM** and then click **Edit**. Click **Indexes And Keys**, and you should be able to see the foreign keys as shown in Figure 4.13.

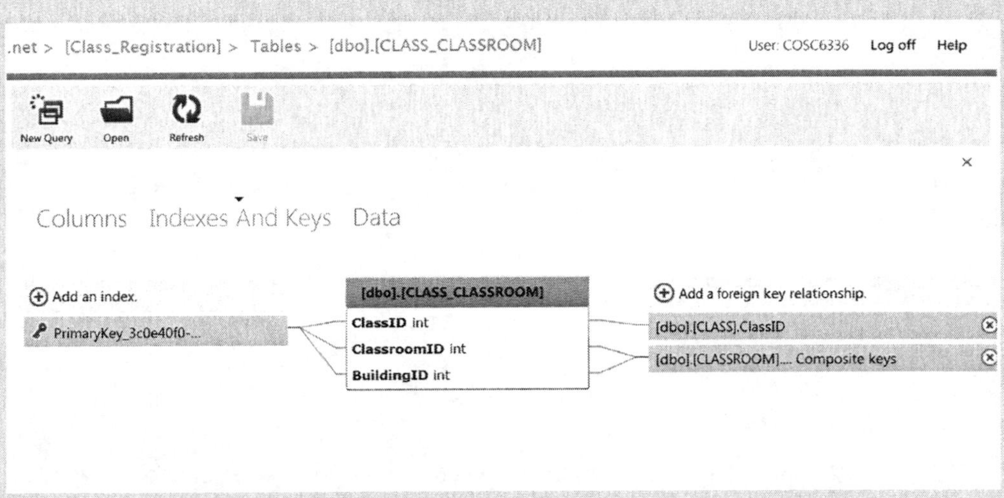

Figure 4.13 Foreign key relationships.

4.5 Manipulating Data in Tables

You can manipulate the data in an existing table with DML commands. You can insert a row of data with the INSERT command, modify data with the UPDATE command, delete data with the DELETE command, and query data with the SELECT command. The following examples show you how to use these commands to manipulate data in a table.

4.5.1 Inserting Data

To insert a new row of data in the table EMPLOYEE, use the following SQL statement:

```
INSERT INTO EMPLOYEE
VALUES(1, 'Liz', 'Chen')
```

As seen from the above SQL statement, the order and data types of the data values listed in the VALUES (…) statement exactly match the column definitions. For example, the data value of the first column is an integer; the first name and last name data values are character strings that should be quoted with single quotes.

4.5.2 Modifying Data

In this example, let us run the following SQL statement that will change the last name Chen to Dean:

```
UPDATE EMPLOYEE
SET LastName = 'Dean'
WHERE LastName = 'Chen'
```

In the above code, WHERE specifies the value to be updated. Without the WHERE clause, all the values in the same column will be updated. The SET keyword is used to set a new value.

4.5.3 Querying Data

The following example shows how to query the information about the employees with the last name Smith:

```
SELECT FirstName, LastName
FROM EMPLOYEE
WHERE LastName = 'Smith'
```

4.5.4 Deleting Data

In the following example, you will delete the row where the employee's last name is Chen:

```
DELETE FROM EMPLOYEE
WHERE LastName = 'Chen'
```

Again, the WHERE clause is necessary to specify which row to be deleted. Otherwise, all rows will be deleted.

ACTIVITY 4.3 POPULATING DATABASE TABLES WITH DATA

After the tables are created, it is time to populate the tables with data. In this section, we will insert data into the tables in the database Computer_Store as well as the tables in the database Class_Registration.

When entering data into the tables, you should first enter the data into the tables without foreign key columns. After the data are entered into the tables without foreign keys, you can populate the tables with foreign key columns. In such a way, the data values entered into foreign key columns can be verified by the foreign key constraint to see if there is a match with the primary keys in the parent tables. If there is no match, you will get an error message.

TASK 1: POPULATE COMPUTER_STORE DATABASE

Follow the steps below to populate the Computer_Store database with SQL statements in Windows Azure SQL Database:

1. Assume that you have logged on to the Windows Azure Management Portal. Select **SQL DATABASES** and the database **Computer_Store**. Click **MANAGE** to log on to the SQL Database portal shown in Figure 4.14.
2. Once the SQL Database portal is opened, click **New Query**. Enter the following SQL statements in the New Query pane. Then, click **Run**.

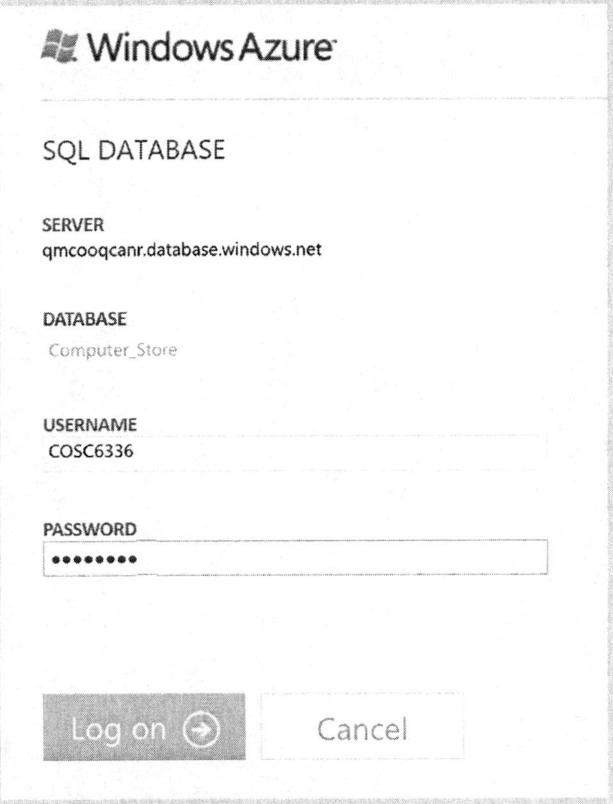

Figure 4.14 Log on to SQL database portal to manage Computer_Store.

```
– - inserting records into table CUSTOMER
INSERT INTO CUSTOMER
VALUES(1,'John','Burge','972-456-5555','214
Nelson','Dallas','TX','75201')

INSERT INTO CUSTOMER
VALUES(2,'Keren','Wu','281-333-1111','345
Bagby','Houston','TX','77002')

INSERT INTO CUSTOMER
VALUES(3,'Dan','Parr','361-111-2222','324
Miori','Victoria','TX','77903')

INSERT INTO CUSTOMER
VALUES(4,'Lisa','Garcia','806-333-1111','874 Wilson','Amorillo',
'TX','79105')

INSERT INTO CUSTOMER
VALUES(5,'Susan','Holly','512-111-2222','4848 Lakeside','Austin',
'TX','78767')
```

```
INSERT INTO CUSTOMER
VALUES(6,'Al','Dean','972-111-3333','1398 International
Rd','Dallas','TX','75201')
INSERT INTO CUSTOMER
VALUES(7,'David','Jouns','281-000-1111','267 College','Houston',
'TX','77487')
INSERT INTO CUSTOMER
VALUES(8,'Bud','Fry','512-234-0000','2396 Anderson','Austin',
'TX','78767')
INSERT INTO CUSTOMER
VALUES(9,'Jane','Young','212-111-4444','1563 Madison','New
York','NY','10159')
INSERT INTO CUSTOMER
VALUES(10,'Robert','Smith','334-555-1111','2995 Post','Montgamery',
'AL','35824')
INSERT INTO CUSTOMER
VALUES(11,'Roy','Munoz','303-333-0000','201 Bellaire','Denver',
'CO','80222')
INSERT INTO CUSTOMER
VALUES(12,'Paul','Sitka','650-555-3333','1240 Villa','Mountain
View','CA','94041')
INSERT INTO CUSTOMER
VALUES(13,'Gary','Sherman','508-333-7777','145 Corporate',
'Cambridge','MA','02142')
INSERT INTO CUSTOMER
VALUES(14,'Larry','Hursh','281-000-1234','1248 Katy
Frwy','Houston','TX','77429')
INSERT INTO CUSTOMER
VALUES(15,'David','Reed','281-444-9999','579 S.
Mason','Houston','TX','77290')
INSERT INTO CUSTOMER
VALUES(16,'John','Shum','281-123-2345','389
Brooks','Houston','TX','76385')
INSERT INTO CUSTOMER
VALUES(17,'Joe','Brand','281-987-1111','2970 Hwy
6','Houston','TX','77638')
INSERT INTO CUSTOMER
VALUES(18,'Eric','Revis','281-567-7890','9108
Travis','Houston','TX','76325')
INSERT INTO CUSTOMER
VALUES(19,'Lilla','White','281-999-1234','1590 Memorial','Houston',
'TX','77389')
INSERT INTO CUSTOMER
VALUES(20,'Frank','Dees','281-888-2345','337 First
St.','Houston','TX','78330')
```

```
INSERT INTO CUSTOMER
VALUES(21,'Aian','Ramos','281-777-1111','466
Sugar','Houston','TX','77449')

INSERT INTO CUSTOMER
VALUES(22,'Mike','Garcia','281-000-2222','1400 Richmond','Houston',
'TX','77562')

INSERT INTO CUSTOMER
VALUES(23,'Dana','Kersh','281-666-7777','8879 Telephone
Rd.','Houston','TX','77541')

INSERT INTO CUSTOMER
VALUES(24,'Jeff','Rose','281-555-1234','735 Tomball','Houston',
'TX','77339')

INSERT INTO CUSTOMER
VALUES(25,'Sam','Parker','281-444-1234','6839 Antoine','Houston',
'TX','77456')

INSERT INTO CUSTOMER
VALUES(26,'Helen','Wood','281-411-1111','179
Greens','Houston','TX','77894')

INSERT INTO CUSTOMER
VALUES(27,'Wanda','Burton','281-012-0123','4221 Gulf
Frwy','Houston','TX','77903')

INSERT INTO CUSTOMER
VALUES(28,'Steve','Perry','281-456-0000','827 Louetta','Houston',
'TX','76450')

INSERT INTO CUSTOMER
VALUES(29,'Jay','Jackson','281-000-1000','1849 Westheimer',
'Houston','TX','76889')

INSERT INTO CUSTOMER
VALUES(30,'Toya','Vela','281-777-2222','163
Fugua','Houston','TX','77398')


– - inserting records into table EMPLOYEE
INSERT INTO EMPLOYEE
VALUES(1, 'Liz', 'Chen')

INSERT INTO EMPLOYEE
VALUES(2, 'Jan','Dean')

INSERT INTO EMPLOYEE
VALUES(3, 'Don','Fry')

INSERT INTO EMPLOYEE
VALUES(4, 'Linda', 'Green')

INSERT INTO EMPLOYEE
VALUES(5, 'Mark','Smith')
```

```
INSERT INTO EMPLOYEE
VALUES(6, 'Mary','Smith')

INSERT INTO EMPLOYEE
VALUES(7, 'Joe','Wyer')

INSERT INTO EMPLOYEE
VALUES(8, 'Bruce','Young')

– - inserting records into table PAYMENT
INSERT INTO PAYMENT
VALUES(1,'Check')

INSERT INTO PAYMENT
VALUES(2,'Master')

INSERT INTO PAYMENT
VALUES(3,'VISA')

INSERT INTO PAYMENT
VALUES(4,'American Express')

INSERT INTO PAYMENT
VALUES(5,'Discover')

– - inserting records into table PRODUCT
INSERT INTO PRODUCT
VALUES(1,'DeskTop')

INSERT INTO PRODUCT
VALUES(2,'Notebook')

INSERT INTO PRODUCT
VALUES(3,'Tablet')

INSERT INTO PRODUCT
VALUES(4,'PDA')

– - inserting records into table ITEM
INSERT INTO ITEM
VALUES(1,3,'PM 2.2 GHz','512MB','60GB','DVD-ROM/CD-RW','14.1″
swivel')

INSERT INTO ITEM
VALUES(2,2,'CM 2.0 GHz','256MB','40GB','DVD-ROM/CD-RW','15″ XGA TFT')

INSERT INTO ITEM
VALUES(3,2,'PM 3.0 GHz','1024MB','100GB','DVD-RAM','15.4″ WXGA TFT')

INSERT INTO ITEM
VALUES(4,2,'PM 3.6 GHz','512MB','40GB','DVD SuperMulti','7.2″ WXGA
TFT')

INSERT INTO ITEM
VALUES(5,2,'PM 3.6GHZ','512MB','60GB','DVD SuperMulti','12.1″ XGA')

INSERT INTO ITEM
VALUES(6,2,'SD 1.5 GHz','512MB','80GB','Bluetooth 2.0','12.1″ XGA')
```

```
INSERT INTO ITEM
VALUES(7,1,'SD 1.25 GHz','256MB','40GB','DVD Combo','')

INSERT INTO ITEM
VALUES(8,2,'SD 1.5 GHz','512MB','80GB','Bluetooth 2.0','15″ XGA')

INSERT INTO ITEM
VALUES(9,1,'SD Dual 2.3 GHz','512MB','250GB','16x SuperDrive DVD','')

INSERT INTO ITEM
VALUES(10,2,'AA 2.2 GHz','512MB','80GB','DVD + -RW','15.4″ WXGA')

INSERT INTO ITEM
VALUES(11,1,'AA 3.2 GHz','1GB','200GB','DVD + -RW','')

INSERT INTO ITEM
VALUES(12,1,'CD 2.0 GHz','512MB','100GB','DVD-ROM/CD-RW','')

INSERT INTO ITEM
VALUES(13,4,'SS 300 MHz','56MB','','','3.5″ Transflective TFT')

INSERT INTO ITEM
VALUES(14,4,'SS 400 MHz','152MB','','','3.5″ Transflective TFT')

INSERT INTO ITEM
VALUES(15,1,'AA 2.6 GHz','512MB','160GB','DVD + -RW','')

INSERT INTO ITEM
VALUES(16,1,'CD 3.4 GHz','512MB','100GB','DVD-ROM/CD-RW','')

INSERT INTO ITEM
VALUES(17,1,'AA 3.2 GHz','1GB','250GB','DVD + -RW','')

INSERT INTO ITEM
VALUES(18,2,'CM 1.40 GHz','256MB','40GB','CD-RW','14.1″ XGA TFT')

INSERT INTO ITEM
VALUES(19,2,'PM 1.6 GHz','256MB','40GB','DVD-ROM/CD-RW','14.1″ XGA
TFT')

INSERT INTO ITEM
VALUES(20,2,'PM 1.50 GHz','512MB','40GB','DVD-ROM/CD-RW','12.1″ XGA
TFT')

— - inserting records into table INVENTORY
INSERT INTO INVENTORY
VALUES(1,1,5,1500)

INSERT INTO INVENTORY
VALUES(2,1,500,1400)

INSERT INTO INVENTORY
VALUES(3,2,2,799)

INSERT INTO INVENTORY
VALUES(4,2,454,749)

INSERT INTO INVENTORY
VALUES(5,3,12,1799)
```

```
INSERT INTO INVENTORY
VALUES(6,3,200,1699)

INSERT INTO INVENTORY
VALUES(7,4,58,1824)

INSERT INTO INVENTORY
VALUES(8,5,56,1999)

INSERT INTO INVENTORY
VALUES(9,6,23,1699)

INSERT INTO INVENTORY
VALUES(10,7,455,499)

INSERT INTO INVENTORY
VALUES(11,8,79,1999)

INSERT INTO INVENTORY
VALUES(12,9,51,2499)

INSERT INTO INVENTORY
VALUES(13,10,222,1040)

INSERT INTO INVENTORY
VALUES(14,11,344,649)

INSERT INTO INVENTORY
VALUES(15,12,450,449)

INSERT INTO INVENTORY
VALUES(16,13,899,299)

INSERT INTO INVENTORY
VALUES(17,14,682,449)

INSERT INTO INVENTORY
VALUES(18,15,739,649)

INSERT INTO INVENTORY
VALUES(19,16,145,409)

INSERT INTO INVENTORY
VALUES(20,17,500,654)

INSERT INTO INVENTORY
VALUES(21,18,130,599)

INSERT INTO INVENTORY
VALUES(22,19,5,1350)

INSERT INTO INVENTORY
VALUES(23,19,100,1300)


— - inserting records into ORDERS
INSERT INTO ORDERS
VALUES(1,1,'2012-02-01')
```

```
INSERT INTO ORDERS
VALUES(2,2,'2012-05-01')

INSERT INTO ORDERS
VALUES(3,3,'2011-02-01')

INSERT INTO ORDERS
VALUES(4,4,'2011-03-01')

INSERT INTO ORDERS
VALUES(5,5,'2011-03-01')

INSERT INTO ORDERS
VALUES(6,6,'2011-04-01')

INSERT INTO ORDERS
VALUES(7,7,'2011-04-01')

INSERT INTO ORDERS
VALUES(8,8,'2012-05-01')

INSERT INTO ORDERS
VALUES(9,9,'2011-05-01')

INSERT INTO ORDERS
VALUES(10,10,'2011-05-01')

INSERT INTO ORDERS
VALUES(11,11,'2011-06-01')

INSERT INTO ORDERS
VALUES(12,12,'2011-06-01')

INSERT INTO ORDERS
VALUES(13,13,'2012-07-01')

INSERT INTO ORDERS
VALUES(14,14,'2012-07-01')

INSERT INTO ORDERS
VALUES(15,15,'2013-08-01')

INSERT INTO ORDERS
VALUES(16,16,'2012-08-01')

INSERT INTO ORDERS
VALUES(17,17,'2011-08-01')

INSERT INTO ORDERS
VALUES(18,18,'2011-09-01')

INSERT INTO ORDERS
VALUES(19,19,'2011-09-01')

INSERT INTO ORDERS
VALUES(20,20,'2012-09-01')

INSERT INTO ORDERS
VALUES(21,21,'2012-10-01')
```

```
INSERT INTO ORDERS
VALUES(22,22,'2011-10-01')

INSERT INTO ORDERS
VALUES(23,23,'2010-11-01')

INSERT INTO ORDERS
VALUES(24,24,'2010-11-01')

INSERT INTO ORDERS
VALUES(25,25,'2010-12-01')

INSERT INTO ORDERS
VALUES(26,26,'2012-12-01')

INSERT INTO ORDERS
VALUES(27,27,'2013-09-11')

INSERT INTO ORDERS
VALUES(28,28,'2009-09-21')

INSERT INTO ORDERS
VALUES(29,29,'2008-10-01')

INSERT INTO ORDERS
VALUES(30,30,'2008-10-06')

INSERT INTO ORDERS
VALUES(31,1,'2008-10-31')

INSERT INTO ORDERS
VALUES(32,2,'2008-11-01')

INSERT INTO ORDERS
VALUES(33,11,'2008-11-07')

INSERT INTO ORDERS
VALUES(34,12,'2008-11-21')

INSERT INTO ORDERS
VALUES(35,13,'2008-12-17')

INSERT INTO ORDERS
VALUES(36,14,'2008-12-21')

– - inserting records into SHIPPING
INSERT INTO SHIPPING
VALUES(1,1,1,'2008-02-01','214 Nelson','Dallas','TX','75201')

INSERT INTO SHIPPING
VALUES(2,2,2,'2008-05-01','345 Bagby','Houston','TX','77002')

INSERT INTO SHIPPING
VALUES(3,3,3,'2008-02-12','324 Miori','Victoria','TX','77903')

INSERT INTO SHIPPING
VALUES(4,4,4,'2008-03-01','874 Wilson','Amorillo','TX','79105')
```

```
INSERT INTO SHIPPING
VALUES(5,5,5,'2008-03-11','4848 Lakeside','Austin','TX','78767')

INSERT INTO SHIPPING
VALUES(6,6,6,'2008-04-01','1398 International
Rd','Dallas','TX','75201')

INSERT INTO SHIPPING
VALUES(7,7,7,'2008-04-11','267 College','Houston','TX','77487')

INSERT INTO SHIPPING
VALUES(8,8,8,'2008-04-15','2396 Anderson','Austin','TX','78767')

INSERT INTO SHIPPING
VALUES(9,9,1,'2008-05-01','1563 Madison','New York','NY','10159')

INSERT INTO SHIPPING
VALUES(10,10,2,'2008-05-11','2995 Post','Huntsville','AL','35824')

INSERT INTO SHIPPING
VALUES(11,11,3,'2008-05-21','201 Bellaire','Denver','CO','80222')

INSERT INTO SHIPPING
VALUES(12,12,4,'2008-05-31','1240 Villa','Mountain
View','CA','94041')

INSERT INTO SHIPPING
VALUES(13,13,5,'2008-06-01','145 Corporate','Cambridge','MA','02142')

INSERT INTO SHIPPING
VALUES(14,14,6,'2008-06-11','1248 Katy Frwy','Houston','TX','77429')

INSERT INTO SHIPPING
VALUES(15,15,7,'2008-06-23','579 S. Mason','Houston','TX','77290')

INSERT INTO SHIPPING
VALUES(16,16,8,'2008-06-25','389 Brooks','Houston','TX','76385')

INSERT INTO SHIPPING
VALUES(17,17,1,'2008-07-01','2970 Hwy 6','Houston','TX','77638')

INSERT INTO SHIPPING
VALUES(18,18,2,'2008-07-11','9108 Travis','Houston','TX','76325')

INSERT INTO SHIPPING
VALUES(19,19,3,'2008-07-21','1590 Memorial','Houston','TX','77389')

INSERT INTO SHIPPING
VALUES(20,20,4,'2008-07-31','337 First St.','Houston','TX','78330')

INSERT INTO SHIPPING
VALUES(21,21,5,'2008-08-01','466 Sugar','Houston','TX','77449')

INSERT INTO SHIPPING
VALUES(22,22,6,'2008-08-05','1400 Richmond','Houston','TX','77562')

INSERT INTO SHIPPING
VALUES(23,23,7,'2008-08-09','8879 Telephone
Rd.','Houston','TX','77541')
```

```
INSERT INTO SHIPPING
VALUES(24,24,8,'2008-08-21','735 Tomball','Houston','TX','77339')

INSERT INTO SHIPPING
VALUES(25,25,1,'2008-09-02','6839 Antoine','Houston','TX','77456')

INSERT INTO SHIPPING
VALUES(26,26,2,'2008-09-08','179 Greens','Houston','TX','77894')

INSERT INTO SHIPPING
VALUES(27,27,3,'2008-09-11','4221 Gulf Frwy','Houston','TX','77903')

INSERT INTO SHIPPING
VALUES(28,28,4,'2009-09-21','827 Louetta','Houston','TX','76450')

INSERT INTO SHIPPING
VALUES(29,29,5,'2008-10-01','1849 Westheimer','Houston','TX','76889')

INSERT INTO SHIPPING
VALUES(30,30,6,'2008-10-06','163 Fugua','Houston','TX','77398')

INSERT INTO SHIPPING
VALUES(31,31,7,'2008-10-31','2995 Post','Huntsville','AL','35824')

INSERT INTO SHIPPING
VALUES(32,32,8,'2008-11-01','201 Bellaire','Denver','CO','80222')

INSERT INTO SHIPPING
VALUES(33,33,1,'2008-11-07','1240 Villa','Mountain
View','CA','94041')

INSERT INTO SHIPPING
VALUES(34,34,2,'2008-11-21','145 Corporate','Cambridge','MA','02142')

INSERT INTO SHIPPING
VALUES(35,35,3,'2008-12-17','145 Corporate','Cambridge','MA','02142')

INSERT INTO SHIPPING
VALUES(36,36,4,'2008-12-21','1248 Katy Frwy','Houston','TX','77429')

INSERT INTO SHIPPING
VALUES(37,33,1,'2008-11-07','1240 Villa','Mountain
View','CA','94041')

INSERT INTO SHIPPING
VALUES(38,34,2,'2008-11-21','145 Corporate','Cambridge','MA','02142')

INSERT INTO SHIPPING
VALUES(39,35,3,'2008-12-17','145 Corporate','Cambridge','MA','02142')

INSERT INTO SHIPPING
VALUES(40,36,4,'2008-12-21','1248 Katy Frwy','Houston','TX','77429')


– - inserting records into ORDER_INVENTORY
INSERT INTO ORDER_INVENTORY
VALUES(1,1,2)
```

```
INSERT INTO ORDER_INVENTORY
VALUES(2,2,2)

INSERT INTO ORDER_INVENTORY
VALUES(3,3,1)

INSERT INTO ORDER_INVENTORY
VALUES(4,4,1)

INSERT INTO ORDER_INVENTORY
VALUES(5,5,1)

INSERT INTO ORDER_INVENTORY
VALUES(6,6,1)

INSERT INTO ORDER_INVENTORY
VALUES(7,7,1)

INSERT INTO ORDER_INVENTORY
VALUES(8,8,1)

INSERT INTO ORDER_INVENTORY
VALUES(9,9,2)

INSERT INTO ORDER_INVENTORY
VALUES(10,10,1)

INSERT INTO ORDER_INVENTORY
VALUES(11,11,2)

INSERT INTO ORDER_INVENTORY
VALUES(12,12,2)

INSERT INTO ORDER_INVENTORY
VALUES(13,13,2)

INSERT INTO ORDER_INVENTORY
VALUES(14,14,2)

INSERT INTO ORDER_INVENTORY
VALUES(15,15,1)

INSERT INTO ORDER_INVENTORY
VALUES(16,16,1)

INSERT INTO ORDER_INVENTORY
VALUES(17,17,1)

INSERT INTO ORDER_INVENTORY
VALUES(18,18,2)

INSERT INTO ORDER_INVENTORY
VALUES(19,19,1)

INSERT INTO ORDER_INVENTORY
VALUES(20,20,1)
```

```
INSERT INTO ORDER_INVENTORY
VALUES(21,21,3)

INSERT INTO ORDER_INVENTORY
VALUES(22,22,1)

INSERT INTO ORDER_INVENTORY
VALUES(23,23,1)

INSERT INTO ORDER_INVENTORY
VALUES(24,1,1)

INSERT INTO ORDER_INVENTORY
VALUES(25,2,1)

INSERT INTO ORDER_INVENTORY
VALUES(26,6,1)

INSERT INTO ORDER_INVENTORY
VALUES(27,7,1)

INSERT INTO ORDER_INVENTORY
VALUES(28,8,1)

INSERT INTO ORDER_INVENTORY
VALUES(29,9,2)

INSERT INTO ORDER_INVENTORY
VALUES(30,10,1)

INSERT INTO ORDER_INVENTORY
VALUES(30,3,1)

INSERT INTO ORDER_INVENTORY
VALUES(31,2,1)

INSERT INTO ORDER_INVENTORY
VALUES(32,4,1)

INSERT INTO ORDER_INVENTORY
VALUES(32,11,1)

INSERT INTO ORDER_INVENTORY
VALUES(33,12,1)

INSERT INTO ORDER_INVENTORY
VALUES(34,12,1)

INSERT INTO ORDER_INVENTORY
VALUES(33,13,1)

INSERT INTO ORDER_INVENTORY
VALUES(35,8,1)

INSERT INTO ORDER_INVENTORY
VALUES(11,14,2)
```

```
INSERT INTO ORDER_INVENTORY
VALUES(12,11,1)

INSERT INTO ORDER_INVENTORY
VALUES(13,12,2)

INSERT INTO ORDER_INVENTORY
VALUES(14,13,1)

INSERT INTO ORDER_INVENTORY
VALUES(36,14,1)


-- inserting records into CUSTOMER_PAYMENT
INSERT INTO CUSTOMER_PAYMENT
VALUES(1,1,'2012-02-01')

INSERT INTO CUSTOMER_PAYMENT
VALUES(2,2,'2012-05-01')

INSERT INTO CUSTOMER_PAYMENT
VALUES(3,3,'2011-02-01')

INSERT INTO CUSTOMER_PAYMENT
VALUES(4,4,'2011-03-01')

INSERT INTO CUSTOMER_PAYMENT
VALUES(5,5,'2011-03-01')

INSERT INTO CUSTOMER_PAYMENT
VALUES(6,1,'2011-04-01')

INSERT INTO CUSTOMER_PAYMENT
VALUES(7,2,'2011-04-01')

INSERT INTO CUSTOMER_PAYMENT
VALUES(8,3,'2012-04-01')

INSERT INTO CUSTOMER_PAYMENT
VALUES(9,4,'2012-05-01')

INSERT INTO CUSTOMER_PAYMENT
VALUES(10,2,'2012-05-01')

INSERT INTO CUSTOMER_PAYMENT
VALUES(11,3,'2011-05-01')

INSERT INTO CUSTOMER_PAYMENT
VALUES(12,2,'2011-05-01')

INSERT INTO CUSTOMER_PAYMENT
VALUES(13,3,'2011-06-01')

INSERT INTO CUSTOMER_PAYMENT
VALUES(14,4,'2011-06-01')

INSERT INTO CUSTOMER_PAYMENT
VALUES(15,5,'2011-06-01')

INSERT INTO CUSTOMER_PAYMENT
VALUES(16,2,'2012-06-01')
```

```
INSERT INTO CUSTOMER_PAYMENT
VALUES(17,3,'2012-07-01')
INSERT INTO CUSTOMER_PAYMENT
VALUES(18,2,'2012-07-01')
INSERT INTO CUSTOMER_PAYMENT
VALUES(19,3,'2012-07-01')
INSERT INTO CUSTOMER_PAYMENT
VALUES(20,2,'2012-07-01')
INSERT INTO CUSTOMER_PAYMENT
VALUES(21,2,'2013-08-01')
INSERT INTO CUSTOMER_PAYMENT
VALUES(22,2,'2012-08-01')
INSERT INTO CUSTOMER_PAYMENT
VALUES(23,2,'2011-08-01')
INSERT INTO CUSTOMER_PAYMENT
VALUES(24,2,'2011-08-01')
INSERT INTO CUSTOMER_PAYMENT
VALUES(25,2,'2011-09-01')
INSERT INTO CUSTOMER_PAYMENT
VALUES(26,2,'2011-09-01')
INSERT INTO CUSTOMER_PAYMENT
VALUES(27,2,'2012-09-01')
INSERT INTO CUSTOMER_PAYMENT
VALUES(28,2,'2012-09-01')
INSERT INTO CUSTOMER_PAYMENT
VALUES(29,2,'2012-10-01')
INSERT INTO CUSTOMER_PAYMENT
VALUES(30,3,'2012-10-01')
INSERT INTO CUSTOMER_PAYMENT
VALUES(1,3,'2011-10-01')
INSERT INTO CUSTOMER_PAYMENT
VALUES(2,3,'2010-11-01')
INSERT INTO CUSTOMER_PAYMENT
VALUES(3,2,'2010-11-01')
INSERT INTO CUSTOMER_PAYMENT
VALUES(4,3,'2010-11-01')
INSERT INTO CUSTOMER_PAYMENT
VALUES(5,3,'2010-12-01')
INSERT INTO CUSTOMER_PAYMENT
VALUES(6,3,'2010-12-01')
```

3. As shown in Figure 4.15, rows are added to the tables in the Computer_Store database.

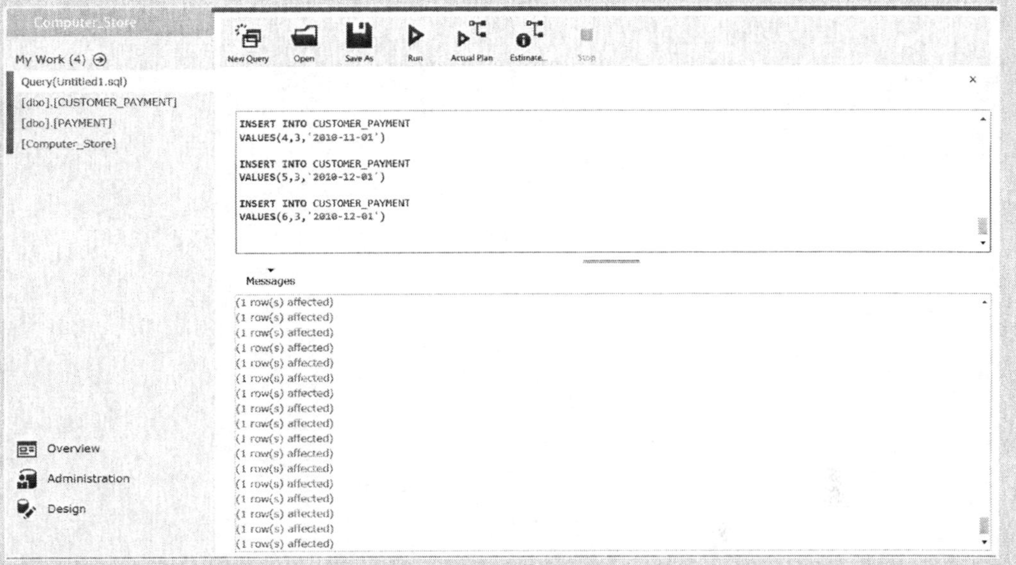

Figure 4.15 Populate Computer_Store database with SQL statements.

TASK 2: POPULATE CLASS_REGISTRATION DATABASE

Follow the steps below to populate the Class_Registration database with SQL statements in Windows Azure SQL Database:

1. Assume that you have logged on to the Windows Azure Management Portal. Select **SQL DATABASES** and the **Class_Registration** database. Click **MANAGE** to log on to the SQL Database portal as shown in Figure 4.16.
2. Once the SQL Database portal is opened, click **New Query**. Enter the following SQL statements in the New Query pane. Then, click **Run**.

```
– - inserting records into BUILDING
INSERT INTO BUILDING (BuildingId, BuildingName)
VALUES(1, 'East')

INSERT INTO BUILDING (BuildingId, BuildingName)
VALUES(2, 'West')

INSERT INTO BUILDING (BuildingId, BuildingName)
VALUES(3, 'South')

INSERT INTO BUILDING (BuildingId, BuildingName)
VALUES(4, 'North')

– - inserting records into FACULTY
INSERT INTO FACULTY (FacultyID, FirstName, LastName)
VALUES(1, 'Fred', 'Smith')

INSERT INTO FACULTY (FacultyID, FirstName, LastName)
VALUES(2, 'Chris', 'Lee')
```

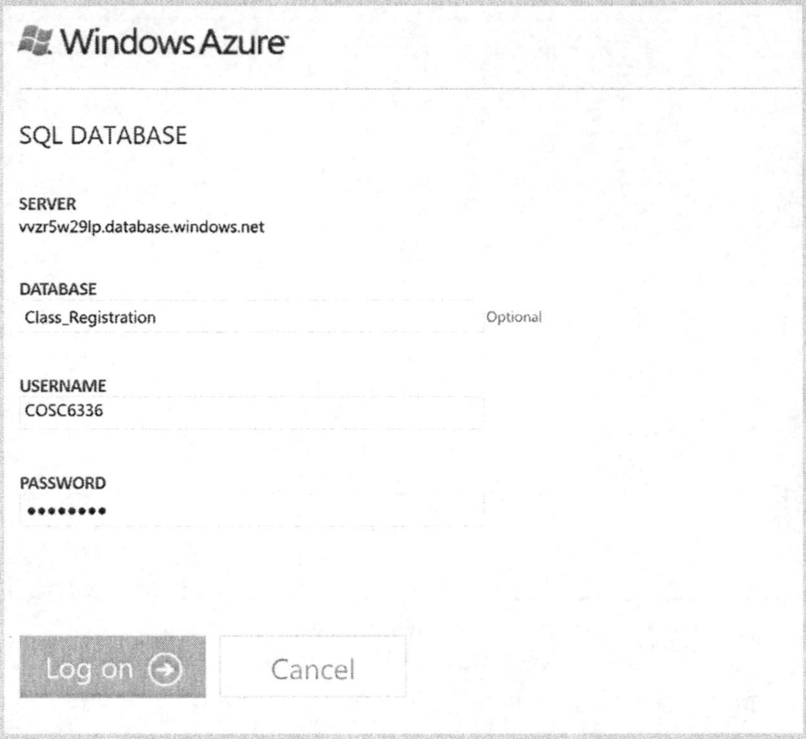

Figure 4.16 Log on to SQL database portal to manage Class_Registration.

```
INSERT INTO FACULTY (FacultyID, FirstName, LastName)
VALUES(3, 'Mary', 'Fry')

INSERT INTO FACULTY (FacultyID, FirstName, LastName)
VALUES(4, 'Jen', 'Garza')

— - inserting records into STUDENT
INSERT INTO STUDENT (StudentID, FirstName, LastName, FacultyID)
VALUES(10, 'Liz', 'Cox', 1)

INSERT INTO STUDENT (StudentID, FirstName, LastName, FacultyID)
VALUES(11, 'Joe', 'Cole', 2)

INSERT INTO STUDENT (StudentID, FirstName, LastName, FacultyID)
VALUES(12, 'Linda', 'Diaz', 1)

INSERT INTO STUDENT (StudentID, FirstName, LastName, FacultyID)
VALUES(13, 'Don', 'Ford', 3)

INSERT INTO STUDENT (StudentID, FirstName, LastName, FacultyID)
VALUES(14, 'Jen', 'Brooks', 4)

INSERT INTO STUDENT (StudentID, FirstName, LastName, FacultyID)
VALUES(16, 'Bruce', 'Cox', 3)
```

```
– - inserting records into COURSE
INSERT INTO COURSE (CourseID, CourseName)
VALUES('ISC2301', 'VB')

INSERT INTO COURSE (CourseID, CourseName)
VALUES('ISC3311', 'Database')

INSERT INTO COURSE (CourseID, CourseName)
VALUES('ISC4301', 'E-Commerce')

INSERT INTO COURSE (CourseID, CourseName)
VALUES('ISC3321', 'Info-Systems')

– - inserting records into TIMEBLOCK
INSERT INTO TIMEBLOCK (TimeID, TimeBlock)
VALUES(1, '9am-12pm')

INSERT INTO TIMEBLOCK (TimeID, TimeBlock)
VALUES(2, '1pm-4pm')

INSERT INTO TIMEBLOCK (TimeID, TimeBlock)
VALUES(3, '7pm-10pm')

– - inserting records into SEMESTER
INSERT INTO SEMESTER(SemesterID, Semester)
VALUES(1, 'Fall')

INSERT INTO SEMESTER(SemesterID, Semester)
VALUES(2, 'Spring')

INSERT INTO SEMESTER(SemesterID, Semester)
VALUES(3, 'Summer')

– - inserting records into DAYS
INSERT INTO DAYS(DayID, WeekDay)
VALUES(1, 'Monday')

INSERT INTO DAYS(DayID, WeekDay)
VALUES(2, 'Tuesday')

INSERT INTO DAYS(DayID, WeekDay)
VALUES(3, 'Wednesday')

INSERT INTO DAYS(DayID, WeekDay)
VALUES(4, 'Thursday')

INSERT INTO DAYS(DayID, WeekDay)
VALUES(5, 'Friday')

INSERT INTO DAYS(DayID, WeekDay)
VALUES(6, 'Saturday')

INSERT INTO DAYS(DayID, WeekDay)
VALUES(7, 'Sunday')

– - inserting records into CLASS
```

```
INSERT INTO CLASS(ClassID, CourseID, Credit, TimeID, DayID,
SemesterID)
VALUES(1000, 'ISC2301', 4, 1, 1, 1)

INSERT INTO CLASS(ClassID, CourseID, Credit, TimeID, DayID,
SemesterID)
VALUES(1001, 'ISC3311', 4, 2, 1, 2)

INSERT INTO CLASS(ClassID, CourseID, Credit, TimeID, DayID,
SemesterID)
VALUES(1002, 'ISC4301', 3, 3, 2, 1)

INSERT INTO CLASS(ClassID, CourseID, Credit, TimeID, DayID,
SemesterID)
VALUES(1003, 'ISC2301', 4, 1, 2, 2)

INSERT INTO CLASS(ClassID, CourseID, Credit, TimeID, DayID,
SemesterID)
VALUES(1004, 'ISC3311', 4, 2, 3, 2)

INSERT INTO CLASS(ClassID, CourseID, Credit, TimeID, DayID,
SemesterID)
VALUES(1005, 'ISC4301', 3, 3, 3, 1)

INSERT INTO CLASS(ClassID, CourseID, Credit, TimeID, DayID,
SemesterID)
VALUES(1006, 'ISC3321', 3, 1, 4, 1)

– - inserting records into CLASSROOM
INSERT INTO CLASSROOM (ClassroomID, BuildingID, Capacity)
VALUES(103, 2, 30)

INSERT INTO CLASSROOM (ClassroomID, BuildingID, Capacity)
VALUES(105, 1, 25)

INSERT INTO CLASSROOM (ClassroomID, BuildingID, Capacity)
VALUES(206, 3, 20)

INSERT INTO CLASSROOM (ClassroomID, BuildingID, Capacity)
VALUES(107, 3, 25)

INSERT INTO CLASSROOM (ClassroomID, BuildingID, Capacity)
VALUES(305, 2, 20)

INSERT INTO CLASSROOM (ClassroomID, BuildingID, Capacity)
VALUES(215, 1, 20)

INSERT INTO CLASSROOM (ClassroomID, BuildingID, Capacity)
VALUES(105, 4, 20)

INSERT INTO CLASSROOM (ClassroomID, BuildingID, Capacity)
VALUES(121, 2, 20)

– - inserting records into STUDENT_CLASS
INSERT INTO STUDENT_CLASS (StudentID, ClassID, Grade)
VALUES(10, 1000, 'A')
```

```
INSERT INTO STUDENT_CLASS (StudentID, ClassID, Grade)
VALUES(11, 1000, 'C')

INSERT INTO STUDENT_CLASS (StudentID, ClassID, Grade)
VALUES(12, 1002, 'B')

INSERT INTO STUDENT_CLASS (StudentID, ClassID, Grade)
VALUES(13, 1000, 'C')

INSERT INTO STUDENT_CLASS (StudentID, ClassID, Grade)
VALUES(14, 1001, 'B')

INSERT INTO STUDENT_CLASS (StudentID, ClassID, Grade)
VALUES(10, 1001, 'A')

INSERT INTO STUDENT_CLASS (StudentID, ClassID, Grade)
VALUES(16, 1000, 'B')

INSERT INTO STUDENT_CLASS (StudentID, ClassID, Grade)
VALUES(13, 1001, 'A')

INSERT INTO STUDENT_CLASS (StudentID, ClassID, Grade)
VALUES(10, 1002, 'A')

INSERT INTO STUDENT_CLASS (StudentID, ClassID, Grade)
VALUES(11, 1006, NULL)

INSERT INTO STUDENT_CLASS (StudentID, ClassID, Grade)
VALUES(12, 1005, NULL)

INSERT INTO STUDENT_CLASS (StudentID, ClassID, Grade)
VALUES(13, 1002, 'C')

INSERT INTO STUDENT_CLASS (StudentID, ClassID, Grade)
VALUES(14, 1002, 'B')

INSERT INTO STUDENT_CLASS (StudentID, ClassID, Grade)
VALUES(10, 1005, NULL)

INSERT INTO STUDENT_CLASS (StudentID, ClassID, Grade)
VALUES(16, 1001, NULL)


– - inserting records into FACULTY_CLASS
INSERT INTO FACULTY_CLASS (FacultyID, ClassID)
VALUES(1, 1000)

INSERT INTO FACULTY_CLASS (FacultyID, ClassID)
VALUES(2, 1001)

INSERT INTO FACULTY_CLASS (FacultyID, ClassID)
VALUES(1, 1002)

INSERT INTO FACULTY_CLASS (FacultyID, ClassID)
VALUES(3, 1000)
```

```
INSERT INTO FACULTY_CLASS (FacultyID, ClassID)
VALUES(4, 1001)

INSERT INTO FACULTY_CLASS (FacultyID, ClassID)
VALUES(1, 1003)

INSERT INTO FACULTY_CLASS (FacultyID, ClassID)
VALUES(3, 1004)

INSERT INTO FACULTY_CLASS (FacultyID, ClassID)
VALUES(2, 1006)

INSERT INTO FACULTY_CLASS (FacultyID, ClassID)
VALUES(3, 1005)

– - inserting records into COURSE_PREREQUISITE
INSERT INTO COURSE_PREREQUISITE (CourseId, Prerequisite)
VALUES('ISC3311', 'ISC2301')

INSERT INTO COURSE_PREREQUISITE (CourseId, Prerequisite)
VALUES('ISC3321', 'ISC3311')

INSERT INTO COURSE_PREREQUISITE (CourseId, Prerequisite)
VALUES('ISC4301', 'ISC3311')

INSERT INTO COURSE_PREREQUISITE (CourseId, Prerequisite)
VALUES('ISC4301', 'ISC3321')


– - inserting records into CLASS_CLASSROOM
INSERT INTO CLASS_CLASSROOM (ClassID, ClassroomID, BuildingID)
VALUES(1000, 103, 2)

INSERT INTO CLASS_CLASSROOM (ClassID, ClassroomID, BuildingID)
VALUES(1001, 105, 1)

INSERT INTO CLASS_CLASSROOM (ClassID, ClassroomID, BuildingID)
VALUES(1002, 206, 3)

INSERT INTO CLASS_CLASSROOM (ClassID, ClassroomID, BuildingID)
VALUES(1003, 107, 3)

INSERT INTO CLASS_CLASSROOM (ClassID, ClassroomID, BuildingID)
VALUES(1004, 305, 2)

INSERT INTO CLASS_CLASSROOM (ClassID, ClassroomID, BuildingID)
VALUES(1000, 121, 2)

INSERT INTO CLASS_CLASSROOM (ClassID, ClassroomID, BuildingID)
VALUES(1001, 107, 3)

INSERT INTO CLASS_CLASSROOM (ClassID, ClassroomID, BuildingID)
VALUES(1006, 215, 1)

INSERT INTO CLASS_CLASSROOM (ClassID, ClassroomID, BuildingID)
VALUES(1005, 105, 4)
```

```
INSERT INTO CLASS(ClassID, CourseID, Credit, TimeID, DayID,
SemesterID)
VALUES(2001, 'ISC3321', 3, 2, 4, 2)
```

3. As shown in Figure 4.17, rows are added to the tables in the database Class_Registration.

Now, you have both the Computer_Store and Class_Registration databases ready for operation on Windows Azure. In later chapters, you will learn how to retrieve information from these databases and develop database applications.

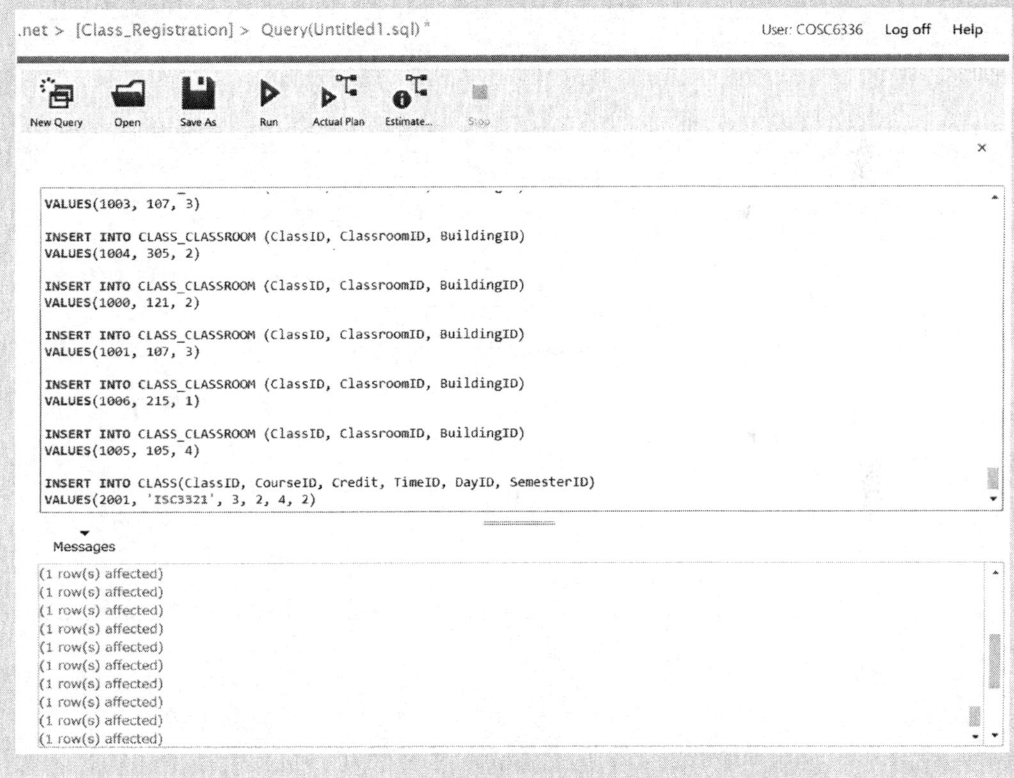

Figure 4.17 Populate Class_Registration database with SQL statements.

4.6 Summary

In this chapter, SQL has been used to implement relational databases. You have learned how to use Data Definition Language (DDL) to create, alter, and delete database objects such as databases, tables, and schemas. You also learned to use Data Control Language (DCL) and Data Manipulation Language (DML) statements to manage database objects. After tables are created, you can enter data into the tables with SQL statements.

Review Questions

1. Explain why SQL is important to database development.
2. What is the SQL extension used in SQL Server?
3. What are the tasks that can be done by DDL?
4. What are the commonly used DDL commands?
5. What are the tasks that can be done by DCL?
6. What are the commonly used DCL commands?
7. What are the tasks that can be carried out by DML?
8. What are the commonly used DML commands?
9. Create the table ORDER(OrderId, OrderDate, ShippingCharge, Total).
10. Write an SQL statement to create a table called COMPUTER with the definition COMPUTER(ComputerId, Maker, Model, Price).
11. Write an SQL statement to create a table with the following information: HARDDRIVE(SerialNumber, Maker, Model, Price).
12. Write an SQL statement to create a table with the following information: ORDER_HARDDRIVE(*SerialNumber*, *OrderId*)
13. Write an SQL statement to create a table with the following information: ORDER_COMPUTER(*OrderId*, *ComputerId*).
14. Alter the table HARDDRIVE by adding a new column Description with CHAR(100) data type.
15. Use the INSERT statement to insert the following information into the table HARDDRIVE:

11111	KEM	TI20GB	168
12293	QVT	SL40GB	243
23412	TTP	FK100GB	405

16. For the table HARDDRIVE, update the price for the hard drive with the serial number 12293 to $220.
17. Use the GRANT statement to grant the insert privilege to public on table HARDDRIVE, and then use the REVOKE statement to remove the insert privilege to public.
18. Insert the following data into the table ORDER created for Question 9:

10	7/9/04	90	1290
11	7/11/04	56	1456
12	7/15/04	78	2078
13	8/1/04	103	1903
14	8/3/04	50	1650
15	8/7/04	90	1896

Insert the following data into the table COMPUTER created for Question 10:

D0001	CQ	DT4135	1200
N0001	DP	NS2190	1400
D0002	CQ	DT6135	1800
N0002	GN	HK4900	1600
N0003	BN	CT1289	2000

Insert the following data into the table ORDER_HARDDRIVE created in Question 11:

10	12293
12	11111
15	23412

Insert the following data into the table ORDER_COMPUTER created in Question 13:

10	D0001
11	N0001
12	N0003
13	D0002
14	N0002
15	D0002

Chapter 5

Importing and Exporting Database Objects

Objectives

- Migrate databases between Windows Azure SQL Database and an on-premises SQL Server
- Move data in and out of a database

5.1 Introduction

Once a database is created, the database administrator will move some existing data into the newly created database, or move some of the data out of the database to support application development. Sometimes, databases need to be copied from one server to another server. For example, the database administrator may need to migrate the databases from an on-premises server to a Windows Azure database server, or migrate them from one data center to another data center.

Moving data in and out of databases can be a challenging process. There will be issues related to user authentication; not everyone can access and manipulate the data. There will be issues related to data formats, and the data formats at the source and the destination may not match exactly. To make things worse, the features supported by an on-premises server may not be supported by a cloud server.

In this chapter, we will introduce several tools for data transport. There are several ways to move data in and out of a database. The commonly used data moving tools by Windows Azure SQL Database are SQL Server Management Studio (SSMS), data-tier applications (DACs), SQL Database Migration Wizard, SQL Server Integration Services (SSIS), and the bulk copy utility bulk copy program (bcp) that copies data between an instance of Microsoft SQL Server and a data file in a user-specified format. In addition to these tools, XML can also be a solution for handling data conversion tasks. With XML, data can be exchanged over heterogeneous computer systems and various programming languages. When sharing data in a multitier database system, XML is often used to represent the data and the structure of the database objects in a common format. In this chapter, we will take a closer look at each of these tools.

5.2 SQL Server Management Studio

With SSMS, the database administrator can manage and develop Windows Azure SQL Database components. SSMS has many different editions. SSMS Express is a minimum edition that works with Windows Azure SQL Database. For database administrators who have experience with SQL Server, managing Windows Azure SQL Database with SSMS will be effortless. A number of GUI tools are included in SSMS. On a client computer, SSMS can be used to connect to Windows Azure SQL Database. SSMS includes a query editor that can be used to edit and execute T-SQL statements, analyze SQL execution plans, and provide statistic information. SSMS allows the database administrator to script out a database object such as a table or a user from one server to another server. The database administrator can use SSMS to migrate databases from Windows Azure SQL Database to an on-premises SQL Server with the tool Generate Script Wizard. When connected to Windows Azure SQL Database, the database administrator can use the set of dialogs provided by SSMS for database maintenance. The database administrator can also launch the Template Explorer to use Windows Azure SQL Database templates to create database objects in Windows Azure SQL Database. Figure 5.1 displays the components in SSMS.

The new SSMS for SQL Server 2012 has added features that can integrate Windows Azure into an on-premises SQL Server. The new SSMS greatly simplifies data migration between Windows Azure SQL Database and an on-premises SQL Server. Its code editor provides a new interface for viewing XML results. In addition, the new SSMS also allows the database administrator to export data to nonrelational data storage such as Blobs.

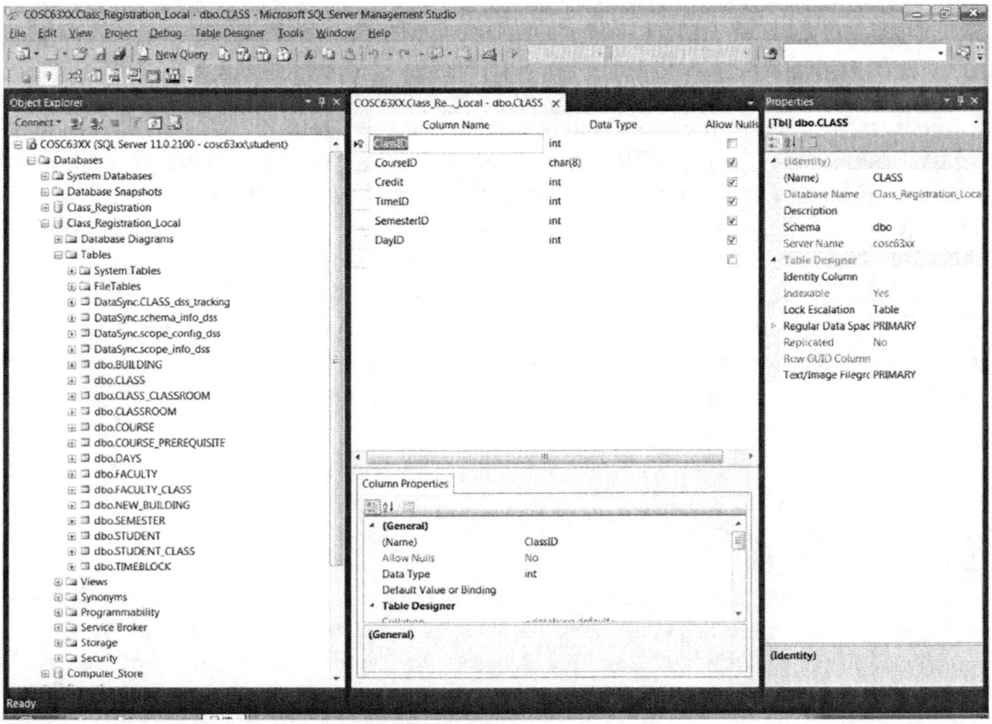

Figure 5.1 SQL Server Management Studio.

ACTIVITY 5.1 MIGRATING DATABASE BETWEEN SQL SERVER AND WINDOWS AZURE SQL DATABASE

In this lab activity, we will use SSMS to migrate the database Computer_Store between Windows Azure SQL Database and a local SQL Server. As the database Computer_Store has been created on Windows Azure SQL Database, the first task is to migrate the database to your local server by generating an SQL script. After the database Computer_Store is migrated to the local server, we will delete the Computer_Store database on Windows Azure SQL Database. Then, we will migrate the database Computer_Store from the local server to Windows Azure SQL Database by using the database import/export tool.

1. Assume that SQL Server 2012 is installed on your virtual machine, myserver, created in Chapter 1. Log on to the Windows Azure Management Portal through the URL https://windows.azure.com.
2. Once you have logged on to the Windows Azure Management Portal, click **VIRTUAL MACHINES**. Select **myserver** and click **CONNECT**. Enter your password for the virtual machine and click **OK** to log in as shown in Figure 5.2.
3. Start SSMS by pressing the **Windows Icon** key and clicking the **SQL Server Management Studio** icon.
4. Similar to Figure 5.3, enter your login information in Windows Azure SQL Database and then click the **Connect** button.
5. After you log on, expand the **Databases** node and right click the database **Computer_Store** and select **Generate Scripts**. On the Introduction page, click **Next**. On the Choose Objects page, make sure the **Script entire database and**

Figure 5.2 Log on to virtual machine.

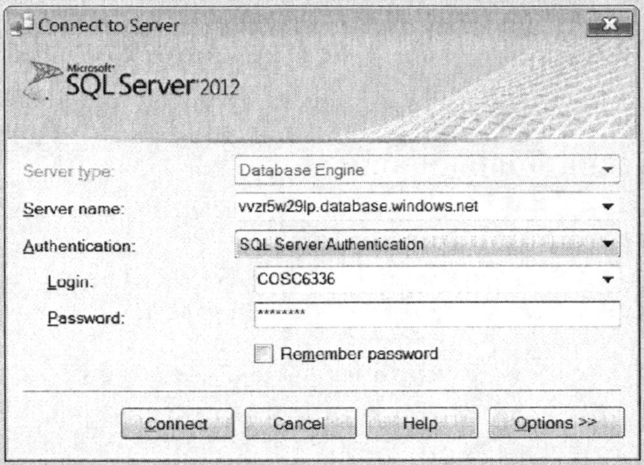

Figure 5.3 Windows Azure SQL Database login.

all database objects option is selected and then click **Next**. On the Set Scripting Options page, click the **Advanced** button and set the **Type of data to script** to **Schema and data** as shown in Figure 5.4. Click **OK** and click **Next**. On the Summary page, click **Next**. After the script is successfully generated, click **Finish**. Then, exit SSMS.

6. Start SSMS again. This time, log on to the local SQL Server as shown in Figure 5.5.

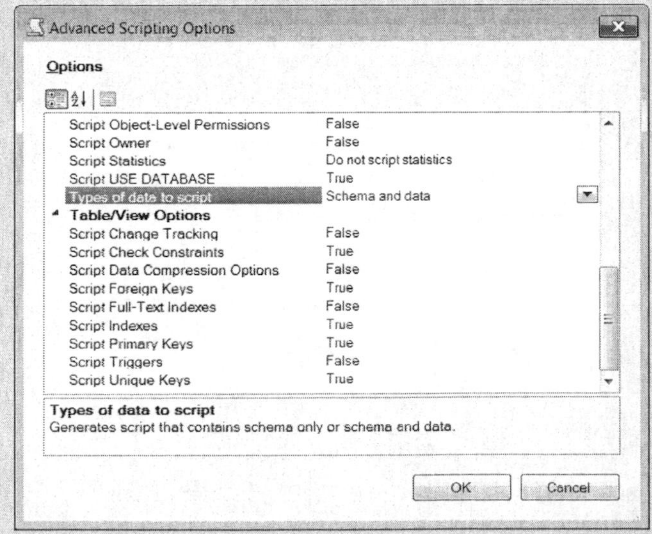

Figure 5.4 Advanced setting for scripting.

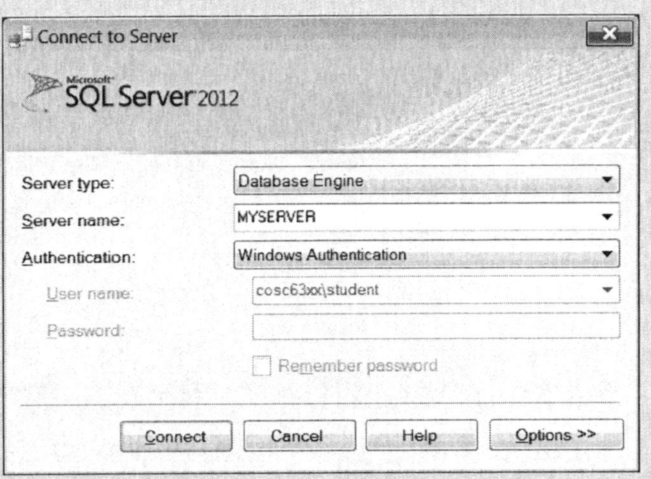

Figure 5.5 Local SQL Server login.

7. In the Documents folder, open the script saved in the previous step. Click **!Execute** on the tool bar to create the database Computer_Store on the local SQL Server.
8. To illustrate the process of migrating the database from the local server to Windows Azure SQL Database, you will need to drop the database Computer_Store from the Windows Azure Management portal.
9. Open the Windows Azure Management Portal, click the **SQL DATABASES** node. Select the database **Computer_Store**. Then, click **DELETE**.
10. After the database Computer_Store is deleted from the Windows Azure Management Portal, open the virtual machine, **myserver**.
11. Start **SQL Server Management Studio**. Expand the **Databases** node to confirm that the database **Computer_Store** has been created on the local computer.
12. To migrate the Computer_Store database to Windows Azure SQL Database. Expand the **Databases** node and right click on the database **Computer_Store**. From the drop-down list, select **Tasks**, and then **Deploy Database to SQL Azure**. On the Introduction page, click **Next**.
13. In the Deployment Settings page, click the **Connect** button. Similar to Figure 5.3, enter your Windows Azure SQL Database server login information and click the **Connect** button.
14. If the connection is successful, you should be able to see the Deployment Settings like the one in Figure 5.6. Notice that the temporary database file has the extension .bacpac. This indicates that we are using another data migration tool called a DAC, which will be covered in the next section.
15. To verify that the database is deployed, open the Windows Azure Management portal, click the **SQL DATABASES** link. You will see that the Computer_Store database is created on Windows Azure.

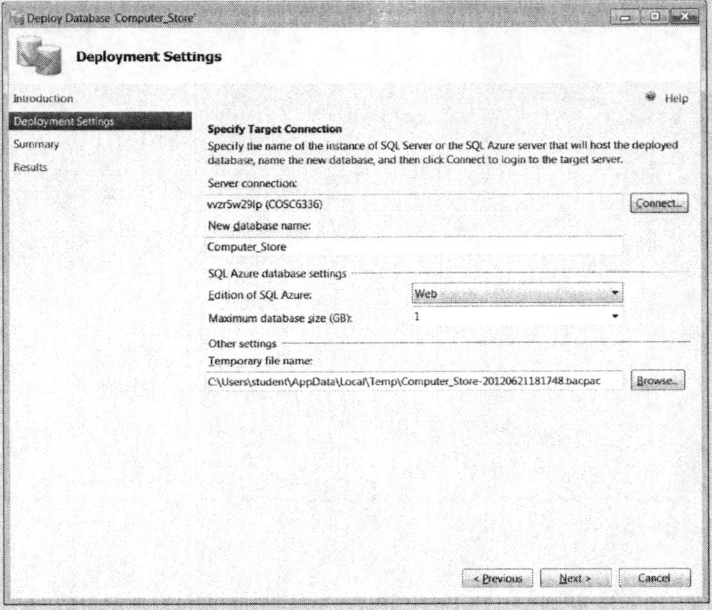

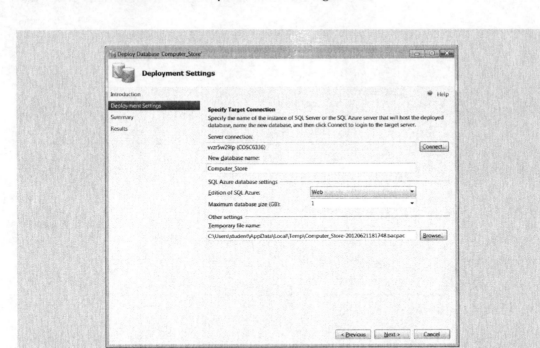

Figure 5.6 Deployment settings.

5.3 Data-Tier Application

During the application development process, typically, two servers are used: one is used for supporting production and one is used for application development. Since the environments in the production server and development server are not exactly the same, some of the database objects and programming scripts that work perfectly on one server may not work on the other server. Databases and their applications are very dynamic. They are often upgraded and modified. The changes made to a database on one server may not work for the database on the other server. To support data transaction in and out of Windows Azure SQL Database, the data management software DAC is developed to help with the moving of database objects between applications and Windows Azure SQL Database. DAC is designed to reduce the hassle in data transaction. DAC handles tasks such as data import/export, data deployment and upgrade, data extraction, and user profile analysis. The following describes how DAC works.

Application developers often request database objects from the production server so that they can keep their applications up-to-date. When a database administrator receives a request for database objects from an application developer, the database administrator will extract the database objects and package the requested database objects with DAC. Both schemas and data are packaged together into a .bacpac file. Schema objects such as logins, users, schemas, tables, columns, constraints, indexes, views, stored procedures, functions, and triggers are packed together with various types of data. To establish a DAC with the existing databases, the database administrator first registers the requested databases to participate in the DAC. Once the databases are registered, the database administrator can then package the databases and deliver the DAC package to the application development server. SSMS supports the DAC operation. With SSMS, the database

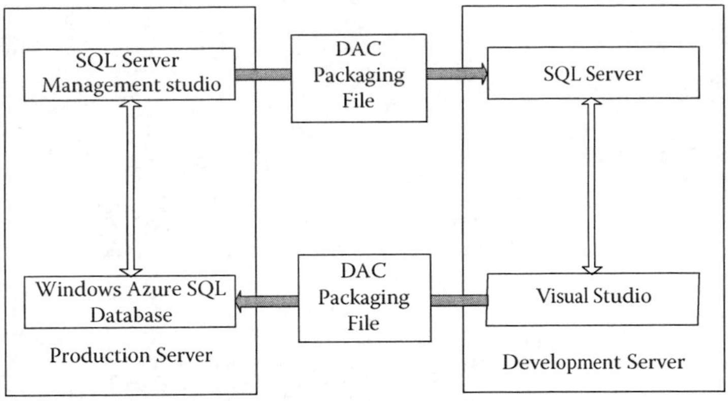

Figure 5.7 DAC deployment.

administrator can package the requested database objects and designate the development server where the package is to be delivered.

Once the DAC package is delivered to the application development server, the data will be imported into the application that is under development. The deployed DAC package will be controlled by the server selection policy, which restricts developers' access to the database objects. The application developers can only access the server instance dedicated to them. Once the application development is completed, the DAC tool included in Microsoft Visual Studio can be used to update the DAC package and deliver the package back to the production server. The application developers integrate the entire DAC package into their project or select only part of the database objects included in the package.

Once a DAC package is deployed on a server, it will upgrade the existing DAC package. If the DAC package does not exist, a new database will be generated on the server, which includes the database objects and the users allowed to access the database. When deployed, the DAC package will generate XML files that contain the metadata of the DAC package and an SQL file that contains the SQL script. During the deployment, the SQL script will be run to generate the database objects, and all the relevant server logins are also created. The applications on the production side can then be upgraded automatically or manually by the database administrator. Before the application can be made available to the public, the database administrator will review the package for production with SSMS. The database administrator will compare the database objects generated by the DAC package with those on the production server to make sure they are consistent. After the review, the database administrator will designate the server instance on the production server. Figure 5.7 illustrates the DAC deployment process.

ACTIVITY 5.2 DEVELOPMENT OF DACS

In this activity, you will learn how to extract, deploy, and upgrade a DAC. The activity starts with database object extraction.

TASK 1: EXTRACTING A DAC FROM A DATABASE

As described earlier, to support application development, you will need to extract database objects and deploy the extracted package to an application development server. The task

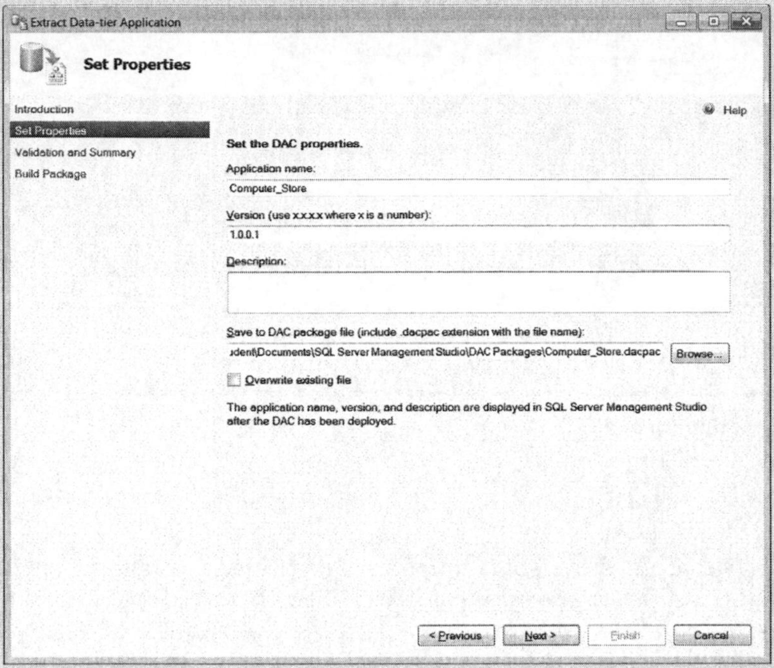

Figure 5.8 DAC property setting.

can be done with the Extract Data-Tier Application Wizard included in SSMS. The wizard retrieves the database objects, validates the content, and packages the database objects into a .bacpac file.

1. To start SSMS, log on to your virtual machine, **myserver.** Press the **Windows Icon** key and click the **SQL Server Management Studio** icon. Similar to Figure 5.2, enter your login information to Windows Azure SQL Database and then click the **Connect** button.
2. After logging on to Windows Azure SQL Database, in Object Explorer, expand the **Databases** node, right click the database **Computer_Store**, select **Tasks**, and then click **Extract Data-tier Application.**
3. On the Introduction page, click **Next** to go to the **Set Properties** page. On this page, set the version to **1.0.0.1** as shown in Figure 5.8. You may also need to record the path to where the packaged .bacpac file is saved such as the one below:
   C:\Users\student\Documents\SQL Server Management Studio\DAC Packages\Computer_Store.dacpac
4. Click **Next** to review the summary information. Click **Next** again to start the extraction and validation process. If the process is successfully completed, click **Finish.**

TASK 2: DEPLOYING A DAC TO VISUAL STUDIO

In this task, you will first create a DAC package from Windows Azure SQL Database. Then, import the packaged database objects to Visual Studio for the application development. For this task, assume that Visual Studio 2012 is installed on your local computer.

Figure 5.9 Log on to Visual Studio 2012.

1. You may need to download and install the new Microsoft SQL Server Data Tools 2012 on your virtual machine if your Visual Studio does not already include the tool. The SQL Server Data Tools can be downloaded from the following website: http://visualstudiogallery.msdn.microsoft.com/96a2f8cc-0c8b-47dd-93cd-1e8e9f34a917

   After the SQL Server Data Tools have been installed, click the **Restart** button.
2. To open Microsoft Visual Studio, press the **Windows Icon** key to open the tile. Then, right-click **Visual Studio 2012** and choose **Run as administrator** as shown in Figure 5.9.
3. Click **New Project**. In the New Project dialog, expand the **Other Languages** node in the Installed Templates pane and then click the **SQL Server** node. Enter the project name as **Computer_Store_DB** shown in Figure 5.10 and click **OK**.
4. After the project is opened, click the **PROJECT** menu and select **Import**. Then, select **Data-tier Application** as shown in Figure 5.11.
5. On the Import Data-tier Application File page, click the **Browse** button next to the Data-tier Application textbox. Navigate to the folder

   C:\Users\student\Documents\SQL Server Management Studio\DAC Packages\Computer_Store.dacpac

   where the packaged file is located. Click **Open** to import the file shown in Figure 5.12. Click **Start** to begin the import process.
6. Then, click **Finish**. To view the imported items, click the drop-down list with a arrow on the menu bar and select **Computer_Store_DB** as shown in Figure 5.13. Expand the dbo node, and then double click **CUSTOMER.sql** under the Tables node.
7. You should have the result shown in Figure 5.14.

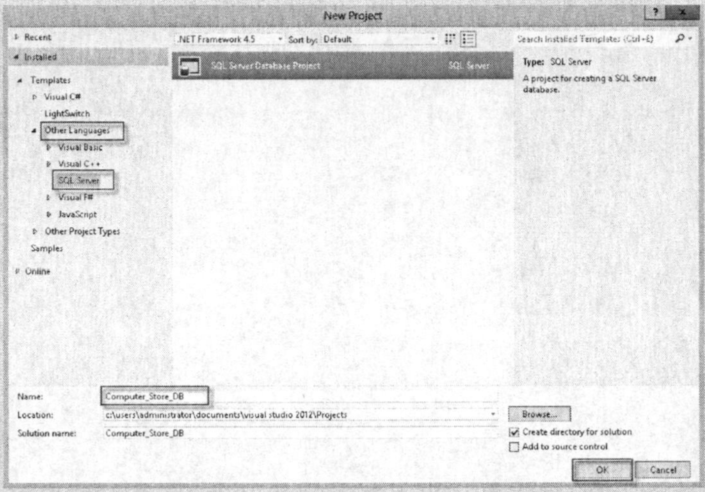

Figure 5.10 Create SQL Server Database project.

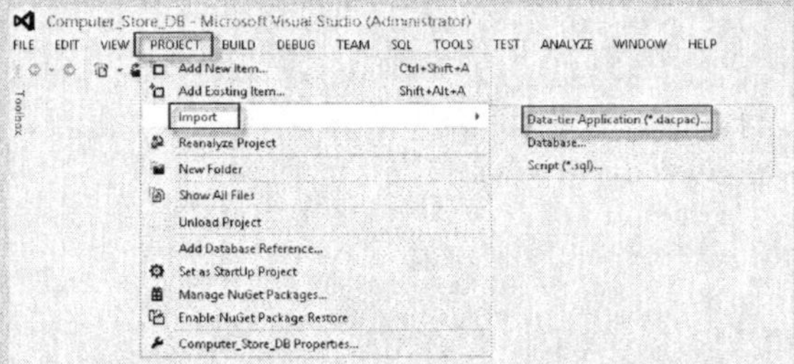

Figure 5.11 Import DAC.

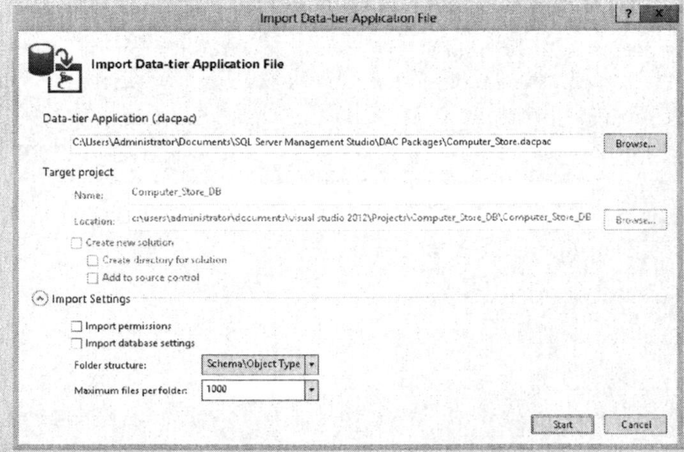

Figure 5.12 Select DAC file for import.

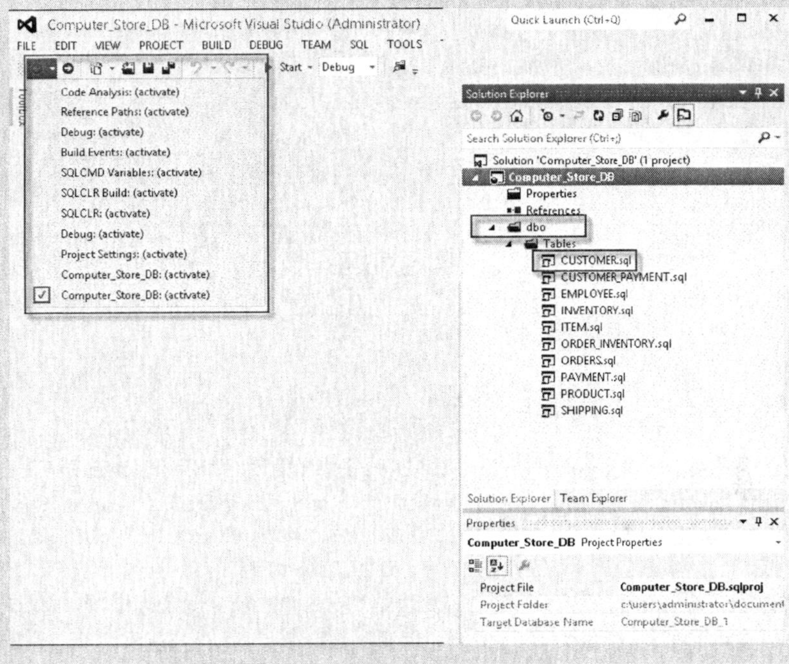

Figure 5.13 Select imported item CUSTOMER.sql.

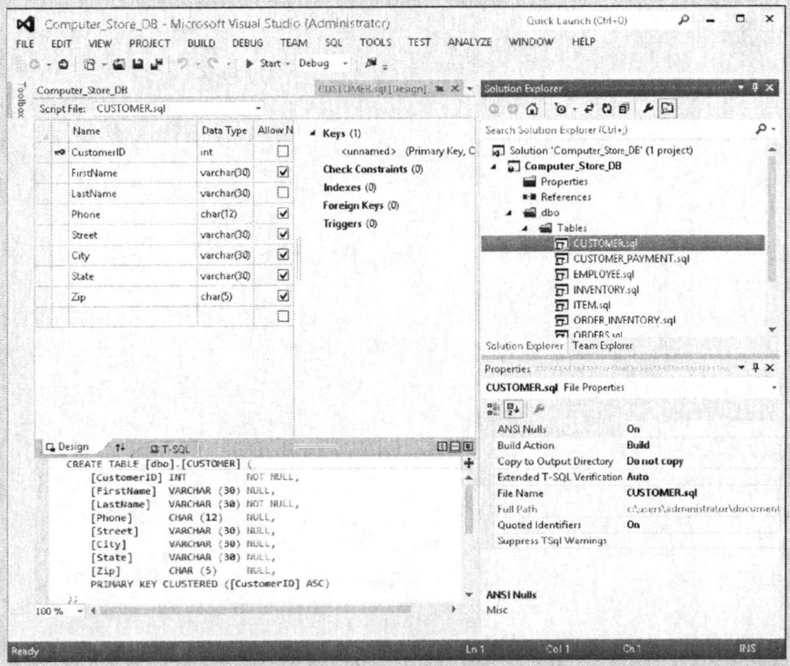

Figure 5.14 Imported DAC package.

5.4 Windows Azure SQL Database Migration Wizard

With Windows Azure SQL Database Migration Wizard, you can migrate SQL Server databases to Windows Azure SQL Database, especially those older versions of databases created on SQL Server 2005 and SQL Server 2008. It allows the database administrator to fully or partially migrate the database schema and data to Windows Azure SQL Database. Before the migration process starts, Windows Azure SQL Database Migration Wizard analyzes the source database for compatibility issues. Once incompatibilities are identified, Windows Azure SQL Database Migration Wizard will allow the database administrator to fix them when possible. To avoid some of the incompatibilities, the database administrator can choose to migrate:

- Database schema and data
- Database schema only
- Data only

The database schema includes database objects such as tables, views, stored procedures, and so on. During the analysis process, Windows Azure SQL Database Migration Wizard creates SQL scripts that create database objects. The database administrator can modify the SQL scripts to resolve incompatibilities. Windows Azure SQL Database Migration Wizard can execute the modified scripts on Windows Azure SQL Database to generate the database that is compatible with Windows Azure SQL Database.

ACTIVITY 5.3 DATABASE MIGRATION WITH SQL AZURE MIGRATION WIZARD

1. Download SQL Azure Migration Wizard from the following website to your virtual machine:
   http://sqlazuremw.codeplex.com/
2. Open the downloaded folder. Double click the file **SQLAzureMW** and click **Extract all** as shown in Figure 5.15. After the extraction is completed, double click the **SQLAzureMW** file again and click **Run** to start the wizard.
3. On the Select Process page, under the title **Analyze/Migrate**, click the option **Database** shown in Figure 5.16.
4. Click **Next** to go to the Connect to Server dialog. Make sure that the server name is **localhost**, the authentication is **Use Windows NT Integrated Security**, and the database is **Master DB** as shown in Figure 5.17. Then, click **Connect.**
5. After the server is connected, on the Select Source page, you will be prompted to select the database for migration. Select the database **Computer_Store**.
6. Click **Next** to go the Choose Objects page. Take the default and click **Next** again.
7. On the Script Wizard Summary Page, click **Next.** When prompted to save the SQL script, click **Yes**.
8. After the SQL script is saved, you will be prompted to configure the connection to Windows Azure SQL Database. Make sure that the server type is **Windows Azure SQL Database**, enter your Windows Azure SQL Database server name, the authentication is **Use a specific user ID and password**, and then enter your user name and password to Windows Azure SQL Database (Figure 5.18). Then click the **Connect** button.

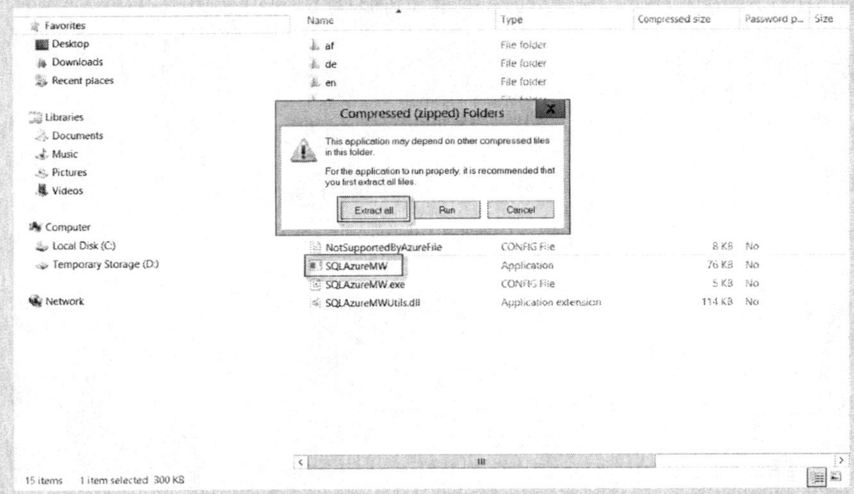

Figure 5.15 Install SQL Azure Migration Wizard.

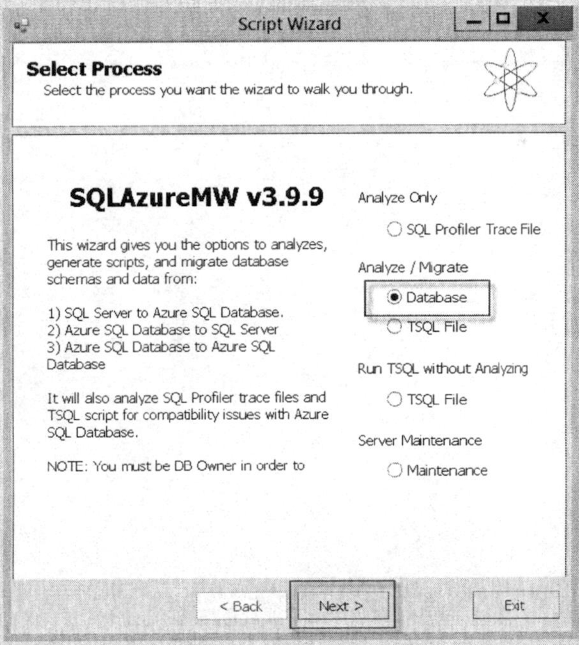

Figure 5.16 Select migration process.

9. Click the **Create Database** button. Enter **Compter_Store_Azure** as the database name. Then click **Create Database**.
10. On the **Setup Target Server Connection** page, click **Next**. Click **Yes** to execute the SQL script.

Figure 5.17 Connect to local server.

Figure 5.18 Connect to Windows Azure SQL Database.

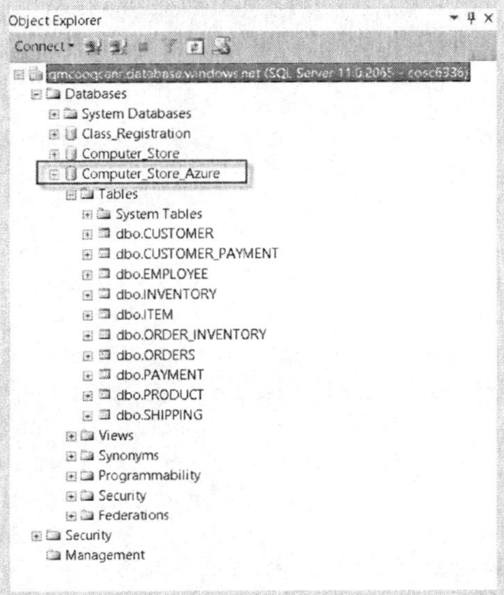

Figure 5.19 Migrated Database Computer_Store_Azure.

11. After the execution is completed, click **Exit**.
12. After logging on to the Windows Azure Management portal through SSMS, you should be able to see the newly migrated database **Computer_Store_Azure** as shown in Figure 5.19.

5.5 Moving Data in and out of Windows Azure SQL Database Using SSIS

SSIS is a tool for integrating and migrating a broad range of data between SQL Servers. SSIS provided by SQL Server can accomplish tasks such as:

- Transferring data from heterogeneous data sources to a database. The data sources may include data stored in Oracle, SQL Server, MS Office, text files, spreadsheets, programming code, and XML files.
- Integrating data with transformation controls that decide how and when to carry out actions like connection, validation, and transformation.
- Providing wizards for importing or exporting database objects. They export multiple data sources and import these data to multiple destinations.
- Providing a GUI designer that can be used to design and implement complicated data transformation. The designer can be used to re-format data. With the designer, database administrators can perform data and character conversions, create calculated columns, and improve lookup performance.

For a relatively simple import or export task, you can use the wizards. For more complicated SSIS constructing tasks, the SSIS designer is the choice. To extend SSIS functionalities to scripts in other programming languages such as C# and Visual Basic, one may consider using the utility SSIS Script.

ACTIVITY 5.4 EXPORTING DATA FROM WINDOWS AZURE SQL DATABASE USING SSIS

As an example, we will export data from the table ORDER_INVENTORY in the database Computer_Store hosted by Windows Azure SQL Database to the same table in the database Computer_Store hosted by the local SQL Server with SSIS. In SQL Server 2012, SSIS is included in SQL Server Data Tools.

1. To start SQL Server Data Tools, press the **Windows Icon** key and click the icon of **SQL Server Data Tools** (Version 2010) as shown in Figure 5.20.
2. To open a new project dialog, click **FILE**, **New**, and **Project**. After the new project dialog is opened, in the **Installed Template** pane, select **Business Intelligence** and select **Integration Services Project** from the Templates pane. Enter **ImportFromCloud** as the project name (Figure 5.21). Click **OK** to create the project.
3. Expand the **Toolbox** on the left-hand side of your screen. In the Toolbox pane, drag and drop the **Execute SQL Task** onto the Design pane as shown in Figure 5.22.
4. Right click the **Execute SQL Task** and select **Edit**. On the General page, click the box next to **Connection Type**, select **ADO.NET**. Also, click the drop-down list on the right side of the **Connection** property and select **New Connection** as shown in Figure 5.23.
5. To create a connection to an SQL Server instance, click the drop-down list on the right side of the **Connection** property and select **New Connection**. When the connection dialog opens (Figure 5.24), the name of the SQL Server is your Windows Azure SQL Database server. For the authentication method, use the **Use SQL Server Authentication** option. Enter your Windows Azure SQL Database login information. Then, select the database **Computer_Store**.

Figure 5.20 Open SQL Server data tools (Version 2010).

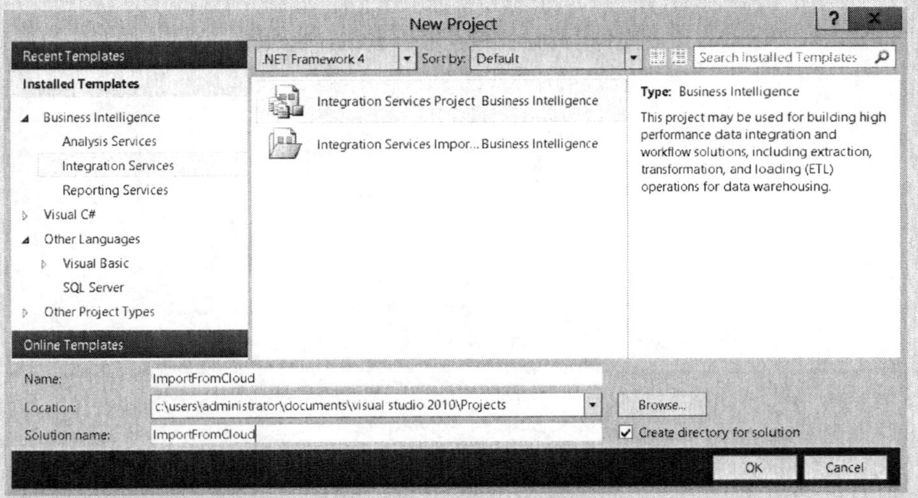

Figure 5.21 New integration services project.

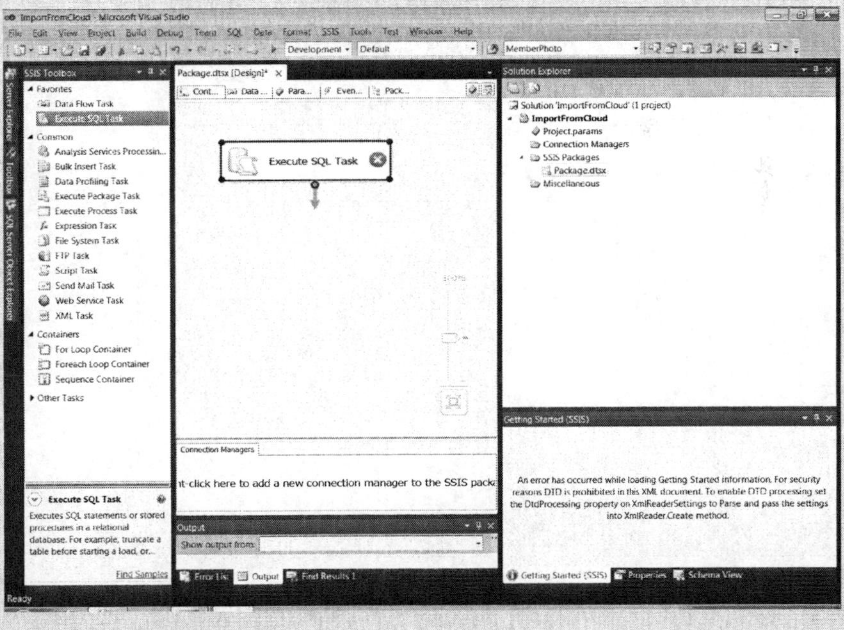

Figure 5.22 Execute SQL task tool.

6. Then, click **Test Connection** and click **OK** twice to save the connection.
7. Click the box on the right side of the **SQL Statement** property, enter the following SQL statement:

```
TRUNCATE TABLE ORDER_INVENTORY
```

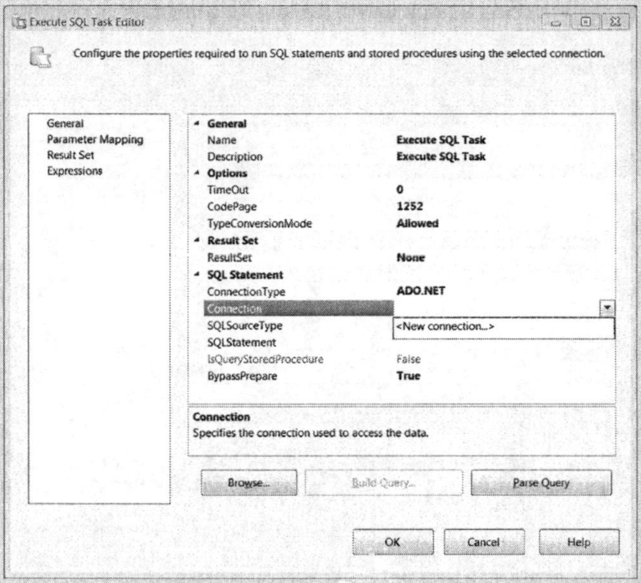

Figure 5.23 Configure connection.

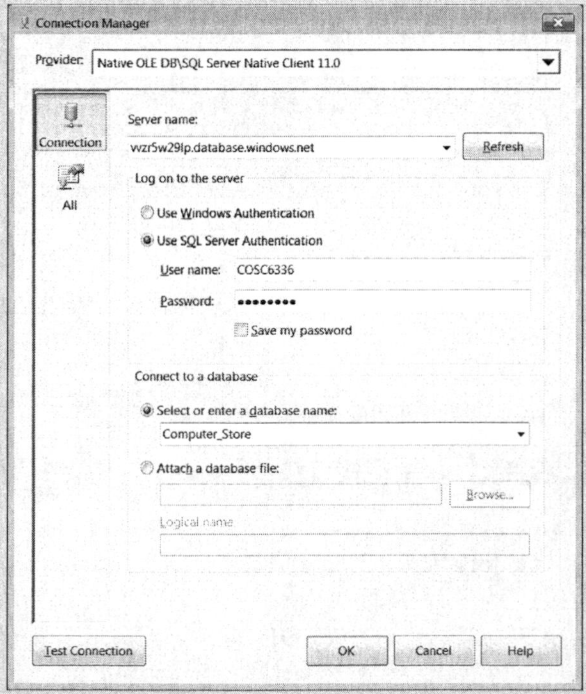

Figure 5.24 Connection properties.

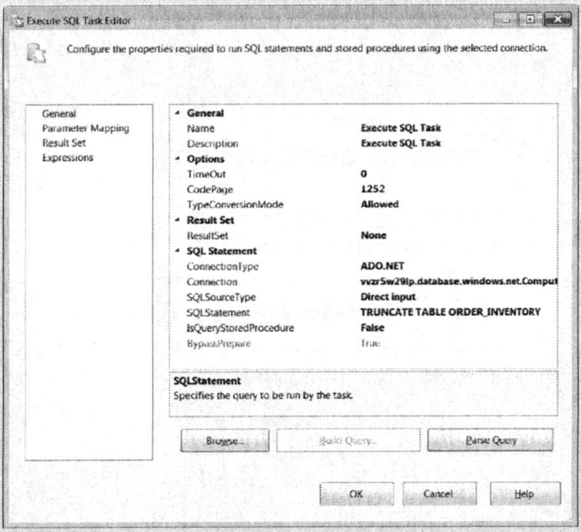

Figure 5.25 Execute SQL task configuration.

Then, click **OK** to save the task (Figure 5.25).

8. Our next task is to create a data flow task that is used to import data from Windows Azure SQL Database to our local database. To do so, drag **Data Flow Task** from the Toolbox pane to the Package pane. Click **Execute SQL Task** and drag the green arrow to **Data Flow Task** as shown in Figure 5.26.

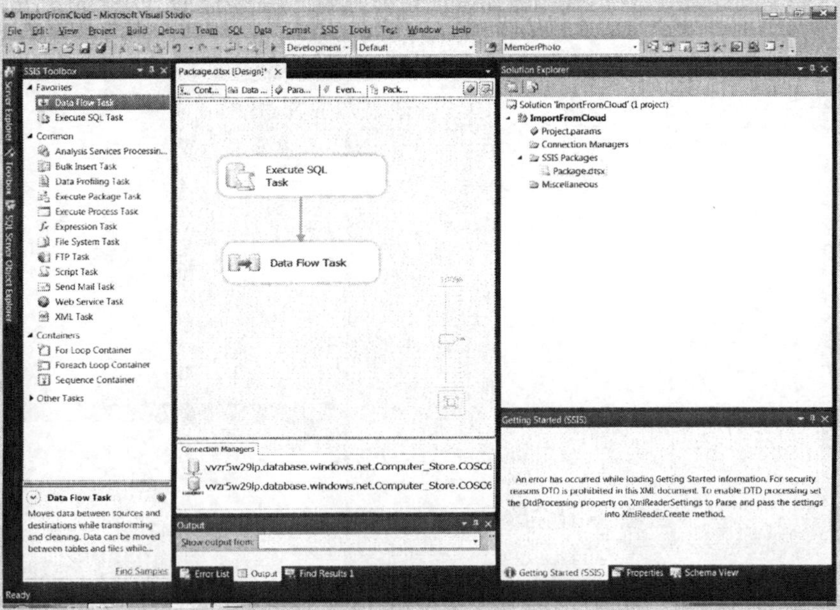

Figure 5.26 Connect tasks.

9. Right click **Data Flow Task** and select **Edit** in the pop-up menu. After the Package Design pane is opened, under the **Other Sources** node, drag **ADO.NET Source** from the Toolbox pane to the Package Design pane as shown in Figure 5.27.
10. Right click on **ADO.NET Source** and select **Edit** from the pop-up menu.
11. In the **Name of the table or the view** drop-down list, select the table named **ORDER_INVENTORY** as shown in Figure 5.28. Click the **Preview** button to make sure that the connection is working. Then, click **OK** to complete the ADO.NET configuration.
12. For the local computer, we can create an OLE DB destination by dragging **OLE DB Destination** under the **Other Destinations** node from the Toolbox pane to the Package Design pane. Click **ADO.NET Source** and drag the green arrow to **OLE DB Destination** as shown in Figure 5.29.
13. Right click **OLE DB Destination** and select **Edit** from the pop-up menu. After OLE DB Destination Editor opens, click the **New** button located on the right-hand side of the OLE DB Connection Manager drop-down list.
14. After the OLE DB Connection Manager dialog is opened, click the **New** button again. In the Connection Manager dialog, select the local SQL Server from the server name drop-down list. Keep the option **Use Winnows Authentication.** Select **Computer_Store** from the Select or enter a database name drop-down list as shown in Figure 5.30. Click **OK** to complete the OLE DB destination connection. Click **OK** to complete the configuration of Connection Manager.
15. Go back to OLE DB Destination Editor, set the Data access mode to **Table or View—fast load** and check **Keep identity.** In the Name of the table or the view drop-down list, select the table **INVENTORY** as shown in Figure 5.31.

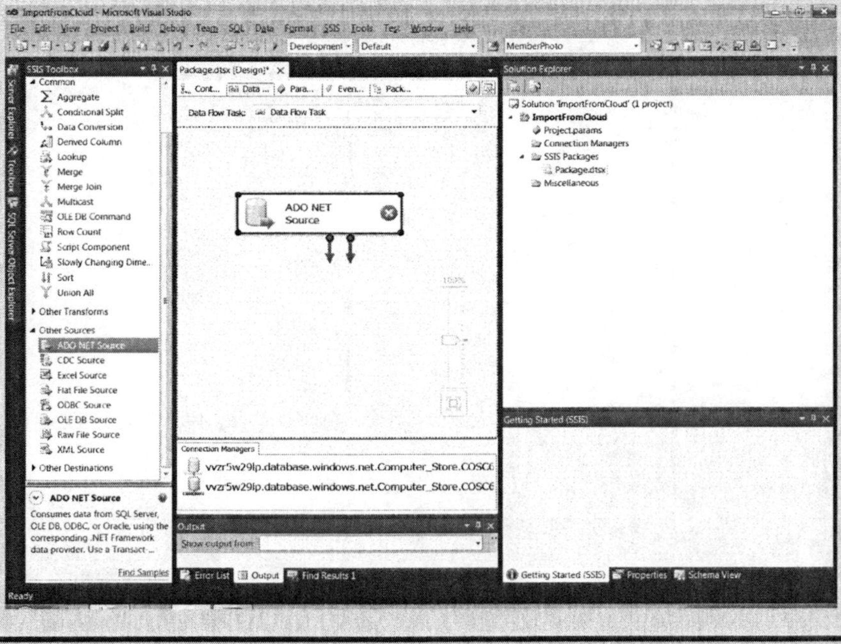

Figure 5.27 ADO.NET source.

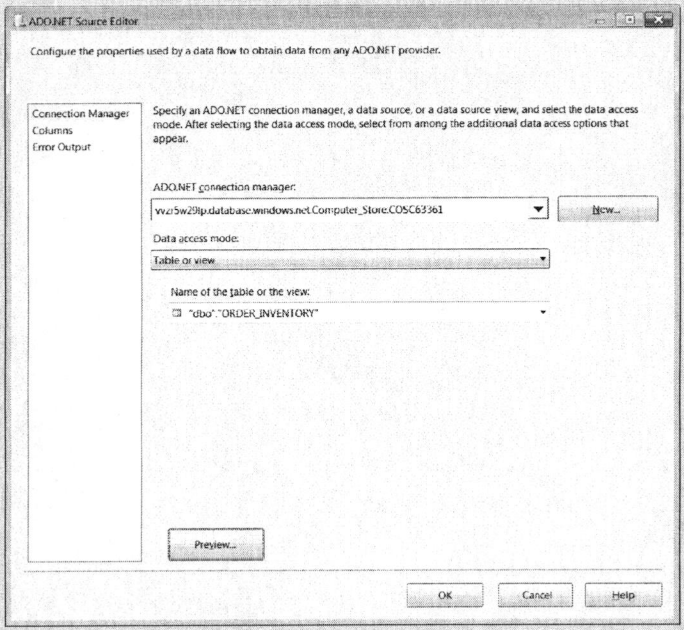

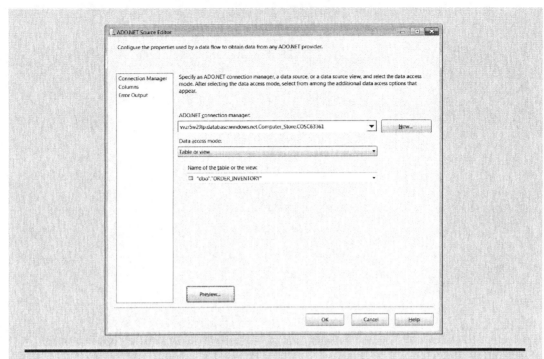

Figure 5.28 ADO.NET source properties.

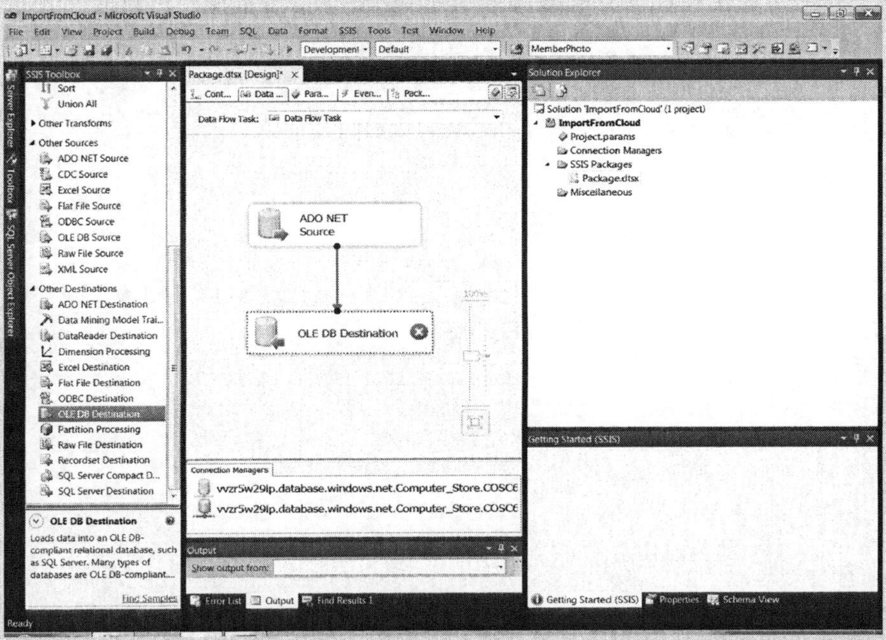

Figure 5.29 Add OLE DB destination.

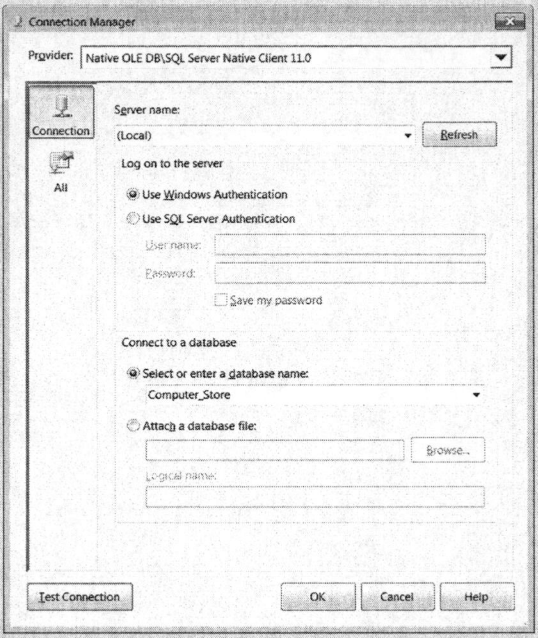

Figure 5.30 OLE DB connection properties.

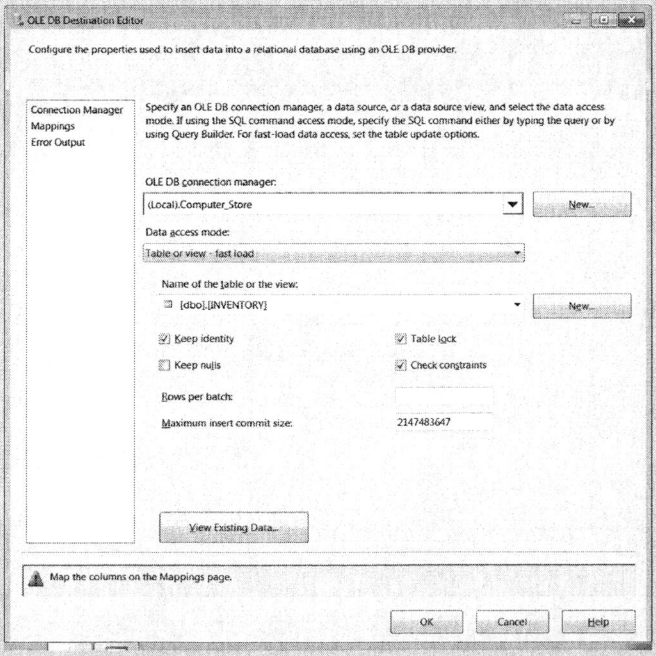

Figure 5.31 OLE DB destination properties.

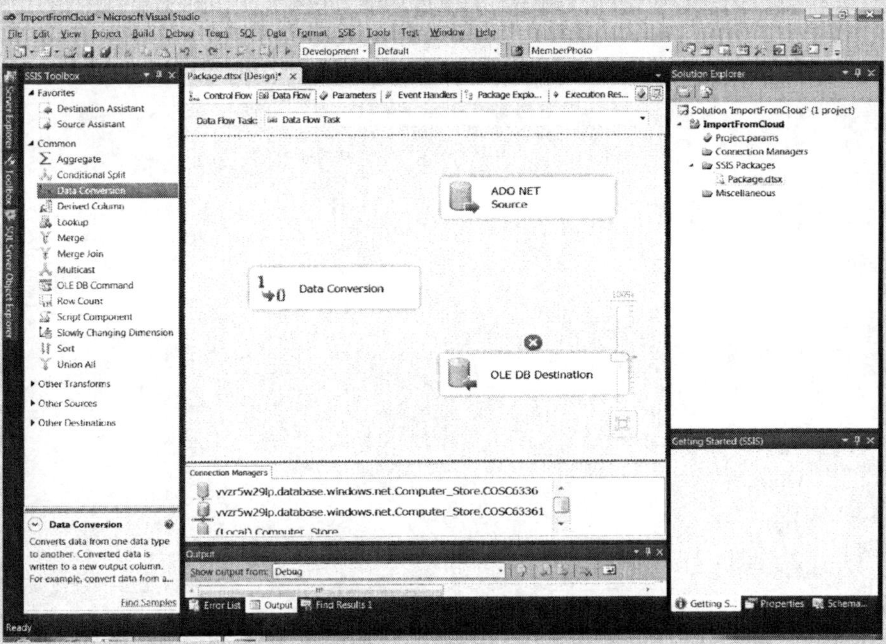

Figure 5.32 Add data conversion tool.

16. Click **Mapping** on the left-hand side of the screen, you will get the default mapping. Take the default mapping and click **OK**.
17. Click the **Control Flow** tab and press the **F5** key. You may see a data conversion error. In this case, click the **Data Flow** tab and drag **Data Conversion** from the Toolbox pane to the Design pane as shown in Figure 5.32.
18. Delete the link from ADO.NET Source to OLE DB Destination and connect **ADO.NET Source** to **Data Conversion**. Right click **Data Conversion** and select **Edit** from the pop-up menu. From the **Available Input Column** list, check **InventoryID**. Change the data type to **Two-byte unsigned integer** as shown in Figure 5.33. Then, click **OK** to finish the configuration of Data Conversion.
19. Drag the green arrow from **Data Conversion** to **OLE DB Destination** to link them. Right click on **OLE DB Destination** and select **Edit**. In OLE DB Destination Editor, click **Mapping**. Delete the link from **InventoryID** to **InventaryID**. Add link from **Copy of InventaryID** to **InventoryID** as shown in Figure 5.34. Click **OK** to close the dialog.
20. Click the **Control Flow** tab and press the **F5** key. If successful, both **Execute SQL Task** and **Data Flow Task** have check marks as shown in Figure 5.35.

This activity demonstrates that SSIS is another convenient data transfer tool. SSIS can be used to transfer data in and out of Windows Azure SQL Database in various detail levels. During the transfer, one can convert a data type and configure the properties of a database object.

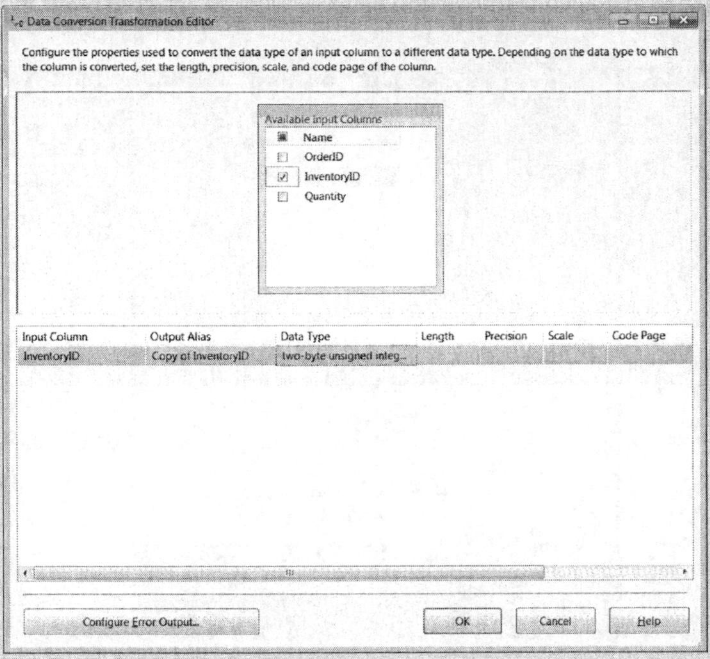

Figure 5.33 Convert input column.

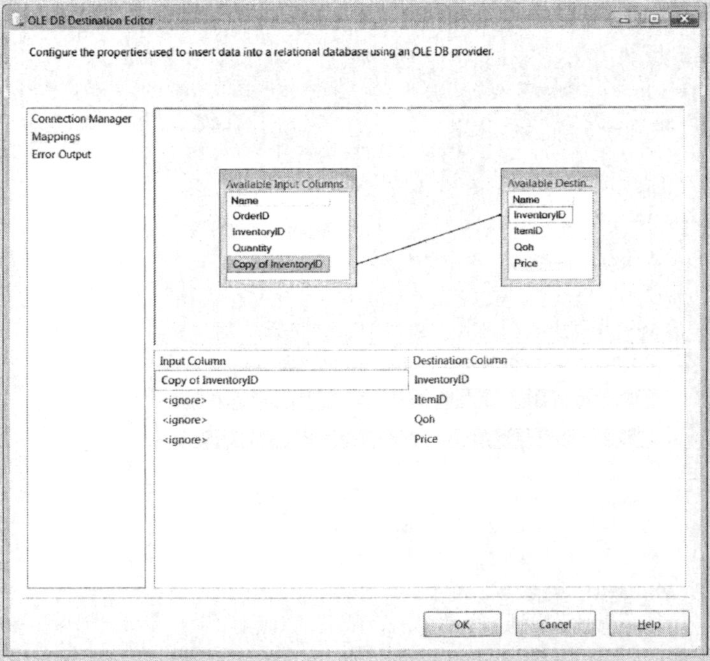

Figure 5.34 Relink primary key and foreign key columns.

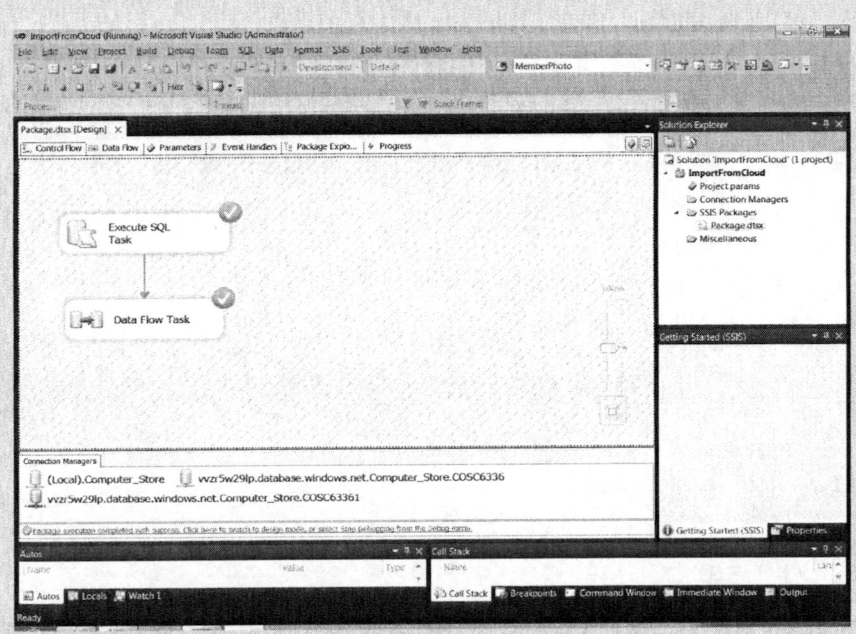

Figure 5.35 Data flow from Windows Azure SQL Database to on-premises SQL Server.

5.6 Import and Export Data with Bulk Copy Program

When you populate tables in a newly created database, data often come from existing data files or databases. Instead of entering data manually, you can import them with data transformation utilities such as the bcp. The bcp utility is a command line utility that is fully supported by SQL Server as well as Windows Azure SQL Database. With the bcp, you can transfer data between relational databases, between a database and a text file, or even with application software such as Microsoft Excel.

When using the bcp for importing or exporting data, the user and the data file should meet the following requirements:

- To use the bcp utility, the user should have the INSERT and SELECT permissions.
- Rows and columns in a data file should be separated by terminators such as Tab and Newline.
- The format of data should be character, unicode, or bcp native format (SQL Server specific).
- The order and the number of columns in a data file do not have to be the same as the SQL Server table.
- The destination table should exist before you can import data.

The bcp utility is only a data transfer utility, which means that it does not migrate database schemas. If the destination table does not exist, the bcp utility will not be able create a destination table for data transfer.

The bcp command has the following general format:

bcp [[db_name.]owner.]table_name | "query" {in | out | format | queryout} datafile_name [-parameter 1] ...[-parameter n]

In the above general format, an item enclosed by a pair of square brackets is optional. The keyword **query** is an SQL statement that generates the export result set. The **{in | out | format | queryout}** expression gives data transfer directions. The vertical bar represents the OR operator. The word **format** indicates that a format file is created. The word **queryout** is used to export the result set returned by an SQL statement or stored procedure. Using the word **–parameter**, you can specify the data format or other options. The commonly used parameters are

[**-m** *max_errors*] [**-f** *format_file*] [**-e** *err_file*]
[**-F** *first_row*] [**-L** *last_row*] [**-b** *batch_size*]
[**-n** *native data type*] [**-c** *char data type*] [**-w** *unicode data type*]
[**-N** *native export for nonchar data or unicode export for char data*]
[**-6** *use 6.x data types*] [**-q** *use quoted identifier*]
[**-C** *code_page*] [**-t** *field_terminator*] [**-r** *row_terminator*]
[**-i** *input_file*] [**-o** *output_file*] [**-a** *packet_size*]
[**-S** *server_name*[*\instance_name*]] [**-U** *login_id*] [**-P** *password*]
[**-T** *use trusted connection to SQL Server*] [**-v** *bcp version*]
[**-k** *preserve null values*] [**-E** *preserve id values*] [**-h** "*hint* [,...*n*]"]

The following activity will demonstrate how to use the bcp for data transfer.

ACTIVITY 5.5 EXPORTING DATA FROM WINDOWS AZURE SQL DATABASE USING BCP

To see how the bcp utility exports and imports data, let us consider an example that will export the data in the table EMPLOYEE to a text file and then import the data from the text file to another table called EMPLOYEE_IMPORT. The following command will be used to export data out of your Windows Azure SQL Database.

```
bcp Computer_Store.dbo.EMPLOYEE out Employee.txt -c -U COSC6336@
vvzr5w29lp -S tcp:vvzr5w29lp.database.windows.net -P password
```

In our example, since the current user is the table owner, the middle part of the three-part table name is missing. That is, the table name is **Computer_Store..EMPLOYEE**. In this example, no query is used. The result set contains the entire table. This example uses the **out** keyword to specify that the data in the table **EMPLOYEE** will be exported to the **Employee.txt** file. The use of **–c** indicates that the data are exported as characters. **–U** is used to specify the user at Windows Azure SQL Database and **–P** specifies the password. **–S** specifies the connection string for the remote Windows Azure SQL Database. You can follow the steps below to run the command in the Windows command prompt.

1. Assume that you are connected to the virtual machine in Windows Azure. To run the command, press the **Windows Icon** key. Right click the **Developer Command** icon on the tile and click **Run as administrator** on the ribbon.
2. Enter the above bcp command and press the **Enter** key. Figure 5.36 shows the export command execution result.

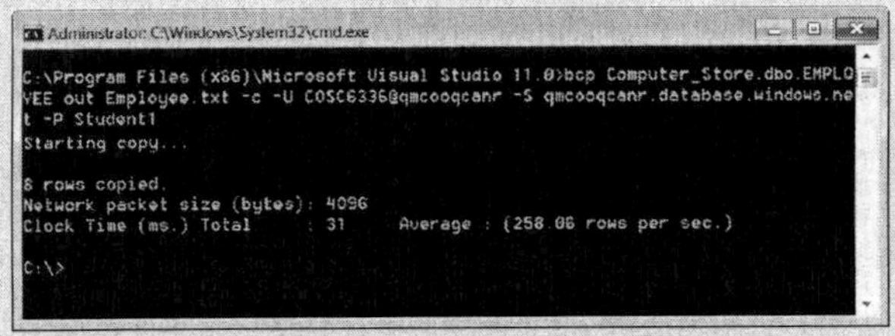
Administrator: C:\Windows\System32\cmd.exe
C:\Program Files (x86)\Microsoft Visual Studio 11.0>bcp Computer_Store.dbo.EMPLOYEE out Employee.txt -c -U COSC6336@qmcooqcanr -S qmcooqcanr.database.windows.net -P Student1
Starting copy...
8 rows copied.
Network packet size (bytes): 4096
Clock Time (ms.) Total : 31 Average : (258.06 rows per sec.)
C:\>

Figure 5.36 Export data with bcp utility.

Figure 5.36 shows that eight rows have been copied to the Employee.txt file.

3. You can view the file Employee.txt in Notepad as shown in Figure 5.37. Press the **Windows Icon** key. Click the **File Explorer** icon. Type **notepad** on the address bar and press the **Enter** key. Open the Employee file in the folder C:\Program Files (x86)\Microsoft Visual Studio 11.0.
4. To perform data import, create a table EMPLOYEE_IMPORT in the database Computer_Store with the same design of the EMPLOYEE table. This can be done by running an SQL statement on your virtual machine. To do so, open SSMS and connect to **MYSERVER** with Windows authentication. Right click at the database **Computer_Store** and select **New Query**. Enter the SQL statement as shown in Figure 5.38 and execute the code.

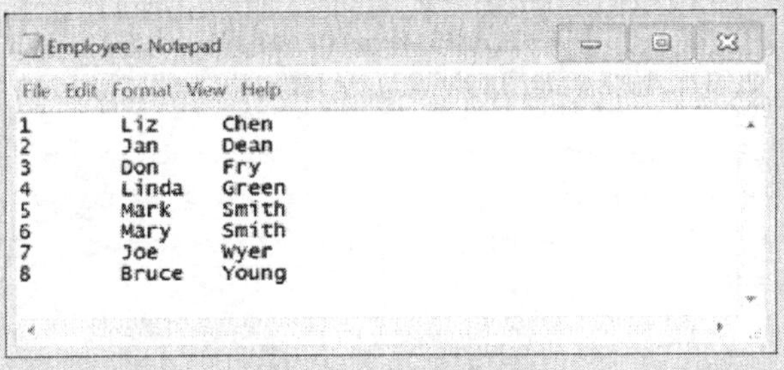
Employee - Notepad
File Edit Format View Help
1 Liz Chen
2 Jan Dean
3 Don Fry
4 Linda Green
5 Mark Smith
6 Mary Smith
7 Joe Wyer
8 Bruce Young

Figure 5.37 Data exported to text file by bcp command.

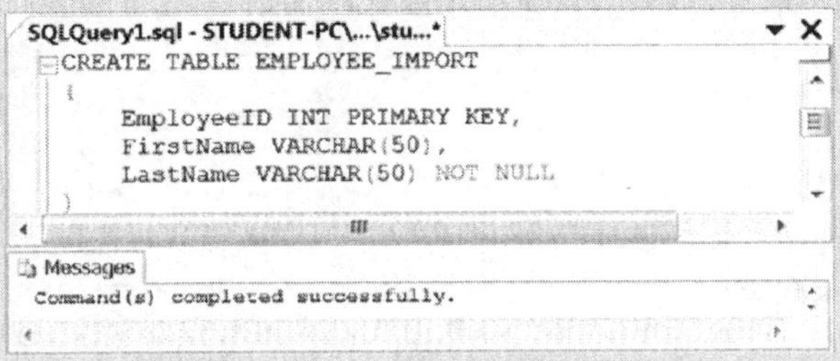
SQLQuery1.sql - STUDENT-PC\...\stu...*
CREATE TABLE EMPLOYEE_IMPORT
(
EmployeeID INT PRIMARY KEY,
FirstName VARCHAR(50),
LastName VARCHAR(50) NOT NULL
)
Messages
Command(s) completed successfully.

Figure 5.38 Create EMPLOYEE_IMPORT table.

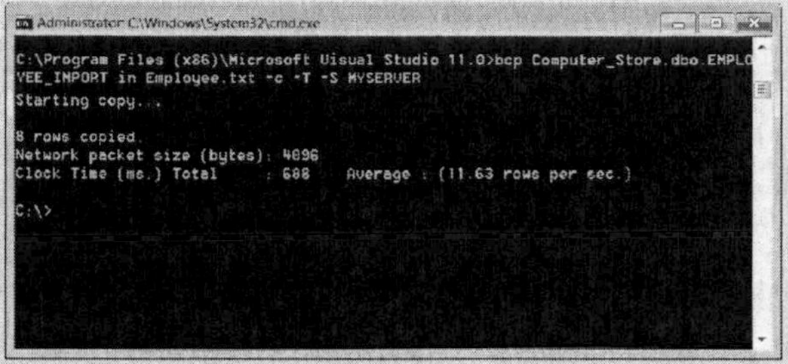
Administrator: C:\Windows\System32\cmd.exe
C:\Program Files (x86)\Microsoft Visual Studio 11.0>bcp Computer_Store.dbo.EMPLOYEE_IMPORT in Employee.txt -c -T -S MYSERVER
Starting copy...
8 rows copied.
Network packet size (bytes): 4096
Clock Time (ms.) Total : 688 Average : (11.63 rows per sec.)
C:\>

Figure 5.39 Import data with bcp command.

5. In the command prompt window, enter the following bcp command, and press the **Enter** key:

   ```
   bcp Computer_Store.dbo.EMPLOYEE_IMPORT in Employee.txt -c -T -S
   COSC63xx
   ```

   –T means that the trusted connection is used to connect to SQL Server, and **–S** refers to the SQL Server instance on the local machine.
6. The execution result is shown in Figure 5.39.

As you can see, eight rows are imported to the table EMPLOYEE_IMPORT.

5.7 Working with XML Data

The data exchange between application software and a database server is a challenge if the application and the database run on computers with different platforms, for example, one running on a Linux machine and the other running on a Windows machine. In the old days, data sent by a client computer would be converted to the format acceptable by the server computer. In today's Internet, there are many different types of data formats. The task of data conversion is extremely difficult. The features of XML can make data conversion easier.

A markup language such as hypertext markup language (HTML) can be used to display information. For example, HTML can display the content on a web page by using a set of predefined tags. The set of HTML tags can be used to specify the location, color, and font of the web page content. HTML can also be used to create some simple form objects. For database applications, HTML has its limitations. HTML has difficulty transferring database objects since there are no predefined tags that can handle database objects.

In the early 1990s, a more powerful markup language, XML, was developed to handle data transactions over the Internet. The World Wide Web Consortium (W3C) established a set of rules that are used to express data formats and structures. Similar to HTML, XML is also a markup language. Unlike HTML, it can define tags for database objects. Therefore, XML has a wide range of application in database development.

When sharing data through the Internet, XML is used to represent the data and structure of database objects in a common format. XML allows information exchange between database applications and database servers. These database applications may be created with heterogeneous application software, operating systems, and database management systems. The databases may be hosted by server running on different platforms.

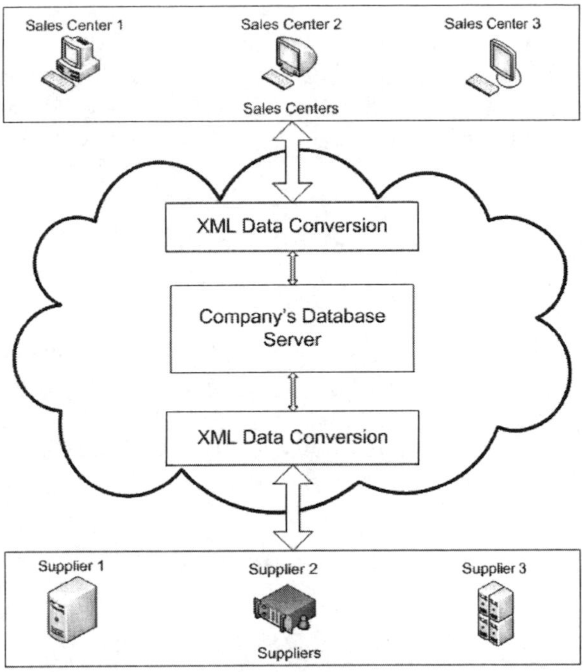

Figure 5.40 Do business over Internet by using XML.

When data are exported from various applications, they can all be formatted to XML data. With the common representation in XML, the data can be exchanged over heterogeneous computer systems and various programming languages. For example, consider the computer store covered in the previous activities. The computer store may have multiple sales centers and may have multiple hardware and software suppliers. Let us assume that the applications such as spreadsheet and forms at each sales center are created with different software from that at the company's headquarters. Meanwhile, the company orders computer parts from various suppliers. The data formats and computer systems used by these suppliers also vary. To meet the requirements for data conversion, the company requires its sales centers to submit their sales information in an XML document and convert computer part order forms to XML files for part suppliers. The business process is illustrated in the Figure 5.40.

In the following section, we will discuss the XML data type and how to store XML data in a database.

5.7.1 Introduction to Extensible Markup Language

Like HTML, XML uses tags to define data formats. XML has the following advantages over HTML:

- XML allows users to create tags to represent database object structures such as views, tables, or stored procedures. It does not depend on a fixed set of predefined tags.
- XML separates the document structure from the content. In this way, the same set of XML data can be used for different applications such as forms, reports, text documents, or spreadsheets.
- XML is platform-independent. Various types of data can be converted to XML data, and then the XML data can be imported to different applications.

Basically, an XML document may include three files. The XML Schema Definition file (.xsd file) contains the definitions of XML document formats, the XML data file (.xml file) contains XML data defined by data types, and the Extensible Stylesheet file (.xsl file) contains the style specifications of the XML data. Brief descriptions of these files are given below.

XML data file (.xml file): An XML document is well defined if it satisfies the following conditions:

- If an element has a value, it must be enclosed by a pair of opening and closing tags such as

  ```
  <element_name> value</element_name>
  ```

  For an element that has no value in it, it can be specified by a single tag such as

  ```
  <element_name/>
  ```

- Subelements must be properly nested. That is, subelement tags must be placed inside the parent element. For example

  ```
  <element_name>
  <sub-element_name> value </sub-element_name>
  </element_name>
  ```

- The value of an attribute should be enclosed by double quotes such as

  ```
  <element_name attribute_name="value"/>
  ```

- An XML document should have a root element, and all other elements are the subelements of the root element. The XML document missing the root element is called a fragment. Some DBMSs also support fragments.
- The name in a tag is case sensitive.

User-defined tags in an XML document are declared in an XML Schema Definition (.xsd) file. The following section will show how user-defined tags are declared in an .xsd file.

XML Schema Definition file (.xsd file): Elements and other XML structures are defined in an XML schema file. The benefits of separating the XML data from the structure are described below:

1. When XML data are transferred from one database application to another, the two applications share the same XML schema file. There is no need to set up a set of rules to convert the data from one format to another. The receiver can completely reconstruct the data through the XML schema file provided by the sender.
2. When we transfer XML data over the Internet, the receiver can check if the data from the sender satisfy a predefined format. An .xsd file can be used to specify the standards for verification.
3. An XML schema can be used to define standards for an entire industry. The standards can be used to verify the format of the data interexchanged within the industry. Industries such as real estate, insurance, banking, and accounting have established their own standards through XML schema files.
4. By using XML schemas, we are able to create more sophisticated database objects such as views and tables with multiple data types.

Extensible Stylesheet file (.xsl file): Unlike HTML, an XML data file does not provide data style formatting information. To specify styles such as color and font, we need to have a document style sheet file, a .xsl file, which provides a set of formatting information about our XML data. Currently, the W3 Consortium splits xsl into two parts, the document transformation part XSLT for formatting and transforming XML documents to HTML and the formatting object part XSL-FO for more sophisticated formatting.

Now that some basic concepts about XML have been introduced, next you will learn about the XML data type and how to store XML data in a database. After that, you will learn how to query XML data with XQuery and display the content by applying the XSLT style sheet.

5.7.2 XML Data Type

SQL Server supports the XML data type, which allows users to store XML documents natively. You can use the XML data type just like you use a data type such as INT or NVARCHAR. The XML data type can be used to declare a variable or to define a column in a CREATE TABLE SQL statement. It can also be used to define the input or output parameters for stored procedures and functions. Documents defined by the XML data type can be managed with DDL SQL statements. The limitation of the XML data type is that you cannot use an XML column as a primary key or foreign key.

The way of declaring an XML variable or an XML column is the same as declaring a Transact-SQL variable or column. For example, to add a new XML column to the table CUSTOMER, use the following SQL statement:

```
ALTER TABLE CUSTOMER
ADD Email XML
```

In the ADD clause, there is no schema collection name; this means that the column Email will not use a schema to validate the XML content. Therefore, we have just added an untyped XML column. You can also declare an XML variable, assign a well-formed XML document to the variable, and then store the XML document in the XML column. The following is the SQL statement to accomplish these tasks:

```
DECLARE @email xml
SET @email='<Email Email="myemail@yahoo.com"/>'
UPDATE CUSTOMER
SET Email=@email
WHERE CustomerID=1
```

You can also insert xml data into a table that has XML columns as shown in the following activity. Besides the untyped XML data, there are typed XML data that are associated with a schema file, which defines the elements and attributes, and specifies the namespace. To use the typed XML data type, you must first create a schema file and register the file in an XML schema collection. Since, at this point, Windows Azure SQL Database does support the typed XML data type, the untyped XML data type will be the main focus of this section.

ACTIVITY 5.6 STORING XML DATA IN WINDOWS AZURE SQL DATABASE

In this activity, you will learn how to create and store untyped XML data. We will create e-mail addresses based on customers' first names and last names, and then insert the e-mail addresses into the CUSTOMER table.

Create and Store XML Data: In the following, the column Email with the XML data type will be added to the table CUSTOMER. Next, an XML variable, email will be created and assigned with the untyped XML data. Then, the data will be inserted into the table CUSTOMER.

1. Start SSMS by pressing the **Windows Icon** key and click the **SQL Server Management Studio** icon on the tile. After the SSMS is opened, right click the database **Computer_Store** and select **New Query**. Similar to Figure 5.2, enter your login information to Windows Azure SQL Database and then click the **Connect** button. Enter the SQL statement shown in Figure 5.41 in the **New Query** editor, and then click the **!Execute** button on the toolbar.
2. To declare the XML variable @email and assign a well-formed XML document to the variable, and then store the XML document in the XML column, enter the code shown in Figure 5.42.
3. To display the inserted XML data, enter the command shown in Figure 5.43.

Store XML E-Mail Addresses: In the following, XML e-mail addresses will be created with the customers' first names and last names in the XML format. Then, the XML e-mail addresses will be stored in the Email column in the CUSTOMER table.

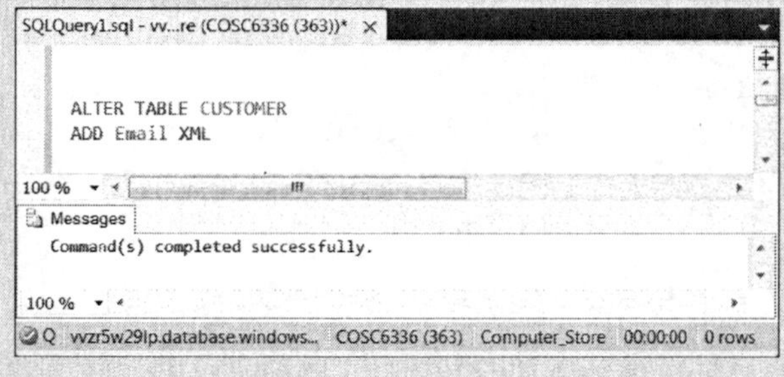

Figure 5.41 Add column with XML data type.

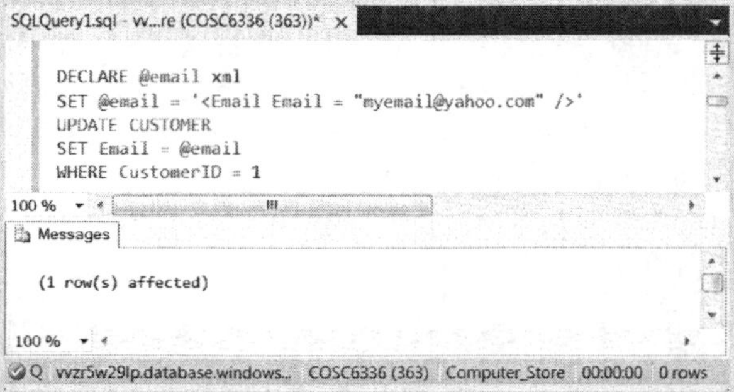

Figure 5.42 Create and store XML data.

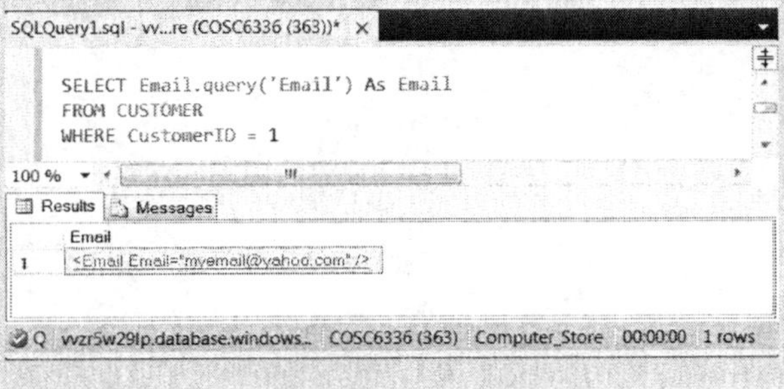

Figure 5.43 Query XML data.

1. To assemble the e-mail addresses with the customers' first names and last names, we need to create a temporary table called CUSTOMER_EMAIL (Figure 5.44).
2. Then, insert the assembled e-mail addresses into the temporary table CUSTOMER_EMAIL as shown in Figure 5.45. The e-mail addresses are assembled with the columns LastName and FirstName of the table CUSTOMER.
3. Next, insert the assembled e-mail addresses into the Email column of the table CUSTOMER as shown in Figure 5.46.
4. The last step is to display the e-mail addresses with the XML method query() as shown in Figure 5.47.

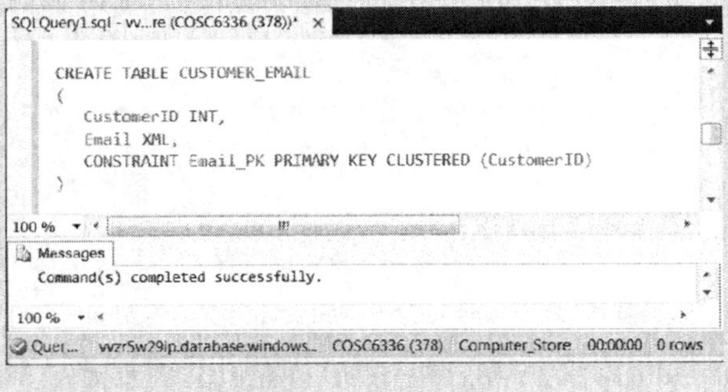

Figure 5.44 Create CUSTOMER_EMAIL table.

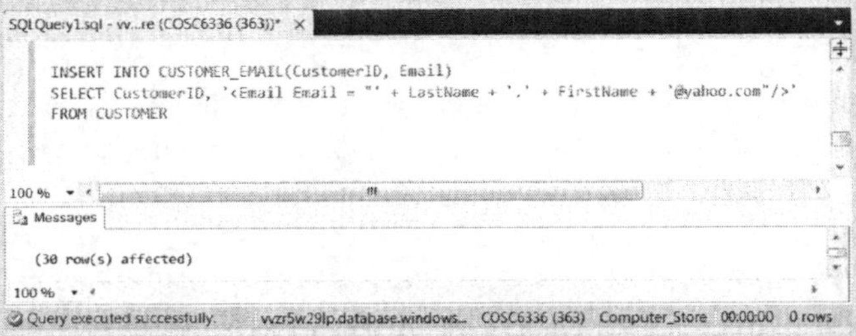

Figure 5.45 Insert e-mail addresses into e-mail column.

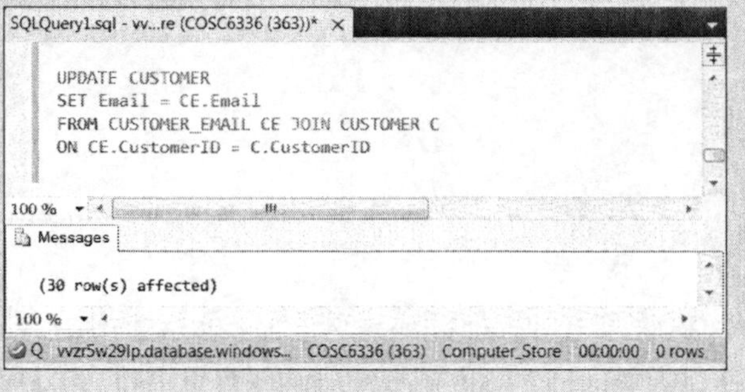

Figure 5.46 Update table CUSTOMER with XML e-mail addresses.

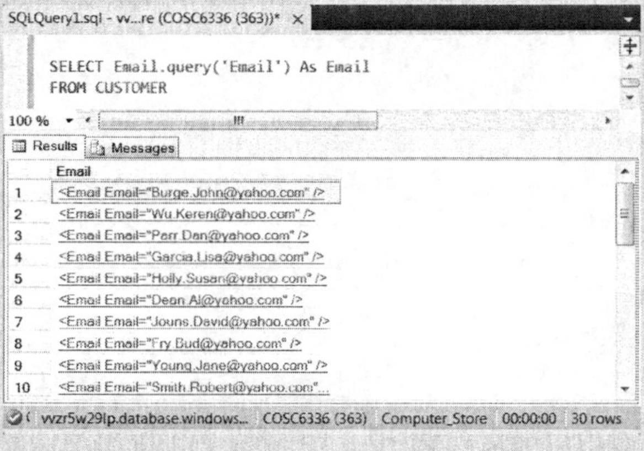

Figure 5.47 Display values in e-mail column.

Owing to the flexible features of XML, it has been widely used in database systems. In this section, we have only covered a small portion of XML and its application. Future versions of Windows Azure SQL Database will support more XML features. Detailed coverage of XML deserves a book on its own. For readers who are interested to know more about XML, they may refer to books that discuss details of XML.

5.8 Summary

This chapter introduces tools used to move data in and out of Windows Azure SQL Database. You have learned how to use SSMS to migrate databases to and from Windows Azure SQL Database. From this chapter, you have gained knowledge about DACs that are used to move databases between database servers and database applications. Through the hands-on activities, you are able to use SQL Azure Migration Wizard to move databases between Windows Azure SQL Database and an on-premises SQL Server. You have learned how to use Microsoft SSIS for controlling data transfer details. With the tool bcp, you are able to copy data from a table hosted by Windows Azure SQL Database to a text file and vice versa. In this chapter, you have also learned how to work with XML data on Windows Azure SQL Database.

Review Questions

1. What tasks can be done with the query editor provided by SSMS?
2. Which tool in SSMS can be used to script out database objects?
3. Name the tool provided by SSMS to search for Windows Azure SQL Database Database template.
4. What features can be used to integrate local SQL Server with Windows Azure?
5. Describe a problem that may occur when you migrate database objects from a production server to an application development server.
6. What tasks can be handled by DAC?
7. What information is packaged into a .bacpac file by DAC?
8. How does the database administrator create a DAC with existing databases?
9. How do application developers manage a DAC package after it is delivered to an application development server?
10. What files are generated by a DAC package after the package is deployed?
11. What should be done by a database administrator before an application can be made available to the public?
12. What do you do with Windows Azure SQL Database Migration Wizard?
13. What options does a database administrator have when migrating database objects?
14. What is SQL Server Integration Services?
15. What tasks can be accomplished with SQL Server Integration Services?
16. What is a bcp utility?
17. What are the requirements for the bcp?
18. What is the general format of a bcp command?
19. What are the advantages of XML?
20. What are the three types of XML files?

Chapter 6

Querying Information in Windows Azure SQL Database

Objectives

- Understand how to extract information with SQL
- Use SQL to query tables in Windows Azure SQL Database

6.1 Introduction

After a database is populated with data, it is ready to provide the data for various database applications. Both database administrators and database application developers need to retrieve information from databases. For example, when developing a web-based class registration form, a database application developer needs to make the class information available to the online form. For database administrators, querying information from databases is also a task performed routinely, for example, querying a log file to retrieve data to rebuild a table deleted accidentally.

There are several ways of querying information from a database. The most commonly used language for querying databases is SQL. In Windows Azure SQL Database, you can also extract information from a database using an XML-based query. In this chapter, you will learn how to write SQL statements to query tables in Windows Azure SQL Database to retrieve useful information.

6.2 Retrieving Data from Tables with SQL

In SQL, getting data stored in a table can be done with a query that consists of three basic parts, SELECT, FROM, and WHERE, shown in the following format:

```
SELECT column_name(s)
FROM table_name(s)
WHERE condition(s)
```

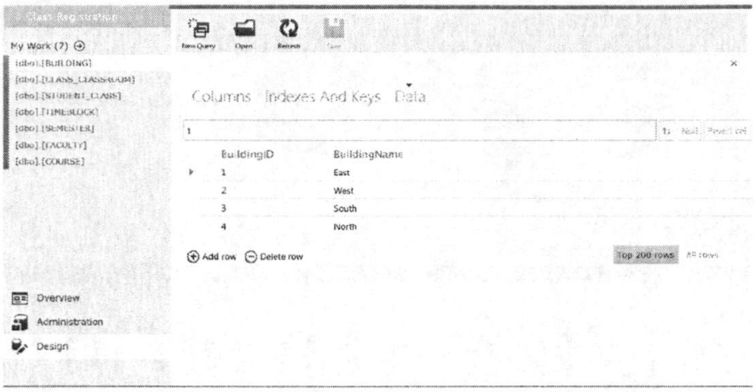

Figure 6.1 Data values in BUILDING table.

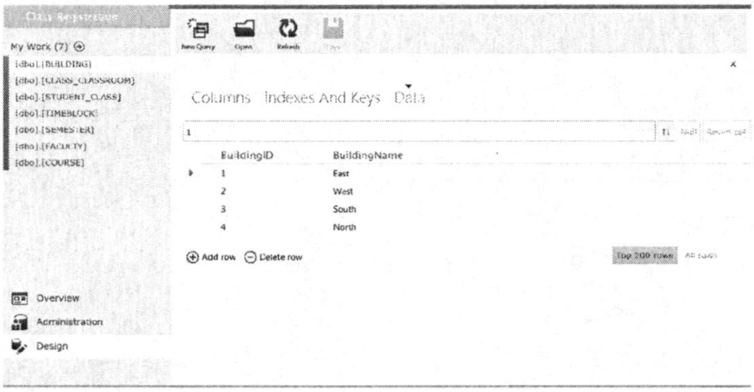

Figure 6.2 Data values in CLASSROOM table.

The SELECT clause is used to specify the column(s) to be selected by a query. The FROM clause is used to specify the table(s) from which the columns are selected. The WHERE clause specifies the condition(s) with which the rows are selected. To better understand the query process, let us examine the data stored in the tables included in a database. The data in the Class Registration database are listed in the tables shown from Figures 6.1 through 6.13.

In this chapter, you will query these tables to retrieve requested information.

6.2.1 Querying Data with SELECT, FROM, and WHERE Statements

Let us start with the SELECT–FROM statement that will return all the data from a table. For example, to display all the information about the students stored in the table STUDENT, you can use the following SQL statement:

```
SELECT *
FROM STUDENT
```

In the above SQL statement, the symbol * means that all columns in the table are selected. Note that the SQL syntax is not case sensitive. The keywords, SELECT and FROM, and the

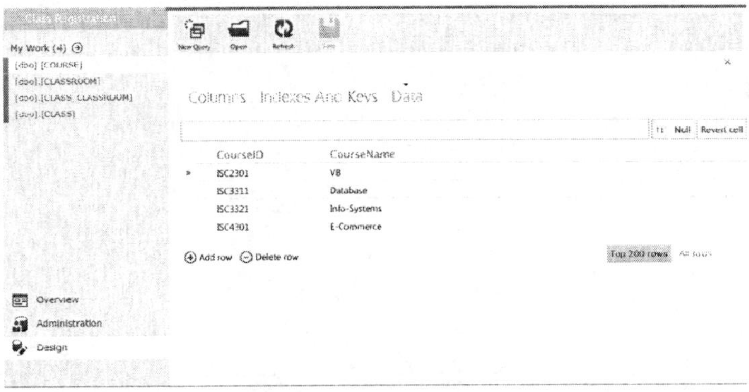

Figure 6.3 Data values in COURSE table.

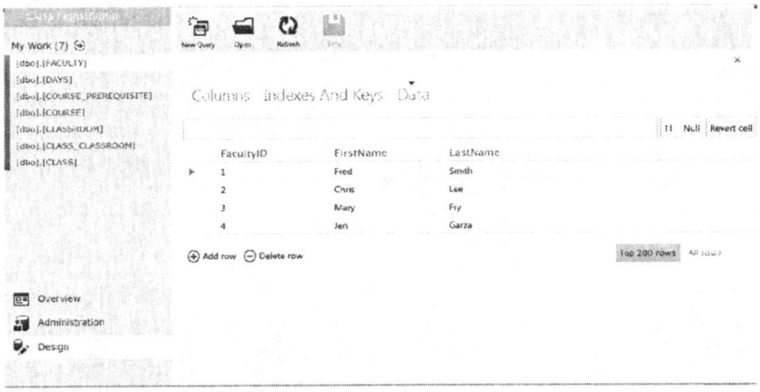

Figure 6.4 Data values in FACULTY table.

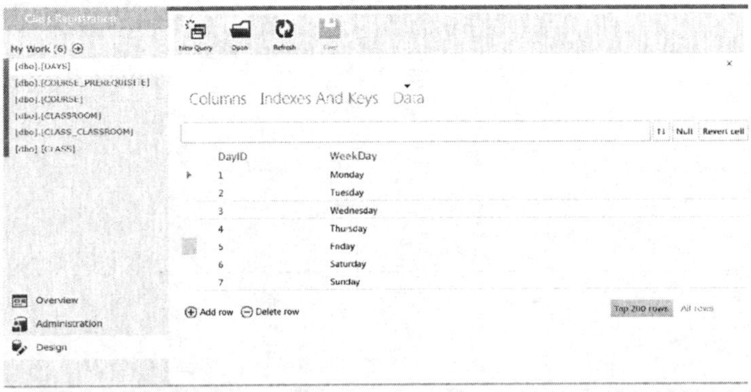

Figure 6.5 Data values in DAYS table.

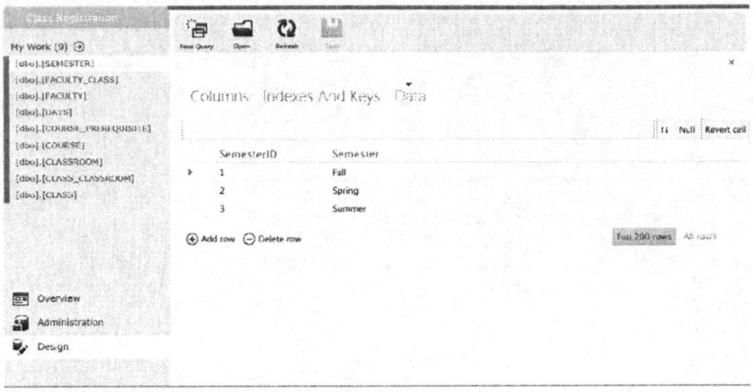

Figure 6.6 Data values in SEMESTER table.

Figure 6.7 Data values in TIMEBLOCK table.

Figure 6.8 Data values in STUDENT table.

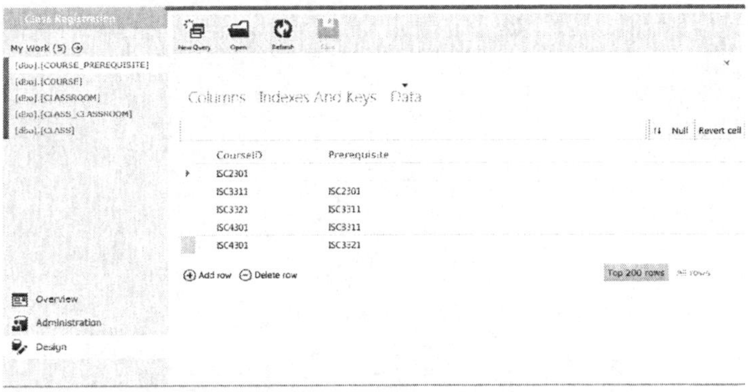

Figure 6.9 Data values in COURSE_PREREQUISITE table.

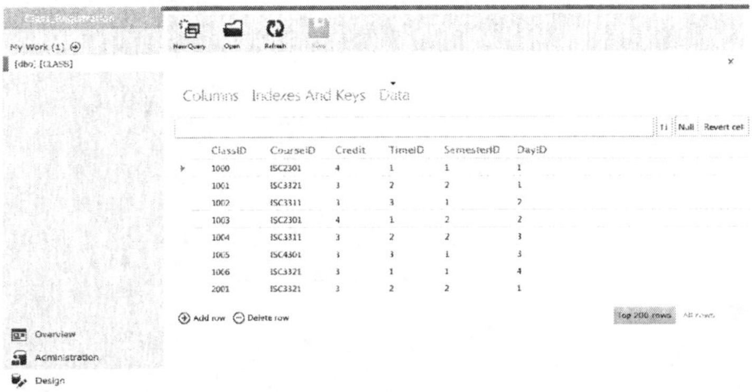

Figure 6.10 Data values in CLASS table.

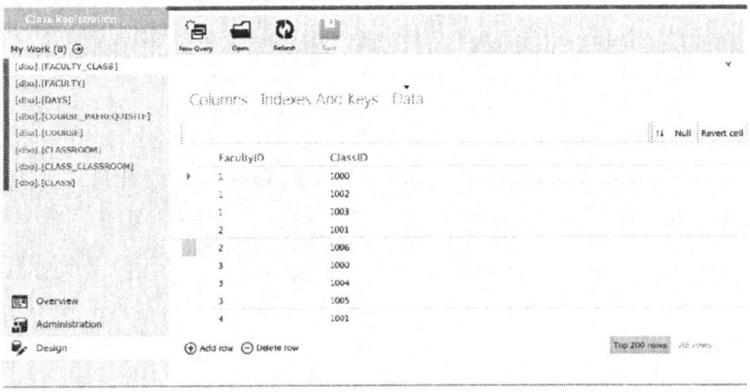

Figure 6.11 Data values in FACULTY_CLASS table.

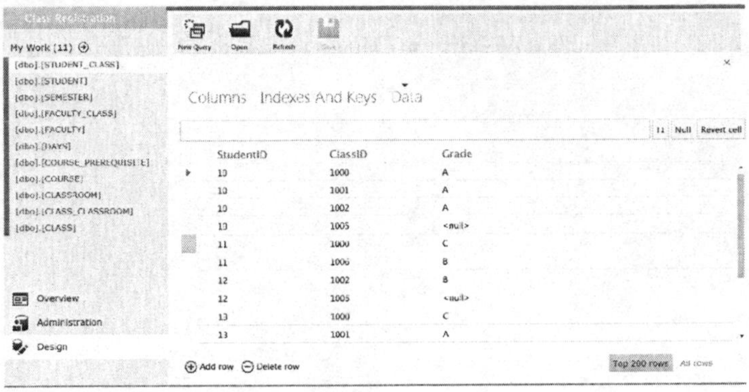

Figure 6.12 Data values in STUDENT_CLASS table.

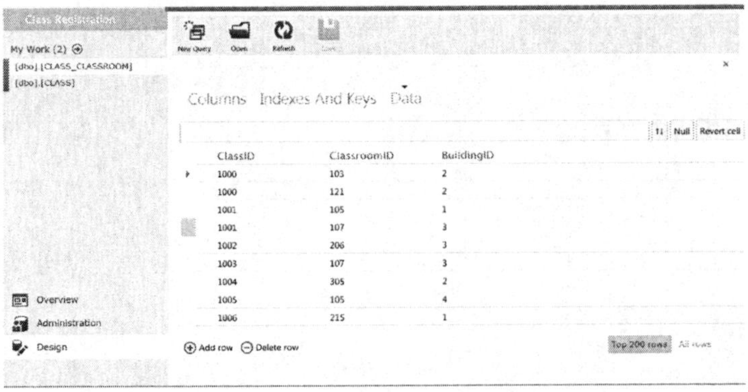

Figure 6.13 Data values in CLASS_CLASSROOM table.

table name STUDENT are capitalized for clarity purposes. Also, you do not have to break the SELECT statement into two lines. If you write the statement as SELECT * FROM STUDENT in a single line, it is perfectly acceptable. Breaking an SQL statement into multiple lines makes it easier to read. The query result is shown in Figure 6.14, which lists the data of every row and every column in the table STUDENT.

To retrieve data in certain rows specified with conditions, the WHERE clause is added to the SELECT statement. The search condition is defined in the WHERE clause. For example, to query the student ids of the students with the last name Cox and their advisors' ids, use the following SQL statement that includes the WHERE clause:

```
SELECT StudentID, FacultyID
FROM STUDENT
WHERE LastName = 'Cox'
```

In this SQL statement, there are other two things that are different from the previous SQL statement. In the SELECT clause, the columns StudentID and FacultyID are specified to indicate that only the data from the StudentID and FacultyID columns are selected. In the WHERE

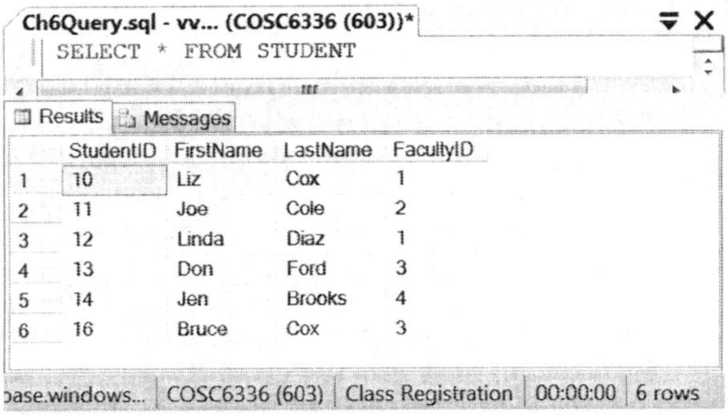

Figure 6.14 Select all columns from STUDENT table.

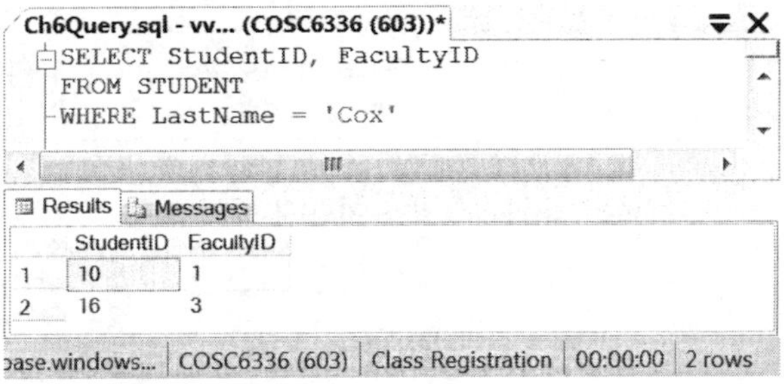

Figure 6.15 Select StudentID and FacultyID for students with last name Cox.

clause, the data type of the LastName column is the character string data type, so the last name Cox should be enclosed with single quotation marks. In SQL Database, single quotes are also used for DATETIME values. For numerical values, no quotation mark is needed. Although SQL statements are not case sensitive, a character string enclosed in the single quotation marks is case sensitive. The search will match exactly what is enclosed in the single quotes. Figure 6.15 shows the query result from the above SQL statement.

In a WHERE clause, search conditions can be defined by operators. There are three types of operators: logical operator, comparison operator, and arithmetic operator. In the following section, you will learn how to use the operators to define search conditions.

6.2.2 Logical Operators

Logical operators are commonly used to combine multiple search conditions or set limits for values to be selected (Table 6.1).

To see how to use these logical operators, consider the following examples. In Figure 6.16, the SQL statement selects the first names and last names of students who have the last name Cox or the last name Diaz.

The above query selects three rows. Two rows match the condition LastName = 'Cox' and one row matches the condition LastName = 'Diaz'. As an example of using the AND operator, let us select the student who has the first name Liz and last name Cox. The SQL statement and the query result are illustrated in Figure 6.17.

Table 6.1 Logical Operators

Logical Operator	*Description*
AND	The data that meet both the search conditions connected by an AND operator will be selected by the query.
OR	The data that meet at least one of the search conditions connected by an OR operator will be selected by the query.
NOT	The data that do not meet the search condition specified by a NOT operator will be selected by the query.
BETWEEN	The data within the range specified by a BETWEEN operator will be selected by the query.
EXISTS	The data will be selected if a subquery in an EXISTS operator returns any rows.
IN	If a value matches at least one of the values specified by an IN operation, the data corresponding to that value will be returned.
IS NULL	The data will be selected if a column in the search condition contains any null (unknown) value.
LIKE	The data will be selected if a given value matches a specific pattern defined in a LIKE operator.

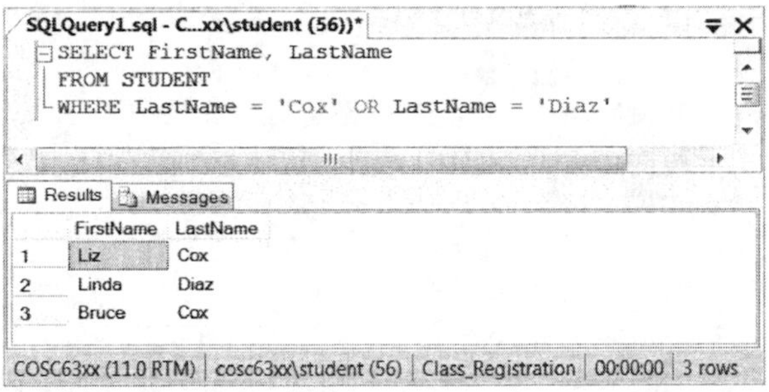

Figure 6.16 Use OR logical operator.

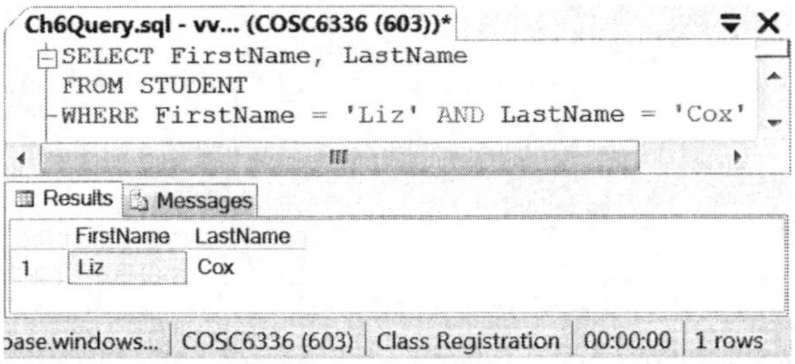

Figure 6.17 Use AND logical operator.

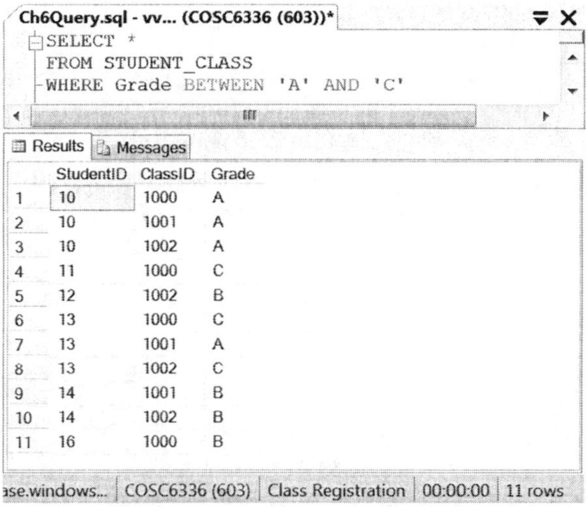

Figure 6.18 Use BETWEEN logical operator.

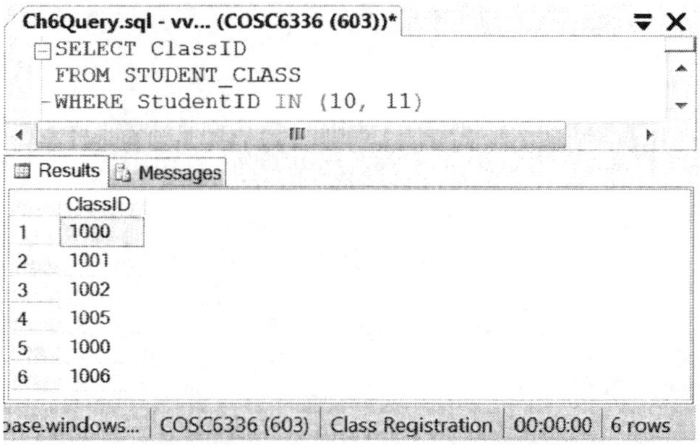

Figure 6.19 Use IN logical operator.

There is only one row that matches both conditions of the AND operator.

The example in Figure 6.18 uses the BETWEEN operator to define the grade range between A and C. The information is about students who have earned the grade C or better.

The next example shows the use of the IN operator. Like the OR operator, if a value matches one of the values specified by the IN operator, the data corresponding to that value will be selected. In Figure 6.19, classes enrolled by a list of students specified by the IN operator are selected.

Six rows are selected; two rows match the search condition StudentID 11 and the other four rows match the search condition StudentID 10.

The LIKE operator is often used with wildcard operators. The common wildcard operators are shown in Table 6.2.

Figure 6.20 shows how to use a wildcard operator with an example that selects students whose last names start with a letter between A and D.

Table 6.2 Wildcard Operators

Wildcard Operator	*Description*
%	This wildcard operator represents any string of characters, for example, "A%" means any string that starts with A.
_ (Underscore)	This wildcard operator represents any single character; for example, "A_" is any two-letter string that starts with A.
[]	This wildcard operator specifies a range of characters, for example, "A[a–c]" means any two-letter string that starts with A and ends with a or b or c.

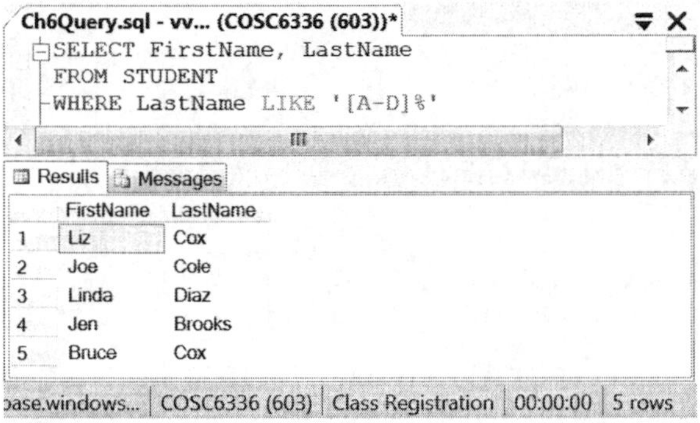

Figure 6.20 Use LIKE operator with wildcard.

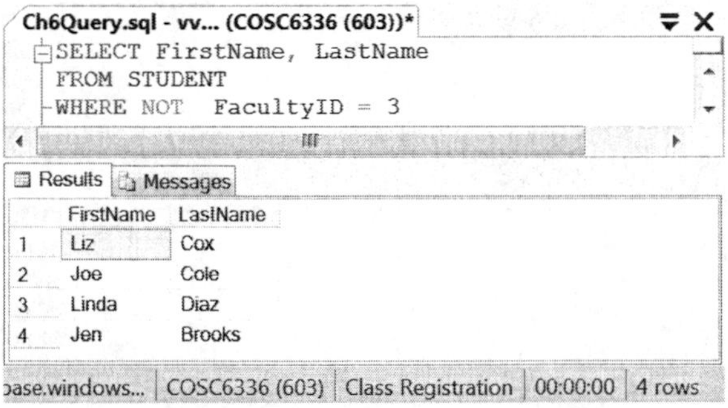

Figure 6.21 Use NOT logical operator.

Five students with their last names starting from A to D are selected. In the next example, we are going to use the NOT operator to select students who are not advised by the faculty member with the faculty id 3 (Figure 6.21).

Students who are advised by the faculty member with the id 3 are not included in the output of the query.

Any combination of the three logical operators (AND, OR, and NOT) can be used to select data with more complicated search conditions. For example, if you want to select the ids of the

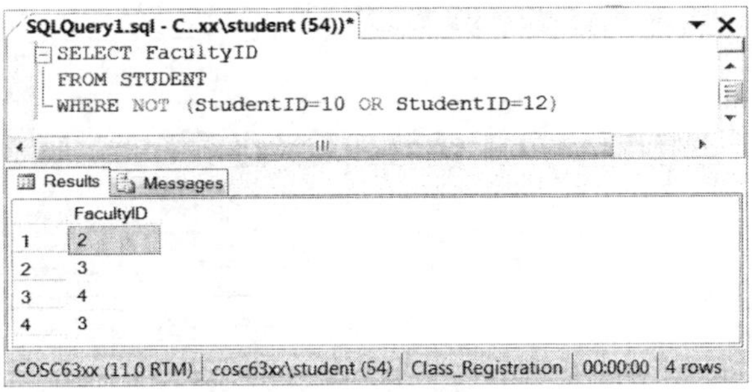

Figure 6.22 Combination of NOT and OR logical operators.

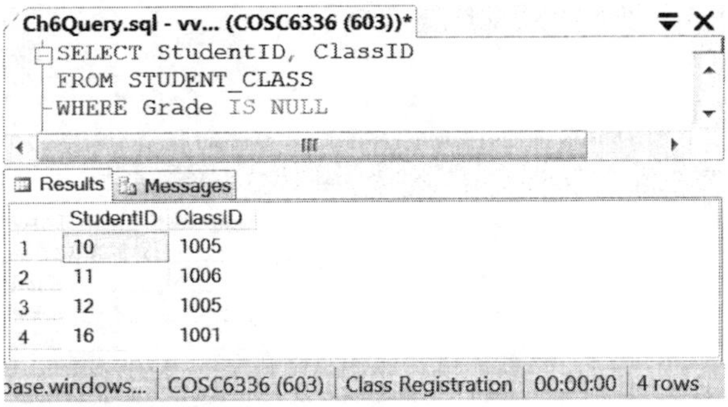

Figure 6.23 IS NULL operator.

advisors who are not advising the students with the student id 11 or with the student id 12, use the query in Figure 6.22.

By using IS NULL in the WHERE clause, you can find null values in a given column. The example in Figure 6.23 finds the null values in the column Grade and selects the corresponding student ids and class ids.

Be aware that NULL is not equal to 0 or empty space. NULL means unknown.

6.2.3 Comparison Operators

Comparison operators are often used to compare two sets of values. Table 6.3 shows commonly used comparison operators.

The operators <> and ! = are equivalent. Both are not-equal-to operators. To demonstrate the use of a comparison operator, consider a query that selects the ids of faculty members who advise students with student ids greater than or equal to 12. The selection result is shown in Figure 6.24.

When comparing two strings, the comparison is based on the order of the American Standard Code for Information Interchange (ASCII) character set, which contains 256 characters. In an ascending order, the numerical characters are in order of 0–9 and the English letters are arranged as A–Z, a–z. When comparing date values with the format dd/mm/yy or dd/mm/yyyy, the comparison starts from the year value, not the date value. The comparison of money values is the same as that of numbers. The example in Figure 6.25 selects the data that are stored in the LastName column and are greater than or equal to the last name Diaz.

Table 6.3 Comparison Operators

Comparison Operator	*Description*
>	a > b, a is greater than b
<	a < b, a is less than b
> =	a >= b, a is greater than or equal to b
< =	a <= b, a is less than or equal to b
<>	a <> b, a is not equal to b
! =	a ! = a, a is not equal to b

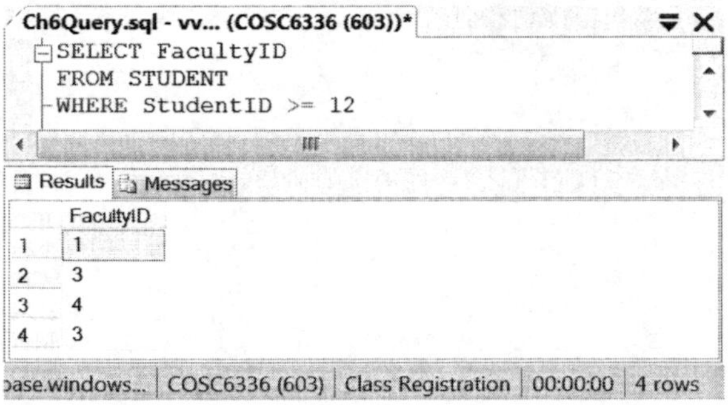

Figure 6.24 Use >= comparison operator.

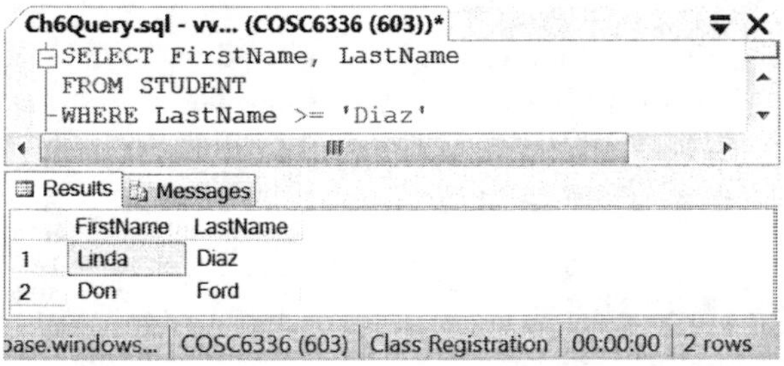

Figure 6.25 Use comparison operator on character string.

6.2.4 Arithmetic Operators

These operators can perform mathematical operations on values of the numeric data type (Table 6.4).

To demonstrate the use of arithmetic operators, consider the following example that selects the classrooms that have a capacity greater than or equal to 110% of the minimum capacity, which is 20 (Figure 6.26).

Some of the above operators can also be used with keywords such as UPDATE and DELETE. For example, after the classrooms are remodeled in the building with the id 2, the capacities of its

Table 6.4 Arithmetic Operators

Arithmetic Operator	*Description*
+	Addition
–	Subtraction
*	Multiplication
/	Division

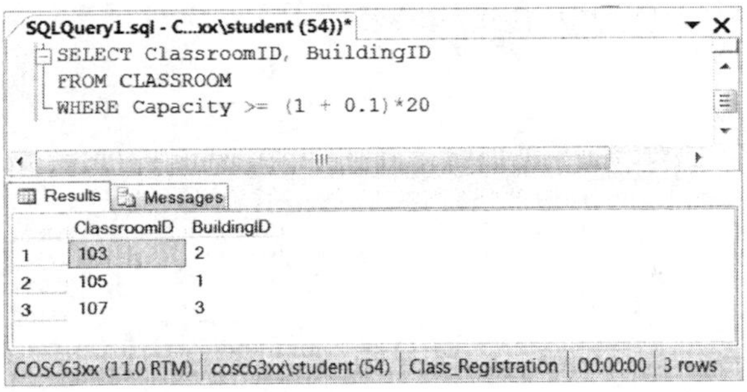

Figure 6.26 Use arithmetic operators.

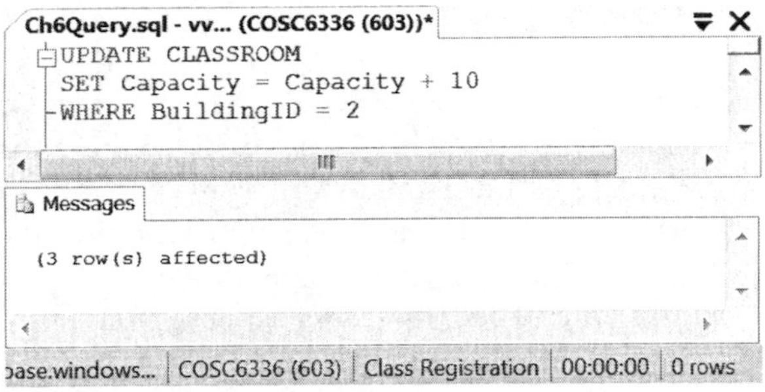

Figure 6.27 Use arithmetic operator in UPDATE statement.

classrooms are increased by 10. You can update the capacities for these classrooms with the code shown in Figure 6.27.

The operators DISTINCT, ORDER BY, TOP, UNION, and PIVOT can be used to reorganize the records selected by the SELECT-FROM-WHERE statement. You can use the operator DISTINCT to eliminate duplicated rows, and use ORDER BY to sort the result in an ascending or descending order. For example, to select the list of distinct student last names in a descending order, use the code in Figure 6.28.

In the above query, with the keyword DESC, the ORDER BY clause sorts the output in a descending order. For ORDER BY, the ascending order is the default.

The keyword TOP can be used to select the top-ranked values. For example, to select classrooms with two of the highest capacities, you can use the code shown in Figure 6.29.

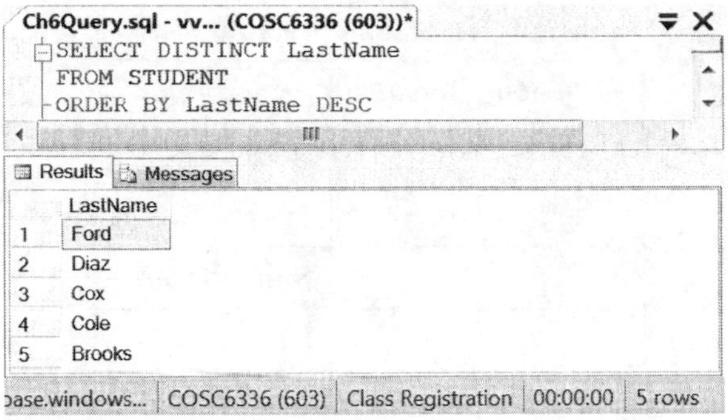

Figure 6.28 Use DISTINCT and ORDER BY.

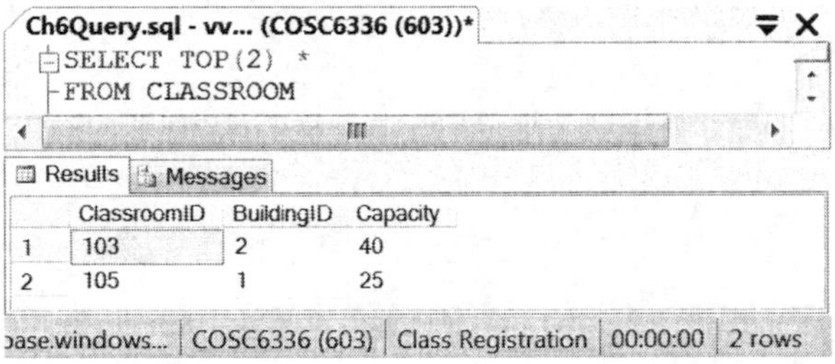

Figure 6.29 Use TOP.

To combine the outputs from two different queries, you can use the UNION keyword. To see how UNION works, consider the example in Figure 6.30. In this example, UNION is used to combine the faculty member with the id 1 and the students advised by this faculty member.

The PIVOT keyword can be used to categorize a set of records returned from a SELECT statement in a cross-classification table. For example, to find out how many As, Bs, Cs, Ds, and Fs are earned by each student, you can run the SQL statement displayed in Figure 6.31.

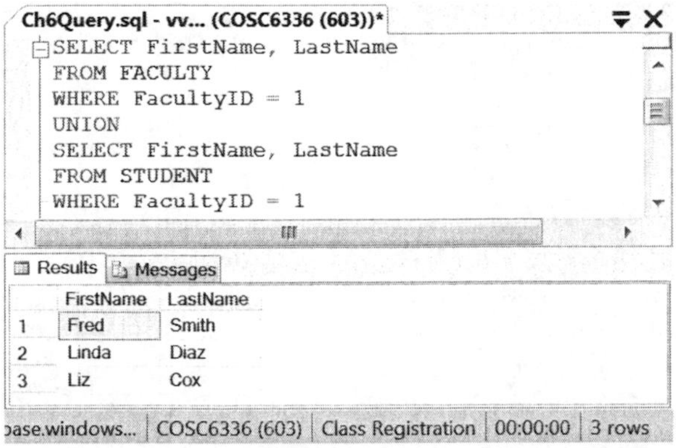

Figure 6.30 Use UNION.

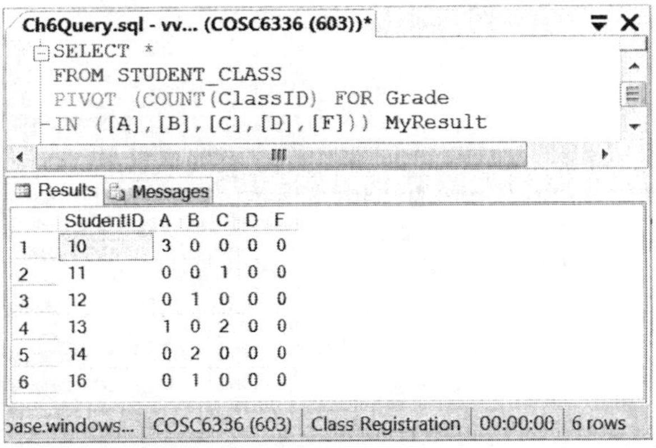

Figure 6.31 Use PIVOT.

The code in Figure 6.31 uses the built-in function COUNT to count the number of elements in each category. Details about built-in functions will be given later in this chapter. The word MyResult at the end of the SQL statement is the name of the pivot table, which can be used for other data analysis tasks.

At this point, you have learned most of the commonly used operators through examples. For querying tasks that involve more than one table, subqueries or the JOIN keyword can be used. In the next section, you will learn how to use subqueries.

6.3 Subqueries

The search condition in a WHERE clause may depend on the result returned by a subquery. The result set returned by a subquery will be used as the search condition in the main query. The output returned by a subquery may include one or more values. If the output has only a single value, the = operator is used to match the comparison value in the WHERE clause. If the output returned by a subquery contains more than one value, the IN or EXIST operator should be used to handle the multiple valued output. The example in Figure 6.32 selects database classes. Since the class and course information are from two different tables, a subquery is used to retrieve the course

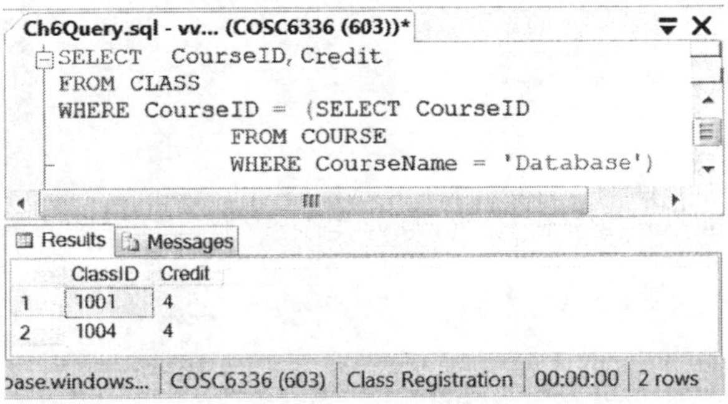

Figure 6.32 Use subquery that returns single value.

information as the intermediate result. Based on the output of the subquery, the main query will return the information about the classes.

Notice that you must enclose the subquery within parentheses. The = operator in the WHERE clause is used since only a single value is returned by the subquery. Sometimes, a subquery returns multiple values. In such a case, the IN operator should be used in the search condition. The next example in Figure 6.33 shows that two different student ids match the last name Cox returned by the subquery. Therefore, the IN operator is used in the WHERE clause.

To select data from more than two tables, more than two subqueries can be used to accomplish the task. You can use an AND operator to relate two subqueries, or nest a subquery in another subquery. To illustrate the use of a nested query, let us consider the scenario where we need to select students who got an A grade in the Database class. This task can be accomplished by a nested query that uses its innermost subquery to return the course id that matches the course name Database. The first intermediate subquery returns the classes that teach Database. The next intermediate subquery returns a list of students who got an A grade from the classes. The outermost query will return the information about those selected students. The query and its result are listed in Figure 6.34. Note that in a nested query, the innermost subquery is executed first and the outermost query is executed last.

The logical operator EXISTS can be used in the WHERE clause to verify if there is any output returned by a subquery. EXISTS will return a True or False value. If the output of the subquery contains one or more values, the search condition in the WHERE clause becomes true; otherwise, the search condition is false. The logical operator NOT EXISTS is just the opposite of EXISTS. In Figure 6.35, if Garza is an advisor, the query will return the information about his student(s).

You need to pay attention to several things in the above query. First, the alias S stands for the table STUDENT and F stands for FACULTY. The aliases are used to distinguish between the two FacultyIDs in the subquery's WHERE clause. The subquery will check if any faculty id from the STUDENT table in the main query matches the id of the faculty who has the last name Garza in the FACULTY table. This leads to the second thing that you need to pay attention to. When using EXISTS or NOT EXISTS with a subquery, you should link the table in the subquery and the table in the main query with a matching condition in the WHERE clause, for example, the condition S.FacultyID = F.FacultyID in Figure 6.35.

Figure 6.33 Use subquery that returns multiple values.

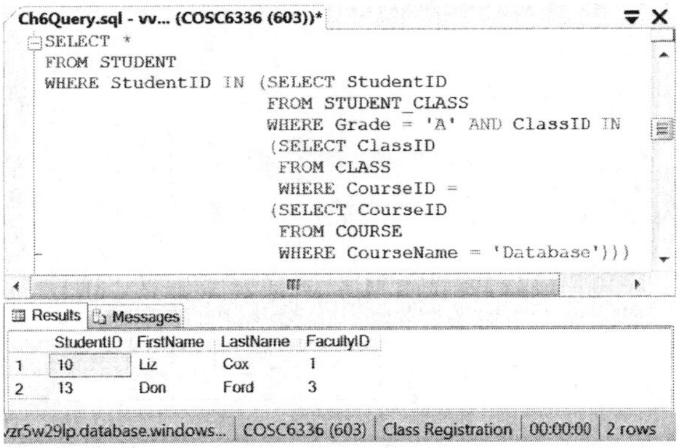
Ch6Query.sql - vv... (COSC6336 (603))*
SELECT *
FROM STUDENT
WHERE StudentID IN (SELECT StudentID
FROM STUDENT_CLASS
WHERE Grade = 'A' AND ClassID IN
(SELECT ClassID
FROM CLASS
WHERE CourseID =
(SELECT CourseID
FROM COURSE
WHERE CourseName = 'Database')))
Results
Messages
StudentID FirstName LastName FacultyID
1 10 Liz Cox 1
2 13 Don Ford 3
COSC6336 (603)
Class Registration
00:00:00
2 rows

Figure 6.34 Use nested queries.

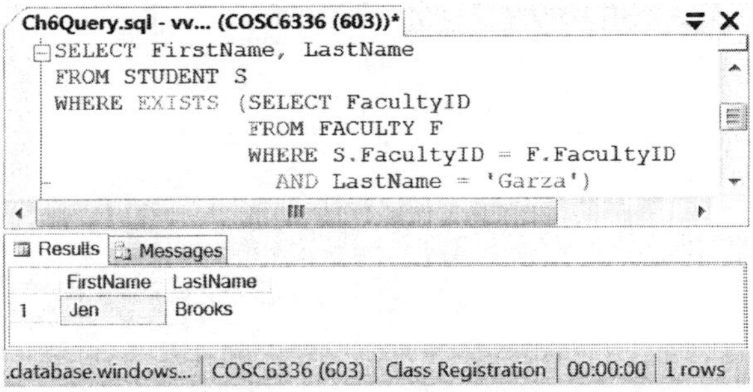
Ch6Query.sql - vv... (COSC6336 (603))*
SELECT FirstName, LastName
FROM STUDENT S
WHERE EXISTS (SELECT FacultyID
FROM FACULTY F
WHERE S.FacultyID = F.FacultyID
AND LastName = 'Garza')
Results
Messages
FirstName LastName
1 Jen Brooks
.database.windows...
COSC6336 (603)
Class Registration
00:00:00
1 rows

Figure 6.35 Use EXISTS with subquery.

With operators such as EXISTS and NOT EXISTS, you can apply subqueries to generate the following sets of data selected from two original tables:

- **Intersection**: Contains rows that exist in both original tables
- **Difference**: Contains rows only in the first original table but not in the second original table (not including the rows in both tables)
- **Union**: Contains all rows that exist in both the original tables
- **Product**: Contains all the matches that associate every row of the first table with every row of the second table

For example, the intersection of CLASS and DAYS is the set of days on which classes are scheduled. Figure 6.36 shows the intersection generated with the EXISTS operator.

Similar to the above example, the difference of DAYS and CLASS should contain those days that have not been assigned. Figure 6.37 displays the difference generated with the NOT EXISTS operator.

As shown in Figure 6.37, Friday, Saturday, and Sunday are the elements in DAYS but not the elements in CLASS. The set of elements is the difference.

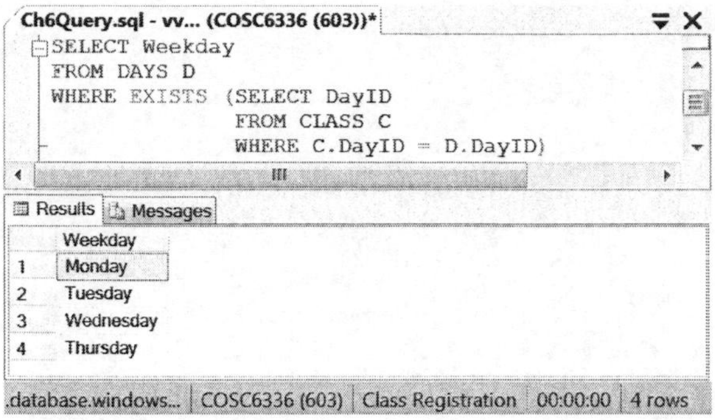

Figure 6.36 Use EXISTS to create intersection.

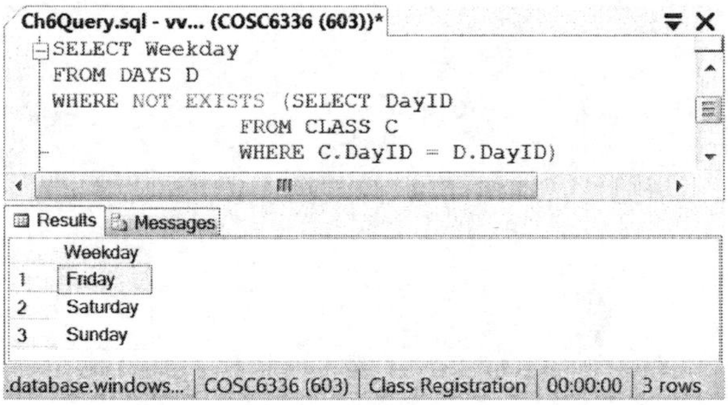

Figure 6.37 Use NOT EXISTS to create difference.

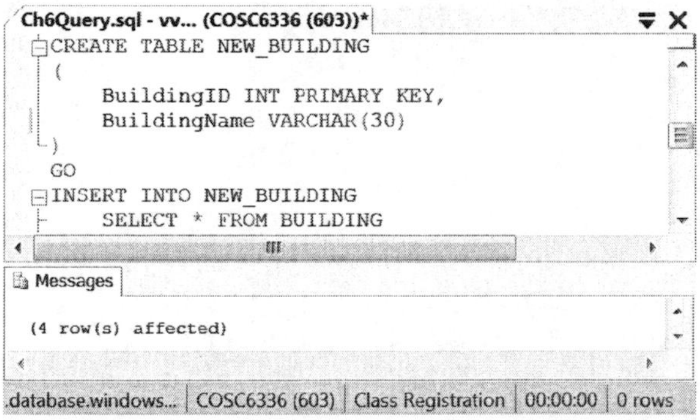

Figure 6.38 Copy data from one table to another with subquery.

Another useful application of a subquery is to populate a table by copying data from another table. The example in Figure 6.38 shows how the table NEW_BUILDING is populated with the data stored in the table BUILDING.

Note that, for the subquery used in the INSERT statement, you do not need to enclose it within parentheses. As mentioned before, the JOIN keyword can also be used in a query involving multiple tables. In the following section, we are going to query information from tables that are joined together.

6.4 Joining Multiple Tables with SQL

If two tables are related with a primary–foreign key pair, you can join them by matching the values in the primary key and the foreign key. To do so, you need to add a join condition in the WHERE clause to match the values of the primary key column and the foreign key column. The columns in the join condition must have the same domain. The following statement shows a query with join conditions:

```
SELECT column1, column2, ...
FROM table1, table2, ...
WHERE table1.column = table2.column, ...
```

In this query, join conditions are used to merge the rows from two or more tables. In SQL Database, tables can also be joined by specifying table names in the FROM clause with the keyword JOIN. It may be clearer if we separate join conditions from search conditions by placing join conditions in the FROM clause and search conditions in the WHERE clause. The following query shows how to separate the join conditions from the search conditions:

```
SELECT column1, column2, ...
FROM table1 JOIN table2 ON table1.column = table2.column
WHERE search_condition
```

Joins can be further categorized as inner join, outer join, or self-join. Like most DBMS packages on the market, SQL Database supports the inner join, left outer join, right outer join, and self-join.

6.4.1 Inner Join

The most commonly used join is the inner join. For two tables to join, they must share a common column such as a primary–foreign key pair. Each value in the column from the first table is used to match the values in the related column from the second table. The inner join only uses the values that have an exactly match in the join condition. As an example, let us suppose that we want to retrieve information about the students along with the classes they have taken. To accomplish this task, we use the StudentID column in the join condition as shown in Figure 6.39.

In the output, the students and class information are printed if the students whose id values in the STUDENT table match the id values in the STUDENT_CLASS table. In the WHERE clause, the common column StudentID is used in the join condition. To indicate the tables the StudentID column belongs to, the aliases of the tables are placed in front of StudentID. Another way to join the two tables is to specify the inner join in the FROM clause as shown below:

```
SELECT FirstName, LastName, ClassID, Grade
FROM STUDENT S JOIN STUDENT_CLASS C
ON S.StudentID=C.StudentID
```

6.4.2 Outer Join

SQL Database supports three types of outer joins: left, right, and full. A **left outer join** includes all rows from the left table, even those with no corresponding rows from the right table. The missing values from the right table are placed with NULL in the output. The example in Figure 6.40

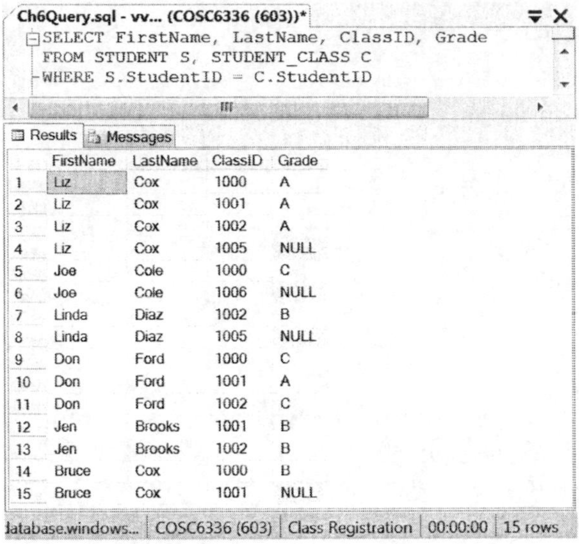

Figure 6.39 Use inner join to select data from two tables.

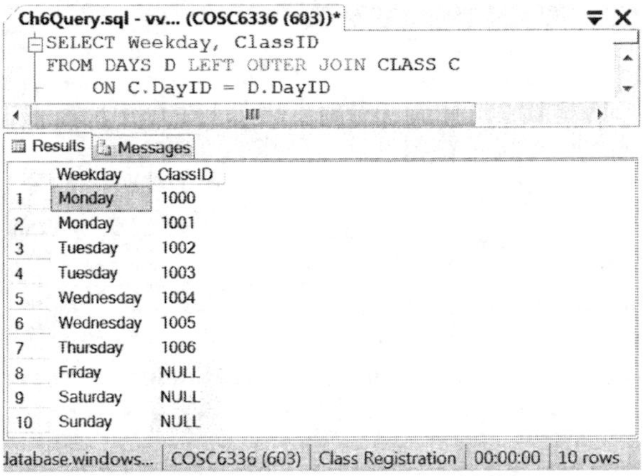

Figure 6.40 Use left outer join to select data from two tables.

selects all the weekdays from the left table that may or may not be assigned classes from the right table.

As you can see, LEFT OUTER JOIN is used to link the two tables. Since no classes are scheduled on Friday, Saturday, and Sunday, the corresponding class id values from the right-hand side table CLASS are NULL.

Reversely, you can use a **right outer join** that includes all rows from the right table and place NULL values in the rows from the left table that do not match the corresponding rows from the right table. When joining two tables with a right outer join, use the phrase RIGHT OUTER JOIN in the query. For a **full outer join**, the selection result includes all rows from both tables no matter if there is a match or not.

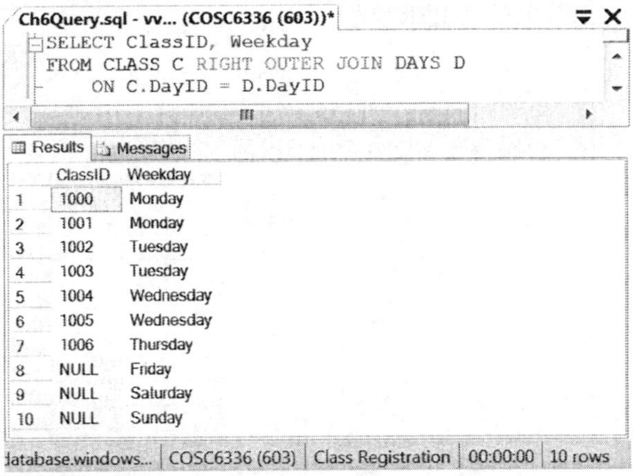

Figure 6.41 Use right outer join to select data from two tables.

To demonstrate the use of a right outer join, let us reverse the tables used in the example for the left outer join. That is, the table CLASS will be the left table and DAYS will be the right table. The output is shown in Figure 6.41.

This time, the NULL values appear on the left-hand side.

In the above, we have used joins to link two tables. In fact, the join method can also be used to join multiple tables. The topic of multiple joins will be covered next.

6.4.3 Multiple Joins

Multiple tables can be joined in the FROM clause. As an example, let us consider a query that will retrieve information, including student names from the table STUDENT, the courses they have taken, and their grades from each class. To get the student names and their grades, we need to join the tables STUDENT and STUDENT_CLASS. To get the course names, we need to first join the table CLASS since CLASS contains both StudentID and CourseID. Then, join the table COURSE. Since data are selected from four different tables, STUDENT, STUDENT_CLASS, CLASS, and COURSE, we join all of them in a query as shown in Figure 6.42.

As you can see, the keyword JOIN is used three times to join the four tables. In the above example, the join conditions are specified in the FROM clause.

6.4.4 Self-Join

There are situations where you need to join a table to itself. For example, if you want to pair the students who are taking the same class, you need to match a given student with another student in the same class. Since both students are from the same table, you need to join the table to itself and use the column ClassID as the common column for the join condition.

Since the tables to be joined are the same, you must distinguish their roles by giving the table two different aliases in the FROM clause. In our example, the aliases C1 and C2 are used to represent the left table and right table, respectively. To be specific, the join condition should look like the one below:

C1.ClassID = C2.ClassID

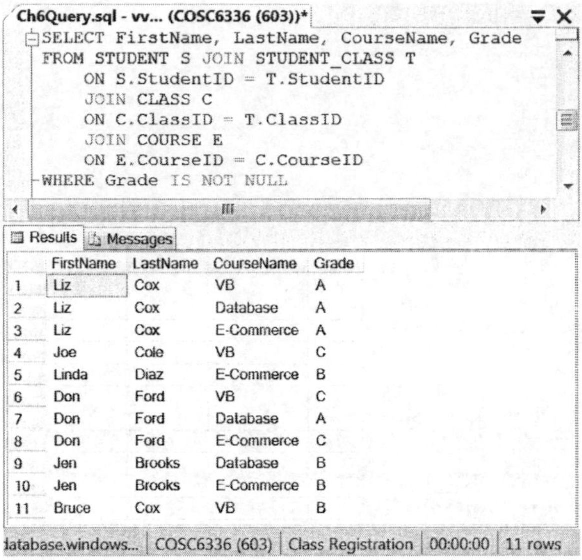

Ch6Query.sql - vv... (COSC6336 (603))*
SELECT FirstName, LastName, CourseName, Grade
FROM STUDENT S JOIN STUDENT_CLASS T
ON S.StudentID = T.StudentID
JOIN CLASS C
ON C.ClassID = T.ClassID
JOIN COURSE E
ON E.CourseID = C.CourseID
WHERE Grade IS NOT NULL
Results
Messages
FirstName LastName CourseName Grade
1 Liz Cox VB A
2 Liz Cox Database A
3 Liz Cox E-Commerce A
4 Joe Cole VB C
5 Linda Diaz E-Commerce B
6 Don Ford VB C
7 Don Ford Database A
8 Don Ford E-Commerce C
9 Jen Brooks Database B
10 Jen Brooks E-Commerce B
11 Bruce Cox VB B
database.windows... COSC6336 (603) Class Registration 00:00:00 11 rows

Figure 6.42 Use multiple inner joins.

As shown in Figure 6.43, to display a pair of students who are enrolled in the same class in the output, you need to do two things. First, you need to get a list of students whose names will appear first in the name pair. To do this, you should match the student ids in the STUDENT table to the student ids in the table STUDENT_CLASS with the alias C1. Then, you need to get a list of students whose names will appear secondly in the name pair. To do so, you need to match the student ids in the same STUDENT table to the student ids in the table STUDENT_CLASS with the alias C2. Two aliases S1 and S2 are used to distinguish the STUDENT table. The join conditions look like the following:

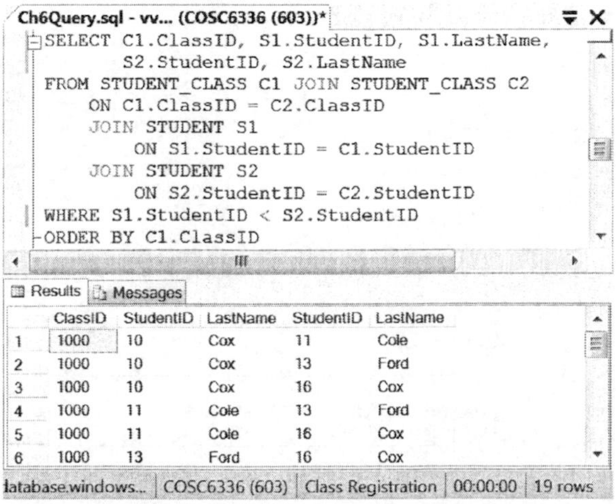

Ch6Query.sql - vv... (COSC6336 (603))*
SELECT C1.ClassID, S1.StudentID, S1.LastName,
S2.StudentID, S2.LastName
FROM STUDENT_CLASS C1 JOIN STUDENT_CLASS C2
ON C1.ClassID = C2.ClassID
JOIN STUDENT S1
ON S1.StudentID = C1.StudentID
JOIN STUDENT S2
ON S2.StudentID = C2.StudentID
WHERE S1.StudentID < S2.StudentID
ORDER BY C1.ClassID
Results
Messages
ClassID StudentID LastName StudentID LastName
1 1000 10 Cox 11 Cole
2 1000 10 Cox 13 Ford
3 1000 10 Cox 16 Cox
4 1000 11 Cole 13 Ford
5 1000 11 Cole 16 Cox
6 1000 13 Ford 16 Cox
database.windows... COSC6336 (603) Class Registration 00:00:00 19 rows

Figure 6.43 Use self-join to select data.

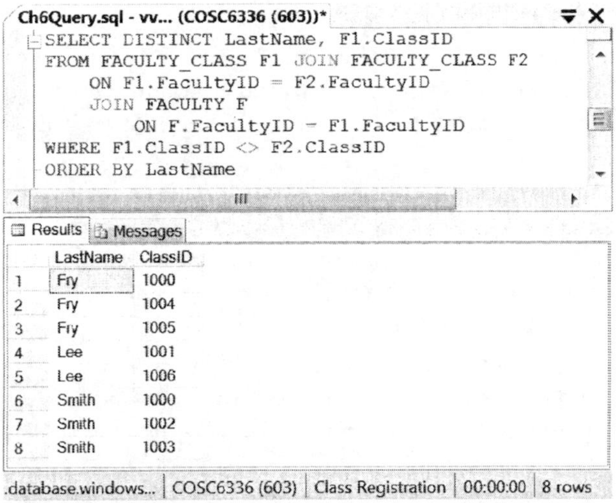

Figure 6.44 Find repeated values by using self-join.

S1.StudentID = C1.StudentID
S2.StudentID = C2.StudentID

To eliminate duplicates such as the pairs (Smith, Green) and (Green, Smith), the WHERE clause should include a search condition as shown below:

S1.StudentID < S2.StudentID

As shown in the output, the classmates are all paired up.

Another use of self-join is to locate repeated values in a column. For example, you can use self-join to find the last names of faculty members who teach more than one class. The self-join illustrated in Figure 6.44 will accomplish the task. The aliases F1 and F2 are used to distinguish the same table FACULTY_CLASS in the self-join. The following condition

F1.ClassID <> F2.ClassID

is used to eliminate faculty members who only teach one class.

As you can see in the output of the query, Fry and Smith each teaches three classes. Lee teaches two classes. Garza's name is not on the list since she teaches one class.

In addition to operators, subqueries, and table joins, SQL also provides built-in functions to enhance the database query process. The descriptions of these built-in functions will be given in the next section.

6.5 SQL Built-In Functions

SQL Database provides a function library where built-in functions are categorized into three types: aggregate, rowset, and scalar. You will first learn about the aggregate functions.

6.5.1 Aggregate Functions

Aggregate built-in functions perform some calculations on a set of rows. They are used with SELECT, GROUP BY, or HAVING statements. The commonly used aggregate functions are COUNT, AVG, SUM, MAX, and MIN. Table 6.5 lists the commonly used aggregate functions, their usage, and related examples.

The aggregate functions in Table 6.5 are also scalar functions. That is, they all return a single value. These built-in functions can be used in a SELECT clause and a WHERE clause. For example, if you want to find out which classroom has the largest capacity, try the query in Figure 6.45 that uses the MAX function in the WHERE clause.

As you can see, the classroom 103 has the largest capacity, which is 40. The next example illustrates how a built-in function can be used in a SELECT clause. In Figure 6.46, the COUNT function is used to count how many students are currently enrolled in the Database class.

The output of the query shows the number of students enrolled in the Database class.

When built-in functions are used in a SELECT clause, which includes columns and functions, the set of values returned from a column usually do not match the single value returned by a function. For example, the following query will generate an error since four rows will be selected from ClassroomID and only a single value will be returned from MIN(Capacity).

```
SELECT ClassroomID, MIN(Capacity)
FROM CLASSROOM
```

Table 6.5 Built-In Aggregate Functions

Function	*Usage*	*Example*
COUNT	Counts how many nonnull rows are in a given column	SELECT COUNT(GPA) FROM ENROLLMENT
SUM	Sums the values in a given numerical column	SELECT SUM(GPA) FROM ENROLLMENT
MAX	Finds the maximum value in a given numerical column	SELECT MAX(GPA) FROM ENROLLMENT
MIN	Finds the minimum value in a given numerical column	SELECT MIN(GPA) FROM ENROLLMENT
AVG	Calculates the average for the values in a given numerical column	SELECT AVG(GPA) FROM ENROLLMENT

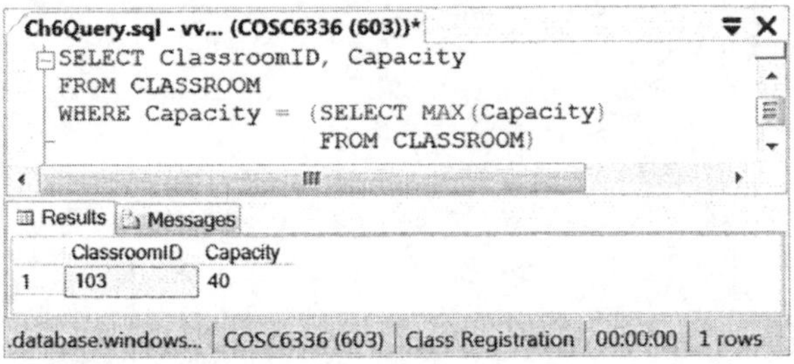
Ch6Query.sql - vv... (COSC6336 (603))*
SELECT ClassroomID, Capacity
FROM CLASSROOM
WHERE Capacity = (SELECT MAX(Capacity)
FROM CLASSROOM)
Results
Messages
ClassroomID Capacity
1 103 40
.database.windows... COSC6336 (603) Class Registration 00:00:00 1 rows

Figure 6.45 Use built-in function in subquery.

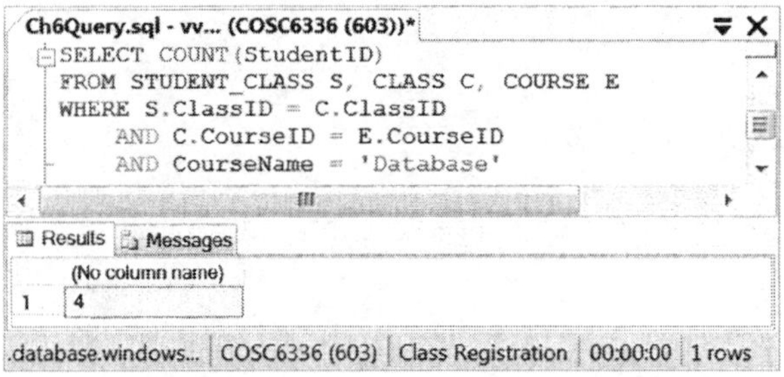
Ch6Query.sql - vv... (COSC6336 (603))*
SELECT COUNT(StudentID)
FROM STUDENT_CLASS S, CLASS C, COURSE E
WHERE S.ClassID = C.ClassID
AND C.CourseID = E.CourseID
AND CourseName = 'Database'
Results
Messages
(No column name)
1
4
.database.windows...
COSC6336 (603)
Class Registration
00:00:00
1 rows

Figure 6.46 Use built-in function COUNT.

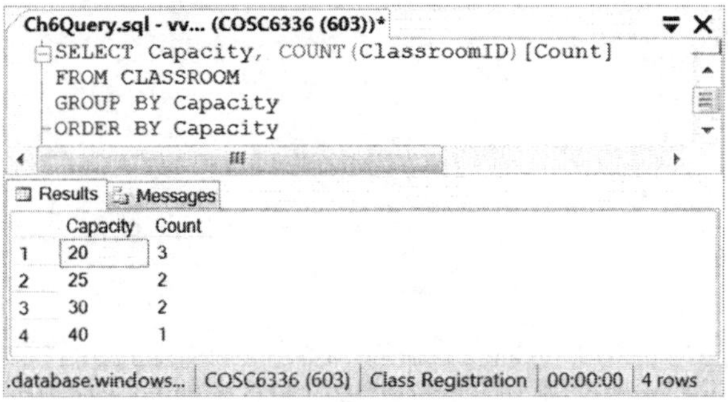
Ch6Query.sql - vv... (COSC6336 (603))*
SELECT Capacity, COUNT(ClassroomID)[Count]
FROM CLASSROOM
GROUP BY Capacity
ORDER BY Capacity
Results
Messages
Capacity Count
1 20 3
2 25 2
3 30 2
4 40 1
.database.windows...
COSC6336 (603)
Class Registration
00:00:00
4 rows

Figure 6.47 Use built-in function with GROUP BY.

However, mixing columns and functions in a SELECT clause will not generate an error if a GROUP BY clause is used. GROUP BY puts the rows with the same data value from a column in a group and the function will return a value for each group. In such a case, the correct output will be displayed. Figure 6.47 shows a query that selects the capacity and counts the number of classroom ids that have the same capacity. The GROUP BY clause includes the Capacity column since the grouping is based on classroom capacity.

As indicated in Figure 6.47, three classrooms have the capacity of 20, two classrooms have the capacity of 25, two classrooms have the capacity of 30, and one classroom has the capacity of 40. Notice that column used by the GROUP BY clause should be the same column in the SELECT clause.

When using the GROUP BY clause, you cannot use the WHERE clause to specify the search condition. Instead, you should use the HAVING clause. HAVING selects only certain groups out of all the groups specified by the GROUP BY clause. As an example, let us use a search condition that returns the first names and last names of students who are enrolled in more than one class (see Figure 6.48).

Figure 6.48 shows the students who are enrolled in more than one class.

In the above, we have discussed some commonly used built-in aggregate functions. Next, you will learn how to use scalar functions.

6.5.2 Scalar Functions

A scalar function returns a single value. The aggregate functions discussed earlier are a type of scalar functions. The commonly used scalar functions are GETDATE, DATEDIFF, ROUND,

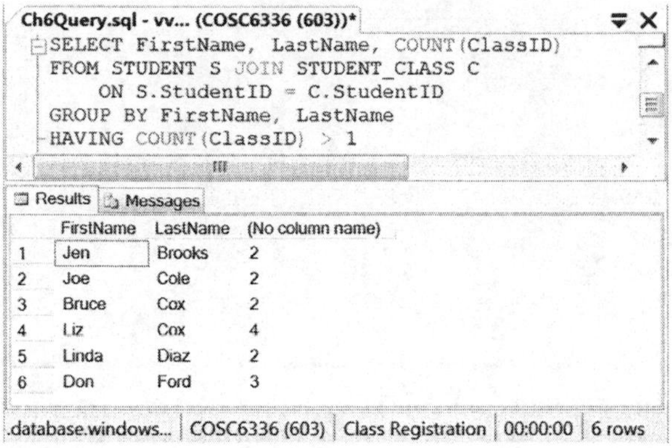

Figure 6.48 Use HAVING with GROUP BY.

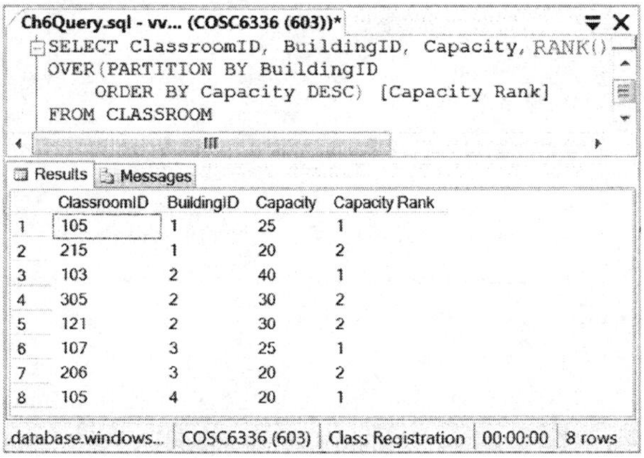

Figure 6.49 Use scalar function RANK.

and RANK. The RANK function returns the rank for each record in a result set from a query. For example, Figure 6.49 shows that the classrooms in each building are ranked based on their capacities. The ranking of capacities is in a descending order per building.

By now, you have learned how to use various built-in functions in query statements. The SQL Database function library includes many other built-in functions. A complete coverage of the built-in functions is beyond the scope of this book. You can find more information about the built-in functions through the SQL Database Help menu. Besides these built-in functions, users can also create user-defined functions. We will discuss user-defined functions in the next chapter.

ACTIVITY 6.1 QUERYING DATA WITH SQL

To query information from the tables, you can either directly log on to the Windows Azure SQL Database portal at https://*yourserver*.database.windows.net or connect the SSMS to the Windows Azure SQL Database server. Since we are able to access Windows Azure SQL

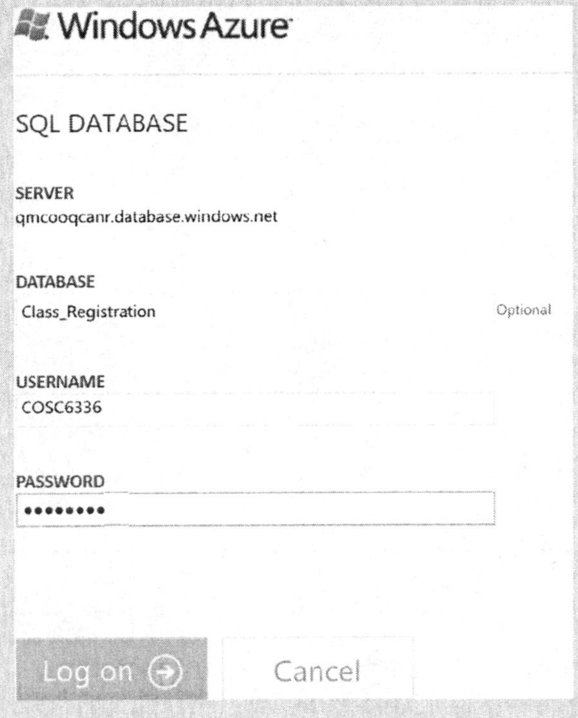

Figure 6.50 Log on to SQL database server through web browser.

Database anytime and anywhere, this hands-on activity will be carried out in Windows Azure SQL Database. The following illustrates how to connect to the Windows Azure SQL Database server and query the tables in the database Class_Registration:

1. On your local computer, log on to Windows Azure through the URL
   https://*yourserver*.database.windows.net
   where yourserver is your SQL Database server name. Enter the database name **Class_Registration.** Then, enter your user name and password to log on to Windows Azure SQL Database as shown in Figure 6.50. Once you have logged on, click the **New Query** icon at the upper-left corner of your screen.
2. Example 1: To select the information about the buildings, you can use the following SELECT statement:

   ```
   SELECT * FROM BUILDING
   ```

   Click the **Run** icon to execute the query. The result is shown in Figure 6.51.
3. Example 2: In the next exercise, you will select the students whose last names begin with a letter between D and T. Enter the below query.

   ```
   SELECT FirstName, LastName
   FROM STUDENT
   WHERE LastName Like '[D-T]%'
   ```

   Highlight the code and click **Run**. The result is shown in Figure 6.52.

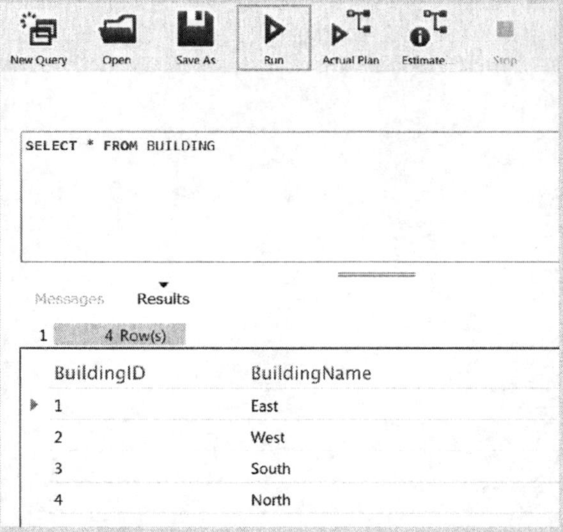

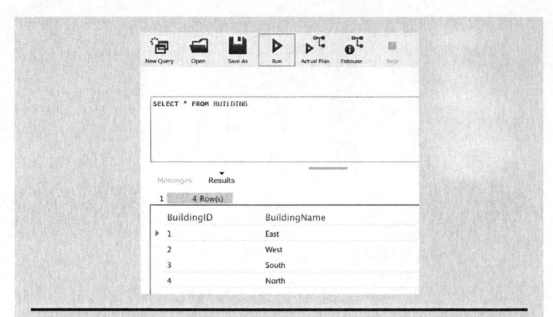

Figure 6.51 Query information about building.

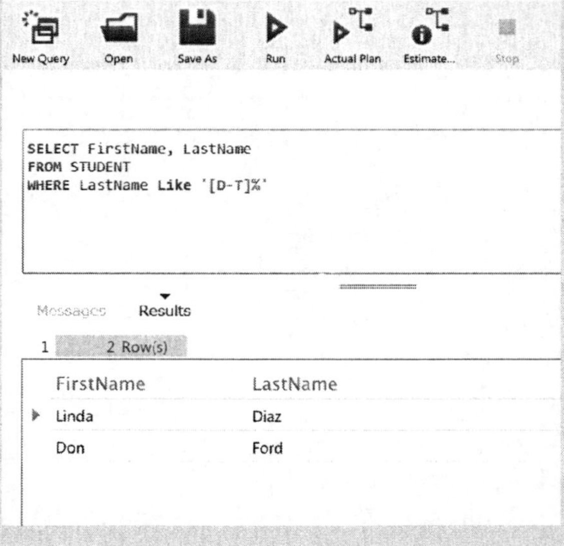

Figure 6.52 Use LIKE operator with wildcard.

4. Example 3: With a subquery, select the name(s) of the faculty member(s) who advise(s) the student whose first name is Liz. Enter the below query.

```
SELECT FirstName, LastName
FROM FACULTY
WHERE FacultyID IN (SELECT FacultyID
FROM STUDENT
WHERE FirstName = 'Liz')
```

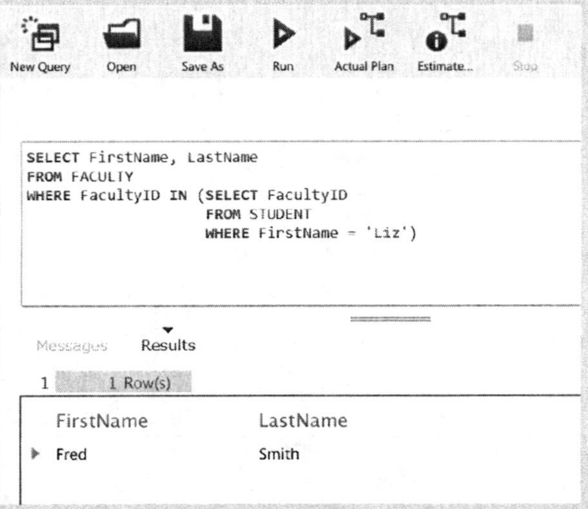

Figure 6.53 Use IN with subquery that may return multiple values.

Highlight the code and click **Run**. The result of the query is shown in Figure 6.53.

5. Example 4: Select the students who have completed the course VB and got an A grade by using a nested subquery. Enter the below query.

```
SELECT FirstName, LastName
FROM STUDENT
WHERE StudentID IN (SELECT StudentID
FROM STUDENT_CLASS
WHERE Grade = 'A' AND
ClassID IN (SELECT ClassID
FROM CLASS
WHERE CourseID = 'ISC2301'))
```

Highlight the code and click **Run**. The result of the query is shown in Figure 6.54.

6. Example 5: Select the first name(s) and last name(s) of the student(s) advised by Professor Garza by using the EXISTS operator. Enter the below query.

```
SELECT FirstName, LastName
FROM STUDENT S
WHERE EXISTS (SELECT *
FROM FACULTY F
WHERE S.FacultyID = F.FacultyID AND
F.LastName = 'Garza')
```

Highlight the code and click **Run**. The result of the query is shown in Figure 6.55. Notice that, to relate the main query and subquery, you need to add the condition S.FacultyID = F.FacultyID, where S is the alias for the STUDENT table and F is the

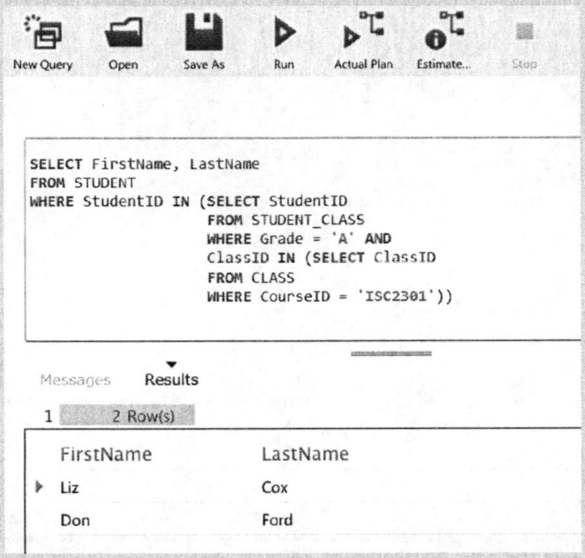
New Query
Open
Save As
Run
Actual Plan
Estimate...
Stop
SELECT FirstName, LastName
FROM STUDENT
WHERE StudentID IN (SELECT StudentID
FROM STUDENT_CLASS
WHERE Grade = 'A' AND
ClassID IN (SELECT ClassID
FROM CLASS
WHERE CourseID = 'ISC2301'))
Messages
Results
1
2 Row(s)
FirstName
LastName
Liz
Cox
Don
Ford

Figure 6.54 Use nested subquery.

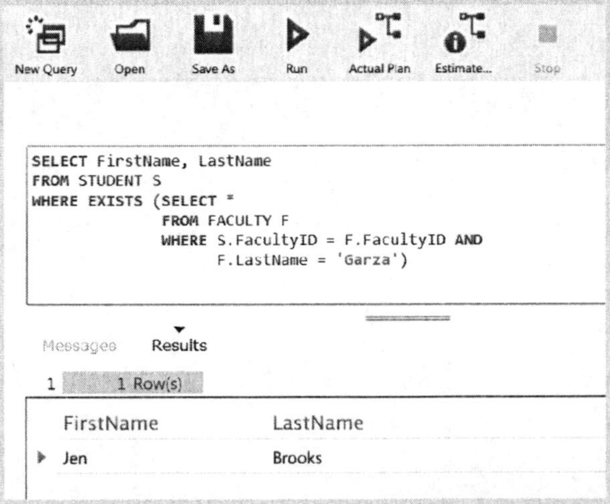
New Query
Open
Save As
Run
Actual Plan
Estimate...
Stop
SELECT FirstName, LastName
FROM STUDENT S
WHERE EXISTS (SELECT *
FROM FACULTY F
WHERE S.FacultyID = F.FacultyID AND
F.LastName = 'Garza')
Messages
Results
1
1 Row(s)
FirstName
LastName
Jen
Brooks

Figure 6.55 Use EXISTS with subquery.

alias for the FACULTY table. The use of aliases can avoid retyping of the entire table names.

7. Example 6: Select the first names and last names of the students along with the courses taken by these students by using the inner join. Enter the below query.

```
SELECT DISTINCT FirstName, LastName, CourseName
FROM STUDENT S, STUDENT_CLASS T, CLASS C, COURSE R
WHERE S.StudentID=T.StudentID AND
T.ClassID=C.ClassID AND
C.CourseID=R.CourseID
```

Since the tables STUDENT and COURSE are not directly linked, two additional tables STUDENT_CLASS and CLASS are used to link the table STUDENT to the table COURSE. Highlight the code and click **Run**. The result of the query is shown in Figure 6.56.

8. Example 7: Select the semesters and classes by using a left outer join to see if any of the semesters offer no class. Enter the following query:

```
SELECT Semester, ClassID
FROM SEMESTER S LEFT OUTER JOIN CLASS C ON
S.SemesterID=C.SemesterID
```

Highlight the code and click **Run**. The result of the query is shown in Figure 6.57. You can see in Figure 6.57 that no class is offered during the summer.

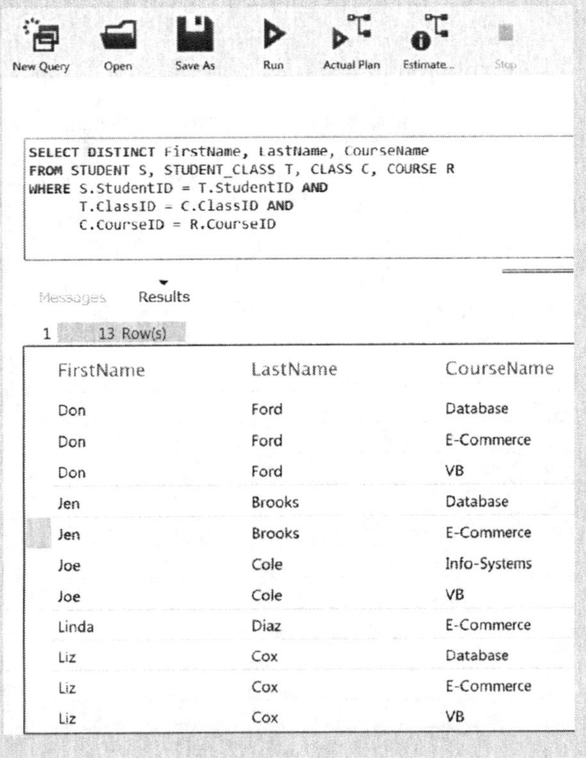

Figure 6.56 Use inner join to select data from multiple tables.

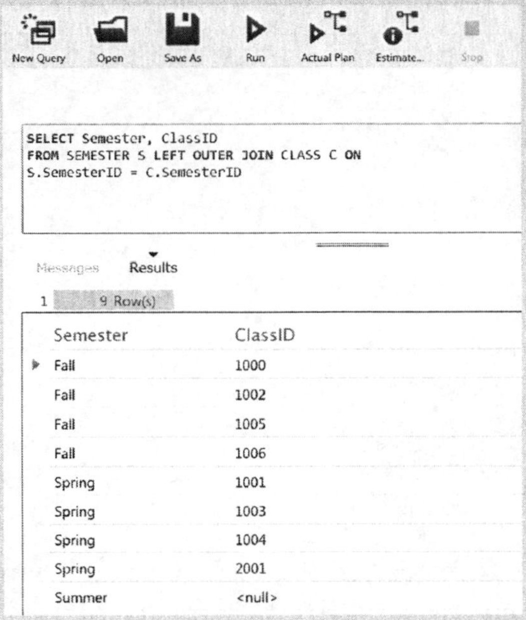

Figure 6.57 Use left outer join to select data from two tables.

9. Example 8: Display the last names of the faculty members who advise more than one student by using the self-join. Enter the following query:

```
SELECT F.LastName, COUNT(S.StudentID) As [Number of Advisees]
FROM ((FACULTY F JOIN STUDENT S ON F.FacultyID=S.FacultyID)
JOIN STUDENT T ON S.FacultyID=T.FacultyID
AND S.StudentID <> T.StudentID)
GROUP BY F.LastName
```

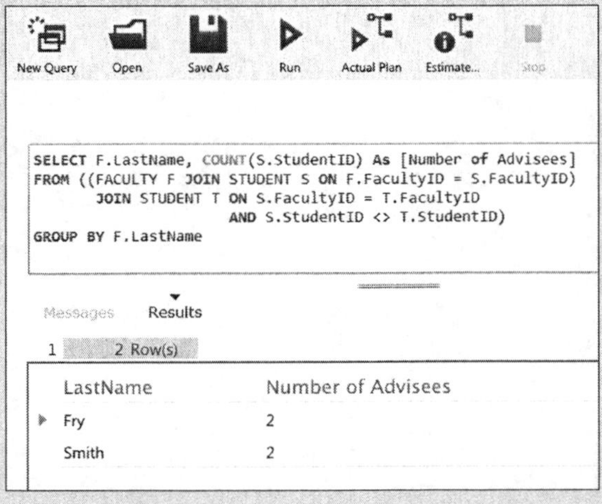

Figure 6.58 Use self-join.

The condition `S.StudentID <> T.StudentID` is used to prevent the same student ID from being counted twice. Highlight the code and click **Run**. The result of the query is shown in Figure 6.58.

10. Example 9: This example shows another way to display the last names of the faculty members who advise more than one student. Enter the following query:

```
SELECT F.LastName, COUNT(S.StudentID) As [Number of Advisees]
FROM FACULTY F JOIN STUDENT S ON F.FacultyID=S.FacultyID
GROUP BY F.LastName
HAVING COUNT(S.StudentID) >1
```

Highlight the code and click **Run**. The result of the query is shown in Figure 6.59. When GROUP BY is used, HAVING replaces the WHERE clause.

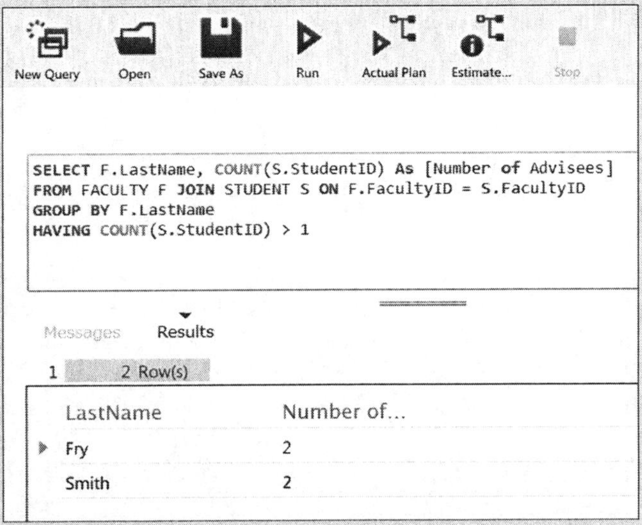
New Query
Open
Save As
Run
Actual Plan
Estimate...
Stop
SELECT F.LastName, COUNT(S.StudentID) As [Number of Advisees]
FROM FACULTY F JOIN STUDENT S ON F.FacultyID = S.FacultyID
GROUP BY F.LastName
HAVING COUNT(S.StudentID) > 1
Messages
Results
1
2 Row(s)
LastName
Number of...
Fry
2
Smith
2

Figure 6.59 Use HAVING clause with GROUP BY.

6.6 Summary

This chapter covers topics of retrieving information from the data stored in a database. At the beginning, we examined the data stored in the tables of the database Class_Registration. Then, through examples, you learned how to query information from database tables by using a combination of the three basic statements: SELECT, FROM, and WHERE. You learned how to query database tables with the logical operators AND, OR, NOT, IN, EXISTS, NOT EXISTS, IS NULL, DISTINCT, BETWEEN, and LIKE. Examples were also used to show how to use the comparison operators and arithmetic operators to query information from a database. To better display retrieved data, the DISTINCT, ORDER BY, HAVING, GROUP BY, and TOP operators were used to organize data outputs.

To retrieve information from multiple tables, subqueries and the JOIN clause were used. Several examples were given to demonstrate how to use subqueries to obtain data selected in an intersection, difference, union, and product. A subquery was used in an INSERT statement to copy data from a table to a new table with the same structure. You also learned how to join tables so that you can retrieve information from multiple tables. A join can be classified as an inner join, left outer join, right outer join, full outer join, or self-join. A number of examples were given to show how to use various joins. A couple of self-join examples were used to help you better understand the concept and application of the self-join.

You have also learned how to use built-in functions to perform calculations. We have discussed commonly used aggregate functions such as COUNT, SUM, MAX, MIN, and AVG. Scalar functions including GETDATE, DATEDIFF, ROUND, and RANK were also introduced. As a query gets more and more complicated, it is important to write more efficient code and execute the code in a more efficient way. In the next chapter, you will write SQL code as programming units such as stored procedures, triggers, and views. You will learn how to reuse previously created stored procedures and functions.

Review Questions

To answer the following questions, you need to use the data from Figures 6.1 through 6.13. For each question below, show the result by executing the query in the New Query editor.

1. Execute an SQL statement to display all the columns in the table CLASSROOM.
2. Execute an SQL statement to display the columns FirstName and LastName in the table STUDENT where the student has the first name Bruce and last name Cox.
3. Execute an SQL statement to display all the students who have the grades between C and A.
4. Execute an SQL statement to display the last names of the faculty members who teach either VB or Database.
5. Execute an SQL statement to display the first names and last names of the students with the last names starting with A, B, or C.
6. Execute an SQL statement to display the student id(s) of the student(s) who have not enrolled in either the ISC3321 class or the ISC4301 class.
7. Execute an SQL statement to display the last names of the students whose ids are between 11 and 15.
8. Execute an SQL statement to display the classroom capacity that is less than or equal to half that of the classroom 103.
9. Execute an SQL statement to display the names of the students who have enrolled in the VB classes in a descending order.
10. Execute an SQL statement to display the student's last name and his/her faculty advisor's name for the student whose id is 10 with the UNION operator.
11. Execute an SQL statement to display the faculty members' name(s) who advise the student(s) who has/have the last name Cox.
12. Execute an SQL statement to display the first name(s) and last name(s) of the student(s) whose faculty advisor is Smith and who is/are enrolled in the VB class.
13. Execute a nested query statement to display the student name(s) and course name(s) from which the student(s) received an A grade.

14. By using the EXISTS operator, execute an SQL statement to display the first names and last names of the students who are enrolled in the ISC2301 class.
15. By using the NOT EXISTS operator, execute an SQL statement to display the names of the courses not required by the Database course.
16. By using an inner join, display the students' names along with their faculty advisors' names.
17. By using the RIGHT OUTER JOIN operator, execute an SQL statement to display classes and semesters to see if any of the semesters in which no class is offered.
18. By using a self-join, display the names of students who have enrolled in more than one class.
19. Find out how many students are advised by each faculty member.
20. By using the HAVING clause, display the last names of the students who have enrolled in more than one class and display how many classes the students have been enrolled.

Chapter 7

Windows Azure SQL Database Procedures and Functions

Objectives

- Learn programming extensions
- Create and use stored procedures, functions, and triggers

7.1 Introduction

Previously, you learned how to create and manage database objects and query information from a database. You accomplish those tasks by executing SQL statements one at a time. Sometimes, for more complicated management and query tasks, you may need to execute multiple SQL statements together or run a group of SQL statements repeatedly. A group of SQL statements that can be executed together is called an SQL procedure. The current standard ANSI SQL does not support procedural SQL programs. Many DBMS vendors provide their own versions of procedural SQL to extend the standard ANSI SQL. Windows Azure SQL Database provides Transact-SQL (T-SQL) as the extension of the standard ANSI SQL. In this chapter, you will learn about various programming units such as stored procedures, user-defined functions, and triggers created with procedural SQL.

7.2 SQL Programming Extensions

To meet the requirements of procedural programming, Transact-SQL allows us to declare variables, control the execution of code with flow-control structures, and handle errors. Some of these extensions will be discussed in this section. In later sections, these extensions will be used in various SQL programs.

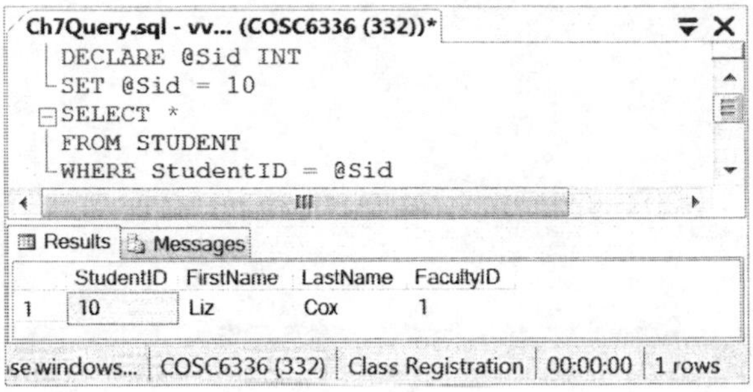
Ch7Query.sql - vv... (COSC6336 (332))*
DECLARE @Sid INT
SET @Sid = 10
SELECT *
FROM STUDENT
WHERE StudentID = @Sid
Results
Messages
StudentID FirstName LastName FacultyID
1 10 Liz Cox 1
se.windows... COSC6336 (332) Class Registration 00:00:00 1 rows

Figure 7.1 Declare and use variable.

7.2.1 Variables

A variable is used to hold data values during the process of SQL program execution. After a variable is declared, you can assign a value to it. The value in a variable can be dynamically modified. Variables can be used in an SQL statement. In a procedure, a variable can be used to hold a returned value from a function call or used in a flow-control structure. The use of variables will be illustrated throughout this chapter. Let us start with a simple example where a variable is created and assigned a student id value. After the variable is assigned a value, the example shows how to use the variable in a SELECT statement. The @ sign indicates that a name is used for a variable (Figure 7.1).

As shown in Figure 7.1, the variable @Sid is declared as an INT type, which is a data type provided by Transact-SQL. Besides built-in data types, Transact-SQL allows users to define their own data types. You can create complicated user-defined data types with struct in C# or with Structure in VB .NET and use these data types in SQL statements.

7.2.2 Flow-Control Structures

As mentioned before, multiple SQL statements are included in an SQL procedure. Usually, the order of execution of multiple SQL statements may not be sequential, meaning that the order of execution is the same as the order in which the code appears in the program. Sometimes, you may need to run a certain part of the code repeatedly. Sometimes, you may execute a certain part of the code based on a given condition. To control the code execution order, Transact-SQL provides several flow-control structures. The commonly used flow-control keywords are shown in Table 7.1.

To illustrate the use of the flow-control keywords, let us consider an example, which includes a WHILE loop and an IF…ELSE structure. In this example, we will move the classes from Monday to Tuesday. That is, the class 1000 that teaches the course ISC2301 and the class 1001 that teaches ISC3311 will be moved to Tuesday. Based on the Information Systems department's regulation, no two classes should teach the same course on the same day. Therefore, we need to check Tuesday's class schedule to see if there are classes that teach the same course. If so, move one of the classes that teach the same course to Wednesday. Repeat the same process for Wednesday and Thursday to make sure that no two classes teach the same course on the same day. A WHILE loop will be used to loop through each weekday. Inside each loop, if it is Monday, we will simply move Monday's classes to Tuesday. Otherwise, we will check if there are two classes that teach the same course on

Table 7.1 Flow-Control Keywords and Descriptions

Keyword	*Description*
WHILE	It defines a loop structure. A block of SQL statements within the loop structure will be executed repeatedly while a given condition continues to be met.
BEGIN...END	It defines a block of SQL statements.
BREAK	While a given condition is met, exit a WHILE loop. For embedded WHILE loops, exit the innermost WHILE loop first.
CONTINUE	When a given condition is met, continue the executions in a WHILE loop.
IF...ELSE	When the IF condition is met, the block of SQL statements under the IF clause is executed. Otherwise, the block of SQL statements under the ELSE clause is executed.
RETURN	Exit the processing of the SQL statements unconditionally and return to the calling program.
GOTO *label*	Jump to the SQL statement labeled by the keyword *label* and continue to process other SQL statements from there.
WAITFOR	Delay a statement execution until a specified time.

the same day. If so, the class with a larger id number will be moved to the next day. The following are the SQL statements that can be used to accomplish the task:

```
Declare @Count INT
SET @Count = 1
WHILE (@Count < 5)
BEGIN
      IF (@Count = 1)
      BEGIN
            UPDATE CLASS
            SET DayID = DayID + 1
            WHERE DayID = 1
      END
ELSE
      BEGIN
            UPDATE CLASS
            SET DayID = DayID + 1
            WHERE ClassID = (SELECT MAX(ClassID)
                        FROM CLASS
                        WHERE CourseID IN (SELECT CourseID
                              FROM CLASS
                              GROUP BY CourseID, DayID
                              HAVING COUNT(CourseID) > 1))
      END
      SET @Count = @Count + 1
END
```

In this example, we first declare the variable @Count, which is used as the counter for the WHILE loop. The initial value of @Count is set to 1. The WHILE loop is used to check all four weekdays' classes. The BEGIN...END keywords are used to enclose a block of SQL Statements for the WHILE loop. Inside the WHILE loop, if the value in the counter is equal to 1, which is Monday, all the classes will be moved to Tuesday by adding 1 to DayID. If the value of the counter is not equal to 1 and there are duplicated classes on the same day (meaning COUNT(CourseID) > 1), the DayID value of the class with the largest class id will be increased by 1. The innermost subquery groups the classes by CourseID and DayID. In the HAVING clause, the built-in function COUNT is used to count the number of elements in each group specified by the GROUP BY clause. If the count of a course id is larger than 1, the course id will be returned by the subquery. In the outer subquery, the built-in function MAX is used to select the largest class id corresponding to the returned course id. Based on the returned class id from the outer subquery, the SET clause increases the value of DayID. For the IF...ELSE structure, if the code block contains more than a one-line statement, BEGIN...END is needed to enclose all the statements. The last SET clause in the WHILE loop is used to increase the counter so that the next loop will process the next day's classes.

As a procedural programming language, Transact-SQL allows users to create functions and procedures. In the next section, you will learn how to create and manage user-defined procedures and functions.

7.3 Procedures and Functions

To execute a set of SQL statements together automatically, you can place these SQL statements in a **function** or **procedure**. Procedures are often used to perform activities while a function is used to return a value. A procedure can have multiple input and output parameters. To run a procedure, you need to explicitly use the keyword EXEC, and you cannot directly run a procedure in a query. In contrast, Transact-SQL functions can be used within a query. A function can take multiple input parameters but will only return a single output. The function output can be returned to a variable or used by clauses such as FROM and WHERE. Let us start with functions.

7.3.1 Functions

There are two types of functions: built-in functions and user-defined functions.

- Built-in functions are prebuilt in Transact-SQL. These functions cannot be modified by the user.
- User-defined functions are created by database users with the CREATE FUNCTION command. A user-defined function can only return a single value or a table and does not have an output parameter.

The built-in functions were discussed in Chapter 6. In this chapter, our main focus is on user-defined functions.

When a user-defined function returns a single value, it is classified as a **scalar function**. If a user-defined function returns a table, it is called a **table function** or **table-valued function**. A user-defined function can be created by the CREATE FUNCTION statement with the following format:

```
CREATE FUNCTION [owner_name.] function_name
([{@parameter_name [AS] scalar_parameter_data_type[= default]}[,...n]])
```

```
RETURNS scalar_return_data_type
[WITH < function_option> [[,]...n]]
[AS]
BEGIN
        function_body
        RETURN scalar_expression
END
```

7.3.1.1 Scalar Functions

With the CREATE FUNCTION statement, you can create a scalar function that returns a scalar value. The data type of the returned scalar value can be **bigint**, **money**, **sql_variant**, or other data types. The sql_variant data type allows a variable to store values of different data types such as **int**, **decimal**, **char**, **binary**, and **nchar**. As an example, let us create a user-defined function that calculates the total credits earned by a given student. The input parameter is the student id. Based on the input parameter, we will retrieve all the classes taken by the student and then return the sum of the course credits. The code is illustrated in Figure 7.2, which also demonstrates how the function is used in a query.

The function has one input parameter @Sid. The returned data type is sql_variant. The SQL statements are enclosed by the keyword BEGIN and END. In the SQL statement block, we first define a variable @Total and use it to store the returned value from the built-in function SUM, which has the column Credit as the input parameter. The query is used to select the credits earned by the student specified by the input parameter. After the total credits are calculated, the function returns the value stored in @Total. The data type for the variable @Total is INT, which can be accepted by the returned type sql_variant. Figure 7.2 shows that a user-defined function can be used in a SELECT statement.

7.3.1.2 Table Functions

A user-defined function returns a **result set**, which is the result returned from an SQL statement in the function. A result set can be used by a query and is treated as a table. User-defined table

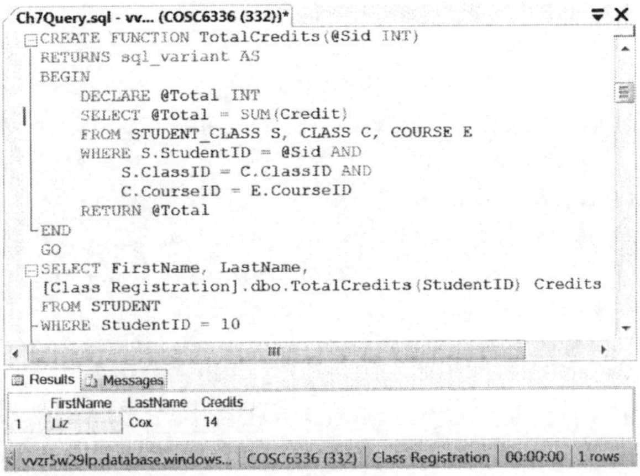
Ch7Query.sql - vv... (COSC6336 (332))*
CREATE FUNCTION TotalCredits(@Sid INT)
RETURNS sql_variant AS
BEGIN
DECLARE @Total INT
SELECT @Total = SUM(Credit)
FROM STUDENT_CLASS S, CLASS C, COURSE E
WHERE S.StudentID = @Sid AND
S.ClassID = C.ClassID AND
C.CourseID = E.CourseID
RETURN @Total
END
GO
SELECT FirstName, LastName,
[Class Registration].dbo.TotalCredits(StudentID) Credits
FROM STUDENT
WHERE StudentID = 10
Results
Messages
FirstName
LastName
Credits
1
Liz
Cox
14
vvzr5w29lp.database.windows...
COSC6336 (332)
Class Registration
00:00:00
1 rows

Figure 7.2 Create and use user-defined scalar function.

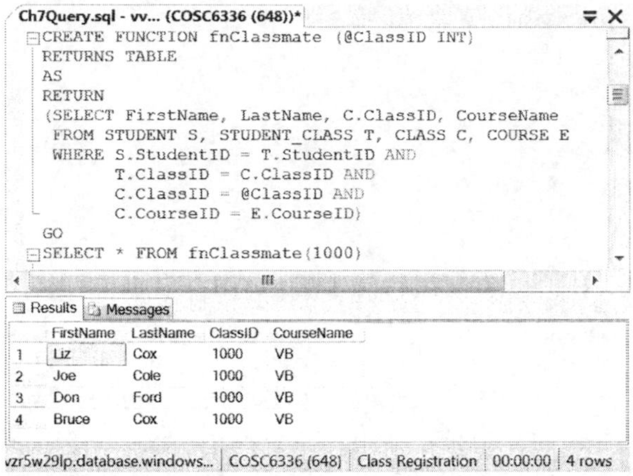
Ch7Query.sql - vv... (COSC6336 (648))*
CREATE FUNCTION fnClassmate (@ClassID INT)
RETURNS TABLE
AS
RETURN
(SELECT FirstName, LastName, C.ClassID, CourseName
FROM STUDENT S, STUDENT_CLASS T, CLASS C, COURSE E
WHERE S.StudentID = T.StudentID AND
T.ClassID = C.ClassID AND
C.ClassID = @ClassID AND
C.CourseID = E.CourseID)
GO
SELECT * FROM fnClassmate(1000)
Results
Messages
FirstName LastName ClassID CourseName
1 Liz Cox 1000 VB
2 Joe Cole 1000 VB
3 Don Ford 1000 VB
4 Bruce Cox 1000 VB
vzr5w29lp.database.windows... COSC6336 (648) Class Registration 00:00:00 4 rows

Figure 7.3 Create and use user-defined inline table function.

functions can be categorized into two types: **inline function** and **multistatement function**. For an inline table function, the returned result set is generated by a single SELECT statement. In a multistatement table function, a TABLE variable is used to store the rows returned from the multiple SELECT statements.

To illustrate the use of inline table functions, let us consider a user-defined table function that returns a result set that contains the information about a group of students who are enrolled in the same class that teaches VB. The function and its application in a query are illustrated in Figure 7.3.

The function fnClassmate returns a table constructed from four tables: STUDENT, STUDENT_CLASS, CLASS, and COURSE. The keyword RETURNS indicates the returned data type is TABLE. There is no need of BREAK…END since there is only one query in the code block. Notice the difference between the keywords RETURNS and RETURN. RETURN is used to exit the function unconditionally after the query is executed. As shown in Figure 7.3, the function is used as a table in the FROM clause.

To illustrate the use of a multistatement function, consider the example that returns information about a given student and his/her classmates. The difference between this example and the previous example is that the function in this example uses a student id as the input parameter. That is, at the beginning, we do not know which class the student is enrolled in. In this function, we need to first query the class information based on the given student id. Then, we will query the classmate information based on the class id selected from the previous SQL statement. A multistatement table function can be used to accomplish this task. The example is displayed in Figure 7.4.

Another difference between an inline function and a multistatement function is that the returned table variable in a multistatement function must be explicitly defined. @INFO is the returned table variable explicitly defined in Figure 7.4. The BEGIN…END keywords enclose two SQL statements. The first one inserts information about a student, his/her class(es), and course(s) into the table variable @INFO based on the input parameter @Sid. The second INSERT statement inserts information about the students and classes based on the class ids inserted by the previous INSERT statement. The condition S.StudentID <> I.StudentID is used to avoid the duplicated row about the student already inserted by first INSERT statement.

To view the result, call the function fnClassmateInfo in a FROM clause shown in Figure 7.5.

Ch7Query.sql - vv... (COSC6336 (648))*

```
CREATE FUNCTION fnClassmateInfo (@Sid INT)
RETURNS @INFO
TABLE(StudentID INT, ClassID INT, CourseName VARCHAR(30))
AS
BEGIN
    INSERT @INFO
    SELECT StudentID, C.ClassID, CourseName
    FROM STUDENT_CLASS S, CLASS C, COURSE E
    WHERE S.StudentID = @Sid AND
          S.ClassID = C.ClassID AND
          C.CourseID = E.CourseID
    INSERT @INFO
    SELECT S.StudentID, C.ClassID, E.CourseName
    FROM @INFO I, STUDENT_CLASS S, CLASS C, COURSE E
    WHERE I.ClassID = S.ClassID AND
          S.StudentID <> I.StudentID AND
          S.ClassID = C.ClassID AND
          C.CourseID = E.CourseID
    RETURN
END
```

Messages

```
Command(s) completed successfully.
```

vvzr5w29lp.database.windows... | COSC6336 (648) | Class Registration | 00:00:00 | 0 rows

Figure 7.4 Create user-defined multistatement table function.

Ch7Query.sql - vv... (COSC6336 (448))

```
SELECT * FROM fnClassmateInfo(10)
```

Results | Messages

	StudentID	ClassID	CourseName
1	10	1000	VB
2	10	1001	Info-Systems
3	10	1002	Database
4	10	1005	E-Commerce
5	11	1000	VB
6	12	1002	Database
7	12	1005	E-Commerce
8	13	1000	VB
9	13	1001	Info-Systems
10	13	1002	Database
11	14	1001	Info-Systems
12	14	1002	Database
13	16	1000	VB
14	16	1001	Info-Systems

5w29lp.database.windows... | COSC6336 (448) | Class_Registration | 00:00:00 | 14 rows

Figure 7.5 Use user-defined multistatement table function.

As shown in Figure 7.5, the student with id 10 enrolled in the classes 1000, 1001, 1002, and 1005. Therefore, all the information about the students in those classes is displayed.

7.3.1.3 APPLY Operator

Sometimes you may want to match the result set returned by a table-valued function to specified rows of another table. For example, you may want to find the classmates for each class listed in the table CLASS. To do so, you can apply the table-valued function fnClassmate against each row in the table CLASS by using the APPLY operator. There are two types of APPLY: CROSS APPLY and OUTER APPLY. CROSS APPLY only returns those rows in the table CLASS that are related to the result set returned by the function fnClassmate. OUTER APPLY returns all rows in the CLASS table, even if a class has no student. NULL will be returned if there is no match from the table-valued

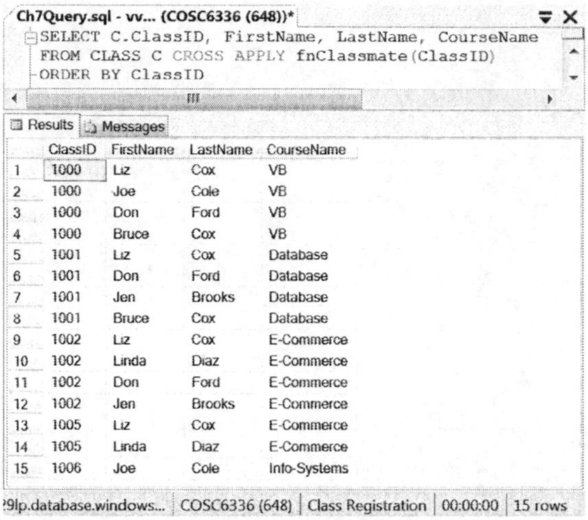

Ch7Query.sql - vv... (COSC6336 (648))*
SELECT C.ClassID, FirstName, LastName, CourseName
FROM CLASS C CROSS APPLY fnClassmate(ClassID)
ORDER BY ClassID
Results
Messages
ClassID FirstName LastName CourseName
1 1000 Liz Cox VB
2 1000 Joe Cole VB
3 1000 Don Ford VB
4 1000 Bruce Cox VB
5 1001 Liz Cox Database
6 1001 Don Ford Database
7 1001 Jen Brooks Database
8 1001 Bruce Cox Database
9 1002 Liz Cox E-Commerce
10 1002 Linda Diaz E-Commerce
11 1002 Don Ford E-Commerce
12 1002 Jen Brooks E-Commerce
13 1005 Liz Cox E-Commerce
14 1005 Linda Diaz E-Commerce
15 1006 Joe Cole Info-Systems
9lp.database.windows... COSC6336 (648) Class Registration 00:00:00 15 rows

Figure 7.6 Use apply operator.

function. As shown in Figure 7.6, the way to use an APPLY operator is similar to the use of a JOIN operator. The function fnClassmate returns the student and course information for each class.

7.3.2 Procedures

Unlike functions, procedures do not explicitly return a value. No keyword RETURN is used in a procedure to return a value. Often, procedures are stored and executed on a database server. This kind of procedure is called a **stored procedure**. Stored procedures play an important role in database management and application due to the following advantages:

- A stored procedure can be shared by multiple database applications, and it can be accessed by many users with proper privileges.
- Since stored procedures are already executable files, they can be called by a database application without reparsing the code. Therefore, using stored procedures can improve database performance.
- Written by experienced programmers and optimized by DBMSs, stored procedures have fewer programming errors and run faster.
- Being installed on servers, stored procedures are better protected by server security measures.
- When a database application calls a stored procedure for a certain activity, only the final computation results are returned to the database application. Therefore, using stored procedures generate less network traffic.

Stored procedures are used to accomplish various tasks. Usually, you can use stored procedures to do the following things:

- Perform database management tasks such as adding a user login.
- Calculate complicated logics requested by a database application.
- Invoke other stored procedures or functions.

- Provide data to database applications.
- Create and submit events to Windows Azure SQL Database for processing.

Stored procedures can be categorized into five different types:

- **System Stored Procedures**: System stored procedures are built-in stored procedures and their names often start with sp_. They are used for database administration, security management, and for providing system data to database applications. You cannot drop the built-in procedures.
- **Local Stored Procedures**: These procedures are created by users and are stored on databases created by the users. They are used to accomplish user-defined database tasks.
- **Temporary Stored Procedures**: As the name indicates, they are temporary local procedures. When the database server is shut down or when the database connection is terminated, they will be deleted.
- **Extended Stored Procedures**: Written in other programming languages such as C, these stored procedures can be compiled as dynamic link library (DLL) files.
- **Remote Stored Procedures**: These procedures can be executed remotely.

7.3.2.1 Creating and Executing Stored Procedures

You can create a procedure with the CREATE PROCEDURE statement in the New Query editor. As an example, let us create a procedure that calculates enrollment. If the number of students enrolled in a given class is less than the classroom capacity, print the number of available seats. Otherwise, print the message 'No seat is available'. Figure 7.7 shows the Transact-SQL statements for creating the procedure.

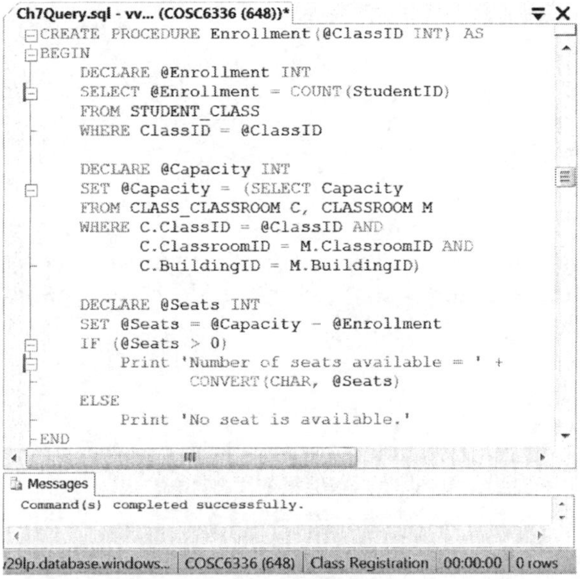

Ch7Query.sql - vv... (COSC6336 (648))*
CREATE PROCEDURE Enrollment(@ClassID INT) AS
BEGIN
DECLARE @Enrollment INT
SELECT @Enrollment = COUNT(StudentID)
FROM STUDENT_CLASS
WHERE ClassID = @ClassID
DECLARE @Capacity INT
SET @Capacity = (SELECT Capacity
FROM CLASS_CLASSROOM C, CLASSROOM M
WHERE C.ClassID = @ClassID AND
C.ClassroomID = M.ClassroomID AND
C.BuildingID = M.BuildingID)
DECLARE @Seats INT
SET @Seats = @Capacity - @Enrollment
IF (@Seats > 0)
Print 'Number of seats available = ' +
CONVERT(CHAR, @Seats)
ELSE
Print 'No seat is available.'
END
Messages
Command(s) completed successfully.
29lp.database.windows... | COSC6336 (648) | Class Registration | 00:00:00 | 0 rows

Figure 7.7 Create procedure with Transact-SQL statements.

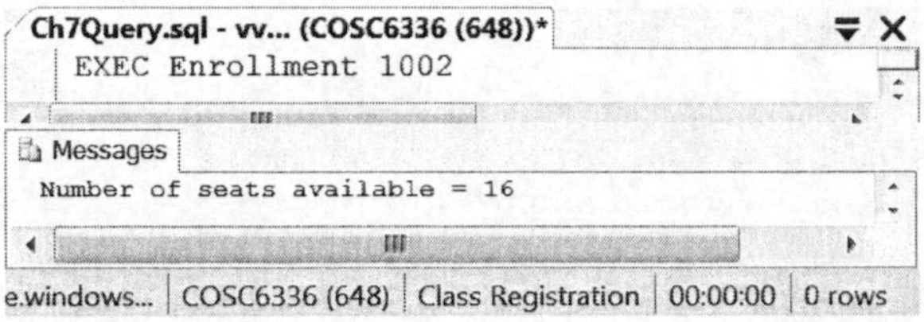

Figure 7.8 Execute procedure.

For a given class id, the first query in the procedure counts the number of students in a class and assigns the number of students to the variable @Enrollment. The second query assigns the capacity of the classroom used for the class to the variable @Capacity. The variable @Seats is declared and assigned the difference between @Capacity and @Enrollment. If the value in @Seats is >0, the number of available seats is printed on the screen. Otherwise, the message 'No seat is available' is printed on the screen. The build-in function CONVERT is used to convert the integer value in the variable @Seats to a string of characters.

To execute a procedure, you need to use the keyword EXEC. Figure 7.8 shows the result of the execution for the stored procedure Enrollment.

7.3.2.2 Modifying and Deleting Stored Procedures

The code in Figure 7.7 can cause a problem. By the department rules, a class may use two classrooms. For example, the VB class uses a classroom for lectures and another classroom for lab work. In such a case, the query in the following code:

```
DECLARE @Capacity INT
        SET @Capacity= (SELECT Capacity
        FROM CLASS_CLASSROOM C, CLASSROOM M
        WHERE C.ClassID=@ClassID AND
                C.ClassroomID=M.ClassroomID AND
                C.BuildingID=M.BuildingID)
```

will select two capacity values that cannot be assigned to the single value variable @Capacity. When passing the ClassID 1000 to the procedure, you will get an error message. You can fix the problem by modifying the procedure with the keyword ALTER as shown in Figure 7.9 where the above code is changed to

```
DECLARE @Capacity INT
        SELECT @Capacity=MIN(Capacity)
        FROM CLASS_CLASSROOM C, CLASSROOM M
        WHERE C.ClassID=@ClassID AND
                C.ClassroomID=M.ClassroomID AND
                C.BuildingID=M.BuildingID
```

in which the built-in function MIN is used to select and return the smallest capacity to the scalar variable @Capacity.

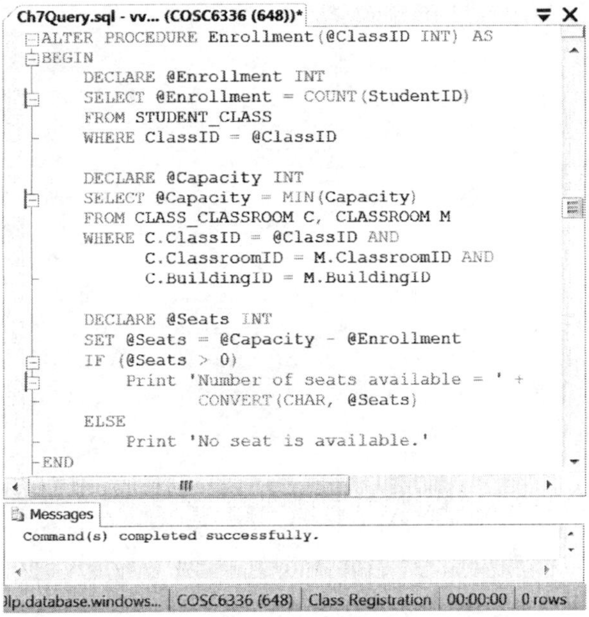

Figure 7.9 Modify procedure.

Execute the procedure again by passing the class id 1000. This time, it should have no error message. The result is shown in Figure 7.10.

If a user-defined procedure is no longer needed, you can delete the procedure with the DROP PROCEDURE statement (Figure 7.11).

In the next section, you will learn a special kind of procedure that does not take input parameters.

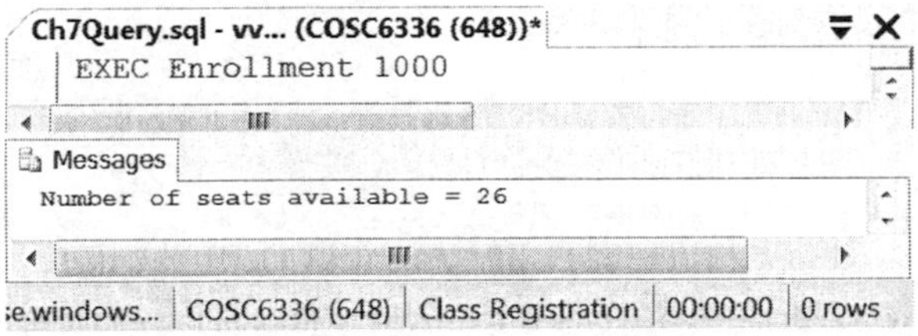

Figure 7.10 Execute procedure with class id 1000.

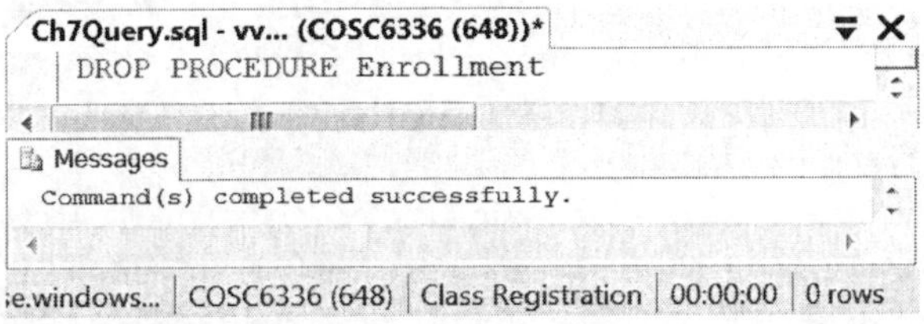

Figure 7.11 Drop procedure.

7.4 Triggers

A special kind of stored procedure is called a **trigger**. When invoked by DML and DDL commands, triggers are executed automatically. The way of executing a trigger is different from that of executing a stored procedure. A trigger can only be fired (executed) when valid data modification events such as INSERT, UPDATE, or DELETE occur, or valid data definition events such as CREATE, ALTER, or DROP occur. Triggers cannot be fired manually.

Triggers are widely used in database maintenance and in implementing database application logic. For example, if the enrollment of a class is small, by the university regulation, the class should be canceled. In this case, you need to remove the class information from the table CLASS and from other related tables in the database Class_Registration. To accomplish this task, you can create a trigger to automatically delete the class from tables such as CLASS, STUDENT_CLASS, and FACULTY_CLASS. Here, triggers play an important role in keeping database integrity. The following are tasks that can be accomplished by triggers:

- When running a database application, implement the application logic dynamically.
- When a change is made in a table, modify related values in other associated tables.
- When an error occurs during a transaction, roll back the transaction.
- When table content is modified by a DML command, display warning messages.
- Before table content is modified, verify if a new data value complies with the integrity constraint in associated tables.
- During the execution of a function or a procedure, invoke external programs.
- Modify the content of a view that is constructed on multiple tables.
- Carry out complex data constraints that may be difficult to implement at the database design stage.
- Respond to events caused by DDL commands such as creating, altering, or dropping a database object.

Triggers are created on a table or view. When creating triggers, you need to keep the following rules in mind:

- A trigger created on one table cannot be recreated on another table with the same name.
- Triggers cannot be created on system tables or temporary tables.
- Triggers do not accept input parameters.
- Too many triggers created on a single table may slow down database performance.
- A trigger can be fired by either DML or DDL commands.

Triggers can be categorized based on the time they are fired and the type of command they respond to. A trigger can be fired either before or after a change is made to a table or view. If a trigger is fired before a change is made, it is called an **INSTEAD OF** trigger. Instead of performing an activity specified by an SQL statement, the INSTEAD OF trigger performs other activities specified by preprogrammed SQL statements in the trigger. For example, a foreign key constraint requires that values in the foreign key must have a corresponding value in the parent key. To delete a value in the parent key, instead of simply deleting the value that may cause an integrity constraint violation, the INSTEAD OF trigger can be used to first delete all the rows with the corresponding foreign key values in the child table. For each table or view, you can only create one INSTEAD OF trigger.

When a trigger is fired after a change is made to an underlying table or view, it is called an **AFTER** trigger. This kind of trigger can be used to enhance the modification done by a DML or DDL command. For example, after a new class is added to the table CLASS, an AFTER trigger should be used to update the class information in related tables such as FACULTY_CLASS and STUDENT_CLASS. Multiple AFTER triggers can be created on a single table. You cannot create AFTER triggers on a view or temporary table. The default trigger type is AFTER.

When a trigger is fired by a DDL command, it is called a **DDL** trigger. DDL triggers are used for auditing and logging. A DDL trigger can be created either on the entire database server or on the current database. A DDL trigger cannot be an INSTEAD OF trigger. You can write a DDL trigger in either Transact-SQL or the programming languages included in .NET.

7.4.1 Creating, Modifying, and Deleting Triggers

You can create a trigger using the New Query editor. The syntax for creating a trigger is given below:

```
CREATE TRIGGER trigger_name
ON associated_table_names or associated_view_names
FOR trigger_types
AS
      Transact-SQL_statement_as_the_trigger_body
```

You may use AFTER or INSTEAD OF to replace FOR. After the keyword AFTER or INSTEAD OF, you can add any combination of INSERT, UPDATE, and DELETE. For example, after a student is added to the STUDENT table, an AFTER trigger can be used to display the time when the enrollment is completed. The definition of the trigger is shown in Figure 7.12. Notice that the built-in function RTRIM is used to trim the empty space on the right-hand side. The built-in function GETDATE is used to return the time when the student is added to the STUDENT table.

To test the trigger RegistrationInfo, let us add a new student Mark Lopez to the STUDENT table. His student id is 15 and his advisor's faculty id is 2. The trigger is fired by the INSERT statement shown in Figure 7.13.

You can use ALTER TRIGGER to modify an existing trigger. For example, suppose that you also want to print the information about the student's advisor, modify the trigger as shown in

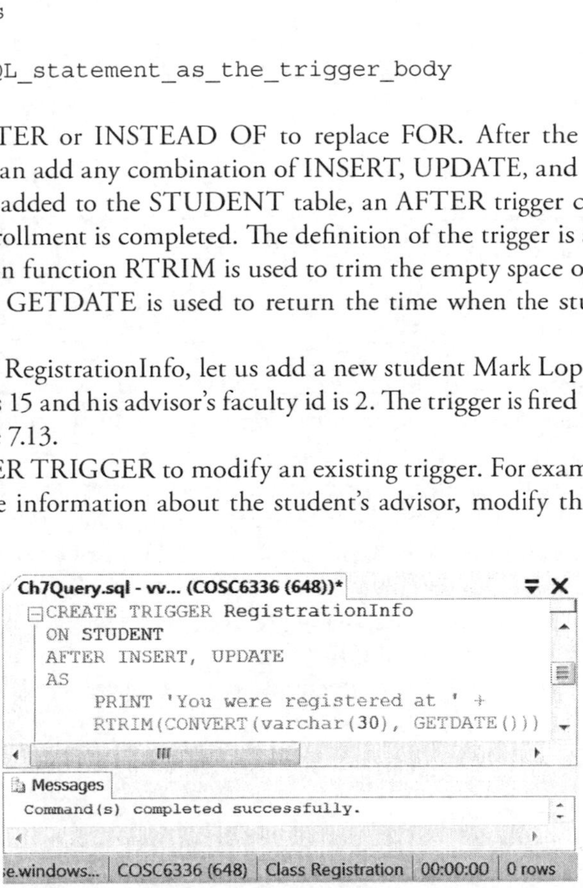
Ch7Query.sql - vv... (COSC6336 (648))*
CREATE TRIGGER RegistrationInfo
ON STUDENT
AFTER INSERT, UPDATE
AS
PRINT 'You were registered at ' +
RTRIM(CONVERT(varchar(30), GETDATE()))
Messages
Command(s) completed successfully.
e.windows...
COSC6336 (648)
Class Registration
00:00:00
0 rows

Figure 7.12 Create trigger.

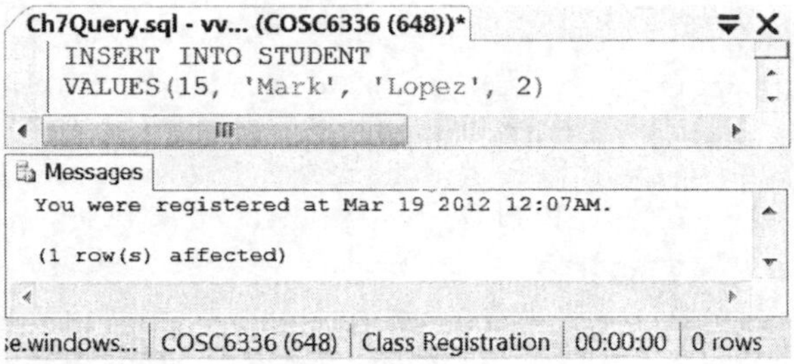
Ch7Query.sql - vv... (COSC6336 (648))*
INSERT INTO STUDENT
VALUES(15, 'Mark', 'Lopez', 2)
Messages
You were registered at Mar 19 2012 12:07AM.
(1 row(s) affected)
e.windows... | COSC6336 (648) | Class Registration | 00:00:00 | 0 rows

Figure 7.13 Test AFTER trigger.

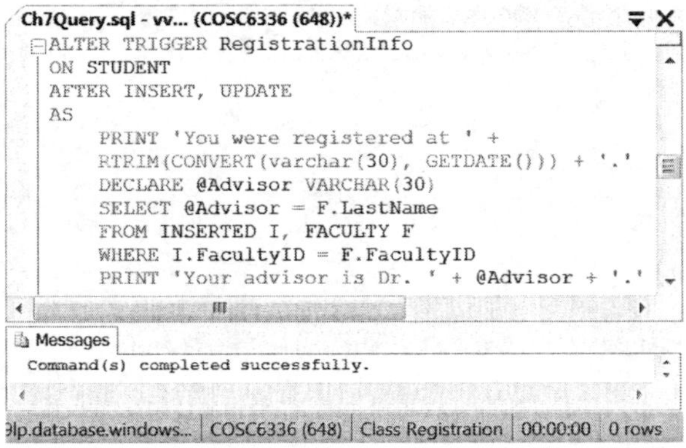
Ch7Query.sql - vv... (COSC6336 (648))*
ALTER TRIGGER RegistrationInfo
ON STUDENT
AFTER INSERT, UPDATE
AS
PRINT 'You were registered at ' +
RTRIM(CONVERT(varchar(30), GETDATE())) + '.'
DECLARE @Advisor VARCHAR(30)
SELECT @Advisor = F.LastName
FROM INSERTED I, FACULTY F
WHERE I.FacultyID = F.FacultyID
PRINT 'Your advisor is Dr. ' + @Advisor + '.'
Messages
Command(s) completed successfully.
lp.database.windows... | COSC6336 (648) | Class Registration | 00:00:00 | 0 rows

Figure 7.14 Modify trigger using ALTER TRIGGER.

Figure 7.14 where a logical table INSERTED is used. When a trigger fires, transactions are logged in the logical tables such as INSERTED or DELETED. These are pseudo tables that can be used for database maintenance and dynamic modification of data values. An insert event will generate the INSERTED logic table that contains the record set that has been inserted. A delete event will generate the DELETED logic table that contains the deleted record set. An update event will generate both the INSERTED and DELETED logic tables that contain the original record set in the DELETED table and the modified record set in the INSERTED table. In this example, we use the FacultyID value to search for the faculty member's last name.

To test the modified trigger, let us register another student Sarah Hudson with FacultyID 2. Figure 7.15 shows the test result of the modified trigger.

You can use the DROP TRIGGER statement to delete a trigger from a database. For example, to delete the RegistrationInfo trigger, use the SQL statement in Figure 7.16.

The syntax for triggers fired by DDL commands is given below:

```
CREATE TRIGGER trigger_name
ON ALL SERVER or DATABASE
AFTER DDL_DATABASE_LEVEL_EVENTS or event_types
AS
      Transact-SQL_statement_as_the_trigger_body or EXTERNAL NAME
```

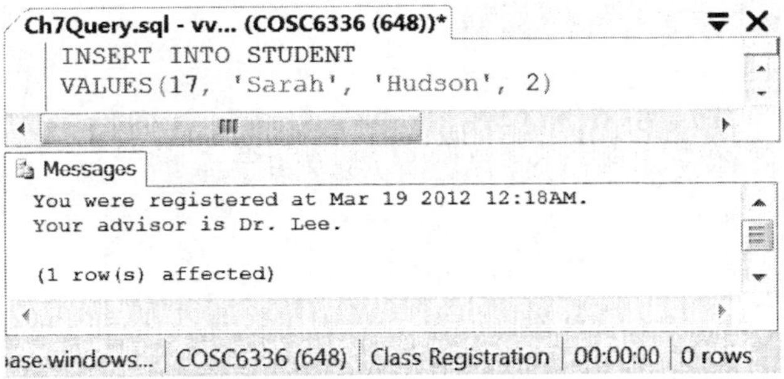

Figure 7.15 Test modified AFTER Trigger.

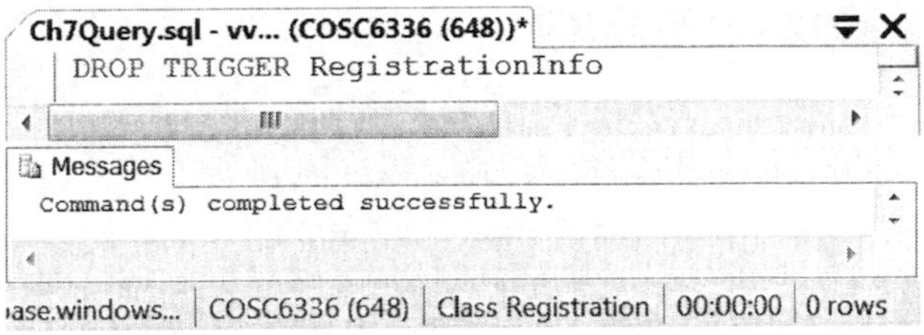

Figure 7.16 Delete trigger using DROP TRIGGER.

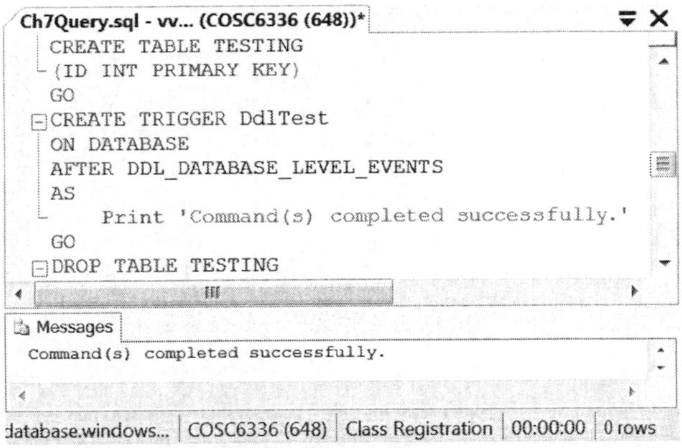

Figure 7.17 Create and test DDL trigger.

In the above syntax, the capital letter words are the actual keywords used in the statement, and lower case words are meanings of the content. To illustrate the use of DDL triggers, we will first create a table TESTING. Then, create a DDL trigger fired by the DROP_TABLE event. The SQL statement DROP TABLE is then used to test the DDL trigger. Figure 7.17 shows how a DDL trigger is created and used with the DDL command DROP TABLE.

7.4.2 Using Triggers

Now, we will discuss how triggers are used in database management and business logic implementation through examples. Triggers will be used to enforce business constraints and implement application logic dynamically to keep database integrity.

7.4.2.1 Validating Business Constraints

Here, we will use a trigger to verify if a student has met the prerequisite requirement before he/she enrolls in a new class. Before a student and class information can be added to the table STUDENT_CLASS, an AFTER trigger is used to query the courses that have been taken by the student and then compare the prerequisite of the course to be taken. If there is a match, add the student and class id to the table STUDENT_CLASS. If not, print the message to inform the student that he/she cannot enroll in the class. The SQL statement below shows the definition of the trigger:

```
CREATE TRIGGER VerifyPrerequisite
ON STUDENT_CLASS AFTER INSERT, UPDATE
AS
IF(('ISC2301' NOT IN (SELECT C.CourseID
                          FROM INSERTED I, CLASS C
                          WHERE I.ClassID=C.ClassID))
AND
      (SELECT CourseID
      FROM (SELECT CourseID
            FROM STUDENT_CLASS T, INSERTED I, CLASS C
            WHERE T.StudentID=I.StudentID AND
                  T.ClassID=C.ClassID) W
      WHERE NOT EXISTS (
            SELECT Prerequisite
            FROM CLASS C, INSERTED I, COURSE_PREREQUISITE P
            WHERE C.ClassID=I.ClassID AND
                  C.CourseID=W.CourseID AND
                  W.CourseID=P.CourseID)
      ) IS NULL)
BEGIN
      PRINT 'The prerequisite is not fulfilled.'
      ROLLBACK
END
```

In the above code, an IF structure is used to verify if a student has met the required prerequisite. If a student is enrolled in the class that teaches ISC2301, which has no prerequisite, the trigger will not do anything. Otherwise, the condition after AND in the IF structure will verify if the prerequisite courses have been taken. To accomplish this task, we use the NOT EXISTS operator to match the set of courses taken by the student with the set of prerequisite courses. The subquery in the FROM clause selects all the courses taken by the student. The subquery in the NOT EXISTS operator selects all prerequisite courses of the course specified by the class id and stored in the INSERTED table. If the intersection of the record sets selected by the above two subqueries is empty, it means that none of the courses taken by the student matches the prerequisite, the message 'The prerequisite is not fulfilled.' is printed on the screen, and the insert transaction

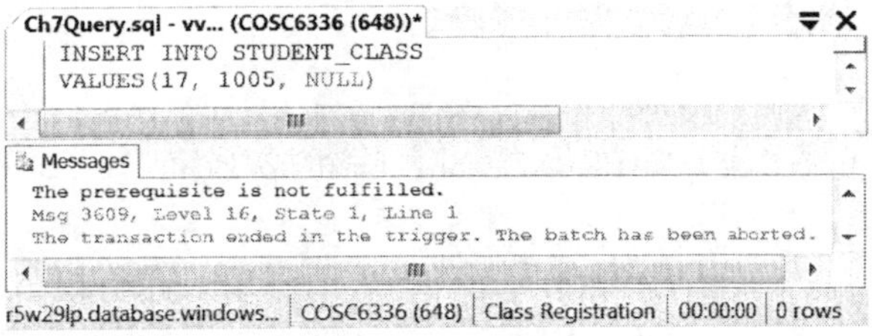
Ch7Query.sql - vv... (COSC6336 (648))*
INSERT INTO STUDENT_CLASS
VALUES(17, 1005, NULL)
Messages
The prerequisite is not fulfilled.
Msg 3609, Level 16, State 1, Line 1
The transaction ended in the trigger. The batch has been aborted.
r5w29lp.database.windows... COSC6336 (648) Class Registration 00:00:00 0 rows

Figure 7.18 Test constraint trigger.

is rolled back. To verify if the trigger works, run the code in Figure 7.18. Since the student with the id 18 has not taken the prerequisite for the course ISC4301 specified by the class id 1005, the insert operation is rolled back.

7.4.2.2 Implementing Dynamic Application Logic

Here, we will create a trigger to calculate the cumulative GPA whenever a student and his/her class information is inserted or updated in the table STUDENT_CLASS. In this trigger, we will assign the A grade the number 4.0, B grade the number 3.0, C grade the number 2.0, D grade the number 1.0, and F grade the number 0.0. Then, the trigger will calculate the average for all the classes completed by the student. The calculation result will be displayed on the screen. The code to implement this application logic is given below:

```
CREATE TRIGGER CalculateGPA
ON STUDENT_CLASS AFTER INSERT, UPDATE
AS
BEGIN
     SELECT S.StudentId, AVG(CASE S.Grade
     WHEN 'A' THEN 4.0
     WHEN 'B' THEN 3.0
     WHEN 'C' THEN 2.0
     WHEN 'D' THEN 1.0
     WHEN 'F' THEN 0.0
     WHEN NULL THEN 0.0 END) [Cumulative GPA]
     FROM STUDENT_CLASS S, INSERTED I
     GROUP BY S.StudentID, I.StudentID
     HAVING S.StudentID = I.StudentID
END
```

In the above code, an AFTER trigger is created on the table STUDENT_CLASS. The built-in function AVG is used to calculate the cumulative GPA. The function AVG takes the result returned by a CASE operator as the input parameter. The CASE operator is used to convert letter grades to decimal numbers. Because the aggregate function AVG is in the SELECT clause with the column StudentID, GROUP BY is used to match the GPA of each student. The HAVING clause is used to match the student id in the STUDENT_CLASS table with the student id just inserted. To test the trigger, run the UPDATE statement given in Figure 7.19.

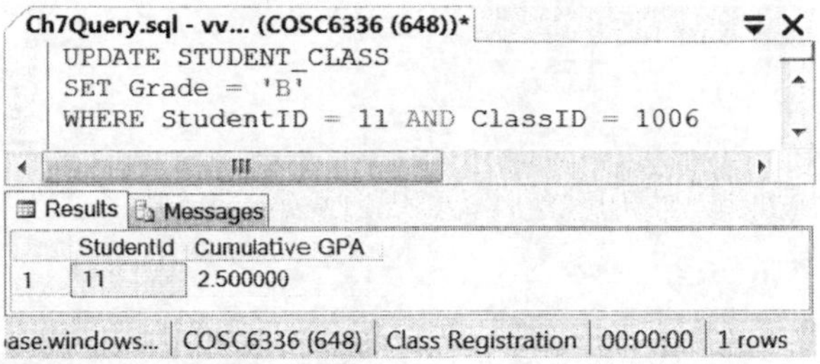

Figure 7.19 Test trigger implementing dynamic logic.

In the SQL statement in Figure 7.19, the grade in the class with the id 1006 taken by the student with the id 11 was changed from NULL to B. After the change, the student's cumulative GPA is 2.5.

7.4.2.3 Keeping Database Integrity

Another important application of triggers is to ensure that referential integrity is kept after data have been inserted, deleted, or updated. As an example, let us consider the following situation. By the university regulation, if the enrollment of a class is small, the class should be canceled. In this case, you need to remove the class information from the table CLASS and other related tables in the database Class_Registration. When deleting a class from the table CLASS, an INSTEAD OF trigger will be used to remove the rows referencing the deleted class from other related tables CLASS_CLASSROOM, STUDENT_CLASS, and FACULTY_CLASS. The SQL statement below creates the trigger called KeepIntegrity to accomplish this task:

```
CREATE TRIGGER KeepIntegrity
ON CLASS
INSTEAD OF DELETE AS
BEGIN
      DELETE STUDENT_CLASS
      WHERE ClassID IN (SELECT ClassID FROM DELETED)
      DELETE FACULTY_CLASS
      WHERE ClassID IN (SELECT ClassID FROM DELETED)
      DELETE CLASS_CLASSROOM
      WHERE ClassID IN (SELECT ClassID FROM DELETED)
      DELETE CLASS
      WHERE ClassID IN (SELECT ClassID FROM DELETED)
END
```

Instead of deleting the class in the table CLASS, which may cause an error on violating the referential constraints, the above trigger first deletes those rows in the tables STUDENT_CLASS, FACULTY_CLASS, and CLASS_CLASSROOM, which are referencing the ClassID values stored in the table DELETED and then deletes the corresponding row in the table CLASS.

To test the trigger, let us delete the classes that have no student enrolled in them. The DELETE statement in Figure 7.20 can accomplish this task.

In the subquery, a RIGHT JOIN operator is used to make sure that the classes with no student are included so that the HAVING clause can identify these classes. Without RIGHT

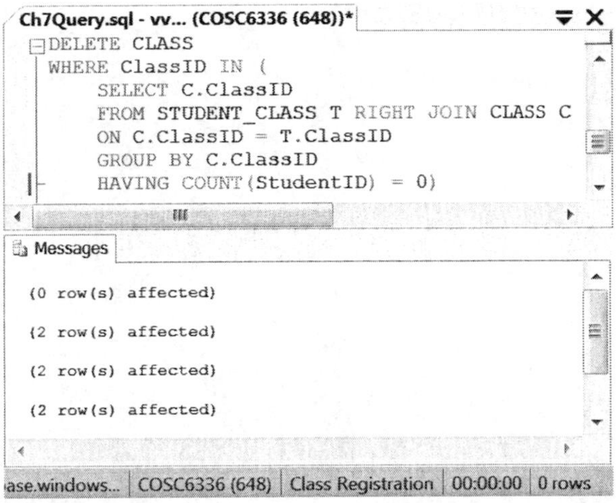
Ch7Query.sql - vv... (COSC6336 (648))*
DELETE CLASS
WHERE ClassID IN (
SELECT C.ClassID
FROM STUDENT_CLASS T RIGHT JOIN CLASS C
ON C.ClassID = T.ClassID
GROUP BY C.ClassID
HAVING COUNT(StudentID) = 0)
Messages
(0 row(s) affected)
(2 row(s) affected)
(2 row(s) affected)
(2 row(s) affected)
ase.windows... COSC6336 (648) Class Registration 00:00:00 0 rows

Figure 7.20 Test trigger KeepIntegrity.

JOIN, only classes with students will be selected. As shown in Figure 7.20, no row is deleted from STUDENT_CLASS since each class has at least one student.

ACTIVITY 7.1 FUNCTIONS, STORED PROCEDURES, AND TRIGGERS

Transact-SQL provided by Windows Azure SQL Database has some procedural programming components such as variables, user-defined functions, and flow-control structures. The following lab activity will show you how to create and use functions, procedures, and triggers.

TASK 1: CONNECT TO WINDOWS AZURE SQL DATABASE

Use the following steps to open the Windows Azure SQL Database Management Portal:

1. On your local computer, log on to Windows Azure through the URL: https://*yourserver*.database.windows.net
   where yourserver is your SQL Database server name.
2. Enter the database name **Class_Registration**. Then, enter your user name and password to log on to Windows Azure SQL Database.
3. Once you have logged on, click the **New Query** icon at the upper-left corner of your screen.

TASK 2: USER-DEFINED TABLE FUNCTIONS

There are two types of table-valued functions, **inline function** and **multistatement function**. The following steps demonstrate how to create a multistatement function:

1. To illustrate the use of multistatement function, consider the case where, for a given student, we first insert the student's information such as the student id, last name,

and class id. Then, based on the inserted student id, the function finds the student's classmates in each class he/she is enrolled. Enter the following code in **New Query**.

```
CREATE FUNCTION fn_StudentInfo (@Sid int)
RETURNS @INFO TABLE (StudentID int, LastName char(20) NOT NULL,
ClassID int)
AS
BEGIN
 INSERT @INFO
  SELECT S.StudentID, S.LastName, C.ClassID
  FROM STUDENT S, CLASS C, STUDENT_CLASS T
  WHERE S.StudentID=@Sid AND S.StudentID=T.StudentID
  AND T.ClassID=C.ClassID
 INSERT @INFO
  SELECT S.StudentID, S.LastName, C.ClassID
  FROM STUDENT S, @INFO I, CLASS C, STUDENT_CLASS T
  WHERE I.ClassID=C.ClassID AND T.ClassID=C.ClassID AND
        T.StudentID=S.StudentID AND S.StudentID <> @Sid
 RETURN
END
```

2. Highlight the code and click **Run**. As shown in Figure 7.21, the function fn_StudentInfo is successfully created.
3. To see how the function works, enter the following SQL statement:

```
SELECT * FROM fn_StudentInfo(11)
```

Highlight the code and click **Run**. Figure 7.22 shows that the function returns the last names and ids of the students who are the classmates of the student with the id 11.

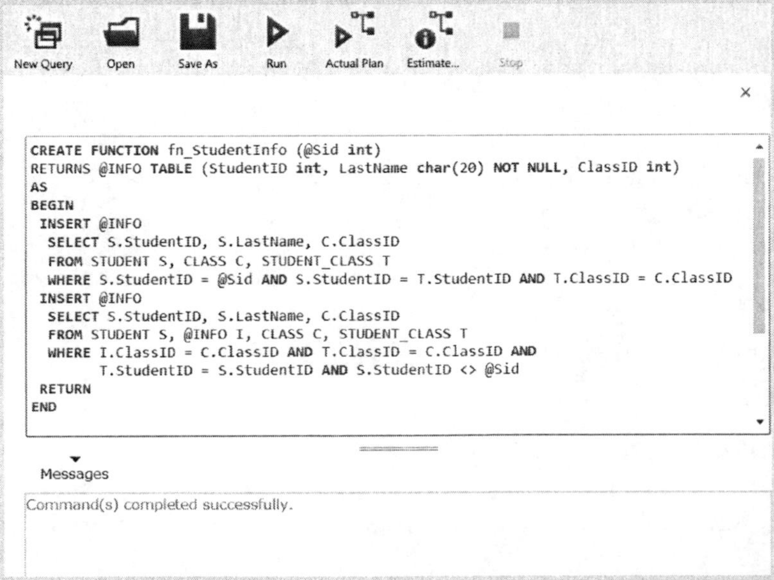
New Query
Open
Save As
Run
Actual Plan
Estimate...
Stop
CREATE FUNCTION fn_StudentInfo (@Sid int)
RETURNS @INFO TABLE (StudentID int, LastName char(20) NOT NULL, ClassID int)
AS
BEGIN
INSERT @INFO
SELECT S.StudentID, S.LastName, C.ClassID
FROM STUDENT S, CLASS C, STUDENT_CLASS T
WHERE S.StudentID = @Sid AND S.StudentID = T.StudentID AND T.ClassID = C.ClassID
INSERT @INFO
SELECT S.StudentID, S.LastName, C.ClassID
FROM STUDENT S, @INFO I, CLASS C, STUDENT_CLASS T
WHERE I.ClassID = C.ClassID AND T.ClassID = C.ClassID AND
T.StudentID = S.StudentID AND S.StudentID <> @Sid
RETURN
END
Messages
Command(s) completed successfully.

Figure 7.21 Function fn_StudentInfo.

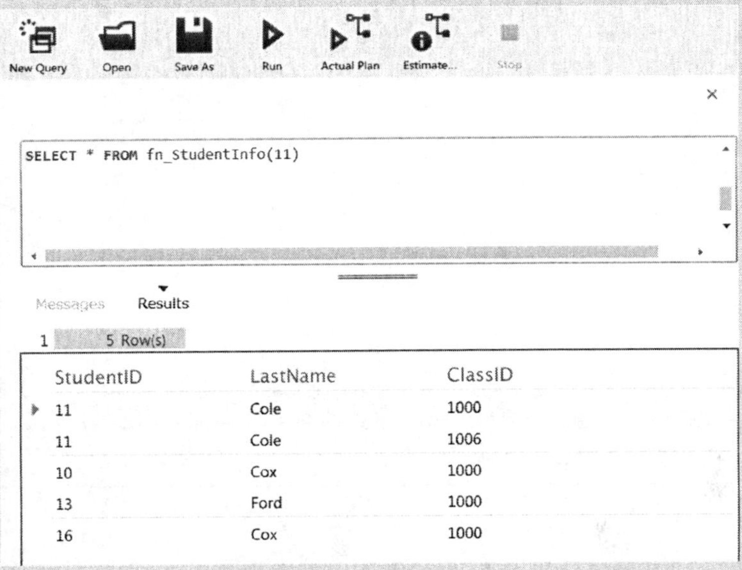

Figure 7.22 Execute function fn_StudentInfo.

TASK 3: CREATE, MODIFY, AND EXECUTE STORED PROCEDURES

To create a stored procedure, you can execute the CREATE PROCEDURE statement in New Query.

1. Enter the SQL statements below in the New Query editor:

```
CREATE PROCEDURE Grade_Change (@Sid INT, @Grade char, @ClassID
INT) AS
        UPDATE STUDENT_CLASS
        SET Grade = @Grade
        WHERE StudentID = @Sid AND ClassID = @ClassID
```

2. Highlight the code and click **Run**. As shown in Figure 7.23, the procedure Grade_Change is successfully created.
3. To modify a stored procedure, use the steps below. Type the following code in the New Query editor:

```
ALTER PROCEDURE Grade_Change (@Sid INT, @Grade char, @ClassID
INT) AS
        UPDATE [Class_Registration].[dbo].[STUDENT_CLASS]
        SET Grade = @Grade
        WHERE StudentID = @Sid AND ClassID = @ClassID
        PRINT 'The grade is changed.'
```

4. Highlight the code and click **Run**. As shown in Figure 7.24, the procedure Grade_Change is successfully altered.

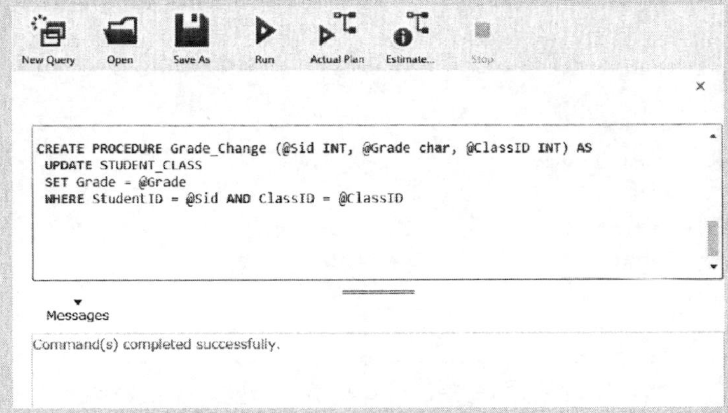
New Query
Open
Save As
Run
Actual Plan
Estimate...
Stop
CREATE PROCEDURE Grade_Change (@Sid INT, @Grade char, @ClassID INT) AS
UPDATE STUDENT_CLASS
SET Grade = @Grade
WHERE StudentID = @Sid AND ClassID = @ClassID
Messages
Command(s) completed successfully.

Figure 7.23 Create stored procedure.

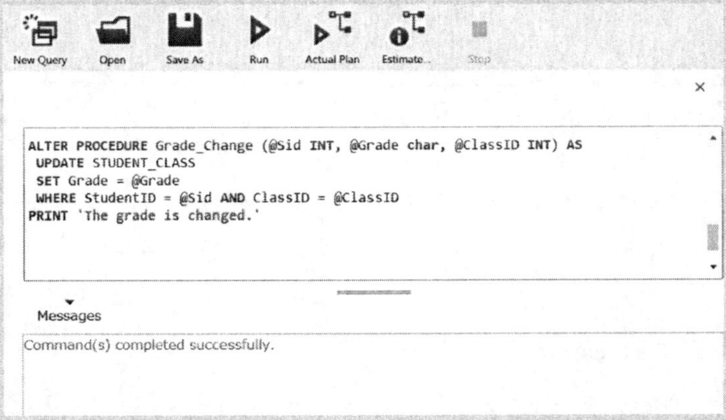
New Query
Open
Save As
Run
Actual Plan
Estimate...
Stop
ALTER PROCEDURE Grade_Change (@Sid INT, @Grade char, @ClassID INT) AS
UPDATE STUDENT_CLASS
SET Grade = @Grade
WHERE StudentID = @Sid AND ClassID = @ClassID
PRINT 'The grade is changed.'
Messages
Command(s) completed successfully.

Figure 7.24 Alter stored procedure.

5. In the New Query pane, enter and execute the code for the trigger **VerifyPrerequisite** and **CalculateGPA** given in the Application of Triggers section. Then, enter the following SQL code in the New Query editor to execute the procedure Grade_Change. Notice that before the execution of the procedure, the triggers on the table STUDENT_CLASS are disabled because they may block the execution of the procedure. The triggers can be enabled after the procedure is executed.

```
ALTER TABLE STUDENT_CLASS DISABLE TRIGGER VerifyPrerequisite,
CalculateGPA
GO
EXEC Grade_Change 10, 'A', 1005
```

6. Highlight the code and click **Run.** As shown in Figure 7.25, the message indicates that the grade is changed for the class with the id 1005 taken by the student with id 10.

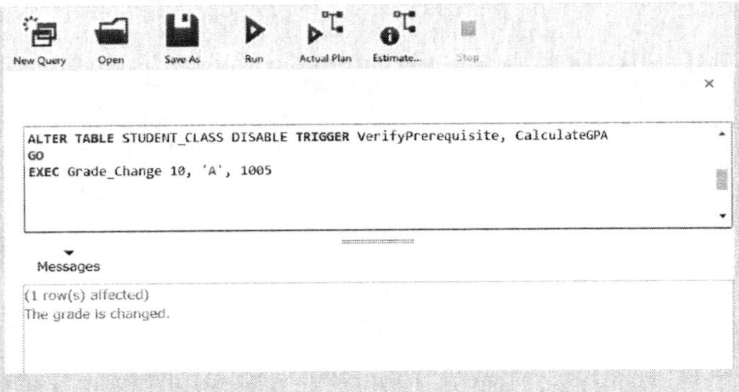
New Query
Open
Save As
Run
Actual Plan
Estimate...
ALTER TABLE STUDENT_CLASS DISABLE TRIGGER VerifyPrerequisite, CalculateGPA
GO
EXEC Grade_Change 10, 'A', 1005
Messages
(1 row(s) affected)
The grade is changed.

Figure 7.25 Execute stored procedure.

TASK 4: CREATE AND TEST TRIGGERS

You can create a trigger in the New Query editor. For example, after a student is added or updated to the STUDENT table, we want to print out an acknowledgment message to display the completing time of the enrollment.

1. Assume that the Windows Azure SQL Database Management Portal is still open. Enter the following SQL code in the New Query editor:

```
CREATE TRIGGER Registration_Info
ON STUDENT
AFTER INSERT, UPDATE
AS
   PRINT 'The student is added at'+
   RTRIM(CONVERT(varchar(30), GETDATE())) + '.'
```

2. Highlight the code and click **Run**. As shown in Figure 7.26, the trigger Registration_Info is successfully created.

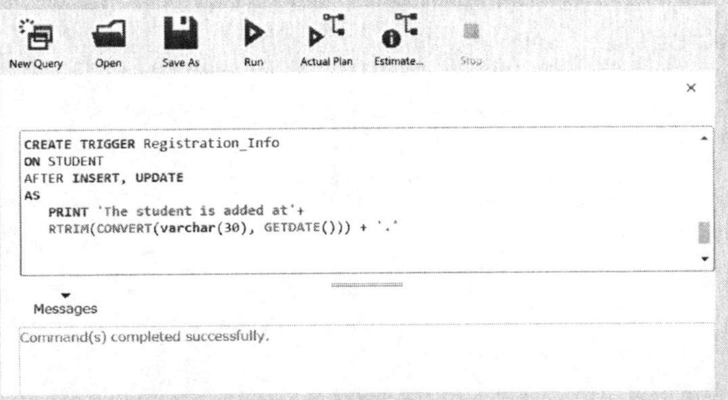
New Query
Open
Save As
Run
Actual Plan
Estimate...
CREATE TRIGGER Registration_Info
ON STUDENT
AFTER INSERT, UPDATE
AS
PRINT 'The student is added at'+
RTRIM(CONVERT(varchar(30), GETDATE())) + '.'
Messages
Command(s) completed successfully.

Figure 7.26 Create trigger.

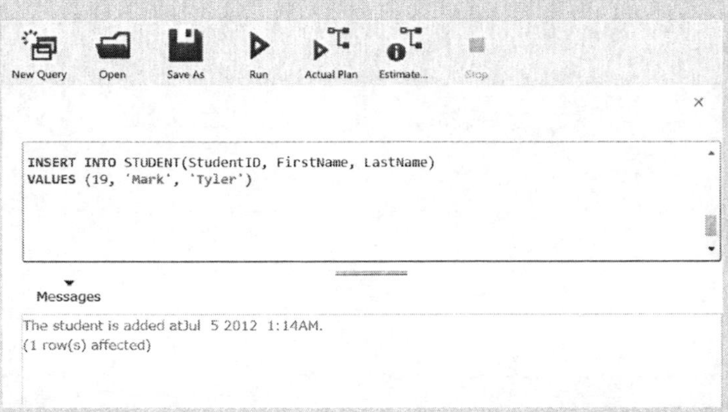
New Query
Open
Save As
Run
Actual Plan
Estimate...
Stop
INSERT INTO STUDENT(StudentID, FirstName, LastName)
VALUES (19, 'Mark', 'Tyler')
Messages
The student is added atJul 5 2012 1:14AM.
(1 row(s) affected)

Figure 7.27 Message sent by trigger.

3. To test the trigger we have just created, we add a new student to the STUDENT table with the student id 19, and the name Mark Tyler with the following SQL statement:

```
INSERT INTO STUDENT(StudentID, FirstName, LastName)
VALUES (19, 'Mark', 'Tyler')
```

4. Highlight the code and click **Run**. As shown in Figure 7.27, the trigger Registration_Info returns a message to indicate that the student is added. However, as seen in the message, it needs a space between the words **at** and **Jul**.
5. You can use the ALTER TRIGGER statement to modify the existing trigger. To add a space between **at** and **Jul** in the message, use the following statement:

```
ALTER TRIGGER registration_info
ON STUDENT
AFTER INSERT, UPDATE
AS
   PRINT 'The student is added at ' +
         RTRIM(CONVERT(varchar(30), GETDATE())) + '.'
```

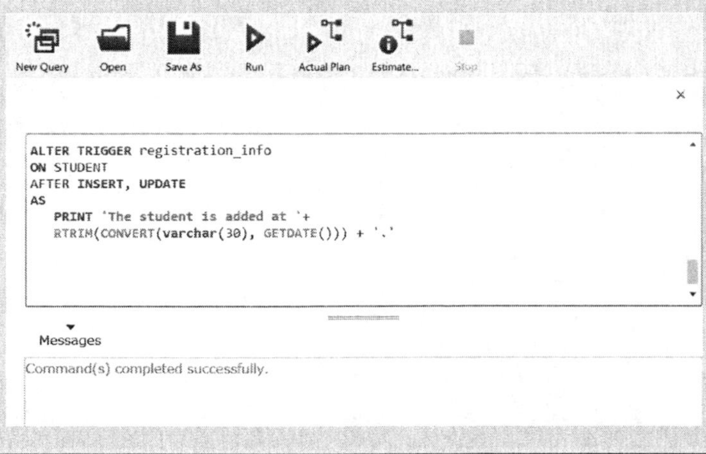
New Query
Open
Save As
Run
Actual Plan
Estimate...
Stop
ALTER TRIGGER registration_info
ON STUDENT
AFTER INSERT, UPDATE
AS
PRINT 'The student is added at '+
RTRIM(CONVERT(varchar(30), GETDATE())) + '.'
Messages
Command(s) completed successfully.

Figure 7.28 Alter trigger.

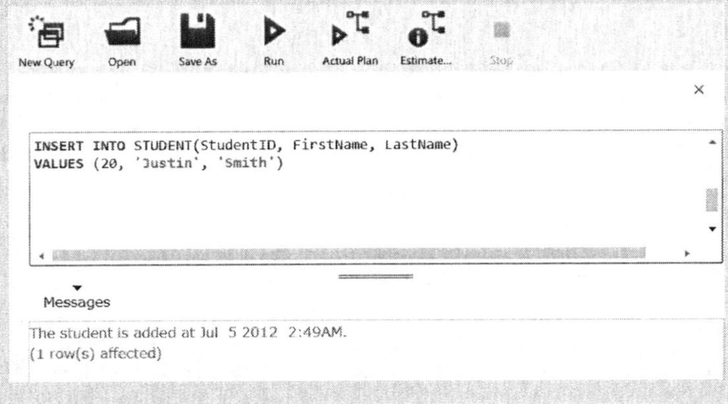

Figure 7.29 Updated message from trigger.

6. Highlight the code and click **Run**. As shown in Figure 7.28, the trigger Registration_Info is successfully altered.
7. Insert another student with the following SQL statement. As shown in Figure 7.29, the message has the added space between the words **at** and **Jul**.

To illustrate the use of the logic tables INSERTED and DELETED, consider the following tasks:

TASK 5: VERIFY DATABASE INTEGRITY

In this task, suppose that you want to insert or update the table STUDENT_CLASS. After STUDENT_CLASS is updated, a trigger Class_Checking is created to check if a class inserted to the table STUDENT_CLASS exists in the table CLASS.

1. To create the trigger Class_Checking, enter the following SQL code in the New Query editor:

```
CREATE TRIGGER Class_Checking
ON STUDENT_CLASS INSTEAD OF INSERT, UPDATE
AS
   SET NOCOUNT ON
   IF ((SELECT COUNT(C.ClassID)
        FROM INSERTED I, CLASS C
        WHERE C.ClassID=I.ClassID)=0)
     BEGIN
        PRINT 'Note: The class does not exist. No change!'
        ROLLBACK
     END
ELSE
     INSERT STUDENT_CLASS
     SELECT * FROM INSERTED
```

2. Highlight the code and click **Run**. As shown in Figure 7.30, the trigger Class_Checking is successfully created.

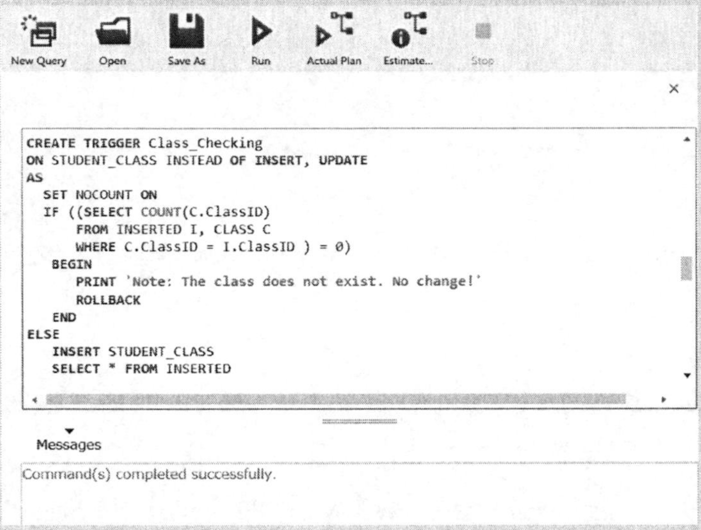
New Query
Open
Save As
Run
Actual Plan
Estimate...
Stop
CREATE TRIGGER Class_Checking
ON STUDENT_CLASS INSTEAD OF INSERT, UPDATE
AS
SET NOCOUNT ON
IF ((SELECT COUNT(C.ClassID)
FROM INSERTED I, CLASS C
WHERE C.ClassID = I.ClassID) = 0)
BEGIN
PRINT 'Note: The class does not exist. No change!'
ROLLBACK
END
ELSE
INSERT STUDENT_CLASS
SELECT * FROM INSERTED
Messages
Command(s) completed successfully.

Figure 7.30 Create trigger Class_Checking.

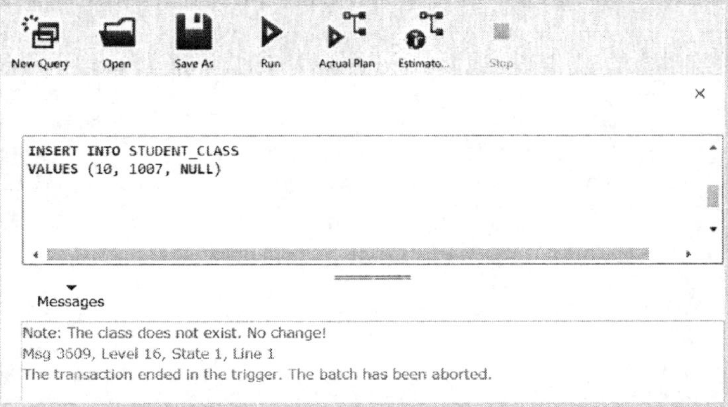
New Query
Open
Save As
Run
Actual Plan
Estimate...
Stop
INSERT INTO STUDENT_CLASS
VALUES (10, 1007, NULL)
Messages
Note: The class does not exist. No change!
Msg 3609, Level 16, State 1, Line 1
The transaction ended in the trigger. The batch has been aborted.

Figure 7.31 Prevent unlisted class from being entered.

3. To verify that the trigger prevents a class not listed in table CLASS from being entered in the table STUDENT_CLASS, enter the following SQL statement to insert the class 1007 for the student with the id 10:

```
INSERT INTO STUDENT_CLASS
VALUES (10, 1007, NULL)
```

4. Highlight the code and click **Run**. As shown in Figure 7.31, the trigger Class_Checking prevents the class 1007 from being entered to the STUDENT_CLASS table because it is not listed in the CLASS table.
5. In contrast, if a class does exist in the CLASS table, the trigger will allow it to be inserted to the STUDENT_CLASS table (Figure 7.32).

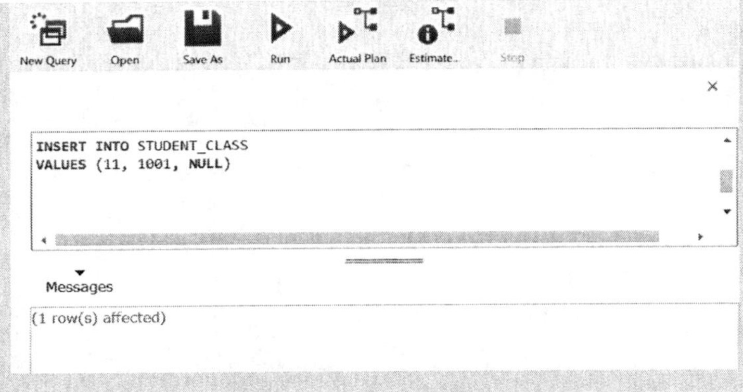

Figure 7.32 Enter class listed in CLASS table.

TASK 6: VALIDATE BUSINESS CONSTRAINTS

Triggers are used to ensure that business constraints are met. Assume that the university requires a student to get approval from his or her advisor if the student decides to withdraw all his/her classes taken in one semester. In the next example, a trigger is used to prevent the database from deleting the last class before getting the approval.

1. To create the trigger Drop_Class, enter the following SQL code in the New Query editor:

```
CREATE TRIGGER Drop_Class
ON STUDENT_CLASS AFTER DELETE
AS
DECLARE @ClassCount As INT
BEGIN
   SELECT @ClassCount = Count(*)
      FROM STUDENT_CLASS S, DELETED D
      WHERE D.StudentID = S.StudentID
   IF (@ClassCount = 0)
   BEGIN
      PRINT 'Need approval to drop the last class.'
      ROLLBACK
   END
END
```

2. Highlight the code and click **Run**. As shown in Figure 7.33, the trigger Drop_Class is successfully created.
3. To verify that the trigger prevents a student from dropping all the classes before getting approval, enter the following SQL statement to delete all classes for the student with the id 12:

```
DELETE STUDENT_CLASS
WHERE StudentID = 12
```

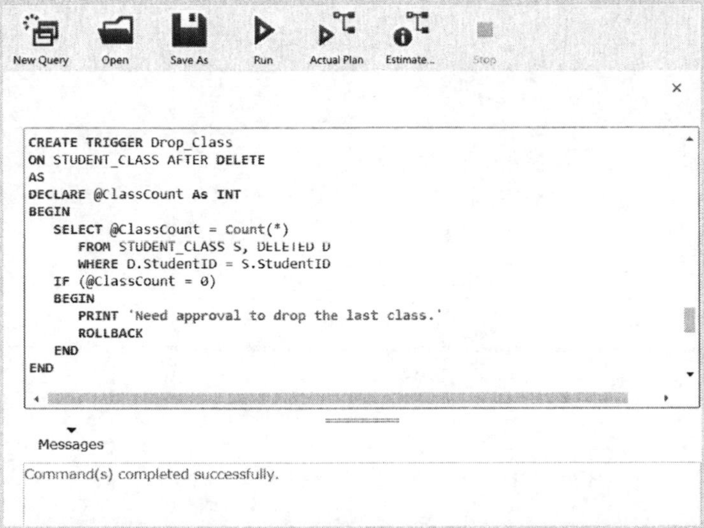
New Query
Open
Save As
Run
Actual Plan
Estimate...
Stop
CREATE TRIGGER Drop_Class
ON STUDENT_CLASS AFTER DELETE
AS
DECLARE @ClassCount As INT
BEGIN
SELECT @ClassCount = Count(*)
FROM STUDENT_CLASS S, DELETED D
WHERE D.StudentID = S.StudentID
IF (@ClassCount = 0)
BEGIN
PRINT 'Need approval to drop the last class.'
ROLLBACK
END
END
Messages
Command(s) completed successfully.

Figure 7.33 Create Drop_Class trigger.

4. Highlight the code and click **Run**. As shown in Figure 7.34, the trigger Drop_Class prevents the student with the id 12 from withdrawing all the classes without approval.

In this hands-on activity, six tasks are carried out to demonstrate how to create, use, and manage user-defined functions, stored procedures, and triggers. You have also learned how to use the logical tables INSERTED and DELETED to implement INSTEAD OF and AFTER triggers.

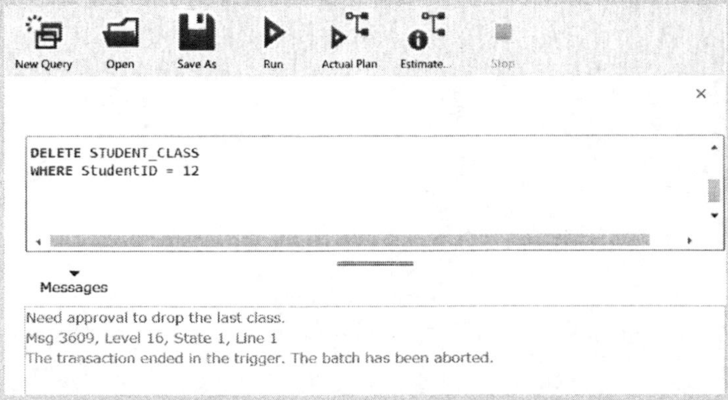
New Query
Open
Save As
Run
Actual Plan
Estimate...
Stop
DELETE STUDENT_CLASS
WHERE StudentID = 12
Messages
Need approval to drop the last class.
Msg 3609, Level 16, State 1, Line 1
The transaction ended in the trigger. The batch has been aborted.

Figure 7.34 Test Drop_Class trigger.

7.5 Summary

In this chapter, you have learned some programming extensions. You have used Transact-SQL to create, execute, and test functions, stored procedures, and triggers. Examples were used to illustrate how to declare and use variables, and use flow-control structures. In this chapter, the advantages of stored procedures and triggers have been discussed in detail. Through hands-on practice, you have learned to create, execute, and test stored procedures and triggers. To further understand the importance of triggers, you have developed various trigger applications in database maintenance and implementation of business logic. There is much more to Transact-SQL. In the next chapter, we will discuss the concepts and applications of some other important database objects such as View, Index, and Cursor.

Review Questions

1. Why do we need variables in SQL code?
2. Why do we need flow-control structures in SQL code?
3. Name eight flow-control structures and describe how to use them.
4. State the difference between a function and a procedure.
5. What types of data can the sql_variant hold?
6. Create a user-defined function that updates the capacity of a classroom on a given new capacity. Use an UPDATE clause to demonstrate the usage of your function. Run your SQL statements in Windows Azure SQL Database.
7. Create a user-defined function that calculates the total classroom capacity for the East building. Use an UPDATE clause to demonstrate the usage of your function. Run your SQL statements in Windows Azure SQL Database.
8. Describe table-valued user-defined functions.
9. For a given student id, create an inline table function to return a course taken by the student. Use a SELECT statement to show the result. Run your SQL statements in Windows Azure SQL Database.
10. What are the advantages of a stored procedure?
11. How is a stored procedure used?
12. Where can a trigger be used?
13. What do we need to be careful about when using a trigger?
14. How can an INSTEAD OF trigger be used? Give an example.
15. What are the tasks that an AFTER trigger can accomplish?
16. What is the default trigger type?
17. How can a trigger be executed?
18. Explain what the logical tables INSERTED and DELETED do.
19. Create an AFTER trigger on the CLASSROOM table. The trigger will display a message to indicate that a new classroom is added. Use an INSERT statement to demonstrate the use of the trigger. Run your SQL statements in Windows Azure SQL Database.
20. Create an INSTEAD OF trigger to verify if the building code is correct when adding a new classroom to the table CLASSROOM. Use an INSERT statement to demonstrate the use of the trigger. Run your SQL statements in Windows Azure SQL Database.

Chapter 8

Windows Azure SQL Database Views, Indexes, and Federations

Objectives

- Develop views for database applications
- Create and manage indexes
- Work with federations

8.1 Introduction

After a database is created, the next step is to develop database applications such as forms and reports. Database applications are used to display and manage the data extracted from various data sources such as databases or spreadsheets. In the previous chapter, several SQL programming units such as functions, procedures, and triggers are introduced. These programming units in general include multiple SQL statements to accomplish tasks such as extracting information from databases, managing database objects, and dynamically responding to certain events. In this chapter, more database SQL programming units such as views, indexes, and federations will be introduced. These SQL programming units are used for improving the performance and scalability.

Often, a database application extracts data from databases, displays data for front-end users, or saves new data or modified data back to the databases. For many interaction-intensive applications, using tables directly will generate frequent table searching and updating that hold back database performance. It is also not secure to allow the front-end users to directly access a database through a database application. The SQL programming unit, **view**, can be developed to improve the database performance by precollecting the data needed for a database application. A view can be used to carry out calculations, which significantly reduce the database performance if they are done on tables. If database applications directly communicate with views, not tables, this will improve performance and security.

Index is another database object used to improve database performance. Like an index at the end of a book, indexes are created on tables or views to improve data search performance. Besides improving search performance, indexes are also used for sorting rows in a table and enforcing uniqueness.

When multiple database applications try to access the same database object, the performance can be significantly reduced. A solution to the overload problem is to divide a database object into multiple parts and distribute the parts to multiple server nodes. Based on the needs of the front-end users, their requests can be sent to different servers. **Federation** is the technology used to balance workload. With the federation, it is possible to expand and shrink database objects according to needs.

In this chapter, we will discuss all the three units. Some hands-on activities on these units will also be given in this chapter. We begin with views.

8.2 Views

After a database is populated with data, the next step is to get ready to support database applications. A view is a database object that collects data from various data sources for a database application such as a form used by front-end users. To support database applications, you can first create views and then bind the views to the applications. The use of views simplifies the way a database application interacts with a database. A view can be created by selecting data from one or multiple data sources, such as tables from one or more databases, other views, calculated values, or even data from spreadsheets. You may consider a view as a virtual table. It looks like a single table and can be used as a single table. An SQL statement that selects data from a view is just like an SQL statement that selects data from a table. The advantages of using views are summarized below:

- Views are more secure. Views limit the database management activities such as inserting, deleting, and updating tables directly by front-end users. A view only provides data that are necessary for an application.
- Views improve the performance. Data stored in a view are ready for an application to use. There is no need for the application to search various data sources to obtain the data. Usually, tables are not used to store calculated values, which may hold back performance. A view can have all the columns needed for calculation and a calculated column that stores calculation results.
- Views simplify data manipulation tasks. When a table name is changed, one can redefine the view to use the new table name; there is no need to modify the code in every database application that is tied to the view.

Owing to these advantages, views are widely used with database applications. Next, you will learn how to create and manage the views.

8.2.1 Create Views

Like creating other database objects, you can use the CREATE VIEW statement to create a view. The syntax for creating a view is given below:

```
CREATE VIEW [db_name.] [owner.] view_name [(column [,...n])]
[WITH < view_attribute > [,...n]]
```

```
AS
select_statement
[WITH CHECK OPTION]
< view_attribute > ::=
{ENCRYPTION|SCHEMABINDING|VIEW_METADATA}
```

The meanings of the parameters and options are the following:

- *View_name* specifies the name of a view
- *Column* defines a specified name to be used by a column
- WITH CHECK OPTION ensures that the modified data are visible in the modified view
- *Select_statement* is a block of SQL statements that queries data for a view
- ENCRYPTION encrypts columns in a system table
- SCHEMABINDING binds a view with a specific database schema
- VIEW_METADATA returns metadata information about a view

When creating a view, the following restrictions may apply:

- The name of a view must be unique within the database.
- The query used to create a view cannot contain the keywords ORDER BY, COMPUTE, and INTO.
- If a view contains columns that are derived from an arithmetic expression, a built-in function, a constant, or columns from different tables with the same column names, you must explicitly assign the names to these columns.

To illustrate the use of the CREATE VIEW statement, let us consider an example that selects detailed information about a class. Figure 8.1 displays the code and the content in the view.

You can use the ALTER VIEW statement to modify the definition of a view. To delete a view, use the DROP VIEW statement.

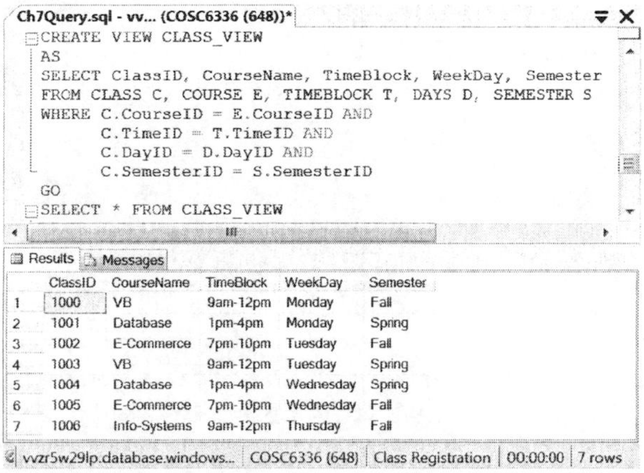

Figure 8.1 Create CLASS_VIEW.

8.2.2 Modify Views

When making a change to a view, you can use the ALTER VIEW statement. ALTER VIEW does not alter the existing indexes, stored procedures, or triggers created for the view. The syntax for the ALTER VIEW statement is

```
ALTER VIEW [db_name.] [owner.] view_name [(column [,...n])]
[WITH<view_attribute> [,...n]]
AS
select_statement
[WITH CHECK OPTION]
< view_attribute>:: =
{ENCRYPTION|SCHEMABINDING|VIEW_METADATA}
```

The definitions of the keywords in the ALTER VIEW statement are similar to those of the CREATE VIEW statement.

8.2.3 Modify Data in a View

One of the advantages of a view is that it limits front-end users' direct use and modification of data in tables. Through a view, however, a user may be able to insert, update, and delete data of the underlying tables according the following rules:

- If a view is constructed on a single table and it meets all the restrictions listed below, the underlying table is updateable (including insert, update, and delete).
- For a multiple-table-based view, the data of the underlying tables can only be modified by an INSTEAD OF trigger defined on the view.

For a single-table-based view, to make the underlying table updateable, you need to meet the following restrictions on the SQL statement that creates the view:

- If the underlying table contains columns defined as NOT NULL, all the NOT NULL columns should be included in the view.
- If the WITH CHECK OPTION clause is used in the CREATE VIEW statement, you cannot delete a row from the view.
- If a view contains calculated columns, the underlying table cannot be modified through the view.

When you modify data through a view, the modification should maintain the data constraints and integrity constraints imposed on the underlying table. For example, to illustrate the modification of data in an underlying table, let us create a view on the STUDENT table, change the last name Brooks to Parker, and then query the underlying table STUDENT to see the change.

In Figure 8.2, the last name of the student with id 14 is changed to Parker. As mentioned earlier, if a view has a calculated column, you cannot modify data through the view for the underlying table. To illustrate this, consider NEW_STUDENT_VIEW in Figure 8.3.

Note that modifying a view may cause its dependent database objects such as triggers or stored procedures to become invalid. If this happens, you need to modify its stored procedures or triggers accordingly.

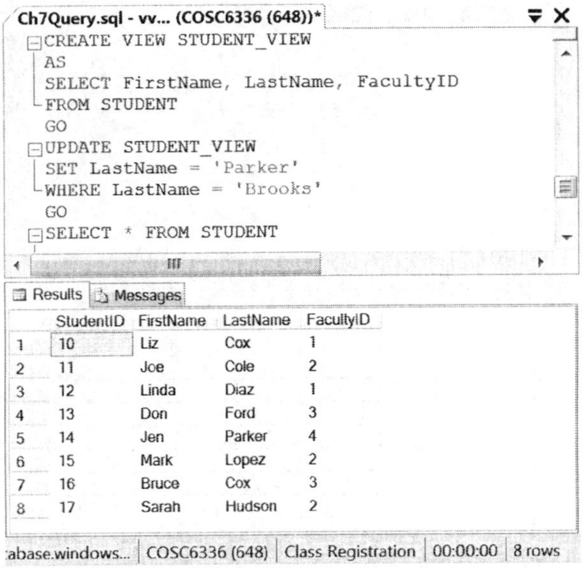

Figure 8.2 Modify data through view based on single table.

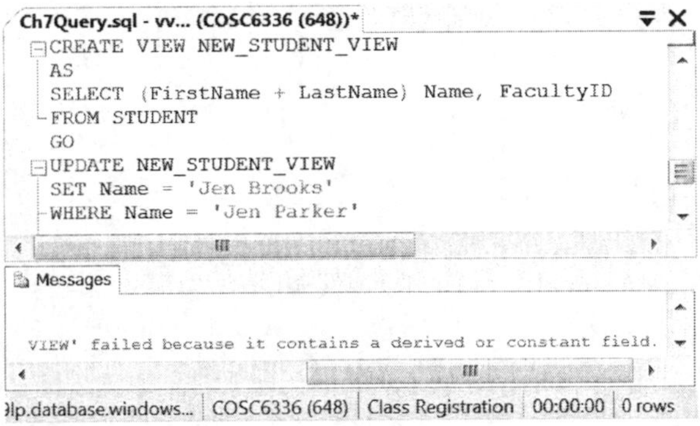

Figure 8.3 Modify data through view with calculated column.

8.2.4 Drop Views

Views that are no longer needed can be deleted from a database with an SQL statement. Like deleting a table, the DELETE statement is used to delete the content of a view. To delete the data as well as the structure of a view, you can use the SQL statement DROP VIEW.

ACTIVITY 8.1 CREATING, MANAGING, DROPPING VIEWS

You can create a view by using the CREATE VIEW statement in the **New Query** editor of SQL Server Management Studio or in Windows Azure SQL Database. Suppose that you want to create views by using the Windows Azure SQL Database portal to collect student information such as student names, classes that the students are enrolled in, the students' advisors, and so on. These views can be created by selecting the data from the tables STUDENT, CLASS, FACULTY, and STUDENT_CLASS as shown in the following tasks.

TASK 1: CREATING VIEW USING SQL DATABASE

Let us create a view called STUDENT_ADVISOR_VIEW.

1. On your local computer, log on to Windows Azure through the URL
   https://*yourserver*.database.windows.net
   where yourserver is your SQL Database server name.
2. Enter the database name **Class_Registration**. Then, enter your user name and password to log on to Windows Azure SQL Database.
3. Once you have logged on, click the **New Query** icon at the upper-left corner of your screen.
4. Enter the following SQL statement to create the view STUDENT_ADVISOR_VIEW:

```
CREATE VIEW STUDENT_ADVISOR_VIEW
AS
    SELECT S.FirstName, S.LastName, F.LastName As [Advisor]
    FROM STUDENT S JOIN FACULTY F ON S.FacultyID=F.FacultyId
```

5. Highlight the code and click **Run**. As shown in Figure 8.4, the view STUDENT_ADVISOR_VIEW is successfully created.
6. To see how the view works, enter the following SQL statement:

```
SELECT * FROM STUDENT_ADVISOR_VIEW
```

Highlight the code and click **Run**. Figure 8.5 shows that the view returns the full names of the students with their advisors' last names.

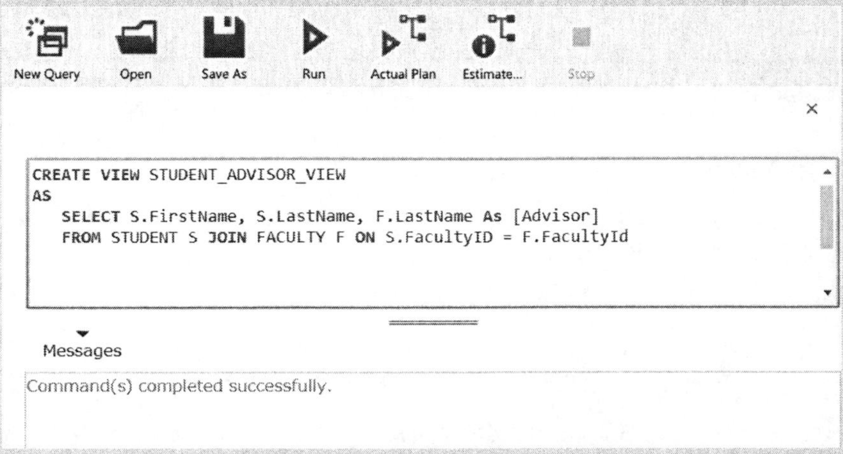
New Query
Open
Save As
Run
Actual Plan
Estimate...
Stop
CREATE VIEW STUDENT_ADVISOR_VIEW
AS
SELECT S.FirstName, S.LastName, F.LastName As [Advisor]
FROM STUDENT S JOIN FACULTY F ON S.FacultyID = F.FacultyId
Messages
Command(s) completed successfully.

Figure 8.4 Create STUDENT_ADVISOR_VIEW.

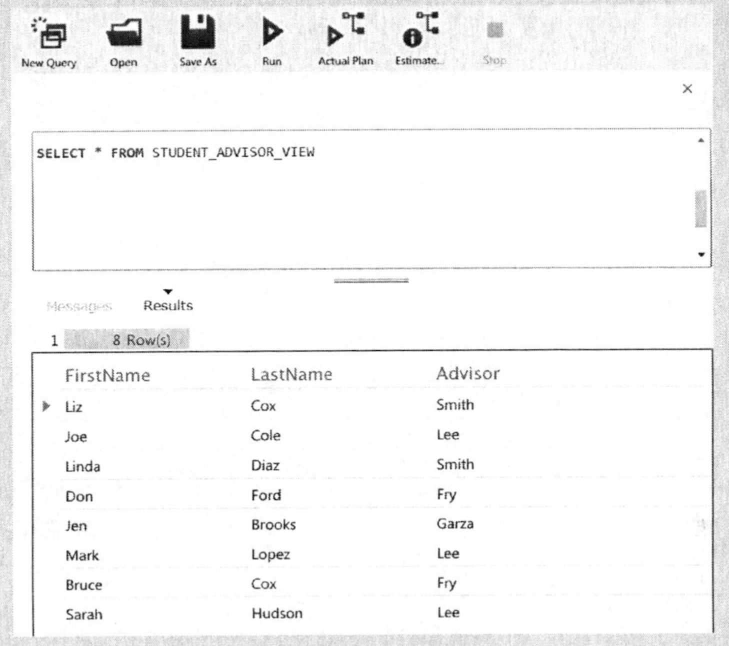

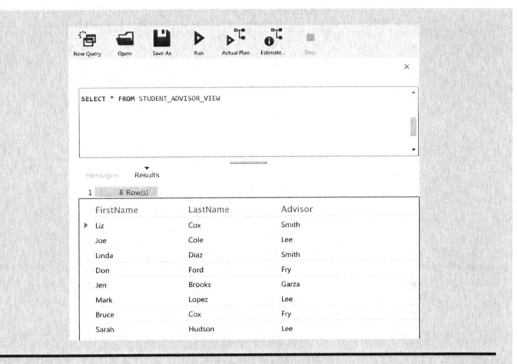

Figure 8.5 STUDENT_ADVISOR_VIEW.

TASK 2: ALTERING VIEW

You can modify a view by using the ALTER VIEW statement in the New Query editor. For example, you can add a column called GPA. The following is the modification to STUDENT_ADVISOR_VIEW:

1. Assume that the Windows Azure SQL Database portal is still open. Enter the following SQL statement to alter the view STUDENT_ADVISOR_VIEW:

```
ALTER VIEW STUDENT_ADVISOR_VIEW
AS
SELECT S.FirstName, S.LastName, F.LastName As [Advisor],
AVG(CASE T.Grade
WHEN 'A' THEN 4.0
WHEN 'B' THEN 3.0
WHEN 'C' THEN 2.0
WHEN 'D' THEN 1.0
WHEN 'F' THEN 0.0 END) [GPA]
FROM ((STUDENT S JOIN FACULTY F ON S.FacultyID=F.FacultyId)
  JOIN STUDENT_CLASS T ON T.StudentID=S.StudentID)
GROUP BY F.LastName, S.LastName, S.FirstName
```

2. Highlight the code and click **Run**. As shown in Figure 8.6, the view STUDENT_ADVISOR_VIEW is successfully modified.

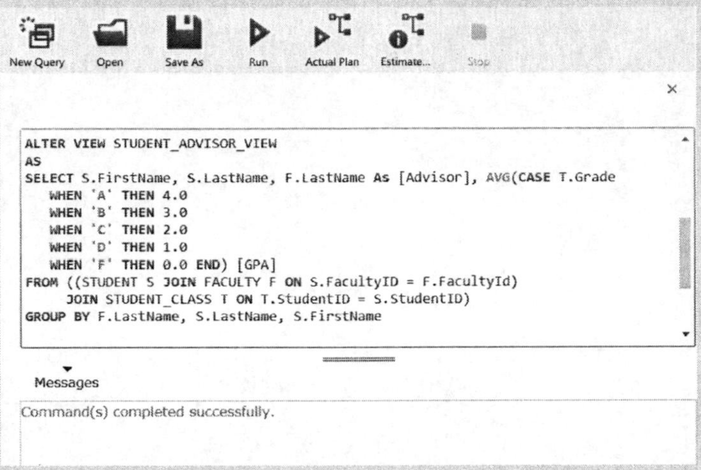
New Query
Open
Save As
Run
Actual Plan
Estimate...
Stop
ALTER VIEW STUDENT_ADVISOR_VIEW
AS
SELECT S.FirstName, S.LastName, F.LastName As [Advisor], AVG(CASE T.Grade
WHEN 'A' THEN 4.0
WHEN 'B' THEN 3.0
WHEN 'C' THEN 2.0
WHEN 'D' THEN 1.0
WHEN 'F' THEN 0.0 END) [GPA]
FROM ((STUDENT S JOIN FACULTY F ON S.FacultyID = F.FacultyId)
JOIN STUDENT_CLASS T ON T.StudentID = S.StudentID)
GROUP BY F.LastName, S.LastName, S.FirstName
Messages
Command(s) completed successfully.

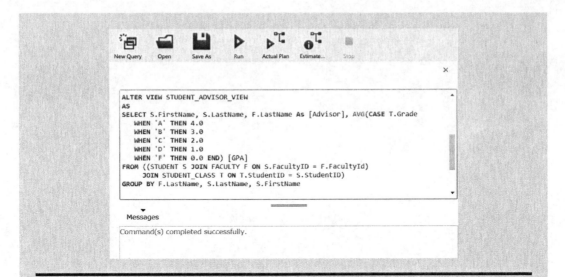

Figure 8.6 View modification.

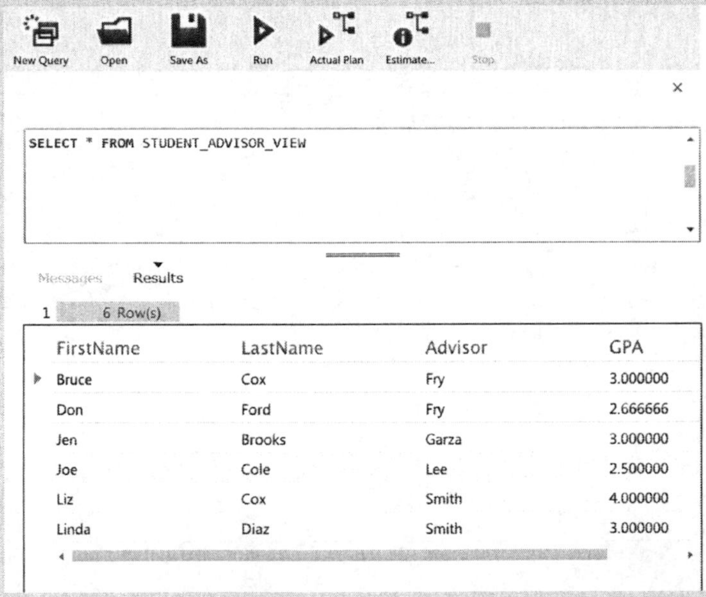
New Query
Open
Save As
Run
Actual Plan
Estimate...
Stop
SELECT * FROM STUDENT_ADVISOR_VIEW
Messages
Results
1
6 Row(s)
FirstName LastName Advisor GPA
Bruce Cox Fry 3.000000
Don Ford Fry 2.666666
Jen Brooks Garza 3.000000
Joe Cole Lee 2.500000
Liz Cox Smith 4.000000
Linda Diaz Smith 3.000000

Figure 8.7 Modified STUDENT_ADVISOR_VIEW.

3. To test the modified view, enter the following SQL statement in the New Query editor:

```
SELECT * FROM STUDENT_ADVISOR_VIEW
```

4. Highlight the code and click **Run**. Figure 8.7 shows that the view returns the information, including the students' names, advisors' names, and the student GPAs.

TASK 3: MODIFYING DATA IN VIEW

To see how the data being modified in a view will impact the underlying table, let us work on the following task. In this activity, we first create a new view STUDENT_GRADE_VIEW based on a single table STUDENT_CLASS. We then perform insert, update, and delete activities on the view. We will check to see if the changes are also made to the underlying table. Next, we will modify the view STUDENT_ADVISOR_VIEW, which has a calculated column and see if the change can be made to this kind of view.

1. Assume that the Windows Azure SQL Database portal is still open. Enter the following SQL statement to create the view Student_GRADE_VIEW:

```
CREATE VIEW STUDENT_GRADE_VIEW
AS
SELECT *
FROM STUDENT_CLASS
```

2. Highlight the code and click **Run**. As shown in Figure 8.8, the view STUDENT_GRADE_VIEW is successfully created.
3. Now, we will perform several modifications. We first insert a row with the following SQL statement:

```
INSERT INTO STUDENT_GRADE_VIEW
VALUES(11, 1005, 'B')
```

4. Highlight the code and click **Run**. To see what has happened in the view STUDENT_GRADE_VIEW, enter the following query statement. As shown in Figure 8.9, the new role is added to the view. (In Figure 8.9, the GO keyword is to separate the two statements so that they can be executed together.)

```
SELECT * FROM STUDENT_GRADE_VIEW
```

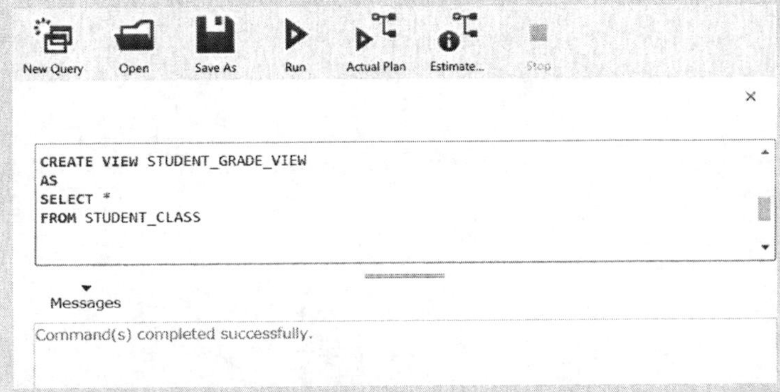
New Query
Open
Save As
Run
Actual Plan
Estimate...
Stop
CREATE VIEW STUDENT_GRADE_VIEW
AS
SELECT *
FROM STUDENT_CLASS
Messages
Command(s) completed successfully.

Figure 8.8 Create view based on single table.

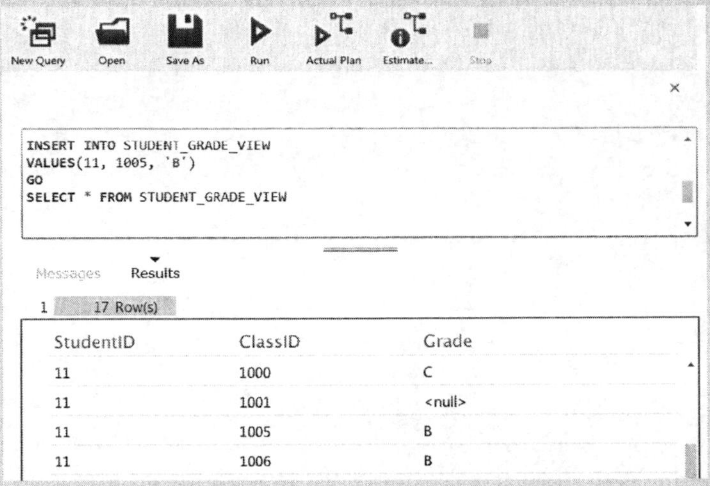

Figure 8.9 Insert new row to STUDENT_GRADE_VIEW.

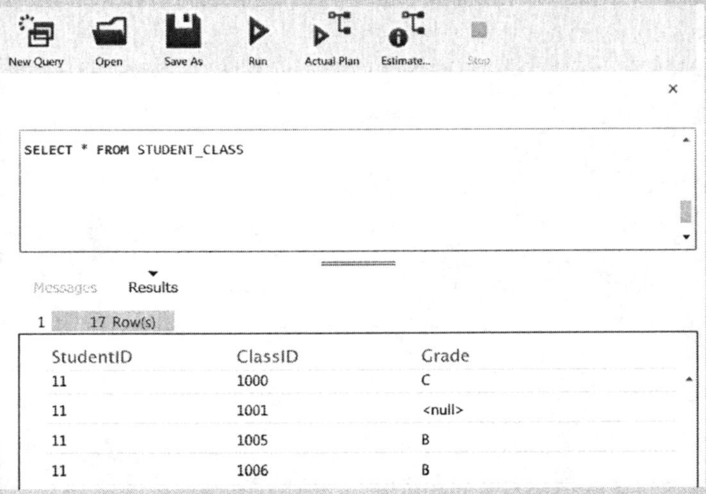

Figure 8.10 New row being inserted in STUDENT_CLASS table.

5. To see the change made to the table STUDENT_CLASS, run the following SQL statement:

```
SELECT * FROM STUDENT_CLASS
```

6. As shown in Figure 8.10, the row is also inserted in the table STUDENT_CLASS.
7. Next, delete the newly inserted row with the following SQL statement:

```
DELETE STUDENT_GRADE_VIEW
WHERE StudentID=11 AND ClassID=1005
```

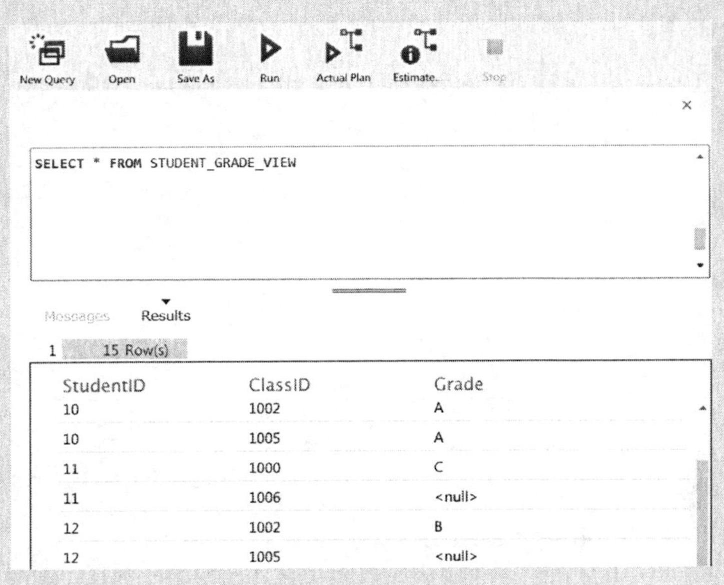

Figure 8.11 New row being deleted from STUDENT_GRADE_VIEW.

8. Highlight the code and click **Run**. To see what has happened to the view STUDENT_GRADE_VIEW, enter the following query statement. As shown in Figure 8.11, the new role is deleted from the view.
9. To verify if the row is deleted from the table STUDENT_CLASS, run the SELECT * FROM STUDENT_CLASS statement. The result shown in Figure 8.12 indicates that the row is no longer in the table STUDENT_CLASS.

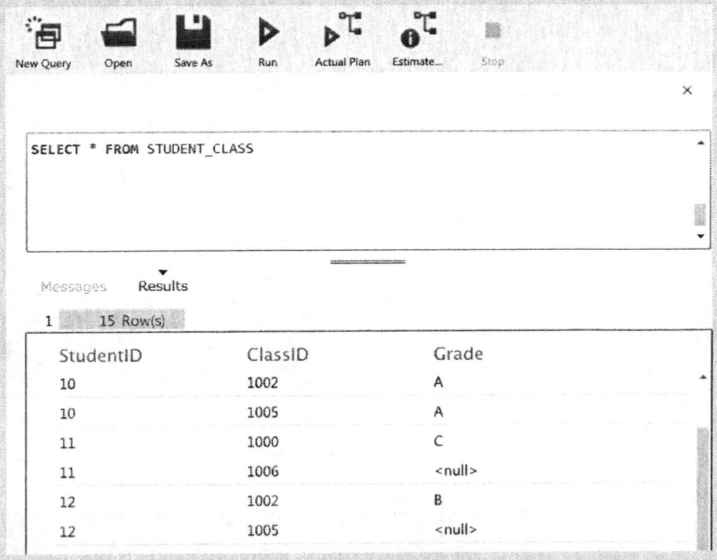

Figure 8.12 New row being deleted from STUDENT_CLASS table.

10. To see how updating a view will impact the underlying table, enter the following SQL statement. Before the execution of the UPDATE SQL statement, you need to use the ALTER TABLE statement to disable the triggers created on the table STUDENT_CLASS. Later, you can enable the triggers.

```
ALTER TABLE STUDENT_CLASS DISABLE TRIGGER Class_Checking, Drop_
Class
GO
UPDATE STUDENT_GRADE_VIEW
SET GRADE = 'A'
WHERE StudentID = 11 AND ClassID = 1000
```

11. Figure 8.13 shows that the update is done.
12. To check if the table is updated accordingly, enter the SQL statement as shown in Figure 8.14. As seen in Figure 8.14, the table STUDENT_CLASS is updated.
13. In the next step, we will update the view STUDENT_ADVISOR_VIEW (which contains a calculated column) with the following SQL statement:

```
UPDATE STUDENT_ADVISOR_VIEW
SET GPA = 3.0
Where FirstName = 'Don' AND LastName = 'Ford'
```

14. Figure 8.15 shows that the update is prevented because the view contains a calculated column.

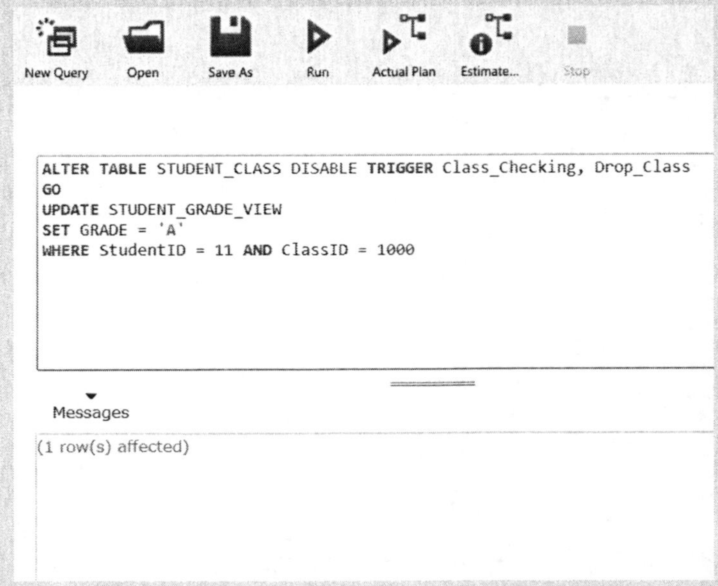
New Query
Open
Save As
Run
Actual Plan
Estimate...
Stop
ALTER TABLE STUDENT_CLASS DISABLE TRIGGER Class_Checking, Drop_Class
GO
UPDATE STUDENT_GRADE_VIEW
SET GRADE = 'A'
WHERE StudentID = 11 AND ClassID = 1000
Messages
(1 row(s) affected)

Figure 8.13 Update STUDENT_GRADE_VIEW.

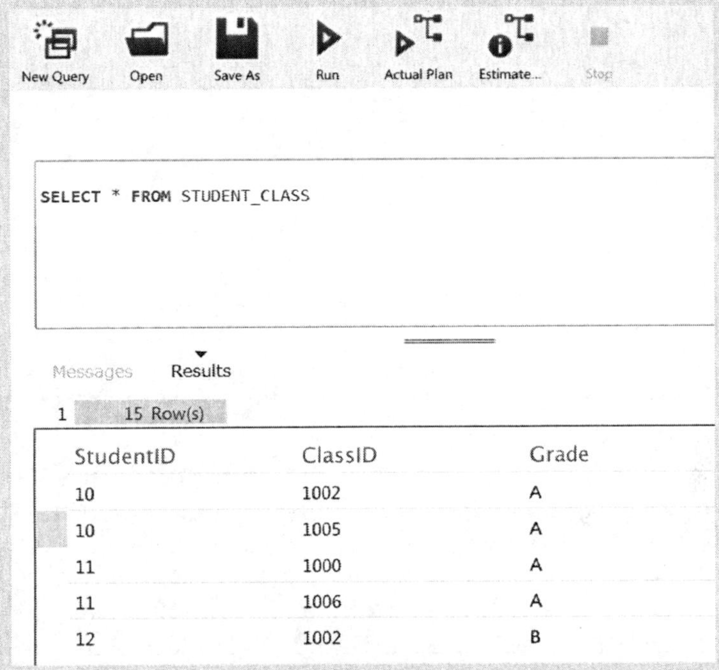

Figure 8.14 Updated STUDENT_CLASS table.

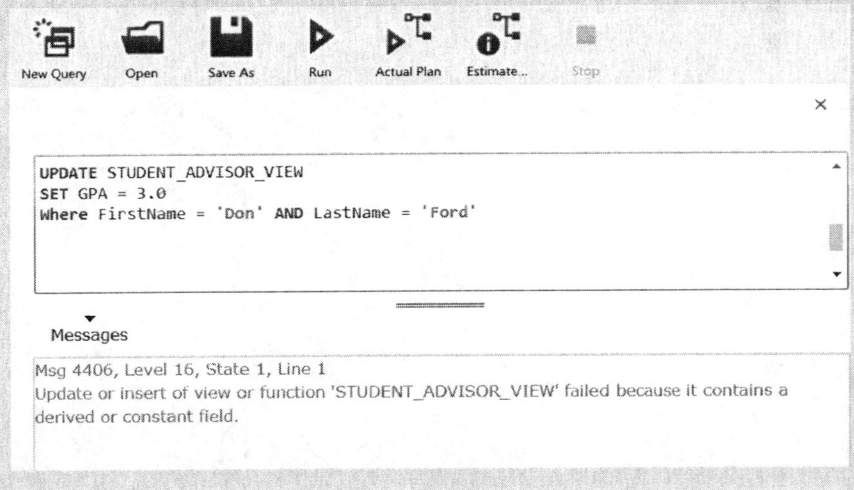

Figure 8.15 Update being prevented for view with calculated column.

TASK 4: DROPPING VIEWS

There are two ways to drop a view. You can drop a view by using the GUI tool provided by Windows Azure SQL Database or by the SQL statement DROP VIEW. To drop a view from the GUI tool, follow the below steps:

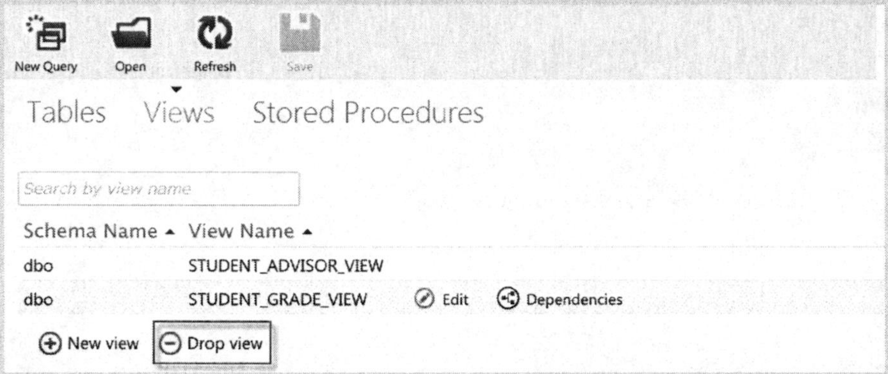

Figure 8.16 Drop view with GUI tool.

1. Assume that the Windows Azure SQL Database portal is still open. Click the **Design** icon on the left-hand side of your screen. Then, click the **Views** tab. You should be able to see the existing views. Select the view **STUDENT_GRADE_VIEW** and click the **Drop view** button as shown in Figure 8.16. Then Click **OK**.
2. Another way to drop the view is to use the DROP VIEW statement. To drop the view Student_GRADE_VIEW, enter the following SQL statement:

   ```
   DROP VIEW STUDENT_GRADE_VIEW
   ```

3. Highlight the code and click **Run**. As shown in Figure 8.17, the view is dropped successfully.
4. To verify that STUDENT_GRADE_VIEW is dropped, log off Windows Azure SQL Database and log on again. Click the **Design** icon and click the **Views** tab. As shown in Figure 8.18, the view STUDENT_GRADE_VIEW is not there anymore.

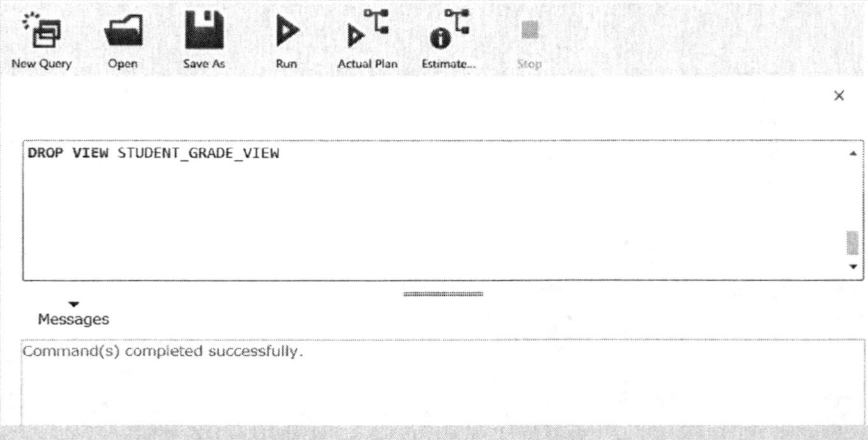

Figure 8.17 Drop view with SQL statement.

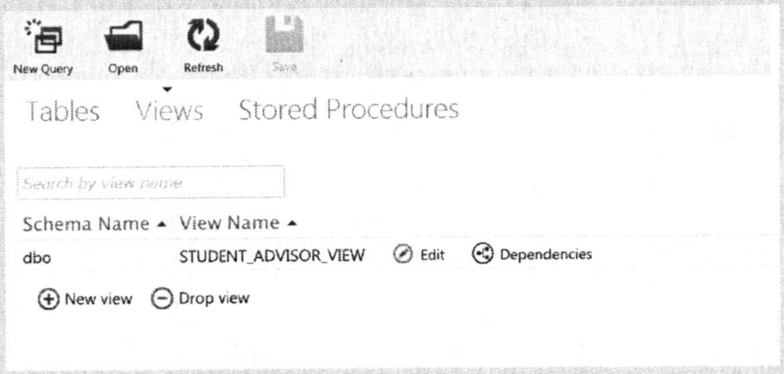

Figure 8.18 Verify that view is dropped.

8.3 Indexes

As more and more data are stored in a database, tables and views can grow very large. To search for a piece of information in a large table or view can be time consuming. Indexes are created on tables or views to speed up the search. Indexes are helpful for improving the query performance in the following scenarios:

- The searching condition in a WHERE clause is used to match values in a column to a specific value. In these cases, if an index is created on a column involved in a search condition, it will significantly improve performance.
- When joining two tables with a foreign key column, a join condition is used to match a value in the primary key column to values in the foreign key column. The use of an index in the matching process will certainly improve performance.
- When sorting values in a column, an index created on the column will speed up the sorting process.

On a table or a view, multiple indexes can be created. However, in some situations, too many indexes may not improve query performance. Reindexing occurs whenever data in an indexed column are modified or the structure of the column is changed. Reindexing slows down performance. Therefore, it is not a good idea to create too many indexes on a frequently updated table.

Indexes are created on a balance tree or **B-tree**, which is a data structure covered by a data structure course in the computer science curriculum. Based on how an index is stored on the B-tree, there are two types of indexes: **clustered index** and **nonclustered index**. A clustered index places each row in a table directly on the leaf node of the B-tree. A nonclustered index places the reference to each row in a table on the leaf node. The clustered index has better performance since data can be accessed directly on a B-tree. When a table is created, Windows Azure SQL Database automatically creates a clustered index on the primary key. Owing to the nature of the cloud, database files are automatically placed on multiple drives. Therefore, there is no need to specify the file groups and create partitions while creating an index. Thus, SQL statements that create indexes on Windows Azure SQL Database will not support the options such as Fillfactor in a nonclustered index, file group, or partition.

An index is called a **composite index** if it includes multiple columns, such as a clustered index on a combination primary key. In general, a composite index requires that each row in the combination must be unique. However, the uniqueness is not required for a single column on which a clustered index is created because the clustered index enforces the uniqueness by creating an associated sorting column containing only unique values.

8.3.1 Create Indexes

One way to create an index is to use the SQL statement CREATE INDEX. The CREATE INDEX syntax has many optional parameters as shown below:

```
CREATE [UNIQUE] [CLUSTERED|NONCLUSTERED] INDEX index_name
ON [table_name | view_name] (column_name [ASC | DESC] [,...n])
[INCLUDE (column_name [,...n])]
[WHERE <filter_predicate>]
[WITH [index_property] [,...n]]
```

In the above syntax, the notation [,...*n*] is used to indicate that multiple columns or multiple options can be listed. The keyword INCLUDE is used to include the name of the column in which the rows are placed on the leaf nodes. The filter_predicate in the WHERE clause includes the conditions joint with logical operators such as AND, IN, and OR, and comparison operators such as

```
{IS|IS NOT| = |<> | ! = |> | >=| !>| < |<=| ! < }
```

The *index_property* in the WITH clause can be any of the following:

```
{
IGNORE_DUP_KEY = {ON|OFF} |
    DROP_EXISTING = {ON | OFF} |
    STATISTICS_NORECOMPUTE = {ON | OFF} |
    ONLINE = {ON | OFF}
}
```

If the ONLINE parameter is set to ON, it allows the database administrator to manage an index while it is used by another DML SQL statement. The example displayed in Figure 8.19 is used to create a nonclustered index on the column CourseID, include the column TimeID, and turn ONLINE to ON.

If the column CourseID is included in the conditions of a WHERE clause, the column CourseID after the keyword ON is used to form the key of the index Course_Index. The index key will be used to search the primary table CLASS to find the rows that satisfy the conditions

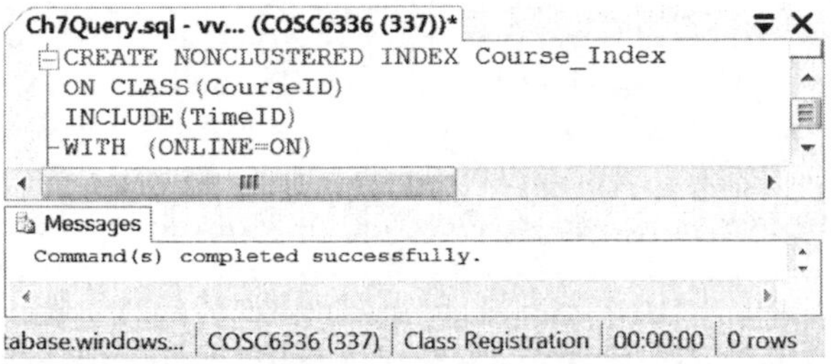
Ch7Query.sql - vv... (COSC6336 (337))*
CREATE NONCLUSTERED INDEX Course_Index
ON CLASS(CourseID)
INCLUDE(TimeID)
WITH (ONLINE=ON)
Messages
Command(s) completed successfully.
tabase.windows... | COSC6336 (337) | Class Registration | 00:00:00 | 0 rows

Figure 8.19 Create index with CREATE INDEX statement.

in the WHERE clause. The column in the INCLUDE clause can be used to search a record set returned by a SELECT clause.

8.3.2 Manage Indexes

After an index is created, you can view, modify, and delete it. SQL Database provides several ways to manage existing indexes. The SQL Statement ALTER INDEX can be used to rebuild, disable, or modify an existing index. With ALTER INDEX, you do not need to drop the existing index and recreate it to defragment. The syntax of ALTER INDEX is given below:

```
ALTER INDEX {index_name | All}
  ON [table_name | view_name] (column_name [ASC | DESC] [,...n])
{REBUILD [WITH [rebuild_index_option] [,...n]] |
  DISABLE |
  SET (<set_index_option> [,...n])}
```

In the above syntax, [,...*n*] is used to indicate that multiple columns or multiple options can be listed. The meanings of the keywords in the ALTER INDEX statement are as follows:

- REBUILD: Rebuilds an index by dropping and recreating an existing index
- DISABLE: Makes an index temporarily unavailable
- SET: Sets options for accessing and maintaining indexes

The parameter *rebuild_index_option* for the keyword REBUILD has similar options as *index_property* in the WITH clause in the CREATE INDEX statement, except the DROP_EXISTING option. Therefore, you cannot use ALTER INDEX to drop an existing index. The parameter *set_index_option* has the following options:

```
{
    IGNORE_DUP_KEY = {ON|OFF} |
    STATISTICS_NORECOMPUTE = {ON|OFF}
}
```

8.3.3 Remove Indexes

If an index is no longer used, you can remove it by using the DROP INDEX statement, which has the following syntax:

```
DROP INDEX index_name
ON {table_or_ view_name}
```

You may need to add the name of the schema and table in front of the index name to make sure that the right index gets dropped. The notation [,...*n*] indicates that you can drop multiple indexes. In Figure 8.20, the index Course_Index defined on the table CLASS is removed.

The stored procedures **sp_help** and **sp_helpindex** can be used to obtain information about an index. For example, if you want to know the information about indexes created for the table CLASS, enter and execute the SQL statement in Figure 8.21.

As shown in Figure 8.21, the stored procedure sp_helpindex returns one index. The index is the index PK_CLASS_CB1927A001738BAC, which is created by Windows Azure SQL Database automatically when the table CLASS is created.

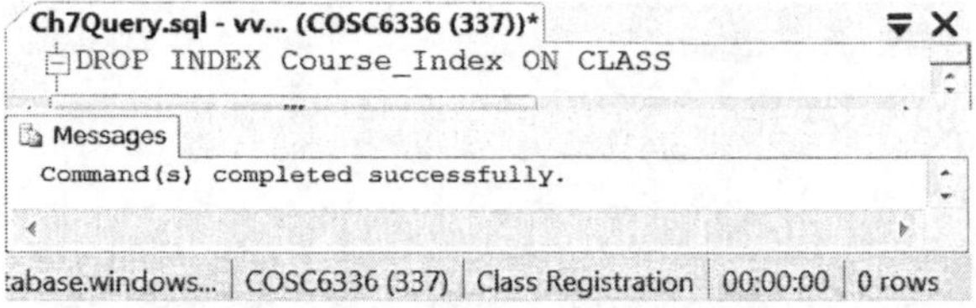

Figure 8.20 Remove index by DROP INDEX statement.

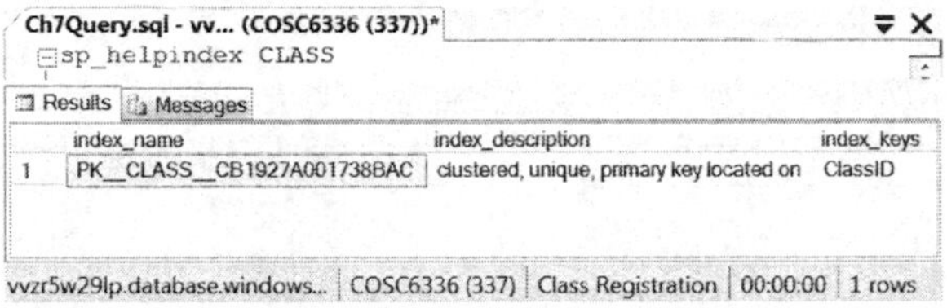

Figure 8.21 Indexes created for CLASS table.

ACTIVITY 8.2 CREATING AND REMOVING INDEXES

For a large table or a view, the use of an index can speed up searching and sorting. In this activity, you will learn how to create an index and how to use the index to improve performance. Suppose that we want to create an index with an SQL statement on Windows Azure SQL Database. Follow the steps below to accomplish this task:

1. On your local computer, log on to Windows Azure SQL Database portal through the URL
   https://*yourserver*.database.windows.net
   where yourserver is your SQL Database server name.
2. Enter the database name **Class_Registration**. Then, enter your user name and password to log on to Windows Azure SQL Database.
3. Once you have logged on, click the **New Query** icon at the upper-left corner of your screen.
4. First, let us exam the performance of the following SQL statement before indexing:

```
SELECT ClassID, CourseName
FROM COURSE, CLASS
GROUP BY CourseName, ClassID
```

5. Highlight the code and click the **Actual Plan** tab. After the SQL statement is executed, click the link **Query Plan**. As shown in Figure 8.22, the sorting takes a lot of workload while executing the query.
6. To view the cost of the SELECT statement, double click the SELECT node. As shown in Figure 8.23, the total cost for the SELECT statement is 0.0184056.
7. To improve the performance, enter the following SQL statement to create an index on the table COURSE. The column CourseName will be used as the index to improve sorting.

```
CREATE INDEX Class_Index on COURSE(CourseName)
```

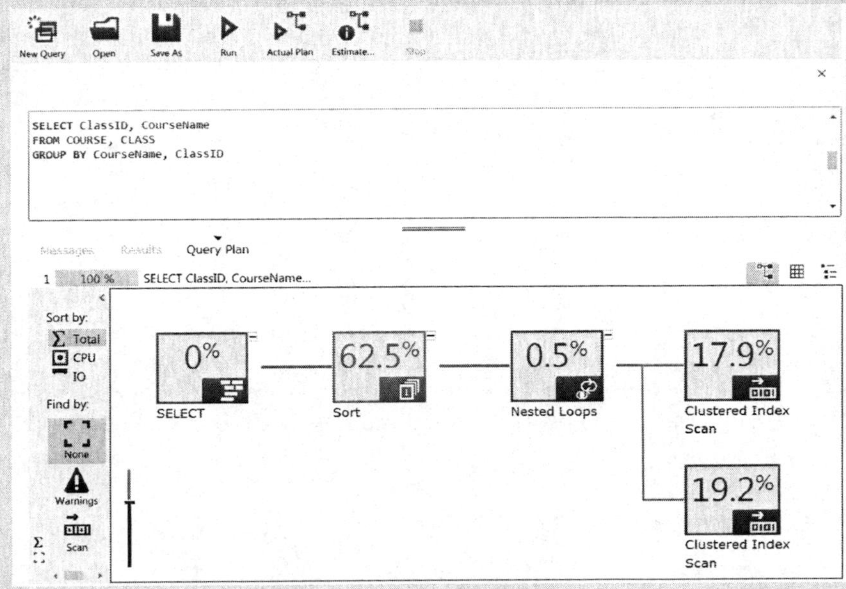

Figure 8.22 Workload distribution before indexing.

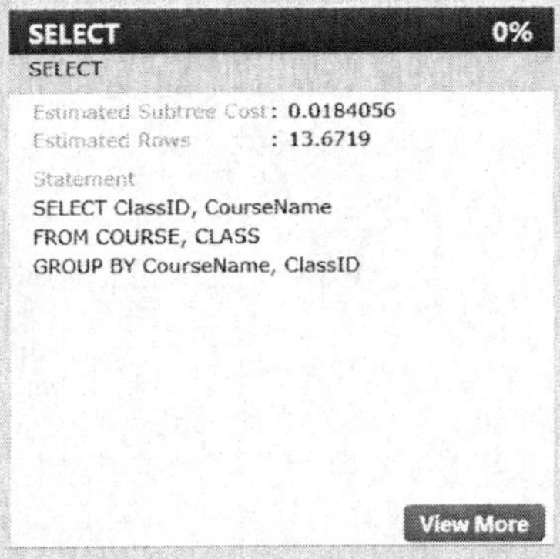

Figure 8.23 Cost before indexing.

8. Highlight the code and click the **Run** tab. As shown in Figure 8.24, the index Class_Index is successfully created.
9. After the index is created, highlight the following SQL Statement and click the **Actual Plan** tab again:

```
SELECT ClassID, CourseName
FROM COURSE, CLASS
GROUP BY CourseName, ClassID
```

10. As shown in Figure 8.25, the workload on sorting is no longer a major factor of the execution.

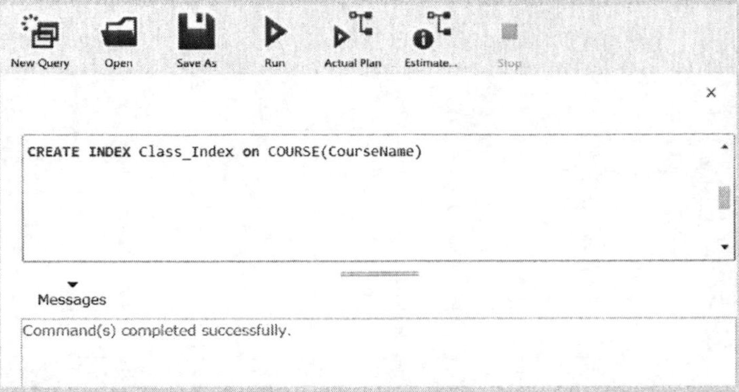

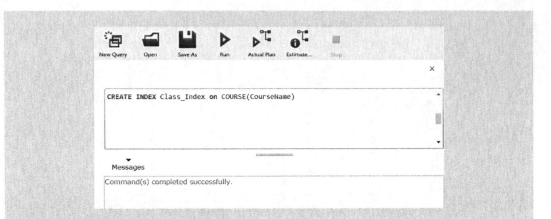

Figure 8.24 Create Class_Index.

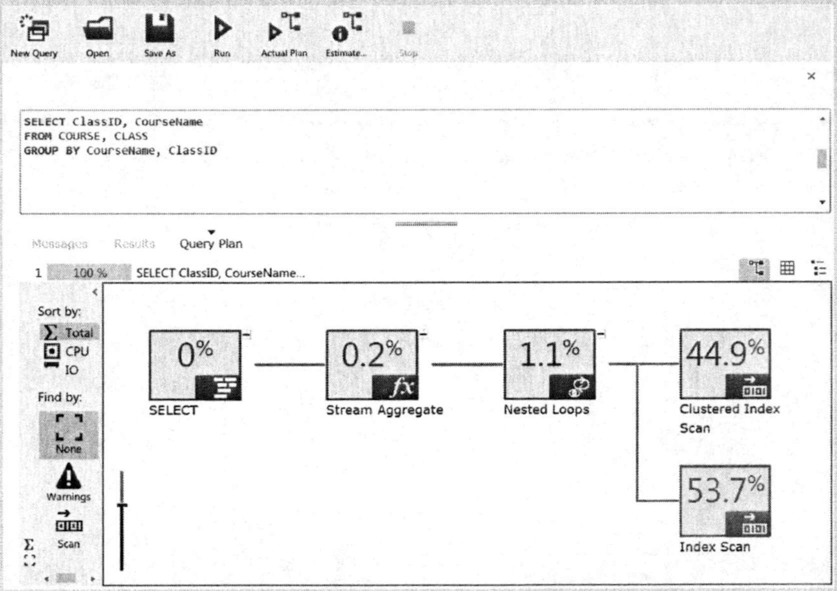

Figure 8.25 Workload distribution after indexing.

11. To view the cost of the SELECT statement after indexing, double click the SELECT node. As shown in Figure 8.26, the total cost for the SELECT statement is 0.000731994, which is over 25 times better.
12. The last step is to drop the index with the following SQL statement:

```
DROP INDEX class_Index ON COURSE
```

13. Highlight the SQL Statement and click **Run**. Figure 8.27 shows that the index is dropped successfully.

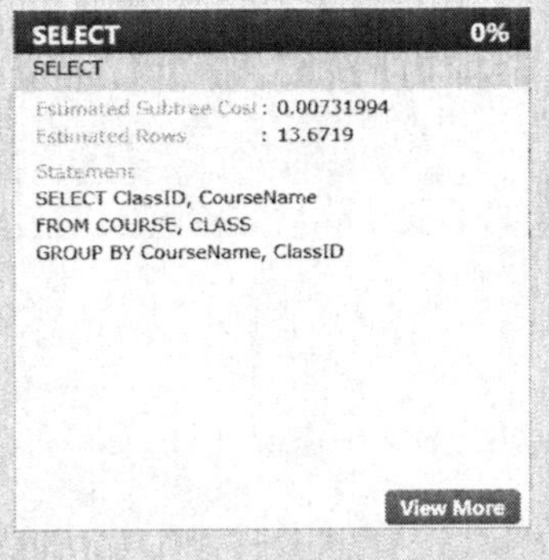

Figure 8.26 Cost after indexing.

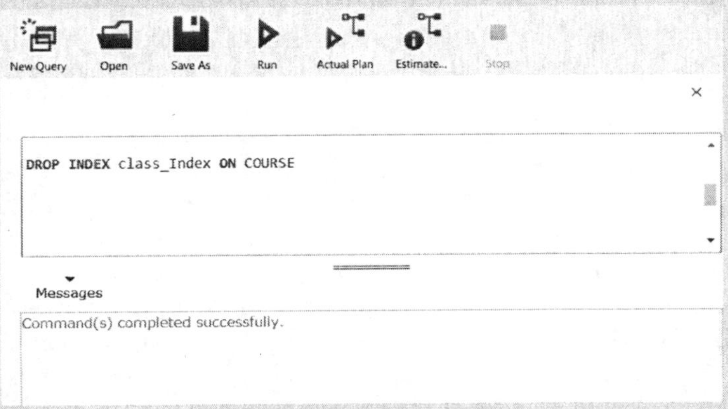

Figure 8.27 Drop index.

8.4 Federations

Federations in Windows Azure SQL Database can be used to improve performance and to achieve better scalability. When multiple applications are accessing a single data source, they may cause a data I/O bottleneck. One way to ease the bottleneck is to split a database object such as a table and place each part into different partitions. Windows Azure SQL Database Federation is a collection of the partitions of one or more database objects. With federations, database administrators are able to systematically build and manage partitions. The processing of a federation is also known as "sharding." The following are some terminologies often used in the federation technology:

- **Federation distribution key**: It contains the values used for specifying partitions. The key values must be the types of INT, BIGINT, UNIQUEIDENTIFIER, or VARBINARY (up to 900 bytes).
- **Federation scheme**: It defines the federation distribution key to determine how the data are distributed to different partitions contained in a federation.

- **Federation members**: They are the partitions of a federation. Each federation member will be implemented on an SQL database, which is physically separated from other SQL databases.
- **Federation atomic unit**: It is a set of related database objects such as tables stored in one federation member. A federation atomic unit is labeled with a specific federation key value. The database objects in an atomic unit are bound together by the federation key assigned to the atomic unit.
- **Federated table**: It is a table with its partitions distributed across multiple federation members.
- **Reference table**: It is a table with no partitioned rows. It contains reference information and is used for lookup purposes.
- **Federation root**: It is the database that contains federations and federation directory. Federation members can be accessed through the federation root. As a federation root, the database may also contain global data such as users, passwords, roles, or other application-specific data.

Partition members are physically separated. Each of the partition members is implemented as a database named with a federation key. As an example, Figure 8.28 illustrates the federations built in a federation root.

Windows Azure SQL Database provides an ideal environment for implementing the federations. In the SQL Database environment, the physical IT infrastructure is highly scalable. If needed, federation members can be built across hundreds or even thousands of databases. SQL Database manages the physical IT infrastructure, which hosts those databases. Without spending time on physical infrastructure management, database administrators and application developers are able to focus on the development of federations over the logical databases. The Windows Azure Management Portal can be used for federation deployment and management. Also, a federation built in SQL Database is highly available. It can be accessed anywhere and anytime. SQL Database provides the 99.9% service-level agreement (SLA) to ensure high availability. It also helps with rebalancing of a federation by adding or removing federation members based on the workload.

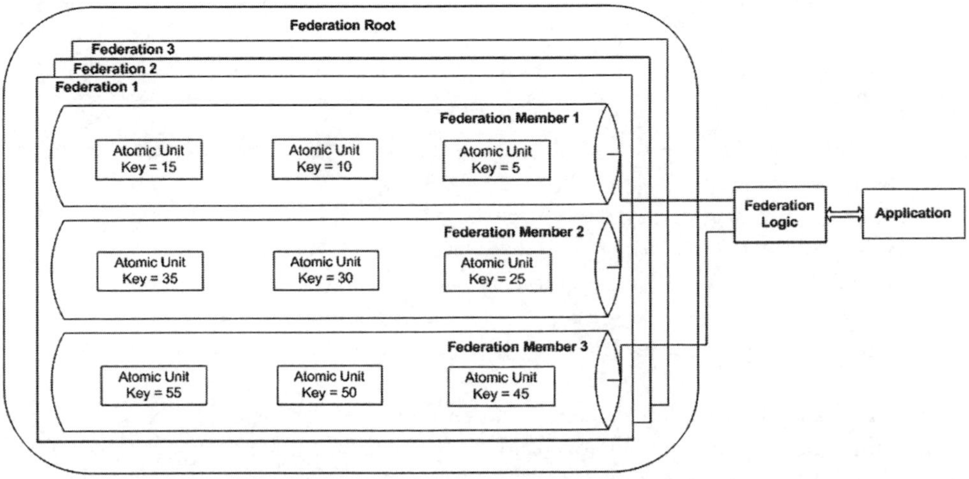

Figure 8.28 Federation architecture.

8.4.1 Federation Design

Although federations can be used for better performance and scalability, it also creates complication for database development and management. When database objects are distributed to multiple federation members, it posts challenges for updating, querying, and altering these database objects. Before implementing a federation, you need to answer the following questions:

- How should the database objects be partitioned?
- What value should be used as the federation key?
- What should be stored in a federation atomic unit?
- How can data be distributed evenly across federation members?
- How should data from multiple federation members be joined to support an application?
- How should we run functions, stored procedures, and other programming units across multiple federation members?
- How should changes made by an application be saved to federation members?
- How should we manage changes in table structures across multiple federation members?
- How should we keep referential integrity when the parent table and child table are stored in different federation members?
- How should we manage user accounts as federation members are dynamically added and removed?

These questions reveal the challenges in designing federations. To answer these questions, one may consider adopting a few design strategies shown below.

8.4.1.1 Generating Federation Key

A federation key should be chosen so that related rows from related tables are stored in one federation member. This kind of design enables the use of related data to be selected from one federation member to reduce the complexity of the query. Federation keys can be generated with the following methods:

- **Sequential Big Integer**: Use sequential big integers as federation keys. Assign each federation atomic unit a sequential big integer as the key. All database objects such as tables within that atomic unit will be labeled with the key. The use of sequential big integer can avoid duplicated federation keys.
- **Globally Unique Identifier (GUID)**: A GUID is the unique identification number assigned by the operating system to each database object. The use of the GUID can guarantee the uniqueness. However, it will cause complication in key management.
- **Keys Generated by Programming Unit**: Federation keys can also be generated with a computer program. To meet a particular purpose, a designer can define the keys with specified range and specially designed hashing function.

8.4.1.2 Database Operations across Multiple Federation Members

For multiple federation members, database operations such as querying, accessing, and updating databases can be designed with the following strategies:

- Design queries that can be distributed across multiple federation members. Then, combine the query results together.
- For better performance, run distributed queries at once on multiple federation members. For testing and for simplicity, run the distributed queries sequentially.
- After the results of a distributed query are returned, the results are reassembled and the reassembled results are returned to the application that issues the query. For testing, a partial result from each of the federation members can be returned.
- Extract data from multiple federation members into a standard database before executing a function or stored procedure.

8.4.1.3 Data Distribution across Multiple Federation Members

To decide how to distribute database objects to multiple federation members, consider the following strategies:

- Store all the global data in separate nonfederated databases.
- After an atomic unit has been stored in a federation member, its federation key can be stored in a nonfederated database for later lookup.
- If sequential big numbers are used as federation keys, distribute the atomic units across based on prespecified ranges of federation keys. The ranges can be defined as subsets of sequential big numbers.
- If GUIDs are used as federation keys, use a hashing algorithm to convert the GUIDs to numerical numbers and distribute atomic units according the range of the numerical numbers.
- To distribute atomic units evenly and automatically, one may consider distributing those units in a rotational manner. The difficulty of the method is that it will not know where to locate a specific atomic unit unless the same atomic unit is distributed to every federation member in the same federation.
- For better performance and easier management, an atomic unit can be distributed to each of the federation members. Newly inserted data can then be written to the atomic unit hosted by each of the federation members. In such a way, multiple applications are able to access the atomic unit simultaneously through different federation members.

8.4.1.4 Applications and Federation Logic

Applications access federations through federation logic. The following are some design strategies related to applications and federation logic implementation:

- Use programming units to maintain relationships and import/export data across multiple federation members.
- Use a single user account to create multiple federation members, which share the same security credentials.
- To allow an application to connect to multiple federation members simultaneous, a connection management pool should be created in the application. In SQL database, ADO.NET is the technique for carrying out connection management pooling.
- Applications supported by a federation should not be designed to rely on data transactions between two federation members. The applications should not join two database objects

from two different federation members. In addition, the applications should not check referential integrity across multiple federation members.
- For scalability, applications should be so designed that they are able to rebalance the workload by splitting and merging of federation members.
- Applications should be so designed that they are able to propagate structure changes made in a database object to all other federation members.

In addition to the above design strategies, you may consider using virtual federations to simulate physical federations for scalability and flexibility. Also, to ease the difficulties in federation management, you may consider using a denormalized table that includes data from several related tables.

8.4.2 Federation Implementation with T-SQL

T-SQL can be used to create a federation root and federations hosted by the federation root. With T-SQL, database administrators can also create federation members, atomic units, and establish connections to federations. They can also manage federations with T-SQL. The following are some commonly used federation-related SQL statements.

SQL Statement for Creating Federation Root: Since a federation root is a database that hosts a set of federations, the SQL statement for creating a federation root is the same as the statement for creating a database as shown below:

```
CREATE DATABASE [database_name]
```

SQL Statement for Creating Federation: After connecting to a federation root, enter the following SQL statement:

```
CREATE FEDERATION
      federation_name (distribution_name <data_type> RANGE)
```

The above SQL statement is described below:

- **federation_name**: It is the name of the federation to be created. The name of the federation should be unique within a federation root.
- **distribution_name**: It is the name of the federation key. As an identifier, the name should be unique and is limited to 128 unicode characters.
- **data_type**: It is the data type for the federation key. The data type can be INT, BIGINT, UNIQUEIDENTIFIER, or VARBINARY(*n*), where *n* can be a maximum of 900.
- **RANGE**: It defines a partition with a range value.

SQL Statement for Altering Federation: To modify a federation, use the following SQL statement:

```
ALTER FEDERATION federation_name
{
   SPLIT AT (distribution_name=boundary_value)
   |DROP AT ([LOW|HIGH] distribution_name=boundary_value)
}
```

The above SQL statement is described below:

- **boundary_value**: This value is used to redefine partitions. The type of the value should be consistent with the data type of the federation key.
- **SPLIT AT**: At the boundary value, split a federation member to two new federation members. The atomic units with the federation key less than the boundary_value are moved to one of the new federation members and the rest of the atomic units are moved to the other new federation member.
- **DROP AT**: Drop the federation members identified by the boundary_value. When LOW is used, drop the federation members below the boundary value and extend the range of the federation members above the boundary_value to include the federation keys of the dropped federation members. When HIGH is used, drop federation members below the boundary_value and extend the range of the federation members above the boundary_value to include the federation keys of the dropped federation members.

SQL Statement for Dropping Federation: To drop a federation, use the following SQL statement:

```
DROP FEDERATION federation_name
```

SQL Statement for Connecting to Federation: To connect to a federation, you need to first connect to the database served as the federation root. After connect to the federation root, reset the federation root with the SQL statement below:

```
USE FEDERATION ROOT WITH RESET
```

Then, use the following SQL statement to connect to the federation:

```
USE FEDERATION federation_name (distribution_name = value)
    WITH FILTERING = {ON|OFF}, RESET
```

The above SQL statement is described below:

- **value**: It is used to identify the federation member to be connected to.
- **WITH FILTERING = ON|OFF**: When OFF is set, the entire federation is connected. When ON is set, the federation member assigned with the value is connected. ON is the default choice. When ON is set, applications are able to connect to a particular atomic unit in a federation member automatically.
- **RESET**: This keyword is required to reset the connection explicitly.

SQL Statement for Creating Federated Table: After connecting to a federation, the following SQL statement can be used to create a federated table:

```
CREATE TABLE
    [schema_name.] table_ame
        ({ <column_definition> | <computed_column_definition>}
        [< table_constraint > ] [,...n])
FEDERATED ON (distribution_name = column_name)
```

In the above statement, the **FEDERATED ON** clause specifies that the table to be created is a federated table. It applies the distribution constraint defined by the distribution_name to the federation keys contained in the federation column named by the column_name.

SQL Statement for Viewing Federation: After connecting to a federation root, you can view the structure of a federation. To do so, use the following SQL statement to retrieve the federation root metadata:

```
SELECT db_name() [db_name]
SELECT * FROM sys.federations
SELECT * FROM sys.federation_distributions
SELECT * FROM sys.federation_member_distributions ORDER BY federation_id,
range_low;
```

The above SQL statement is described below:

- **sys.federations**: It is the system view that contains the names and ids of the federations.
- **sys.federation_distributions**: It is the system view that contains the distribution names and distribution types used by the federations. It also contains data-type-related information such as data type id, max length, precision, and so on.
- **sys.federation_member_distributions**: It is a system view that contains the distribution information about federation members in a federation. It includes the member ids, distribution names, and range_low and range_high values.

With these SQL statements, the database administrator is able to create and manage federations on Windows Azure SQL Database.

ACTIVITY 8.3 WINDOWS AZURE SQL DATABASE FEDERATION

In this activity, you will create a federation called Class_Federation. You will create and manage a federated table. You will also learn how to work with both federated and nonfederated tables. To create a federation, follow the below steps.

TASK 1: CREATING NEW FEDERATION

As time goes on, the table CLASS can grow into a large table. It is a good candidate for being a federated table. Suppose that you want to create a federation on the table CLASS in the database Class_Registration, follow the below steps to get started:

1. On your local computer, log on to Windows Azure through the URL https://windows.azure.com. Click the **SQL DATABASES** node.
2. On the **sql databases** page, click **New**. Click **SQL DATABASES**. Click **CUSTOM CREATE** to open the **Specify database settings** page.
3. On the **Specify database settings** page, type **ClassDB** for NAME. Then, select your server as shown in Figure 8.29. Click the check mark to create the database.
4. After the database is created, select the database **ClassDB**. Then, click **MANAGE** in the Database section to open the Windows Azure SQL Database Portal.

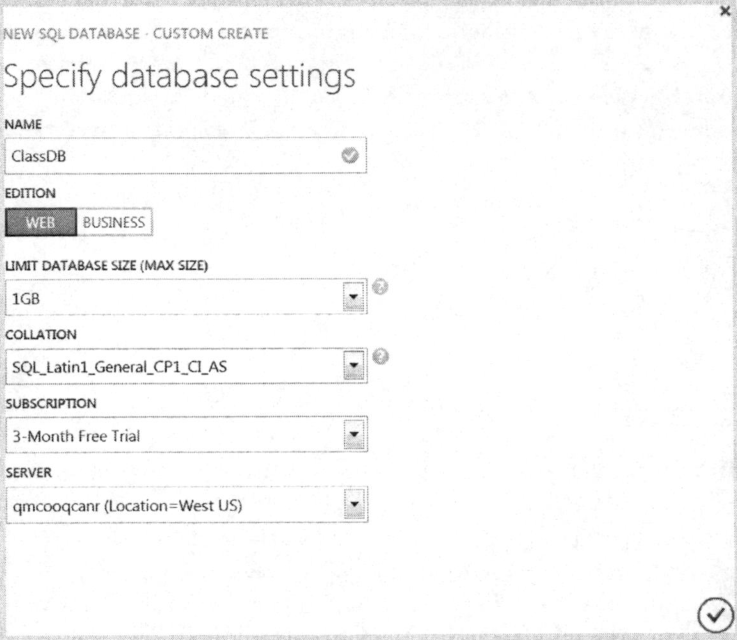

Figure 8.29 Create new database.

5. Enter your user name and password to log on to Windows Azure SQL Database.
6. Once you have logged on to your database, click the **New** icon on the ribbon to open the page for creating a new federation.
7. As shown in Figure 8.30, in the Create a Federation in ClassDB page, enter **Class_Federation** for Name, **ClassID** for Distribution Name, keep **bigint** for Distribution Data Type, and **RANGE** for Distribution Type. Then, click the **Save** button. The newly created federation will be shown on the right-hand side of your screen.

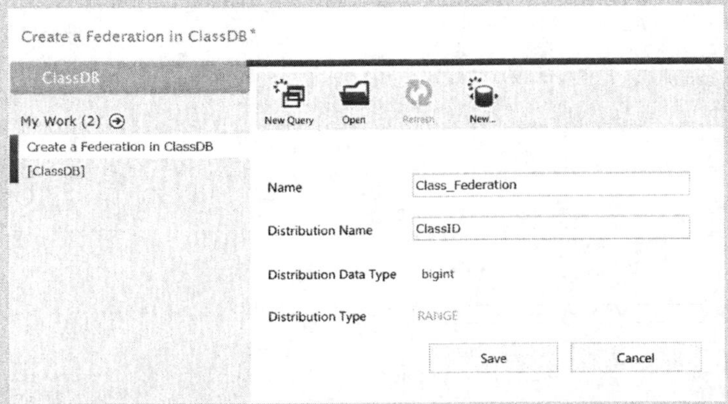

Figure 8.30 Create new federation.

TASK 2: CREATING FEDERATED AND NONFEDERATED TABLES

In this task, you will create a federated table, CLASS, with the FEDERATED ON property. You will also create several nonfederated tables COURSE, TIMEBLOCK, SEMESTER, and DAYS. These tables will be placed across all of the federation members. The following are the steps to create these tables:

1. On the Federation Administration page, click the icon → next to the **Class_Federation** link under the title Federation.
2. As shown in Figure 8.31, click the cell labeled **LOW** to open a context menu.
3. In the context menu, select **Query** and then click **Create Federated Table** to open the Query editor.
4. In the Query editor, enter the following SQL code and click the **Run** button on the ribbon:

```
CREATE TABLE COURSE
(
 CourseID CHAR(8) PRIMARY KEY,
 CourseName VARCHAR(30)
)
GO
CREATE TABLE DAYS
(
 DayID INT PRIMARY KEY,
 WeekDay VARCHAR(30)
)
GO
 CREATE TABLE SEMESTER
(
 SemesterID INT PRIMARY KEY,
 Semester VARCHAR(30)
)
GO
 CREATE TABLE TIMEBLOCK
(
 TimeID INT PRIMARY KEY,
 TimeBlock VARCHAR(30)
)
GO
 CREATE TABLE CLASS
(
 ClassID BIGINT PRIMARY KEY,
 CourseID CHAR(8),
 Credit INT,
 TimeID INT,
 SemesterID INT,
 DayID INT,
 CONSTRAINT Class_TimeId_fk FOREIGN KEY (TimeId)
   REFERENCES TIMEBLOCK (TimeId),
 CONSTRAINT Class_CourseId_fk FOREIGN KEY (CourseId)
```

```
  REFERENCES COURSE (CourseId),
CONSTRAINT Class_SemesterId_fk FOREIGN KEY (SemesterId)
  REFERENCES SEMESTER (SemesterId),
CONSTRAINT Class_DayId_fk FOREIGN KEY (DayId)
  REFERENCES DAYS (DayId)
)
FEDERATED ON ([ClassID] = ClassID)
```

5. The execution is shown in Figure 8.32.

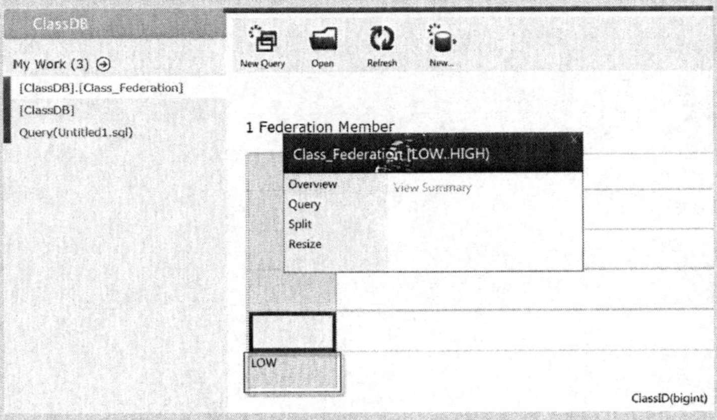
ClassDB
My Work (3)
[ClassDB].[Class_Federation]
[ClassDB]
Query(Untitled1.sql)
New Query
Open
Refresh
New...
1 Federation Member
Class_Federation [LOW..HIGH)
Overview
Query
Split
Resize
View Summary
LOW
ClassID(bigint)

Figure 8.31 Open context menu.

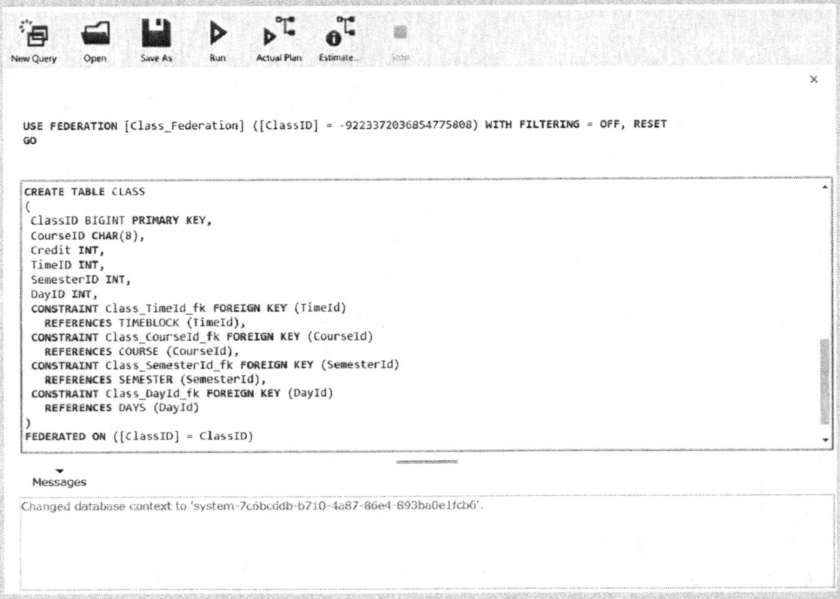
New Query
Open
Save As
Run
Actual Plan
Estimate...
USE FEDERATION [Class_Federation] ([ClassID] = -9223372036854775808) WITH FILTERING = OFF, RESET
GO
CREATE TABLE CLASS
(
ClassID BIGINT PRIMARY KEY,
CourseID CHAR(8),
Credit INT,
TimeID INT,
SemesterID INT,
DayID INT,
CONSTRAINT Class_TimeId_fk FOREIGN KEY (TimeId)
REFERENCES TIMEBLOCK (TimeId),
CONSTRAINT Class_CourseId_fk FOREIGN KEY (CourseId)
REFERENCES COURSE (CourseId),
CONSTRAINT Class_SemesterId_fk FOREIGN KEY (SemesterId)
REFERENCES SEMESTER (SemesterId),
CONSTRAINT Class_DayId_fk FOREIGN KEY (DayId)
REFERENCES DAYS (DayId)
)
FEDERATED ON ([ClassID] = ClassID)
Messages
Changed database context to 'system-7c6bcddb-b710-4a87-86e4-693ba0e1fcb6'.

Figure 8.32 Create federated table.

TASK 3: INSERTING DATA TO TABLES

After the tables are created, our next step is to insert data to those tables by following the below steps:

1. In the **ClassDB** pane on the left-hand side of your screen, click the link **[ClassDB].[Class_Federation]** and select **Query** on the context menu. Then, select **New Query** to open the New Query editor.
2. Enter the following SQL code and click the **Run** button on the ribbon:

```
--- inserting records into COURSE
INSERT INTO COURSE (CourseID, CourseName)
VALUES('ISC2301', 'VB')

INSERT INTO COURSE (CourseID, CourseName)
VALUES('ISC3311', 'Database')

INSERT INTO COURSE (CourseID, CourseName)
VALUES('ISC4301', 'E-Commerce')

INSERT INTO COURSE (CourseID, CourseName)
VALUES('ISC3321', 'Info-Systems')


--- inserting records into TIMEBLOCK
INSERT INTO TIMEBLOCK (TimeID, TimeBlock)
VALUES(1, '9am-12pm')

INSERT INTO TIMEBLOCK (TimeID, TimeBlock)
VALUES(2, '1pm-4pm')

INSERT INTO TIMEBLOCK (TimeID, TimeBlock)
VALUES(3, '7pm-10pm')


--- inserting records into SEMESTER
INSERT INTO SEMESTER(SemesterID, Semester)
VALUES(1, 'Fall')

INSERT INTO SEMESTER(SemesterID, Semester)
VALUES(2, 'Spring')

INSERT INTO SEMESTER(SemesterID, Semester)
VALUES(3, 'Summer')


--- inserting records into DAYS
INSERT INTO DAYS(DayID, WeekDay)
VALUES(1, 'Monday')

INSERT INTO DAYS(DayID, WeekDay)
VALUES(2, 'Tuesday')

INSERT INTO DAYS(DayID, WeekDay)
VALUES(3, 'Wednesday')
```

```
INSERT INTO DAYS(DayID, WeekDay)
VALUES(4, 'Thursday')

INSERT INTO DAYS(DayID, WeekDay)
VALUES(5, 'Friday')

INSERT INTO DAYS(DayID, WeekDay)
VALUES(6, 'Saturday')

INSERT INTO DAYS(DayID, WeekDay)
VALUES(7, 'Sunday')


--- inserting records into CLASS
INSERT INTO CLASS(ClassID, CourseID, Credit, TimeID, DayID,
SemesterID)
VALUES(201101, 'ISC2301', 4, 1, 1, 1)

INSERT INTO CLASS(ClassID, CourseID, Credit, TimeID, DayID,
SemesterID)
VALUES(201102, 'ISC3311', 4, 2, 1, 2)

INSERT INTO CLASS(ClassID, CourseID, Credit, TimeID, DayID,
SemesterID)
VALUES(201103, 'ISC4301', 3, 3, 2, 1)

INSERT INTO CLASS(ClassID, CourseID, Credit, TimeID, DayID,
SemesterID)
VALUES(201104, 'ISC2301', 4, 1, 2, 2)

INSERT INTO CLASS(ClassID, CourseID, Credit, TimeID, DayID,
SemesterID)
VALUES(201105, 'ISC3311', 4, 2, 3, 2)

INSERT INTO CLASS(ClassID, CourseID, Credit, TimeID, DayID,
SemesterID)
VALUES(201106, 'ISC4301', 3, 3, 3, 1)

INSERT INTO CLASS(ClassID, CourseID, Credit, TimeID, DayID,
SemesterID)
VALUES(201107, 'ISC3321', 3, 1, 4, 1)

INSERT INTO CLASS(ClassID, CourseID, Credit, TimeID, DayID,
SemesterID)
VALUES(201201, 'ISC2301', 4, 1, 1, 1)

INSERT INTO CLASS(ClassID, CourseID, Credit, TimeID, DayID,
SemesterID)
VALUES(201202, 'ISC3311', 4, 2, 1, 2)

INSERT INTO CLASS(ClassID, CourseID, Credit, TimeID, DayID,
SemesterID)
VALUES(201203, 'ISC4301', 3, 3, 2, 1)
```

```
INSERT INTO CLASS(ClassID, CourseID, Credit, TimeID, DayID,
SemesterID)
VALUES(201204, 'ISC2301', 4, 1, 2, 2)

INSERT INTO CLASS(ClassID, CourseID, Credit, TimeID, DayID,
SemesterID)
VALUES(201205, 'ISC3311', 4, 2, 3, 2)

INSERT INTO CLASS(ClassID, CourseID, Credit, TimeID, DayID,
SemesterID)
VALUES(201206, 'ISC4301', 3, 3, 3, 1)

INSERT INTO CLASS(ClassID, CourseID, Credit, TimeID, DayID,
SemesterID)
VALUES(201207, 'ISC3321', 3, 1, 4, 1)
```

TASK 4: SPLITTING FEDERATED TABLE

With the command SPLIT, you can split the rows in a federated table and place the partitions into two federation members. Assume that you want to divide the ClassIDs into two partitions. The first one contains the ClassIDs starting with 2011 and the second one contains the ClassIDs starting with 2012. Therefore, the split point can be chosen as 201199. Follow the below steps to split the rows in the CLASS table:

1. Assume that the Query editor is still open, in the **ClassDB** pane on the left-hand side of your screen, click the link **[ClassDB].[Class_Federation]**, and select **Split** on the context menu. Enter the split point 201199 as shown in Figure 8.33. Then, click the **Split** button.
2. Click the **Refresh** button on the ribbon. You should be able to see a new federation member labeled as 201199 shown in Figure 8.34.

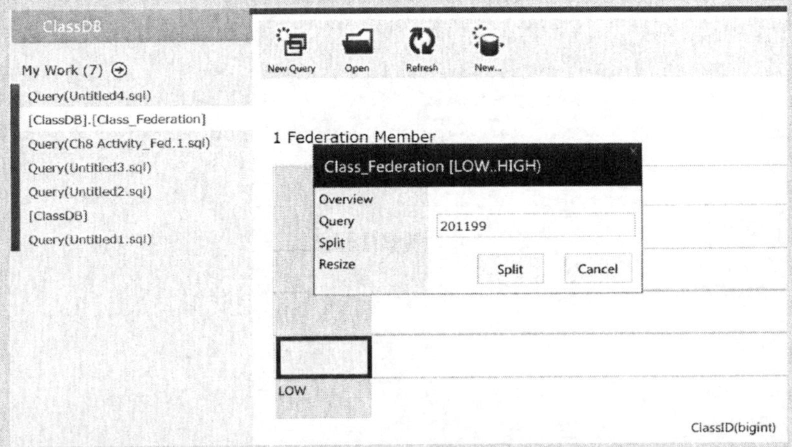

Figure 8.33 Split federated table.

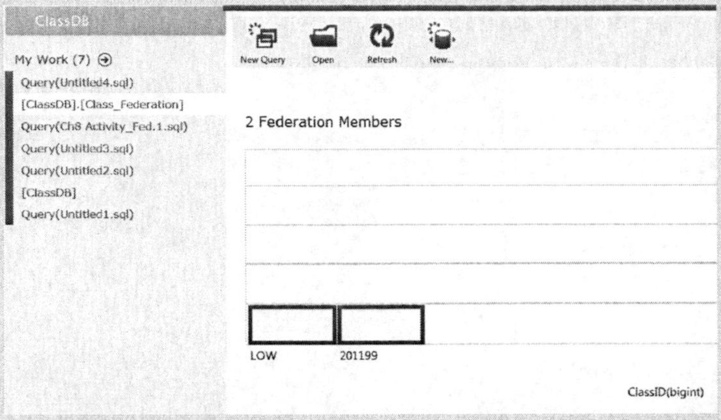

Figure 8.34 New federation member.

TASK 5: QUERYING FEDERATED TABLE

To illustrate the effect of the splitting of a federated table, you will query the federated table on different federation members. You will also query the federation metadata to reveal the structure of the federation members. Follow the below steps to carry out the query:

1. Assume that the Query editor is still open. In the **ClassDB** pane on the left-hand side of your screen, click the link **[ClassDB].[Class_Federation]**. Click the column labeled **LOW** to open the context menu. Select **Query** on the context menu. Then, select **New Query** to open the New Query editor.
2. Enter the following SQL code and click the **Run** button on the ribbon:

```
SELECT * FROM CLASS
```

3. The result of the query is shown in Figure 8.35 where the rows stored on the first federation member are selected. This is due to the fact that the federation key range is (-9223372036854775808, 201199).
4. To query the federated table stored on the second federation member, in the **ClassDB** pane on the left-hand side of your screen, click the link **[ClassDB].[Class_Federation]**. As shown in Figure 8.36, click the column labeled as **201199** to open the context menu.
5. Select **Query** on the context menu. Then, select **New Query** to open the New Query editor. Notice that, this time, in the USE FEDERATION statement, the ClassID starts from 201199.
6. Enter the following SQL code and click the **Run** button on the ribbon:

```
SELECT * FROM CLASS
```

7. The result of the query is shown in Figure 8.37 where the rows stored on the second federation member are selected.
8. By setting the property FILTERING as ON in the USE FEDERATION statement, you will have more control on what to query. For example, you can limit the range of

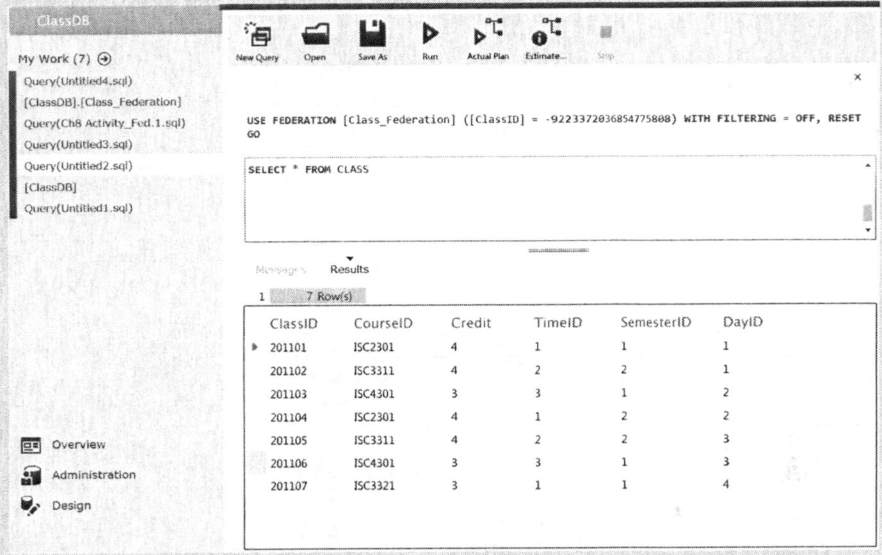

Figure 8.35 Query federated table on first federation member.

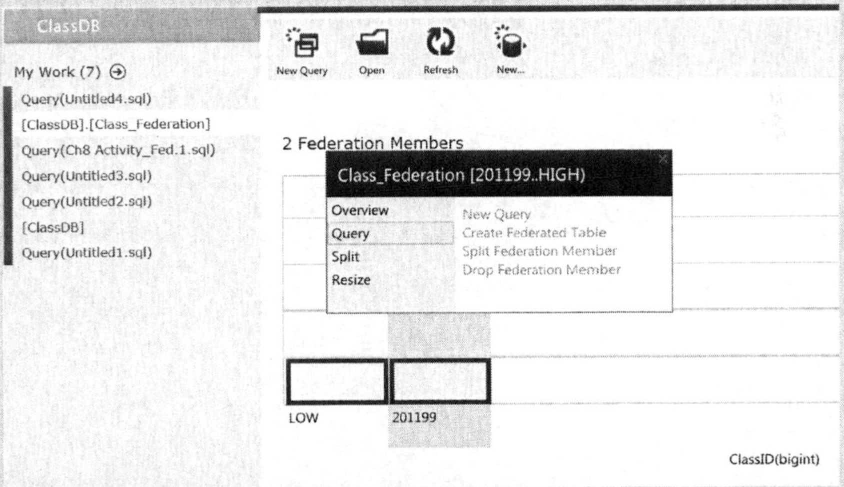

Figure 8.36 Work on second federation member.

a selection to a specific class id. To do so, click the **New Query** button on the ribbon and enter the following SQL code:

```
USE FEDERATION [Class_Federation] ([ClassID] = 201205) WITH
FILTERING = ON, RESET
GO
SELECT * FROM CLASS
```

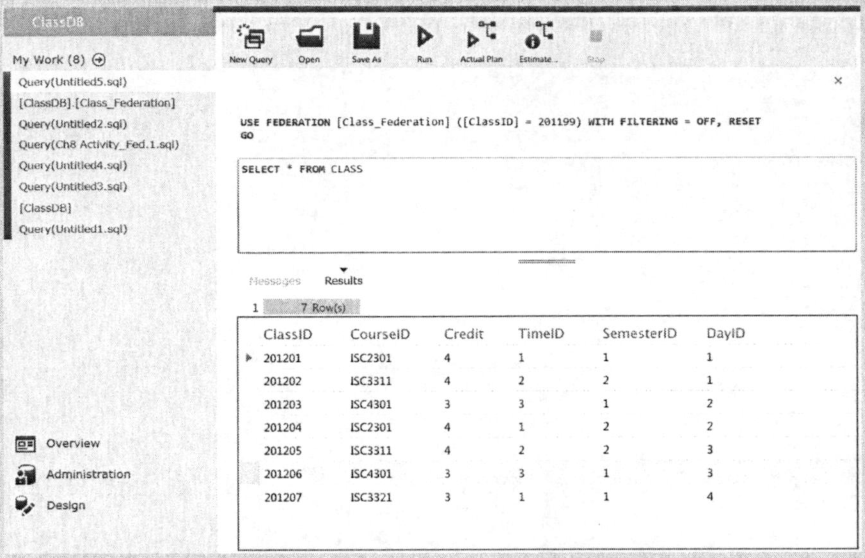

Figure 8.37 Query federated table on second federation member.

9. Highlight the code and click the **Run** button on the ribbon. The query result is shown in Figure 8.38 where only one row with ClassID 201205 is selected.
10. To view the structure of the federation member, you can query the metadata stored in the built-in view sys.federation_member_distributions with the following SQL statement in the **New Query** pane:

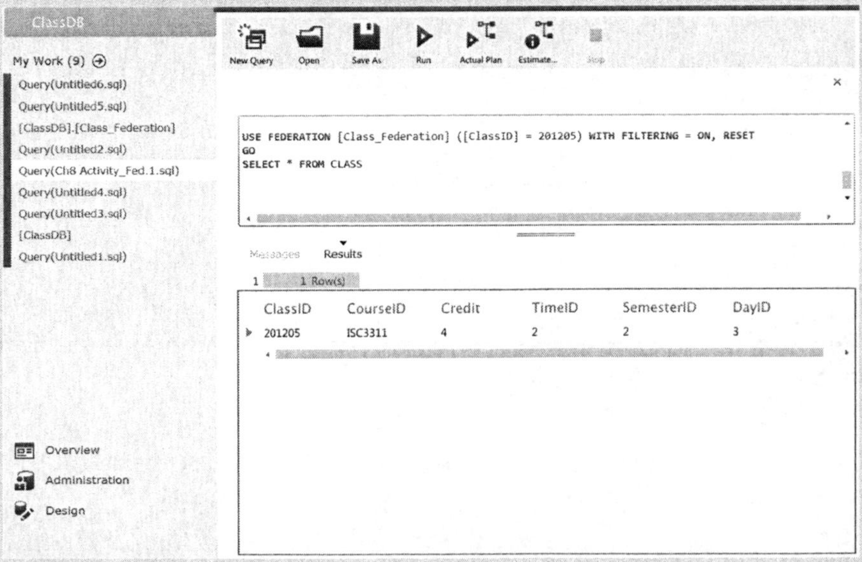

Figure 8.38 Query federated table with FILTERING = ON.

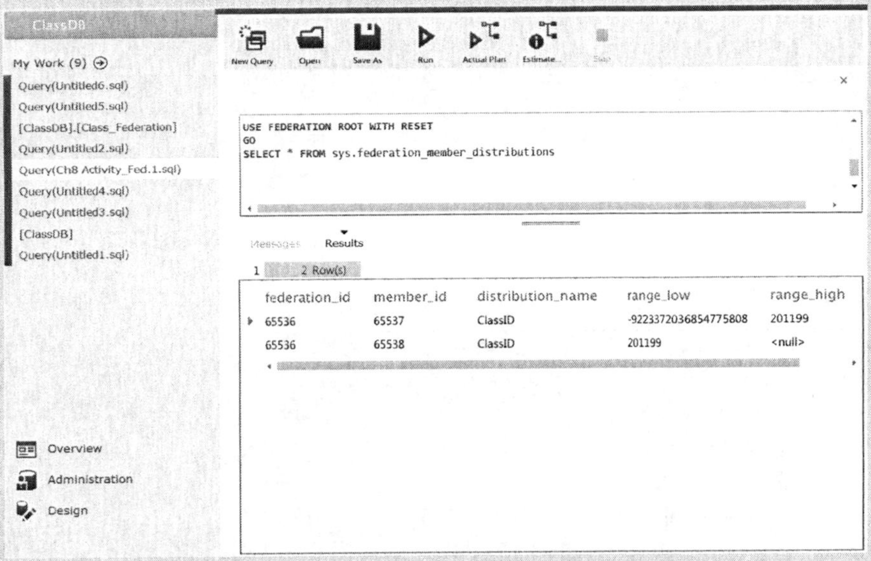

Figure 8.39 Query federation member metadata.

```
USE FEDERATION ROOT WITH RESET
GO
SELECT * FROM sys.federation_member_distributions
```

11. Enter the above code in the New Query editor, highlight the code, and click the **Run** button on the ribbon. The query result is shown in Figure 8.39 where the information about the two federation members is listed.

Through the above steps, you have learned how to create a federation. In that federation, a federated table is created and is split into two partitions. Queries of the federated table can be controlled by the distribution ids. By changing the range of the distribution ids, one is able to select the rows on a specific federation member. The metadata about the federation members can be viewed by the database administrator.

8.5 Summary

This chapter covers the concepts and hands-on practice about views, indexes, and federations. These programming units are used for improving scalability and performance.

This chapter gives detailed descriptions of the benefits of views to support database applications. The hands-on activity of views demonstrates how to create, modify, and drop views. It also shows how the modification of a view impacts the underlying table.

The concepts of indexes are also discussed in this chapter. The index hands-on activity illustrates that the index use can significantly improve the performance of a cloud-based database.

Federations are important to databases on the cloud due to the size limit on each individual database. For business use, each SQL database is limited to 50 GB in size. For other usage, an

SQL database is limited to 1 GB. To expand the database size beyond the limit and to improve performance, the federation technology can get the job done. This chapter discusses the concepts of federations. It also includes some design strategies to fully take advantage of the federation technology. For creating and managing federations, this chapter introduces a set of SQL statements. In the federation hands-on activity, we have created and managed a federation for the database ClassDB. The hands-on activity illustrates how to query information from different federation members.

Review Questions

1. What are the advantages of using views in database applications?
2. How can indexes be used to improve query performance?
3. In what situations will indexes not improve performance?
4. What are the restrictions when creating a view?
5. When can a view be updated?
6. What are the restrictions for modification operations on a view?
7. In the New Query editor, create a view FACULTY_CLASS_VIEW, including all rows from the single table FACULTY_CLASS. Perform the insert, delete, and update operations to demonstrate the modifications on the table FACULTY_CLASS through the view.
8. What is a clustered index? What is the advantage of the clustered index?
9. What is a nonclustered index?
10. What is a composite index?
11. In the New Query editor, create an index called Faculty_Index on the Name column in FACULTY the table.
12. Why do federations play an important role in database application development?
13. What is a federation?
14. Why do we need federations?
15. What is a federation key?
16. What command is used to split a federated table?
17. What is a federation member?
18. What is an atomic unit?
19. What is a federation table?
20. What types of data can be used to generate federation keys?

Chapter 9

Database Application Development

Objectives

- Create forms
- Design user interfaces

9.1 Introduction

Once an SQL database is made available on Windows Azure, it is time to develop database applications. Through these applications, users can interact with the database to perform tasks such as importing and exporting data, enforcing constraints and security, and implementing business logic.

To assist users in dealing with the data stored in databases, various database applications are created. Forms are used to enter, display, and update data stored in a database. Reports are used to present information. Data stored in a database can also be used for data analysis and for decision making. A database application provides a GUI environment where controls and menus are created for data manipulation.

Database applications can be created with programming languages such as VB.NET, C#.NET, ASP.NET, Java, or scripting languages such as JavaScript, PHP, and Pearl, or enhanced SQL languages such as Transact-SQL. Microsoft Visual Studio is a commonly used database application development package. It provides an integrated environment that supports multiple programming languages. Microsoft Access is a DBMS mainly for small businesses or personal database use. It is also a good application development tool for creating forms and reports.

Database applications can greatly benefit from the cloud computing platform. With the hardware, network and license-related issues are taken care of by the cloud provider and the application developers can focus on developing the database applications. These database applications can be deployed on the Internet so that they are available to anyone who has the permission to access them.

In this chapter, you will learn various ways to create and manage database applications. You will also learn how to use these applications to access data and how to use these applications to manage database objects on Windows Azure.

9.2 Database Application Design

A database application development process, in general, may include three phases including design, development, and deployment. The descriptions of these phases are given below:

- **Design**: The design phase starts with the requirement analysis. It investigates the needs and constraints from a business process. The design phase also collects information about the IT infrastructure used to support an application. On the basis of the result of the analysis, the application designer will be able to identify the actions to be implemented in an application and the GUIs for processing the data stored in a data source. After the actions and GUIs are determined, the application designer will decide which platform the application will run on and which tools will be used to create the application.
- **Develop**: In this phase, the database application will be developed based on the specifications established in the design phase. Microsoft Visual Studio and SQL Server can be used to create the programming units for implementing the actions and GUIs. The components related to network communication will be added to the application. The remote data access mechanisms will also be properly configured in the development phase.
- **Deploy**: In the deployment phase, the database application will first be tested before it can be deployed to front-end users. The programming units and GUIs should function flawlessly. During the testing, the application developers need to make sure that the network functionality and remote access all work properly. If there are errors, the application developer and the database administrator should work together to fix the problems before the application can be deployed to the public. Once the application is deployed, it is necessary to provide training, instructional documents, and technical support for the front-end users.

To further improve the application, it is necessary to get feedback from the users. The users' feedback can then be used as a guideline for further improvement. The new version of the application should address the users' feedback.

9.2.1 Application Design

To make database applications meet the requirements of a business process, our first task is to understand the business process. A good understanding of the business process often leads to good database application designs.

The first step to accomplish this task is to identify data entry and data updating activities in the business process. For example, for class registration, we can identify the following data entry and updating tasks:

- Students need to fill out the online class registration forms.
- The registration office needs to update the students' class schedules.
- The students' grades need to be updated each semester.

- Faculty teaching assignments need to be updated.
- Each new student will be assigned a faculty member as his/her advisor.
- The course descriptions need to be updated each semester, and so on.

The next step is to identify the information that needs to be presented to front-end users. For example

- The students need to view their grade reports.
- Before class registration, the students need to know the course prerequisites.
- The dean needs to view the faculty's teaching loads.
- The Admissions Office needs to view the class schedule.
- Faculty members need to view the teaching schedule, and so on.

To assist the front-end users to accomplish these tasks, many GUIs can be developed to allow the front-end users to manipulate data without using SQL commands. GUIs are also used by database administrators for database management. A GUI consists of labels and controls such as buttons and text boxes. For database applications, forms and reports are the two types of commonly used GUI.

Before developing a GUI, let us examine some GUI examples for database applications and get to know the features provided by each of the controls.

Form: A form can be used to help front-end users to insert data into a database or update the existing data in an existing database. Figure 9.1 shows a set of controls commonly used in a form.

When working with an electronic form, front-end users are able to enter data through a text box. In a combo box, the users can select an item from the drop-down list and edit the selected item. They can start an action by clicking the command button. They can also make a choice

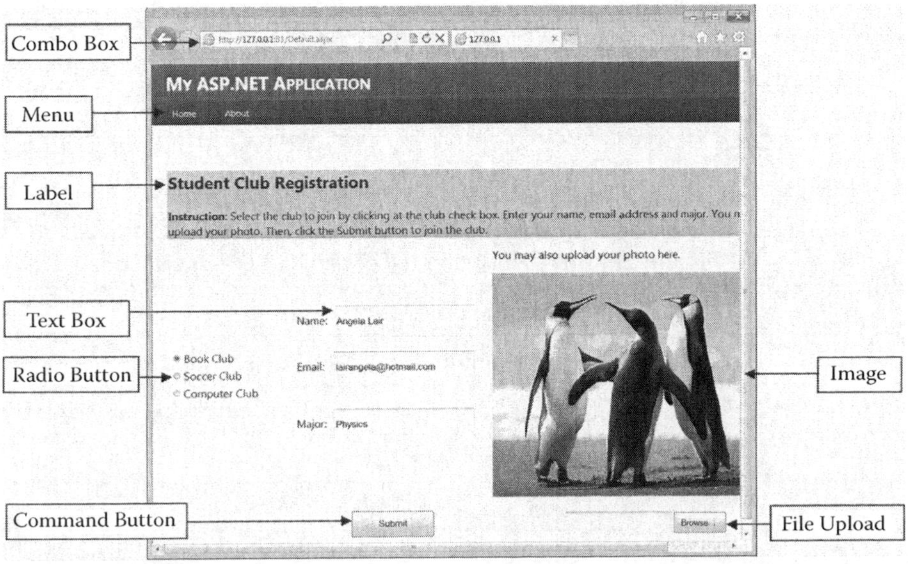

Figure 9.1 Form.

through the radio button control. The users are able to upload an image file with the file upload control and present the image in a picture box. With the form, the front-end users do not have to know SQL statements such as INSERT, UPDATE, and DELETE for data management. The controls on the form are linked to a data source such as a relational database. The data presented on the form are extracted from the linked database. Modifications made to the data on the form are saved to the corresponding tables in the back-end database. In Figure 9.1, several commonly used controls are displayed. These application controls are used to help the front-end users to manipulate data. Table 9.1 describes a list of controls.

Report: Report is another important database application that is used to display data extracted from a database in a certain format. Similar to a form, a report contains controls and graphics. Unlike a form, the main task of a report is to display data. A report may include some components such as Report Header, Page Header, Detail, Page Footer, and Report Footer. To make it easier to read, a report is often divided into several sections. In such a case, a report may have multiple header components, multiple detail sections, and multiple footer components. Figure 9.2 shows an example of a report.

The report in Figure 9.2 has a binding navigator that is used to navigate through each student. The binding navigator has a tool strip interface that contains items such as Save and Print. Each student's grade and other class-related information are displayed in a table.

Table 9.1 Descriptions of Controls

Control Name	*Description*
Binding Navigator	This control is used to navigate data sets displayed in a form or report.
Check Box	This control allows users to select options in a list of check boxes.
Combo Box	This control can be used to display and edit a drop-down list of items.
Command Button	This control triggers an action such as starting, stopping, or interrupting a process.
FormView	This control is used to display and edit a single record in a table.
GridView	This control can be used to display data in a customizable grid.
Image	The image control is a repository for images.
Label	The label control can be used to display text as a label.
List Box	This can be used to display a list of text and graphical items.
Menu Strip	This control provides custom menus.
Picture Box	This control displays pictures in a frame.
Radio Button	This control allows users to select an option by clicking at a radio button.
Table	This control lays out its content in a table.
Text Box	This control can be used to display and edit text.
Tool Strip	This control creates tool bars.

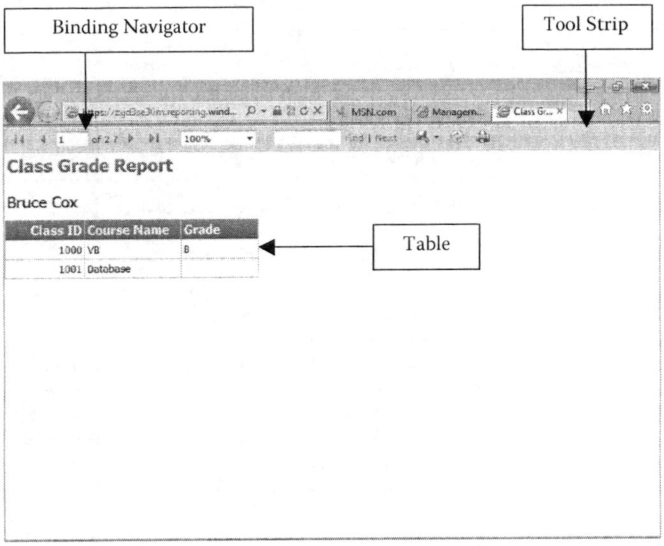

Figure 9.2 Report.

General Design Guidelines: There are some general guidelines about how a GUI should be properly designed so that it is easy to use and properly reflects the view structure. These guidelines are listed below:

- The locations of controls should be convenient for application users. For example, place the related controls together and use a frame to surround these controls.
- A GUI should be designed to help front-end users avoid mistakes. For example, a text box for entering e-mail should verify if the text entered has the correct e-mail address format.
- The design of a GUI should reflect the structure of an underlying table, view, or stored procedure. That is, the names of the columns from the same table should be placed close to each other in a form.
- In the case that an application needs to display detailed information related to an item displayed on the main form or main report, a subform or subreport should be created. The content displayed on the subform or subreport should be consistent with content on the main form.
- The ultimate goal of the GUI design is to create a form or a report that reduces the anxiety of front-end users and helps them process data stored in a database. The database application developer may have to modify the original design many times based on users' feedback.

9.2.2 GUI Design

The GUI design is commonly carried out with the following procedure:

- Identify the input and output of an application, and then design a GUI that can be used to enter the input and display the output.
- Specify the data source connection mechanism.
- Identify actions involved in data manipulation, and then write code to implement these actions.

Table 9.2 Input and Output

Input	*Output*
A class schedule	Updated class schedule
A selected class	Selected class info that will be displayed on a subform
Changes made to a selected class	Status after saving the edited class

Table 9.3 Action Descriptions

Event	*Action*
Click Select button	Select a class to update or delete
Click New link	Insert a new class
Click Edit link	Update class info
Click Delete link	Delete a class from the class schedule
Click Insert link	Insert a new or updated class to the database
Click Cancel link	Not save a new or updated class to the database

As an example, let us consider designing a form for class schedule management. The form can be used for inserting, updating, and deleting classes. This form allows the staff members at the Admissions Office to extract data from the database Class_Registration and display the class schedule in a GridView control. A staff member can also update or delete a selected class. When a class is selected for updating, a subform is opened for the staff member to change the schedule. According to the description of the form, we can identify the input and output shown in Table 9.2.

In Table 9.3, a set of actions are defined.

According to the input/output and the actions identified in Tables 9.2 and 9.3, one possible GUI can be designed as shown in Figure 9.3.

The design has three sections. The first section contains the form title and the instruction on using the form. The second section contains the GridView control and FormView control. The GridView control is used to display the class schedule and to select a class so that its information can be displayed in the FormView. The FormView contains text boxes to display the selected class information. The FormView control also includes links for editing the form content. When the updated form content is saved, the current status will be displayed in the status label placed in the bottom section.

9.3 Database Application Development

As mentioned previously, many tools are available for creating forms. To create database applications for Windows Azure SQL Database, the choice is Microsoft Visual Studio that includes three components, integrated development environment (IDE), Windows Azure SDK, and Microsoft .NET Framework, which can significantly simplify the development of database applications.

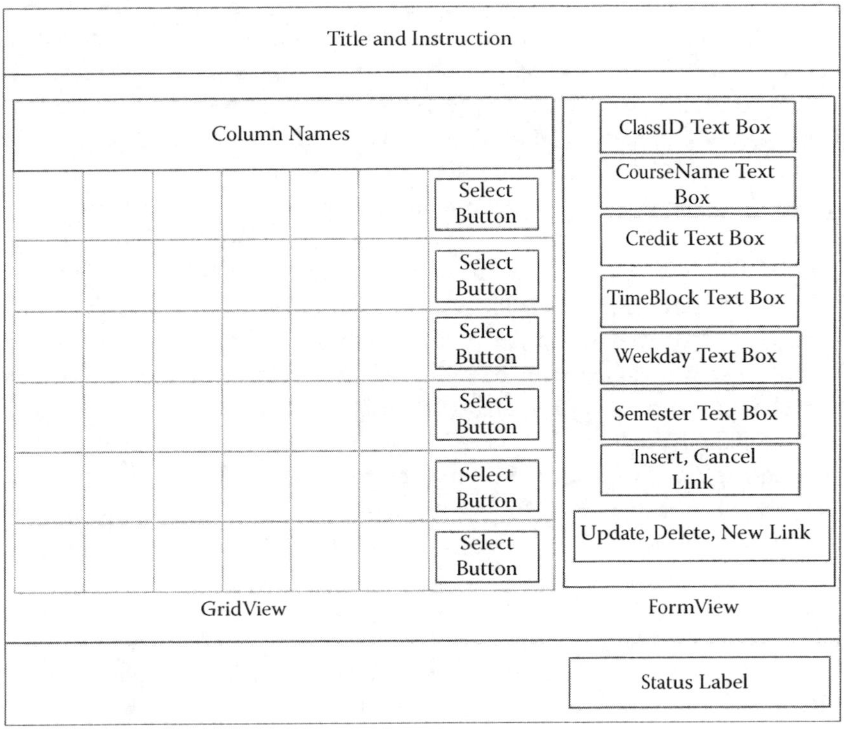

Figure 9.3 GUI design.

The IDE allows application developers to create mixed-language projects. It also allows different programming languages to share the tools. It provides various tools for building Windows applications, web applications, XML web services, desktop applications, and mobile applications.

When creating forms, the IDE supports various programming languages such as Visual Basic, Visual C#, ASP.NET, and Visual C++. It is designed to fully integrate with the Windows Azure SDK. Windows Azure SDK provides a set of tools for running, testing, debugging, and tuning database applications before the applications are deployed to Windows Azure.

Microsoft.NET Framework provides a library of code packages, including data access, database connectivity, cryptography, network communication, user interface, and web application development. The tools provided by .NET Framework are used for developing network capable applications such as web forms and reports.

9.3.1 Form Development

In this chapter, based on the GUI design, Microsoft Visual Studio will be used to create a GUI given in Figure 9.3. The programming language C# included in Visual Studio will be used to implement the actions listed in Table 9.3. Since C# provides the templates used to handle those events listed in Table 9.3, the effort on programming can be reduced significantly.

Among the tools provided by Visual Studio, Forms Designer is particularly useful for developing forms. Forms Designer provides a platform for the database application developer to create forms. It provides various form controls such as text box, combo box, dialog box, menu strip, buttons, and many other controls. The application developer can drag these controls from the Toolbox to Forms Designer. The code units implementing these controls are included in the .NET Framework class library. Once all of the controls are added, the application developer can change properties of the controls such as changing a control's name or size. The application developer needs to specify the data source for some of the controls if these controls need to present data extracted from a database. The application developer also needs to add code for implementing actions triggered by a control such as the command button.

The development process starts with dragging the controls from the Toolbox to the Designer pane. Position these controls according to the design shown in Figure 9.3. Figure 9.4 presents the GUI design of the Class Schedule Management form implemented with Visual Studio.

The next step is to name the controls shown in Figure 9.4 and then set the properties for these controls. Table 9.4 gives the names of the controls and the properties configured for these controls.

After the GUI is implemented, your next task is to implement the actions with a programming language. In this chapter, C# is the programming language to be used. As shown in Figure 9.4, the event will be generated by clicking the Select button, and the Update, Delete, or New links. The FormView also includes two other links Insert and Cancel. C# provides the built-in methods to handle these events. Table 9.5 lists the methods to be used for the Class Schedule Management form.

As seen in Table 9.5, most of the actions are handled by the built-in methods. The methods provided by C# take care of the data source connection. They update the data source according to which the link has been clicked. They also maintain the relationship between the GridView and FormView. The main coding task for the application developer is to write the code to update the message of the Status label. On the data source side, the database administrator needs to prepare a data set used as the input of the GridView. For the GridView and FormView controls, we may need to add some SQL statements to carry out tasks such as update, delete, and insert data into the

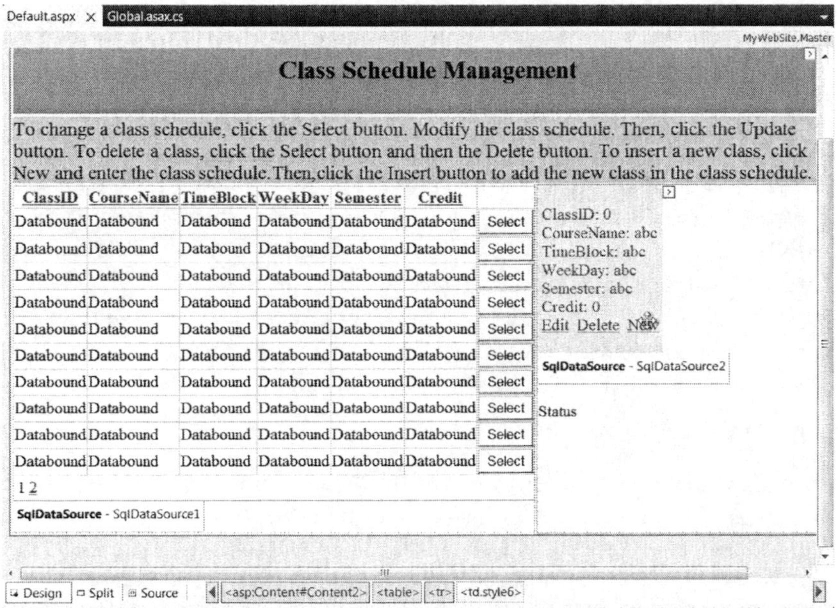
Default.aspx
Global.asax.cs
MyWebSite.Master
Class Schedule Management
To change a class schedule, click the Select button. Modify the class schedule. Then, click the Update button. To delete a class, click the Select button and then the Delete button. To insert a new class, click New and enter the class schedule. Then, click the Insert button to add the new class in the class schedule.
ClassID CourseName TimeBlock WeekDay Semester Credit
Databound Databound Databound Databound Databound Databound Select
1 2
SqlDataSource - SqlDataSource1
ClassID: 0
CourseName: abc
TimeBlock: abc
WeekDay: abc
Semester: abc
Credit: 0
Edit Delete New
SqlDataSource - SqlDataSource2
Status
Design
Split
Source
<asp:Content#Content2> <table> <tr> <td.style6>

Figure 9.4 GUI design in visual studio.

Table 9.4 Control Specifications

Control Name	*Property*	*Configuration*
GridView1	AllowPaging	True
	AllowSorting	True
	AutoGenerateColumns	False
	DatakeyName	ClassID
	DatasourceID	SqlDataSource1
	Width	680 px
lblStatus	Text	Status
Table1	Frame	Border
	Style	Width: 100%
	Width	160 px
FormView1	DataSourceID	SqlDataSource2
	DatakeyName	ClassID
	Height	200 px
	CellPadding	4
	ForeColor	#333333

Table 9.5 Action Implementation

Event	*Method to Use*	*Action*
Clicking the Delete, Update, and New links in FormView1	FormView1_ItemDeleted()	Delete a record in the data source and write a message to the Status label.
	FormView1_ ItemUpdated()	Update a record in the data source and write a message to the Status label.
	FormView1_ ItemInserted()	Insert a record in the data source and write a message to the Status label.
Clicking the Insert and Cancel links in FormView1	FormView1 uses the built-in Insert method	Update the data source with the edited content.
	FormView1 uses the built-in Cancel method	Not to update the data source.
Clicking the Select button in GridView1	GridView1 uses the built-in Select method	Select a record and pass it to FormView1 for editing.

database Class_Registration. We will discuss how to develop a data source in Activity 9.1, where we will also create the Class Schedule Management form.

9.3.2 Report Development

For the development of reports, we can use the powerful cloud-based reporting service Microsoft Windows Azure SQL Reporting, which is built on SQL Server Reporting Services technologies. Azure SQL Reporting provides tools for creating, managing, and displaying reports. It also allows qualified developers to access the data source. With the tools provided by SQL Reporting, developers are able to perform the authoring and publishing of reports.

With the cloud-based SQL Reporting service, application developers are able to rapidly create highly scalable reports. Windows Azure SQL Reporting supports various data sources and works within the Microsoft Visual Studio.NET environment. Through a set of application programming interfaces (APIs), these reports can also be embedded in other database applications. Visual Studio provides the Report Viewer control, which can be used to embed a report in a database application such as a web form.

Through the cloud, the reports are widely available to front-end users and application developers. The reports are hosted on a report server with a fully qualified URL. The users can view the reports through a browser or through the SQL Reporting portal.

In the Windows Azure Management Portal, you can find the SQL Reporting Management portal as shown in Figure 9.5.

In the SQL Reporting Management portal, you can find the report server information including the fully qualified server URL, the server administrator's URL, the region in which the server was created, and the percentage of space used by the reporting service. The portal also includes the

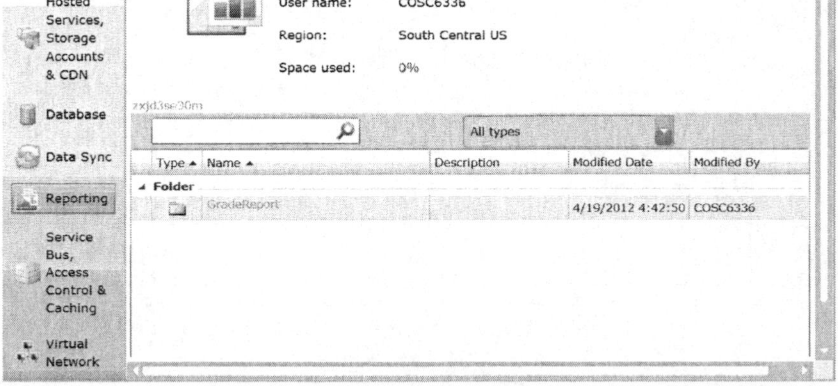

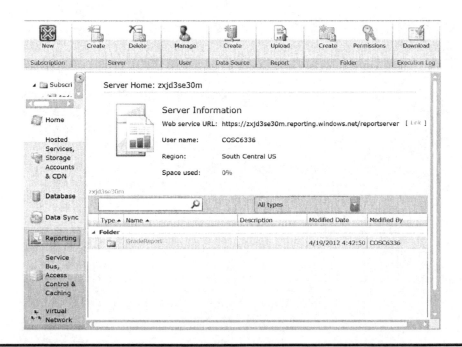

Figure 9.5 SQL reporting management portal.

folders that contain the data sources and reports. With the SQL Reporting Management portal, the application developer can perform the following tasks:

- Create a subscription for the reporting service.
- Create an SQL Reporting server to host reports.
- After the report server is created, create users on the server and assign these users with different permission levels.
- Upload reports to the report server so that the reports can be accessed by front-end users.
- Run, update, and download reports.
- Create folders for report organization.
- Create and edit data sources for the reports.
- Monitor the usage of the reports.

In the next chapter, we will accomplish some of the tasks with the SQL Reporting Management portal after the Windows Azure computing environment is introduced.

ACTIVITY 9.1 DEVELOPING WEB FORM

In this activity, we will first create the Class Schedule Management form for managing the class schedule. To make the form a web form so that front-end users can access it through a web browser, we will create the form with ASP.NET, which is provided by Microsoft Visual Studio. The following steps will achieve our goals:

TASK 1: CREATE ASP.NET WEB FORM

1. Assume that Microsoft Visual Studio is installed on the virtual machine created in Chapter 1. To log on to the virtual machine, you need to log on to the Windows Azure Management Portal through your web browser. After you have logged in, click **VIRTUAL MACHINES**. Select the server **myserver**, which is created in Chapter 1 and click **CONNECT**. Then, log on to the virtual machine with your user name and password.
2. After you have logged in, press the **Windows Icon** key and right click the icon **Visual Studio 2012** on the tile. Click **Run as administrator**.
3. To create a new project, click the **New Project** link. In the **Recent Templates** pane on the left-hand side of the screen, click **Web** and select **ASP.NET Web Forms Application** in the template pane. Rename the project as **MyWebForm** (Figure 9.6). Then, click **OK** to create the project.
4. Click **SQL Server Object Explorer** on the left-hand side of the screen. In the SQL Server Object Explorer, click the **Add Server** icon. On the Connect to Server dialog, enter the information about the server name, authentication, login, and password as shown in Figure 9.7. Then, click **Connect**. Note that your server name should be different from the server name qmcooqcanr listed in Figure 9.7.
5. The next task is to create a web page, which will be used to manage the data. To do so, in the Solution Explorer, right click on the **MyWebForm** node and select **Add**

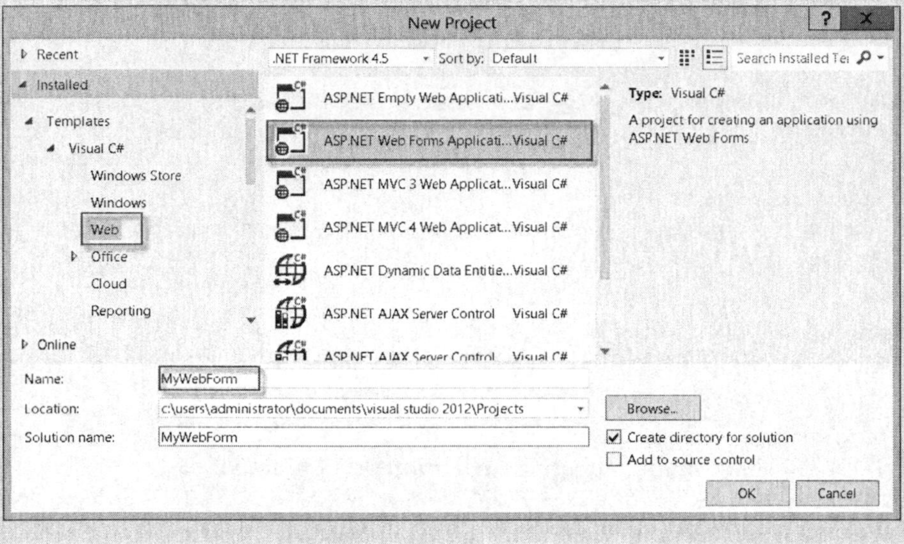

Figure 9.6 Create ASP.NET application.

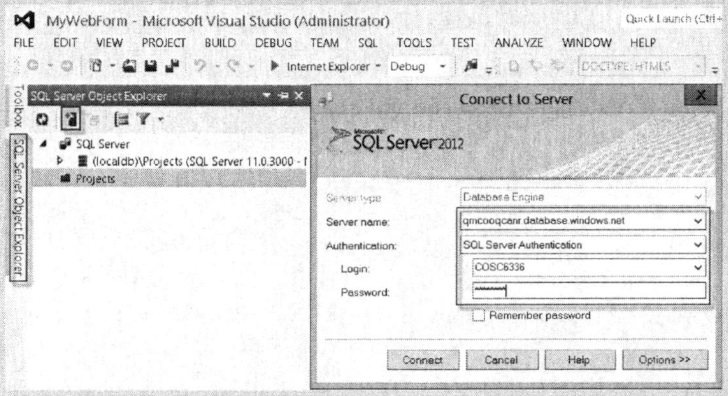

Figure 9.7 Connect to SQL Azure server.

| **New Item**. In the **Installed Templates** pane, select **Web**. Click **Master Page** and name the page as **MyWebSite.Master** (Figure 9.8). Then, click **Add**.

6. Once the MyWebSite.Master page is created, the original default page Default.aspx can be deleted. Right click **Default.aspx** and select **Delete**.
7. Next, let us add a web form. To do so, right click the project **MyWebForm** in the Solution Explorer pane and select **Add | New Item**. In the **Installed Templates** pane, select **Web**. Click **Web Form using Master Page** and name the form as **Default.aspx** (Figure 9.9). Then, click **Add**.
8. On the Select a Master Page dialog, select **MyWebSite.Master** and click **OK**.

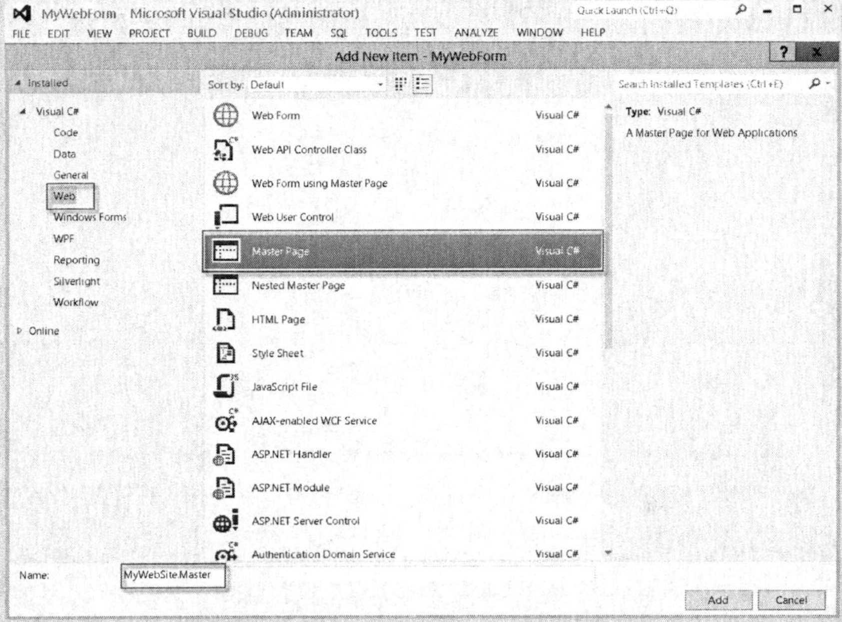

Figure 9.8 Create main web page.

Figure 9.9 Create web form using master page.

9. On the Master page, you can add the title for your web form. To do so, double click **MyWebSite.Master** in the Solution Explorer pane. Add the following code as shown in Figure 9.10:

```
<h1> Class Schedule Management Web Page </h1>
```

Figure 9.10 Add web form title.

TASK 2: GUI DESIGN

Your next task is to design the web form by adding some controls.

1. In the **Default.aspx** window, click the **Design** button to switch to the design view. Expand the **Toolbox** on the left-hand side of the screen. Then, expand the **HTML** section and drag the **Table** control to the **ContentPlaceHolder**. You should have the table design shown in Figure 9.11.

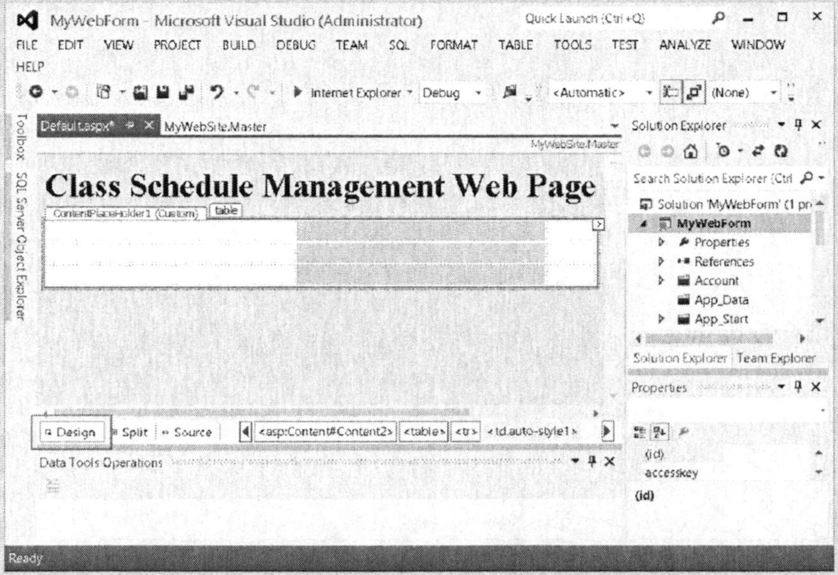

Figure 9.11 Add table control.

2. Select the first two cells on the first row of the HTML table, right click the selected row and select **Modify**, and then **Merge** (Figure 9.12). For merged cells, you can change the background color. To do so, in the **Properties** pane at the bottom-right of your screen, select **Style** and double click the **[...]** sign. In the Modify Style dialog, change the color to silver as shown in Figure 9.13.
3. Type the instruction as Instruction: **To change a class schedule, click the Select button. Modify the class schedule. Then, click the Update button. To delete a class, click the Select button. Then, click the Delete button. To insert a new class, click**

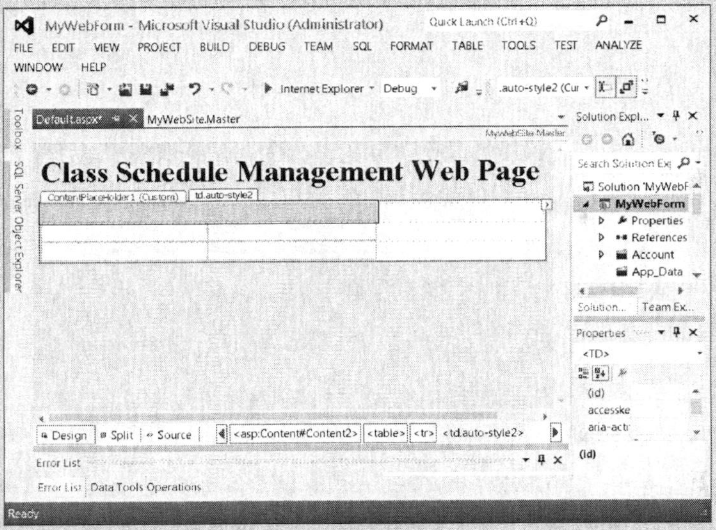

Figure 9.12 Merge cells.

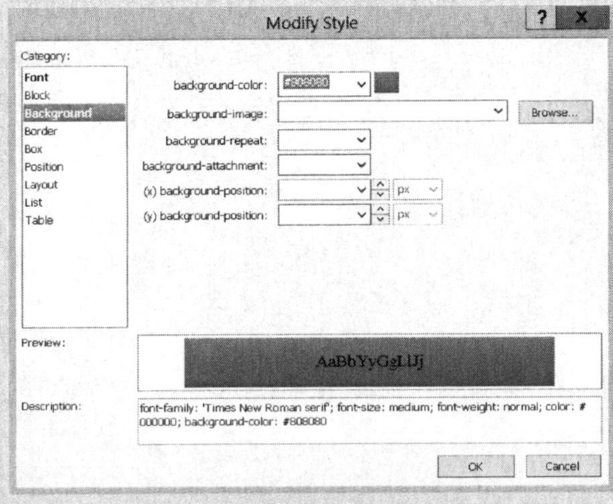

Figure 9.13 Configure background color.

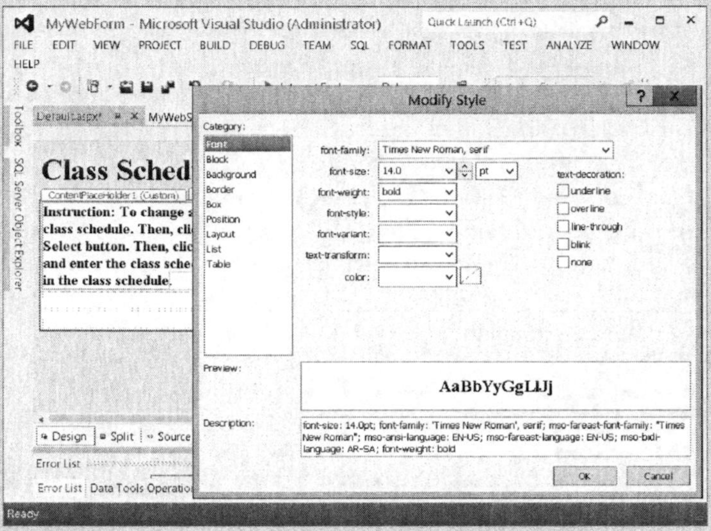

Figure 9.14 Modify font.

New and enter the class schedule; then click the Insert button to add the new class in the class schedule.

4. Highlight the text entered at the previous step. In the **Properties** pane, select **Style** and click the **[...]** sign to open the Modify Style dialog. In the Modify Style dialog, you may change the font size to **14 pt** and the font weight to **bold** as shown in Figure 9.14. Then click **OK**.
5. Select the entire table. Double click the icon next to Style to open the Modify Style dialog. Set the **Position** property as shown in Figure 9.15.

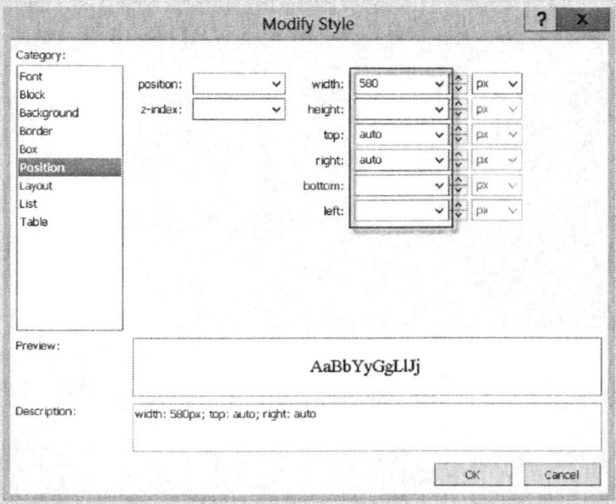

Figure 9.15 Configure position.

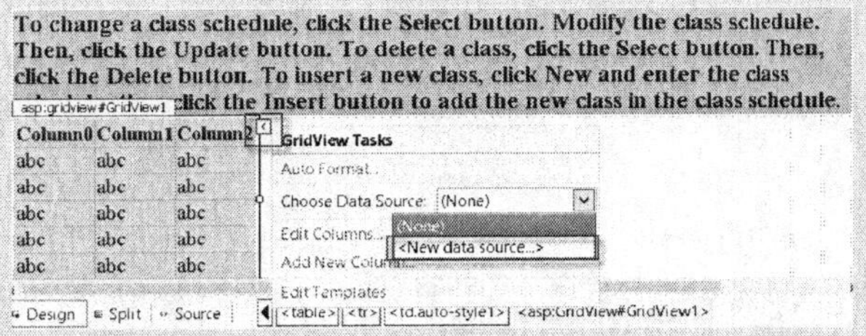

Figure 9.16 Configure new data source for GridView.

6. In the **Toolbox**, expand the **Data** section, drag a **GridView** control to the first cell of the second row. Click the smart tab > which is located at the up-right corner of the GridView. In the **Choose Data Source** drop-down list, select **New Data Source** as shown in Figure 9.16.
7. After the **New Data Source** dialog is opened, select the **SQL Database** icon and then click the **OK** button. On the **New Connection** drop-down list, select **Microsoft SQL Server** in the Data source pane and select**.NET Framework Data Provider for SQL Server** in the Data provider drop-down list as shown in Figure 9.17. Then, click **Continue.**
8. Enter the connection information to your Windows Azure SQL Database as shown in Figure 9.18. Then, click **OK.**
9. Click Next twice to go to the **Configure, the Select Statement** page. Then, click the option **Specify a custom SQL statement or stored procedure.** Then, click **Next.**

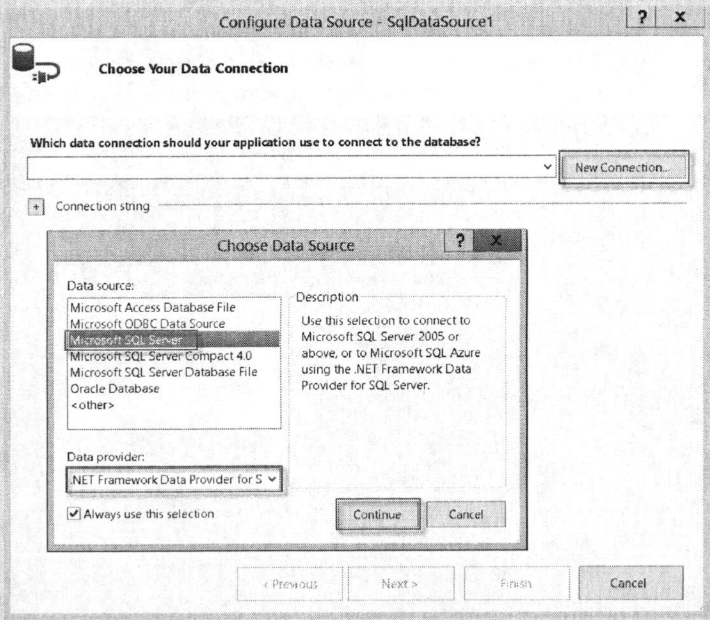

Figure 9.17 Configure data source for GridView.

Figure 9.18 Configure connection.

10. On the Define Custom Statements or Stored Procedure page, click the **Query Builder** button. In the Query Builder dialog, add the tables **CLASS**, **COURSE**, **SEMESTER**, **DAYS**, and **TIMEBLOCK**. Then, select the columns **ClassID**, **CourseName**, **TimeBlock**, **WeekDay**, **Semester**, and **Credit**. Click **Execute Query** to make sure that the query is working properly as shown in Figure 9.19. Then, click **OK**.

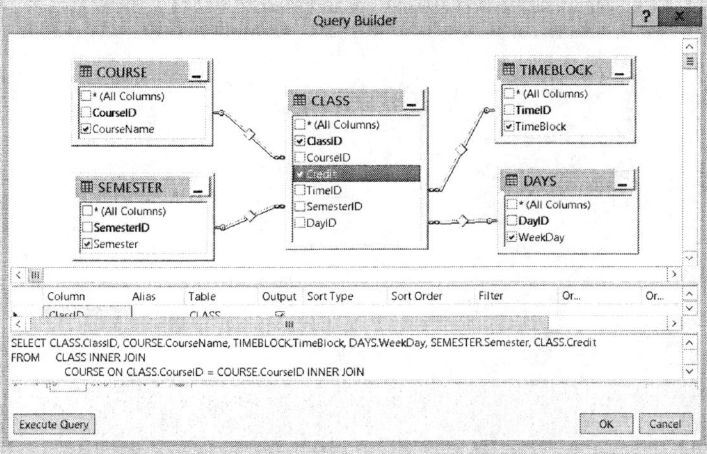

Figure 9.19 Create SELECT statement.

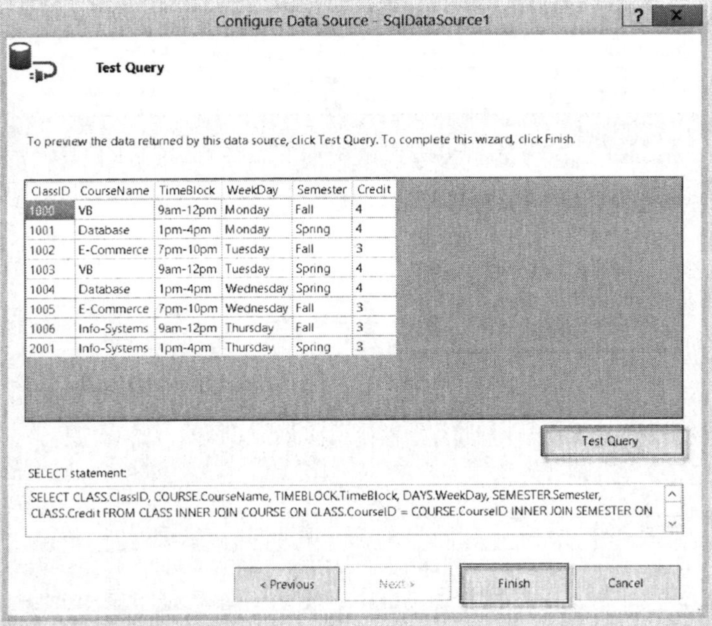

Figure 9.20 Data set for GridView.

11. Click **Next** to go to the Test Query page. Click the **Test Query** button; you will have the class information displayed as shown in Figure 9.20. Then, click **Finish**.
12. Assume that the GridView is still displayed on your screen, click the smart tag > and select **Edit Columns** as shown in Figure 9.21.
13. When the Fields dialog is opened, in the Available fields pane, expand **CommandField**, choose **Select**, and click the **Add** button. In the CammandField properties pane, specify **ButtonType** as **Button** and make sure that **ShowSelectButton** is **True**. Then, click **OK** (Figure 9.22).
14. Select the **GridView1** property in the Properties pane located at the lower-right corner of your screen. Specify **DataKeyName** as **ClassID** as shown in Figure 9.23.

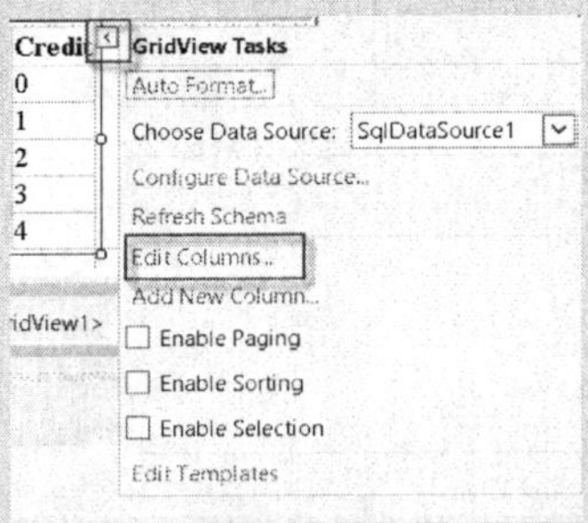

Figure 9.21 Edit columns in GridView.

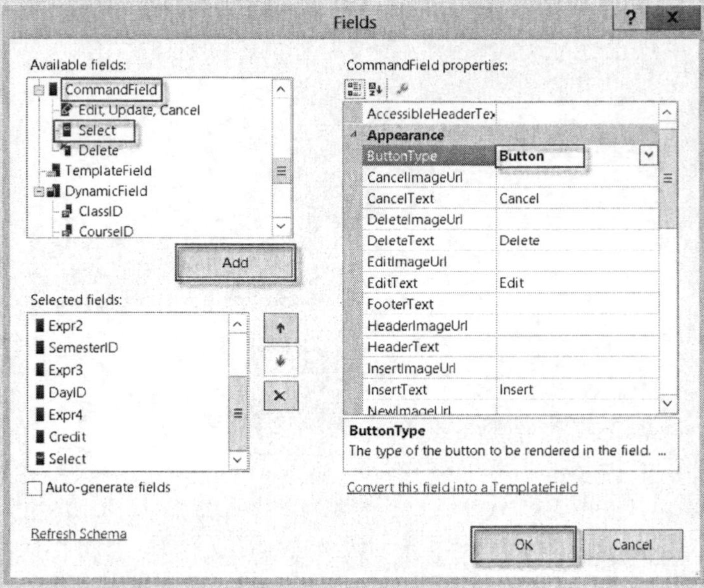

Figure 9.22 Field configuration.

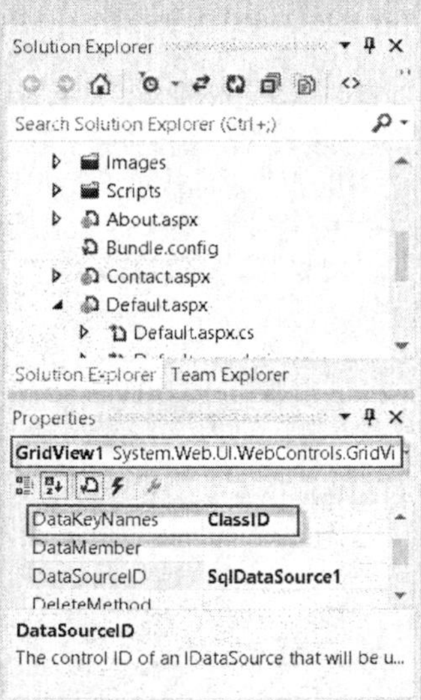

Figure 9.23 Specify DataKeyNames.

15. In the Toolbox, select the **FormView** in the Data section and drag the **FromView** to the second cell in the second row of the HTML table. Click the smart tag > and select **Choose Data Source** as shown in Figure 9.24. In the **Choose Data Source** drop-down list, select **New data source**.

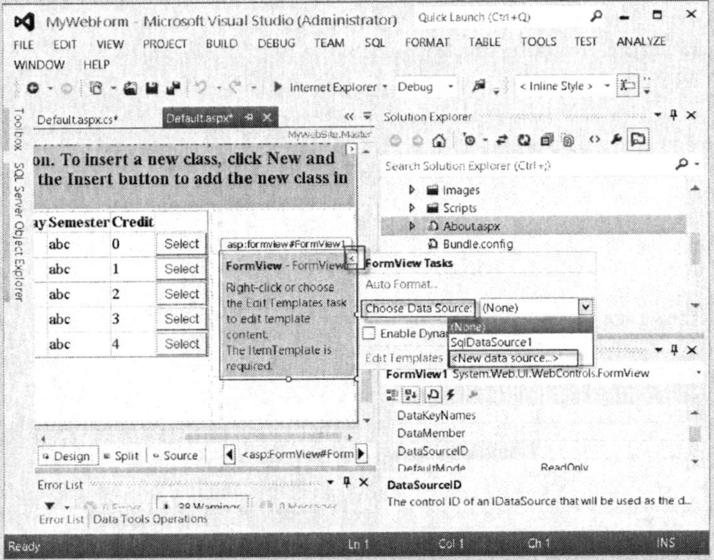

Figure 9.24 Configure data source for FormView.

16. In the Choose a Data Source Type page, select **SQL Database** as shown in Figure 9.25. Then, click **OK**. Notice that the name of the new data source is **SqlDataSource2**.
17. On the Choose Your Data Source page, select the data source **Class_Registration ConnectionString**, which is created in the previous steps as shown in Figure 9.26. Then, click the **Next** button.

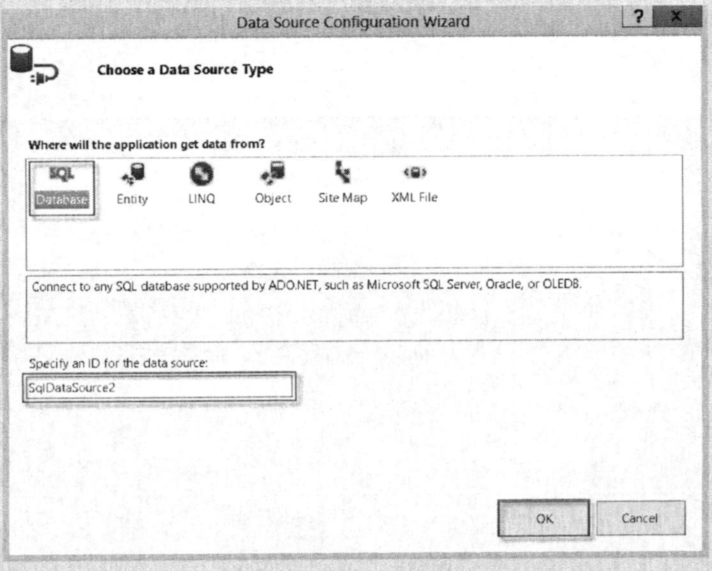

Figure 9.25 Configure data source for FirmView.

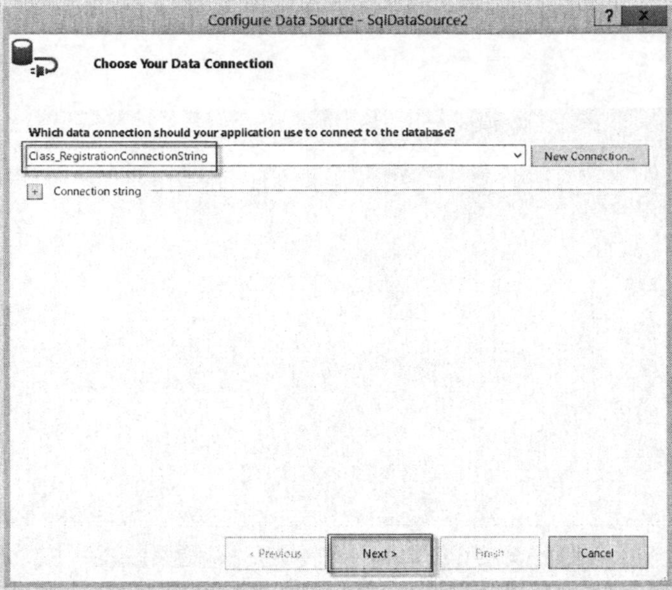

Figure 9.26 Choose data connection.

18. On the Configure the Select Statement page, select the option **Specify a custom SQL statement or stored procedure** and then click **Next.**
19. On the Define Custom Statements and Stored Procedures page, click the **Query Builder** button. In the Query Builder dialog, add the tables **CLASS**, **COURSE**, **SEMESTER**, **DAYS**, and **TIMEBLOCK**. Then, select the columns, **ClassID**, **CourseName**, **TimeBlock**, **WeekDay**, **Semester**, and **Credit** as shown in Figure 9.19. Click **Execute Query** to make sure that the query is working properly. Then, click **OK**.
20. In the SQL statement pane, make sure that the SELECT tab is selected and add the selection condition

```
WHERE CLASS.ClassID = @ClassID
```

to the SQL statement generated by Query Builder as shown in Figure 9.27.

21. Click the **UPDATE** tab and enter the following code as shown in Figure 9.28:

```
UPDATE CLASS
SET    CourseID = (SELECT CourseID FROM COURSE
       WHERE CourseName = @CourseName),
       TimeID = (SELECT TimeID FROM TIMEBLOCK
       WHERE TimeBlock = @TimeBlock),
       SemesterID = (SELECT SemesterID FROM SEMESTER
       WHERE Semester = @Semester),
       DayID = (SELECT DayID FROM [DAYS]
       WHERE [WeekDay] = @WeekDay),
       Credit = @Credit
WHERE ClassID = @original_ClassID
```

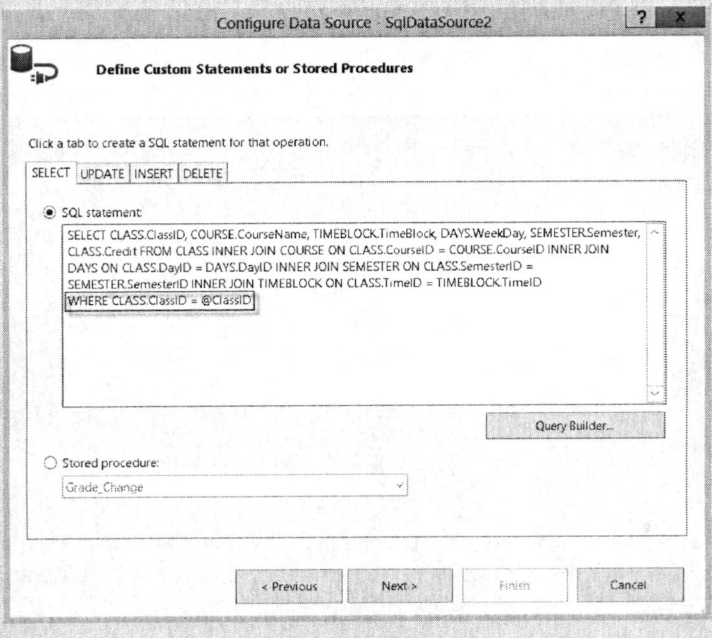
Configure Data Source - SqlDataSource2
Define Custom Statements or Stored Procedures
Click a tab to create a SQL statement for that operation.
SELECT
UPDATE
INSERT
DELETE
SQL statement:
SELECT CLASS.ClassID, COURSE.CourseName, TIMEBLOCK.TimeBlock, DAYS.WeekDay, SEMESTER.Semester, CLASS.Credit FROM CLASS INNER JOIN COURSE ON CLASS.CourseID = COURSE.CourseID INNER JOIN DAYS ON CLASS.DayID = DAYS.DayID INNER JOIN SEMESTER ON CLASS.SemesterID = SEMESTER.SemesterID INNER JOIN TIMEBLOCK ON CLASS.TimeID = TIMEBLOCK.TimeID
WHERE CLASS.ClassID = @ClassID
Query Builder...
Stored procedure:
Grade_Change
< Previous
Next >
Finish
Cancel

Figure 9.27 Configure SELECT tab.

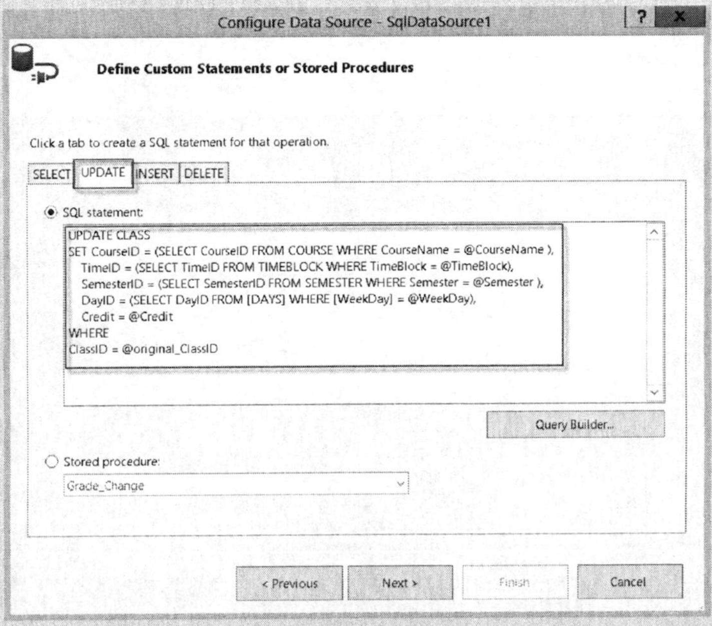
Configure Data Source - SqlDataSource1
Define Custom Statements or Stored Procedures
Click a tab to create a SQL statement for that operation.
SELECT
UPDATE
INSERT
DELETE
SQL statement:
UPDATE CLASS
SET CourseID = (SELECT CourseID FROM COURSE WHERE CourseName = @CourseName),
TimeID = (SELECT TimeID FROM TIMEBLOCK WHERE TimeBlock = @TimeBlock),
SemesterID = (SELECT SemesterID FROM SEMESTER WHERE Semester = @Semester),
DayID = (SELECT DayID FROM [DAYS] WHERE [WeekDay] = @WeekDay),
Credit = @Credit
WHERE
ClassID = @original_ClassID
Query Builder...
Stored procedure:
Grade_Change
< Previous
Next >
Finish
Cancel

Figure 9.28 Configure UPDATE tab.

22. Click the **INSERT** tab and enter the following code as shown in Figure 9.29:

```
INSERT INTO CLASS
(ClassID, CourseID, Credit, TimeID, SemesterID, DayID)
SELECT @ClassID,
(SELECT DISTINCT CourseID FROM COURSE WHERE CourseName=@
CourseName),
@Credit,
(SELECT DISTINCT TimeID FROM TIMEBLOCK WHERE TimeBlock=@
TimeBlock),
(SELECT DISTINCT SemesterID FROM SEMESTER WHERE Semester=@
Semester),
(SELECT DISTINCT DayID FROM [DAYS] WHERE [WeekDay]=@WeekDay)
```

23. Click the **DELETE** tab and enter the following code as shown in Figure 9.30:

```
DELETE CLASS
WHERE ClassID=@original_ClassID
```

24. Click **Next** to go to the **Define Parameters** page. In the **Parameter source** drop-down list, select **Control**. In the **ControlID** drop-down list, select **GridView1** as shown in Figure 9.31.

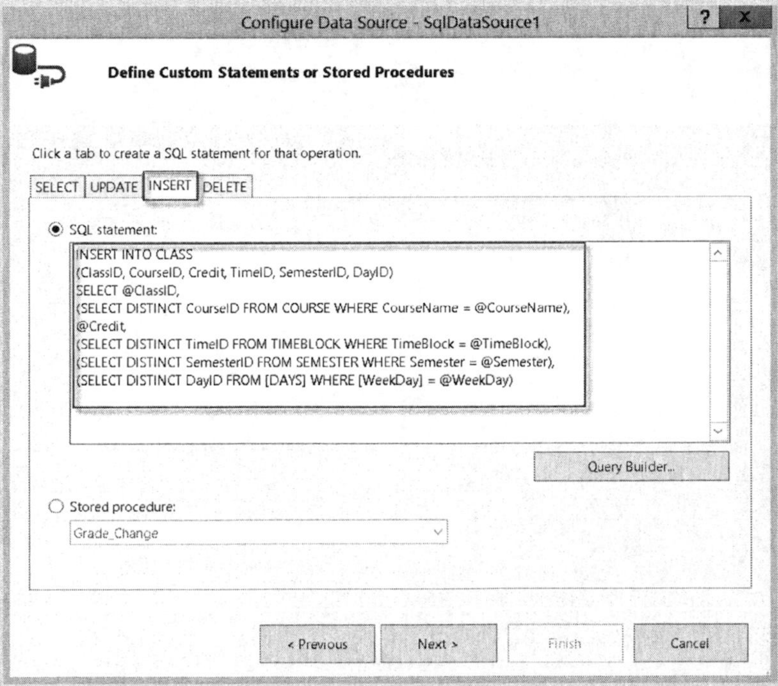

Configure Data Source - SqlDataSource1
Define Custom Statements or Stored Procedures
Click a tab to create a SQL statement for that operation.
SELECT
UPDATE
INSERT
DELETE
SQL statement:
INSERT INTO CLASS
(ClassID, CourseID, Credit, TimeID, SemesterID, DayID)
SELECT @ClassID,
(SELECT DISTINCT CourseID FROM COURSE WHERE CourseName = @CourseName),
@Credit,
(SELECT DISTINCT TimeID FROM TIMEBLOCK WHERE TimeBlock = @TimeBlock),
(SELECT DISTINCT SemesterID FROM SEMESTER WHERE Semester = @Semester),
(SELECT DISTINCT DayID FROM [DAYS] WHERE [WeekDay] = @WeekDay)
Query Builder...
Stored procedure:
Grade_Change
< Previous
Next >
Finish
Cancel

Figure 9.29 Configure INSERT tab.

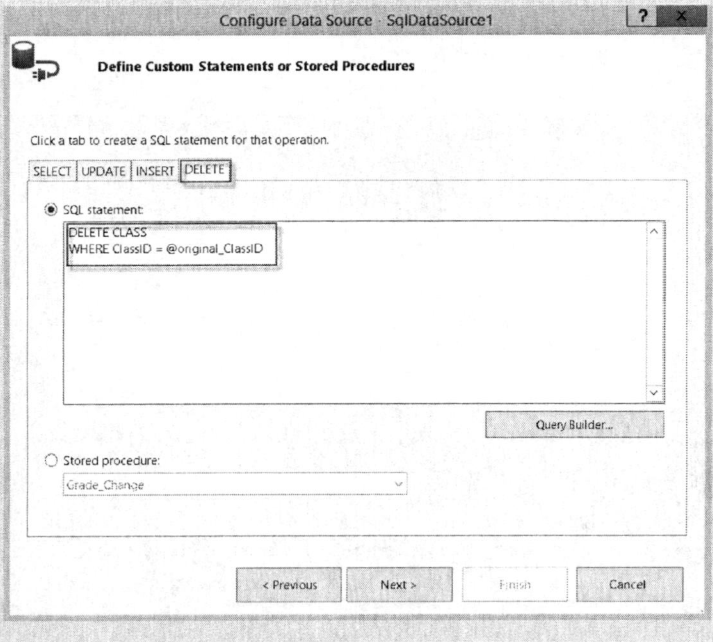

Figure 9.30 Configure DELETE tab.

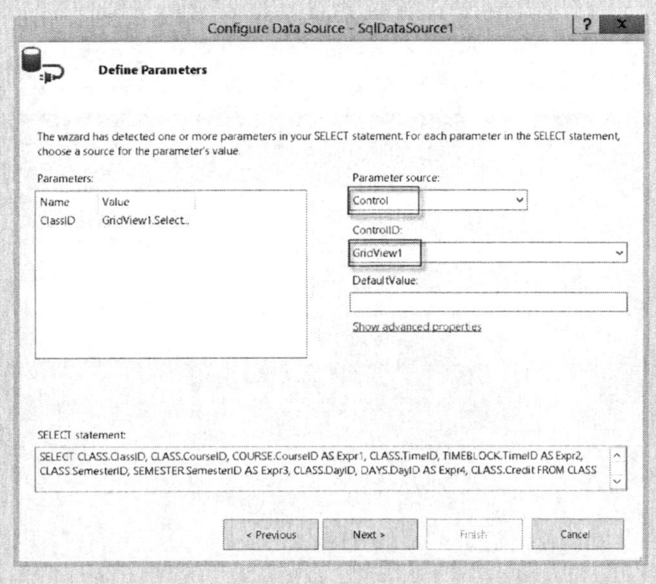

Figure 9.31 Define parameters.

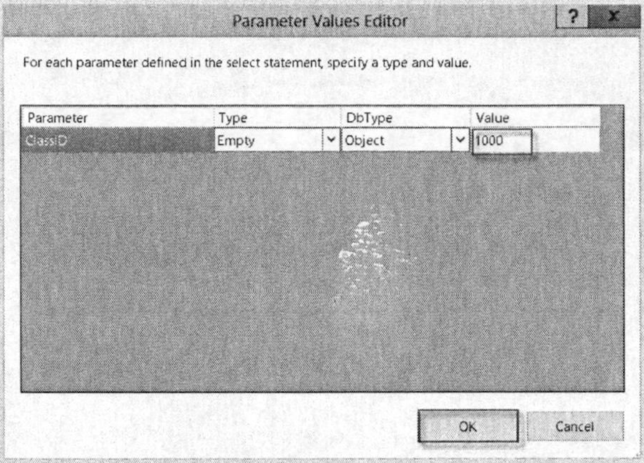

Figure 9.32 Specify parameter value.

25. Click **Next** to go to the **Test Query** page. Click the **Test Query** button. Enter 1000 as the value of the parameter shown in Figure 9.32. Then, click **OK**. You will see that the specified record is selected. Click **Finish** to complete the parameter configuration.
26. In the Properties pane, select **SqlDataSource2** in the **Properties** drop-down list. Specify **ConflictDetection** as **CompareAllValues** and **OldValuesParamterFormatString** as **original_{0}** as shown in Figure 9.33. The specification of these properties enforces the optimistic concurrency control.
27. Now, select **FormView1** in the Properties pane and make sure that the data key name is set as **ClassID** (Figure 9.34).
28. In the Design window, space down one line below SqlDataSource2. From the **Standard** section of the Toolbox, drag the **Label** control to the line below SqlDataSource2. Specify the **ID** property as **lblStatus** (Figure 9.35) and the **Text** property as **Status.**

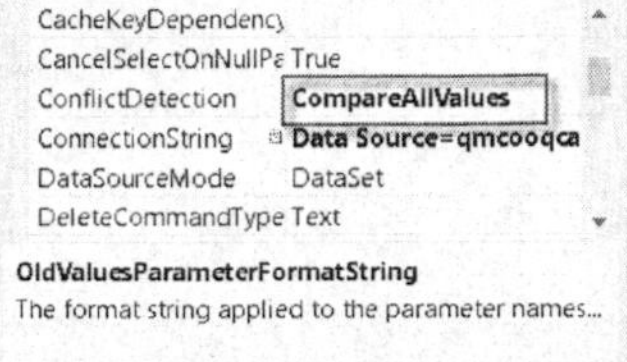

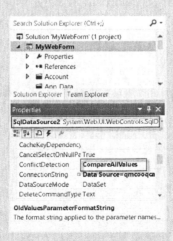

Figure 9.33 Configure SqlDataSource2 properties.

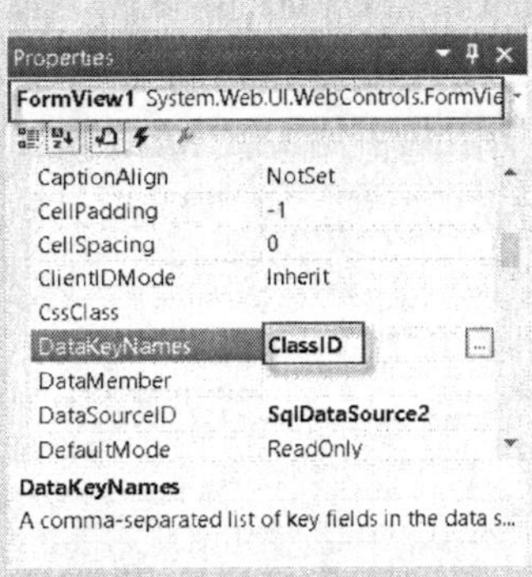

Figure 9.34 Configure FormView1 properties.

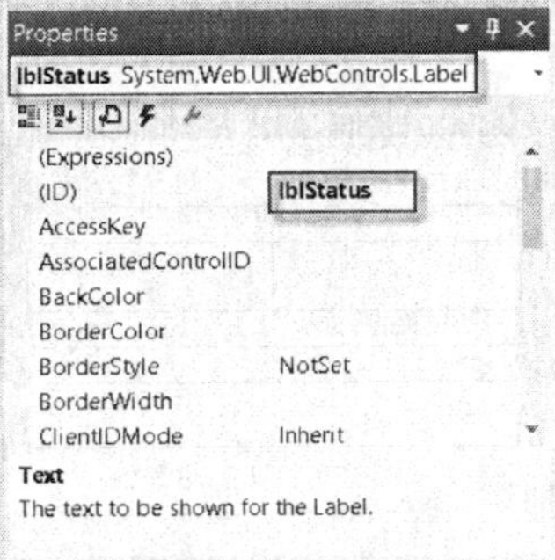

Figure 9.35 Configure label properties.

TASK 3: IMPLEMENT ACTIONS

At this point, the web form has been designed. The next task is to add code to implement some actions to be performed by the web form. To do so, follow the steps below:

1. The first action is to make the FormView display the first record presented in the GridView while loading the web form. To do so, we need to make the SelectedIndex of the GridView to be set as 0. In the Solution Explorer pane, double click the file **Default.aspx.cs** to open it. Rewrite the code for the Page_Load function with the code

```
protected void Page_Load(object sender, EventArgs e)
{
    if(!IsPostBack)
      GridView1.SelectedIndex=0;
}
```

   as shown in Figure 9.36.
2. To display the status of the update action, add the following code for the FormView1_ItemUpdated method as shown in Figure 9.37:

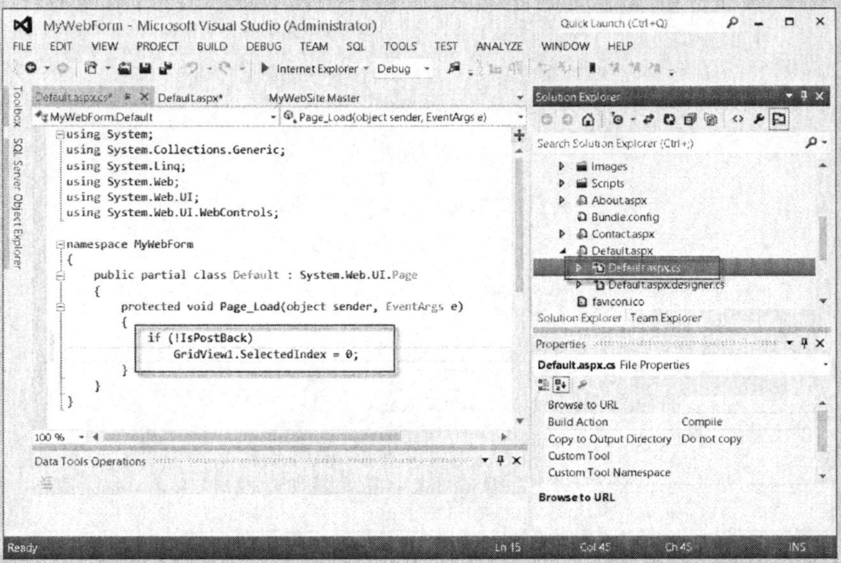
MyWebForm - Microsoft Visual Studio (Administrator)
FILE EDIT VIEW PROJECT BUILD DEBUG TEAM SQL TOOLS TEST ANALYZE WINDOW HELP
Default.aspx.cs* Default.aspx* MyWebSite.Master
MyWebForm.Default
Page_Load(object sender, EventArgs e)
using System;
using System.Collections.Generic;
using System.Linq;
using System.Web;
using System.Web.UI;
using System.Web.UI.WebControls;
namespace MyWebForm
{
public partial class Default : System.Web.UI.Page
{
protected void Page_Load(object sender, EventArgs e)
{
if (!IsPostBack)
GridView1.SelectedIndex = 0;
}
}
}
Solution Explorer
Images
Scripts
About.aspx
Bundle.config
Contact.aspx
Default.aspx
Default.aspx.cs
Default.aspx.designer.cs
favicon.ico
Properties
Default.aspx.cs File Properties
Browse to URL
Build Action Compile
Copy to Output Directory Do not copy
Custom Tool
Custom Tool Namespace
Data Tools Operations
Ready

Figure 9.36 Page_Load code.

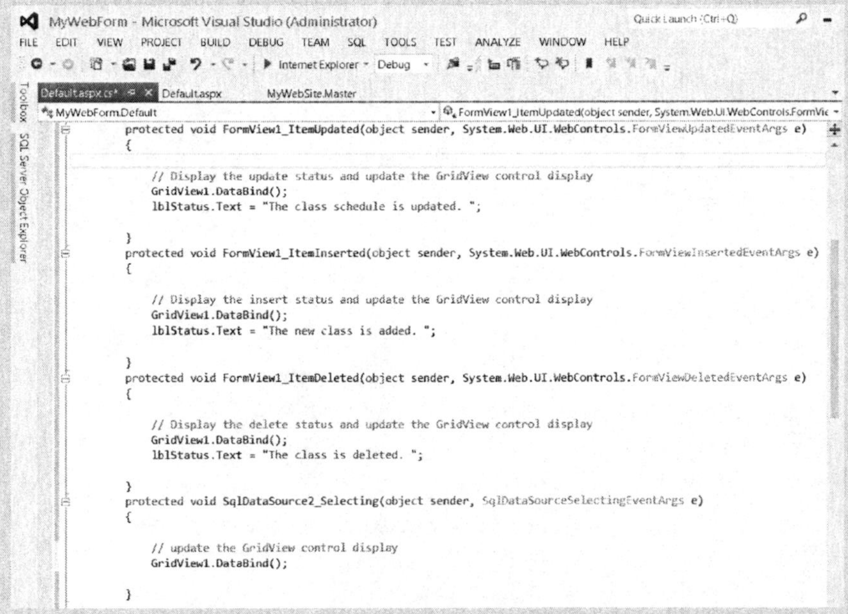
MyWebForm - Microsoft Visual Studio (Administrator)
FILE EDIT VIEW PROJECT BUILD DEBUG TEAM SQL TOOLS TEST ANALYZE WINDOW HELP
Default.aspx.cs* Default.aspx MyWebSite.Master
MyWebForm.Default
protected void FormView1_ItemUpdated(object sender, System.Web.UI.WebControls.FormViewUpdatedEventArgs e)
{
// Display the update status and update the GridView control display
GridView1.DataBind();
lblStatus.Text = "The class schedule is updated. ";
}
protected void FormView1_ItemInserted(object sender, System.Web.UI.WebControls.FormViewInsertedEventArgs e)
{
// Display the insert status and update the GridView control display
GridView1.DataBind();
lblStatus.Text = "The new class is added. ";
}
protected void FormView1_ItemDeleted(object sender, System.Web.UI.WebControls.FormViewDeletedEventArgs e)
{
// Display the delete status and update the GridView control display
GridView1.DataBind();
lblStatus.Text = "The class is deleted. ";
}
protected void SqlDataSource2_Selecting(object sender, SqlDataSourceSelectingEventArgs e)
{
// update the GridView control display
GridView1.DataBind();
}

Figure 9.37 Code for implementing activities.

```
protected void FormView1_ItemUpdated(object sender,
System.Web.UI.WebControls.FormViewUpdatedEventArgs e)
{
  //Display the update status and update the GridView control
display
  GridView1.DataBind();
  lblStatus.Text = "The class schedule is updated.";
}
```

3. To display the status of the insert action, add the following code for the FormView1_ItemInserted method as shown in Figure 9.37:

```
protected void FormView1_ItemInserted(object sender,
System.Web.UI.WebControls.FormViewInsertedEventArgs e)
{
  //Display the insert status and update the GridView control
display
  GridView1.DataBind();
  lblStatus.Text = "The new class is added.";
}
```

4. To display the status of the delete action, add the following code for the FormView1_ItemDeleted method as shown in Figure 9.37:

```
protected void FormView1_ItemDeleted(object sender,
System.Web.UI.WebControls.FormViewDeletedEventArgs e)
{
  //Display the delete status and update the GridView control
display
  GridView1.DataBind();
  lblStatus.Text = "The class is deleted.";
}
```

5. To update the GridView control, add the following code for the SqlDataSource2_Selecting method as shown in Figure 9.37:

```
protected void SqlDataSource2_Selecting(object sender,
SqlDataSourceSelectingEventArgs e)
{
  //Update the GridView control display
     GridView1.DataBind();
}
```

6. The actions update, insert, and delete are triggered by clicking the Update, Delete, and Insert links. When clicking one of these links, a corresponding event will be generated. The event handler onItemInserted, onItemUpdated, or onItemDeleted is used to process a related event. As shown in Figure 9.38, you need to modify the Default.aspx file by adding three event handlers:

```
onItemInserted = "FormView1_ItemInserted"
onItemUpdated = "FormView1_ItemUpdated"
onItemDeleted = "FormView1_ItemDeleted"
```

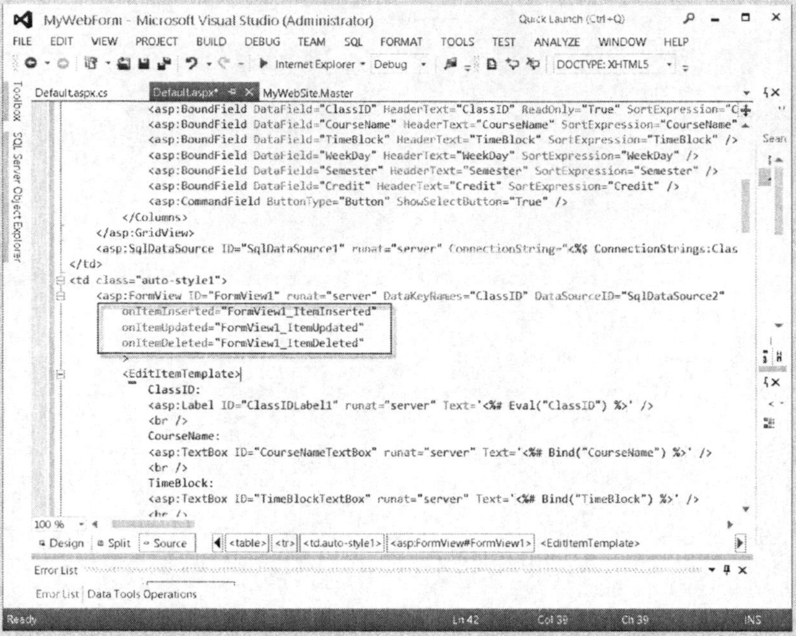
MyWebForm - Microsoft Visual Studio (Administrator)
Default.aspx.cs
Default.aspx*
MyWebSite.Master
onItemInserted="FormView1_ItemInserted"
onItemUpdated="FormView1_ItemUpdated"
onItemDeleted="FormView1_ItemDeleted"
<EditItemTemplate>
ClassID:
<asp:Label ID="ClassIDLabel1" runat="server" Text='<%# Eval("ClassID") %>' />
CourseName:
<asp:TextBox ID="CourseNameTextBox" runat="server" Text='<%# Bind("CourseName") %>' />
TimeBlock:
<asp:TextBox ID="TimeBlockTextBox" runat="server" Text='<%# Bind("TimeBlock") %>' />

Figure 9.38 Default.aspx file.

7. The completed web form design is shown in Figure 9.39.
8. Run the project by clicking the **Start Debuging** icon, which is the green arrow on the toolbar. You should have the web page shown in Figure 9.40.

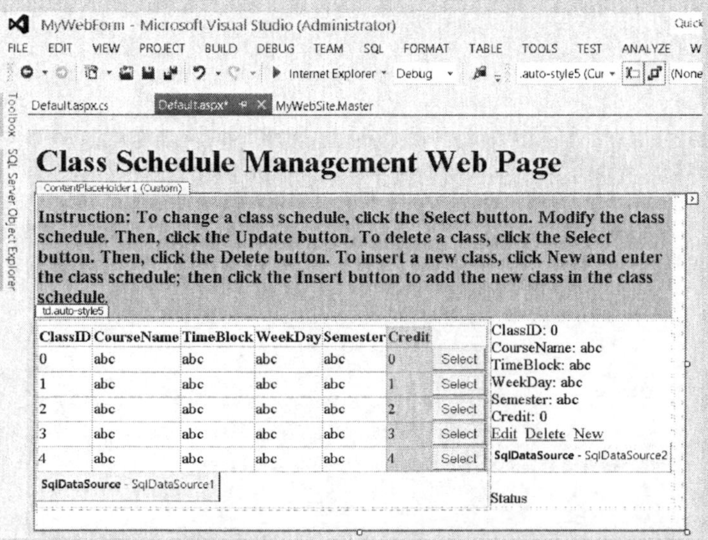
MyWebForm - Microsoft Visual Studio (Administrator)
Class Schedule Management Web Page
Instruction: To change a class schedule, click the Select button. Modify the class schedule. Then, click the Update button. To delete a class, click the Select button. Then, click the Delete button. To insert a new class, click New and enter the class schedule; then click the Insert button to add the new class in the class schedule.
ClassID CourseName TimeBlock WeekDay Semester Credit
ClassID: 0
CourseName: abc
TimeBlock: abc
WeekDay: abc
Semester: abc
Credit: 0
Edit Delete New
SqlDataSource - SqlDataSource1
SqlDataSource - SqlDataSource2
Status

Figure 9.39 Form design.

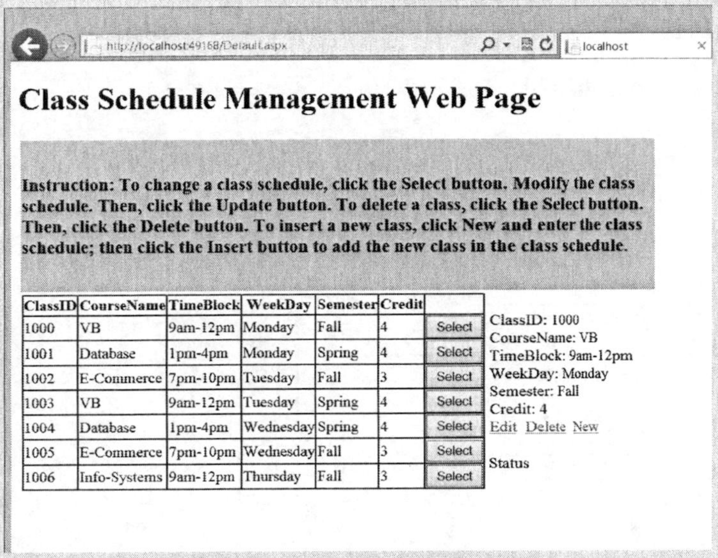

Figure 9.40 Class management web page.

9. To test an insert action, click the **New** link in the form section. You will be prompted to enter the information about a new class shown in Figure 9.41.
10. After the class information is entered, click the **Insert** link. You should be able to see the update on the web form as shown in Figure 9.42.
11. To test the update action, select the class with the id 1001 and click the **Edit** link and change the **Timeblock** to **7pm–10pm** as shown in Figure 9.43.

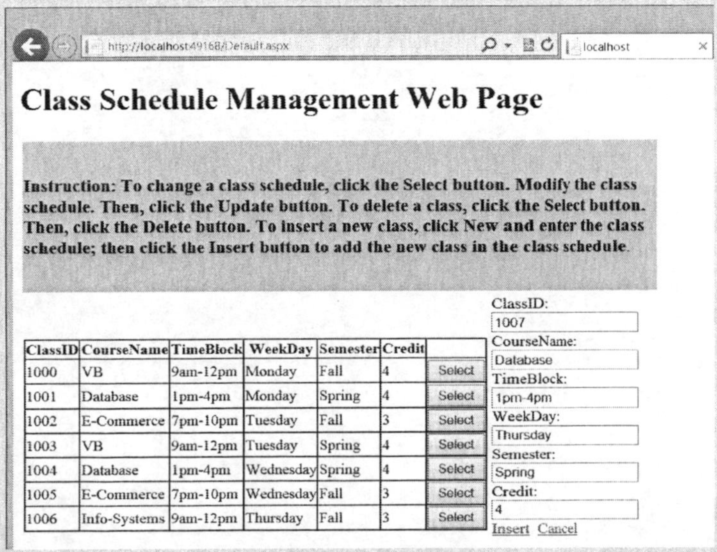

Figure 9.41 Enter information about new class.

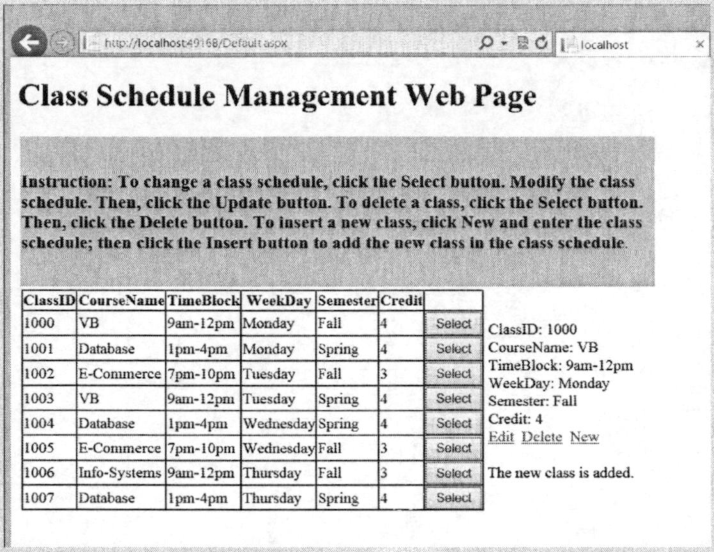

Figure 9.42 New class added.

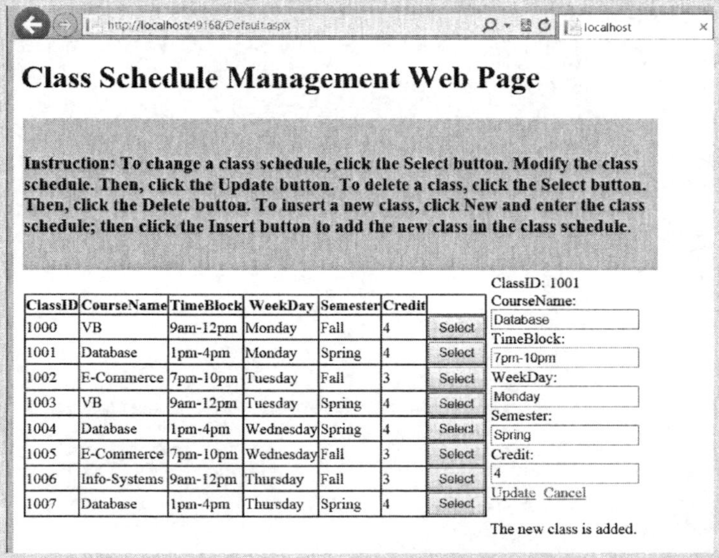

Figure 9.43 Modify class information.

12. Click the **Update** link; you should be able to see that the TimeBlock is updated to **7pm–10pm** as shown in Figure 9.44.
13. To test the Delete action, click the Select button in the row with Class ID as 1007. Click the **Delete** link. You will see that the class with the id 1007 is deleted as shown in Figure 9.45.

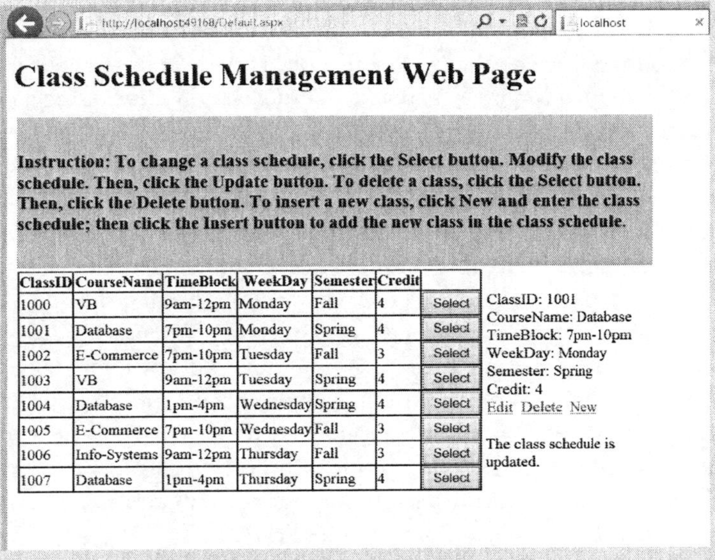

Figure 9.44 Class schedule updated.

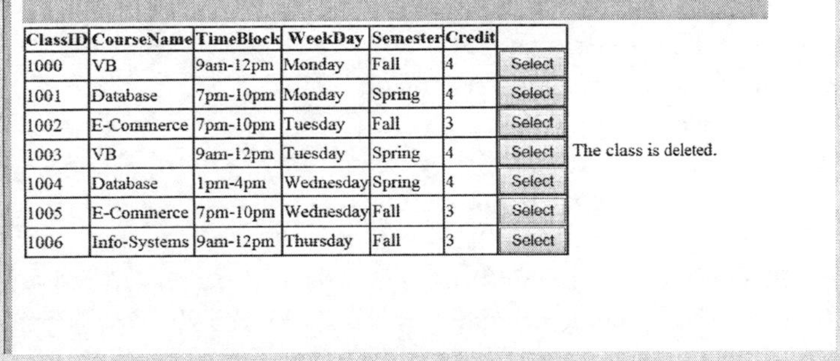

Figure 9.45 Class deleted.

Once a form is created with Visual Studio, it is ready to be deployed to Windows Azure. With the tools of the Windows Azure SDK, Visual Studio provides an ideal environment for testing and deploying the database applications. The next chapter will talk about the deployment of database applications after the in-depth discussion of Windows Azure.

9.4 Summary

In this chapter, you have learned about the design and development of database applications such as forms. A good database application design starts with requirement analysis. Carefully analyzing users' needs and requirements is the key to successfully developing a database application. Some commonly used application design guidelines have been introduced. We have also discussed the procedure of designing a GUI. Some of commonly used GUI controls have also been introduced.

In this chapter, Microsoft Visual Studio has been used for the quick development of forms. Visual Studio provides many convenient tools for developing database applications; these tools usually need only a few clicks to get the job done. By working through the hands-on activity, you have built a form against some tables in the Class_Registration database.

In a real-life business environment, a database can be accessed by many remote users through a network. Windows Azure provides an environment so that an application project can be developed by many application developers who are located in different parts of the world. Once a database application is deployed to Windows Azure, it is accessible through a web browser. Application development and deployment can greatly benefit from the cloud platform. In the next chapter, you will learn the deployment of cloud-based database applications.

Review Questions

1. Describe the three phases used by a database application development process.
2. What are forms and reports for?
3. Explain the role of an Image control.
4. Explain the role of a Label control.
5. Explain the role of a Text Box control.
6. Explain the role of a Combo Box control.
7. Explain the role of a GridView control.
8. Explain the role of a Menu Strip control.
9. Explain the role of a Picture Box control.
10. Explain the role of a Command Button control.
11. Explain the role of a FormView control.
12. How can a form be designed to make it convenient for the user?
13. Give an example to show how to design a GUI to help users avoid making mistakes?
14. How can a GUI be designed to reflect the structure of a data source?
15. Give an example where the main/subform or main/subreport structure is appropriate.
16. What are the three components provided by Visual Studio that can simplify the development of database applications?
17. Explain how the integrated development environment (IDE) can be used in application development.
18. What tasks can be accomplished by Microsoft.NET Framework?
19. How can application developers benefit from Forms Designer?
20. What can be done with the SQL Reporting Management portal?

Chapter 10

Windows Azure and Deployment of Applications to the Cloud

Objectives

- Understand the Windows Azure
- Understand the Windows Azure SDK
- Deploy the database applications to Windows Azure

10.1 Introduction

Traditionally, the development of database systems has been done in the Windows server environment. Microsoft SQL Server has been used to create and manage databases. Microsoft Visual Studio provides various tools to develop applications. Windows Server has been used to host databases and applications. It provides security protection and allows remote access. Similar to the Windows Server platform, Windows Azure also provides the environment where IT professionals can develop and manage databases and applications. Therefore, IT professionals who are familiar with the Windows development environment will have no difficulty working in the Windows Azure development environment. The database design tools, database application software, and database management utilities are about the same between SQL Server and Windows Azure SQL Database. IT professionals can continue to use the theory and skills used in the Windows Server development environment. The difference is that Windows Azure is a cloud-based application development environment. Unlike the Windows Server development environment, it is not necessary to develop an IT infrastructure to support the development environment. There is no initial labor cost spent on IT infrastructure development and management. However, users need to pay monthly for the storage and server usage on Windows Azure. Windows Azure provides a highly available development environment. Developers can work on their projects from anywhere and at any time. Additional database capacity can be added as desired until the subscription limit is reached. The data may be distributed to multiple servers on Windows Azure for better scalability and performance.

In this chapter, more details about Windows Azure are given. First, the infrastructure of Windows Azure is briefly described to obtain the whole picture. Previously, the Windows Azure Management Portal has been used to develop databases on Windows Azure. However, we did not go over the rest of the components provided by the portal. This chapter provides more information about Windows Azure and the Windows Azure SDK. It also reviews the process of creating a cloud-based application. The emphasis is on deploying the applications to a cloud environment. It provides two hands-on activities. The first one is to deploy the web form created in the previous chapter. The second one is to develop a cloud-based reporting service.

10.2 Windows Azure

In this section, we will first take a look at how Windows Azure is structured. Then, we will examine the features provided by Windows Azure.

10.2.1 Windows Azure Structure

Windows Azure is built on a set of nodes, each of which includes data storage devices and numbers of computers installed in a blade enclosure. The computers installed in the blade enclosure at each node carry the computation workload. These nodes are interconnected with high-speed wires and switches called fabric and are controlled by a unit called Fabric Controller (FC). During the development of applications, an FC unit monitors, provisions, and manages servers and resources for the nodes in Windows Azure. The FC unit takes work orders from Windows Azure customers and selects the nodes to handle the work orders. After the work is completed, the FC returns the results back to the Windows Azure customers. The FC works with another unit called Load Balancer to make sure that none of the nodes is overworked. Through routers, the Windows Azure customers are able to interact with the Load Balancer and FC. The Windows Azure architecture is illustrated in Figure 10.1.

The FC, Load Balancer, and Nodes together are also called Azure Fabric. Various cloud services have been developed on top of Azure Fabric.

Windows Azure stores its data in data centers across the world. Windows Azure customers are able to remotely access these data centers. If the data are stored in multiple data centers, application developers can use Windows Azure Traffic Manager to manage the network traffic among data centers. Windows Azure also allows customers to access the data stored on an on-premises server through an application on Windows Azure.

The free Windows Azure SDK package is available for developing and testing the applications on local computers. It includes the compute emulator and storage emulator to provide a development environment that is similar to the one on Windows Azure. On a local computer, the compute service and storage service can be created with the compute emulator and storage emulator. The Windows Azure SDK also includes tools for testing the applications created on local computers and deploying the applications to Windows Azure.

An application can be deployed at the staging level or production level. At the staging level, an application developer can develop an application and test it in Windows Azure. When the application is ready, it can be published as a cloud service to the public. At that point, the application

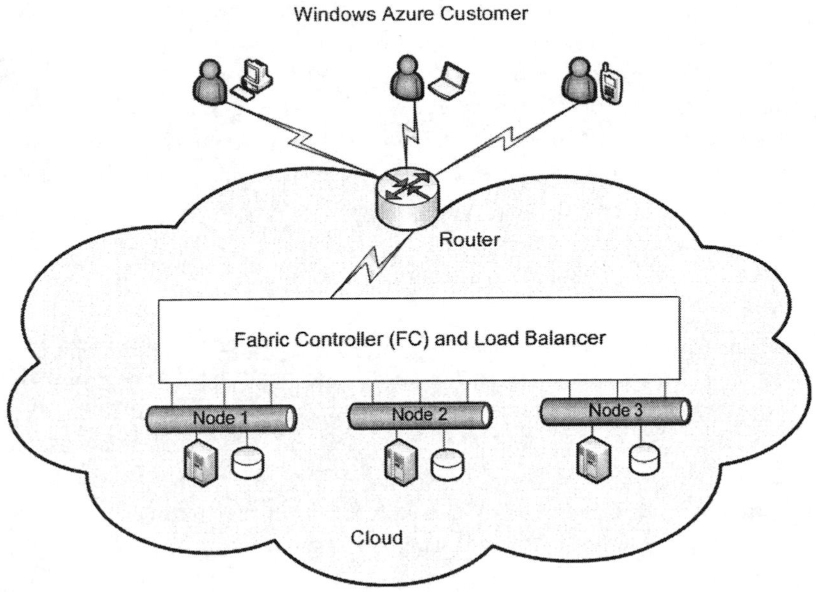

Figure 10.1 Windows Azure architecture.

is at the production level and ready for its customers. The application developer can continue to improve the application with Windows Azure based on the customers' feedback.

10.2.2 Windows Azure Management Portal

There are several ways to access Windows Azure for developing, deploying, and managing the cloud services. The Windows Azure Management Portal is one of the user interfaces for accessing the Windows Azure.

The Windows Azure Management Portal can be used to view, manage, and monitor the development of cloud services, virtual networks, and data storage. All the development and management tools are web based. Application development tasks such as creating and managing websites, virtual machines, cloud services, virtual networks, storage, and SQL Database instances can all be done in a single portal. The Windows Azure Management Portal can be accessed from anywhere and at anytime through the Internet. With the Management Portal, you are able to accomplish the following tasks:

- **Provide SaaS**: Through the portal, application developers can create application software and make it available to their customers. With the application software, customers can support their own online business.
- **Provide IaaS**: Windows- and Linux-based virtual machines that form IT infrastructures can be deployed and managed with the portal.
- **Provide PaaS**: To support the collaboration in application development, the portal provides a platform that consists of Web roles and Worker roles, Service Bus, Storage, Workflow, Content Delivery Network (CDN), and Media Services. Through the portal, application developers around the world can participate in the development process. Tools such as Team Foundation Server (TFS) and Git are also available to support collaborative software

development projects. For large-scale application development, application developers are also able to rely on the source control technology.

- **Develop SQL Database Projects**: Through the user interface provided by the portal, database administrators are able to provision SQL Database servers and logins, configure firewalls, and create SQL Databases. After logging on to the portal, the database administrators can perform management tasks such as altering and deleting tables, views, and stored procedures, and authoring and executing the Transact-SQL queries.
- **Create Storage Service**: The portal allows application developers to create storage accounts, and create and manage Windows Azure Storage, including Blob Storage, Table Storage, and Queue Storage.
- **Develop and Host Websites**: The portal allows application developers to create and run websites on Windows Azure. Tools such as WebMatrix and the Visual Studio SDK are available to help with website configuration and deployment. With tools such as TFS and Git, a team project can be directly published to a website. One can also view the dependencies between a data source such as SQL Database and a website. When needed, the website and the data source can be scaled simultaneously to meet the requirement.
- **Monitor Services**: Through the portal, one is able to monitor cloud services, websites, storage, and virtual machines. Tools are available for detecting the problems in applications, and generating reports and analyses about an operation process. Windows Azure can even alert users about resource usage and billings.
- **Provide Help Information**: The portal provides the help information and the status information for a long process.
- **Get Quick Start on Application Development**: The portal provides galleries of images, templates, virtual machines, and default options to help application developers get a quick start instead of starting from scratch.
- **Deploy Applications in Integrated Developing Environment**: The portal is able to deploy websites or cloud services developed in Microsoft Visual Studio 2010, Visual Studio 2012, and WebMatrix. It can also deploy applications developed with the cross-platform of Node.js, Java, and PHP.
- **Work with Integrated Management API**: To build services that can make various resources available on web pages for distribution, the representational state transfer (REST) approach is adopted by Windows Azure. With REST, different types of hypermedia can relate to each other. The Windows Azure Management REST API is provided to help application developers create web-based applications that are able to share Windows Azure resources. Based on the REST approach, the API provides an integrated management API across Windows Azure. The integration management API allows developers to work on content management, workflow, and content integration applications through a single set of programming interfaces.

Figure 10.2 summarizes the tasks that can be accomplished by the Windows Azure Management Portal.

The Windows Azure Management Portal is so designed that it is accessible from various devices. After the Windows Azure Management Portal is opened, you should be able to work on the sections shown in Figure 10.3.

- **Main Menu**: It allows users to access all the information about the Windows Azure platform.
- **Service Menu**: It allows users to create new services and resources.

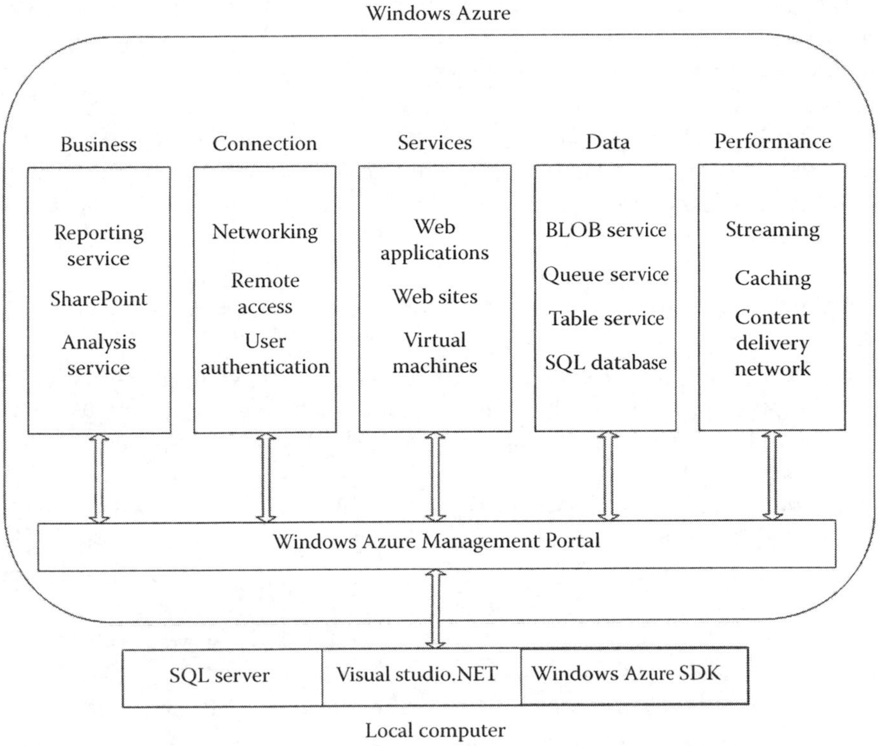

Figure 10.2 Windows Azure Management Portal functionalities.

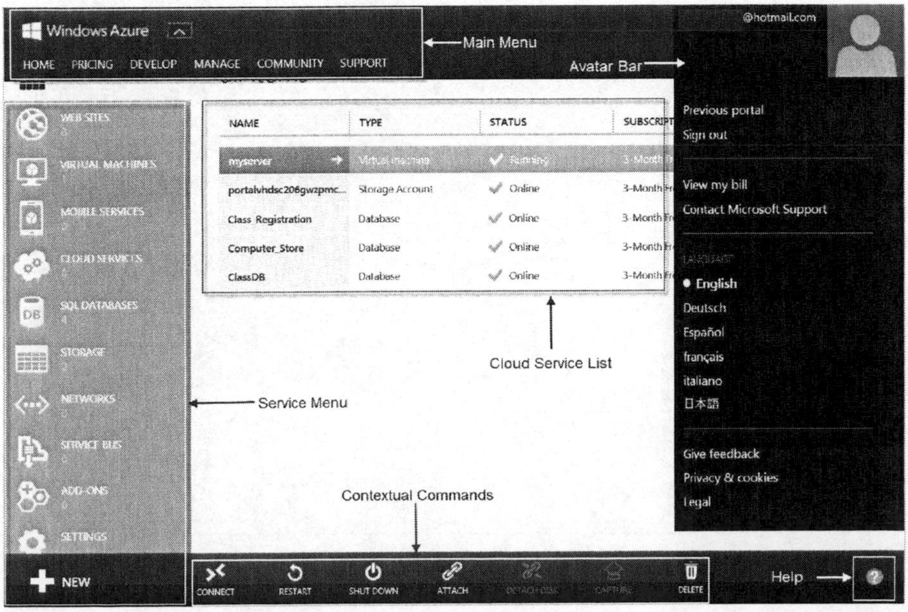

Figure 10.3 Windows Azure Management Portal.

- **Contextual Commands**: This section provides a set of command icons depending on what service a user is working with.
- **Cloud Service List**: It displays a set of services created by the user.
- **Help**: It provides help information.
- **Avatar Bar**: It provides more details about other services. The Previous portal link reviews more services that are not listed on the main portal directly. On the Avatar bar, users can find billing information and support information. Users can also specify the language used by the Windows Azure Management Portal.

After the Previous portal is opened, it displays with the following sections (Figure 10.4):

- **Ribbon**: This section lists actions one can take based on the element selected in the Navigation section. For example, when Database is selected in the Navigation pane, the Database section in the ribbon becomes active. The buttons such as Create, Drop, and Manage become available to the database administrator.
- **Navigation**: This section displays different types of functionalities provided by Windows Azure. The main functionalities are listed in the lower half of the Navigation pane. The subareas of the selected main functionality are listed in the upper half of the Navigation pane. For example, if the Database link is selected in the lower half of the Navigation pane, the nodes related to Database, such as Subscriptions and database servers under Subscriptions, appear in the upper half of the Navigation pane.
- **List**: This section lists items based on the selected navigation button. For example, when Database is selected, a list of databases is displayed in the List section.
- **Properties**: This section displays the properties associated with the selected item in the Navigation section. For example, when the database server vvzr5w29lp is selected, the properties of the server are displayed in the properties section.

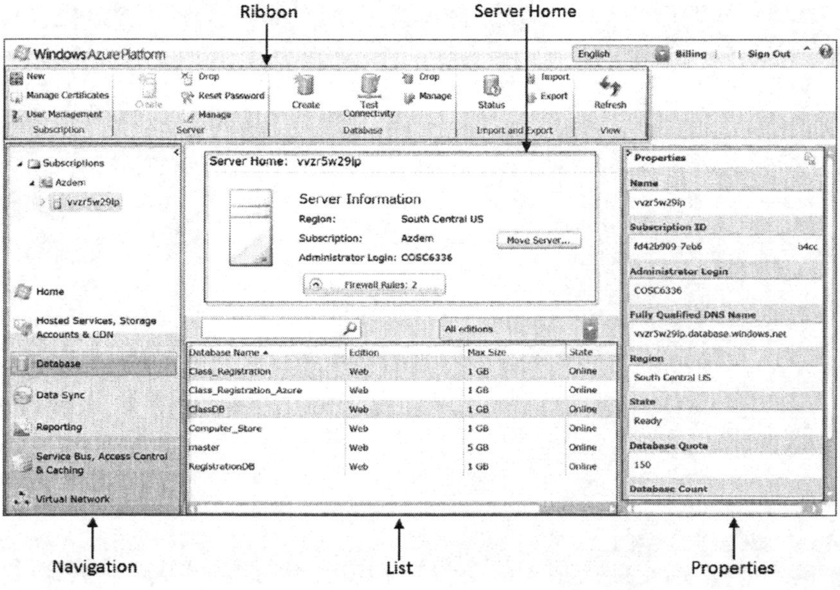

Figure 10.4 Sections of previous portal.

- **Server Home**: This section displays the information of the server, which hosts the databases. In this example, the information about the administrator, the location of the server, and the subscription is displayed.

The main category of the Navigation pane includes items such as Hosted Services, Storage Accounts & CDN, Database, Data Sync, Reporting, Service Bus, Access Control & Caching, and Virtual Network. The following paragraphs describe these items:

Hosted Services: A cloud application runs in a hosted service created on Windows Azure. A hosted service, in general, can be used to host business applications such as website hosting, e-mail servers, backups, data warehousing, and so on. When created on Windows Azure, a hosted service can take advantage of the cloud so that it can support a wide range of collaboration and interconnectivity. The configuration of a hosted service is kept in XML configuration files. Figure 10.5 illustrates the components included in a hosted service.

A web-based application that runs in Windows Azure as a hosted service requires two components, a web-based front-end user interface and a background process that handles the maintenance work. In Windows Azure, these two components are named as the Web role and the Worker role. The Web role is the web-based front-end application. The Worker role is the application running in the background to support the Web role. There is another role called the VM role that runs a virtual machine, which is created on a virtual hard disk (VHD). Virtual machines simplify the support of SaaS, PaaS, and IaaS. Developers can design and implement virtual machines on local computers and then upload them to a hosted service. On these virtual machines, developers can install application software such as SQL Server, Microsoft Office, and SharePoint on Windows Azure. A virtual machine supports both Windows Server and Linux operating systems. Once a virtual machine is loaded into the VM role and executed, the developer can manage it through the VM role. The VM role can be used to help the migration of local applications to Windows Azure, or help with the installation of an operating system on a virtual machine. An application that runs as a hosted service on Windows Azure is required to implement one or more types of roles. Windows Azure creates multiple instances of a role and stores these instances across different physical machines. In such a way, if one of these role instances fails, the application can still keep running correctly.

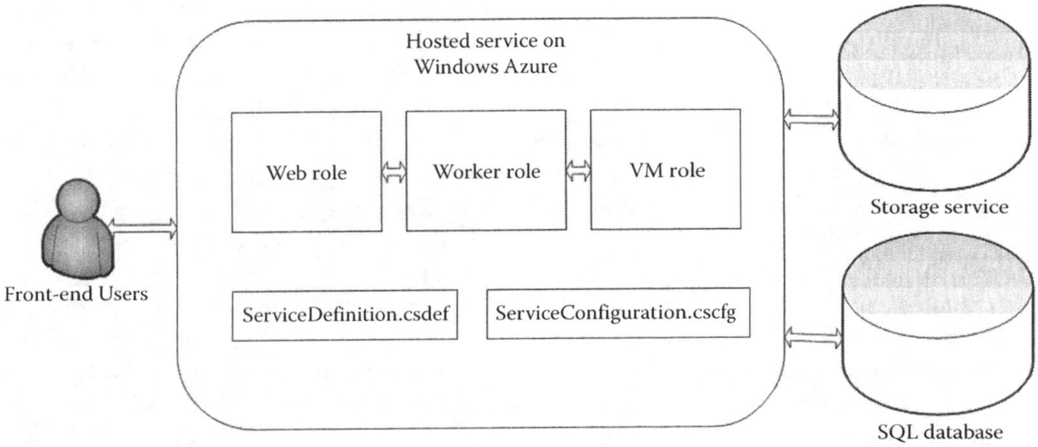

Figure 10.5 Hosted service.

A hosted service includes two configuration files: ServiceDefinition.csdef and Service Configuration.cscfg. The ServiceDefinition.csdef file contains the configuration settings and the application metadata used by Windows Azure Fabric. The settings defined in the ServiceDefinition.csdef file determine the roles and resources of a cloud application. The ServiceConfiguration.cscfg file is used to specify the parameters for the configuration settings. This file is used by Windows Azure to determine how the application should run. These two files are packaged with a cloud application during the deployment process.

An application that runs on Windows Azure as a hosted service communicates with data storage for data processing. The data storage is replicated to improve the reliability. There are two types of data storage: Windows Azure Storage or SQL Database. Windows Azure Storage such as Table Storage, Blob Storage, and Queue Storage are used to handle very large volumes of data. SQL Database can be used for data with complex relationships.

The interaction between two role instances is managed by the Queue service. When a Web role gets a work request from a front-end user, the Web role creates a message containing the work request and stores the message in the Queue storage where the message will be replicated multiple times for better fault tolerance. A Worker instance picks up the message from Queue storage and handles the request from the front-end user. Once the job is done, the message is removed from the Queue storage by the Worker role.

Content Delivery Network: The CDN is a technology used by Internet service providers (ISPs) to deliver web pages and audio and video data. The CDN is designed to be used with blob content. In Windows Azure, the CDN can deliver web content rapidly to a large number of users by replicating the content to data centers closer to the end users. With the CDN, the users are able to access the web content and other applications from the local data centers.

Storage Account: With a storage account, an application developer is able to access the Windows Azure Storage services including Blob services, Queue services, and Table services.

Data Sync: Data Sync is a cloud-based data synchronization service. When data are transferred between SQL Database on Windows Azure and an on-premises database, this service synchronizes the data so that the data can be shared by the databases on both sides of the transaction.

Access Control: Access control service (ACS) is used to authenticate and authorize users to access web applications and services. Instead of creating your own authentication system that is specific to your application, you can use ACS to set the service so that the users are permitted in a specific domain where the application belongs. The service can be integrated with other authentication mechanisms such as the Directory service commonly used by an enterprise for user authentication and authorization. It can also be integrated with web identities such as those in Windows Live ID, Google, Yahoo!, and Facebook.

Service Bus: Service Bus allows applications to communicate from various locations. It enables secure messaging and data transactions among distributed and hybrid applications. With Service Bus, applications on Windows Azure are able to communicate with on-premises applications without creating a complex firewall and security infrastructure. It supports network security protocols and is able to accommodate load variations.

Reporting: This service allows application developers to develop and publish reports by using data stored in SQL Database. These reports can be viewed and managed through a web browser. They can also be viewed through an application. By using the same technologies as SQL Server Reporting Services, the service also provides tools that are similar to those included in the technologies provided by SQL Server Reporting Services.

Caching: The Caching service is used to accelerate web applications' performance. The Caching service consists of a large number of cache clusters on Windows Azure. Developers can specify the amount of memory needed for the Cashing service. The Caching service is flexible. The amount of memory for caching can be scaled up or down based on the needs. The Caching service is also highly available and has no management overhead for its users. On Windows Azure, the Caching service automatically partitions the cache to improve the performance and reliability.

Virtual Network: Virtual Network enables developers to create private networks used to link virtual machines in the cloud. With the Virtual Network service, developers can assign IP addresses to virtual machines and configure the virtual network gateway. Virtual Network allows the developer to develop the naming service for the virtual machines and role instances. It also allows the developer to create a network that connects the virtual machines in the cloud as well as the computers in the on-premises network so that they appear to be on the same network. The protocol IPSec is used to establish the connection between Windows Azure and the on-premises network. The Virtual Network service can also accomplish some network administration tasks.

10.3 Windows Azure SDK

The Windows Azure SDK is a software package used to run, test, debug, and fine-tune the applications before the applications can be deployed to Windows Azure. The Windows Azure development environment contains two services: computer service and storage service. The compute service is also called the hosted service that does the computation work and the storage service stores the data in the format of Blob, Queue, or Table. The Windows Azure SDK is designed to emulate these two services. To emulate the two cloud services on local computer, the Windows Azure SDK provides the following tools:

- **Windows Azure compute emulator**: On the local computer, this tool emulates the cloud environment for testing the applications.
- **Windows Azure storage emulator**: On the local computer, this tool emulates Windows Azure Storage used to store application data.
- **CSPack**: This is a command-line tool used for preparing an application for deployment. When an application is ready to be deployed, the developer can use this tool to create a package for deployment.
- **CSUpload**: This is a command-line tool used for uploading VHD files and service certificates to Windows Azure. VHD is used as the hard drive of a virtual machine.
- **CSEncrypt**: This is a command-line tool used for encrypting the passwords for remote desktop connections.
- **CSRun**: This is a command-line tool used for running the application packages with the Windows Azure compute emulator.
- **DSinit**: This is a command-line tool used for initializing the Windows Azure storage emulator environment locally.

10.3.1 Windows Azure Compute Emulator

The Windows Azure compute emulator provides an environment similar to the cloud environment on the local computer so that the application developer can build and test an application before it can be deployed to Windows Azure. Through the Windows Azure compute emulator, the application developer is able to configure a cloud service, manage the cloud service, and manage the role instances.

The Windows Azure compute emulator does not include all the services that are available on Windows Azure. Although most of the services are able to run on the Windows Azure compute emulator, it may require additional effort to run some advanced services. In addition, the Windows Azure compute emulator has a few other limits listed below:

- Each deployment requires a minimum of one role.
- Each deployment can have a maximum of 25 roles.
- Each deployment can have a maximum of 25 input endpoints. These input endpoints are accessible from the Internet. Through these input endpoints, incoming requests can be routed to dedicated web applications.
- Each deployment can have a maximum of 25 internal endpoints. The internal endpoints are used for communication inside the application.
- Each deployment can have a maximum of 20 cores. A core allows users to control and expose their own web servers.

Windows Azure Compute Emulator Networking: If an application uses a web role as its user interface, it is required that IIS 7.0 with ASP.NET be enabled on the local computer. The newer version of the Windows Azure SDK includes a lightweight and self-contained version of IIS called IIS Express, which is optimized for web application development. IIS Express has all the web server features that are necessary for developing the web applications. In addition, the following features are added to IIS Express to ease web application development:

- IIS Express does not require the administrator permission to perform most of the tasks; for example, no administrator permission is necessary for installation.
- On the same computer, multiple application developers can work on IIS Express independently.

When an application is deployed on a local computer, the Windows Azure compute emulator assigns a web role a loopback IP address starting from 127.0.0.1:81, where 81 is the default port number. The IP address 127.0.0.1:81 is used as the endpoint for data communication. If a role has 25 endpoints, each endpoint will be assigned with an IP address ranging from 127.0.0.1:81 to 127.0.0.25:81. If the port number 81 has been used by others, the Windows Azure compute emulator increases the port number by one and tries it again. The application developer will be informed once the new port number is adopted.

10.3.2 Windows Azure Storage Emulator

Windows Azure provides three types of storage: tables, blobs, and queues. On the local SQL Server, the Windows Azure storage emulator creates storage that is similar to those three types of the storage. When developing an application on your local computer, the emulated storage will be used to store data for the application on your local computer. The storage can be used as a testing environment for the applications that will use the Windows Azure storage services after deployment.

During the development of an application on the local computer, the application will connect to a database instance for data transaction. By default, the database instance created by the storage emulator is SQL Server Express LocalDB. The application developer can also configure the storage emulator to use the database instance on the local SQL Server instead of LocalDB.

The storage emulator creates a public known account on the emulated storage for testing the application that is under development. The account only works for the local emulation environment. When the storage emulator gets started for the first time, the initialization process creates a database in the LocalDB instance. The initialization process also reserves the HTTP port for the local storage. When switching to a different database instance, the tool DSInit can be used to reinitialize the database instance.

10.3.3 Application Development with Windows Azure SDK

Similar to the process of developing an ASP.NET application, the process of developing a cloud application also includes three phases: design, development, and deployment. In addition, to make an application a cloud-based application, application developers need to address issues in the areas of remote access, multiple tenants, project participation, asynchronous processing, and even billing mechanism. Figure 10.6 illustrates a flowchart of an application development process.

10.3.3.1 Windows Azure Application Design

The cloud platform is particularly suitable for those applications that tend to have usage spikes in a short period of time and those applications that are accessible around the world. For applications that require variable computing resources according to time and geographical locations, the cloud also provides an ideal environment.

The first step of a development process is to design an application that meets the business requirements. The design draws an architectural overview of the application. It also provides strategies for adopting the cloud platform. The design addresses issues in making the application available around the world to support multiple customers (multiple tenants). It also addresses issues related to remote access such as the application's URL for remote access, security measures, the geographic locations of the data centers, and so on. For a large application, the design also addresses participation issues.

The developer needs to design various web, worker, and VM roles if any of them will be used in the application. The developer should also show how to create these roles and the tasks carried out by these roles. When the application is shared by multiple groups of users for different tasks, the developer can create a separate web role for each task. Although the application has one URL,

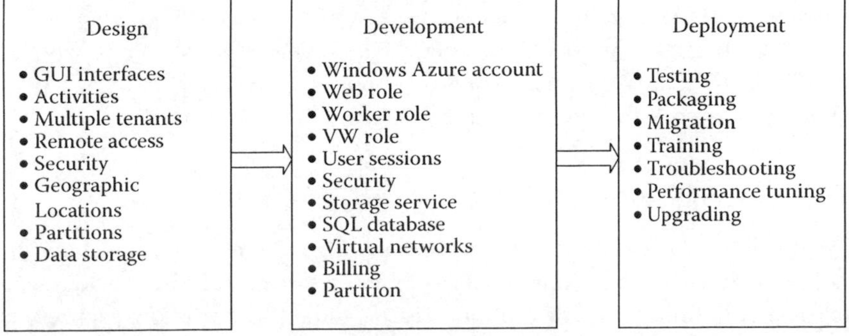

Figure 10.6 Windows Azure application development process.

each Web role of the application can have its own port number. Separating Web roles allows the developer to manage each task independently.

To process the data used in an application, the storage service should be specified in the design phase. The design needs to decide whether to use SQL Database or to use Windows Azure Storage. If SQL Database is used to support the application, the database should be designed as discussed in the previous chapters. If Windows Azure Storage is used to support the application, the developer needs to specify how Table Storage, Blob Storage, and Queue Storage will be used in the application. During the design process, the developer should specify how to form PartitionKey and RowKey. The design and implementation of Windows Azure Storage will be discussed in Chapter 11.

An application may be required to set up an authentication system for remote access. Different permissions may be needed for different types of users. For example, a large enterprise may require the authentication system be integrated with the company's on-premises authentication system. A small company may use the authentication created with the application. Individual users may want to use Windows Live ID. Before the application is created, the developer should address these issues according to the user's requirements.

Since an application including its Web role, Worker role, and VM role will be replicated in Windows Azure automatically, one does not have to put in a lot of effort on backup and restore. In contrast, if customers require data transactions between Windows Azure and the on-premises server, the developer needs to consider how data should be transferred and how to protect the data during a transaction.

10.3.3.2 Windows Azure Application Development

To develop an application that is truly global and is able to deal with the immense peak demand, it needs an IT infrastructure that is powerful enough to support such a peak demand. The cost for this kind of IT infrastructure can be huge. It also requires an experienced team to manage such an infrastructure.

The cloud platform provides an ideal environment to hold such applications. The applications hosted by a cloud environment are truly global. The cloud provider is responsible for managing and maintaining the IT infrastructure. The infrastructure built by a cloud provider is able to scale up the resources to handle the peak demand. When the demand is low, the resources can be released to lower the cost.

As shown in Figure 10.7, application developers can develop Windows Azure applications with two approaches. They can create applications on local computers first. When an application is developed with the Windows Azure emulators on a local computer, the application can be tested with the Windows Azure SDK. After the application is tested, it can then be deployed to Windows Azure. Once it is deployed, the application developer can manage the Windows Azure application through the Windows Azure Management Portal. Application developers can also develop and manage applications directly through the Windows Azure Management Portal.

10.3.3.3 Developing Applications on Local Computers

There are many application development software packages available. Visual Studio is one such software available to develop applications on local computers. Visual Studio provides a cloud development tool package, Windows Azure Tools for Visual Studio. With this tool package, application developers can build, debug, and deploy services and applications for the cloud. Windows Azure Tools for Visual Studio can also help application developers to deploy applications to Windows

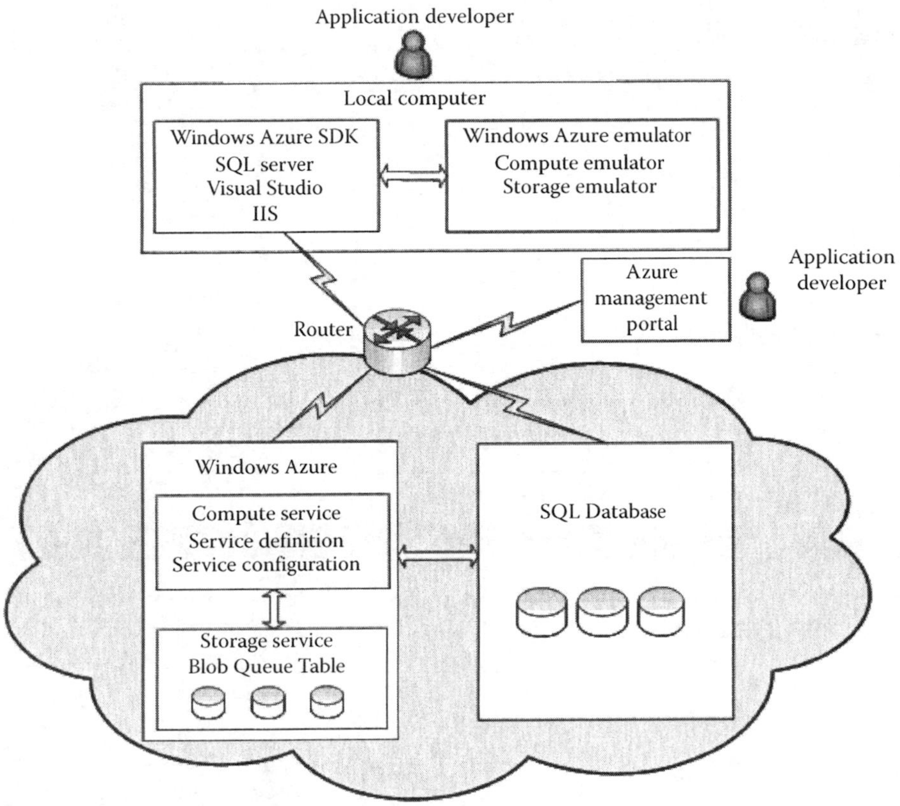

Figure 10.7 Windows Azure application development environment.

Azure and manage them after deployment. Figure 10.8 shows the Visual Studio dialog used to create a new cloud-based application.

It is recommended to run the Windows Azure compute emulator and the Windows Azure storage emulator in the 64-bit edition of the Windows operating system. .NET Framework 3.5 SP1 or later should be installed. If an application uses Web roles, the IIS service should be started before an application development process can be started. The following IIS components are added for running the Windows Azure application.

10.3.3.4 Role Definition and Configuration

A cloud project created with Visual Studio includes two configuration files: ServiceDefinition.csdef and ServiceConfiguration.cscfg. These files are packaged with your Windows Azure application and deployed to Windows Azure. The ServiceDefinition.csdef file defines the roles contained in an application. The ServiceConfiguration.cscfg file specifies the values for the configurations defined in the ServiceDefinition.csdef file. This file also specifies the number of instances to run for each role.

When creating multiple websites hosted by a single hosted service, the developer needs to create multiple Web roles according to the design. These Web roles can be defined in the ServiceDefinition.csdef file. Some of the websites can be used for application management by the administrators. Some of the websites can be made available to customers who are subscribers of the application

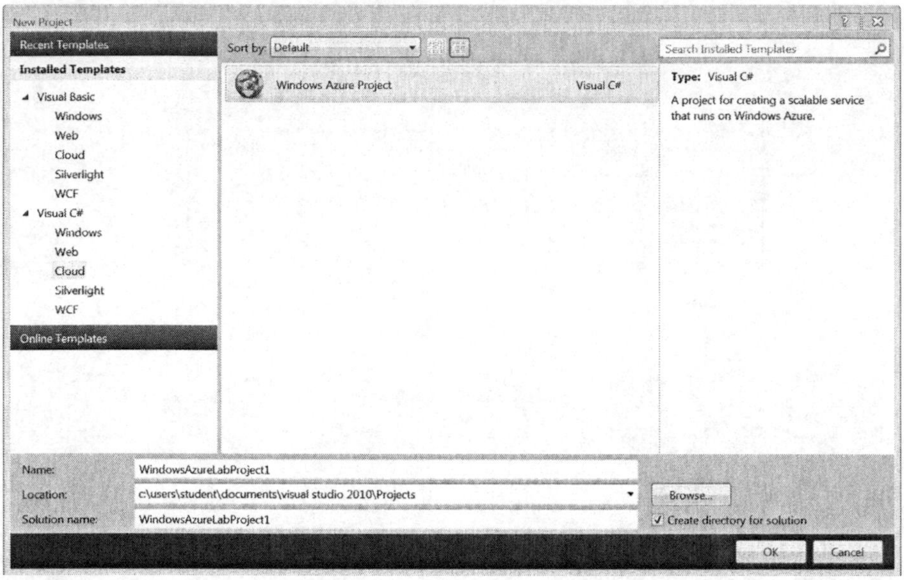

Figure 10.8 New cloud project.

with the permission that allows the customers to adopt the application for their own needs. These customers can integrate their own authentication system with the one provided by Windows Azure. The customers can also use these websites to transfer data between Windows Azure and the on-premises server. In addition, some of the websites are accessible by the public with a limited permission. An example of a Web role definition in the ServiceDefinition.csdef file is given below:

```
<?xml version="1.0" encoding="utf-8"?>
<ServiceDefinition name="MyWebFromService" xmlns="http://schemas.
microsoft.com/ServiceHosting/2008/10/ServiceDefinition">
  <WebRole name="MyWebForm" vmsize="Small">
    <Sites>
      <Site name="Web">
        <Bindings>
          <Binding name="Endpoint1" endpointName="Endpoint1"/>
        </Bindings>
      </Site>
    </Sites>
    <Endpoints>
      <InputEndpoint name="Endpoint1" protocol="http" port="80"/>
    </Endpoints>
    <Imports>
      <Import moduleName="Diagnostics"/>
    </Imports>
  </WebRole>
</ServiceDefinition>
```

In the file, a Web role MyWebForm is defined. vmsize is the size assigned by Windows Azure for the VM role instances. The definition of the Web role defines a website, an endpoint that is the entry point for such as a web page to enter the service, and an Import that is used to import modules to the current running application. The protocol defined in the endpoint is http. For better security, you can specify SSL as the network protocol. The port number is 80. You can specify a different port number. <import moduleName="Diagnostics"> is used to enable diagnostics with the storage.

In addition to the Web role definition, the ServiceDefinition.csdef file can also be used to define LoadBalancerProbes, NetworkTrafficRules, VirtualMachineRole, and WorkerRole with the below code:

```
<LoadBalancerProbes>
    ...
</LoadBalancerProbes>
<NetworkTrafficRules>
    ...
</NetworkTrafficRules>
<VirtualMachineRole ...>
    ...
</VirtualMachineRole>
<WorkerRole ...>
    ...
</WorkerRole>
```

The following is the content of the corresponding ServiceConfiguration.cscfg file, which specifies the values for the configuration defined in the ServiceDefinition.csdef file:

```
<?xml version="1.0" encoding="utf-8"?>
<ServiceConfiguration serviceName="MyWebFromService" xmlns="http://
schemas.microsoft.com/ServiceHosting/2008/10/ServiceConfiguration"
osFamily="1" osVersion="*">
  <Role name="MyWebForm">
    <Instances count="1"/>
    <ConfigurationSettings>
      <Setting
name="Microsoft.WindowsAzure.Plugins.Diagnostics.ConnectionString" value=
"DefaultEndPointProtocol=https; AccountName=mywebform; Accountkey=..."/>
    </ConfigurationSettings>
  </Role>
</ServiceConfiguration>
```

The root element ServiceConfiguration has one attribute that specifies the serviceName, which is required. The name of the service should match the name of the service defined in the ServiceDefinition.csdef file. The ServiceConfiguration element has one child element Role, which matches the number of roles defined in the ServiceDefinition.csdef file. The Role element also has a required name attribute. The value of the name attribute matches the WebRole name in the definition file. The Role element can have three child elements:

- **Instances**: This element specifies the number of role instances to be created.
- **ConfigurationSettings**: This element can be used to set the connection string. It specifies the number of Setting elements. The name attribute specifies the name of the connection string and the value attribute specifies the properties of the connection string.
- **Certificates**: This element specifies the optional certificates associated with a role.

10.3.3.5 Authentication

For the implementation of authentication to access an application, ACS is the tool that can be used to accomplish the task. ACS provides authentication service to control the access to the application and service. With ACS, the web application and web service can easily authenticate users and manage users' permissions. By providing the authentication service, it saves application developers' time and effort. If needed, the authentication system can be integrated with an enterprise's authentication or a third-party authentication system such as Windows Live ID and Google ID. The third-party authentication service can be configured in ACS so that ACS trusts the security tokens issued by the third party.

The integration with other authentication systems can be implemented in the application. For example, developers can use IAuthorizationFilter included in Visual Studio to define the methods that are required for user authorization. They can also make use of the Microsoft Active Directory Federation security token service for user authentication. The Active Directory Federation security token service is a component provided by the Windows Server 2008 operating system. It can authenticate a user to multiple web applications with web single-sign-on (SSO) technologies. The service allows users to securely access applications running on the cloud from virtually everywhere. During the development of an application, the developer can use the FederatedPassiveSignIn control to redirect users to a federated security token service and to process security tokens issued by that service. To use the third-party authentication system, the application redirects the authentication request to the third-party authentication provider.

10.3.4 Windows Azure Application Deployment

After an application is tested and debugged on a local computer, it is ready to be deployed to Windows Azure. To prepare the deployment, the properties of the application need to be reconfigured so that it is suitable for running on Windows Azure.

Testing: The deployment process starts with testing. Tools such as Windows Azure Diagnostics and Microsoft IntelliTrace can be used for testing. With IntelliTrace, developers can test role instances. This tool provides extensive debugging information about the test. The information includes the key code execution and environment data collected during the execution of the application. For cloud-based applications, the testing should focus on the consistencies such as deadlock on a database when it is accessed by multiple roles. Identifying the performance bottleneck is another common testing task. Security is another area that should be tested thoroughly. When migrating a database from SQL Server on a local computer to SQL Database on Windows Azure, make sure not to use SQL Server features that are not supported by SQL Database.

Packaging Application: Before an application can be deployed to Windows Azure, it needs to be packaged into a .cspkg file. Then, the .cspkg file is uploaded to Windows Azure along with the service configuration file. There are three ways to package an application: using the Visual Studio user interface, using the CSPack Command-Line tool, and running the MSBuild command in the Microsoft Visual Studio command prompt.

If Visual Studio is installed on your local computer, you will be able to package an application by using the packaging tool found on the menu. Once the application is packaged, you can then upload the packaged file to Windows Azure.

When you install the Windows Azure SDK, the CSPack tool is installed by default. With CSPack, the application developer can package the application in the command prompt. The application package, which is used to run the application as a cloud service, includes the application files and the service model files. Two files, service definition file and service configuration file, are used by CSPack to define the contents of the package. Before using the CSPack command, you may need to configure the contents in these two files.

MSBuild is another tool that can be used to package an application. You need to run the MSBuild command in the Microsoft Visual Studio command prompt. The MSBuild command relies on its XML schema file to control the packaging.

Managing Application: Windows Azure provides various management tools for managing, monitoring, and debugging applications. REST is a type of architecture designed for large-scale network software by using web protocols and technologies. With REST-based interfaces, the management task can be done through web browsers. Developers can use Windows Azure Diagnostics to collect diagnostic data from an application running in Windows Azure. With the collected diagnostic data, developers can accomplish many management tasks such as troubleshooting, performance tuning, monitoring running processes, resource usage analysis, and activity auditing. When deploying applications from local computers to the cloud, Windows Azure allows the developer to update the roles to adapt to the cloud computing environment. The developer can stop an application for fixing a bug. Then, redeploy the application after the bug is fixed. With Windows Azure, developers can use a staging development process to avoid application downtime. When upgrading an application to a new version, an in-place upgrade can be used by the developer to replace a running application without interrupting the application's operation. To make the upgrading process go smoothly, the developer should consider a strategy to update the application without interrupting the service.

ACTIVITY 10.1 DEPLOYING WEB FORM TO WINDOWS AZURE

In the last chapter, you created the web form application, Class Schedule Management. To deploy this application to Windows Azure, you should first reconfigure the application to make it suitable for Windows Azure. Then, the application can be deployed with the tools provided by Visual Studio.

1. To log on to the virtual machine, you need to log on to the Windows Azure Management Portal through your web browser. After logging in, click **VIRTUAL MACHINES**. Select the server **myserver** and click **CONNECT**. Then, log on to the virtual machine with your user name and password.
2. After logging in, press the **Windows Icon** key and right click the icon **Visual Studio 2012** on the tile. Click **Run as administrator**.
3. Click the link **MyWebForm** to open the project. Right click on the **MyWebForm** solution link in the **Solution Explorer** pane. Select **Add Windows Azure Cloud Service Project** (Figure 10.9).
4. After the **New Windows Azure Project** dialog is added, expand the **MyWebForm.Azure** node. You should be able to see the default Web role **MyWebForm** shown in Figure 10.10. The role points to the web form MyWebForm built earlier.
5. To set the **MyWebFrom.Azure** project as the startup project, right click the project and select **Set as StartUp Project** as shown in Figure 10.11.
6. Click the **Start Debugging** icon to run the cloud project. You should be able to see the Class Management web page in your browser as shown in Figure 10.12.

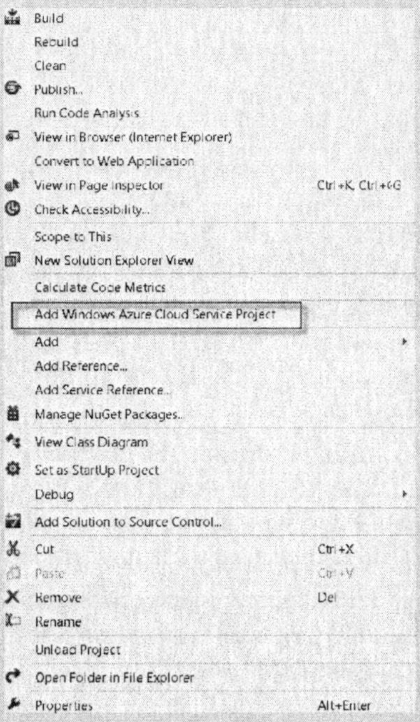

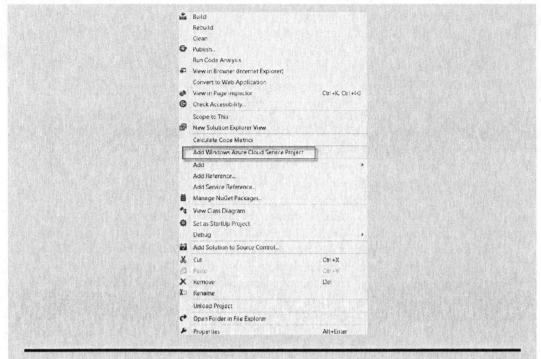

Figure 10.9 Add Windows Azure Cloud Service Project.

Figure 10.10 Create New Windows Azure Project.

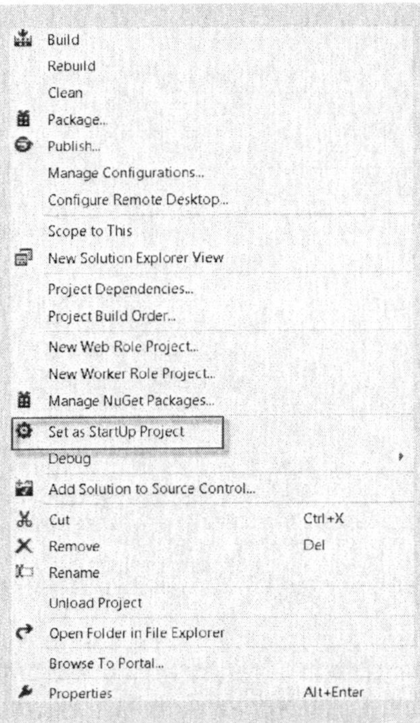

Figure 10.11 Set MyWebForm.Azure as StartUp Project.

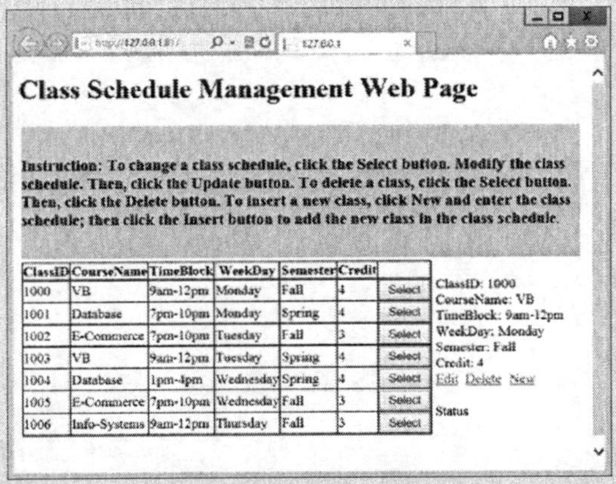

Figure 10.12 Class management web page on local computer.

Notice that the URL of the web page is http://127.0.0.1:81. This means that the web page has not been published to Windows Azure yet. Close the web page and get ready to publish the web page to Windows Azure.

7. To configure the role MyWebForm, double click the MyWebForm role. When the configuration page is opened, change the number of instances to 2 as shown in Figure 10.13. The two instances are used to improve the performance and provide the redundancy.

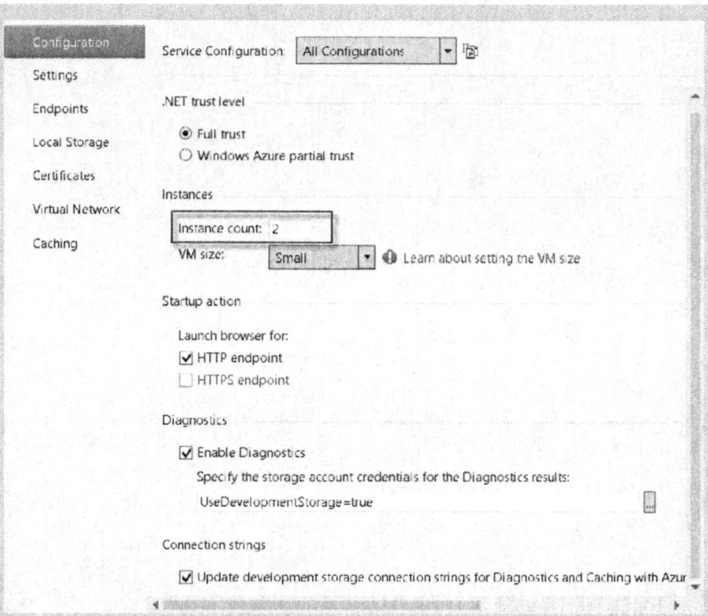

Figure 10.13 Configure MyWebForm role.

8. To publish MyWebForm to the cloud, you need the information about your Windows Azure account. To get the account information, log on to your **Windows Azure Management Portal**. Click the **STORAGE** service and click the name of your storage subscription. Then click **MANAGE KEYS** on the Contextual Command bar as shown in Figure 10.14.

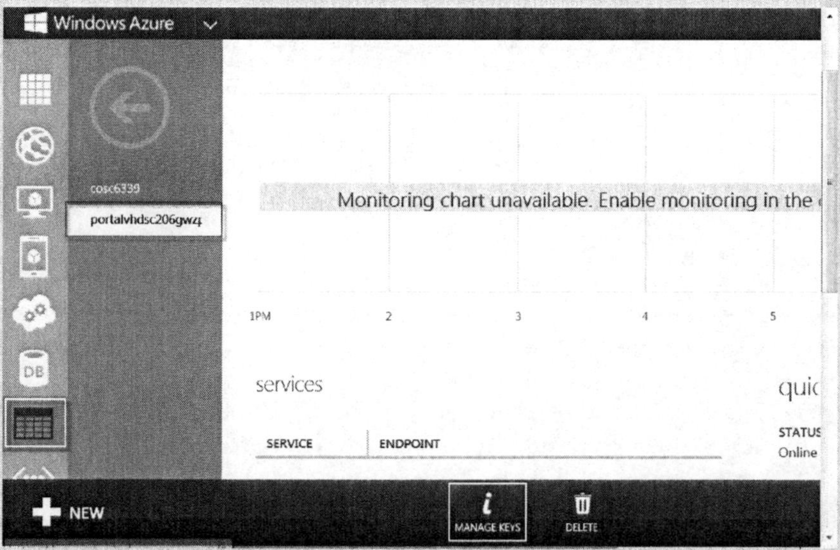

Figure 10.14 Manage keys.

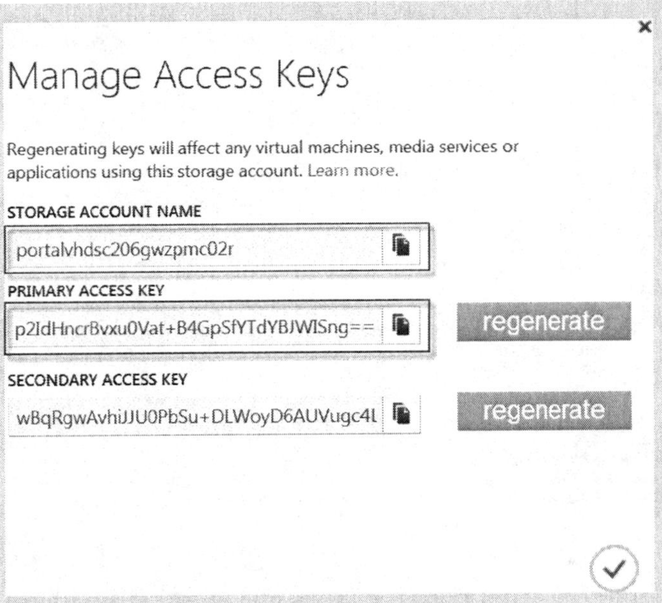

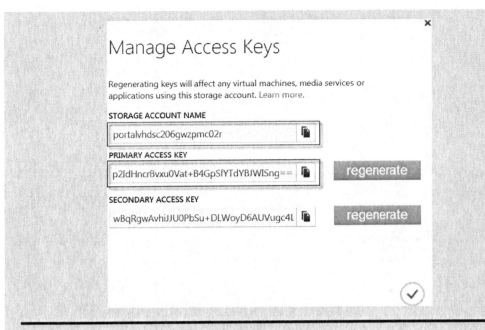

Figure 10.15 Storage account name and primary access key.

9. In the **Manage Access Keys** dialog as shown in Figure 10.15, record the storage account name and the primary access key.
10. After the storage account name and the primary access key are recorded, you can enter the information to the role configuration dialog. Assume that the role configuration dialog is still open as shown in Figure 10.13. Click **Settings** and click the **Add Setting** tab. Enter the setting name as **MyConnection** and select **Connection String** in the Type drop-down list. Then, click the ellipsis button [. . .] as shown in Figure 10.16.

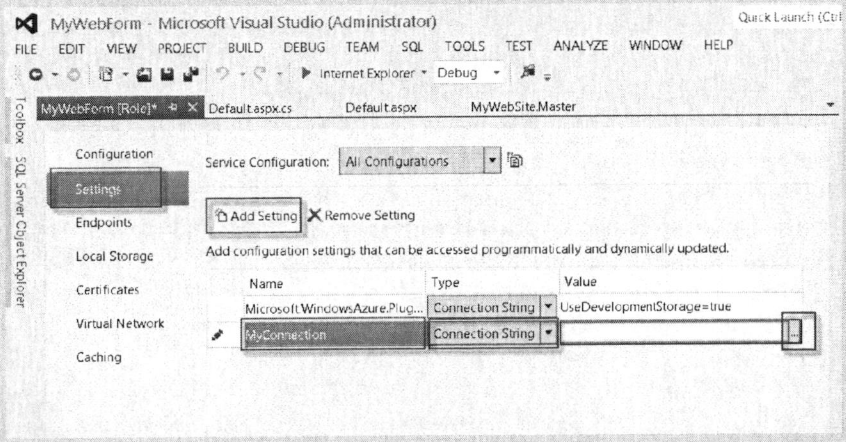

Figure 10.16 Add connection string.

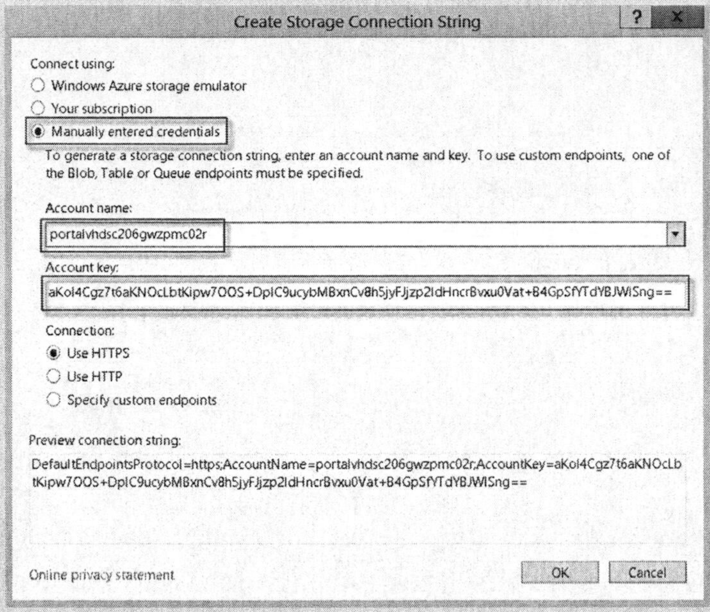

Figure 10.17 Configure connection string.

11. Once the Create Storage Connection String dialog is opened, click the option **Manually Entered Credentials.** Then, enter the recorded account name and account key as shown in Figure 10.17. Then, click **OK.**
12. After the connection string is configured, you are ready to publish MyWebForm to the cloud. Right click the cloud project **MyWebForm.Azure** and select **Publish**. On the Windows Azure Publish Sign In page, click the link **Sign in to download credentials** as shown in Figure 10.18.
13. When prompted, enter the e-mail address used for your Windows Azure Management Portal. Assume that you have a Hotmail e-mail account. Click the link **Sign in Hotmail.com.** Enter the password for your Windows Azure Management Portal and log on to the portal. The download web page is opened as shown in Figure 10.19. Then, click the **Save** button.
14. Click **View Downloads.** You should be able to see the downloaded file saved to the Downloads folder as shown in Figure 10.20. Then, click **Close.**
15. After the file is downloaded, click the **Import** button shown in Figure 10.18. Navigate to the **Downloads** folder and select the downloaded **PUBLISHSETTINGS** file as shown in Figure 10.21. Then, click **Open.**
16. Click Next to go to the **Windows Azure Publish Settings** page. When prompted, type a name for a Windows Azure cloud service and select a location as shown in Figure 10.22. Then, click **OK.**
17. The newly created cloud service appears on the **Windows Azure Publish Settings** page as shown in Figure 10.23. Choose **Staging** from the Environment drop-down

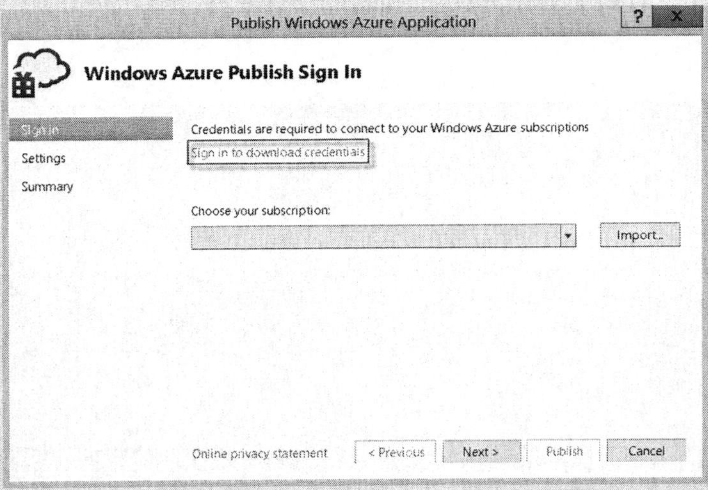
Publish Windows Azure Application
Windows Azure Publish Sign In
Sign in
Settings
Summary
Credentials are required to connect to your Windows Azure subscriptions
Sign in to download credentials
Choose your subscription:
Import...
Online privacy statement
< Previous
Next >
Publish
Cancel

Figure 10.18 Windows Azure Publish Sign In.

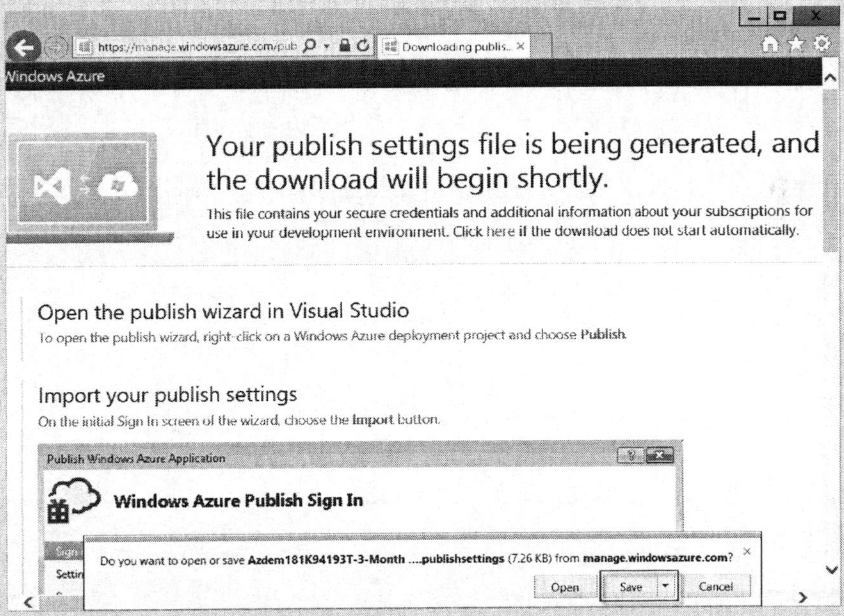
https://manage.windowsazure.com/pub
Downloading publis...
Windows Azure
Your publish settings file is being generated, and the download will begin shortly.
This file contains your secure credentials and additional information about your subscriptions for use in your development environment. Click here if the download does not start automatically.
Open the publish wizard in Visual Studio
To open the publish wizard, right-click on a Windows Azure deployment project and choose Publish.
Import your publish settings
On the initial Sign In screen of the wizard, choose the Import button.
Publish Windows Azure Application
Windows Azure Publish Sign In
Do you want to open or save Azdem181K94193T-3-Month ....publishsettings (7.26 KB) from manage.windowsazure.com?
Open
Save
Cancel

Figure 10.19 Download web page.

list. By choosing Staging, you deploy the application to a test environment. You can change to the production environment after the test. To allow remote access to the Web role, check **Enable Remote Desktop for all roles.**

18. In the Remote Desktop Configuration dialog, enter the user name and password as shown in Figure 10.24. Then, click **OK.**

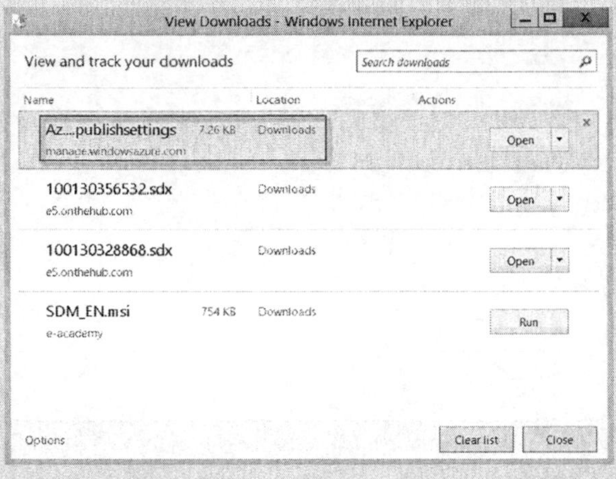

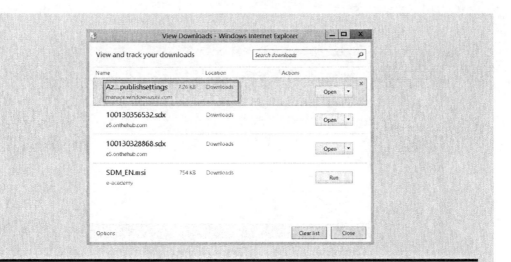

Figure 10.20 View downloaded file.

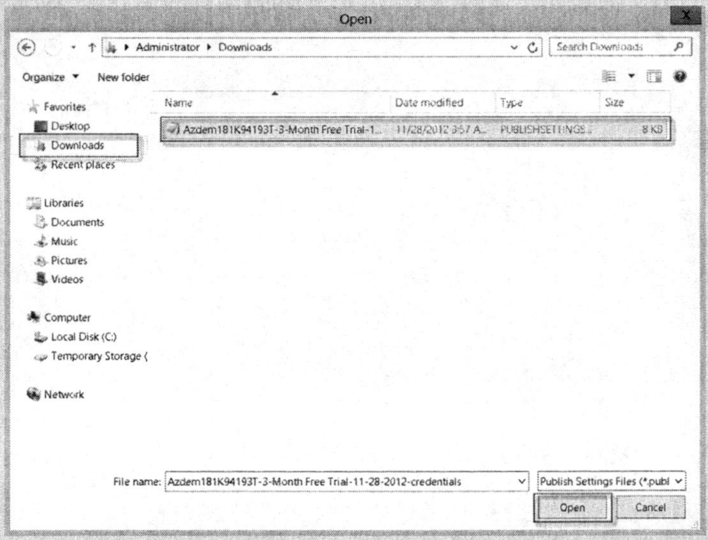

Figure 10.21 Open downloaded file.

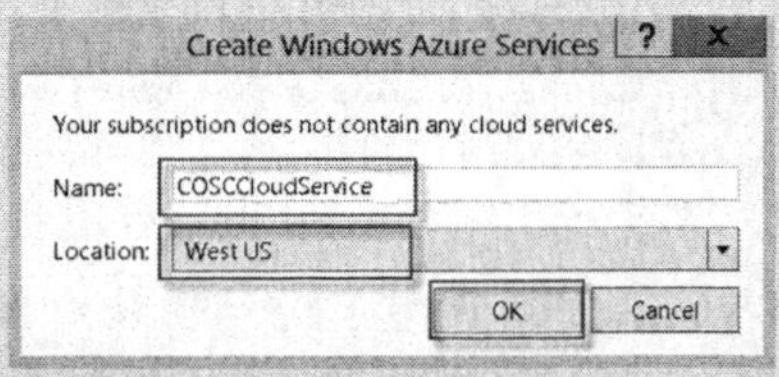

Figure 10.22 Create cloud service.

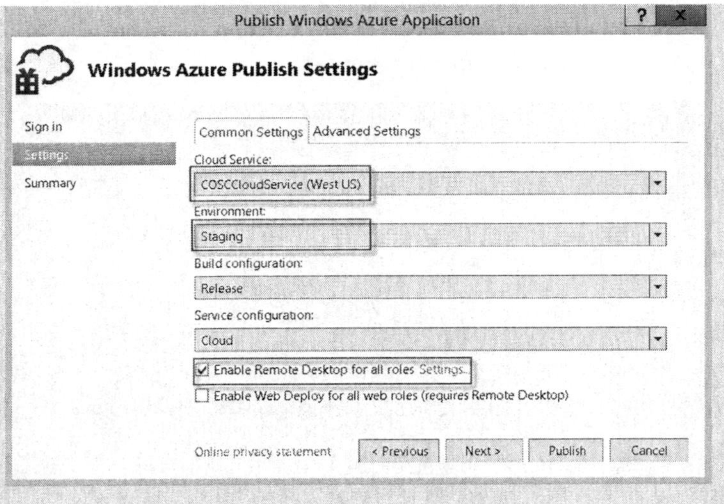

Figure 10.23 Configure publish settings.

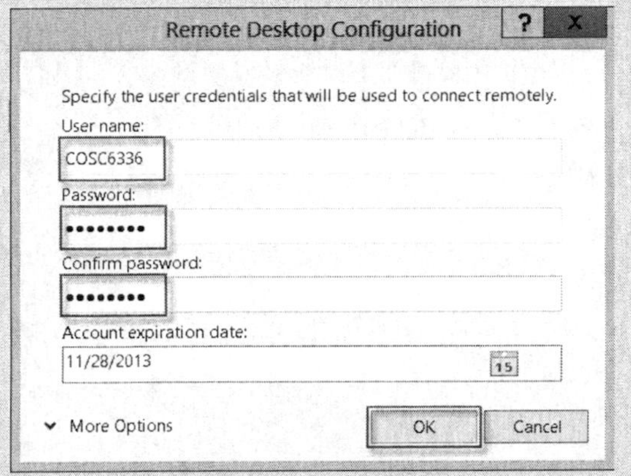

Figure 10.24 Configure remote desktop.

19. Click **Next** to go to the summary page. Review the summary and click **Publish** as shown in Figure 10.25.
20. You can view the result of the publishing in the output window as shown in Figure 10.26. To view the published web form, click the URL for the website.
21. You should be able to see your web form as shown in Figure 10.27. Notice that the URL is not your local computer.

Once it is published to Windows Azure, the web form will be accessible anytime and anywhere. It can also take advantage of the scalability of Windows Azure.

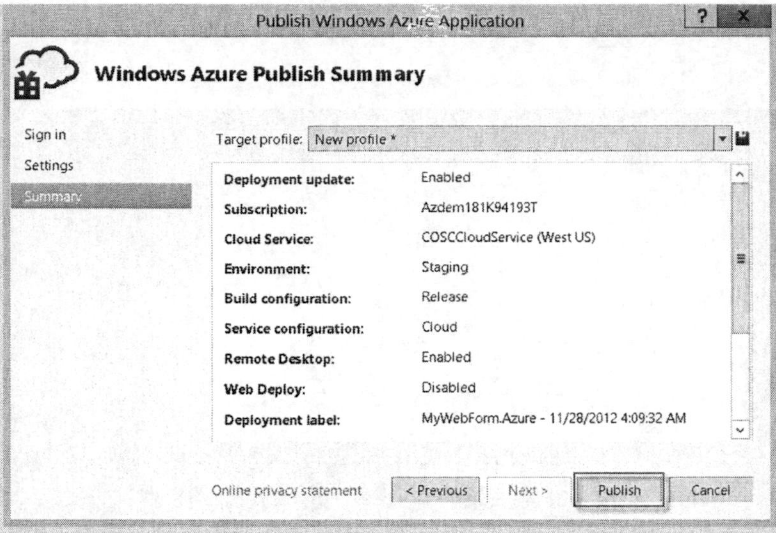

Figure 10.25 Publish application.

Figure 10.26 Result of publishing.

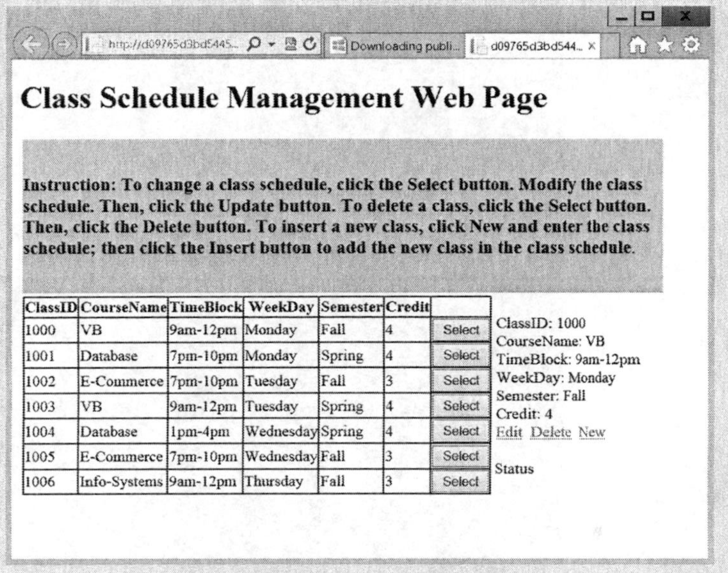

Figure 10.27 Class management web page on Windows Azure.

ACTIVITY 10.2 CREATING REPORT WITH WINDOWS AZURE SQL REPORTING

In this activity, we will create a reporting service by using Reporting Services. The first task is to create a report server on Windows Azure.

TASK 1: CREATE REPORTING SERVER ON WINDOWS AZURE

1. Log on to Windows Azure through the URL http://windows.azure.com.
2. After signing in to Windows Azure, open the Avatar bar by clicking the account icon at the upper-right corner of your screen. Then click **Previous portal** as shown in Figure 10.28.
3. Once the Previous Windows Azure Management Portal is opened, click the link **Reporting** on the left-hand side of your screen. To create a reporting server, click the **Create** icon in the Server section on the Ribbon.
4. On the Create an SQL Azure Reporting Server dialog, enter **your subscription** and the preferred **region code** as shown in Figure 10.29.
5. Then, click **Next** to enter the user name and password for the SQL Reporting server. Then, click **Finish**.
6. On the Management Portal, click the **Subscription** link on the left-hand side of your screen; you should be able to see the newly created reporting server (Figure 10.30).
7. Click the link to the web service URL of the reporting server to open the reporting server portal shown in Figure 10.31. Record the connection string for future use.

Figure 10.28 Open previous portal.

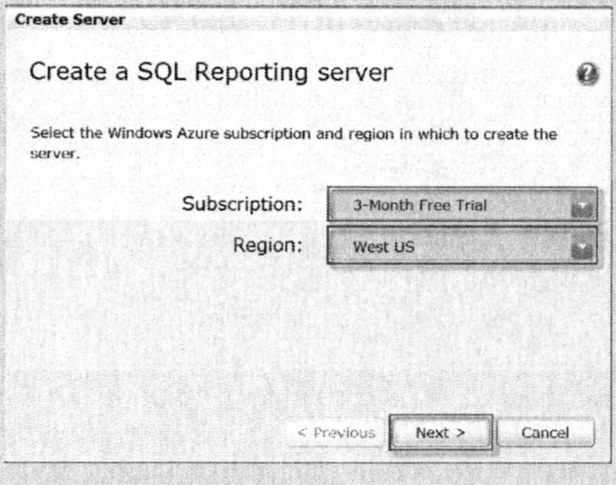

Figure 10.29 Create SQL reporting server.

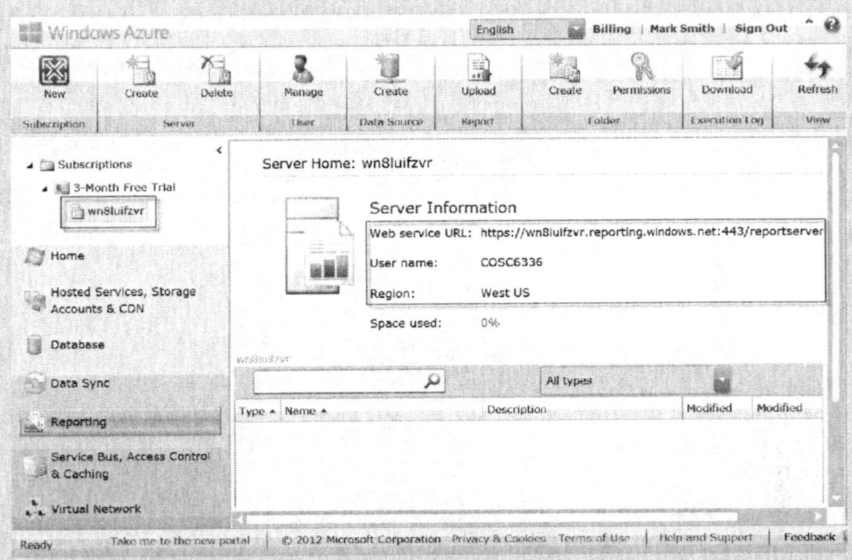

Figure 10.30 Display SQL reporting server.

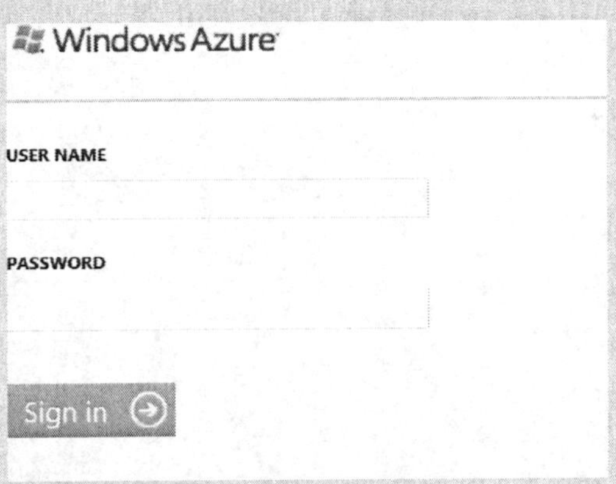

Figure 10.31 Windows Azure SQL reporting portal.

TASK 2: CREATE REPORT WITH SQL SERVER DATA TOOLS

Our next task is to create a new report project with SQL Server Data Tools. Although Visual Studio can be used to create some simple reports, for more sophisticated reports, you need the reporting tool provided by Business Intelligence.

1. You need to go back to the new Windows Azure Management Portal by clicking the link **Take me to the new portal** as shown in Figure 10.32.
2. From the new Windows Azure Management Portal, connect to your virtual machine. Press the **Windows Icon** key. When the tile is opened, right-click **SQL Server Data Tools 2010** and select **Run as administrator** as shown in Figure 10.33.

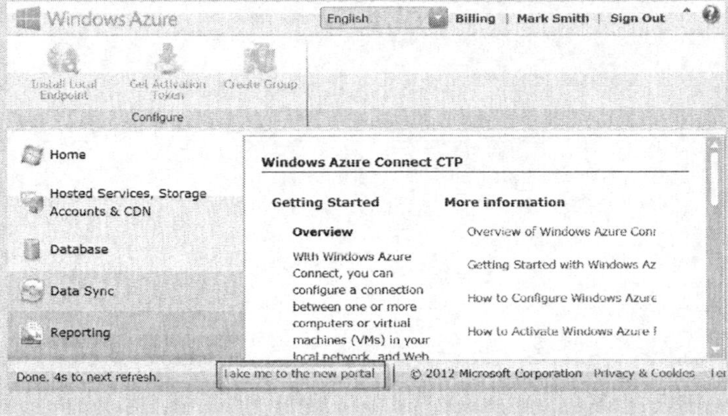

Figure 10.32 Go to New portal.

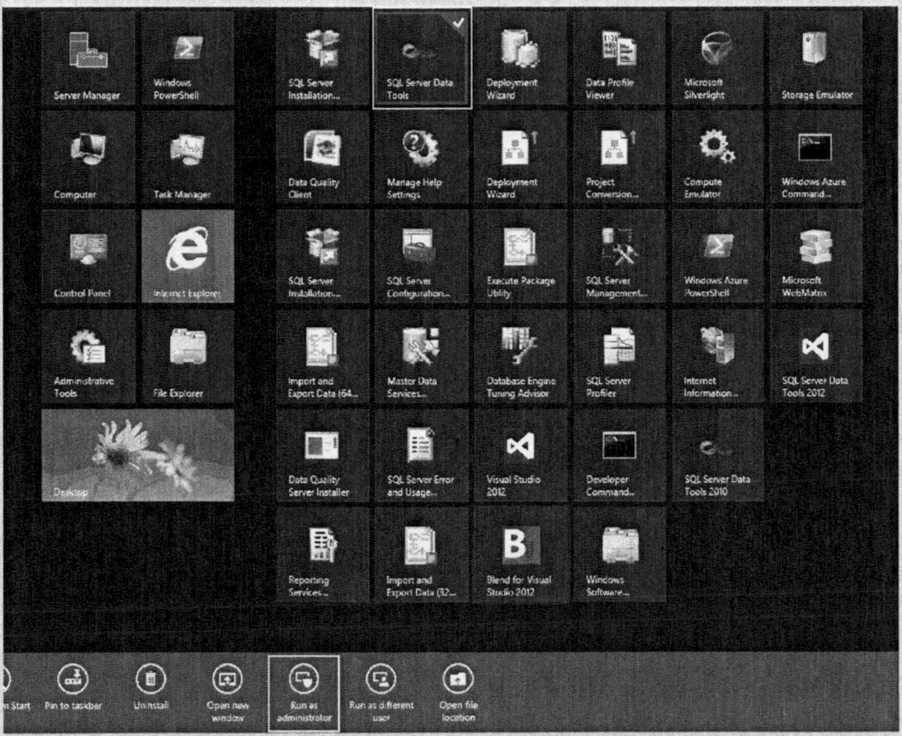

Figure 10.33 Start SQL server data tools.

3. To open a new project dialog, click **File**, **New**, and **Project**. After the new project dialog is opened, in the **Project types** pane, select **Business Intelligence** and select **Report Server Project** from the Templates pane. Enter the project name **GradeReport** as shown in Figure 10.34. Click **OK** to create the project.

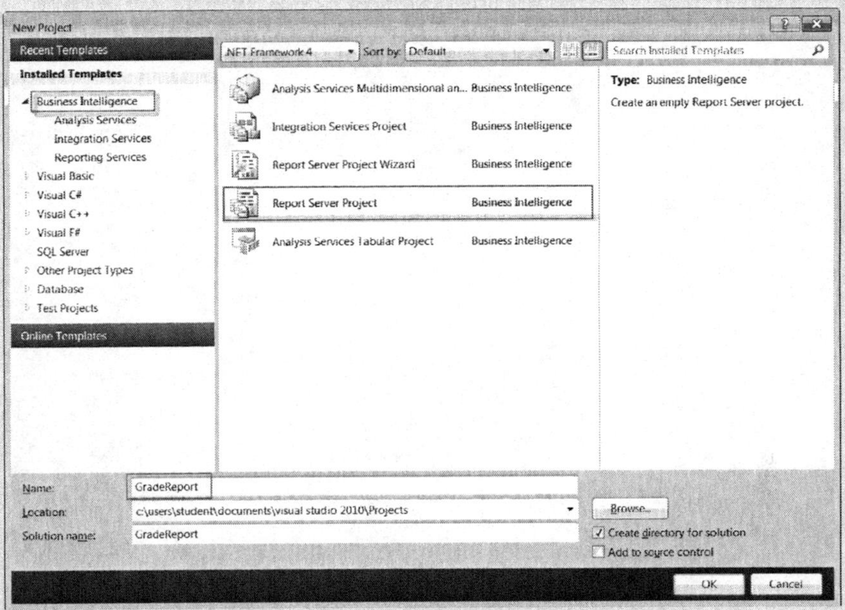

Figure 10.34 GradeReport project.

4. On the Welcome to Report Wizard page, click **Next** to go to the Select Data Source page. Name the new data source as **SQLDBDataSource** and specify **Microsoft SQL Azure** in the **Type** drop-down list.
5. Click the **Edit** button to open the **Connection Properties** dialog. In the Server name combo box, enter the name of your Windows Azure SQL Database Server. Select the option **Use SQL Server Authentication** and enter the user name and password. You may also click the check box **Save my password**. In the **Select or enter a database name** combo box, specify the database **Class_Registration** as shown in Figure 10.35. Click the **Test Connection** button to verify if the connection is successful. Then, click **OK**.
6. You will be prompted to enter the user name and password for the data source SQLDBDataSource. For example, you may use the user name **COSC6336** and password **Student1** (Figure 10.36). Then, click **OK**.
7. On the **Design the Query** page, click the **Query Builder** button. Expand the **Tables** node. Select the tables **CLASS**, **COURSE**, **STUDENT**, and **STUDENT_CLASS**. Click the button **Auto Detect** to establish the relationships among these tables. Then, remove the rest of the columns except the columns **FirstName**, **LastName**, **CourseName**, **ClassID**, and **Grade** as shown in Figure 10.37. Click the **Run Query** icon; you should be able to see the data selected by the query. Then, click **OK** to complete the construction of the query.
8. Click **Next** twice to go to the Select the Report Type page. Take the default type **Tabular**.
9. Click **Next** to go to the Design the Table page. Select **FirstName** and click **Page >**, select **LastName** and click **Page >**, select **CourseName**, **ClassID**, and **Grade**, and then click **Details >** as shown in Figure 10.38.

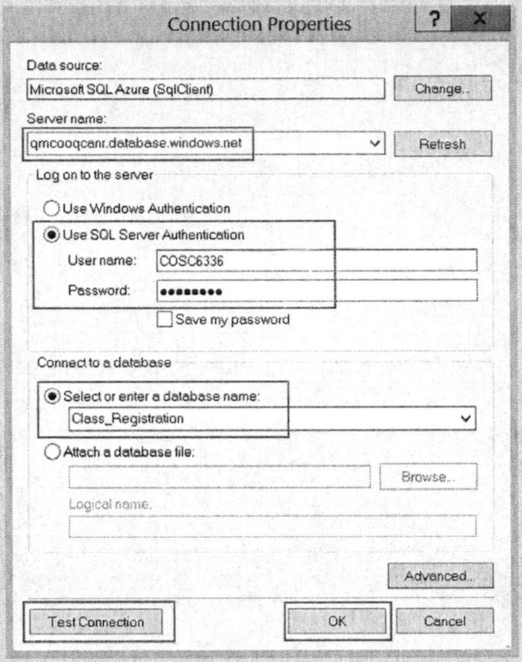

Figure 10.35 Configure connection properties.

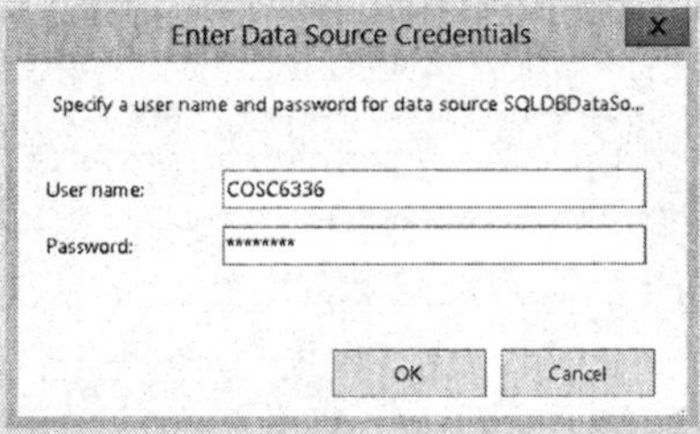

Figure 10.36 Enter data source credentials.

10. Click **Next** to go to the **Choose the Table Style** page. Select the **Slate** style.
11. Click **Next** twice to go to the Completing the Wizard page. Enter the report name as **Class Grade Report**, and then click **Finish**.
12. In the design window, highlight the page title **Class Grade Report**, right click on it, and select **Text Property** on the pop-up menu. Click **Font** and change the font size to **16**.
13. Drag the **FirstName** placeholder from the FirstName Text Box to the **LastName** Text Box, and place the **FirstName** placeholder in the left-hand side of the **LastName** placeholder.
14. Drag the **FirstName** and the **LastName** text boxes toward to the title **Class Grade Report** to reduce the distance between the title and the rest of the content on

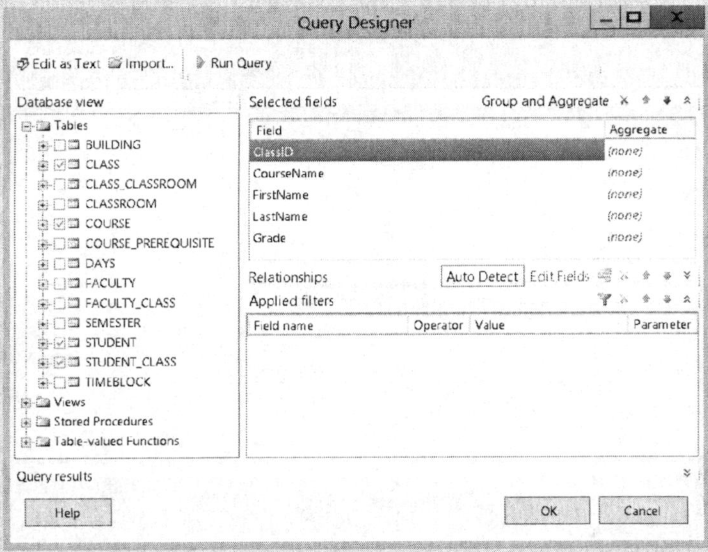

Figure 10.37 Design query.

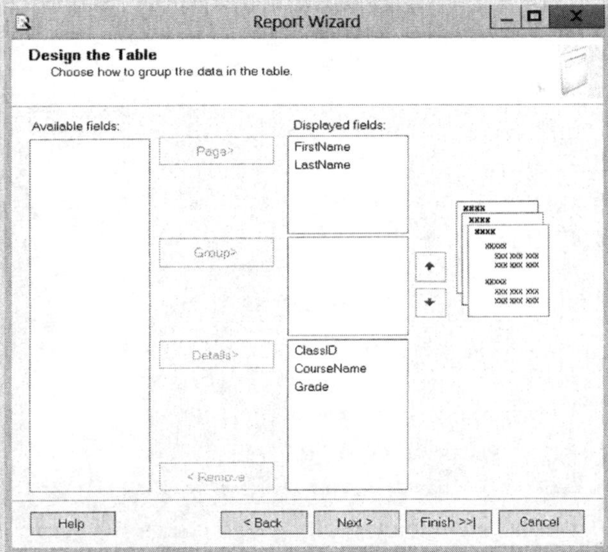

Figure 10.38 Design table in report wizard.

the report. Similarly, move the placeholder of ClassID, CourseName, and Grade toward to the FirstName and LastName Text boxes to reduce the space as shown in Figure 10.39.

15. Right click the **FirstName** placeholder and select **Placeholder Properties** on the pop-up menu. Click **Font** and set the color to **Black**. Similarly, change the font size to **14pt**

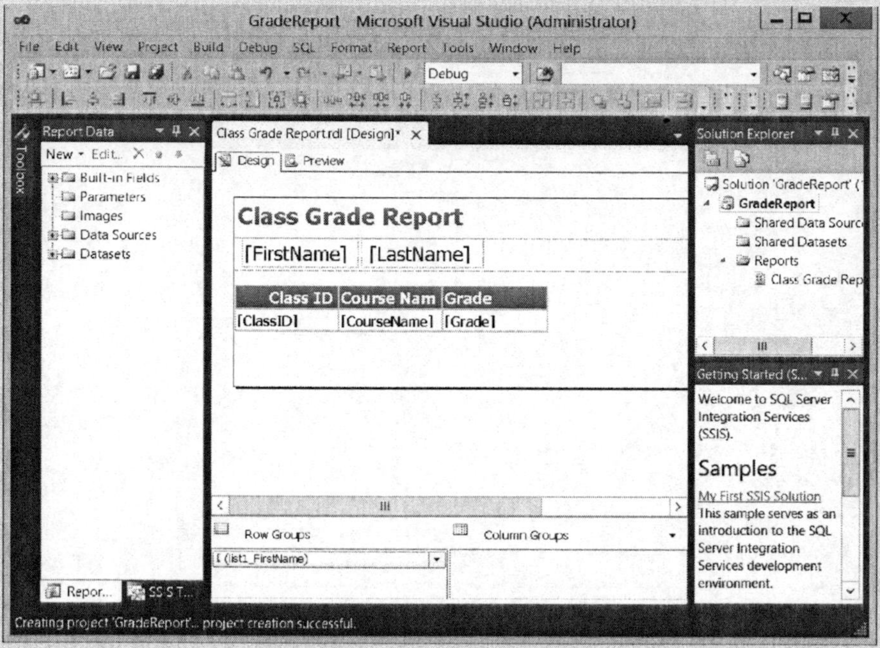

Figure 10.39 Design report.

as shown in Figure 10.40. Also, adjust the FirstName's Alignment to the right and LastName's Alignment to the left.

16. Click the **Preview** tab. Enter your user name and password; for example, enter the user name **COSC6336** and password **Student1**, and then click the **View Report** button to display the report as shown in Figure 10.41.

TASK 3: DEPLOY REPORT TO WINDOWS AZURE

1. You can now deploy the newly created report to the Windows Azure so that it will be available to readers on the Internet. To do so, right-click the **GradeReport** project in Solution Explore and select **Properties** on the pop-up menu.
2. In the GradeReport Property Pages dialog, double click the **TargetServerURL** property and enter the report server name recorded in earlier activities as shown in Figure 10.42. The report URL looks something like https://wn8luifzvr.reporting.windows.net/ReportServer/
3. Make sure that **StartItem** has the report **Class Grade Report.rdl** file selected as shown in Figure 10.42.
4. Click **OK** to complete the configuration. To deploy the report, right click the **GradeReport** project and select **Deploy** on the pop-up menu. Enter the user name and password for your report server in the Report Services Login dialog and then click **OK** to deploy the report.
5. To see the deployed report, in your browser, enter the URL https://wn8luifzvr.reporting.windows.net/ReportServer/

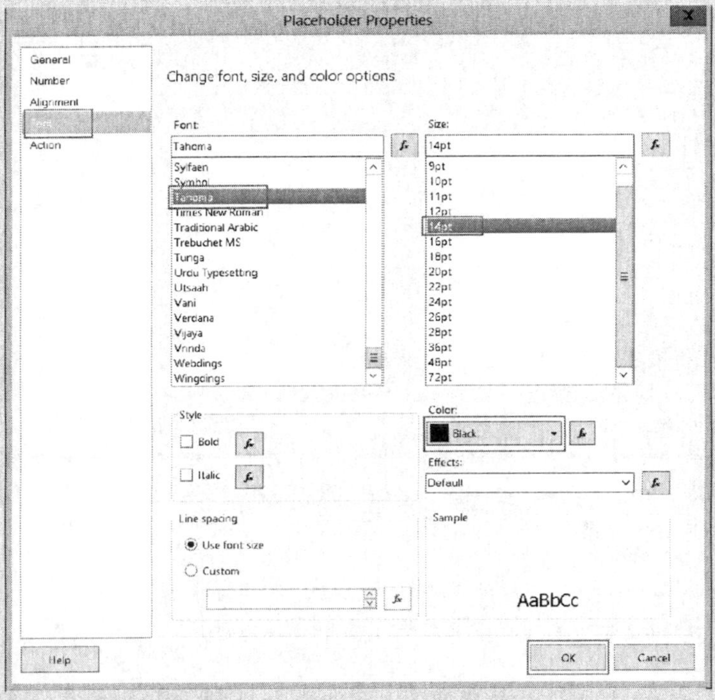

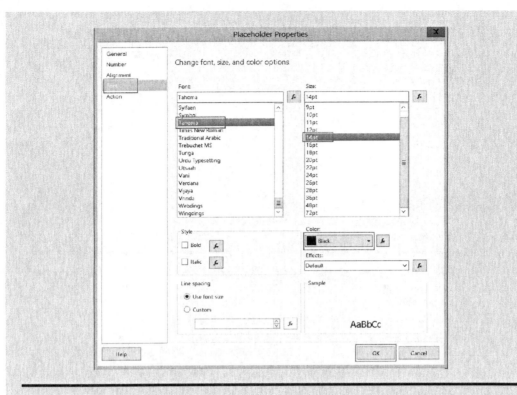

Figure 10.40 Font configuration.

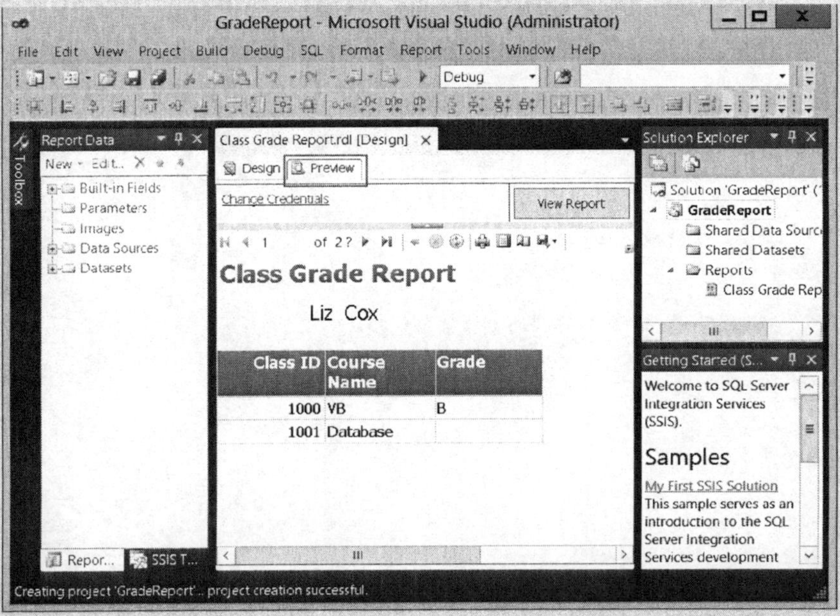

Figure 10.41 Preview Class Grade Report.

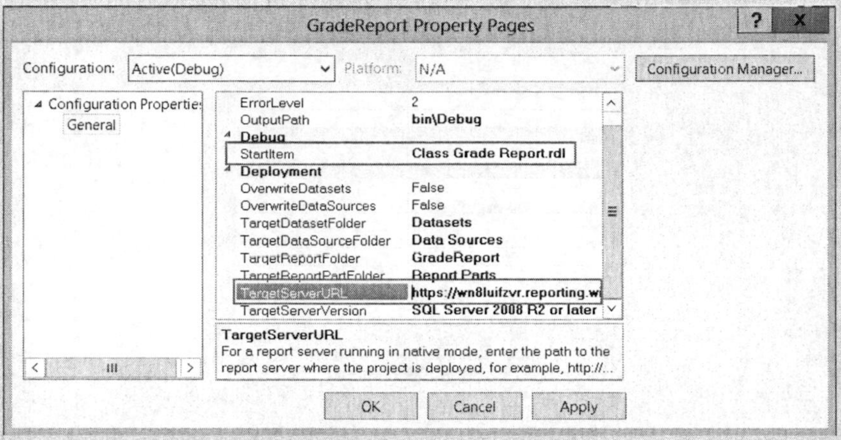

Figure 10.42 Configure report properties for report deployment.

6. Then, log on to the **report server portal** created earlier. Double click the link **GradeReport** and enter your user name and password for the data source. Then, click **Class Grade Report** to open the report as shown in Figure 10.43.
7. Save and exit the report server portal, the Windows Azure Management Portal, and the GradeReport project in SQL Server Data Tools.

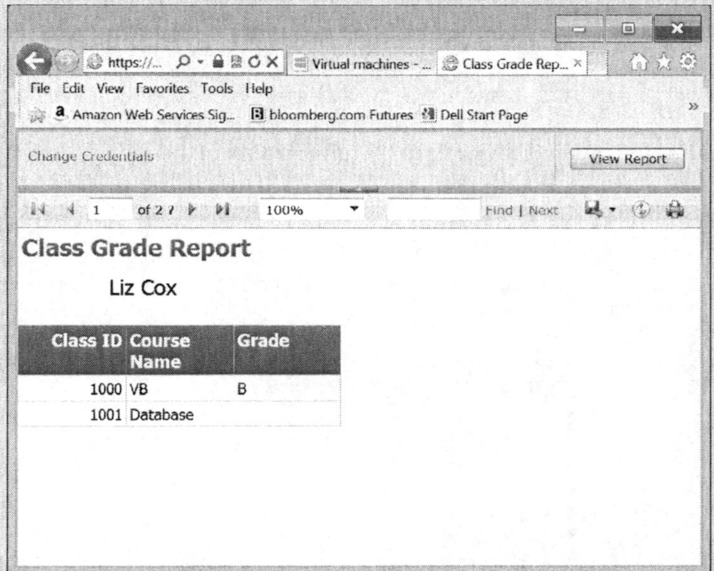

Figure 10.43 Deploy Class Grade Report.

In this section, a cloud-based report server has been created with the Window Azure Management Portal. SQL Server Data Tools is used to create a new report that uses SQL Database as its data source. Once the newly created report is deployed to the report server, it can be accessed through a web browser by users with the proper permission.

10.4 Summary

This chapter explores Windows Azure and the Windows Azure SDK. The Windows Azure SDK can provide a cloud development environment on a desktop computer. Without connecting to the Internet, application developers can develop, test, and debug an application on a local computer before deploying the application to Windows Azure. After the application is fully tested and is ready to be deployed to Windows Azure, it only requires a few clicks to accomplish the task. In this chapter, applications developed locally are deployed to Windows Azure to make them cloud-based applications. Once deployed to the cloud, these applications can be accessed through the web browser. To illustrate the deployment process, this chapter demonstrates the process of deploying web forms and reports to Windows Azure.

Review Questions

1. How is Windows Azure structured?
2. How does the Fabric Controller (FC) work?
3. What tasks can be accomplished by the Windows Azure SDK?
4. What tasks can be accomplished with the Management Portal?
5. Describe the Ribbon section in the Windows Azure Management Portal.
6. Describe the Navigation area in the Windows Azure Management Portal.
7. Describe the Properties section in the Windows Azure Management Portal.
8. What is a hosted service?
9. What is a Web role?
10. What is a Worker role?
11. What is a VM role?
12. What does the ServiceDefinition.csdef file do?
13. What do you do with the ServiceConfiguration.cscfg file?
14. Describe access control service (ACS).
15. Describe how Reporting Services work.
16. What tasks can be accomplished by the Windows Azure compute emulator?
17. What are the limits of the Windows Azure compute emulator?
18. What tasks can be accomplished by the Windows Azure storage emulator?
19. What are the three packaging tools mentioned in this chapter?
20. What is Representational State Transfer (REST)?

Chapter 11

Windows Azure Storage

Objectives

- Understand the Windows Azure storage
- Use the Table storage
- Use the Blob storage
- Use the Queue storage

11.1 Introduction

So far, you have accomplished the tasks of developing databases in Windows Azure SQL Database. The SQL Database has been used to support applications such as forms and reports. On the other hand, there are some applications that need to work with a large amount of nonrelational data. For example, some of the web applications need to store dozens of terabytes of audio and video binary data into storage, which does not require complex joins, integrity constraints, and stored procedures. These applications require data to be quickly stored and queried. In such a case, the nonrelational data storage such as Windows Azure storage may be a good choice. In this chapter, our focus is on Windows Azure storage and the deployment of web and worker roles.

11.2 Windows Azure Storage Services

The Windows Azure storage services include three components: the Windows Azure Table service for efficiently storing a large amount of data, the Windows Azure Queue service for the storage of messages, and the Windows Azure Blob service for the storage of large binary objects such as video and audio files. The Windows Azure provides storage for Windows Azure Blobs, Tables, and Queues. Once a Windows Azure storage account is created for a user, the storage services will be accessible by one or more applications owned by the user. Unlike local storage, the Windows Azure storage services are accessible anywhere and anytime.

Windows Azure Table Storage: The Windows Azure storage services offer Table storage, which is for storing nonrelational data. The Table storage data service stores all the records in a table. These records may belong to different entities. The Table storage uses keys to distinguish these records from one entity to another entity. The meaning of the word "table" in the Table storage service is a bit different from the table used in a relational database. In a relational database, rows in a table have the same number of columns. The data in a column have the same data type. Also, there are no duplicated rows in a relational database table. In a relational database, tables are related with primary/foreign key pairs. Unlike the relational database, there is no relationship to link two different entities in the Table storage. Multiple entities are simply placed in the same table. Therefore, the rows in a Table storage table may have different numbers of columns. The advantage of the Table storage is that it is more scalable and has better performance. It costs less to store data in the Table storage. The disadvantage is that the Table storage is difficult to work with for many application developers. Data in the Table storage is less portable when compared with data stored in a relational database. Both SQL Database and the Table storage can be used for storing, processing, and analyzing the data. However, for customers with high needs on scalability, the Table storage is the choice. On the other hand, when there are complex data transactions and portability is a concern, SQL Database should be considered.

In the Table storage, data in a table are structured with rows and columns. Rows in the Table storage are also called entities and columns are called properties. A Windows Azure entity can have as many as 255 properties. That is, each row/entity in the Table storage can have as many as 255 columns/properties. Among the 255 properties, three of them are required. These three properties are defined in Table 11.1.

The commonly used data types in Windows Azure are the subset of data types defined by ADO.NET Data Services as shown in Table 11.2.

Windows Azure Blob Storage: The Windows Azure Blob storage is used to store the binary contents. It also provides inexpensive storage. An application can store a large amount of binary data such as video and audio data in the Blob storage. The Blob storage can also be used to backup large files. Even an entire Windows file system used by an application can be stored in the Blob storage. There are two types of Blob storage available. When creating Blob storage, one needs to specify the type of the Blob storage. Each type has its own set of features as described in the following:

- *Block Blob*: A block blob consists of a set of blocks. Each block is identified by its block ID. The maximum block size is 4 MB and each block can be different in size. A block blob can

Table 11.1 Required Properties

Property Name	*Description*
Partition key	A table can be partitioned based on the partition key, which is used to uniquely identify partitions. A partition can be used to represent a set of related entities. It can also be used for load balancing and scaling out since a partition can be placed on multiple storage nodes. The size of each partition key is limited to 1 kB.
Row key	It is used to uniquely identify rows/entities within a table. The partition key and row key are used to uniquely identify each row in a Table storage. The size of each row key is limited to 1 kB.
Timestamp	It is used for time-related activities such as sorting and auditing.

Table 11.2 Data Types in Table Storage

Data Types	*Description*
Edm.Binary	It defines an array of bytes up to 64 kB in size. Edm stands for Entity Data Model.
Edm.Boolean	It defines a Boolean value.
Edm.DateTime	It defines a 64-bit value in UTC (coordinated universal time).
Edm.Double	It defines a 64-bit floating point value.
Edm.Guid	It defines a 128-bit globally unique identifier.
Edm.Int32	It defines a 32-bit integer.
Edm.Int64	It defines a 64-bit integer.
Edm.String	It defines a UTF-16-encoded string up to 64 kB in size. UTF stands for unicode transformation format.

have as many as 50,000 blocks, and the maximum size of a block blob is 200 GB. By using blocks, a large block blob can be efficiently uploaded to a cloud. The block blob is optimized for upload and download streaming.

- *Page Blob*: A page blob consists of 512-byte pages. It is optimized for random read and write operations. The maximum size of a page blob is 1 TB. When creating a page blob, one needs to specify the maximum size for the page blob to grow. When writing content to the page blob, one may write the content to one or more pages. The page blob can be used to implement NTFS Virtual Hard Drive, which can be mounted by applications on the Windows Azure platform. The snapshots of the blob can be used for backup. The blob can also be cached at the nearby data center for fast data access.

Windows Azure Queue Storage: The Queue storage service is used to store a large number of messages. The service processes message between applications. It can pass messages from a Windows Azure Web role to a Windows Azure Worker role. The stored messages can be accessed from anywhere through network protocols such as HTTP or HTTPS. The messages are processed in a first-in first-out (FIFO) manner. The stored messages can be processed asynchronously. By default, the size of a message is limited to 8 kB. Although there is no limit on the number of messages that can be stored in the Queue storage, there is a time limit. Messages will be deleted after a week in the Queue storage. The life cycle of a message is described below:

- A message is added to the Queue storage.
- When one application is reading the message, the message is marked as invisible until the message is deleted or a specified reading interval is reached.
- The message gets deleted if the message stays in the Queue storage for longer than the TTL or a specified reading interval is reached.

A message has four main properties that specify the message ID, message visibility, receiving receipt, and the lifetime of the message.

Remote Access: Users can access cloud-based storage space through remote access. The Windows Azure Table service and the Windows Azure Blob service use various remote access tools such as Representational State Transfer (REST) APIs and Language Integrated Query (LINQ).

11.3 Use of Table Storage

In this section, you will learn how to use the Windows Azure Table storage. The Table storage will be used to store student information generated by a web form. As an example, let us consider the Student Club web page that uses the Table storage to store the information about club members. The web page can be used for students to register for a club. This form will allow a student to select a club that the student likes. To register for a club, the student needs to enter the contact information. He or she can also upload his or her photo along with the contact information. After the student clicks the Submit button, the form should display a message to welcome the new club member and the contact information of the fellow club members. According to the description of the form, we can identify the input and output shown in Table 11.3.

In Table 11.4, a set of actions are defined.

According to the input/output and the actions identified in Tables 11.3 and 11.4, a possible GUI interface can be designed as shown in Figure 11.1.

Table 11.3 Control Description

Input		*Output*	
Input	*Control Used*	*Output*	*Control Used*
Selection of a Club	Radio button	Welcome message	Label
Name, e-mail, and major	Text boxes	A list of contact info	Grid View
Student's photo	Picture box	Student's photo image	Image

Table 11.4 Action Description

Event	*Action*
Click radio button	Assign the value of the ratio button as the one clicked.
Click submit button	Save the selected club, the student's name, e-mail, and major to a table. Display message. Query the club members and display the members' contact info. Retrieve the binary file and display the photo image.
Click browse button	Allow user to search for the image file on the local computer. Upload student's photo to binary storage.

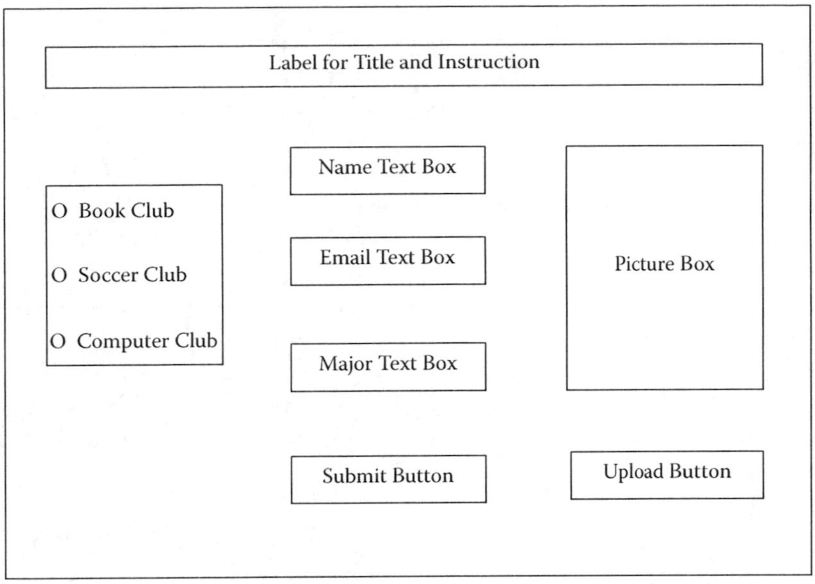

Figure 11.1 GUI interface design.

ACTIVITY 11.1 USING TABLE STORAGE

This activity includes four tasks. The descriptions of these tasks are given below:

- **Task 1: Create Student Club ASP.NET Project**: This task creates an ASP.NET project that includes a GUI interface and a web role.
- **Task 2: Create Data Source for Student Club Web Page**: This task defines and creates the data model for the StudentClub application. At the end of this task, the users will be able to insert student information into the Table storage through the ASP.NET application.
- **Task 3: Storage Account Configuration**: This task configures authentication information for the storage account.
- **Task 4: Develop Student Club Web Page and Process User Input**: This task further develops the Student Club web page and link the web page to the data source.

TASK 1: CREATE STUDENT CLUB ASP.NET PROJECT

Assume that Windows Azure SDK has been installed on your machine. To create an ASP.NET application, follow the steps below:

1. Log on to the Windows Azure Management Portal through your web browser. After you have logged in, click the link **VIRTUAL MACHINES**. Select the server **myserver** that is created in Chapter 1 and click **CONNECT**. Then, log on to the virtual machine with your user name and password.

2. Start Microsoft Visual Studio by pressing the **Windows Icon** key, right click **Visual Studio 2012** on the tile, and click the context command **Run as administrator**. Once Microsoft Visual Studio 2012 is opened, click **FILE | New | Project** on the top-left part of the screen.
3. Within the **Installed Templates** pane, expand the **Visual C#** node, and then click **Cloud**. Click **Windows Azure Cloud Service** project. In the Name field, change the name to **StudentClub.** The **New Project** dialog should look similar to the one in Figure 11.2. Click **OK** to close the New Project dialog.
4. After the New Windows Azure Cloud Service dialog is opened, select **ASP.NET Web Role**, which is a framework for building scalable web applications, and then click **>** to add a web role to the **Windows Azure Cloud Service solution** pane. Select the new role in the **Windows Azure Cloud Service solution** pane, click the **pencil** icon and rename the role as **StudentClub_WebRole** (Figure 11.3). Click **OK** to create the new ASP.NET project.

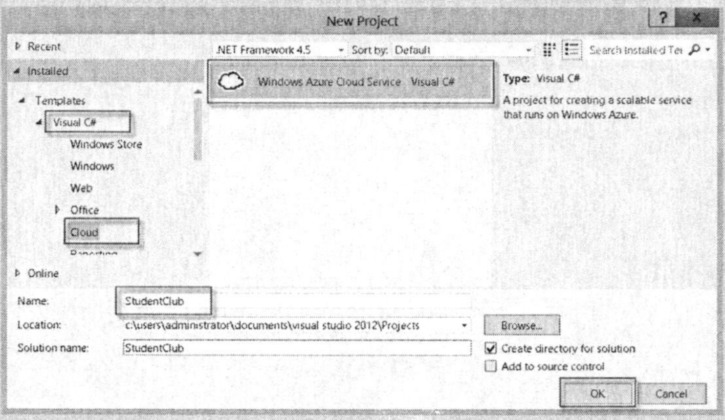

Figure 11.2 StudentClub Project dialog.

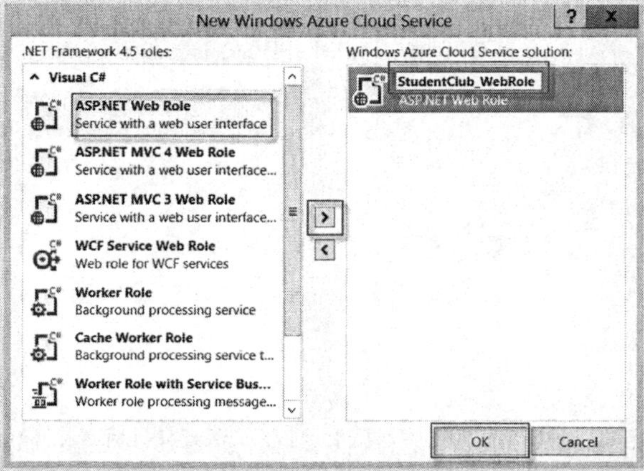

Figure 11.3 New Windows Azure Cloud Service dialog.

5. In the Solution Explorer pane, you should be able to see that StudentClub_WebRole is created under Roles node. A web role can be used to construct the front end of a web service. The web role will be referenced by a Windows Azure cloud service, which includes three files: ServiceDefinition.csdef, ServiceConfiguration.Cloud.cscfg, and ServiceConfiguration.Local.cscfg. The file ServiceDefinition.csdef contains the metadata that define Windows Azure. ServiceConfiguration.Cloud.cscfg and ServiceConfiguration.Local.cscfg are the configuration files that specify the settings for the cloud version of service and local version of service. The file Default.aspx is automatically opened. The Default.aspx file can be used to display messages to the users who interact with the application. As for the Student Club cloud service, you will need to delete the web page automatically added by Microsoft Visual Studio. To do so, right click **Default.aspx** and select **Delete**. You will create your own Default.aspx file in the next step.
6. To create a main web page for the student club, right click **StudentClub_WebRole** in Solution Explorer and choose **Add | New Item** in the menu. In the **Add New Item** dialog, choose the item type of **Visual C# | Web | Web Form using Master Page** and set its name to be **Default.aspx** and click **Add**. On the Select a Master Page dialog, click **OK**.
7. In the Default.aspx window, click the **Design** button to switch to the design view. Expand the **Toolbox** on the left-hand side of your screen. Then, expand the **HTML** section and drag the **Table** control to the **MainContent** area.
8. Highlight the first three cells in the first row, right click at them and select **Modify | Merge**. In the merged cell, type the following instruction and change the font size to **Large** on the menu bar:

   Instruction: Click the club radio button to select the club to join. In the textboxes, enter your name, e-mail, and major. You may also upload your photo. Then, click the Submit button to join the club.
9. From the **Standard** section of the **Toolbox**, drag the **RadioButtonList** control to the cell at the second row and first column. Click the smart tag and select **Edit Items**. Once ListItem Collection Editor is opened, add three items and name them as **Book Club**, **Soccer Club**, and **Computer Club** as shown in Figure 11.4. Then, click **OK**.
10. From the **Data** section, drag one **ObjectDataSource** control to the cell at the third row and the first column.
11. From the **Standard** section, drag three **Label** and three **Textbox** controls to the cell at the second row and the second column.
12. From the **Standard** section, drag one **Button** control to the cell at the third row and the second column.
13. From the **Standard** section, drag one **FileUpload** control to the cell at the third row and the third column.
14. From the **Standard** section, drag one **Label** control and one **Image** control to the cell at the second row and the third column. Then, configure the controls as shown in Table 11.5.
15. In the Solution Explorer dialog, right click the **StudentClub_WebRole** and select **View in Page Inspector** as shown in Figure 11.5.

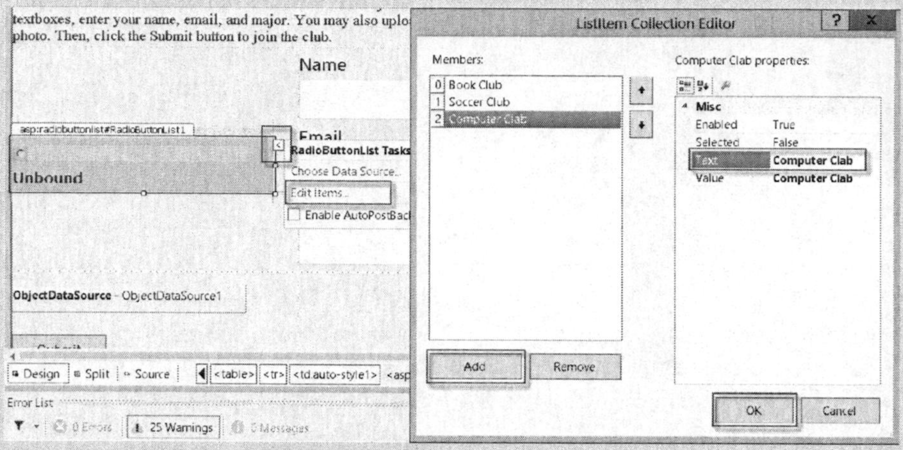

Figure 11.4 Configuration of radio button.

16. After the Page Inspector dialog is opened, click the **Inspect** tab at the left-bottom part of your screen. Then, click **your logo here** in the title area. In the **HTML** code, change the header to **Student Club Web Page**. Similarly, open the file **Site.Master** and change the header to **Student Club Web Page** as shown in Figure 11.6.
17. Rearrange the controls so that the design of Student Club web page looks like the one in Figure 11.7.
18. To run the project, click **Start Debugging** on Visual Studio's **Debug** menu. A browser will be launched on the local machine to display the computing result as shown in Figure 11.8. The computation is done by the compute emulator included in the Windows Azure SDK package. The local computer is used by the compute emulator to emulate the Windows Azure environment. The browser on your local computer is used to view the running instance in the Windows Azure environment.

TASK 2: CREATE DATA SOURCE FOR STUDENT CLUB WEB PAGE

For data communication between services, the Table storage accommodates Windows Communication Foundation (WCF). Through the context class TableServiceContext, WCF Data Services is able to access the data stored in the Table storage. This task will implement the class derived from TableServiceContext to define the data model for the StudentClub application. Then, a data model will be created for the entities used by the StudentClub application. At the end of this task, the users will be able to insert student information into the Table storage through the ASP.NET application.

1. To include the class library that contains WCF Data Services, you need to create a new project. Assume that Visual Studio 2012 is still open, click **FILE | Add | New Project.** Under the **Visual C#** node in the **Installed Templates** pane, expand the **Windows** node and select the **Class Library** template. Rename the project as **StudentClub_Info** as shown in Figure 11.9 and then click **OK**.
2. To add the references to WCF Data Services, right click the **StudentClub_Info** project node in the Solution Explorer pane and select **Add Reference.** Enter the reference

Table 11.5 Control Specifications for Student Club Web Page

Control Name	*Properties*	*Configuration*
Label1	Text	Name
	Font size	14
	Font color	Black
Label2	Text	E-mail
	Font size	14
	Font color	Black
Label3	Text	Major
	Font size	14
	Font color	Black
Label4	Text	Upload your photo here
	Font size	14
	Font color	Black
TextBox_1	ID	TextBox_Name
	Height	40 px
	Width	200 px
TextBox_2	ID	TextBox_Email
	Height	40 px
	Width	200 px
TextBox_3	ID	TextBox_Major
	Height	40 px
	Width	200 px
Button1	Text	Submit
	Width	120 px
	Height	40 px
FileUpdate1	Height	32 px
RadioButtonList1	ForeColor	Black
	Width	160 px
	TextAlign	Left
Image1	Height	180 px
	Width	200 px

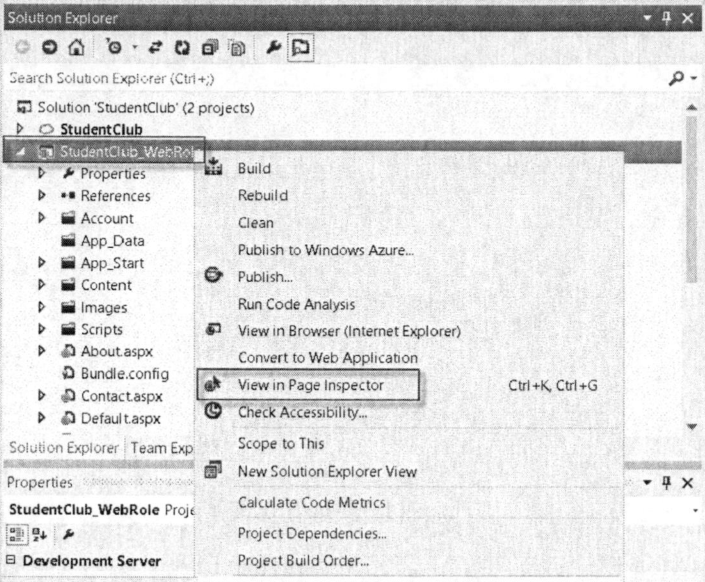

Figure 11.5 View in Page Inspector.

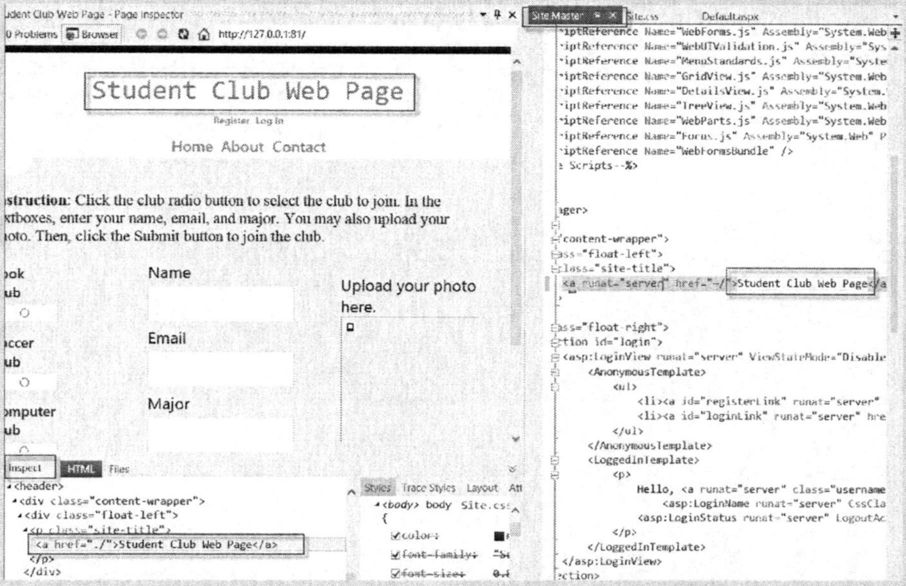

Figure 11.6 Header configuration.

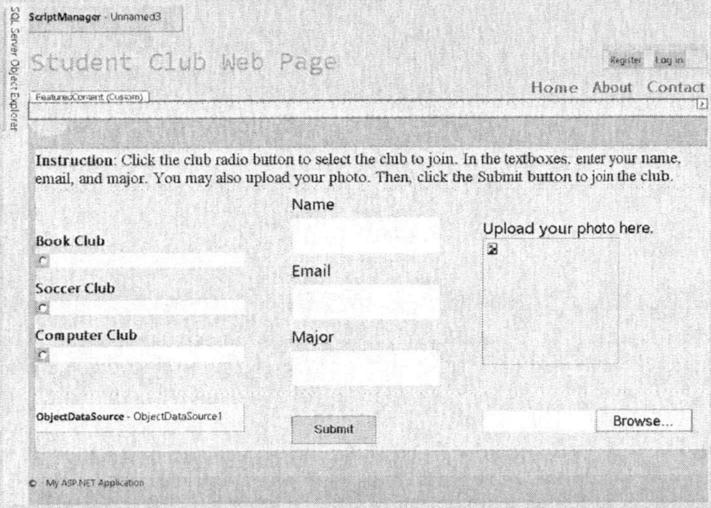
ScriptManager - Unnamed3
Student Club Web Page
Register Log in
Home About Contact
Instruction: Click the club radio button to select the club to join. In the textboxes, enter your name, email, and major. You may also upload your photo. Then, click the Submit button to join the club.
Name
Upload your photo here.
Book Club
Email
Soccer Club
Computer Club
Major
ObjectDataSource - ObjectDataSource1
Submit
Browse...

Figure 11.7 Design of Student Club web page.

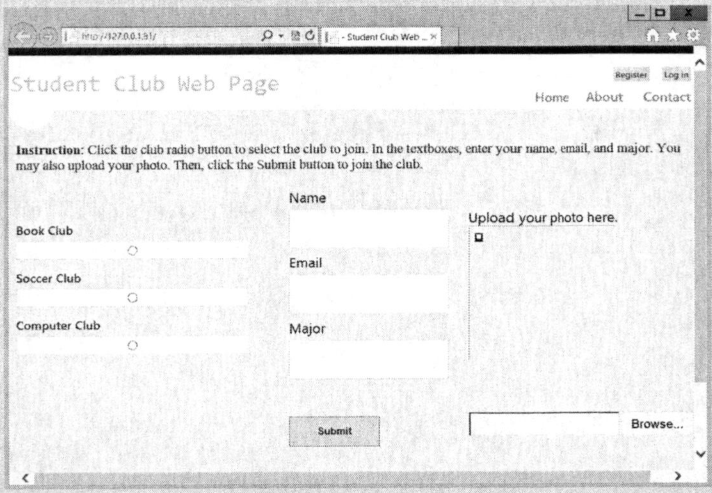
Student Club Web Page
Register Log in
Home About Contact
Instruction: Click the club radio button to select the club to join. In the textboxes, enter your name, email, and major. You may also upload your photo. Then, click the Submit button to join the club.
Name
Upload your photo here.
Book Club
Email
Soccer Club
Computer Club
Major
Submit
Browse...

Figure 11.8 Student Club web page.

System.Data.Services.Client in the search box and press **Enter**, check the newly searched reference shown in Figure 11.10 and then click **OK**. Similarly, add the references **Microsoft.WindowsAzure.StorageClient** for using the Windows Azure storage services and **Microsoft.WindowsAzure.ServiceRuntime** for retrieving the connection string.

3. The specification of columns/properties in a table will be defined in a class called schema class. In the schema class, you will define the names of the properties and the initial values assigned to the properties. To create the schema class, you need to delete the default class **Class1** by right clicking at it and select **Delete**. Then, right click at the

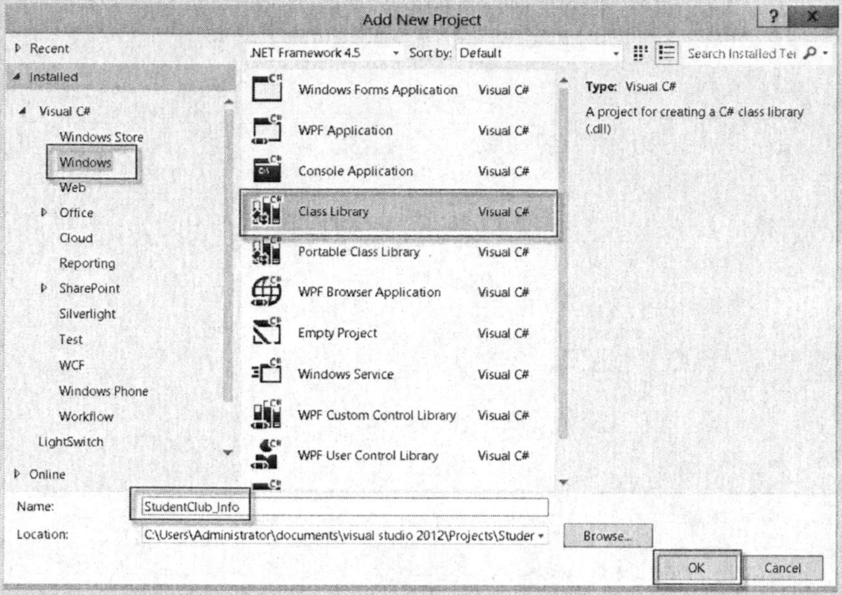

Figure 11.9 Add StudentClub_Info project.

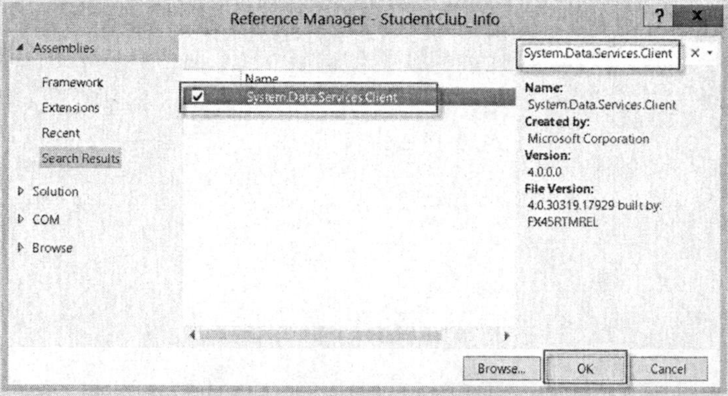

Figure 11.10 Add reference System.Data.Services.Client.

StudentClub_Info project, select **Add**, and then **Class**. In the **Add New Item** dialog, change the name to **StudentClubEntry1.cs** and click **Add** as shown in Figure 11.11.

4. After the **StudentClubEntry1.cs** file is opened, at the top of the file, you need to add more references required by the schema class StudentClubEntry1. The StudentClubEntry1 class is derived from the built-in class TableServiceEntity. You need to write the code for the StudentClubEntry1 class to define the columns, also called properties, for the Table storage. In StudentClubEntry1, you will also initialize the properties Rowkey and PartitionKey with the following code:

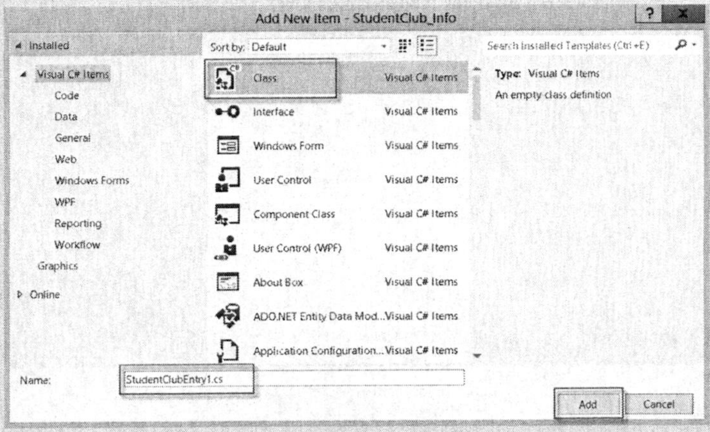

Figure 11.11 Add class StudentClubEntry1.cs.

```
using System;
using System.Collections.Generic;
using System.Linq;
using System.Text;
using Microsoft.WindowsAzure.StorageClient;
namespace StudentClub_Info
{
public class StudentClubEntry1 : Microsoft.WindowsAzure.
StorageClient.TableServiceEntity
{
  public StudentClubEntry1()
  {
  //The default constructor is needed for ObjectDataSource.
}

//Define the columns for the Table storage.
  public StudentClubEntry1(string memberClub, string
memberEmail)
  {

  //Initialize Rowkey by email and PartitionKey by club name
  RowKey=memberEmail;
  PartitionKey=memberClub;
}

//Add more columns in the Table storage.
  public string Name {get; set;}
  public string Major {get; set;}
  public string Photo {get; set;}
}
}
```

5. After the properties are defined in the schema class, a class called context class will be created so that an application is able to instantiate its own Table storage by using the definition specified in the schema class. To be able to use the services provided by WCF Data Services, the context class is so constructed that it will be derived from the class TableServiceContext, which itself is derived from another WCF Data Service class DataServiceContext. The TableServiceContext class can be used to manage the credentials and retry policy. In a context class, the public property of the type IQueryable <SchemaClass> is used to expose a table specified by the schema class to an application. To create the context class, right-click the **StudentClub_Info** project, and select **Add | New item.** In the **Add New Item** dialog, select the **Code** category and then select the **Class** template. Change the class name to **StudentClubContext.cs** and click **Add**. Add the following code in the class StduentClubContext.cs:

```
using System;
using System.Collections.Generic;
using System.Linq;
using System.Text;
using Microsoft.WindowsAzure;
using Microsoft.WindowsAzure.StorageClient;
namespace StudentClub_Info
{

public class StudentClubContext : Microsoft.WindowsAzure.
StorageClient.TableServiceContext
{
//Default constructor used to initialize the base class with
//storage account access information.
  public StudentClubContext(string baseAddress,
  Microsoft.WindowsAzure.StorageCredentials credentials)
  : base(baseAddress, credentials)
  {}

//Define the property that returns the StudentClubEntry table.
  public IQueryable<StudentClubEntry1> StudentClubEntry1
  {
  get
  {
  return this.
CreateQuery<StudentClubEntry1>("StudentClubEntry1");
  }
}
}
}
```

6. After the table is returned in the context class, you need to create a data source class that implements data source objects to provide the data to the controls on the application's web page and to allow the front-end users to interact with the Table storage. To do so, right click the **StudentClub_Info** project and select **Add | New item**. In

the **Add New Item** dialog, select the **Code** category and select the **Class** template. Change the name of the class to **StudentClubDataSource.cs** and click **Add**. After the StudentClubDataSource.cs file is opened, enter the following code:

```
using System;
using System.Collections.Generic;
using System.Linq;
using System.Text;
using Microsoft.WindowsAzure;
using Microsoft.WindowsAzure.StorageClient;
using Microsoft.WindowsAzure.ServiceRuntime;

namespace StudentClub_Info
{
public class StudentClubDataSource
{

//Declaring the storageAccount object to store account info.
  private static CloudStorageAccount storageAccount;

//Declaring the Context object to expose tables to an
//application.
  private StudentClubContext context;

//The constructor is used to initializes storage account info
//and creates a table with the defined schema.
  static StudentClubDataSource()
  {
  //Instantiate the storageAccount object with data
//connection string
  storageAccount =
  CloudStorageAccount.FromConfigurationSetting("DataConnectionSt
ring");

  //Creating a table with the storageAccount and Context
//objects
  CloudTableClient.CreateTablesFromModel(
        typeof(StudentClubContext),
        storageAccount.TableEndpoint.AbsoluteUri,
        storageAccount.Credentials);
}

//initializing the data source.
  public StudentClubDataSource()
  {
  //Initialize context using account info.
  this.context =
        new StudentClubContext(storageAccount.TableEndpoint.
AbsoluteUri,
  storageAccount.Credentials);

  //Initialize retry update policy.
  this.context.RetryPolicy = RetryPolicies.Retry(3,
```

```
    TimeSpan.FromSeconds(1));
  }
  ///Insert new entries in the StudentClubEntry table.
    public void AddStudentClubEntry(StudentClubEntry1 newItem)
    {
    this.context.AddObject("StudentClubEntry1", newItem);
    this.context.SaveChanges();
  }
  //Retrieve info about the students enrolled in the same club.
    public IEnumerable<StudentClubEntry1>
  GetStudentClubEntries(string memberClub)
    {
    var results = from s in this.context.StudentClubEntry1
                  where s.PartitionKey == memberClub
                  select s;
    return results;
  }
  }
  }
```

TASK 3: CONFIGURE STORAGE ACCOUNT

To use the Windows Azure storage services, you need to provide the authentication information for the storage account. The authentication information such as the username and password will be specified in the connection string used by the StudentClubContext class.

1. To specify the connection string, expand the **StudentClub** node. Under the **Roles** node, double click **StudentClub_WebRole** in the Solution Explorer pane. After the Properties dialog is opened, click the **Settings** link. In the **Name** column, enter **DataConnectionString**, and specify **Connection String** as the Type shown in Figure 11.12.
2. In the Value column, click the ellipsis button labeled with the icon **[...]**. After the **Storage Account Connection String** dialog is opened, select the option **Windows Azure storage emulator** to use the local Windows Azure storage emulator and then click **OK**. Later, to deploy the project to Windows Azure, the connection string will be changed here.

TASK 4: DEVELOP STUDENT CLUB WEB PAGE AND PROCESS USER INPUT

In the previous section, you have created the data source to support the Student Club web page. With the classes created in the previous section, the users will be able to access the data stored in the Table storage. In this section, you will continue to develop the Student Club web page and link the web page to the data source.

1. First, to link the data source to the web page, you need to reference the StudentClub_Info project in the web role. To do so, right click the project **StudentClub_WebRole** in Solution Explorer and select **Add Reference**. Expand the Solution node and click

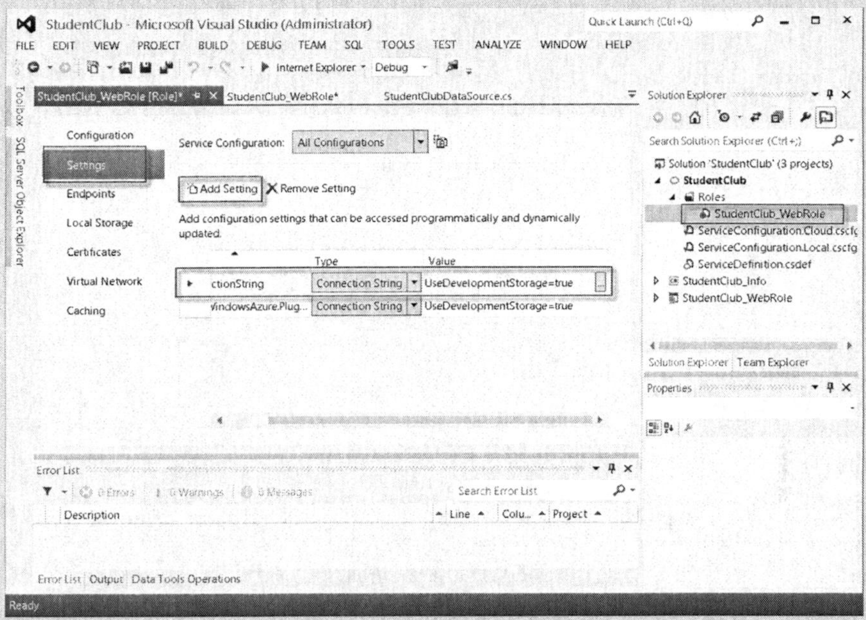

Figure 11.12 Configure DataConnectionString.

Projects, and then check the **StudentClub_Info** project as shown in Figure 11.13, and then click **OK**.

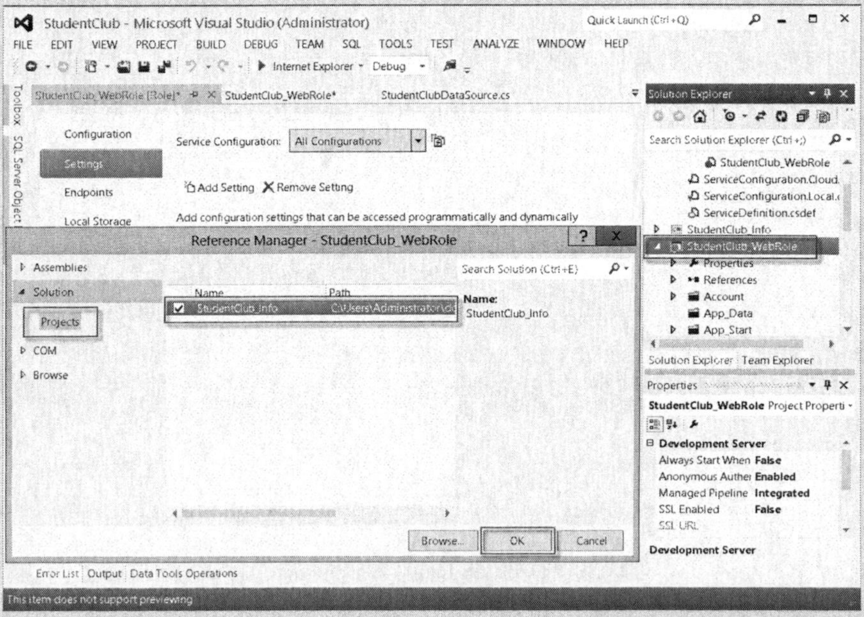

Figure 11.13 Add reference StudentClub_Info.

2. To implement the activities, double click the button **Submit** in the Design view of the Default.aspx file. After the Default.aspx.cs file is opened, insert the following code. The code also includes the definition of the Blob storage and Queue storage. The Blob storage and Queue storage will be covered in the next two sections.

```
using System;
using System.IO;
using System.Net;
using Microsoft.WindowsAzure;
using Microsoft.WindowsAzure.ServiceRuntime;
using Microsoft.WindowsAzure.StorageClient;
using System.Collections.Generic;
using System.Linq;
using System.Web;
using System.Web.UI;
using System.Web.UI.WebControls;
using StudentClub_Info;

namespace StudentClub_WebRole
{
public partial class Default : System.Web.UI.Page
{
  private static bool storageInitialized=false;

//Declare a CloudBobClient type of object.
  private static CloudBlobClient blobStorage;

//Declare a CloudQueueClient type of object.
  private static CloudQueueClient queueStorage;

  protected void Page_Load(object sender, EventArgs e)
  {

}
  private void StorageInit()
  {
  if (storageInitialized)
  {
        return;
  }
  //Initialize an account instance with connection string.

  var
  storageAccount = CloudStorageAccount.FromConfigurationSetting("
DataConnectionString");
  //Create blob container for images.
//Do not use Upper case for container name.
  blobStorage = storageAccount.CreateCloudBlobClient();
  CloudBlobContainer
  container = blobStorage.GetContainerReference("memberphoto");
  container.CreateIfNotExist();
```

```
    //Create the queue client queueStorage and then the queue.
    //Do not use Upper case for container name.
    queueStorage = storageAccount.CreateCloudQueueClient();
    CloudQueue queue = queueStorage.GetQueueReference("myqueue");
    queue.CreateIfNotExist();

    //Change container permission to public access.
    var permissions = container.GetPermissions();
    permissions.PublicAccess = BlobContainerPublicAccessType.
Container;
    container.SetPermissions(permissions);

    storageInitialized = true;
}

    protected void Button1_Click(object sender, EventArgs e)
    {

    if (FileUpload1.HasFile)
    {
          StorageInit();

    //Upload the image to blob storage.
          string uniqueBlobName = string.Format("memberphoto/
image_{0}{1}", Guid.NewGuid().ToString(), Path.
GetExtension(FileUpload1.FileName));
          string Club = RadioButtonList1.SelectedValue.ToString();
          string Email = Email = TextBox_Email.Text.ToString();

    //Retrieve blob reference.
          CloudBlockBlob
          blob = blobStorage.GetBlockBlobReference(uniqueBlobN
ame);
    //Set blob properties and upload the file to the blob.
          blob.Properties.ContentType = FileUpload1.PostedFile.
ContentType;
          blob.UploadFromStream(FileUpload1.FileContent);
          System.Diagnostics.Trace.TraceInformation("Uploaded
image '{0}' to blob storage as '{1}'", FileUpload1.FileName,
uniqueBlobName);

    //Create an new entry for table storage.
          StudentClubEntry1 entry = new StudentClubEntry1(Club,
Email)
          {
          Name = TextBox_Name.Text.ToString(),
          Major = TextBox_Major.Text.ToString(),
          Photo = blob.Uri.ToString()

    };
    //Insert a new entry in table storage.
          StudentClubDataSource ds = new StudentClubDataSource();
          ds.AddStudentClubEntry(entry);
```

```
        System.Diagnostics.Trace.TraceInformation("Added entry
{0}-{1} in table storage for guest '{2}'", entry.PartitionKey,
entry.RowKey, entry.Name, entry.Major, entry.Photo);
        Image1.ImageUrl = entry.Photo;

  //queue a message.
        var queue = queueStorage.GetQueueReference("myqueue");
        var message = new
        CloudQueueMessage(String.Format("{0},{1},{2}", entry.
PartitionKey, entry.RowKey, entry.Name));
        queue.AddMessage(message);
  }
}
}
}
```

3. To run the project, you need to set up the environment for the configuration publisher. To do so, double click the file **Global.asax.cs** in Solution Explorer under **StudentClub_WebRole**. After the file is opened, insert the following two namespace declarations as well as the code for the function **void Application_Start(object sender, EventArgs e)** as shown below:

```
using System;
using System.Collections.Generic;
using System.Linq;
using System.Web;
using System.Web.Security;
using System.Web.SessionState;
using Microsoft.WindowsAzure;
using Microsoft.WindowsAzure.ServiceRuntime;

namespace StudentClub_WebRole
{
public class Global : System.Web.HttpApplication
{
  void Application_Start(object sender, EventArgs e)
  {
  //Code that runs on application startup.
  Microsoft.WindowsAzure.CloudStorageAccount.SetConfigurationSet
tingPublisher((configName, configSetter) =>
  {
        configSetter(RoleEnvironment.GetConfigurationSettingVal
ue(configName));

  });
}
  void Application_End(object sender, EventArgs e)
  {
  //Code that runs on application shutdown.
}
  void Application_Error(object sender, EventArgs e)
```

```
    {
    //Code that runs when an unhandled error occurs.
  }
    void Session_Start(object sender, EventArgs e)
    {
    //Code that runs when a new session is started.
  }
    void Session_End(object sender, EventArgs e)
    {
    //Code that runs when a session ends.
    //Note: The Session_End event is raised only when
  //the sessionstate mode
    //is set to InProc in the Web.config file.
  //If session mode is set to StateServer
    //or SQLServer, the event is not raised.
  }
  }
```

4. To try the project, click the **Internet Explorer** icon on the tool bar. The Student Club web page will be displayed as shown in Figure 11.14. Click the **Book Club** radio button and enter information about the name, e-mail, and major (Figure 11.14). Then, click the **Submit** button. At this step, you may not see anything since the Windows Azure storage emulator may not be active yet. We will demonstrate this in the next activity.

As you can see in Figure 11.14, there is no photo yet. Since photos are often stored as binary code, we will use the Blob storage to store the photos in the next section.

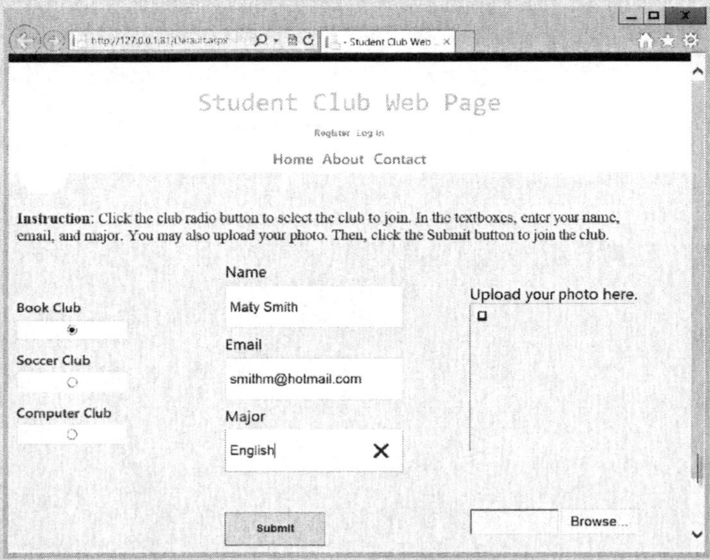

Student Club Web Page
Home About Contact
Instruction: Click the club radio button to select the club to join. In the textboxes, enter your name, email, and major. You may also upload your photo. Then, click the Submit button to join the club.
Name
Maty Smith
Email
smithm@hotmail.com
Major
English
Book Club
Soccer Club
Computer Club
Upload your photo here.
Browse...
Submit

Figure 11.14 Student Club web page.

11.4 Use of Blob Storage

Blob stands for "binary large object." In Windows Azure, the Blob storage can be used to store large amounts of unstructured data such as image files. Windows Azure allows users to store as much as 100 TB Blob data. The Blob storage service consists of a storage account, container, and Blob. To store and access Blob data, the user needs to create a Blob storage account in Windows Azure. A storage account can host many containers and one container can host many Blobs. The binary files will be stored in one of the Blobs. The Blob can be categorized into two types: block Blob and page Blob. The size of a block Blob can be up to 200 GB. The size of a page Blob can be up to 1 TB.

In the previous activity, you have created a Blob storage account when creating an account for using the Windows Azure storage emulator. To connect the Blob storage service from an application, you will first need to establish the account by initiating an object of the type CloudStorageAccount with the connection string to your Windows Azure account. Once the connection is established, you will need to initiate an object of the CloudBlobClient type. This object will be able to retrieve the references of containers and the Blobs stored in these containers. With the CloudBlobClient object, the user can also create containers if they do not already exist.

To upload a file to a specific Blob, you will first need to get the reference of the container that contains the Blob. The default permission for a container is Private. For public access, you may need PublicAccess. Through the container, you will be able to get Blob's reference. With the reference of the container, you can also list the information about the Blobs hosted by the container with the method ListBlobs. Once you have Blob's reference, you can then upload the files to that Blob with the UploadFromStream method. By using the reference of the Blob, you can download the Blob with the DownloadToStream, DownloadToFile, DownloadByteArray, or DownloadText methods to transfer the Blob contents to various types of local files. With the Blob reference, you can also delete the Blob with the Delete method.

To use the Blob storage service in our project, you need to declare the CloudBlobClient type object for the class StudentClub in the Default.aspx.cs file. You may also set the Boolean variable storageInitialized to false control the initialization process.

```
//Declare the CloudBobClient type of the object.
private static bool storageInitialized = false;
private static CloudBlobClient blobStorage;
```

You also need to add the code in the initialization method to create a container and Blob.

```
      //Create blob container for images.
//Do not use Upper case for container name.
      blobStorage = storageAccount.CreateCloudBlobClient();
      CloudBlobContainer container = blobStorage.GetContainerReference("m
emberphoto");
      container.CreateIfNotExist();
      //Change container permission to public access.
      var permissions = container.GetPermissions();
      permissions.PublicAccess = BlobContainerPublicAccessType.Container;
      container.SetPermissions(permissions);
```

The code has been added to the Default.aspx.cs file in Activity 11.1.

ACTIVITY 11.2 USING BLOB STORAGE

In this activity, you will first create a container and Blob. Next, you will implement the actions behind the command button to upload the images. Then, you will test and view the content stored in the Blob storage.

1. As the code for creating the Blob service has been added in Task 4 of Activity 11.1, this activity will continue from Activity 11.1. To try the project, you need to first start the Windows Azure storage emulator and compute emulator. Assume that the virtual machine is still connected. Press the **Window Icon** key on the tile; click the icons of **Storage Emulator** and **Compute Emulator** (Figure 11.15).
2. To demonstrate the process of uploading photos to the Blob storage, you may need to copy and paste some publicly available images to your virtual machine. For example, from your local computer, you can copy some images such as **Penguins.jpg** in the Windows 7 local folder **C:\Users\Public\Pictures\Sample Pictures** to the folder **C:\Users\Pictures** on your virtual machine as shown in Figure 11.16.
3. On the virtual machine, assume the Design window of the Default.aspx file is still open. Click the **Internet Explorer** icon on the tool bar. The Student Club web page will be displayed. Click the **radio button** to select a club and enter the information about **Name**, **Email**, and **Major**. Now, click the **Browse** button. You will be prompted to upload the image file from your virtual machine. For testing purposes, let us open the **Penguins.jpg** file in the folder **C:\Users\Pictures**. Then, click the **Submit** button. You should have the web page shown in Figure 11.17.

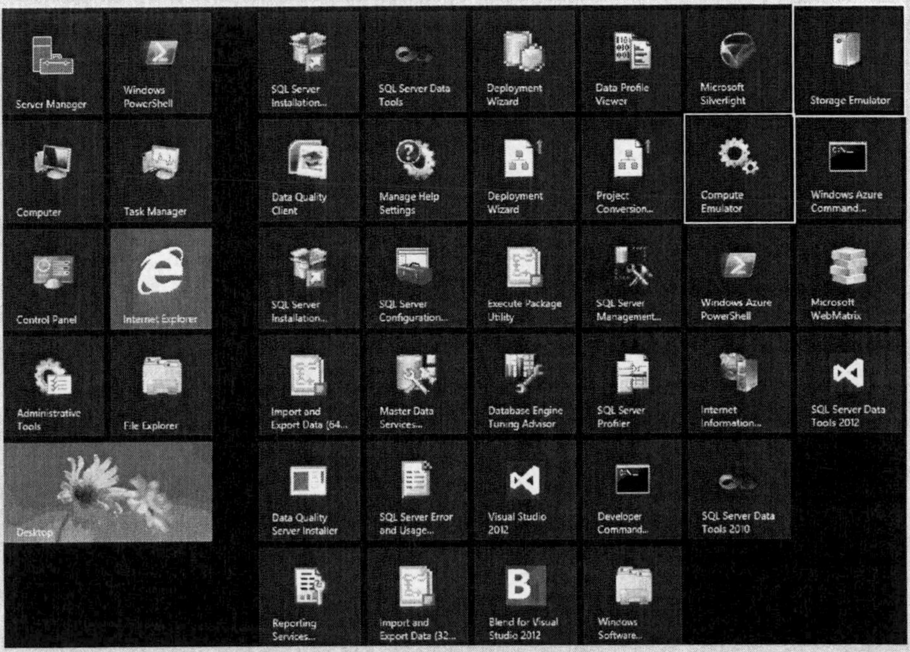

Figure 11.15 Start storage emulator and compute emulator.

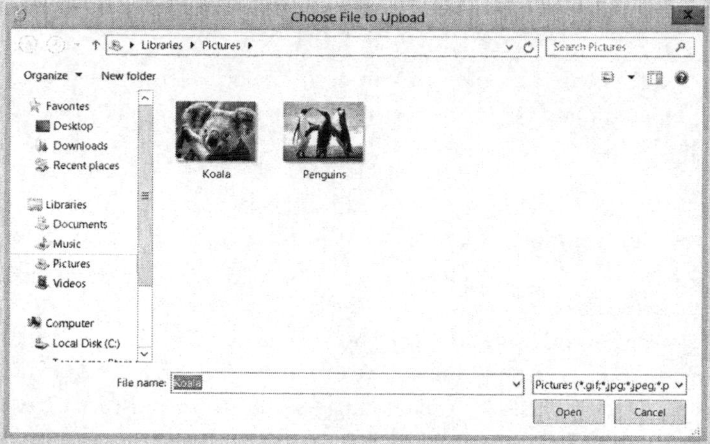

Figure 11.16 Copy and paste images to virtual machine.

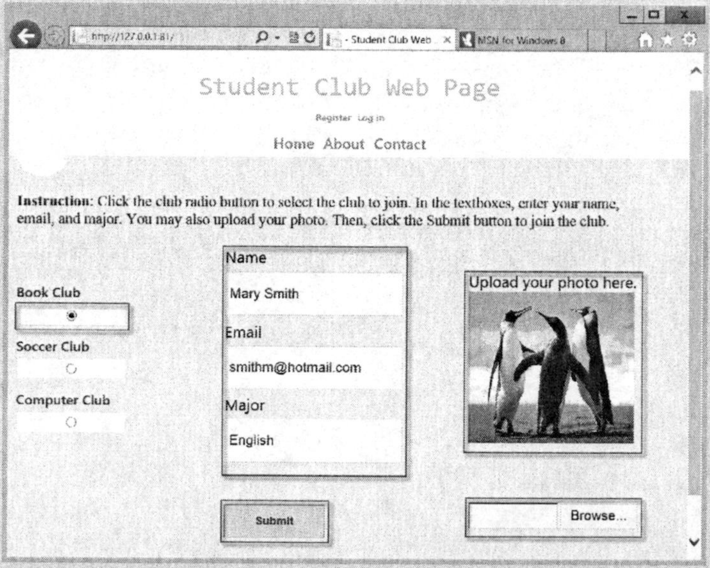

Figure 11.17 Submit information.

4. After the Penguins.jpg file is uploaded to the Blob storage. To view the content in the Blob storage, you need to connect to the Windows Azure storage emulator. To do so, click the **TOOLS** Menu and select **Connect to Server** as shown in Figure 11.18.
5. Expand the **Server Explorer** node on the left-hand side of your screen. Then, expand the node **Windows Azure Storage**, and the node **Blobs**. You should be able to see the Blob storage **memberphoto**. To view the data stored in the Blob storage, double click **memberphoto** and you should be able to see the data shown in Figure 11.19.

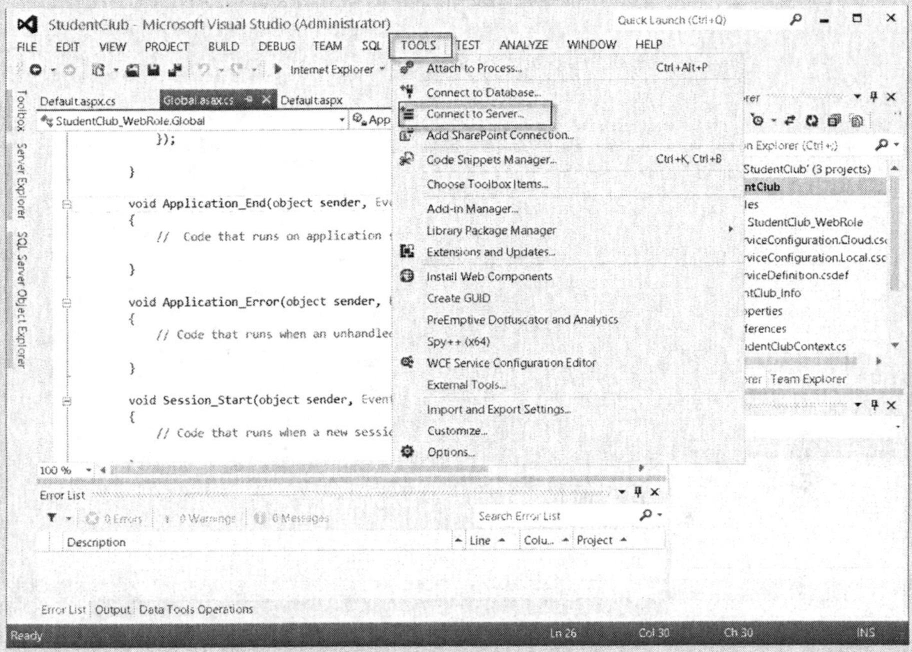

Figure 11.18 Connect to Windows Azure Storage Emulator.

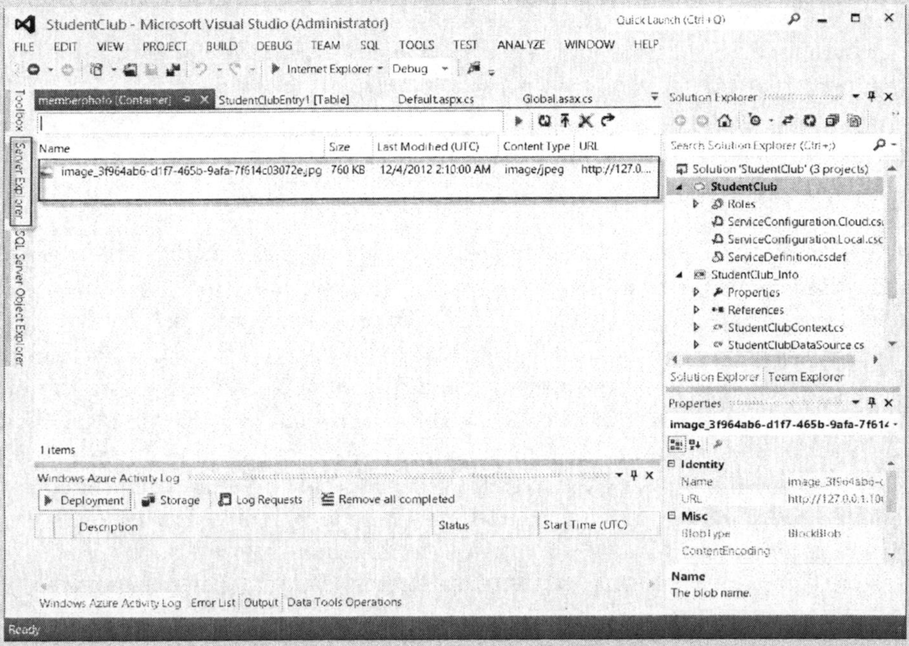

Figure 11.19 Files stored in Blob storage.

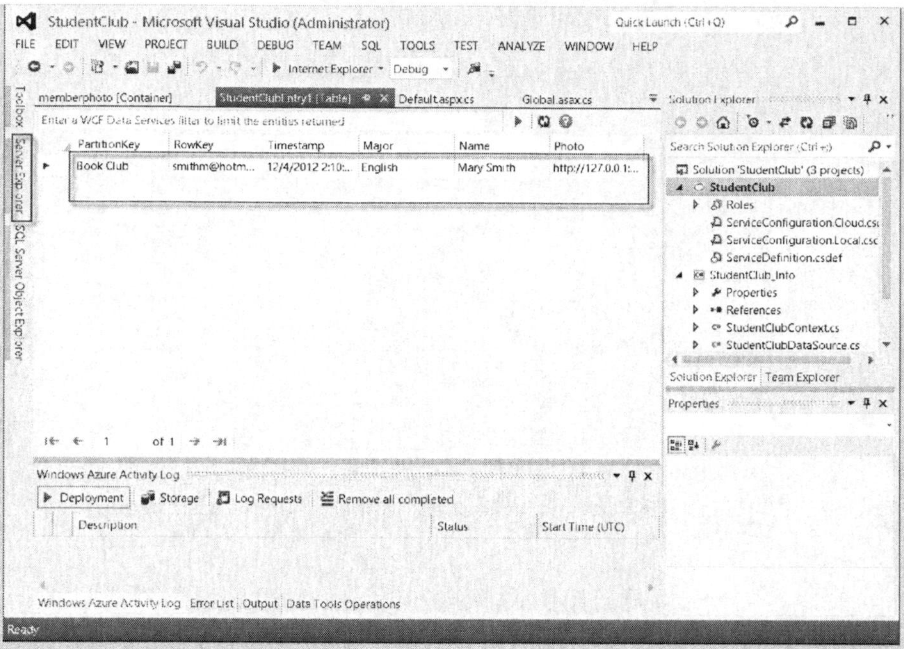

Figure 11.20 Content stored in Table storage.

6. To view the content in the files stored in the Table storage, expand the **Server Explorer** node on the left-hand side of your screen. Then, expand the **Windows Azure Storage** node, and the **Tables** node. You should be able to see the Table storage **StudentClubEntry**. To view the data stored in the Table storage, double click **StudentClubEntry** and you should be able to see the data shown in Figure 11.20.

11.5 Use of Queue Storage

The Windows Azure Queue storage is used to temporarily store messages that will be passed from one Windows Azure component to another component, for example, from a Windows Azure Web role to a Windows Azure Worker role. A Queue storage account can hold as much as 100 TB data in the Queue storage. The size of a single message can be up to 64 kB. Like the Blob storage, the Queue storage also has three components: storage account, queues, and messages stored in a queue. A message stored in a queue can be accessed through a URL assigned to the message.

When the storage account was created in the previous activity for the Windows Azure storage emulator, the Queue storage was also created. In the previous activity, you also initiated the object of the CloudStorageAccount type with a connection string to your Windows Azure account.

To get a reference object for a queue, you need to initiate a CloudBlobClient object with the following code:

```
CloudQueueClient queueClient = storageAccount.CreateCloudQueueClient();
```

With the **queueClient** object, you can get the reference to a queue and create the queue with the following code if it does not exist:

```
CloudQueue queue=queueClient.GetQueueReference("queue_name");
queue.CreateIfNotExist();
```

To insert a message into an existing queue, you need to create the message with the method CloudQueueMessage() and then add the message to the existing queue with the following code:

```
CloudQueueMessage message=new CloudQueueMessage("message_content");
queue.AddMessage(message);
```

You can modify the content of a message stored in a queue. In the process, you will first get the message with the method GetMessage(). Next, modify the message with the method SetMessageContent(). Then, update the message with the method UpdateMessage(). The code for changing the content of a message is given below:

```
CloudQueueMessage message=queue.GetMessage();
message.SetMessageContent("Modified_Message") ;
queue.UpdateMessage(message,
TimeSpan.FromSeconds(0.0),MessageUpdateFields.Content |
MessageUpdateFields.Visibility);
```

With the PeekMessage method, you can peek at the next message in a queue with the following code:

```
CloudQueueMessage peekedMessage=queue.PeekMessage();
```

You can delete a message from a queue with the method DeleteMessage(). The process can be done in two steps. You first retrieve the message with the method GetMessage(). Then, delete the message with the method DeleteMessage(). The code for deleting a message from a queue is given below:

```
CloudQueueMessage Message=queue.GetMessage();
queue.DeleteMessage(Message);
```

You can also delete a queue and all the messages contained in it with the method Delete(). The following is the code for deleting an entire queue:

```
CloudQueue queue=queueClient.GetQueueReference("queue_name");
queue.Delete();
```

ACTIVITY 11.3 USING QUEUE STORAGE

This activity will illustrate the use of Queue storage. The web role will be used to create a message and upload the message to the queue. The message includes a new member's information including the new member's name, e-mail, club, and major. A worker role will be created to process the message by reading the message in the queue, find out which club the new member is enrolled, and retrieve the information about the students who enrolled in the same club. The activity will accomplish the following task:

- **Task 1: Add Worker Role to Process Queue Messages:** The task creates a worker role.

TASK 1: ADD WORKER ROLE TO PROCESS QUEUE MESSAGES

To process a message, you need to add a worker role project. To do so, follow the following steps:

1. Assume that the StudentClub project is still open. Open the **Default.aspx.cs** file and make sure that the code sections `//Declare a CloudQueueClient type of object` and `//queue a message` are added as shown in Task 4 of Activity 11.1.
2. In **Solution Explorer**, right click the **Roles** node under the StudentClub project, select **Add** and then **New Worker Role Project.** In the Add New Role Project dialog, select the **Worker Role** category and name the **Worker Role** template as **StudentClub_WorkerRole** as shown in Figure 11.21, and then click **Add**.
3. To add a reference to StudentClub_Info, right click the **StudentClub_WorkerRole** project and select **Add Reference**. Click the **Projects** tab, select **StudentClub_Info** and then click **OK** as shown in Figure 11.22.
4. To specify the connection string, double click the role **StudentClub_WorkerRole** in the Solution Explorer pane and click **Properties**. After the Properties dialog is opened, click the **Settings** link. Click the **Add Setting** tab. In the **Name** column, enter **DataConnectionString**, and specify the Type as **Connection String**. Click the ellipsis button labeled with the icon **[...]** as shown in Figure 11.23.
5. After the **Storage Account Connection String** dialog is opened, select the option **Windows Azure storage emulator** to use the local Windows Azure storage emulator and then click **OK**.
6. Double click the **WorkerRole.cs** file of the StudentClub_WorkerRole project and insert the following namespace declaration:

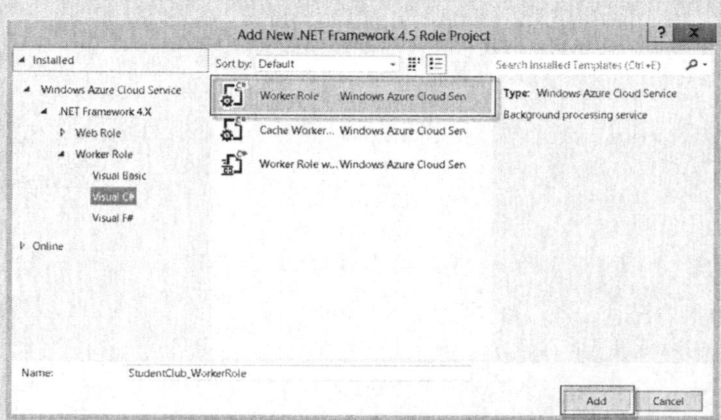

Figure 11.21 Create worker role.

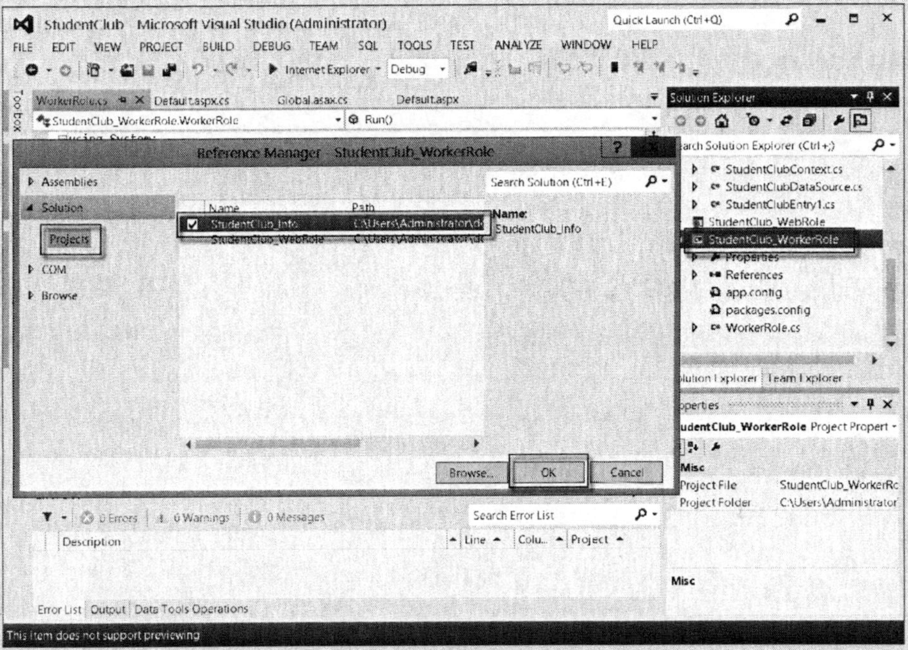

Figure 11.22 Add reference to StudentClub_WorkerRole.

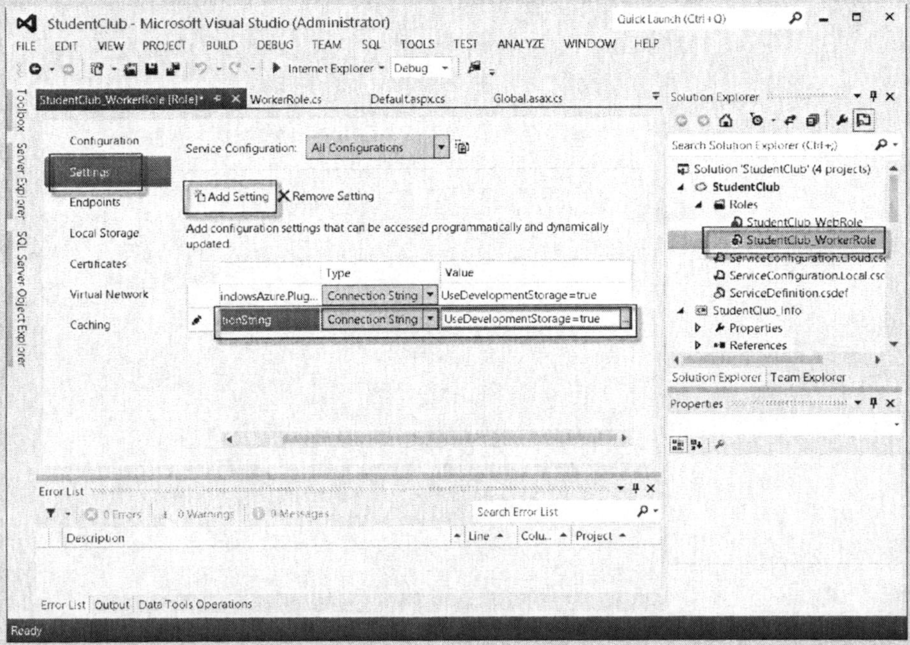

Figure 11.23 Configure connection string.

```
using System;
using System.Collections.Generic;
using System.Diagnostics;
using System.Linq;
using System.Net;
using System.Threading;
using Microsoft.WindowsAzure;
using Microsoft.WindowsAzure.Diagnostics;
using Microsoft.WindowsAzure.ServiceRuntime;
using Microsoft.WindowsAzure.StorageClient;
using StudentClub_Info;

namespace StudentClub_WorkerRole

{
    public class WorkerRole : RoleEntryPoint
    {
        private CloudQueue queue;

        public override void Run()
        {
            //This is a sample worker implementation.
            //Replace with your logic.
            Trace.TraceInformation("Listening for queue
messages...");

            while (true)
            {
                //Retrieve the message from the queue.
                CloudQueueMessage msg = queue.GetMessage();
                if (msg != null)
                {
                    //Parse the message retrieved from the queue.
                    var messageParts = msg.AsString.Split(new char[]
{',’});
                    var partitionKey = messageParts[0];
                    var rowkey = messageParts[1];
                    var membername = messageParts[2];

                    //Retreive entries in table storage.
                    StudentClubDataSource ds = new StudentClubData-
Source();
                    ds.GetStudentClubEntries(partitionKey);

                    //Remove the message from the queue.
                    queue.DeleteMessage(msg);
                }
                else
                {
                    System.Threading.Thread.Sleep(1000);
                }
            }
        }
```

```
        public override bool OnStart()
        {
            //Set the maximum number of concurrent connections.
            ServicePointManager.DefaultConnectionLimit = 12;
            //Retrieve the storage account configuration.
            //Make sure to add DataConnectionString.
            //Set WorkerRole Properties.
  CloudStorageAccount.SetConfigurationSettingPublisher((configN
  ame, configSetter) =>
            {
  configSetter(RoleEnvironment.GetConfigurationSettingValue(config
  Name));
            });
            var storageAccount = CloudStorageAccount.FromConfigurat
  ionSetting("DataConnectionString");
            //Initialize queue storage.
            CloudQueueClient
            queueStorage = storageAccount.CreateCloudQueueClient();
            queue = queueStorage.GetQueueReference("myqueue");
            Trace.TraceInformation("Creating container and
  queue...");
            bool storageInitialized = false;
            while (!storageInitialized)
            {
                //Create a message queue.
                queue.CreateIfNotExist();
                storageInitialized = true;
            }
            return base.OnStart();
        }
    }
}
```

7. Once the StudentClubDataSource object ds is initiated with the partition key, which is the club name, the data source for the ObjectDataSource control will be filled with information about the students who are enrolled in the same club as the new member. To make sure that ObjectDataSource takes StudentClubDataSource as its data source, in the **Design** window of the file **Dafault.aspx**, click the left arrow at the upper right corner of the **ObjectDataSource** control to open the **ObjectDataSource** task menu and select **Configure Data Source.**
8. In the Choose a Business Object page, select the object **StudentClub_Info. StudentClub DataSource** from the **Choose your business object** dropdown list as shown in Figure 11.24.
9. Click **Next** to go to the **Define Data Methods** page. From the **Choose a method** dropdown list, select the method **GetStudentClubEntries** as shown in Figure 11.25.
10. Click **Next** to go the **Define Parameters** page. From the **Parameter source** dropdown list, select **Control.** From the **ControlID** dropdown list, select **RadioButtonList1**. In the **DefaultValue** textbox, enter **none** as shown in Figure 11.26. Then, click **Finish.**

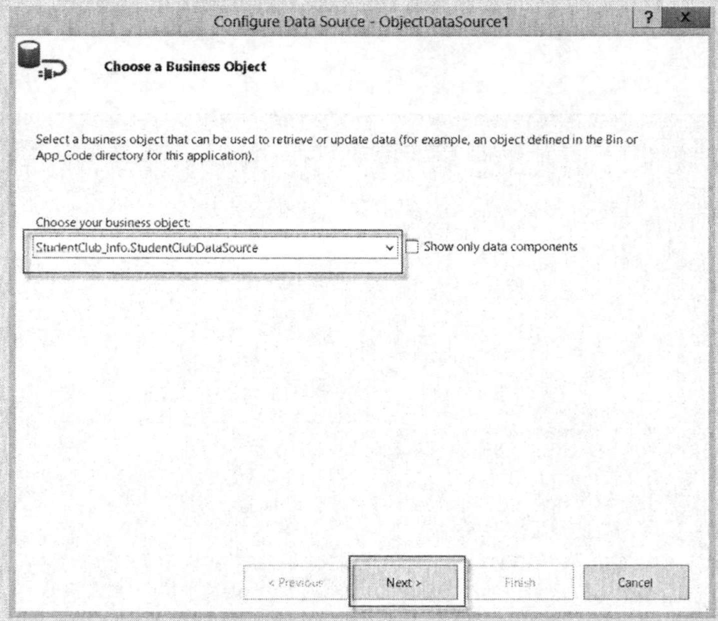

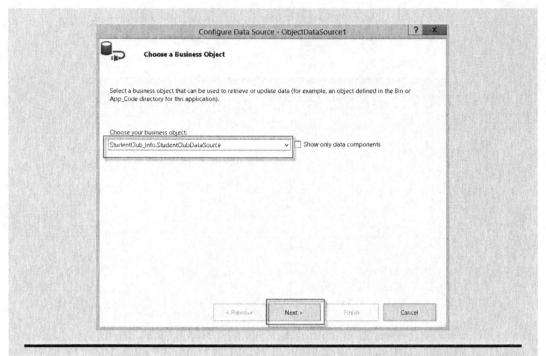

Figure 11.24 Choose business object.

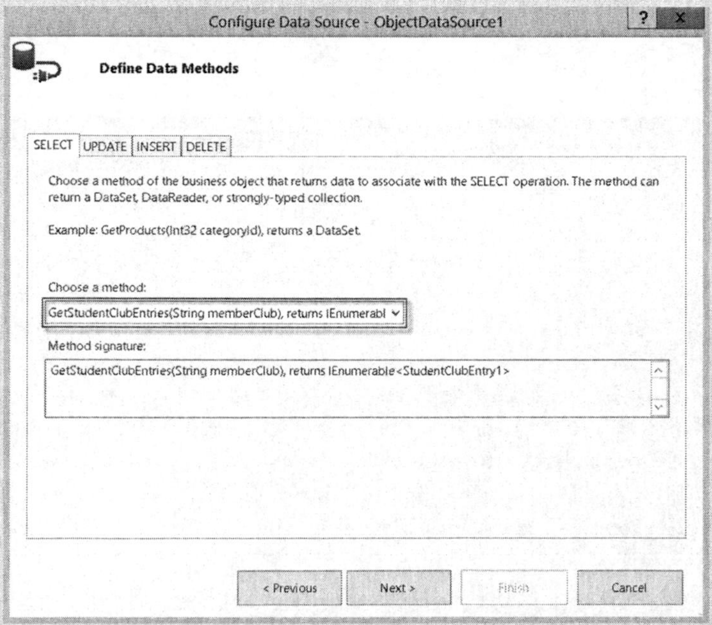

Figure 11.25 Choose method.

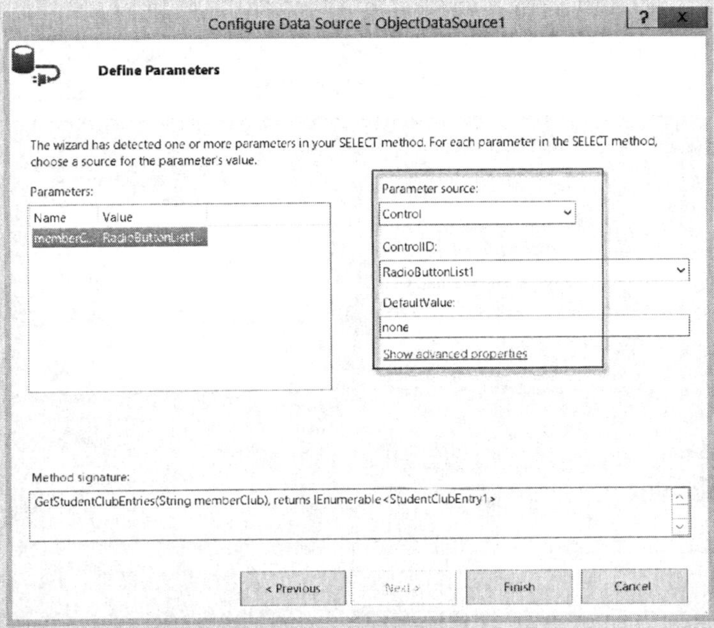

Figure 11.26 Define parameters.

11. Go back to the Design window of Default.aspx. In the Toolbox, from the **Data** section, drag the **GridView** control as shown in Figure 11.27. Click the left arrow at the upper right corner of the **GridView** control to open the **GridView** task menu. Select ObjectDataSource1 from the **Choose Data Source** dropdown list and select **Edit Columns.**
12. In the **Fields** dialog, keep **Name**, **RowKey**, and **PartitionKey** in the **Selected fields** as shown in Figure 11.28. These three columns will be displayed in GridView. Click **OK** to complete the selection of fields.
13. In the **GridView Tasks** menu, click **Auto Format.** In the AutoFormat dialog, click **Simple** as shown in Figure 11.29. Then, click **OK.**
14. In file **Default.aspx**, switch to the **Source** window. Make sure that **BoundField** is specified for the columns **Name**, **RowKey**, and **PartitionKey** as shown in the code below. Also, for the RowKey column, use **Email** as the **HeaderText**; for the PartitionKey column, use **Club** as the **HeaderText** as shown in the following code:

```
<asp:BoundField DataField="Name" HeaderText="Name"/>
<asp:BoundField DataField="RowKey" HeaderText="Email"
                SortExpression="RowKey"/>
<asp:BoundField DataField="PartitionKey" HeaderText="Club"
                SortExpression="PartitionKey"/>
```

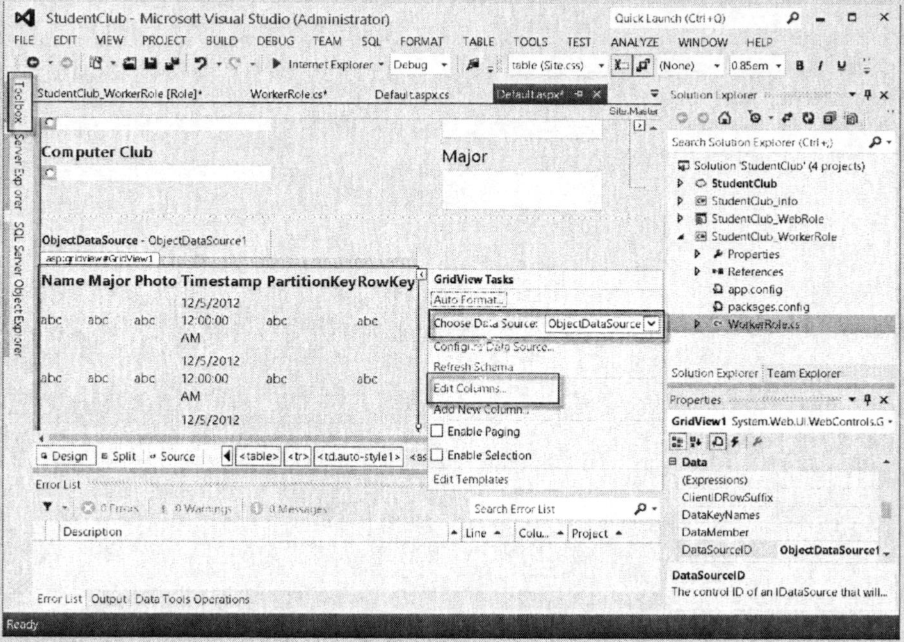

Figure 11.27 Add GridView control.

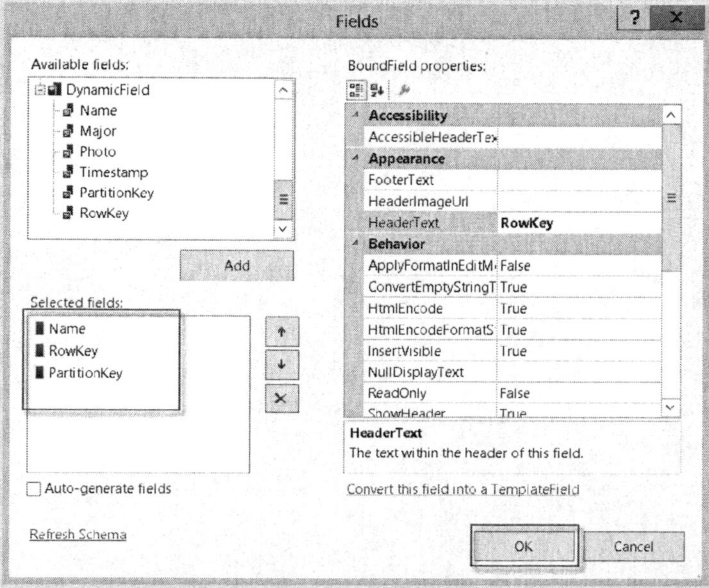

Figure 11.28 Select columns to be displayed in GridView.

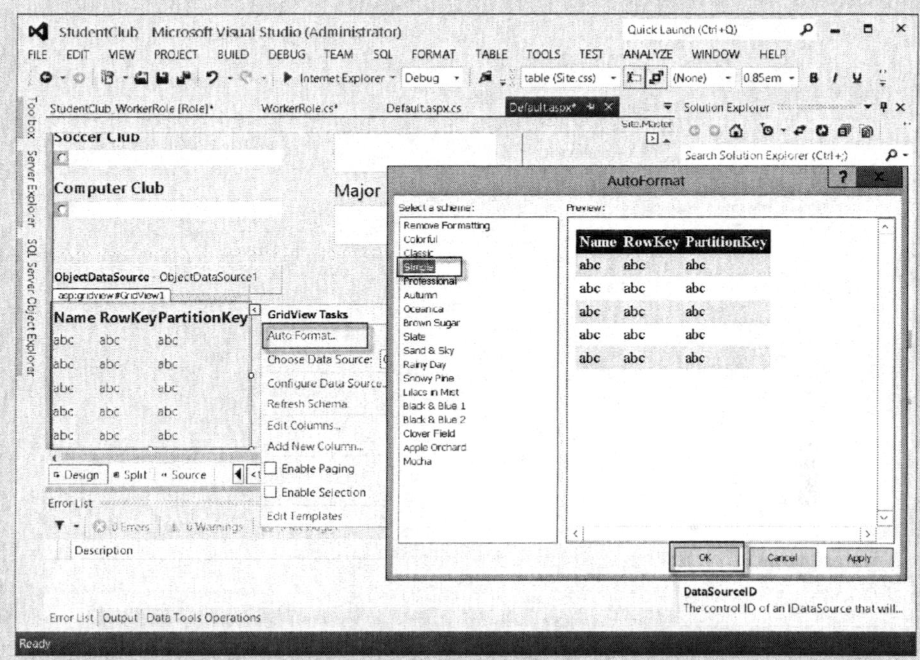

Figure 11.29 Configure AutoFormat.

Make sure that the GridView section looks like the following:

```
<asp:GridView ID = "GridView1" runat = "server"
AutoGenerateColumns = "False" DataSourceID = "ObjectDataSource1" >
```

15. In the Solution Explorer pane, expand the **StudentClub_WebRole** node, Open the **Web.Debug.config** file, and add the following lines in the system.web section (Figure 11.30):

```
<system.web >
<customErrors mode = "Off"/ >
</system.web >
```

16. In the Design window of Default.aspx, add a **Label** control and change the **Text** property to **Club member contact info** (Figure 11.31).
17. Now, run the application, enter the information for the new member as shown in Figure 11.32.
18. Click the **Submit** button. Figure 11.33 shows the web page where Mark joins the computer club and the club members are listed so that Mark can e-mail other members to start the communication.

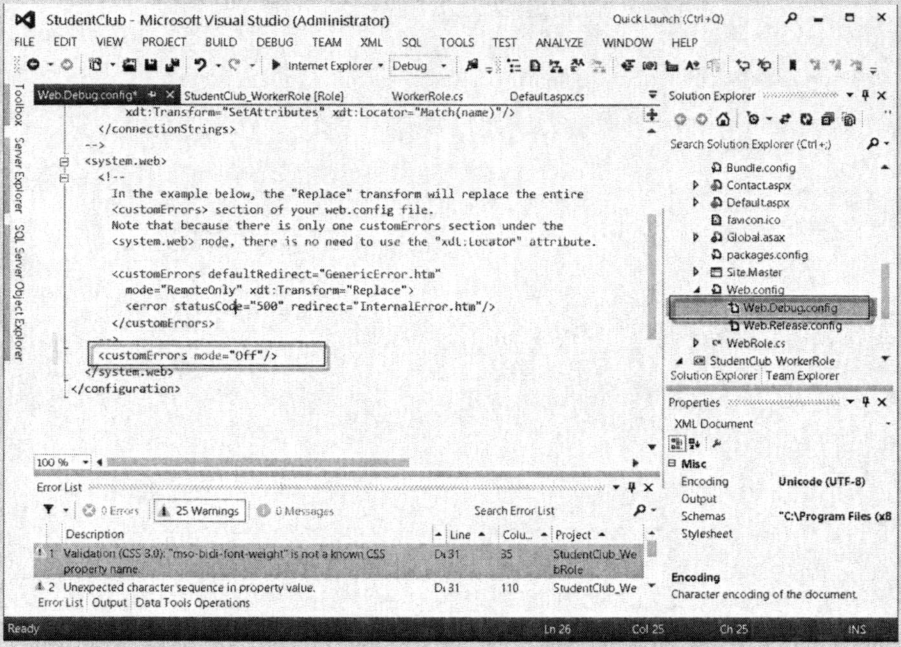

Figure 11.30 Configure Web.Debug.config File.

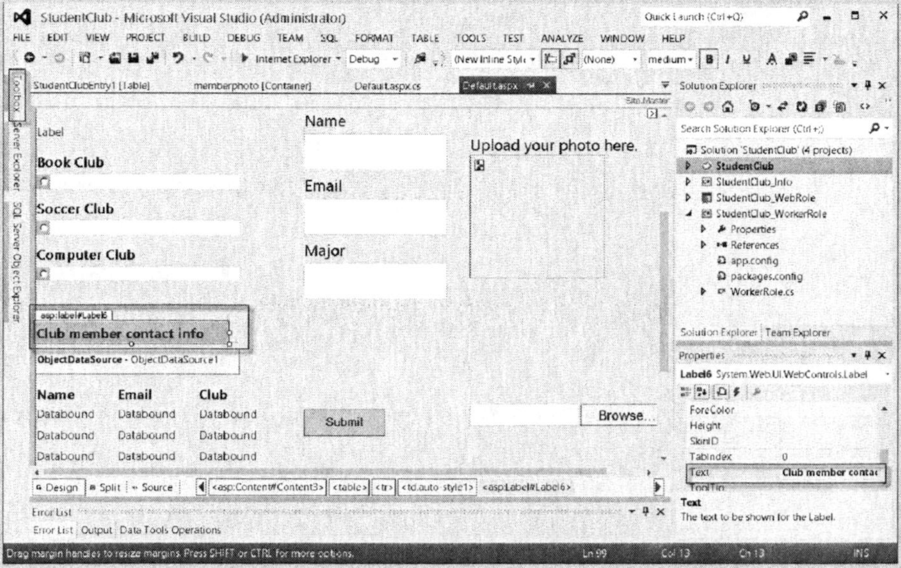

Figure 11.31 Web page design.

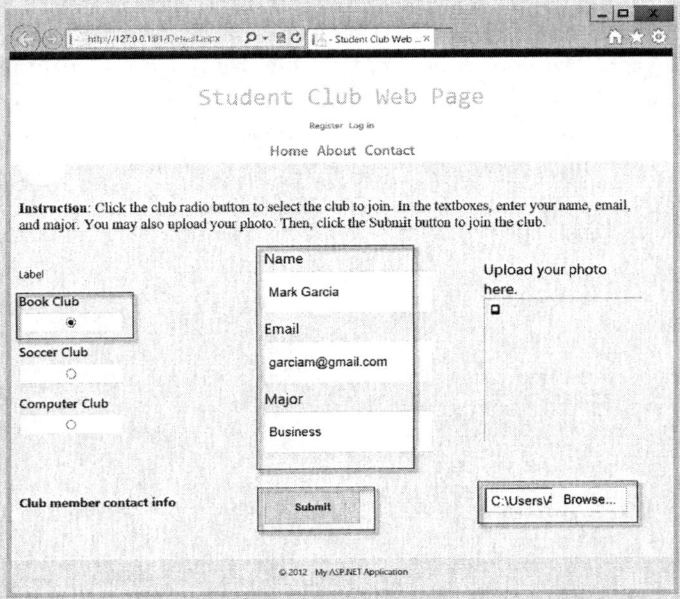

Figure 11.32 Student Club web page.

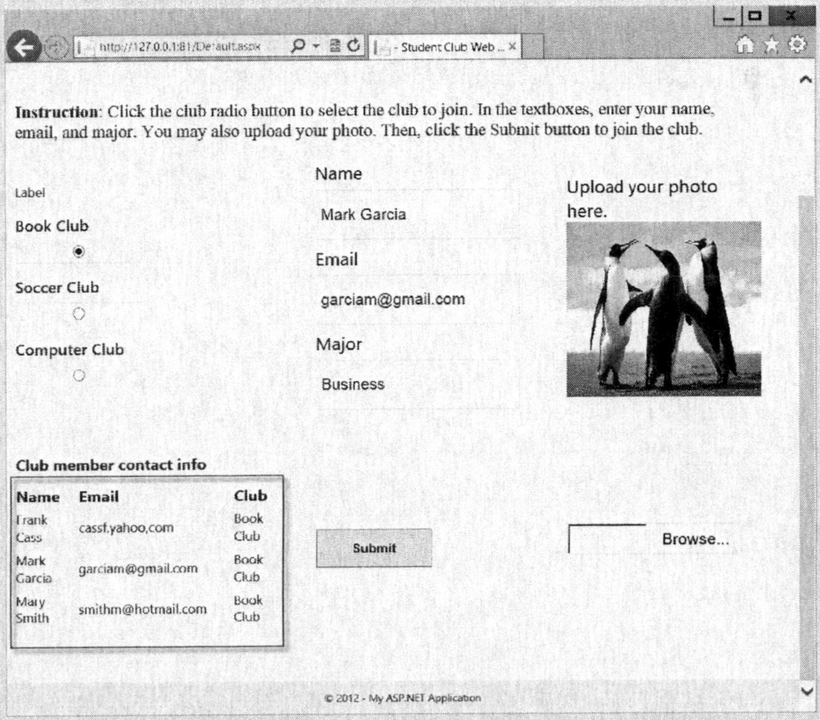

Figure 11.33 Add new member.

11.6 Deploy Applications to Windows Azure

In the previous activities, the local storage is used to emulate the Table storage, Blob storage, and Queue storage. To run the application StudentClub in a true cloud environment, we need to deploy the application to Windows Azure. In the following, you will configure some of the services so that they will be ready for the deployment. The application package will be uploaded to the staging area for further configuration. It will also be tested in the staging area. If everything works as expected, the application package will be promoted to production.

ACTIVITY 11.4 DEPLOYING APPLICATION TO WINDOWS AZURE

During this activity, you will accomplish the following tasks:

- **Task 1: Prepare Compute and Storage Services**: This task verifies the cloud service and storage account on Windows Azure.
- **Task 2: Publish the Application to Windows Azure**: This task first packages the StudentClub application. Then, it publishes the application to Windows Azure.
- **Task 3: Test the Application in the Staging Environment**: Once published, the application will be tested for remote access through the public endpoint.

TASK 1: PREPARE COMPUTE AND STORAGE SERVICES

Assume that you have created a Windows Azure account in the previous lab activities. The first task is to verify that the storage account and the cloud service are created for the Table storage, Blog storage, and Queue storage. Follow the steps below to get started:

1. Log on to your Windows Azure account at the website https://windows.azure.com.
2. Click the **STORAGE** link on the left-hand side of the screen. Select your storage and click **MANAGE KEYS**.
3. Click the **Copy to Clipboard** button next to the Primary access key. Save the key in a file on the desktop of your computer. Do the same to copy the Secondary access key. You may also want to save the name of the storage account as shown in Figure 11.34.
4. To create a new cloud service, click the **CLOUD SERVICE** link on the left-hand side of the screen. Click **NEW** on the left pane and then click **CUSTOM SERVICE**. Click **QUICK CREATE** and enter **service63xx** as URL, specify **West US** as the affinity group, and your subscription is shown in Figure 11.35.

TASK 2: PUBLISH THE APPLICATION TO WINDOWS AZURE

In this task, you will first generate a service package in Visual Studio. Then, you will publish the StudentClub application to the staging environment.

1. In the Windows Azure Management Portal, to log on to the virtual machine, click **VIRTUAL MACHINES**. Select the server **myserver** that is created in Chapter 1 and click **Connect**. Then, log on to the virtual machine with your user name and password.

Figure 11.34 Storage URL.

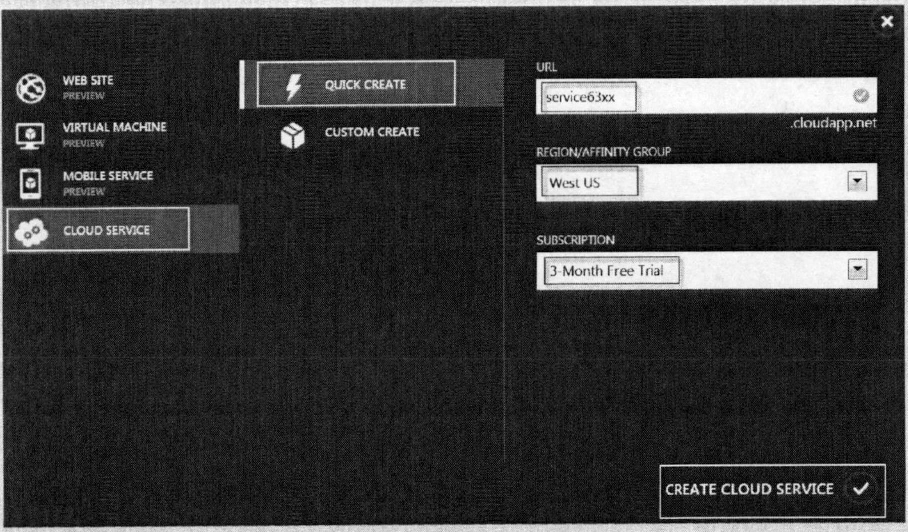

Figure 11.35 Configure cloud service.

2. After you have logged in, press the **Windows Icon** key and right click the icon **Visual Studio 2012** on the tile. Click **Run as administrator**. Then, start the **StudentClub** project.
3. In Solution Explorer, double click the file **ServiceConfiguration.Cloud.cscfg**. After the file is opened, you will see two Role sections, one is StudentClub_WebRole and the other one is StudentClub_WorkerRole. In each of the sections, there will be two Setting sections as shown in Figure 11.36.

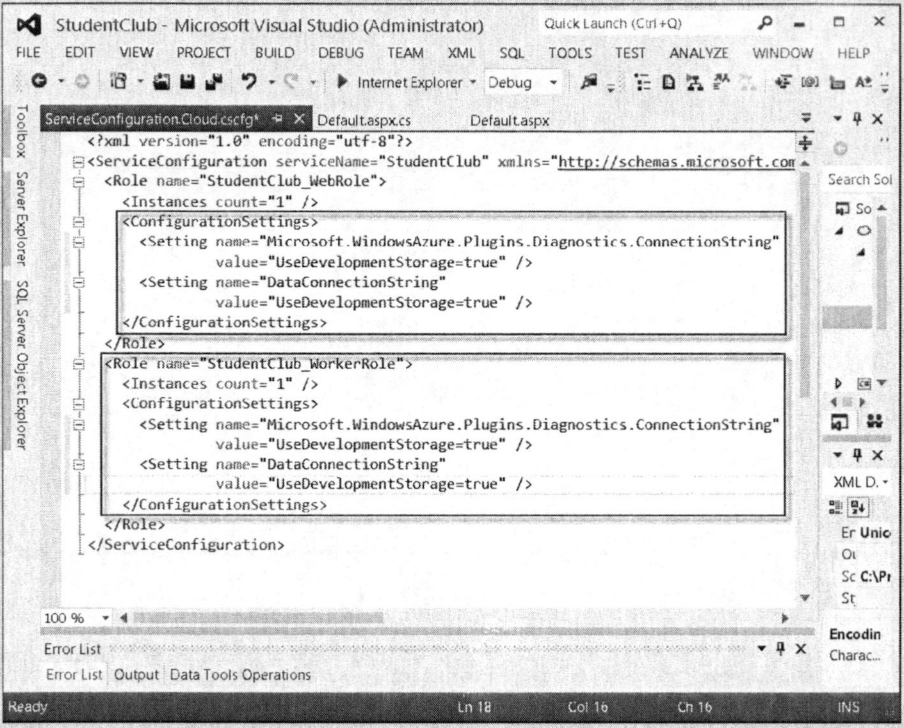

Figure 11.36 ServiceConfiguration.Cloud.cscfg File.

4. Replace the values for the Setting section with the default protocol as https, AccountName as the name of your Windows Azure storage account, and AccountKey as the Primary access key (Figure 11.37).
5. In the Solution Explorer pane, expand the **Roles** node, and then double click **StudentClub_WebRole.** Click the **Settings** link. Select the **Microsoft Windows Azure ...** connection string and click the ellipsis button **[...]** as shown in Figure 11.38.
6. Configure the Connection String type to https for DefaultEndpointsProtocol, specify AccountName to use the name of your Windows Azure storage account, and specify AccountKey to use your Windows Azure Primary access key (Figure 11.39). Then click **OK**. Do the same to configure StudentClub_WorkerRole.
7. To publish to the cloud, right click the **StudentClub** cloud project and select **Package**. In the **Package Windows Azure Application** dialog, select **Cloud** from the **Service configuration** dropdown list and select **Release** from the **Build configuration** dropdown list as shown in Figure 11.40. Then, click **Package**. After the package is built, the StudentClub package will be displayed in Windows Explorer. Record the path to the folder for later use.
8. Assume that you are still on the virtual machine. In the web browser, log on to the **Windows Azure Management Portal**. Click the **CLOUD SERVICE** link and click your newly created cloud service. Click **STAGING** to indicate that the project is to be

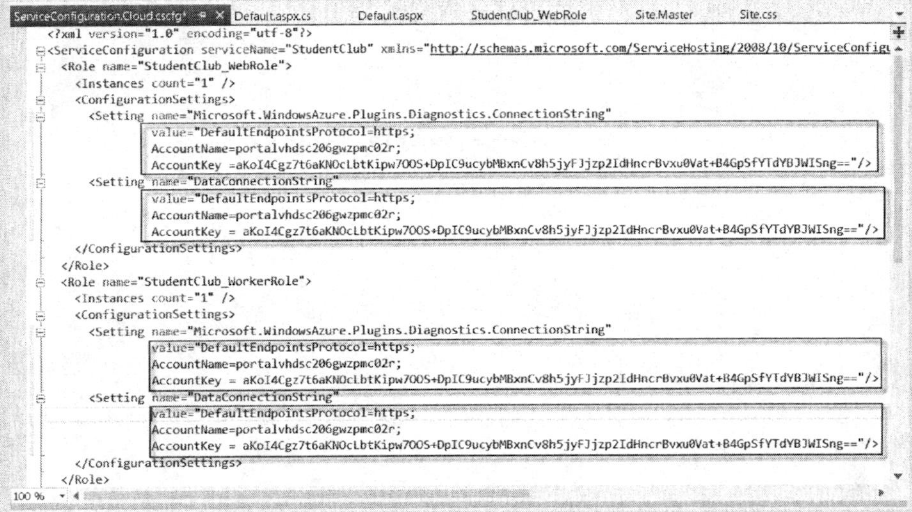
ServiceConfiguration.Cloud.cscfg* Default.aspx.cs Default.aspx StudentClub_WebRole Site.Master Site.css
<?xml version="1.0" encoding="utf-8"?>
<ServiceConfiguration serviceName="StudentClub" xmlns="http://schemas.microsoft.com/ServiceHosting/2008/10/ServiceConfigu
<Role name="StudentClub_WebRole">
<Instances count="1" />
<ConfigurationSettings>
<Setting name="Microsoft.WindowsAzure.Plugins.Diagnostics.ConnectionString"
value="DefaultEndpointsProtocol=https;
AccountName=portalvhdsc206gwzpmc02r;
AccountKey =aKoI4Cgz7t6aKNOcLbtKipw7OOS+DpIC9ucybMBxnCv8h5jyFJjzp2IdHncrBvxu0Vat+B4GpSfYTdYBJWISng=="/>
<Setting name="DataConnectionString"
value="DefaultEndpointsProtocol=https;
AccountName=portalvhdsc206gwzpmc02r;
AccountKey = aKoI4Cgz7t6aKNOcLbtKipw7OOS+DpIC9ucybMBxnCv8h5jyFJjzp2IdHncrBvxu0Vat+B4GpSfYTdYBJWISng=="/>
</ConfigurationSettings>
</Role>
<Role name="StudentClub_WorkerRole">
<Instances count="1" />
<ConfigurationSettings>
<Setting name="Microsoft.WindowsAzure.Plugins.Diagnostics.ConnectionString"
value="DefaultEndpointsProtocol=https;
AccountName=portalvhdsc206gwzpmc02r;
AccountKey = aKoI4Cgz7t6aKNOcLbtKipw7OOS+DpIC9ucybMBxnCv8h5jyFJjzp2IdHncrBvxu0Vat+B4GpSfYTdYBJWISng=="/>
<Setting name="DataConnectionString"
value="DefaultEndpointsProtocol=https;
AccountName=portalvhdsc206gwzpmc02r;
AccountKey = aKoI4Cgz7t6aKNOcLbtKipw7OOS+DpIC9ucybMBxnCv8h5jyFJjzp2IdHncrBvxu0Vat+B4GpSfYTdYBJWISng=="/>
</ConfigurationSettings>
</Role>
100 %

Figure 11.37 Configure Protocol, AccountName, and AccountKey.

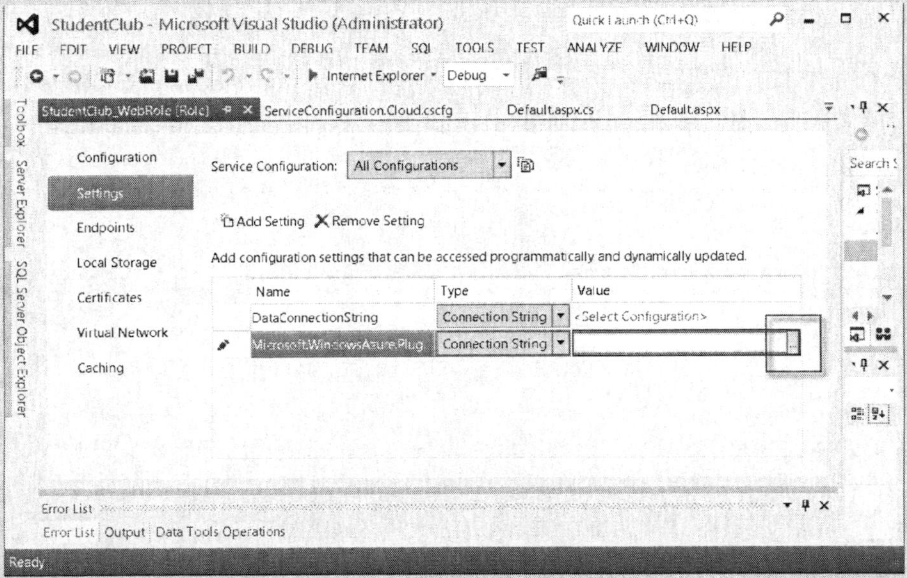
StudentClub - Microsoft Visual Studio (Administrator)
Quick Launch (Ctrl+Q)
FILE EDIT VIEW PROJECT BUILD DEBUG TEAM SQL TOOLS TEST ANALYZE WINDOW HELP
Internet Explorer Debug
StudentClub_WebRole (Role) ServiceConfiguration.Cloud.cscfg Default.aspx.cs Default.aspx
Toolbox Server Explorer SQL Server Object Explorer
Configuration
Settings
Endpoints
Local Storage
Certificates
Virtual Network
Caching
Service Configuration: All Configurations
Add Setting Remove Setting
Add configuration settings that can be accessed programmatically and dynamically updated.
Name Type Value
DataConnectionString Connection String <Select Configuration>
Microsoft.WindowsAzure.Plug Connection String
Error List
Error List Output Data Tools Operations
Ready

Figure 11.38 Configure StudentClub_WebRole.

deployed in the staging environment for testing. To start the deployment process, click the **UPLOAD A NEW STAGING DEPLOYMENT** arrow as shown in Figure 11.41.

9. In the **Create a new Deployment** dialog, name the deployment as **MyDeployment**. For PACKAGE, click **FROM LOCAL**. Navigate to the folder where the StudentClub package is saved and the select the package **StudentClub**. Then, click

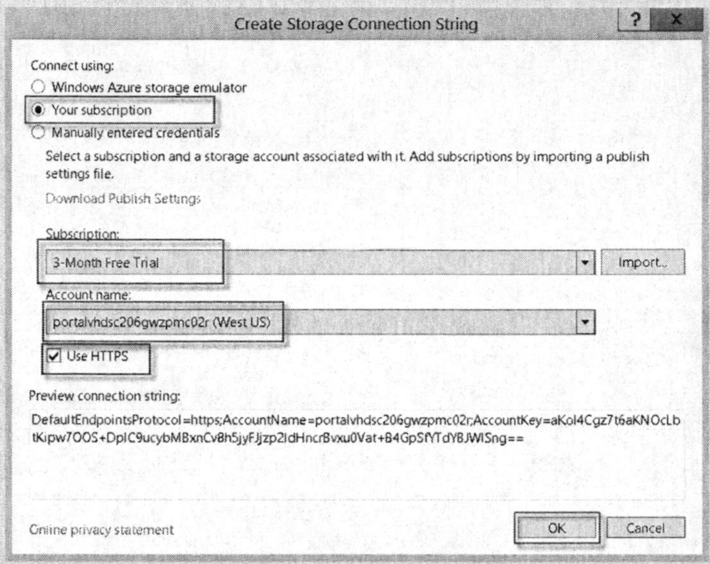

Figure 11.39 Configure Connection String.

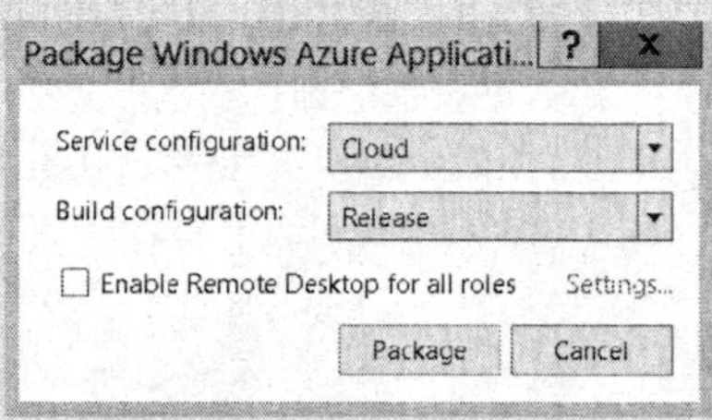

Figure 11.40 Configure package.

Open. For the CONFIGURATION textbox, click **FROM LOCAL** and select **ServiceConfiguration.cloud** in the same folder. Check the option **Deploy even if one or more roles contain a single instance**. Then, click the check box as shown in Figure 11.42.

10. After a few minutes, the StudentClub project should be deployed to Windows Azure as shown in Figure 11.43.

TASK 3: TEST THE APPLICATION IN THE STAGING ENVIRONMENT

After the application is deployed to the staging environment, it can be accessed through the public endpoint. To do so, follow the steps below:

1. Click the link under SITE URL as shown in Figure 11.43. If everything works properly, you should be able to see the application displayed in the browser as shown in Figure 11.44.

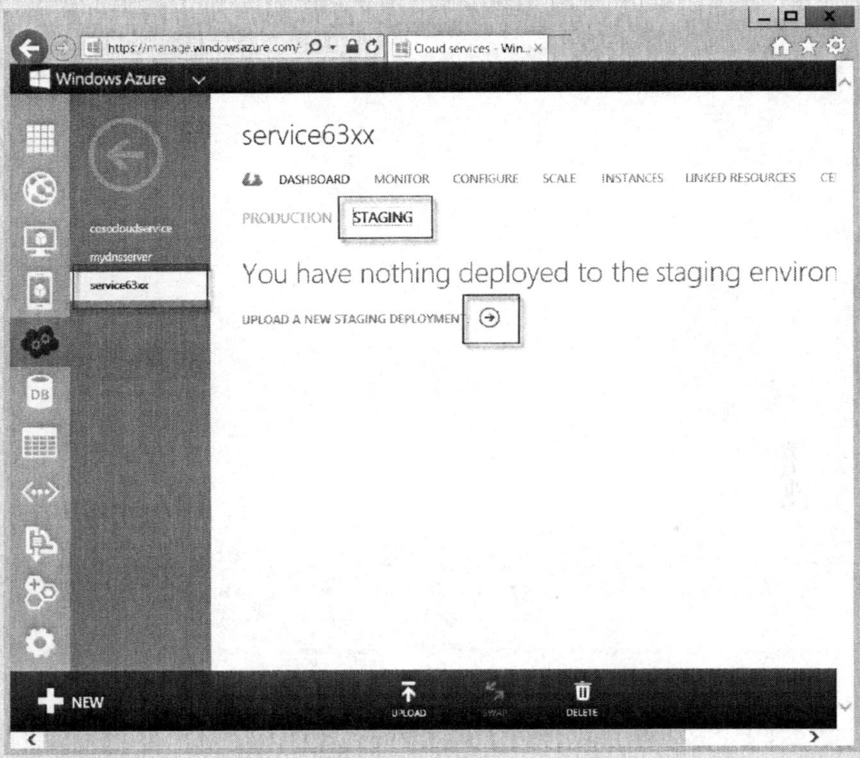

Figure 11.41 New staging deployment.

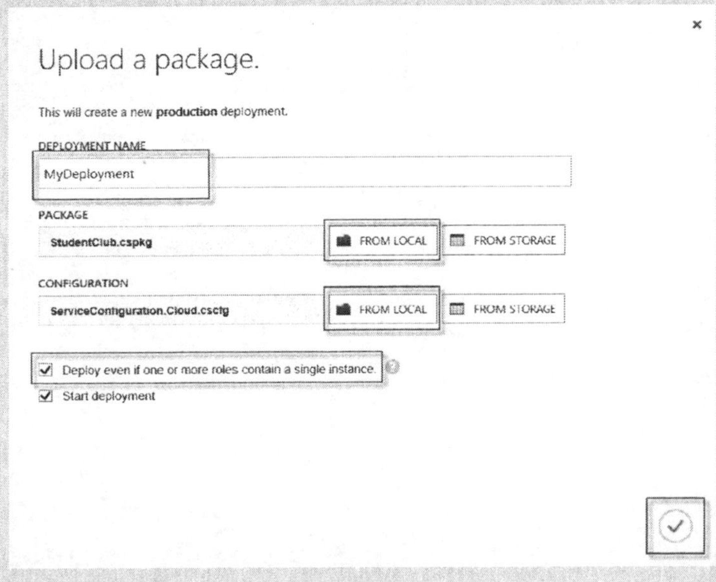

Figure 11.42 Configure deployment package.

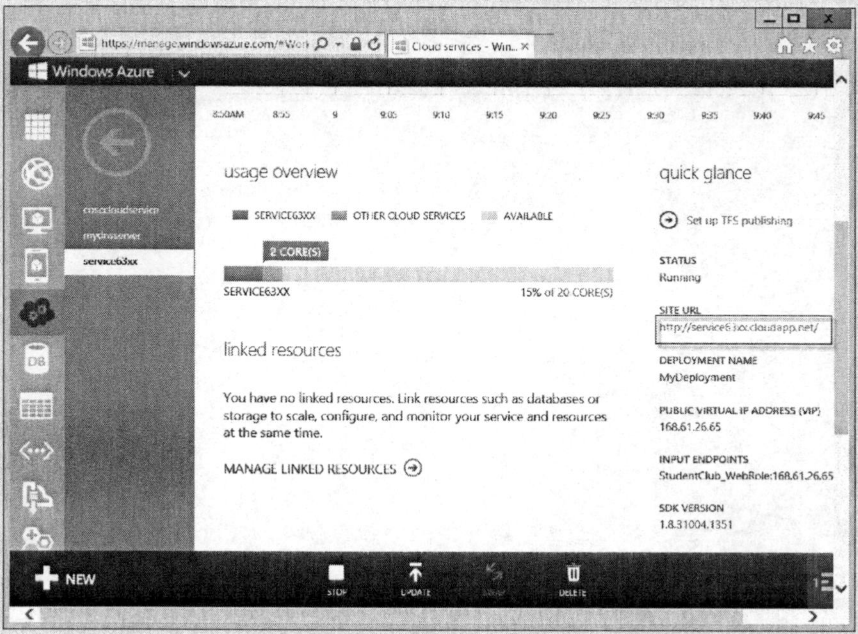

Figure 11.43 MyDeployment.

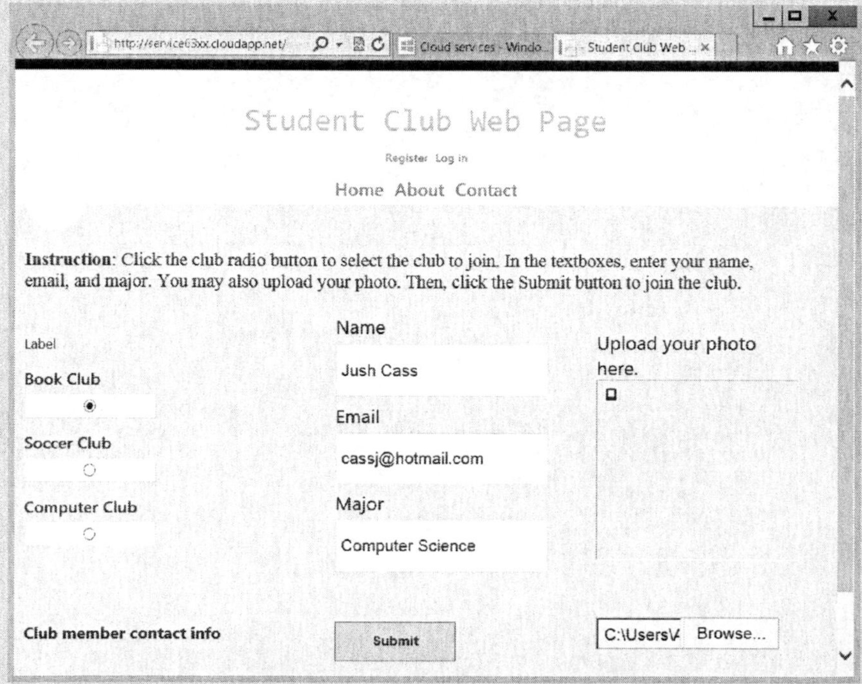

Figure 11.44 StudentClub application in staging environment.

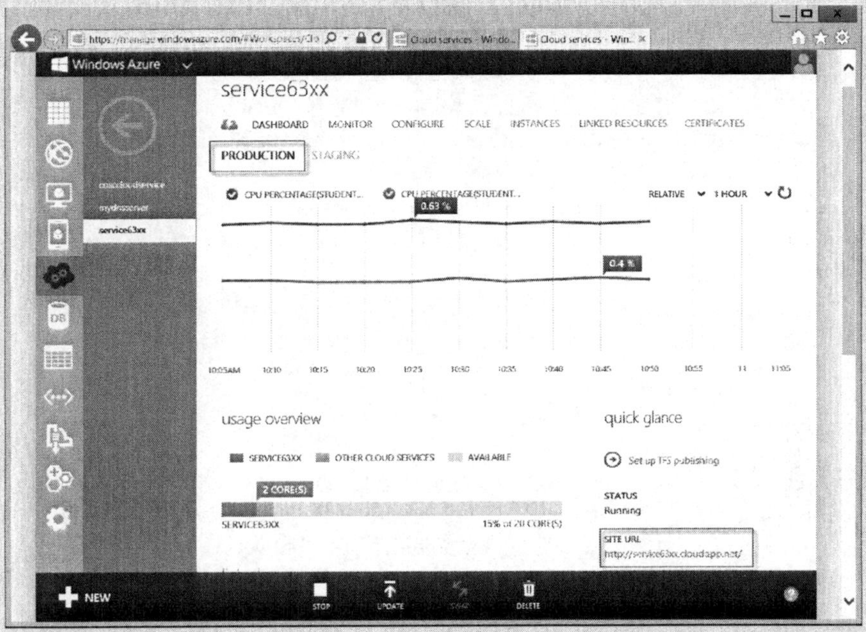

Figure 11.45 Publish to PRODUCTION.

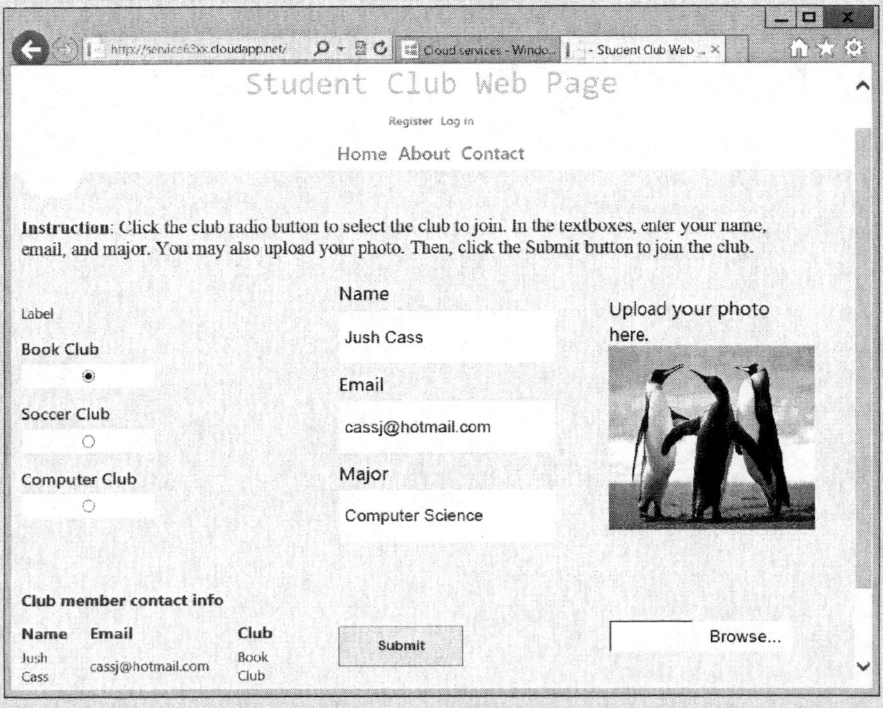

Figure 11.46 Student Club web page.

2. After the testing is successful in the staging environment, navigate to the DASHBOARD of service63xx and click **PRODUCTION** as shown in Figure 11.45.
3. After the project is published, click the link under SITE URL as shown in Figure 11.45. Then, enter the information to join the club. After clicking the **Submit** button, you should have the Student Club web page as shown in Figure 11.46.

The Student Club web page is now available on the Internet. Information entered on the web page will be stored in Windows Azure storage. Students can now enroll in the clubs. As shown in Figure 11.46, after a new member is enrolled in a club, the contact information about the other club members is displayed. So the newly enrolled student can contact the other members.

11.7 Summary

This chapter has discussed Windows Azure storage that provides highly scalable data storage. Three storage services, Table storage, Blob storage, and Queue storage, have been examined in this chapter. The storage services are used to store data generated by the web pages. They also offer cloud-based data services such as data management, data transfer, and data querying to support web applications. To illustrate the usage of these storage services, a web application, the Student Club web page, was created. Three hands-on activities were used to illustrate how to use these storage services. At the end of this chapter, the fourth hands-on activity was used to illustrate how to deploy the web application to Windows Azure so that it is accessible to the students anywhere and anytime.

Review Questions

1. What are the three components of Windows Azure storage services?
2. What are the benefits of Windows Azure storage when compared to local storage?
3. How does Table storage work?
4. Describe the difference between the table of Table storage and the table of a relational database.
5. What is the advantage and disadvantage of the Table storage?
6. What is the entity and property of the Table storage?
7. How many properties can an entity have?
8. What are the three required properties?
9. Describe the Partition key.
10. Describe the Row key.
11. What do you do with the Blob storage?
12. Describe the block blob.
13. Describe the page blob.
14. What do you do with the Queue storage?
15. What is the default size of a message?
16. How long can messages be kept in the Queue storage?
17. What is the life cycle of a message?
18. Which class can be used to define the properties of PartitionKey, RowKey, and TimeStamp?
19. How to connect the Blob storage service from an application?
20. What are the three components of the Queue storage?

Chapter 12

Windows Azure Management

Objectives

- Manage an SQL Database
- Manage the Windows Azure
- Monitor the services

12.1 Introduction

For database administrators, database management is the main job assignment. They need to address issues related to user accounts and security, database backup and restoration, and database performance tuning. A database administrator is responsible for database system update, remote access, security enforcement, database backup and restoration, monitoring and tuning database performance, data analysis for decision making, supporting database applications, and other daily maintenance tasks.

In Windows Azure, the work on managing storage services and SQL Database can be significantly simplified. In the Windows Azure computing environment, database backup and restoration are mostly done by Windows Azure. Database administrators do not need to carry out database backup tasks. An SQL database is automatically replicated to multiple physical servers. The performance tuning on IT infrastructure is done by the cloud provider. There is no need to decide which file should be placed to which hard drive. Also, the cloud provider takes care of most of the antivirus tasks.

In this chapter, we will explore some of the management tools and issues related to the management of Windows Azure storage and SQL Database. Three commonly used tools are available for managing the Windows Azure and Windows Azure SQL Database. As a GUI-based management tool, the Windows Azure Management Portal can be used to manage applications and databases hosted by Windows Azure. As a programming alternative, the Service Management API provides operations that can perform much of the functionality available through the Management Portal. As a command-line tool, Windows Azure Service Management PowerShell provides cmdlets that can perform operations usually done with the Windows Azure Service Management API. With the hands-on activities in this chapter, you will learn about some management tools for SQL Database management, user management, and service monitoring.

12.2 Windows Azure SQL Database Security

When a database is running in the cloud environment, database security becomes the top concern. Your database shares the storage device with other databases. It is exposed to the Internet and is no longer protested by the private network.

To be secure, in general, a database should meet the requirements of confidentiality, integrity, and availability, which are defined in the following:

- **Confidentiality**: Preventing information from being viewed by unauthorized individuals
- **Integrity**: Preventing information from being intentionally or unintentionally altered
- **Availability**: Making sure that information is available to the authorized users when needed

Confidentiality: In the cloud environment, to protect data from unauthorized people, a security policy should clearly define who can access to what information, who should be allowed to do what, and what data should be encrypted. Sensitive data should be encrypted before being transferred over the Internet or be stored in databases. In such a way, even if the ciphertext is captured by hackers, it is not readable without the decryption key. For confidentiality, a well-defined authentication and authorization system should also be in place.

For encryption, Windows Azure SQL Database supports encrypted connections between SQL Database and client applications. Windows Azure SQL Database supports the Tabular Data Stream (TDS) protocol. The protocol is used to securely transfer data between a database server and a client.

.NET libraries include the Cryptographic Service Provider (CSP), which implements the cryptographic standards, algorithms, and functions. CSPs can be used to encrypt data and store the encrypted data in SQL Database, and decrypt data in a Windows Azure application. During the data synchronization, encryption and decryption can also be carried out for the data communication between SQL Database and the database on an on-promises server.

The encryption and decryption can also be implemented with the programming language C# while developing an application. The Advanced Encryption Standard (AES) algorithm or other encryption algorithms are supported by Visual Studio. The security keys used by AES can be programmed with C#. The ciphertext returned by these algorithms can be safely stored in Windows Azure SQL Database. Visual Studio also provides decryption methods.

One can also take advantage of ADO.NET encryption and trusted server certificates. ADO. NET does not pass user IDs and passwords in clear text. You can also set the encrypt property in the connection string to encrypt the communication channel.

Integrity: Although encryption can prevent unauthorized users from reading the content stored in Windows Azure SQL Database, it may not prevent them from altering the stored content. Hashing is the technology to find out if sensitive information is altered by an unauthorized user. The hashing technology can be used for detecting duplicated data, message signatures, and password verification. When transferring or storing passwords or keys, one can use hashing to generate the ciphertext that can never be decrypted. The ciphertext generated by hashing can be compared with another hashing value to detect the difference. For example, if a password has been altered during the transaction, the hashing value of the original password will not match the hashing value of the altered password. In such a way, we can prevent hackers from altering sensitive information. Windows Azure provides tools such as MD5 and SHA to carry out the hashing tasks.

Availability: The availability of a cloud computing environment is usually good. Windows Azure offers 99.9% availability guarantee through its server level agreement. The redundancy provided by Windows Azure is adequate for most of the database systems. Three copies of a database are stored on three different physical servers. One of them is used as the primary database and the other two are used as standby. Windows Azure supports operations that require high scalability. It can handle a large workload in a small time period.

Before implementing security measures to enhance confidentiality, integrity, and availability, you need to create a security policy. Based on the security policy, the developers can select some of the tools to implement their own measures. The policy will serve as a guideline on

- Data encryption and hashing
- Permissions on accessing database objects and on performing database operations at various levels
- Remote access control

The policy should identify the content for encryption or hashing. Security requirements for the data stored in a cloud database and for operations performed on database objects are different depending on the types of users or schemas. The security policy should define the needs of different levels of users. It should also specify remote access control mechanisms and related network security protocols used to protect remote login information.

12.3 Managing Windows Azure SQL Database

As the physical infrastructure of Windows Azure is managed by the cloud provider, which is Microsoft, database administrators can focus their management effort on the management of their databases. The main tasks for the database management are

- Remote access control with firewall
- User Account Management

Remote access control with firewall: A firewall should be implemented to protect your server and database hosted by Windows Azure. The server side firewall configuration can be done in Windows Azure when creating a database server. In the Windows Azure Management Portal, you can create a list of IP addresses to be allowed to access the database server. For illustration purposes, Figure 12.1 shows the firewall configuration that allows a predetermined set of IP addresses ranging from 10.1.1.1 to 10.1.1.255 to access the database server. In real life, your IP address should be different from what is illustrated in Figure 12.1 since 10.x.x.x is not available on the Internet. If the Windows Azure application needs to connect to SQL Database, the firewall should also allow the IP address 0.0.0.0. The list of the approved IP addresses will be stored in the master database. On local computers, the firewall should be configured to allow network communication through the port 1433, which is the port used by SQL Database.

Once a connection request arrives, Windows Azure checks the IP address. The request will be rejected if the IP address is not on the allowed list. If the request is accepted, it will be routed to the primary database server.

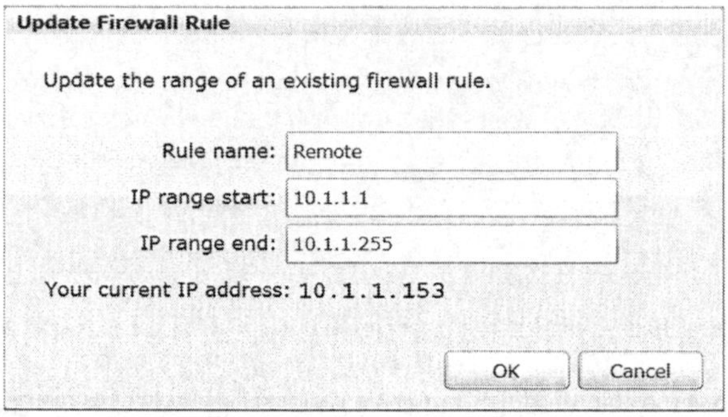

Figure 12.1 Firewall configuration.

You can also create a list of allowed IP addresses directly in the master database by using a stored procedure. For example, to create a firewall rule called myrule to allow IP addresses ranging from 192.168.1.1 to 192.168.1.254 to access your database server on Windows Azure, use the following SQL statement:

```
exec sp_set_firewall_rule N'myrule','192.168.1.1','192.168.1.254'
```

You can also delete a firewall rule with a stored procedure. For example, to delete the firewall rule myrule, use the following SQL statement:

```
exec sp_delete_firewall_rule N'myrule'
```

SQL Database provides SQL statements for firewall management. You can query firewall rules from the sys.firewall.rules table. After being connected to the master database, you can use the following SQL statement to view the firewall rules:

```
SELECT * FROM sys.firewall_rules
```

To run the above SQL statement, you need to first connect to the master database with the administrator's permission. After the connection is allowed, the next task is to carry out the authentication process to verify if the user is allowed to work on the database.

User Account Management: While the SQL Database firewall can be used to prevent connections from some IP addresses, SQL authentication controls users' access to SQL Database. The SQL authentication process in Windows Azure SQL Database is very much the same way as in on-premises SQL Server. To grant a user to access a database, you need to first connect to the master database with the administrator's privilege. Then, you need to create a login for the server itself with an SQL statement.

To configure the users and logins, you need to connect to the master database in Windows Azure SQL Database. You also need to be a member of the LoginManager role or DBManager role for configuring the properties of the users and logins. After connecting to the master database, you can use the following SQL statement to create a login:

```
create login login_name with password='strongpw'
```

where *login_name* and *strongpw* are the login name and password of the login to be created. The password needs to be a strong password. Once a server login is created, you may need to create a user account in a database specified by the login. The following SQL statement creates a user with the login created in the previous SQL statement:

```
create user user_name from login login_name
```

After the user is created, the user can be granted some permission with the following SQL statement:

```
GRANT SELECT
ON BUILDING
TO user_name
```

In the above code, the user is granted the SELECT permission on the table BUILGING. To remove a permission granted to a user, the REVOKE SQL statement can be used to accomplish the task.

Schemas can also be used to grant permissions to users. A schema is a set of database objects assigned to one or more users. For the users who are allowed to access the same set of database objects, you can create a schema to include these database objects. Then, assign the schema to these users. You can grant some permission to the schema instead of granting the permission to each user.

Using strong passwords or keys is another way to make your database safer. When using SQL authentication, a strong password is required. A user name should not include symbols like @. Also, SQL authentication does not support Remote Desktop Connection.

ACTIVITY 12.1 WINDOWS AZURE SQL DATABASE USER MANAGEMENT

For our Class_Registration database created on Windows Azure, only the database owner can access the database. It is recommended that we should design separate database roles for the applications connected to the database and then add the application accounts to those database roles. The following activity demonstrates how to accomplish this task:

1. To follow the recommendation, log on to the **master** database with the URL https://qmcooqcanr.database.windows.net/?langid=en-US#$database=master where qmcooqcanr is the SQL Database server name. Your SQL Database server name should be different. Then, log on to the database as shown in Figure 12.2.
2. In the **New Query** pane, run the following SQL statement. The password has to be strong enough to create the login.

   ```
   create login Smith with password='PWF@rCa$$&/-7'
   go
   ```

3. After the Smith login is created. Click **Log off** to exit the SQL Database Management Portal.
4. Enter the database **Class_Registration** as shown in Figure 12.3 and log in again with your user name and password.
5. In the **New Query** pane, run the following SQL statement:

   ```
   create user Smith from login Smith
   go
   ```

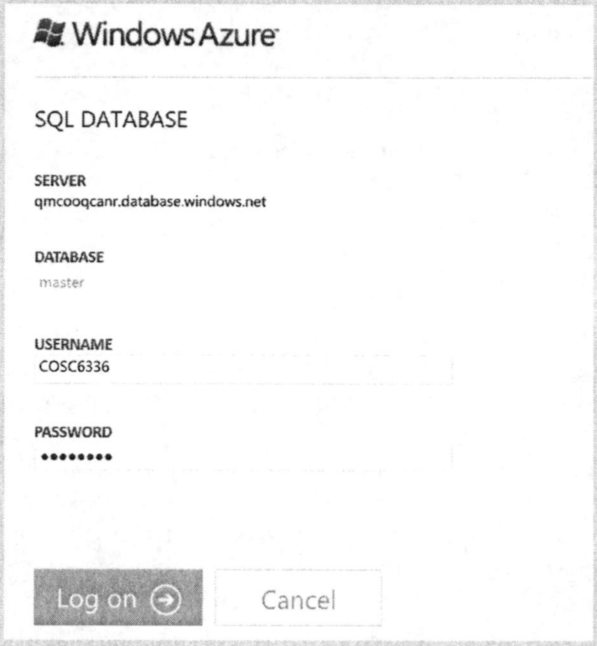

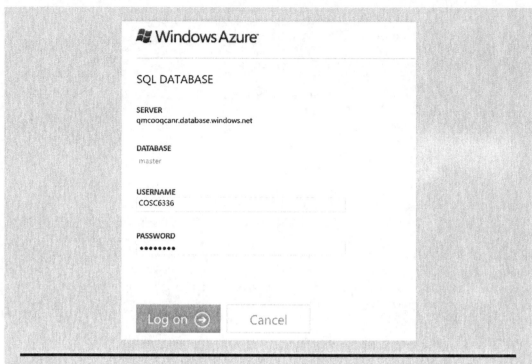

Figure 12.2 Master database login.

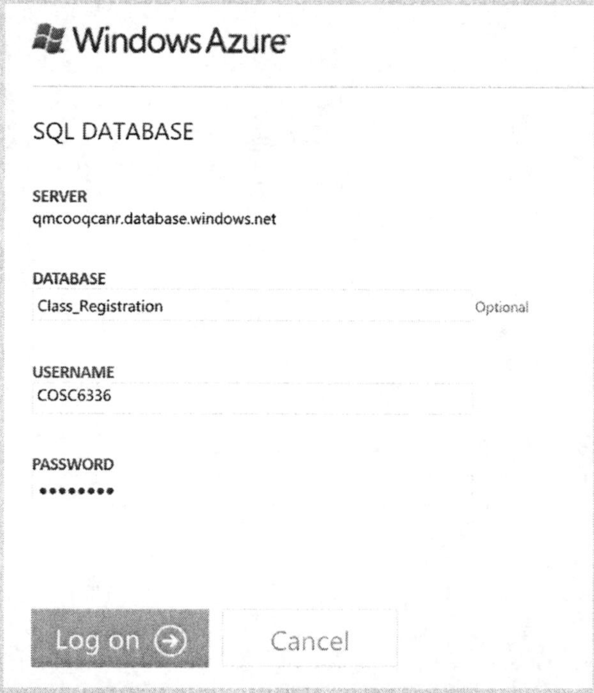

Figure 12.3 Class_Registration database login.

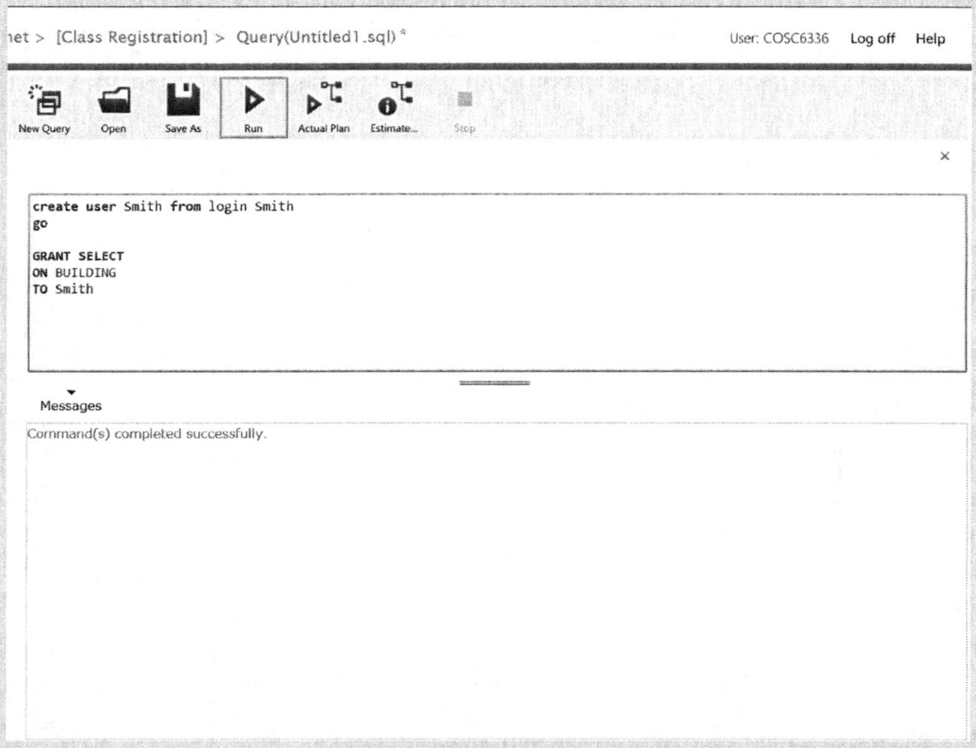

Figure 12.4 Grant permission to user Smith.

6. After the user Smith is created, highlight and run the following SQL statement to grant the SELECT permission to Smith as shown in Figure 12.4:

```
GRANT SELECT
ON BUILDING
TO Smith
```

7. To test the login, log off from the current user. Then, log in with the user **Smith** and password PWF@rCa$$&/-7 to the database **Class_Registration**. In the **New Query** pane, run the following SQL Statement:

```
SELECT * FROM BUILDING
```

8. With the permission granted, Smith should be able to run the SELECT statement as shown in Figure 12.5.
9. However, Smith should not be able to run the UPDATE SQL statement as shown in Figure 12.6.

As illustrated above, user management can be done through SQL statements. More management-related tasks will be discussed in the following sections.

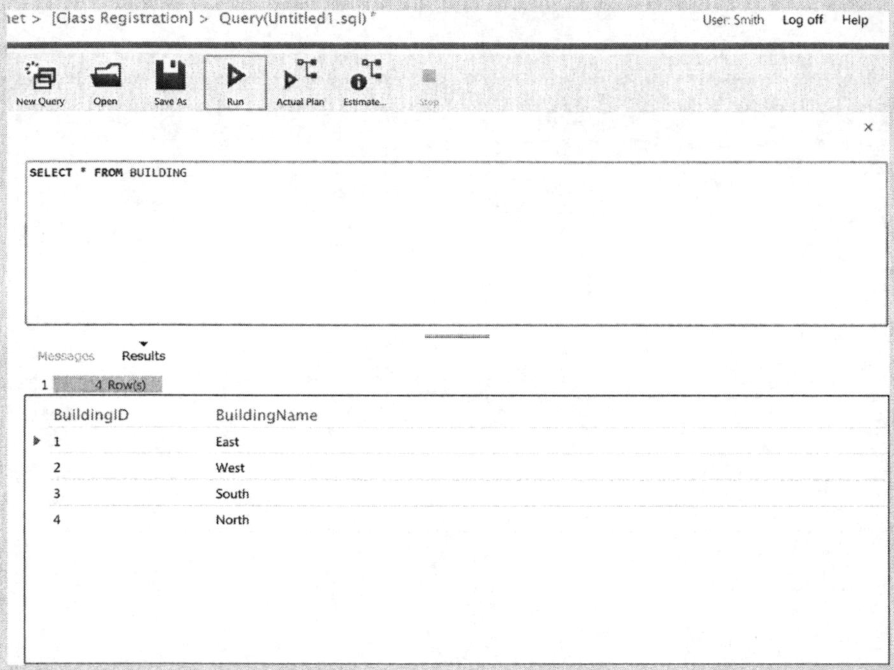

Figure 12.5 Execute SELECT SQL statement.

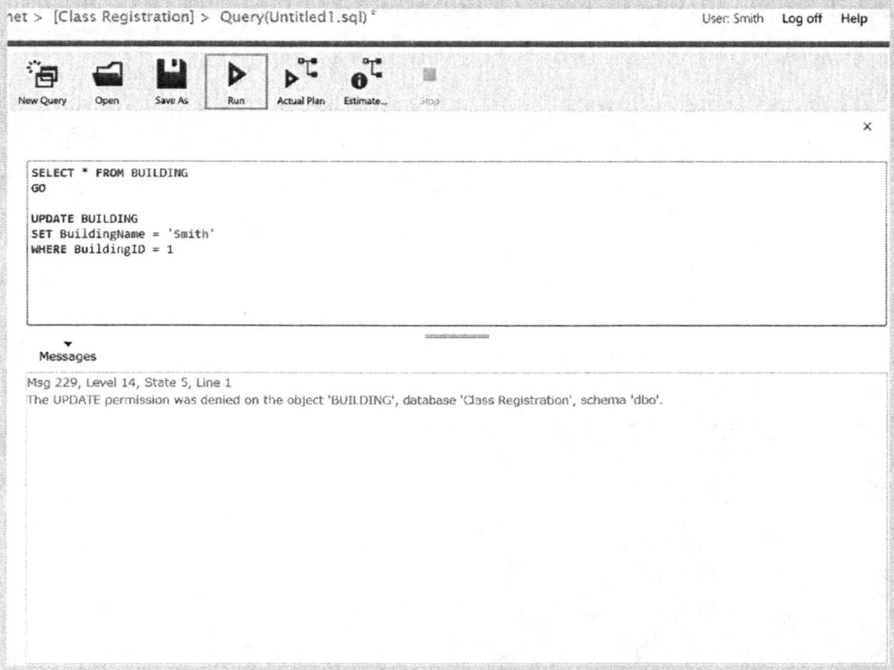

Figure 12.6 Execute UPDATE SQL statement.

While authentication controls users' access to SQL Database, authorization controls permissions to users to access certain database objects and perform contain tasks. In Windows Azure SQL Database, authorization can be implemented through the configuration of users, roles, schemas, and related login properties.

ACTIVITY 12.2 MANAGING SQL DATABASE WITH SCHEMAS

As mentioned earlier, schemas are used to manage database objects and security. A schema can be created by using the command CREATE SCHEMA. To illustrate the creation and use of schemas, let us go through the following steps:

1. In **Internet Explorer**, enter the following URL to the SQL Database Management Portal:
   https://qmcooqcanr.database.windows.net/?langid=en-us#$database=Class_Registration
   Again, you need to change qmcooqcanr to your database server's name.
2. Log on to SQL Database with your user name and password.
3. To create a schema account and add a table ACCOUNT to it, use the following SQL statement in the **New Query** window:

   ```
   CREATE SCHEMA Accounting
     CREATE TABLE ACCOUNT (AccountID INT, Balance MONEY)
   ```

4. You can assign a user with the default schema. For example, the following SQL statement will assign the user Smith with the default schema Accounting and grant Smith the permission to use the ALTER statement. To do so, run the following SQL statement:

   ```
   ALTER USER Smith WITH DEFAULT_SCHEMA = Accounting
   ```

5. Then, run the following SQL statement to create an account for Smith in the Class_Registration database and grant the permission for Smith to alter the schema Accounting.

   ```
   GRANT ALTER ON SCHEMA::Accounting TO Smith
   ```

   When Smith logs on to the Class_Registration database, the default schema for Smith is Accounting. Smith will be the owner of the ACCOUNT table.
6. A fully qualified database object name has the format that contains four parts server.database.schema.object. When missing the names of the server and database, a database object takes the current server and database as default. When missing the name

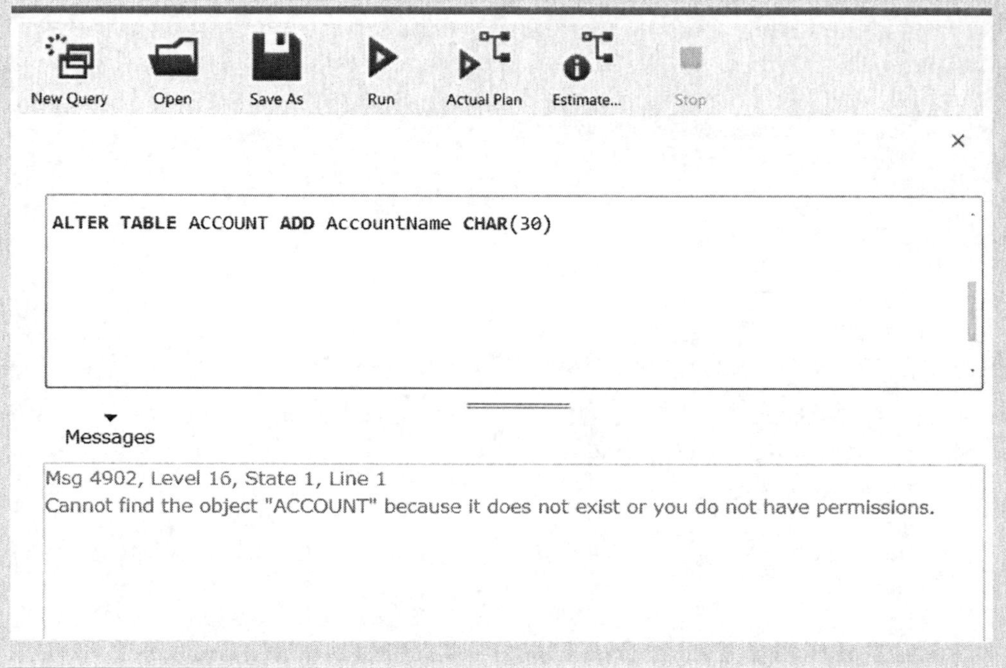
New Query
Open
Save As
Run
Actual Plan
Estimate...
Stop
ALTER TABLE ACCOUNT ADD AccountName CHAR(30)
Messages
Msg 4902, Level 16, State 1, Line 1
Cannot find the object "ACCOUNT" because it does not exist or you do not have permissions.

Figure 12.7 Error caused by missing schema name.

of the schema, the database takes the default schema dbo. Often, an unqualified object name will cause errors. The following example will illustrate the problem with unqualified object names. As shown in Figure 12.7, the following SQL statement produces an error message:

```
ALTER TABLE ACCOUNT ADD AccountName CHAR(30)
```

The error message indicates that the table ACCOUNT does not exist. This is because the missing schema name in the name of the ACCOUNT table causes dbo to be the default schema.

7. However, the table ACCOUNT is built in the schema Accounting. Adding the schema name in front of the table name will solve the problem (Figure 12.8).
8. If Smith is logged on directly to the database Class_Registration, the default schema is Accounting. In this case, no error will be generated when using only the table name ACCOUNT. Let us log on as **Smith** as shown in Figure 12.9.
9. To show that Smith is a qualified user to the schema Accounting, enter the SQL statement

```
ALTER TABLE ACCOUNT ADD LastName CHAR(30)
```

shown in Figure 12.10 and execute it.

Since Smith's default schema is Accounting, using the table name ACCOUNT without attaching the schema name does not generate an error.

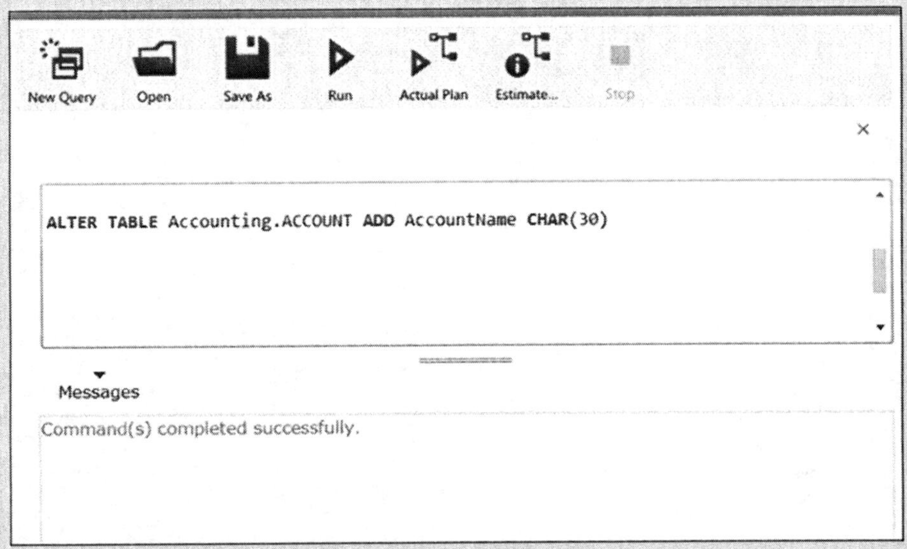

Figure 12.8 No error with fully qualified name.

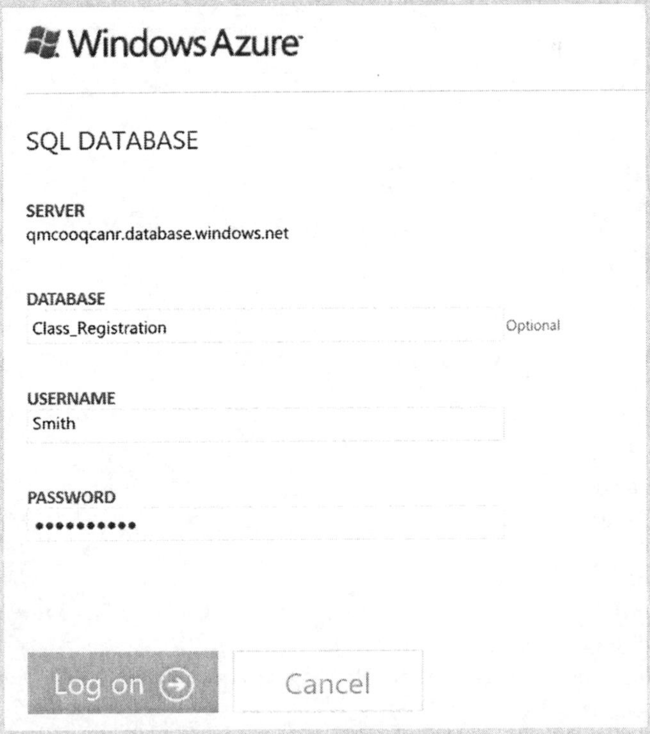

Figure 12.9 Log on to SQL database as user Smith.

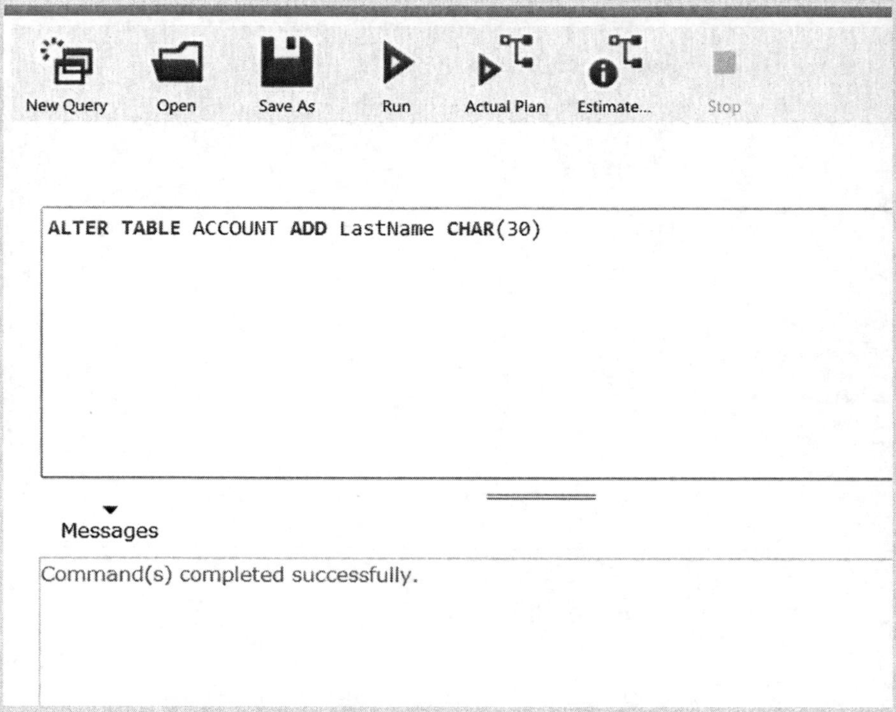

Figure 12.10 No error with table name only.

12.4 Managing Windows Azure

Most of the Windows Azure management tasks can be done in the Windows Azure Management Portal and Windows Azure Service Management API. Created on top of the Azure Service Management API, PowerShell provides a command-lets environment where developers can carry out some management tasks. With the Management Portal, Management API, or PowerShell, developers can perform the following tasks:

- Storage account management
- Cloud service management
- Certificate management
- Affinity group management

Storage Account Management: To use Windows Azure Storage services, you need to first create a storage account with the Management Portal. Figure 12.11 illustrates a storage account with the account name portalvhdsc206gwz$.

As shown in Figure 12.11, the name of the storage account becomes the host name if the URI is for the Blob, Queue, or Table services.

With the Management Portal, developers can create and manage storage accounts. Later, when you create an application that uses storage services such as Blob service, the storage account information need to be entered in the application. To simplify account management, the developer can

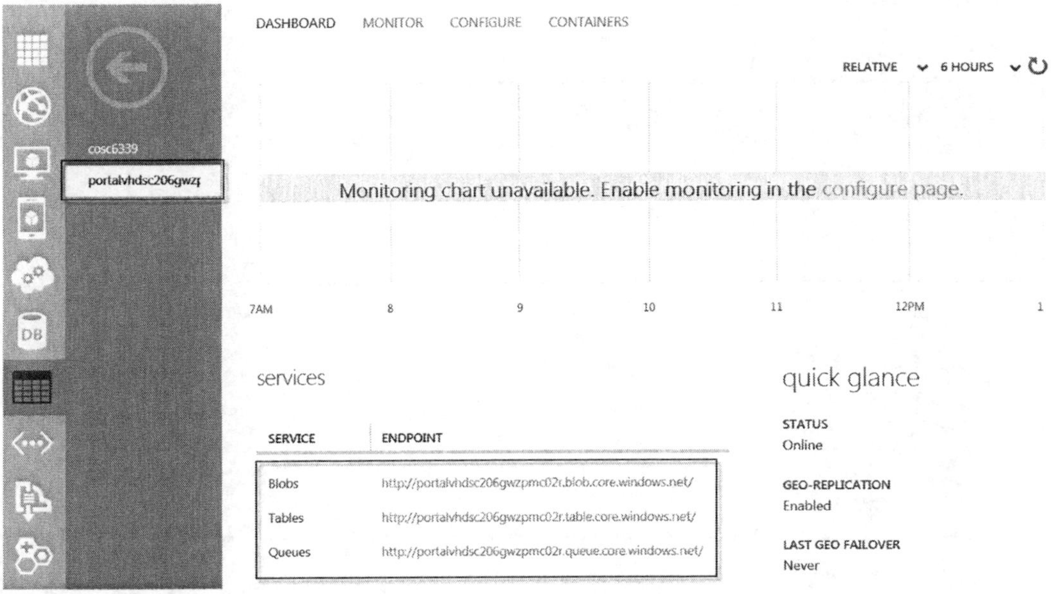

Figure 12.11 Storage account.

create a subdomain for the clients to access the storage service. The developer can also view and regenerate storage access keys in the Management Portal. Once the storage account and subdomain is no longer needed, they can be deleted in the Management Portal.

Cloud Service Management: In Windows Azure, a cloud service is used as a container for the service deployment. In the Management Portal, you can create, deploy, run, suspend, and delete cloud services. Figure 12.12 illustrates the cloud service service63xx and its properties.

As shown in Figure 12.12, the cloud service service63xx hosts a deployment called MyDeployment that contains two roles. The deployment has the public IP address 168.61.26.65. The endpoint of the deployment is StudentClub_WebRole:168.61.26.65:80 through which PCs and mobile devices can access the deployment.

Linked Resource Management: The linked resources can be used to link databases or other resources to your cloud service. With the Windows Azure Management Portal, you can manage the linked resources such as a Windows Azure SQL Database instance. You are able to view and scale the linked resources. You can switch the database between the web edition and Business edition. You can also change the size of a linked database. Figure 12.13 shows the linked resource to the cloud service service63xx.

Certificate Management: When using the Windows Azure SDK tools, the developer can access the Windows Azure resources by using a certificate. When the developer needs to create or manage a cloud service on Windows Azure from Visual Studio, the certificate is used to authenticate the developer. The certificate is also needed if the developer uploads VM roles to Windows Azure with the command-line tool CSUpload. The Windows Azure certificate store can be used to store certificates. By using the Management Portal, you can upload a certificate to the certificate store in a cloud service. For one subscription, as many as 10 certificates can be added to Windows Azure. Figure 12.14 illustrates a certificate upload dialog.

Affinity Group Management: When developing a cloud application, you may want a Blob service to be run with a Queue service. In such a case, if a group of services need to work together

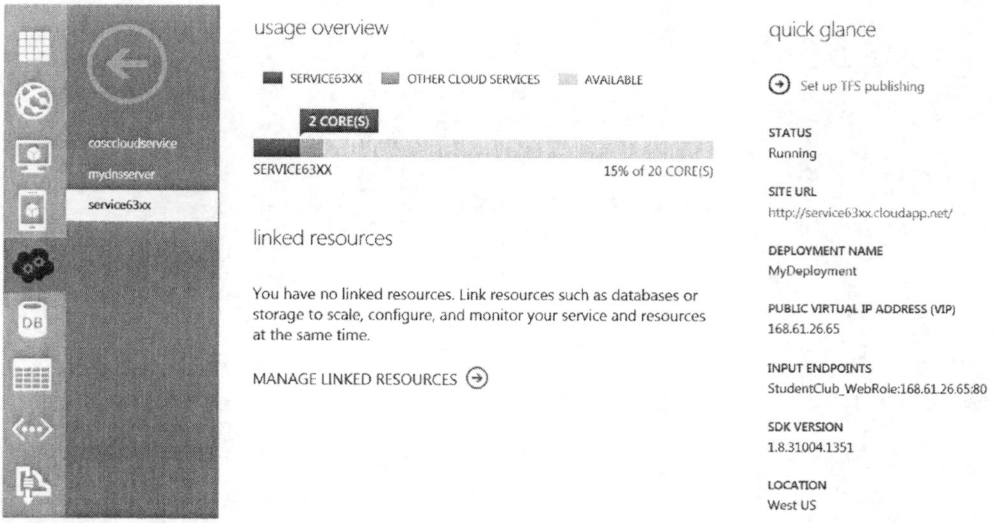

Figure 12.12 Cloud service.

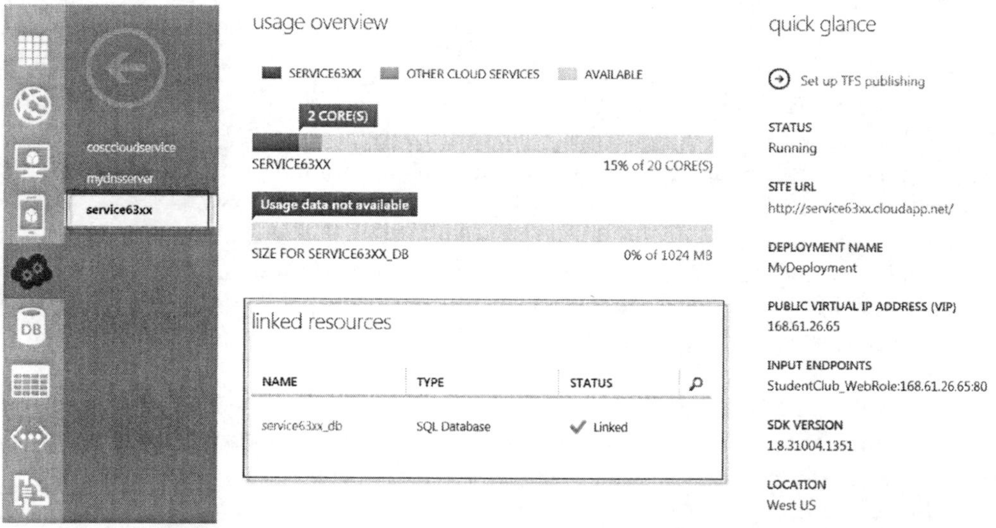

Figure 12.13 Linked resources.

in the same data center, you can group these services to form an affinity group for better performance. Once an affinity group is created, it is available to every cloud service in the same subscription. You can assign the affinity group to a cloud service.

Windows Azure Service Management API: To programmatically access much of the functionalities available through the Management Portal, the developer can consider using the REST-based Windows Azure Service Management API. With the API, developers can create their own or use the existing management utilities. The API allows the developers to manage their Windows Azure deployments, cloud services, affinity groups, and storage accounts. The services and applications

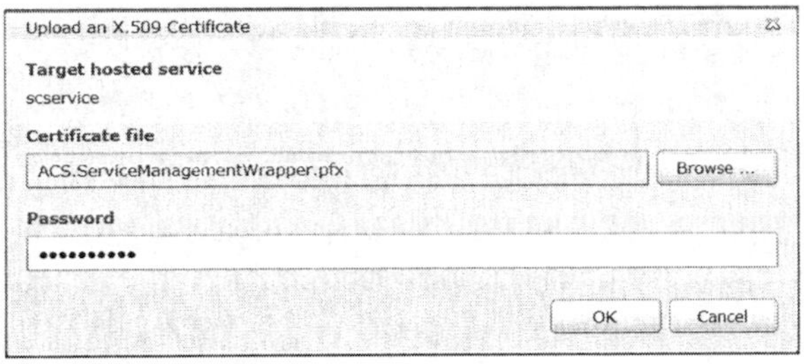

Figure 12.14 Certificate upload dialog.

can access the management services by sending requests for API operations via a secured network protocol such as SSL. The API uses an X.509 certificate to authenticate requests from clients.

The Service Management API can be used to manage the existing storage accounts. Since the API can only be used to manage existing storage accounts, the developer cannot directly create and delete storage accounts with the API. The API cannot change the labels of storage accounts, register or unregister a storage account with a content delivery network (CDN), and register or unregister a custom domain name through a storage account. For the management of existing storage accounts, the API provides the following operations:

- List storage accounts within a subscription
- Get storage account properties
- Retrieve primary and secondary storage account keys
- Regenerate storage account keys

The Service Management API allows you to specify the ways to deploy a service. You can use Staging or Production to deploy a service. However, developers cannot directly create and delete cloud services with the API. The API cannot change the labels of cloud services. For the management of cloud services, the Windows Azure Service Management API provides the following operations:

- List cloud services in a subscription.
- Get properties for a cloud service.
- Create, get, swap, delete, and upgrade deployment.
- Configure deployment properties.
- Update and manage deployments.
- Upgrade cloud services.

For affinity group management, the Windows Azure Service Management API provides the following operations. However, developers cannot directly create and delete a hosted affinity group with the API. The API cannot change the labels of affinity groups.

- List and get properties of affinity groups.

To use a certificate, you need to generate a self-signed certificate with IIS 7 or use the utility makecert in the command window. For certificate management, the Windows Azure Service Management API provides the following operations:

- List, get, add, and delete certificates.

Windows Azure PowerShell: Windows PowerShell is a new type of command-line utility. Unlike the regular command-line utility, PowerShell is a task-based command-line shell and scripting language designed for handling repeatable tasks. Built on the .NET Framework, PowerShell provides greater control and flexibility for system administration. Windows PowerShell includes four types of commands: Cmdlets (Command-Lets), PowerShell Functions, PowerShell Scripts, and native Windows commands. A cmdlet is a single-function command-line tool. There are more than 100 cmdlets in Windows Azure PowerShell. Multiple cmdlets can be combined together to form a script used to handle a complicated task.

With Windows Azure PowerShell, developers can control and automate the deployment and management of the workloads in Windows Azure. PowerShell can also be used to provide virtual machines, set up virtual networks, configure cross-premises networks, and manage cloud services in Windows Azure. For the management of Windows Azure and Windows Azure SQL Database, you can use Windows Azure Management Comlets and Windows Azure SQL Database Comlets. Windows Azure Management Comlets can be used to handle the following tasks:

- Managing subscriptions
- Deploying and managing virtual machines
- Managing virtual networks
- Managing storage accounts
- Deploying and managing cloud services

Windows Azure SQL Database Cmdlets can be used to handle the following tasks:

- Managing SQL Database servers
- Managing SQL Database firewall rules

Figure 12.15 shows some of the cmdlets in Windows Azure PowerShell.

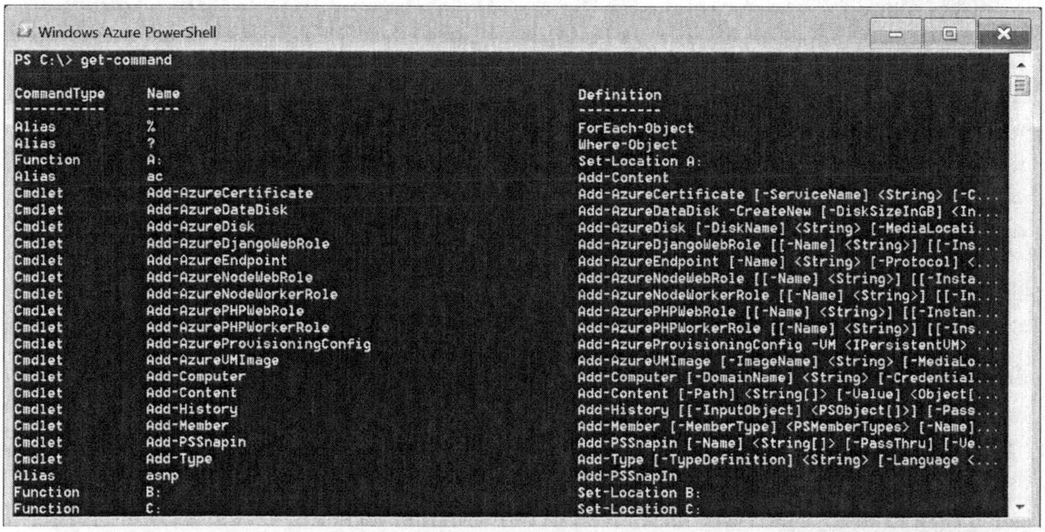
Windows Azure PowerShell
PS C:\> get-command
CommandType Name Definition
----------- ---- ----------
Alias % ForEach-Object
Alias ? Where-Object
Function A: Set-Location A:
Alias ac Add-Content
Cmdlet Add-AzureCertificate Add-AzureCertificate [-ServiceName] <String> [-C...
Cmdlet Add-AzureDataDisk Add-AzureDataDisk -CreateNew [-DiskSizeInGB] <In...
Cmdlet Add-AzureDisk Add-AzureDisk [-DiskName] <String> [-MediaLocati...
Cmdlet Add-AzureDjangoWebRole Add-AzureDjangoWebRole [[-Name] <String>] [[-Ins...
Cmdlet Add-AzureEndpoint Add-AzureEndpoint [-Name] <String> [-Protocol] <...
Cmdlet Add-AzureNodeWebRole Add-AzureNodeWebRole [[-Name] <String>] [[-Insta...
Cmdlet Add-AzureNodeWorkerRole Add-AzureNodeWorkerRole [[-Name] <String>] [[-In...
Cmdlet Add-AzurePHPWebRole Add-AzurePHPWebRole [[-Name] <String>] [[-Instan...
Cmdlet Add-AzurePHPWorkerRole Add-AzurePHPWorkerRole [[-Name] <String>] [[-Ins...
Cmdlet Add-AzureProvisioningConfig Add-AzureProvisioningConfig -VM <IPersistentVM> ...
Cmdlet Add-AzureVMImage Add-AzureVMImage [-ImageName] <String> [-MediaLo...
Cmdlet Add-Computer Add-Computer [-DomainName] <String> [-Credential...
Cmdlet Add-Content Add-Content [-Path] <String[]> [-Value] <Object[...
Cmdlet Add-History Add-History [[-InputObject] <PSObject[]>] [-Pass...
Cmdlet Add-Member Add-Member [-MemberType] <PSMemberTypes> [-Name]...
Cmdlet Add-PSSnapin Add-PSSnapin [-Name] <String[]> [-PassThru] [-Ve...
Cmdlet Add-Type Add-Type [-TypeDefinition] <String> [-Language <...
Alias asnp Add-PSSnapIn
Function B: Set-Location B:
Function C: Set-Location C:

Figure 12.15 PowerShell Cmdlets.

ACTIVITY 12.3 MANAGING WINDOWS AZURE APPLICATIONS WITH POWERSHELL

This activity demonstrates how to use PowerShell to carry out management tasks such as creating an SQL Database server and set a firewall rule. In this activity, create an SQL Database server by following the steps below.

TASK 1: CREATE SQL DATABASE SERVER ON WINDOWS AZURE

1. To open Windows Azure PowerShell, connect to your virtual machine hosted by Windows Azure. Press the **Windows Icon** key and click the **Windows Azure PowerShell** icon on the tile as shown in Figure 12.16.
2. First, you need to download the .publishSettings file by running the following command in PowerShell:

```
Get-AzurePublishSettingsFile
```

3. You will be prompted to log on to your Windows Azure account. Once you have logged in, a web page is opened to provide the instruction on the usage of the .publishSettings file as shown in Figure 12.17.
4. You will be prompted to save the .publishSettings file. Once the file is saved, click the **View Downloads** button to find where the file is downloaded (Figure 12.18). Your .publishSettings file name may be different from the one shown here.

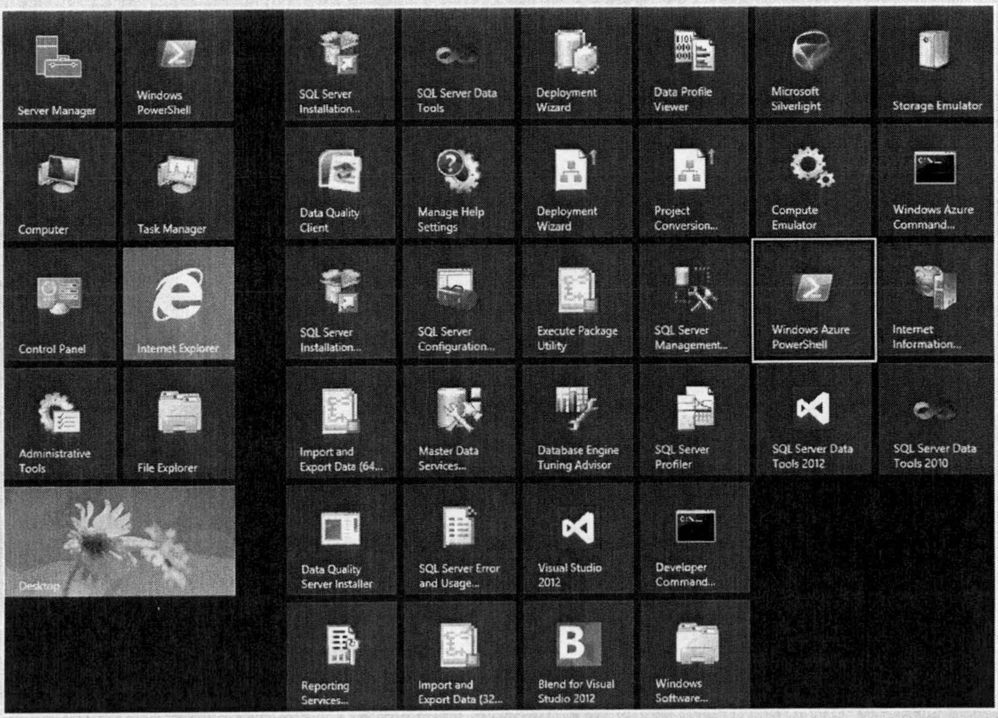

Figure 12.16 Windows Azure PowerShell.

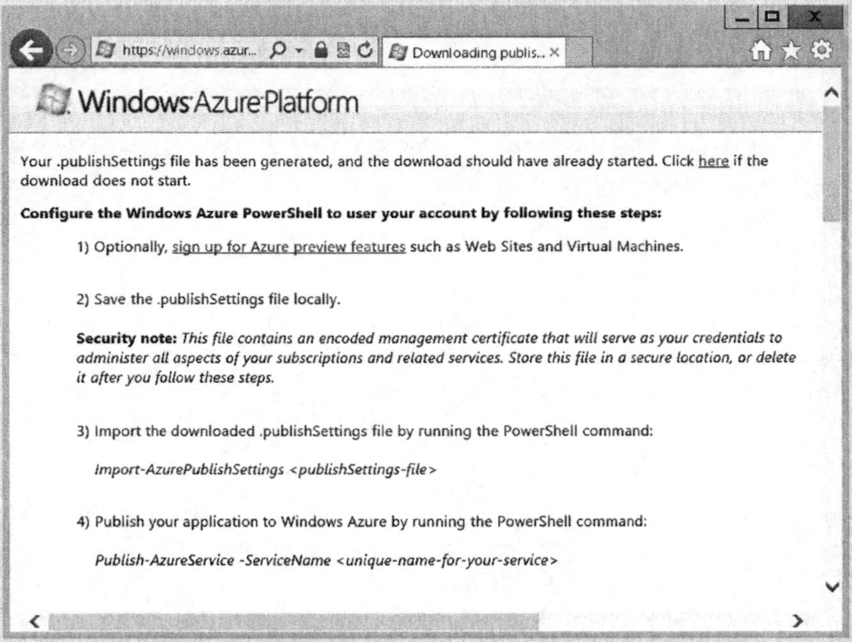

https://windows.azur...
Downloading publis...
Windows Azure Platform
Your .publishSettings file has been generated, and the download should have already started. Click here if the download does not start.
Configure the Windows Azure PowerShell to user your account by following these steps:
1) Optionally, sign up for Azure preview features such as Web Sites and Virtual Machines.
2) Save the .publishSettings file locally.
Security note: This file contains an encoded management certificate that will serve as your credentials to administer all aspects of your subscriptions and related services. Store this file in a secure location, or delete it after you follow these steps.
3) Import the downloaded .publishSettings file by running the PowerShell command:
Import-AzurePublishSettings <publishSettings-file>
4) Publish your application to Windows Azure by running the PowerShell command:
Publish-AzureService -ServiceName <unique-name-for-your-service>

Figure 12.17 Download .publishSettings file.

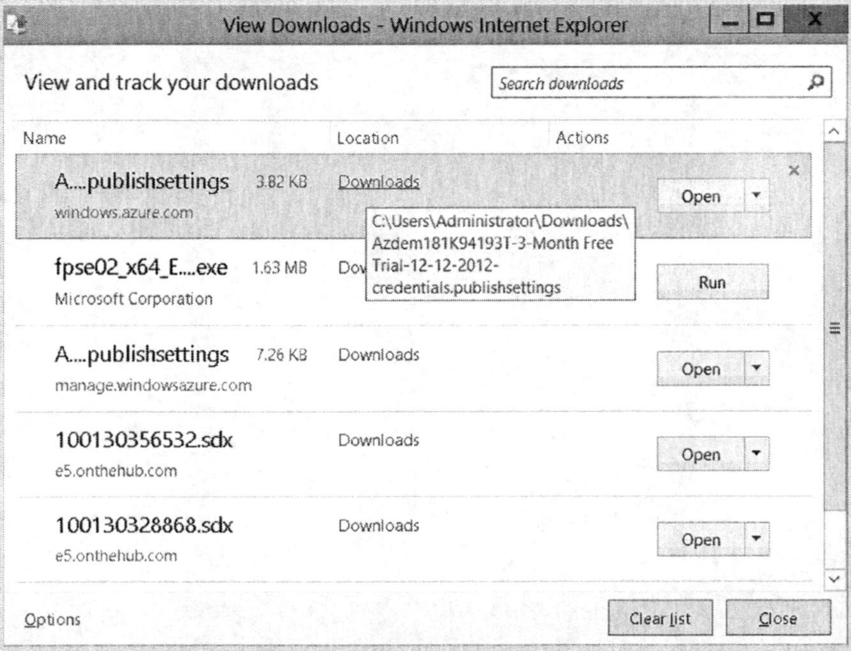

View Downloads - Windows Internet Explorer
View and track your downloads
Search downloads
Name
Location
Actions
A....publishsettings 3.82 KB
windows.azure.com
Downloads
Open
C:\Users\Administrator\Downloads\Azdem181K94193T-3-Month Free Trial-12-12-2012-credentials.publishsettings
fpse02_x64_E....exe 1.63 MB
Microsoft Corporation
Run
A....publishsettings 7.26 KB
manage.windowsazure.com
Downloads
Open
100130356532.sdx
e5.onthehub.com
Downloads
Open
100130328868.sdx
e5.onthehub.com
Downloads
Open
Options
Clear list
Close

Figure 12.18 View downloads.

5. To import the .publishSettings file, run the following command:

```
Import-AzurePublishSettingsFile
"C:\Users\Administrator\Downloads\Azdem181k94193T-3-Month Free
Trial-12-12-2012-credentials.publishsettings"
```

6. To view the subscriptions, run the following command:

```
Get-AzureSubscription
```

7. To select the subscription for your project, for example, run the following command:

```
Select-AzureSubscription '3-Month Free Trial'
```

8. You are now ready to manage your databases. To create an SQL Database server, use the New-AzureSqlDatabaseServer cmdlet shown below:

```
PS C:\> New-AzureSqlDatabaseServer -AdministratorLogin COSC6301 -
AdministratorLoginPassword Student1 -Location "North Central US"
```

9. The result is shown in Figure 12.19. A random name, dwsyklavsf, is assigned as the server name.
10. For the newly created SQL Database server, as an example, you can create a firewall rule to allow the computers with the IP addresses from 129.0.0.0 to 129.255.255.255 to access the SQL Database server on Windows Azure. To create a firewall rule, use the following command:

```
PS C:\> New-AzureSqlDatabaseServerFirewallRule -RuleName MyRule -
ServerName dwsyklavsf -StartIpAddress 129.0.0.0 -EndIpAddress
129.255.255.255
```

The result is shown in Figure 12.20.

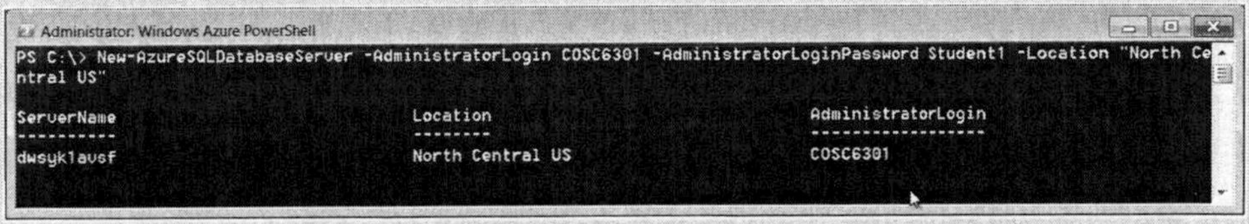
Administrator: Windows Azure PowerShell
PS C:\> New-AzureSQLDatabaseServer -AdministratorLogin COSC6301 -AdministratorLoginPassword Student1 -Location "North Ce
ntral US"
ServerName
Location
AdministratorLogin
dwsyklavsf
North Central US
COSC6301

Figure 12.19 Create new SQL database server in Windows Azure PowerShell.

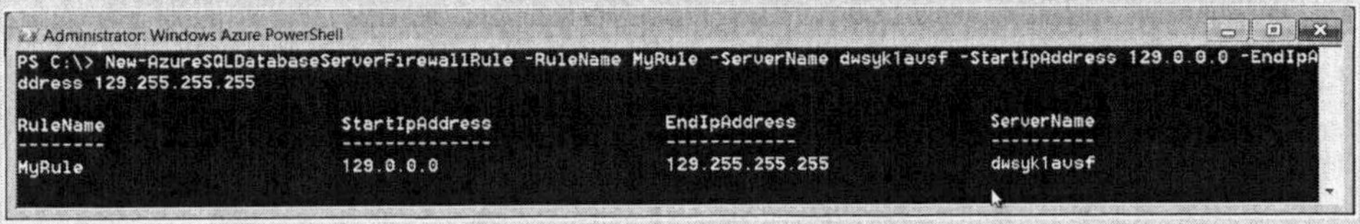
Administrator: Windows Azure PowerShell
PS C:\> New-AzureSQLDatabaseServerFirewallRule -RuleName MyRule -ServerName dwsyklavsf -StartIpAddress 129.0.0.0 -EndIpA
ddress 129.255.255.255
RuleName
StartIpAddress
EndIpAddress
ServerName
MyRule
129.0.0.0
129.255.255.255
dwsyklavsf

Figure 12.20 Create firewall rule with Windows Azure PowerShell.

11. To get the list of SQL Database servers created in your subscription, use the cmdlet Get-AzureSqlDatabaseServer as shown in Figure 12.21. Two servers are listed, one is the server created with the Windows Azure Management Portal in the earlier chapter and the other one is created with Window Azure PowerShell in this chapter.
12. To modify the firewall rule, you can use the following command:

```
PS C:\> Set-AzureSqlDatabaseServerFirewallRule -RuleName MyRule
- ServerName dwsyklavsf -StartIpAddress 64.0.0.0 -EndIpAddress
64.255.255.255
```

    The execution result is shown in Figure 12.22.
13. To remove an SQL Database server, use the Remove-AzureSqlDatabaseServer cmdlet as shown in Figure 12.23.

There are many other operations that can be done through Windows Azure PowerShell. Detailed coverage of PowerShell is beyond the scope of this book. Readers can look for books that are specialized in PowerShell for more information.

Administrator: Windows Azure PowerShell
PS C:\> Get-AzureSQLDatabaseServer
ServerName
Location
AdministratorLogin
dwsyklavsf
North Central US
COSC6301
vvzr5w291p
South Central US
COSC6336

Figure 12.21 Get a list of SQL database servers in Windows Azure PowerShell.

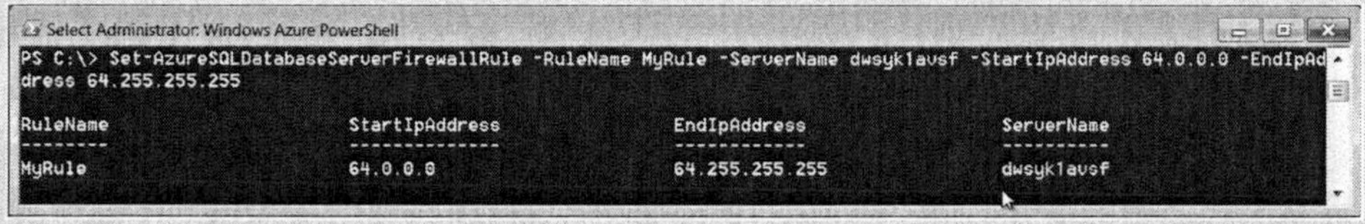
Select Administrator: Windows Azure PowerShell
PS C:\> Set-AzureSQLDatabaseServerFirewallRule -RuleName MyRule -ServerName dwsyklavsf -StartIpAddress 64.0.0.0 -EndIpAd
dress 64.255.255.255
RuleName
StartIpAddress
EndIpAddress
ServerName
MyRule
64.0.0.0
64.255.255.255
dwsyklavsf

Figure 12.22 Update firewall rule with Windows Azure PowerShell.

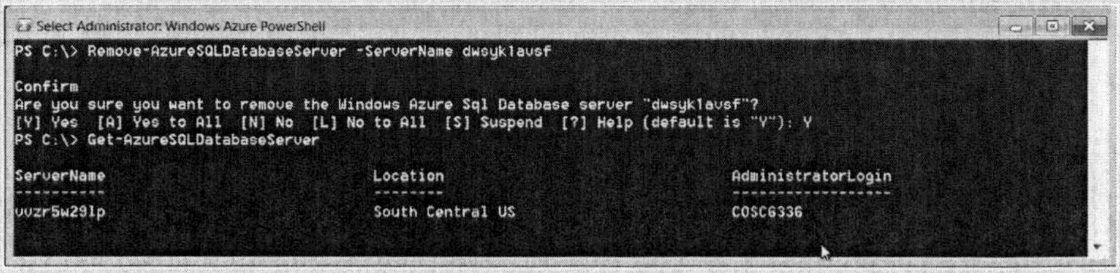
Select Administrator: Windows Azure PowerShell
PS C:\> Remove-AzureSQLDatabaseServer -ServerName dwsyklavsf
Confirm
Are you sure you want to remove the Windows Azure Sql Database server "dwsyklavsf"?
[Y] Yes [A] Yes to All [N] No [L] No to All [S] Suspend [?] Help (default is "Y"): Y
PS C:\> Get-AzureSQLDatabaseServer
ServerName
Location
AdministratorLogin
vvzr5w291p
South Central US
COSC6336

Figure 12.23 Remove SQL database server in Windows Azure PowerShell.

12.5 Monitoring Windows Azure

When applications on Windows Azure are up and running, we need to closely observe the operations. The operation data will be collected and analyzed to diagnose operation problems. Windows Azure provides several tools to help monitor and analyze the operations. The most well-known monitoring tool is the Windows Azure Management Portal. Another tool, Windows Azure Diagnostics, is a programming-based tool, which supports monitoring functionalities.

Monitor with Windows Azure Diagnostics: Windows Azure Diagnostics can be used to accomplish management tasks such as performance management, resource usage analysis, monitoring and auditing network traffic, and debugging and troubleshooting applications on Windows Azure. Diagnostic data can be periodically collected from running role instances. Then, the collected diagnostic data are transferred to Windows Azure storage for further analysis.

To run Windows Azure Diagnostics, you need to first create an XML configuration file and save the configuration file to the Windows Azure Blob storage resource called wad-control-container. In the configuration file, you can configure the items such as the deployment ID, role name, and the instance ID of a role instance. The configuration of Windows Azure Diagnostics can be done with programming code created in a role of an application on Windows Azure. You can also program a local application to remotely perform management tasks. In such a way, you can run and manage Windows Azure Diagnostics on Windows Azure from your local computer.

To use the Diagnostics module in a role, you need to import the module into the service definition file with the following code:

```
<Imports>
  <Import moduleName="Diagnostics"/>
</Imports>
```

Once the Diagnostics module is imported, the diagnostic monitor will be started automatically. The diagnostic monitor runs in Windows Azure and in the Windows Azure compute emulator. With the diagnostic monitor, you can collect diagnostic data for a role instance. To collect the diagnostic data, you need to configure the data source where the diagnostic data are collected. The data source may include the Windows Azure logs, IIS 7.0 logs, IIS failed request trace logs, crash dumps, as well as custom error logs. Information collected by the diagnostic monitor may include:

- Logs about IIS sites
- Logs about Windows Azure diagnostic infrastructure for web roles
- Logs about the information of the RemoteAccess module and RemoteForwarder module
- Logs about web and worker roles' failed requests
- Logs about failed requests to an IIS site, an application or a driver
- Logs of Windows events of web roles
- Logs about performance counters
- Logs about the state of the operating system in the event of a system crash, as well as the information from the customer error logs

There are several ways to collect diagnostic data. You can define a trace element in the configuration XML file in the web role. You can use the trace element during or after application development. Tracing can help you validate the operation flow of an application. For example, you can collect data from the failed request trace logs to check what has caused a failure.

Another way to collect data from an event log is to use the GetDefaultInitialConfiguration method in the programming code. Then, specify a data source such as WindowsEventLog, and call the start method of the class DiagnosticMonitor.

To collect data from the crash dump logs, in the programming code, you first need to ensure that the project references the Microsoft.WindowsAzure.Diagnostics.dll file in the programming code. You then call either the EnableCollection or the EnableCollectionToDirectory method from the CrashDumps class. Then, you can collect the entire crash dump information or specify a subset of the crash dump information.

To collect diagnostic data from a custom log file in a local storage resource, you need to add the LocalResources element into the service definition file with following code:

```
<LocalResources >
   <LocalStorage name = "CustomLogs_Name" sizeInMB = "10"
      cleanOnRoleRecycle = "false"/>
</LocalResources>
```

The attribute cleanOnRoleRecycle is used to specify whether the local storage resource should be wiped clean when a role instance is recycled. In the programming code of your role, include the reference Microsoft.WindowsAzure.Diagnostics. You can then specify the configuration of the Windows Azure diagnostic monitor by creating a DiagnosticMonitorConfiguration object. After you restart the diagnostic monitor, diagnostic data will be collected during the operation.

You can view the collected diagnostic data in Server Explorer of Visual Studio with Windows Azure Tools preinstalled. Once connected to the Windows Azure storage account, you are able to view the content stored in the Blob storage and Table storage. You can also view the diagnostic data stored in the local storage emulator account.

Monitor with Windows Azure Management Portal: The Windows Azure Management Portal provides status values of the deployments in a cloud service. Status values such as Created, Ready, and Active are used to indicate the status of a cloud service, deployment, and subscription. The status values will be displayed in the Management Portal for actions such as creating, updating, starting, and stopping a deployment. The following activity illustrates the monitoring operations provided by the Windows Azure Management Portal.

ACTIVITY 12.4 MONITORING WITH WINDOWS AZURE MANAGEMENT PORTAL

There are two levels of monitoring: minimal monitoring or verbose monitoring. With minimal monitoring, you can monitor CPU percentage, disk read throughput, disk write throughput, and data I/O. Minimal monitoring is easy to set and it does not need your storage account for storing the monitoring data. With verbose monitoring, you can collect additional performance-related information. You can also analyze application operation-related issues. Verbose monitoring requires a storage account for data storage, data transfer, and storage transactions. The use of the monitoring tool in the Windows Azure Management Portal requires that Windows Azure Diagnostics be enabled. The Windows Azure Diagnostics tool is enabled in Visual Studio 2012 by default. In this activity, you are going to use minimal monitoring and verbose monitoring to accomplish the following monitoring tasks:

Task 1: Monitor cloud services
Task 2: Monitor storage services

We begin with cloud service monitoring.

TASK 1: MONITOR CLOUD SERVICES

With the Windows Azure Management Portal, you can set the level of monitoring. If the monitoring level is set to verbose, you can configure the connection strings so that Windows Azure Diagnostics can store the data generated during the monitoring process to your storage account. To configure the diagnostics connection strings, follow the steps below:

1. Log on to the Windows Azure Management Portal through the website https://windows.azure.com with your user name and password.
2. Select the service **service63xx**. Click the **CONFIGURE** menu on the top part of your screen. You should be able to change the level of monitoring as shown in Figure 12.24.
3. Select **VERBOSE** as the monitoring level. You should get the warning that the verbose monitoring level will increase the storage cost. DIAGNOSTICS CONNECTION STRINGS are set to your storage account as shown in Figure 12.25. Click **Save** on the context command bar.
4. Click **MONITOR** on the menu. You should be able to see the display of the default verbose monitoring metrics, CPU PERCENTAGE (STUDENTCLUB_WORKERROLE) and CPU PERCENTAGE (STUDENTCLUB_WEBROLE). To add more monitoring metrics, click **ADD METRICS** as shown in Figure 12.26.

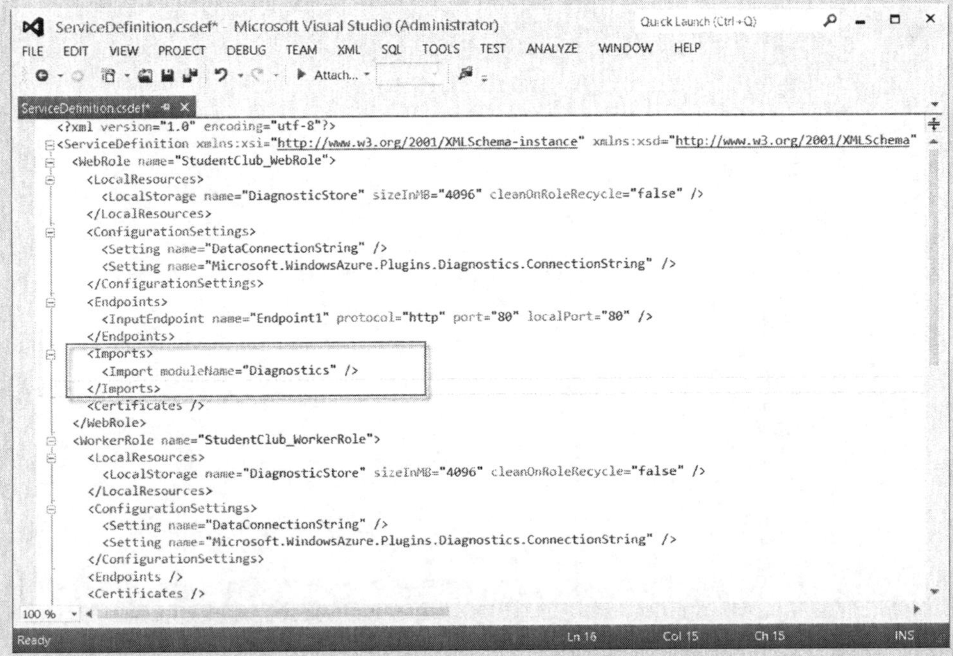
ServiceDefinition.csdef* - Microsoft Visual Studio (Administrator)
Quick Launch (Ctrl+Q)
FILE EDIT VIEW PROJECT DEBUG TEAM XML SQL TOOLS TEST ANALYZE WINDOW HELP
Attach...
ServiceDefinition.csdef*
<?xml version="1.0" encoding="utf-8"?>
<ServiceDefinition xmlns:xsi="http://www.w3.org/2001/XMLSchema-instance" xmlns:xsd="http://www.w3.org/2001/XMLSchema"
<WebRole name="StudentClub_WebRole">
<LocalResources>
<LocalStorage name="DiagnosticStore" sizeInMB="4096" cleanOnRoleRecycle="false" />
</LocalResources>
<ConfigurationSettings>
<Setting name="DataConnectionString" />
<Setting name="Microsoft.WindowsAzure.Plugins.Diagnostics.ConnectionString" />
</ConfigurationSettings>
<Endpoints>
<InputEndpoint name="Endpoint1" protocol="http" port="80" localPort="80" />
</Endpoints>
<Imports>
<Import moduleName="Diagnostics" />
</Imports>
<Certificates />
</WebRole>
<WorkerRole name="StudentClub_WorkerRole">
<LocalResources>
<LocalStorage name="DiagnosticStore" sizeInMB="4096" cleanOnRoleRecycle="false" />
</LocalResources>
<ConfigurationSettings>
<Setting name="DataConnectionString" />
<Setting name="Microsoft.WindowsAzure.Plugins.Diagnostics.ConnectionString" />
</ConfigurationSettings>
<Endpoints />
<Certificates />
100 %
Ready
Ln 16
Col 15
Ch 15
INS

Figure 12.24 Select monitoring level.

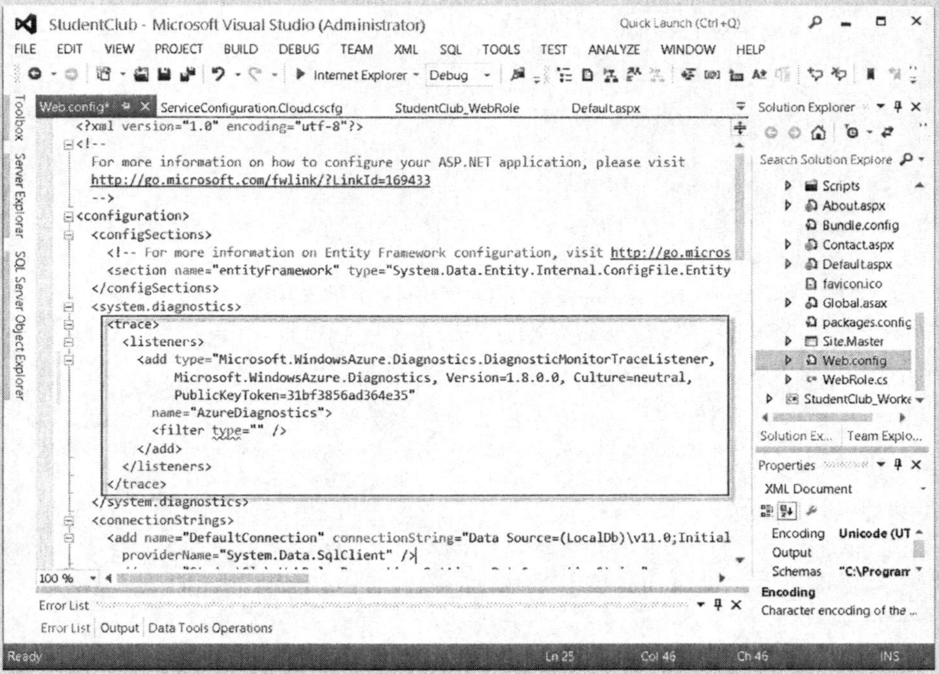

Figure 12.25 Verbose monitoring level.

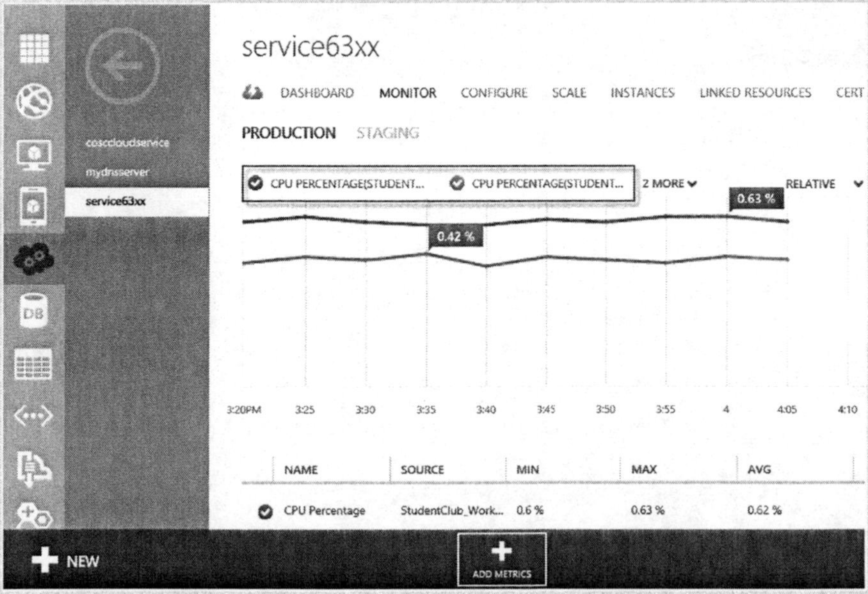

Figure 12.26 Monitor page.

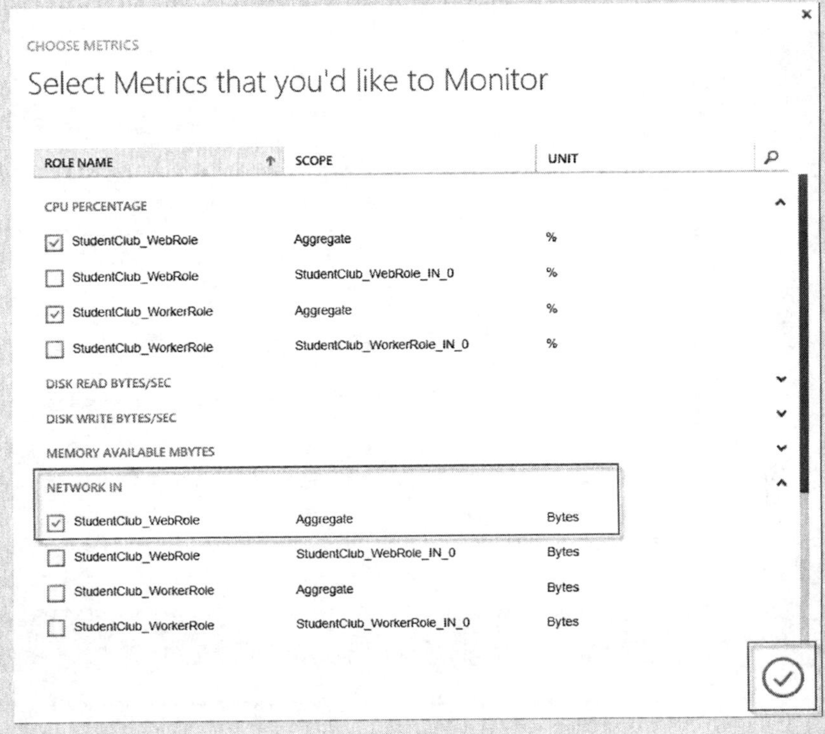

Figure 12.27 Add metric.

5. In the **Select Metrics that you'd like to Monitor** dialog, select the metric, for example, **NETWORK IN** for **StudentClub.WebRole** as shown in Figure 12.27. Then, click the check box.
6. To display the newly added metric, check the metric as shown in Figure 12.28.
7. You can also change the monitoring time range. Figure 12.29 displays the metrics in the 24-h time range.
8. To delete the newly added metric, select the metric and click the context command **DELETE METRIC**.

TASK 2: MONITOR STORAGE SERVICES

With the Windows Azure Management Portal, you can monitor the storage accounts that host the storage services Blob storage service, Queue storage service, and Table storage service. As described earlier, monitoring can be done at the minimal level or verbose level. You can also specify the appropriate data retention policy. The following steps show how to accomplish these tasks:

1. Assume that the Windows Azure Management Portal is still open. Click the STORAGE link and the Storage account you want to monitor. Click the CONFIGURE menu and you should be able to see the options of monitoring levels shown in Figure 12.30.

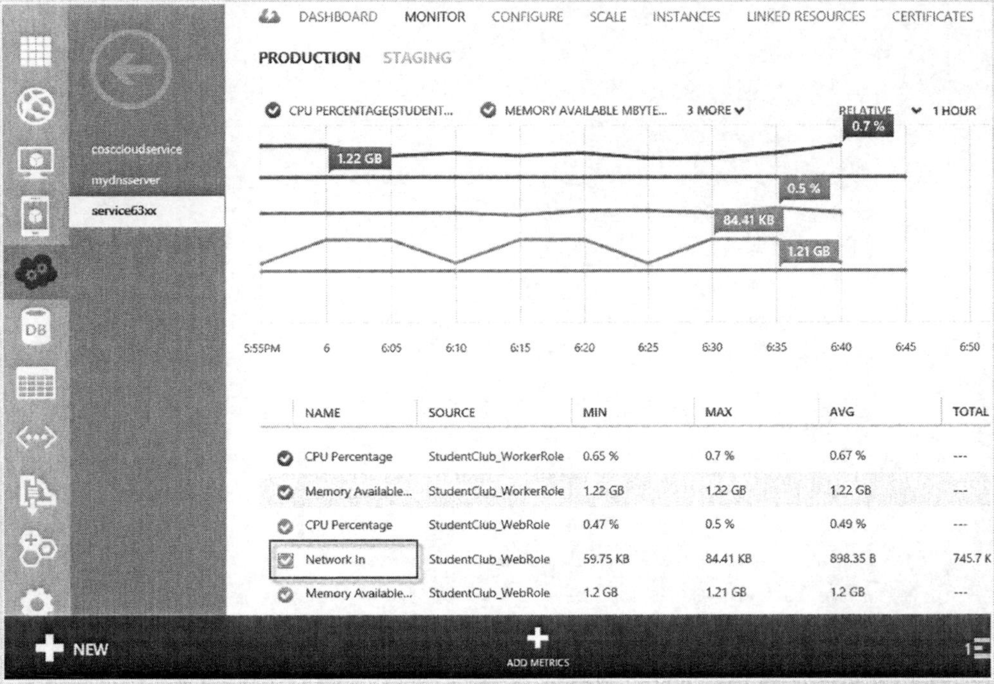

Figure 12.28 Display added metric.

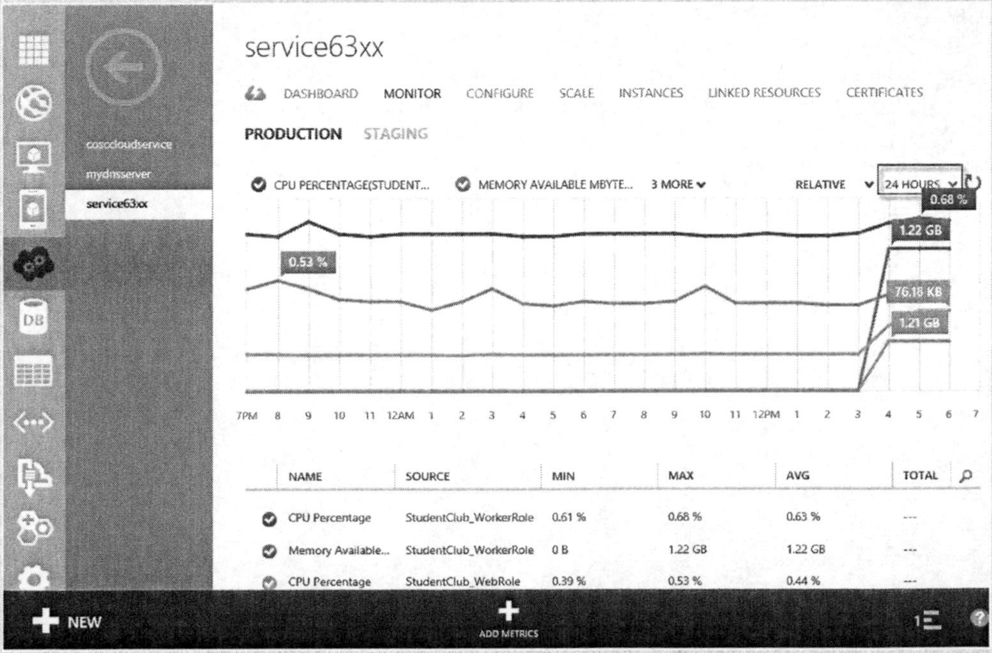

Figure 12.29 Display metrics in a 24-h time range.

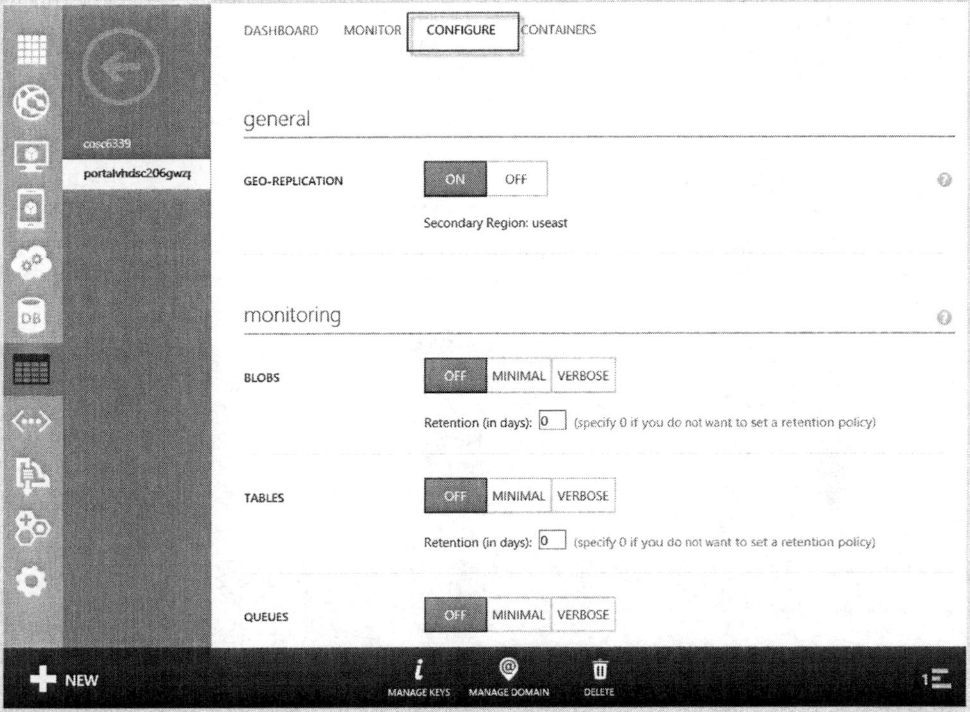

Figure 12.30 Monitoring levels of storage account.

2. Suppose that you would like to monitor the Blob and Table services at the verbose level and the Queue service at the minimal level. Change the settings as shown in Figure 12.31.
3. You can also specify how to log the Blob, Table, and Queue services. On the logging page, specify the logging as shown in Figure 12.32. Then, click the **SAVE** context command.
4. To display the metric, click the **MONITOR** menu. The default metrics are displayed (Figure 12.33).
5. To monitor a new metric, for example, Total Requests, expand the **4 MORE** node on the top part of your screen and select **TOTAL REQUESTS(TABLE)** as shown in Figure 12.34. If you click ADD METRICS, you will see many more metrics available for monitoring.
6. After the Table Requests metric is added, you need to click the icon left to the metric to display the monitoring result as shown in Figure 12.35.
7. You can also change the display time range; for example, you can change the time range from **6 HOURS** to **24 HOURS** as shown in Figure 12.36.

This activity shows that monitoring cloud components can be easily done through the Windows Azure Management Portal. In addition to monitoring cloud services and storage services, you can also use the Windows Azure Management Portal to monitor SQL databases, SQL reports, websites, service buses, and multimedia services.

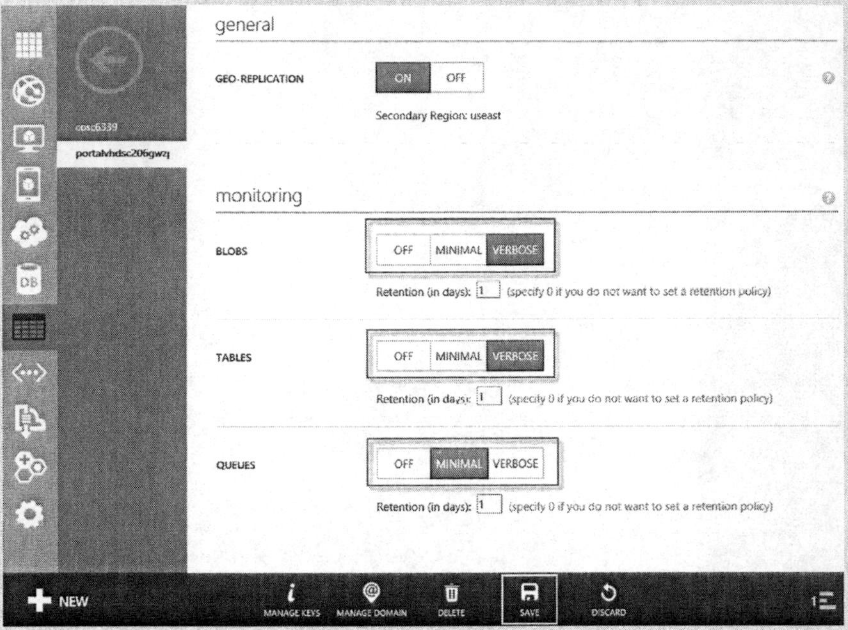

Figure 12.31 Configure monitoring levels.

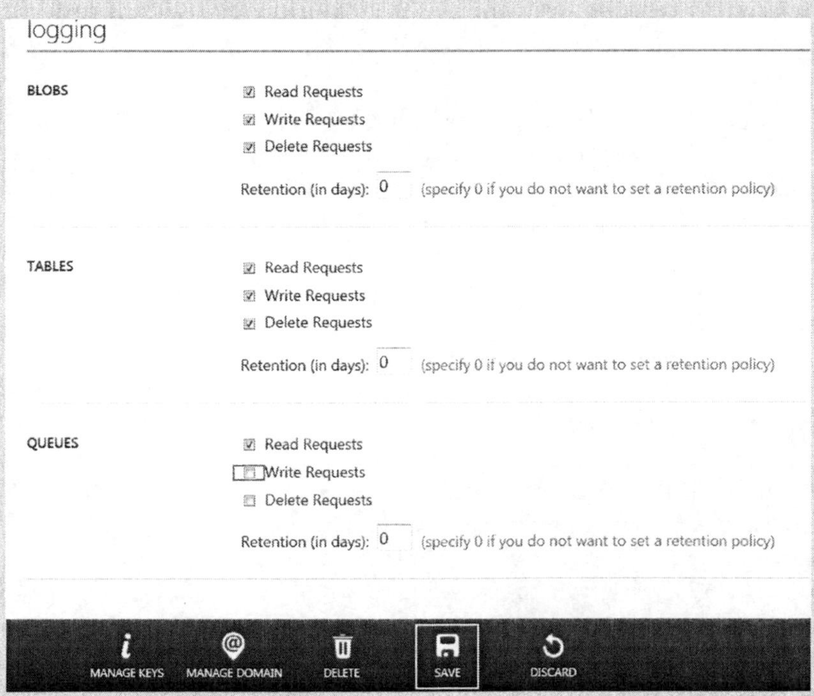

Figure 12.32 Configure logging.

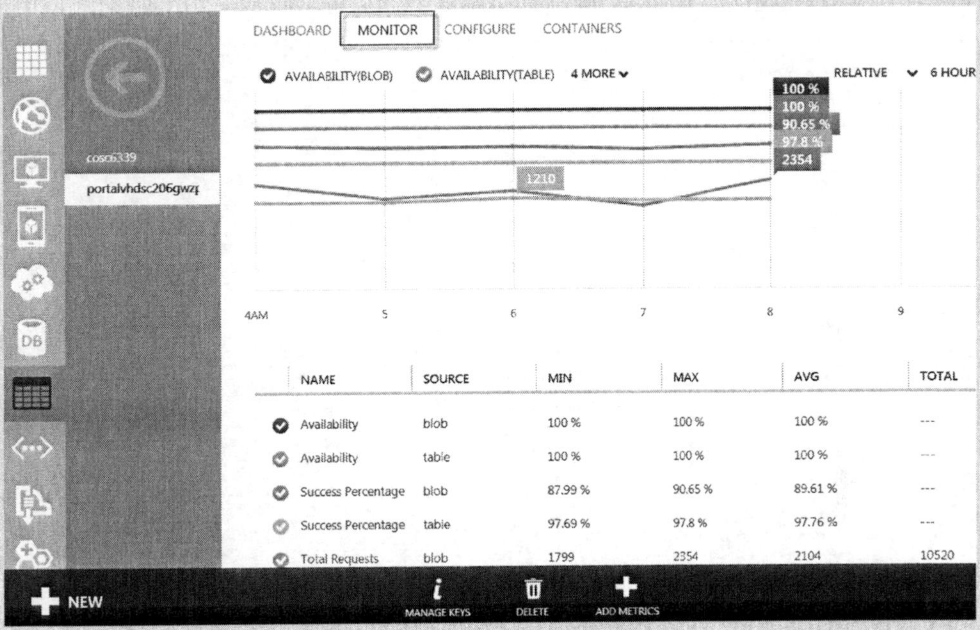

Figure 12.33 Display metrics.

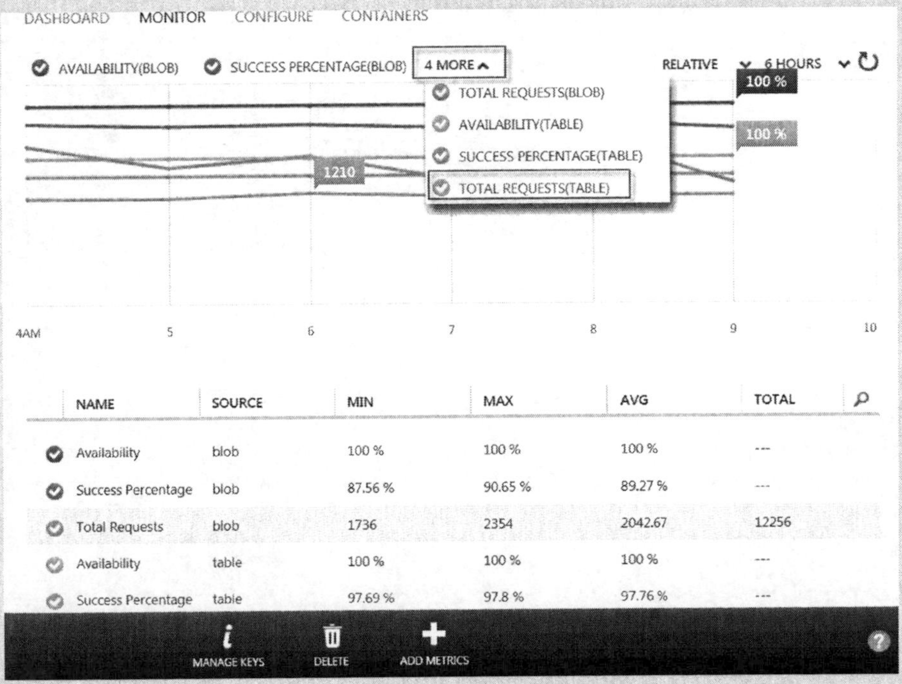

Figure 12.34 Add new metric.

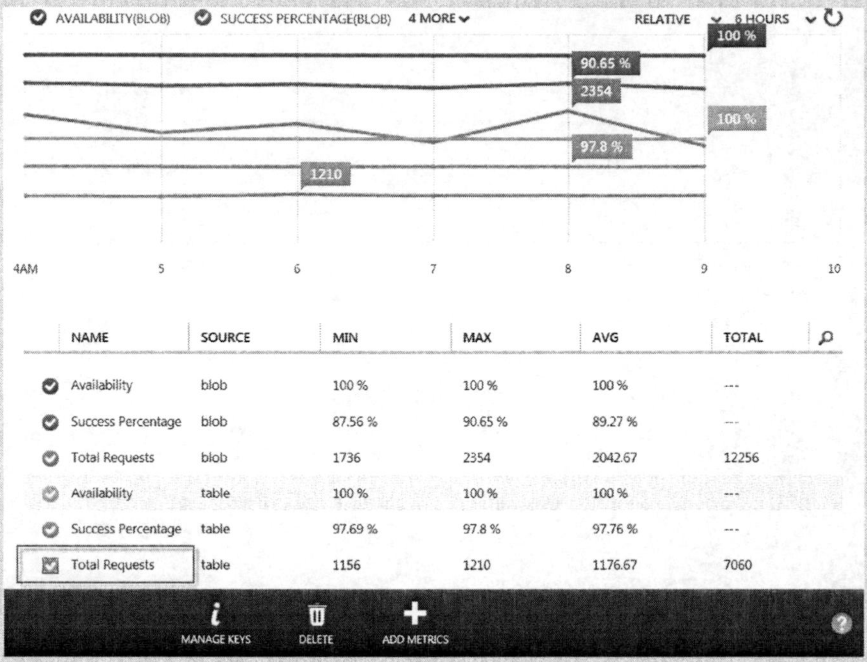

Figure 12.35 Display total requests metric.

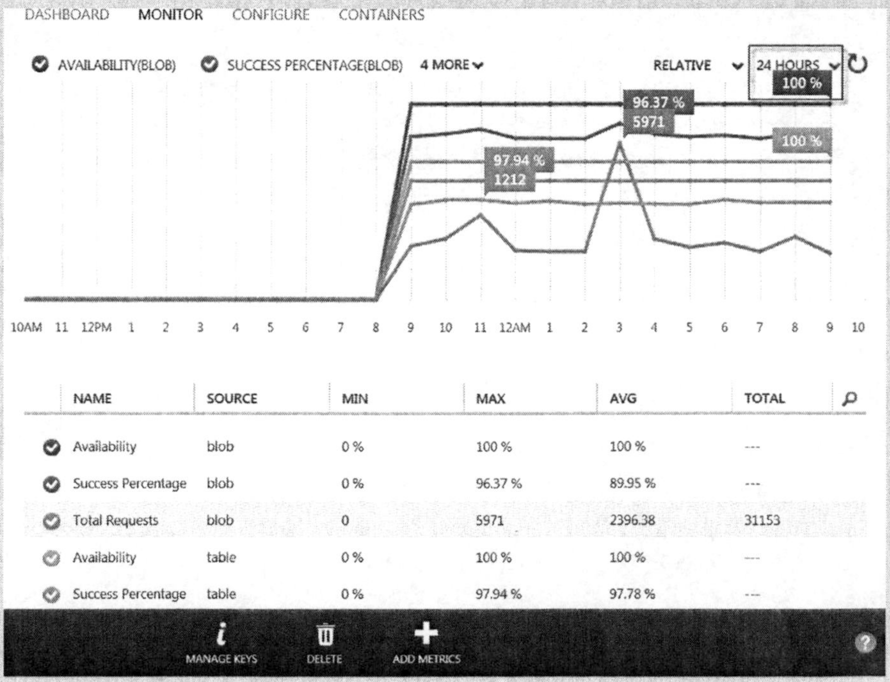

Figure 12.36 Change time range.

12.6 Summary

This chapter covers management-related issues. Security is the top concern for the databases and applications deployed to a cloud environment. This chapter addresses the issues related to confidentiality, integrity, and availability in the cloud environment. The cloud environment makes it easy for database management. Cloud providers take care of the management of infrastructure, security, database backup, and replication. In the cloud environment, the database administrator can focus on the management of the database itself, such as user authentication and authorization. For the management of Windows Azure, the Windows Azure Management Portal and Windows Azure Service Management API are the tools that can accomplish tasks such as the management of storage accounts, cloud services, certificates, and affinity groups. To observe databases and applications running on Windows Azure, we can use Windows Azure Diagnostics, which is a programming-based tool that supports monitoring functionalities. The Windows Azure Management Portal also provides tools to help monitor and analyze operations. To demonstrate how to manage databases and applications in Windows Azure, four hands-on activities are provided. These activities cover the management of database users, storage accounts, as well as service monitoring.

Review Questions

1. What are the three security requirements for databases running in a cloud environment?
2. State the definition of confidentiality.
3. State the definition of integrity.
4. State the definition of availability.
5. Why is security the top concern for a database running in a cloud environment?
6. What do you do with CSP?
7. Why do you need to keep the integrity of the data stored in Windows Azure SQL Database?
8. How can the hashing technology be used to keep integrity?
9. What tools does Windows Azure provide to carry out hashing?
10. What is the technology used to improve the availability of cloud-based database systems?
11. What should be addressed by a security policy?
12. Why is it easier to manage databases in a cloud environment?
13. How to prevent invalid access to your database server and database hosted by Windows Azure?
14. State the difference between authentication and authorization.
15. What tasks can be accomplished by the Windows Azure Management Portal?
16. What do you do with a certificate?
17. Why do you need to create an affinity group?
18. What do you do with the Windows Azure Service Management API?
19. What tasks can be performed by Windows Azure Diagnostics?
20. What monitoring tasks can be accomplished with the Windows Azure Management Portal?

Bibliography

Web Sites

The following web sites are about the recent development of cloud computing-related technologies.

- Web sites that provide comprehensive coverage of some major cloud providers:
  - http://www.ibm.com/solutions/education/cloudacademy/us/en/cloud_academy_3.html
  - http://aws.amazon.com/
  - http://www.apple.com/icloud/
  - http://windows.azure.com
  - https://cloud.google.com/
  - http://windows.microsoft.com/en-US/skydrive/download
- Web sites that provide tutorials of Windows Azure:
  - http://dotnetslackers.com/articles/aspnet/How-Windows-Azure-Works.aspx
  - http://msdn.microsoft.com/en-us/magazine/ff796231.aspx
  - https://docs.google.com/file/d/0B3u3OyCtiYmWNDQ0ZGUxYmItODAwMy00NThlLThjZGMtZjY1MjI0N2IxNzI4/edit?hl=en_GB
  - http://www.microsoft.com/learning/en/us/azure-training.aspx
  - http://msdn.microsoft.com/en-us/library/gg432983.aspx
  - http://content.dell.com/us/en/enterprise/dell-cloud-computing-strategy.aspx
  - http://www.windowsazure.com/en-us/develop/overview/
  - http://www.windowsazure.com/en-us/develop/overview/
  - http://www.windowsazure.com/en-us/develop/other/
  - http://msdn.microsoft.com/en-us/library/ee336235.aspx
  - http://sqlazuremw.codeplex.com/
  - http://social.technet.microsoft.com/wiki/contents/articles/2153.windows-azure-and-sql-database-tutorials-tutorial-3-using-windows-azure-blob-service-en-us.aspx
  - http://social.technet.microsoft.com/wiki/contents/articles/1695.inside-windows-azure-sql-database.aspx
  - http://www.brentozar.com/archive/2009/11/playing-around-with-sql-azure-and-ssms/
  - http://msdn.microsoft.com/en-us/wazplatformtrainingcourse_introtosqlazureforvs2010developers_topic2#_Toc303834957
  - http://msdn.microsoft.com/en-us/gg282147
  - http://www.devproconnections.com/article/windows-azure/how-to-migrate-a-web-application-to-windows-azure-and-sql-azure-130034

- http://www.windowsazure.com/en-us/develop/net/how-to-guides/table-services/
- http://www.tugberkugurlu.com/archive/how-to-use-windows-azure-blob-storage-service-with-asp-net-mvc-web-application
- http://www.windowsazure.com/en-us/develop/net/how-to-guides/queue-service/
- http://www.cse.ust.hk/~lingu/azure/labs/2/2.html
- http://social.technet.microsoft.com/wiki/contents/articles/7556.introduction-to-sql-server-data-tools-ssdt.aspx#SSDT_Installation_Step-By-Step
- http://technet.microsoft.com/en-us/hh352139
- http://msdn.microsoft.com/en-us/library/windowsazure/gg442307.aspx
- http://technet.microsoft.com/en-us/library/ee210526(v=sql.105).aspx
- http://msdn.microsoft.com/en-us/library/windowsazure/hh597460.aspx
- http://www.c-sharpcorner.com/UploadFile/deepak.sharma00/how-to-generate-report-from-shttp://msdn.microsoft.com/en-us/library/windowsazure/hh597460.aspxql-server-database-using-report/
- http://msdn.microsoft.com/en-us/magazine//jj618299.aspx

■ Cloud Resource Web sites:
- https://www.dreamspark.com/Product/Product.aspx?productid=8
- http://content.dell.com/us/en/enterprise/dell-cloud-computing.aspx
- http://www.windowsazure.com/en-us/pricing/free-trial/
- http://www.windowsazure.com/en-us/develop/overview/
- http://blogs.msdn.com/b/sqlazure/
- http://social.technet.microsoft.com/wiki/contents/articles/1571.overview-of-tools-to-use-with-windows-azure-sql-database.aspx
- http://www.vmware.com/solutions/cloud-computing

Books

The following books provide in-depth coverage of cloud computing theories and related technologies.

Crookes, D. *Cloud Computing in Easy Steps*. Warwickshire, UK: In Easy Steps Limited, 2012.

Dudley, R.J. and Duchene, N.A. *Microsoft Azure: Enterprise Application Development*. Birmingham, UK: Packt Publishing Ltd., 2010.

Finn, A., Vredevoort, H., Lownds, P., and Flynn, D. *Microsoft Private Cloud Computing*. Indianapolis, IN: Sybex, 2012.

Jackson, K. *OpenStack Cloud Computing Cookbook*. Birmingham, UK: Packt Publishing, 2012.

Johnson, B. *Professional Visual Studio 2012*. Indianapolis, IN: Wrox, 2012.

Josyula, V. and Orr, M. *Cloud Computing: Automating the Virtualized Data Center (Networking Technology)*. Indianapolis, IN: Cisco Press, 2011.

Klein, S. and Roggero, H. *Pro SQL Azure*. New York, NY: Apress, 2010.

Mehner, P. *Developing Cloud Applications with Windows Azure Storage*. Redmond, WA: Microsoft Press, 2013.

Nielsen, L. *The Little Book of Cloud Computing, 2011 Edition*. Wickford, RI: New Street Communications, LLC, 2011.

Rhoton, J. and Haukioja, R. *Cloud Computing Architected: Solution Design Handbook*. USA: Recursive, Limited, 2011.

Rosenberg, J. and Mateos, A. *The Cloud at Your Service*. Greenwich, CT: Manning Publications, 2010.

Sosinsky, B. *Cloud Computing Bible*. Hoboken, NJ: Wiley, 2011.

Vic Winkler, J.R. *Securing the Cloud: Cloud Computer Security Techniques and Tactics*. Waltham, MA: Syngress, 2011.

Wilder, B. *Cloud Architecture Patterns: Using Microsoft Azure*. Sebastopol, CA: O'Reilly Media, 2012.

Index

E

F

G

H

I

S

T

U

V

X